Welcome to Alaska

Alaska is America's last frontier, with landscapes that stretch out seemingly to infinity. From the lush rain forests of the Southeast to the vast, flat tundra in the north, you can stare in awe at the same things that take an Alaskan's breath away: calving glaciers, volcanic valleys, jagged sea cliffs, the northern lights, and more. Here you can kayak to icebergs, fly over the highest peak in North America, stay out all night celebrating the midnight sun, and spot wildlife from eagles to whales. For lovers of nature, few places exhilarate like Alaska.

TOP REASONS TO GO

★ **Denali National Park:** Whether you're flightseeing, rafting, or on foot, this national park is a must.

★ **Cruising:** Nothing beats the panoramic glacier views from an Inside Passage cruise.

★ **Outdoor Adventures:** Fishing the Kenai and hiking Harding Icefield are just the start.

★ **Denali:** The skyscraping "High One" is the continent's most majestic mountain.

★ **Bears:** When the salmon run, the brown bears of Katmai spring into action.

★ **Crafts:** Aleut weaving and Inupiaq ivory carvings represent Alaska Native traditions.

Contents

Fodor's

ALASKA

Fodor's Features

MAPS

Chapter 1

EXPERIENCE
ALASKA

20 ULTIMATE EXPERIENCES

Alaska offers terrific experiences that should be on every traveler's list. Here are Fodor's top picks for a memorable trip.

1 Juneau and Mendenhall Glacier

Alaska's capital city has a vibrant downtown filled with charming shops, restaurants, and bars, but it's also known for its proximity to the most easily accessible glacier in the state, Mendenhall Glacier. *(Ch. 4)*

2 Bear-Spotting

Magnificent brown bears are found all over southern and interior Alaska, but Kodiak Island and Katmai National Park are the most popular spots for a sighting. *(Ch. 5, 8)*

3 Cruising the Inside Passage

This network of waterways in southeastern Alaska is one of the most-traveled routes for cruise ships, taking passengers past stunning glaciers and to charming small towns. *(Ch. 4)*

4 Kayaking and Rafting

With 365,000 miles of streams and rivers, there are plenty of opportunities for water adventures, whether it's calm kayaking or class IV white-water rafting. *(Ch. 5)*

5 Gold Rush History

The discovery of gold created modern Alaska, bringing thousands north to establish towns like Skagway and Dawson City, which still offer gold-panning tours today. *(Ch. 4, 7)*

6 Whale-Watching

A variety of cetaceans, from gray whales to humpbacks to orcas, are found in Alaskan waters. Prince William Sound and the Inside Passage are prime spots for watching. *(Ch. 4, 5)*

7 Anchorage

Alaska's most populous city is also its most thriving urban center, with impressive cuisine and nightlife, not to mention gorgeous urban trails for hiking and biking. *(Ch. 3)*

8 Denali National Park

Home to North America's tallest mountain, Denali is Alaska's most famous park, and yet remains surprisingly pristine, with plenty of moose, bears, caribou, and wolves. *(Ch. 6)*

9 Native Culture

With 229 federally recognized tribes, Alaska has a thriving Native culture, from Anchorage's Alaska Native Heritage Center to Ketchikan's Saxman Totem Park. *(Ch. 3, 4)*

10 Flightseeing Tours

Not everywhere in Alaska is accessible by road, but small bush planes offer amazing views and unparalleled access to some of the state's most wondrous spots. *(Ch. 5)*

11 Fishing

From Ketchikan to Homer, Alaska is perhaps the best place for fishing in the world. Try your hand at nabbing a salmon or halibut via a chartered boat or fly-fishing. *(Ch. 4)*

12 The Midnight Sun

In summer, some Alaskan regions see nearly 24 hours of sunlight. Take advantage by seeing a midnight baseball game in Fairbanks or attending various festivals. *(Ch. 7)*

13 Fairbanks

Home to the University of Alaska, the state's second largest city is a young, hip college town with plenty of art, culture, breweries, and outdoor activities. *(Ch. 7)*

14 Glacier-Trekking

Alaska is home to nearly 100,000 glaciers like Mendenhall and Matanuska, and a guided glacier trek is the perfect way to explore these otherworldly giants up close. *(Ch. 5)*

15 Dog-Sledding

Mushing is one of Alaska's most popular sports, thanks to the famed Iditarod race from Anchorage to Nome. In the off-season, you can visit dog-sled camps across the state. *(Ch. 8)*

16 Seafood

Dining in Alaska is all about the freshly caught seafood, from Copper River red salmon and halibut cheeks to Dungeness and king crabs. *(Ch. 4, 5, 7)*

17 Wildlife

Wildlife abounds all over Alaska, from bears, moose, caribou, and wolves in Denali to bison, bald eagles, and Dall sheep in various parks and reserves. *(Ch. 6)*

18 Kenai Fjords National Park

To experience Alaska's coastline at its best, visit Kenai Fjords and its impressive array of glaciers and sea life, including orcas, otters, and dolphins. *(Ch. 5)*

19 The Northern Lights

Seeing the stunning greens, purples, and reds of the Aurora Borealis is an unforgettable experience. Visit northern Alaska between October and March for your best chance. *(Ch. 8)*

20 Alaska's Railroads

The best way to see Alaska's towering mountains and wide-open vistas are from the windows of a train, like the famed White Pass and Yukon Railway. *(Ch. 4)*

WHAT'S WHERE

1 **Anchorage.** Containing nearly half of the state's population, Anchorage is Alaska's biggest city. The restaurants, art and history museums, numerous espresso stands, and performing arts have earned the city the sobriquet "Seattle of the North." Alaskans often deride the place as "Los Anchorage," but the occasional moose ambling down a street hints at the wilderness nearby.

2 **Juneau, the Inside Passage, and Southeast Alaska.** Southeast Alaska (or "the Panhandle") includes the state capital (Juneau) and the Lynn Canal (the Inside Passage). The region is speckled with small towns and villages, most accessible only by boat or plane. Haines and Skagway are the only towns along the water route that have roads to "the Outside," while the Inside Passage ties together almost all the populated places in the region. Here fjords snake between the mountains, timbered slopes plunge to rocky shores, and marine life abounds.

3 **The Kenai Peninsula and Southcentral Alaska.** This region offers great fishing, hiking, rafting, kayaking, and wildlife viewing. Visit Seward and Homer on the Kenai Peninsula and dip your paddle into marine wilderness. Kodiak, in the Gulf of Alaska, is known for its green-carpeted mountains and brown bears. Charter outfits take you to remote areas and choice fishing spots.

4 **Denali National Park and Preserve.** Home to Denali—the highest peak in North America— Denali National Park and Preserve comprises 6 million acres of Alaska's best wildlife, scenery, and adventures.

5 **Fairbanks, the Yukon, and the Interior.** Bound by the Brooks Range to the north and the Alaska Range to the south, the Interior is home to a vast expanse of pristine backcountry. The largest city in the region is Fairbanks (gateway to the towns of the Arctic), and includes the Bering Coast and Canada's Yukon Territory.

6 **The Bush.** Inupiaq people share the tundra with the Prudhoe Bay oil fields, brown bears roam Katmai National Park, and prospectors still pan for gold. Except for the Dalton Highway and a few short roads near Nome, the region is essentially roadless. Traveling here requires planning; the reward is true adventure.

What to Eat and Drink in Alaska

BLACK COD

Black cod may be overshadowed by more famous Alaskan seafood like salmon and halibut, but it's still one of the most delicious fresh fishes you can sample here. So oily it's also known as butterfish, black cod is a rich and succulent choice found on many menus throughout the state.

BLUEBERRIES

Berry-picking here is a serious business. People compete with each other for the best spots during the short growing season for the chance to sample fresh, sweet berries. If you can't go berry-picking, look for options like gooseberry pie, wild berry cobbler, and blueberry French toast on menus.

BEER

The craft beer craze has made it to Alaska, and now dozens of microbreweries scattered across the state provide ample tasting opportunities for beer-lovers. Try creations that make use of the native bounty, like beers brewed with spruce tips, an Alaskan specialty since Captain Cook made his first voyage here.

SALMON

Sampling salmon, perhaps Alaska's most famous food, is an essential experience. Throughout the summer, five types of salmon (king, coho, sockeye, chum, and pink) fill Alaska's rivers, beckoning commercial and amateur fishers alike. Many consider Copper River salmon to be some of the best in the world, and there's nothing like trying it fresh. Have it grilled simply and alongside fresh local vegetables. Or try smoked salmon, a quintessential Alaskan snack.

CRABS

Whether it's Dungeness, snow, or king, you'll find crab in any seaside Alaskan town, freshly caught from places like the Aleutian Islands. Get ready to crack open a crab leg and dip the succulent meat in melted butter, one of the most memorable, and tastiest, Alaskan culinary experiences. Be sure to wear a bib, or at least have plenty of napkins.

HALIBUT CHEEKS

Another favorite of amateur fishers (Ketchikan in particular has some excellent waters for halibut fishing), fresh-caught halibut should also be on your must-eat list, and halibut cheeks are a delicate, sweet treat. Cut from the head of the fish, the cheeks are small, oval-shaped, and often compared to scallops in appearance and texture. Try them breaded or sautéed with garlic and butter.

1

REINDEER
These domesticated cousins of caribou were first brought over from Siberia and have since become a popular Alaskan protein. Reindeer store their fat on the outside of their muscles, which results in a lean cut free from the marbling found in other red meats. Pair a side of reindeer sausage with breakfast or savor reindeer meatloaf or burgers at dinner.

SOURDOUGH BREAD
A favorite of those who came to Alaska in search of riches during the Klondike Gold Rush, sourdough bread is created with naturally occurring fermentation instead of baker's yeast. During the Gold Rush, yeast and baking soda were difficult to find, and so a legend was born (sourdough also keeps a lot longer than regular bread). Today items like sourdough pancakes and pastries help keep the Gold Rush spirit alive on menus throughout the state.

KELP
Kelp has been on the menu for Native people along Alaska's southern coast for centuries. Luckily for gourmands, interest has been sparked again and local companies like Barnacle Foods are harvesting and selling it in a variety of forms, including kelp pickles, salsa, and spice mix. Pick some up from an Alaskan grocery store.

AKUTAQ
Don't leave Alaska without experiencing its rich indigenous culture and sampling foods that have been eaten here for centuries. Sometimes called Eskimo ice cream, Akutaq is a dessert traditionally made from whipped animal fat and berries. Today, the dish is often made with Crisco, sugar, and berries.

What to Buy in Alaska

HAND-CRAFTED BOWLS

Birch logs that arrive at the Great Alaskan Bowl Company undergo a 22-step process of shaping, sanding, oiling, and drying until they turn into beautiful objets d'art that ripple with streaks of dark and light grain unique to each piece.

QUIVET HATS

Alaskans excel at inventing ways to keep warm, and the quivet hat is one of their most beloved creations. Quivet is the undercoat of a musk ox that yields a yarn finer than cashmere and eight times warmer than wool. Find hand-knit hats in places like the Oomingmak Musk Ox Co-op.

JADE

Alaska's state gem, jade has long been used by Native people for tools, jewelry, and weapons. There's lots of it to go around—including an entire jade mountain on Alaska's Seward Peninsula—so jade carvings and jewelry can be found in gift shops across the state.

ULU KNIFE

Originally made from rock, slate, or jade with a wooden or bone handle, the ulu is a curved, all-purpose knife originally used by Alaska Natives for everything from making clothes to cutting food to building boats. Today, it's a fun gift with an interesting history as well as a great kitchen tool, often paired with a bowl for dicing and mincing.

XTRATUFS

These dependable rubber boots are quintessential Alaska, owned by nearly every local in a coastal town. Preferred because of their comfort and ability to withstand brutal Alaskan weather, Xtratufs have become a veritable rite-of-passage for Alaskans. In recent years, the boot-maker has paired with Alaskan company Salmon Sisters, releasing more fashionable Xtratufs with colorful, patterned interiors.

SMOKED SALMON

You can't head home without bringing back some of Alaska's most famous seafood. Caught fresh and then filleted, brined, and smoked with a variety of methods, smoked salmon is especially delicious when paired with crackers and/or cheese. It often needs to be kept refrigerated, so be sure to check the package before you put it in your luggage.

TEA

Alaskans can get pretty experimental with their tea. Popular varieties include wild rose and tea made from chaga, an antioxidant-packed fungus that grows on birch trees throughout the north. The Anchorage-based Kobuk Tea Company has been leading this tea brigade for more than 50 years, and at their eclectic downtown store, you can buy all manner of local and international goods; be sure to take home some of their signature Samovar Tea.

GOLD

Alaska's other most famous precious metal is what sent thousands careening north during the Yukon Gold Rush. Today, you can easily buy this prized Alaskan gold or find some yourself on a gold-panning tour. Once you get home, you'll be able to relive the thrill of those first Klondikers as you show off your Alaskan gold.

CHRISTMAS DECORATIONS

It may be July, but that won't stop shoppers from buying Christmas ornaments at the Santa Claus House in North Pole, Alaska. Fifteen minutes south of Fairbanks, the town is decorated for the holidays year-round and offers plenty of items to put you in the holiday spirit. You can even tell your kids that their gifts really did come from the North Pole.

ALASKA NATIVE CRAFTS

Alaska's Native culture is reflected in its abundance of craft traditions, from totem poles to intricate baskets and detailed carvings. Many of these reflect traditions passed down across countless generations. Each of Alaska's Native groups is noted for particular skills and visual-art styles.

Best Outdoor Adventures in Alaska

VIEW THE NORTHERN LIGHTS FROM CHENA HOT SPRINGS

Located 60 miles northeast of Fairbanks, Chena Hot Springs experiences nearly 24 hours of darkness in mid-winter, making it an ideal place to view Aurora Borealis displays. The naturally occurring hot springs are also a welcome relief from air temperatures that reach fifty below zero.

EXPLORE KATMAI NATIONAL PARK

Accessible only by plane, Katmai, known as the land of ten thousand smokes, features a dynamic combination of volcanic activity and coastal brown bears. Float trips, hiking, and kayaking are popular activities, all with a high chance of spotting one of the park's 2,200 bears.

CAMP IN DENALI NATIONAL PARK

Alaska's most popular national park, Denali's wilderness stretches as far as the imagination, and you shouldn't settle for seeing it from a tour bus. Grab your backpack and a bear-proof food container, and head out for a multiday backcountry adventure. Shuttle buses allow you to start your hike anywhere, from the realm of moose and lowland spruces to high alpine tundra among the Dall sheep.

TREK ON MENDENHALL GLACIER

The cruise ship industry has turned downtown Juneau into a thriving summer tourism destination. Get away from the crowds and board a helicopter for the Mendenhall Glacier. A litany of tour options are available, including landings next to glittering blue glacial lakes and dog-sledding tours. Bring your hats, gloves, and snowball fighting skills and experience winter in the middle of summer.

TAKE A FLIGHTSEEING TOUR OVER DENALI

Even if you are lucky enough to glimpse "The High One" from within Denali National Park, there's still nothing like seeing Denali up close. Charter a flightseeing tour out of Healy or Talkeetna and get so close to the continent's highest peak that you can practically feel the ice beneath your feet.

KAYAK IN GLACIER BAY NATIONAL PARK

Millions have traveled to Glacier Bay to see this incredible park forged by ice, and there is no better way to explore it than from your very own kayak. Guided tours and personal rentals are offered by park concessionaires and get you as close to the glaciers as possible.

HIKE THE CHILKOOT TRAIL

Originating just north of Skagway, the Chilkoot Trail became famous as the jumping-off point for the Klondike Gold Rush. Today the well-maintained trail crosses the Canadian border and stretches 33 miles to the old town of Bennett. Guided hikes are available, or you can set out on your own.

BACKPACK IN THE ARCTIC NATIONAL WILDLIFE REFUGE

Meant for those who find a Denali backpacking trip too easy, the Arctic National Wildlife Refuge (known in conservation circles simply as "The Refuge") is a remote, protected body of more than 19 million acres in the northeast corner of the state. It is perhaps best known for the Porcupine Caribou herd, which numbers more than 100,000 animals. An eclectic mix of ecosystems, mountain ranges, plants, and wildlife make this distant but magical piece of the planet an unforgettable sight. If disappearing alone into the largest protected region above the Arctic Circle isn't to your taste, outfitters offer rafting, hiking, and backpacking tours.

Best Wildlife Experiences in Alaska

BALD EAGLES IN HAINES
These majestic birds can be found all over the state, lounging everywhere from the docks of Juneau to the northern villages of the Bush. But the world's largest gathering of bald eagles occurs in southeast Alaska each winter, along the Chilkat River near Haines. Here they build the biggest nests in the world, the largest one to date weighing almost 3 tons.

THE BIG 5 IN DENALI NATIONAL PARK
Denali gives you the best chance to spot the "Big 5" of Alaskan animals. Bears, moose, wolves, caribou, and Dall sheep all live throughout the park in various regions, and sightings happen often. Always be on the lookout (even if you're on a bus tour), and be sure to keep your distance.

HUMPBACK AND ORCA WHALES IN JUNEAU
Whale-watching tours are offered from many coastal towns, but the best leave from Juneau. Here huge humpback whales move in pods, traveling and feeding together. The finale occurs when every whale rockets to the surface for air. You can also often spot majestic orcas traveling with their young.

OTTERS AND SEALS IN GLACIER BAY
Whether you're sailing through Glacier Bay National Park on a large cruise ship or kayaking on a guided tour, keep your eyes out for the many animals that inhabit this area. Otters and harbor seals are often found on the rocky shores, hanging out on ice floes, or swimming in the waters.

IDITAROD SLED DOG RACE

The original Iditarod was a relay of dog teams getting medication to Nome during a diphtheria outbreak in 1925. Today the Iditarod commemorates the history and culture of dog mushing in Alaska. The race begins in early March in Anchorage with the top runners reaching Nome eight to ten days later.

SALMON IN KETCHIKAN

The southeast town of Ketchikan is often referred to as the salmon capital of the world. Head out on a fishing boat to try your luck catching one yourself. Every summer, salmon return to where they were born to spawn and die; seeing them fill the rivers is morbid, but part of the Alaskan circle of life.

BROWN BEARS ON KODIAK ISLAND

Brown bears, or grizzlies, are found throughout the state, from Admiralty Island near Wrangell to Katmai National Park. But one the most accessible places is Kodiak National Wildlife Refuge. Spot them most easily in July and August, feeding along the salmon-filled streams.

BELUGA WHALES AND DOLPHINS IN TURNAGAIN ARM

Turnagain Arm, a waterway in the northwestern part of the Gulf of Alaska, is known for its large tidal ranges (it has the second-highest tides in North America). Driving along it through the Cook Inlet is one of the most scenic road trips in the country. As you head from Anchorage to the Kenai Peninsula, be on constant look-out for the beluga whales and dolphins that regularly swim through these waters; Beluga Point is a popular stop for a photo-op.

CARIBOU IN ARCTIC NATIONAL WILDLIFE REFUGE

Sometimes called the nomads of the north, caribou are long-distance wandering mammals. Within the Arctic National Wildlife Refuge, you'll find the Porcupine Caribou herd, one of the greatest remaining groups of caribou in the world; the herd has ranged between 70,000 and 180,000 over the past decades. Glimpsing these majestic creatures en masse is an unforgettable experience.

Alaska Cruises 101

Alaska is one of cruising's showcase destinations. From traditional loop cruises of the Inside Passage to one-way trips between the Inside Passage and the Gulf of Alaska, traveling by boat allows you to glimpse gorgeous glaciers and visit charming small towns, all places that are otherwise difficult to reach on your own.

WHEN TO GO

Cruise season runs from mid-May to late September. The most popular sailing dates are from late June through August, when warm days are plentiful, wildlife is most visible, and crowds (and prices) are at their highest. In spring, wildflowers are abundant and early fall brings the splendor of autumn colors. Cruising in these low and shoulder seasons will give you discounted fares, better availability of ships and certain cabins, and ports almost completely free of tourists. However, some excursions and establishments may not be open for the season in May or already closed for the season in September.

CRUISE ITINERARIES

Cruise ships typically follow one of two itineraries in Alaska: round-trip Inside Passage loops and one-way Inside Passage--Gulf of Alaska routes. Itineraries are usually seven days, although some lines offer longer trips. The most popular ports of call you'll most likely visit on your cruise are Juneau, Skagway, Ketchikan, and Sitka. Many itineraries also take you through Glacier Bay National Park and to some of Alaska's largest glaciers like Hubbard Glacier.

Smaller ships typically sail from Juneau or other ports, stopping at the popular towns as well as smaller, less visited villages. Some expedition vessels focus on remote beaches and fjords, with few, if any, port calls.

Most cruise lines also offer shore excursions you can book before you board. These activities best capture what a particular port is most known for, and are usually associated with local guides and companies. Not all excursions are available at all times of the year, so double-check your dates if you have anything on your must-do list.

LAND TOURS

Most cruise lines offer the option of independent, hosted, or fully escorted land tours before or after your cruise. Typical land tours can take you to Anchorage, Denali National Park, and/or Fairbanks, and many include a ride aboard the Alaska Railroad. Some cruises lines also offer tours into the Yukon.

BOOKING YOUR CRUISE

As a rule, the majority of cruisers plan their trips four to six months ahead of time. It follows, then, that a four-to-six month window should give you the best pick of sail dates, ships, itineraries, cabins, and flights to the port city. If you're looking for a standard itinerary and aren't choosy about the vessel or dates, you could wait for a last-minute discount, but they are harder to find than in the past.

WHAT'S INCLUDED

Cruise fares typically include accommodation, onboard meals and snacks, and most onboard activities. Not normally included are airfare, shore excursions, tips, soft drinks, alcoholic drinks, specialty dining, or spa treatments. Many cruise lines offer an option to add unlimited alcohol to your trip for an extra cost. Note that because single cabins for solo travelers are nonexistent on cruise ships, those traveling alone may pay twice the advertised per-person rates for a double cabin. Some cruise lines will find roommates of the same sex for singles so that each can travel at the regular per-person rate.

ABOARD THE SHIP

While you'll probably be out and about when your ship docks at a port of call, many itineraries include at least one full day at sea. Regardless of the cruise line, there are always numerous activities to keep you occupied while onboard. There are usually several different restaurants and bars, as well as a spa and several pools (yes, sometimes it does get warm enough to swim in Alaska). There's nightly entertainment, ranging from talent shows to live performances, and most cruise lines also offer different classes, games, and entertainment throughout the day. As a rule, the larger the ship, the more activities are available.

MOST POPULAR CRUISE LINES

Nearly every major cruise line offers multiple itineraires and ships in Alaska, but some of the most popular are Princess Cruises, Holland America, Norwegian Cruise Line, Celebrity Cruises, and Royal Caribbean.

SMALL SHIP CRUISING

Compact expedition-type vessels bring you right up to the shoreline to skirt the face of a glacier and pull through narrow channels where big ships don't fit. You'll see more wildlife and call into smaller ports, as well as some of the better-known towns. Enrichment talks—conducted by naturalists, Alaska Natives, and other experts—are the norm. Small-ship cruising can be pricey, as fares tend to be all-inclusive, but have few onboard charges, and, given the size of the ship, fewer opportunities for spending time on board.

Best Shore Excursions in Alaska

SNORKELING IN KETCHIKAN

With a wet suit and guide, you can spend an hour spying on the cool marine species—including sunflower and blood starfish, sea urchins, and sea cucumbers—that inhabit the calm tide pools and submerged rock walls around Mountain Point.

HELICOPTER GLACIER TREKKING IN JUNEAU

The Juneau Icefield is home to massive glaciers with awesome bright blue crevasses, and can be your landing pad when you take a scenic helicopter tour from Juneau. No experience is required, but you'll need to be in decent physical condition as you strap on mountaineering spikes and other glacier gear and explore two miles or more of steep, uneven, and visually surreal terrain. Some treks even teach you the basics of ice-wall climbing.

ROCK CLIMBING IN SKAGWAY

If you're looking for a physical challenge in the remote Alaskan wilderness, the Klondike Rock Climbing and Rappelling Adventure in Skagway definitely qualifies. After a short hike to the base of granite cliffs in the region's renowned White Pass, you'll learn the proper techniques of rock climbing and rappelling from experienced guides. There are multiple climbing routes to choose from—from easy to very difficult. The payoff is twofold: the awesome views of the Skagway River and surrounding wilderness as well as the exhilaration of rappelling back down to the base.

FISHING IN SITKA

If you love to fish, Sitka is the place to go, thanks to its location on the open ocean; anglers can catch any of five species of Pacific salmon, including prized king salmon, as well as halibut. Opt for a half-day excursion focused on trolling or mooching for salmon or book a full day to also anchor and jig for halibut. Any fish you catch can be processed, frozen, and shipped home for you to enjoy.

ATV TOUR IN KETCHIKAN

Keep your foot on the gas pedal and your eyes on the trail as you navigate an ATV over 10 miles of backcountry rain forest. There's a chance to spot local wildlife—from eagles to deer and bears—as you race over rugged terrain. Enjoy the adrenaline rush of navigating sharp curves, then swap the steering wheel for the passenger seat and enjoy the views of Tongass National Forest (the largest in the country), Behm Canal, and the Inside Passage where your ship is docked.

WHALE-WATCHING IN THE ICY STRAIT

Humpbacks or orcas—do you have a favorite? It doesn't really matter, because during a whale-watching excursion in the Icy Strait, you're likely to see both. How many and how close depends on the month, the weather, and however the whales are feeling that day. But spending three or four hours watching these magnificent creatures surface, splash, spout, bubble-feed, and even breach out of the water from any distance is pretty amazing. Sea lions, dolphins, and even bears are bonus species you might see, so bring your binoculars and have your camera ready.

MISTY FJORDS FLIGHT-SEEING TOUR IN KETCHIKAN

During a Misty Fjords Flightseeing tour, you'll soar above the huge granite cliffs, cascading waterfalls, and unspoiled wilderness of this two million-acre National Monument area located on postcard-perfect Rudyerd Bay. Depending on the tour you book, you might even land on a secluded lake where you can soak in the serenity by stepping onto the pontoon.

DOG SLEDDING ON MENDENHALL GLACIER IN JUNEAU

If you've always wanted to get behind a sled of ready-to-run Alaskan huskies and yell mush, book an authentic dog-sled adventure—even in the middle of summer—by helicoptering from Juneau to a dog sled camp on the icy-blue Mendenhall Glacier. There, you'll meet dozens of resident canines who love to run (as well as their irresistibly cute puppies) and even take the reins yourself to guide your dog team on an exhilarating sled adventure across the snow pack.

WHITE PASS TRAIN AND MOUNTAIN BIKING IN SKAGWAY

Don't let the sedate train ride from Skagway on the vintage White Pass & Yukon Route Railroad fool you. Once you've enjoyed the stunning scenery of the Skagway Valley and arrive at White Pass Summit, it will be time to put on your helmet, straddle your mountain bike, and ride back down—descending almost 3,000 thrilling feet over 15 miles along the Klondike Highway.

BEAR-WATCHING AND FLIGHTSEEING IN KETCHIKAN

Soar high above the wild landscape around Ketchikan in a float plane before landing on a lake at one of several locations where Alaskan black bears (and occasionally brown bears) congregate: Neets Bay (home to the highest black bear population per square mile in North America), Prince of Wales Island (the third-largest island in the U.S. and a known bear habitat), or Misty Fjords.

BEST BETS FOR ALASKA

Fodor's writers and editors have chosen our favorites to help you plan. Search individual chapters for more recommendations.

🍴 RESTAURANTS

BEST FOR ROMANCE

Café Cups, $$$, Ch. 5

Crow's Nest Restaurant, $$$$, Ch. 3

Crush Wine Bistro and Cellar, $$ Ch. 3

Halibut Cove Live, $$$$, Ch. 5

McCarthy Lodge, $$$$, Ch. 5

BEST DINING WITH A VIEW

Crow's Nest Restaurant, $$$$, Ch. 3

The Hangar on the Wharf, $$, Ch. 4

Kingfisher Roadhouse, $$, Ch. 5

The Saltry Restaurant, $$$, Ch. 5

Seven Glaciers, $$$$, Ch. 3

BEST FOR VEGETARIANS

229 Parks Restaurant and Tavern, $$$, Ch. 5

Ginger, $$$, Ch. 3

Organic Oasis, $$, Ch. 3

Rainbow Foods, $, Ch. 4

Thai House, $$, Ch. 6

BEST FOR MEAT-LOVERS

Black Diamond Grill, $$$, Ch. 6

Club Paris, $$$$, Ch. 3

Klondike Rib & Salmon, $$$$, Ch. 7

Old Town Burgers, $$, Ch. 5

BEST FAMILY-FRIENDLY DINING

Black Diamond Grill, $$$, Ch. 6

East Ramp Wood-fired Pizza, $, Ch. 7

Fire Island Rustic Bakeshop, $, Ch. 3

Henry's Great Alaskan Restaurant, $$, Ch. 5

The Potato, $, Ch. 5

Prospector's Historic Pizzeria and Ale House, $$, Ch. 6

BEST FOR SEAFOOD

The Cookery, $$$, Ch. 5

Denali Park Salmon Bake, $$, Ch. 6

Little Mermaid, $$$, Ch. 5

Simon & Seafort's Saloon & Grill, $$$$, Ch. 3

Tracy's King Crab Shack, $$, Ch. 4

Varly's Swiftwater Seafood Café, $$, Ch. 5

BEST FOR BREAKFAST

Diamond C Café, $, Ch. 4

La Baleine, $, Ch. 5

Le Barn Appetit, $$, Ch. 5

Gwennie's Old Alaska Restaurant, $, Ch. 3

Sam's Sourdough Café, $, Ch. 7

Snow City Café, $, Ch. 3

BEST LOCAL FAVORITES

49th State Brewing Company, $$, Ch. 6

The Moose is Loose, $, Ch. 5

Moose's Tooth Pub & Pizzeria, $$, Ch. 3

Ocean View Restaurant, $$, Ch. 4

Starfire, $$, Ch. 4

BEST HISTORIC RESTAURANTS

Ivory Jack's, $$, Ch. 7

Marx Bros. Café, $$$$, Ch. 3

Ms. Gene's Place, $$$, Ch. 5

Pump House Restaurant and Saloon, $$$$, Ch. 7

BEST ICE CREAM

Varly's Ice Cream & Pizza Parlor, $, Ch. 5

Wild Scoops, $, Ch. 3

BEST COFFEE

Alaska Coffee Roasting Company, $, Ch. 7

Bering Tea, $, Ch. 7

Heritage Coffee Company, $, Ch. 4

Highliner Coffee, $, Ch. 4

Midnight Sun Coffee Roasters, $, Ch. 7

BEST UPSCALE ($$$$)

Chart Room, $$$$, Ch. 8

Crow's Nest Restaurant, $$$$, Ch. 3

Klondike Rib & Salmon, $$$$, Ch. 7

Lavelle's Bistro, $$$$, Ch. 7

McCarthy Lodge, $$$$, Ch. 5

Pump House Restaurant and Saloon, $$$$, Ch. 7

BEST MID-RANGE ($$-$$$)

229 Parks Restaurant and Tavern, $$$, Ch. 5

Bar Harbor Restaurant, $$$, Ch. 4

Crush Wine Bistro and Cellar, $$, Ch. 3

Le Barn Appetit, $$, Ch. 5

Ludvig's Bistro, $$$, Ch. 4

BEST ON A BUDGET ($)

Baja Taco, $, Ch. 5

Coastal Cold Storage, $, Ch. 4

The Denali Doghouse, $, Ch. 6

La Baleine, $, Ch. 5

Snow City Café, $, Ch. 3

 BARS

BEST COCKTAILS

Bayview Pub, Ch. 4

The Narrows, Ch. 4

BEST LOCAL FAVORITES

Fairbanks Distilling Company, Ch. 7

Fogcutter Bar, Ch. 4

Harbor View Bar and Grill, Ch. 8

Humpy's Great Alaskan Alehouse, Ch. 3

Pioneer Bar, Ch. 4

BEST BARS WITH LIVE MUSIC

Alice's Champagne Palace, Ch. 5

Howling Dog Saloon, Ch. 7

BEST BREWERIES

49th State Brewing Company, Ch. 3 and 6

Anchorage Brewing Company, Ch. 3

Denali Brewing Company Twister Creek Restaurant, Ch. 5

Glacier Brewhouse, Ch. 3

Silver Gulch Brewing and Bottling Co., Ch. 7

HooDoo Brewing Co., Ch. 7

Skagway Brewing Company, Ch. 4

BEST SPOTS FOR DANCING

Chilkoot Charlie's, Ch. 3

BEST HAPPY HOURS

Kinley's Restaurant & Bar, Ch. 3

BEST HISTORIC BARS

Alaskan Hotel Bar, Ch. 4

Red Dog Saloon, Ch. 4

Red Onion Saloon, Ch. 4

🛏 HOTELS

BEST FOR FAMILIES

Bentley's B&B, $$$, Ch. 8

Chatanika Lodge, $, Ch. 7

Comfort Inn Downtown Ship Creek, $$$, Ch. 3

Tonglen Lake Lodge, $$$$, Ch. 6

Triple J Hotel & Cabins, $$, Ch. 7

BEST B&BS

Alaska's Capital Inn, $$$$, Ch. 4

Aurora Express, $$$, Ch. 7

Denali Dome Home, $$$, Ch. 6

Pioneer Ridge Bed and Breakfast, $$, Ch. 5

BEST VIEWS

The Cliffhanger, $$$$, Ch. 4

The Hotel Alyeska, $$$$, Ch. 3

Hotel Captain Cook, $$$$, Ch. 3

Susitna River Lodging, $$, Ch. 5

Westmark Anchorage Hotel, $$$, Ch. 3

BEST HISTORIC

Alaska's Capital Inn, $$$$, Ch. 4

Gwin's Lodge, $$, Ch. 5

Historic Anchorage Hotel, $$$, Ch. 3

Hotel Halsingland, $$, Ch. 4

Manley Roadhouse, $, Ch. 7

Talkeetna Roadhouse, $, Ch. 5

BEST LOCATIONS

Glacier Bay Lodge, $$$, Ch. 4

Teddy's Inn the Woods, $$, Ch. 5

Susitna River Lodging, $$, Ch. 5

Kennicott Glacier Lodge, $$, Ch. 5

Camp Denali and North Face Lodge, $$$$, Ch. 6

BEST ALL-INCLUSIVE

Favorite Bay Lodge, $$$$, Ch. 4

Silver Salmon Creek Lodge, $$$$, Ch. 5

Waterfall Resort, $$$$, Ch. 4

Wild Strawberry Lodge, $$$$, Ch. 4

Winterlake Lodge, $$$$, Ch. 5

BEST LUXURY ($$$$)

Hotel Captain Cook, $$$$, Ch. 3

Pearson's Pond Luxury Inn and Adventure Spa, $$$$, Ch. 4

Prince William Sound Lodge, $$$$, Ch. 5

Tutka Bay Lodge, $$$$, Ch. 5

Brooks Lodge, $$$$, Ch. 7

BEST MID-RANGE ($$-$$$)

Orca Adventure Lodge, $$, Ch. 5

Teddy's Inn the Woods, $$, Ch. 5

The Inn at Tern lake, $$, Ch. 5

EarthSong Lodge, $$$, Ch. 6

Wedgewood Resort, $$$, Ch. 7

BEST ON A BUDGET ($-$$)

Beach Road House, $, Ch. 4

Colony Inn, $, Ch. 5

Copper River Princess Wilderness Lodge, $, Ch. 5

U.S. Forest Service Cabins, $, Ch. 4

White Sulphur Springs Cabin, $, Ch. 4

Alaska Today

POLITICS

Alaska's politics and policies seem as wild as its vast, untamed acres. From the Iditarod to cabin building, everything in Alaska is steeped in politics—there are more politicians per capita than police officers. The largest state in the nation comes with a seemingly limitless supply of natural resources, and with them come conflict and controversy. Alaska's politics are thus saddled with numerous fiscal and environmental responsibilities, none of which are easily met. Before it entered statehood in 1959, Alaska had been reviled as Seward's Folly; and for nearly 50 years of statehood, it was often overlooked in the political media. Since then, certain instances of kept Alaska politics in the limelight: then-governor Sarah Palin was tapped to be the 2008 presidential running mate, current Senator Lisa Murkowski continues to be an occasional swing vote in the Senate, and an increasing need for Alaskan oil continues to shape climate change policy.

Gas and mining corporations have enormous influence on public policy in Alaska, but not without push-back from environmentalists and subsistence advocates. There are ongoing and highly publicized battles over proposed mines and offshore oil drilling. Also in the media spotlight is the Arctic National Wildlife Refuge (ANWR), 19.2 million roadless acres supporting 45 species of land and marine mammals, 36 species of fish, and 180 species of birds. ANWR is in the northeast corner of the state and has been dubbed the Last Great Wilderness. The only way to get there is by bush plane. In 2015, then-President Obama proposed new protections for parts of ANWR to Congress, which sparked much national and statewide debate. Area 1002, which consists of 1.5 million acres along the refuge's coastal plain, is thought to contain a large supply of oil that the state would like to explore. President Trump is currently making moves to open the refuge for oil drilling, much to the dismay of environmental activists.

ECONOMICS

More than 75 percent of Alaska's revenue is derived from oil extraction. The state is also the nation's leader in commercial fishing, but ranks dead last in number of farms and farm products. There is very little manufacturing in the state. Thus the cost of manufactured goods, produce, and other foodstuffs is considerably higher than in other states.

Because Alaska is predominantly composed of rural villages, thousands of miles from any distribution center, the cost of living is relatively high. In some cities in the Bush, for instance, one can expect to pay $10 for a gallon of milk.

The Permanent Fund Dividend (PFD) is a sacred check that Alaskans receive once a year, and for many in the Bush it can be a lifesaver. In 1977 the fund was created to receive 25% of Alaska's oil royalty income. It was designed to maintain a state income even after the reserves had been tapped out. Residents receive a check every October in amounts that vary from year to year, but are in the ballpark of $1,200. Every bit helps; in recent years, rural and remote Alaska has seen heating fuel go as high as $10 per gallon.

CLIMATE CHANGE

In Alaska few people disagree that the glaciers and permafrost are melting; it's just a fact. Warmer temperatures means new economic opportunities and financial challenges. As the Arctic ice melts, the region is becoming more accessible, which means there is greater possibility for more oil and gas exploration. However, as temperatures rise, so does the ocean. The village of Kivalina, a remote whaling community of almost 400 inhabitants, is under immediate threat as the water rises and the coast erodes. Relocation of Kivalina's residents must happen, but the cost is high both financially and for these people's history and way of life.

Many Native tribes in the Arctic region have begun to adapt to the changes that global warming has impressed upon them. Their hunting patterns have adjusted to new migration times and routes. Unfortunately permafrost, the frozen ground they live upon, is also melting. Towns and villages are sinking, and the cost of relocation could rise into the billions of dollars. Groups like the Army Corps of Engineers, social artists, and political and environmental activists are scrambling to save the villages, the people, and their cultures.

THE ARTS

Visitors are often surprised to find that Alaska is filled with an impressive number of talented contemporary artists. Not only do some of the world's foremost artists, writers, and photographers reside in Alaska, there is equal talent found among those whose work never sees the Outside. For many Alaskans the long, dark winter is a great time to hunker down, season their craft, and prepare to sell their wares in the summer at galleries, museums, and theaters all over the state. In summer, weekend outdoor markets are also an excellent place to find local and Native talent. Look for the "Made in Alaska" sticker or the silver hand symbol for authenticity.

SPORTS

In a state full of renegades and thrill seekers, it is no wonder that the biggest sporting event of the year occasionally requires a racer to permanently relinquish feeling in a finger or foot. The Iditarod Trail Sled Dog Race, a 1,149-mile-long trek, is by far the most popular sporting event in Alaska. It began in 1973 in homage to the brave souls who ventured to Nome in 1925 to take medicine to villagers struck with one of the worst outbreaks of diphtheria ever recorded. Nowadays, more than 100 racers and their packs of canines converge on the ice and snow on the first Saturday in March to race from Anchorage to Nome. The sport is not without controversy; high-profile mushers have come under scrutiny since several groups have made allegations of animal cruelty.

Although Alaskans from all over the state are passionate about their dog mushers, the most popular sport is basketball. Even as far north as Utqiaġvik (where it is most popular), one can find basketball courts both inside and outside. The most popular urban team sport is ice hockey.

Alaska's History

THE FIRST PEOPLE

No one knows for sure when humans first began living in the northwest corner of the North American continent. How and when they arrived is still a subject of great controversy and debate. One popular theory is that 12,000 years ago humans followed the eastern migration of Ice Age mammals over the Bering Land Bridge, a 600-mile-wide stretch of land that connected present-day Alaska to Siberia. To date, the oldest human remains found in Alaska are 11,500 years old, the second-oldest Ice Age remains to be found in the world. Found in Central Alaska near the Tanana River, the remains of a three-year-old girl are thought to be those of an Athabascan ancestral relative.

No matter when humans first arrived, by 1750, there were only 57,300 Native peoples living in Russian Alaska, including Aleuts, Alutiiqs, Yup'iks, Inupiaqs, Athabascan, Tlingit, and Haida; many had been killed by disease and Russian traders. Notably, according to the U.S. Census, today there are more than 100,000 American Indians and Alaska Natives living in the state.

RUSSIANS IN ALASKA

It wasn't until 1741 that Danish navigator Vitus Bering, under Russian rule, made the Alaska region known to to his fellow European explorers. Bering died before he could ever explore the continent further or return to Russia.

Politically speaking, Russia then imposed itself on Alaska to varying degrees. It was the arrival of the promyshlenniki, or fur hunters, that had the biggest impact on the Native cultures. By most accounts, the hunters were illiterate, quarrelsome, hard drinking, and virtually out of control. They penetrated the Aleutian chain and made themselves masters of the islands and their inhabitants,

the Aleuts. Several times the Natives revolted; their attempts were squelched, and they were brutalized.

By 1790 the small fur traders were replaced by large Russian companies. Siberian fur trader Aleksandr Andreyevich Baranov became manager of a fur-trading company and director of a settlement on Kodiak Island in 1791. He essentially governed all Russian activities in North America until 1818, when he was ordered back to Russia. Word was spreading to the Russian government that foreigners, particularly Americans, were gaining a disproportionate share of the Alaskan market. The Russian Navy was ordered to assume control of Alaska, and by 1821 it had barred all foreign ships from entering Alaskan waters. Russia created new policies forbidding any trade with non-Russians and requiring that the colonies be supplied solely by Russian ships.

The 1853 Crimean War between Imperial Russia and Britain and France put a great financial burden on Russia. It fiscally behooved the country to sell Russian Alaska. In 1867, under a treaty signed by U.S. Secretary of State William H. Seward, Alaska was sold to the United States for $7.2 million. On October 18, 1867, the territory officially changed hands. Newspapers around the nation hailed the purchase of Alaska as "Seward's Folly." Within 30 years, however, one of the biggest gold strikes in the world would bring hundreds of thousands of people to this U.S. territory.

THE GOLD RUSH

The great Klondike gold discoveries of 1896 gained national (and worldwide) attention. Due to the depression of 1893, the need for food, money, and hope sparked a gold fever unmatched in history. Men and women alike clamored for information about Alaska, not realizing that the Klondike was in the Yukon Territory of Canada. Perhaps if they'd known their geography, Alaska would never have become the state that it is now.

The most popular route for the gold stampeders was to go entirely by water. It wasn't cheaper, but it was far easier than taking the inland route. They would start in either San Francisco or Seattle, buy passage on a steamship, and disembark more than 1,000 nautical miles later in Skagway, Alaska. No gold was in Skagway, but overnight it became a city of 20,000 miners. Gold-seekers used it as a place to negotiate and get ready for the only part of their journey that would be traversed on foot. The Chilkoot Trail was 35 challenging miles that were too rugged for packhorses. The hardest part of the journey was the climb to the summit, Chilkoot Pass. This climb was known as the Golden Staircase, a ¾-mile hike on a 45-degree incline. Chilkoot Pass was the gateway to Canada and the point at which the Canadian government required each person entering the territory to have at least a year's supply (approximately 1 ton) of food. This is partially why it took most stampeders one to three months to travel this 35-mile stretch. At the base of the Golden Staircase, stampeders had everything they were taking over the pass weighed, and were charged $1 per pound. Once into Canada, they built boats and floated the remaining 600 miles to Dawson City, where the gold rush was taking place. By 1899 the Yukon gold rush was over, however, and the population of Skagway shrank dramatically.

Alaska experienced its own gold strike in Nome, on the Seward Peninsula, in 1898. The fever didn't actually hit until 1900, but, because it did, gold mining all over Alaska began to get national attention.

WORLD WAR II

In 1942, after the United States entered the war, the War Production Board deemed gold mining nonessential to the war effort, and forced gold mining all over the country to come to a halt. Despite this, World War II was financially beneficial to parts of Alaska. Numerous bases and ports were strategically built around the state, and the Alaska Highway was created to help deliver supplies to them.

The only time Alaska had any direct involvement with the war was in June 1942, when the Japanese attacked Attu and Kiska islands in the Aleutian chain. The attack has been recorded in history as an "incident," but it had a great impact on many lives; a few hundred casualties occurred due to friendly fire. Nearly a thousand inhabitants were relocated and many died in the process.

STATEHOOD

On January 3, 1959, "Seward's Folly" became the 49th state in the nation—more than 100 years after Seward first visited. Soon, a mass of investors, bold entrepreneurs, tourists, and land grabbers began to arrive. It's still a new state, far from direct scrutiny by the rest of the nation. With a constantly growing, competitive industry of oil and other natural resources, Alaska has made an identity for itself that resembles that of no other state in the nation. It boasts the second-highest production of gas and oil in the country, is twice the size of the second-largest state, and has millions of lakes, minimal pollution, and endless possibilities.

What to Read and Watch Before Your Trip

ORDINARY WOLVES BY SETH KANTNER

A heartbreaking and beautiful novel from the far north, Seth Kantner's story follows the life of Cutuk Hawcley, who, like Kantner, is raised in a sod igloo in Alaska's Arctic region.

INTO THE WILD BY JON KRAKAUER

Arguably the most controversial and divisive story to come out of the state in the last 25 years, Jon Krakauer's book (and the subsequent 2007 film adaptation) examines the life and travels of Chris McCandless, whose adventures hitchhiking to Alaska and living in Denali National Park eventually led to his demise.

CALL OF THE WILD BY JACK LONDON

Inspired by Jack London's time in the Yukon, this 1903 adventure novel follows a husky named Buck who is kidnapped from his home in California and sent north to become a sled dog.

THE SNOW CHILD BY EOWYN IVEY

Set in the 1920s, *The Snow Child* is the story of a childless homesteading couple whose lives are turned upside down by the sudden appearance of a mysterious little girl who seems capable of surviving alone in the harsh wilderness.

HYPERBOREAL BY JOAN NAVIYUK KANE

Written in both English and the writer's native Inupiaq, Hyperboreal is a collection of poetry that captures the beauty of Alaska's far north.

BLONDE INDIAN BY ERNESTINE HAYES

A real and at times sobering examination of Alaska's Native population since the arrival of Europeans, Ernestine Hayes's memoir is required reading for those wishing to confront the recent struggles and issues of the state.

WILD ALASKA'S NATIONAL PARKS

This documentary from National Geographic provides a great introduction to Alaska's national parks including Denali, Katmai, and Glacier Bay.

BETWEEN EARTH & SKY

From melting permafrost to depleting salmon stocks to whole villages falling into the sea, Paul Allen Hunton's documentary examines Alaska's role on the frontlines of the fight against climate change and what we can do to make this region habitable for the generations to follow.

GRIZZLY MAN

In this acclaimed documentary, Werner Herzog examines the life of Timothy Treadwell, a self-proclaimed grizzly bear expert who spent several summers in the Alaskan Bush communing with and carrying on one-way conversations with multiple bears before being killed by a grizzly in 2003.

BALTO

This 1995 animated classic captures the spirit of adventure and heroism in Alaskan dog-sledding with a very fictionalized tale of the sled dog who led the journey to deliver medicine to Nome, Alaska during the 1925 diphtheria outbreak (the inspiration for the Iditarod).

NORTHERN EXPOSURE

A fish-out-of-water tale of a New York City doctor who finds himself in a quirky small town in Alaska, this television show aired for six seasons in the 1990s and was inspired by the equally quirky town of Talkeetna, Alaska.

DEADLIEST CATCH

This popular documentary series highlights the dangers faced by the fishing crews based in Dutch Harbor, Alaska, as they search for king crabs on the Bering Sea.

Chapter 2

TRAVEL SMART ALASKA

2

Updated by
Amy Fletcher

★ **CAPITAL**
Juneau

👥 **POPULATION**
739,795

💬 **LANGUAGE**
English; multiple Native
languages

$ **CURRENCY**
U.S. dollar

☎ **AREA CODES**
907, 250

⚠ **EMERGENCIES**
911

🚗 **DRIVING**
On the right

⚡ **ELECTRICITY**
120-240 v/60 cycles;
plugs have two or three
rectangular prongs

🕐 **TIME**
Four hours behind New York

🌐 **WEB RESOURCES**
www.travelalaska.com
www.alaskamagazine.com
www.alaskanative.net
www.alaskageographic.org

What You Need to Know Before You Visit Alaska

PLACES CAN BE MUCH MORE DIFFICULT TO REACH THAN YOU THINK.

Most of Alaska's hidden gems are located far from the main highway system, which sometimes means they are completely inaccessible via cars or buses. In addition, many smaller communities and towns don't have runways big enough for standard domestic airplanes. Instead, small bush planes or Alaska state ferries are the best ways to reach these out-of-the-way places. Be aware that ferry service doesn't run every day, and anyone with a fear of flying won't be thrilled by the small planes that typically transfer passengers to these towns. Also keep in mind that except for Skagway and Haines, none of the major cities and towns in southeast Alaska (including the state capital of Juneau) are accessible by roads; they can only be reached via plane, cruise ship, or ferry.

IT CAN BE COLD, EVEN IN THE MIDDLE OF THE SUMMER.

While some places in Alaska's interior can hit the high 80s during the summer, odds are you won't be wearing shorts and t-shirts most of the time. On overcast days or along coastal regions, the temperature rarely cracks 70 degrees. Combine that with a little bit of wind (not uncommon near the water or in the mountains) and things can get downright chilly. Be prepared with plenty of warm layers, including hats and gloves. Also, always be prepared for rain, as sudden storms are common year-round. On the flip side, you should always pack sunscreen, even if the temperature is cool. Sunglasses are also essential, especially when visiting glaciers.

RESPECTING WILDLIFE IS CRUCIAL.

Alaska is indeed as untamed as you might imagine, and sightings of wild animals are common, especially in national and state parks and reserves. Be respectful of any animals you encounter, and be sure to keep your distance as much as possible. If you spot a bear, make your presence known by talking, singing, or clapping (bears don't like noise). If you encounter a bear at close range, don't run. Make yourself as big as possible and talk in a normal voice. If a brown bear attacks you, play dead. If a black bear attacks you, you are better off fighting back with anything you can find.

DON'T GET OVERCONFI-DENT ABOUT YOUR HIKING SKILLS.

Travelers lacking outdoor experience need to take precautions when venturing away from the beaten path in national and state parks. Hiking and camping in Alaska can be an amazing experience, but also challenging and sometimes dangerous. If you lack backcountry experience, hire a guide or go on a guided group tour.

BE PREPARED FOR A LOT OF SUN, OR NONE AT ALL.

The light (or lack thereof) is one of Alaska's most dynamic characteristics. Because of its location on the Earth's axis, during summer, parts of Alaska see nearly 24 hours of daylight (the farther north you go, the more sunlight you get). However, in winter, this means some places have several months of total darkness (luckily this makes for some amazing Northern Lights viewing). Once again, the farther north you go, the more darkness you get.

ALCOHOL MIGHT BE HARD TO FIND.

The drinking age in Alaska is 21, but keep in mind that alcoholism is a devastating problem in many rural areas, and because of this, many Bush communities do not sell it and some do not allow it at all. Check the rules before flying into a Bush community with alcohol, as it is possible to be charged with illegally importing it.

WEED IS LEGAL HERE.

Recreational marijuana became legal in Alaska for people over 21 in 2014. Several dispensaries have opened since then, and visitors are allowed to buy and carry up to one ounce of marijuana at a time. Like with cigarettes, it is still illegal to smoke in most indoor public places and all national parks. Unlike cigarettes, it is still illegal to consume marijuana on public streets (you'll get a $100 fine if you're caught doing so).

THERE ARE TWO STATE HOLIDAYS.

In addition to standard national holidays, Alaska also celebrates Alaska Day on October 18th and Seward's Day on the last Monday in March. Some businesses and government offices might be closed on these days, while others (especially museums and national parks) might be more crowded than usual.

IN SUMMER, MOSQUITOS ARE EVERYWHERE.

Alaskan summers are infamous for their mosquitos. If traveling in the summer, be sure to bring insect repellent; mosquito coils may helpful if you are camping or staying in remote cabins. Head nets can also be a wise purchase.

THERE'S NO SALES TAX (KIND OF).

Alaska does not impose a state sales tax, but individual cities and boroughs have their own taxes (except for Anchorage).

OUTSIDE OF CITY CENTERS, CELL PHONE SERVICE ISN'T ALWAYS RELIABLE.

It can be easy to take access to a cell phone network for granted in the Lower 48, but you'll quickly learn this isn't always the case in Alaska, where remote stretches of highway or treks into the mountains will often take you out of the range of service. Make sure you have physical back-ups of directions, itinerary numbers, and anything else you might need before you leave.

DON'T EXPECT TO SEE EVERYTHING.

Alaska's scenery and wildlife is varied and spectacular, but it's also unpredictable so be wary of unrealistic expectations. Weather, uncooperative animals, and other factors will likely prevent you from seeing everything on your checklist. It's possible you won't see bears or moose during your trip at all or that Denali itself will be covered in clouds. Helicopter and small plane tours are often canceled or postponed due to high wind speeds. Don't let this get you down; the challenge will make the wildlife and views you are lucky enough to experience all the more special.

SEAFOOD IS PLENTIFUL, BUT EXPENSIVE.

Alaska is renowned for its natural resources, but the majority of Alaska's commercially harvested fish is exported. The seafood that remains in the state is mostly marketed to visitors (locals are perfectly happy to go out and catch their own) and priced accordingly.

YOU'LL HAVE A HARD TIME FINDING WILD GAME.

While seafood is attainable, Alaska's wild game like elk and caribou is not so easily sampled. Specific laws forbid its commercial sale; the closest you can get is domesticated reindeer. There's no good way around this restriction (although a rising farm-to-table movement means an increasing number of restaurants offer exotic Alaska-raised meats like yak). Your best bet is to make some friends around the campfire and hope to be offered a sample.

WHEN CAMPING OR HIKING, ALWAYS FILTER UNTREATED WATER.

Alaska has a reputation as a pristine landscape with massive swathes of land untouched by humans. But no matter how clean and pristine your water source may seem, always filter untreated water before drinking it. It may be more time-consuming, but nothing ruins a trip faster than a nasty case of Giardia.

Getting Here and Around

✈ Air Travel

Alaska Airlines is the state's flagship carrier, with year-round service from its Seattle hub to Anchorage, Fairbanks, Juneau, Ketchikan, and Sitka. The airline and its subsidiary, Horizon Air, offer direct flights from Anchorage to a handful of American cities year-round, including Chicago, Las Vegas, Los Angeles, and Portland. Alaska Airlines flies to many other North American cities via Seattle or Portland. Other airlines that fly to and from the Lower 48 include American, Delta, JetBlue, and United. Note, however, that few offer nonstop flights; any nonstop flights to Alaska you do find will most likely be in the summer.

Air travel within Alaska is quite expensive, particularly to Bush destinations where flying is the only option. There are also air taxis that fly between towns or backcountry locations and smaller planes that can take you everywhere from the top of Denali to famed glaciers; these often won't fly in poor weather.

AIRPORTS
Anchorage's Ted Stevens International Airport is Alaska's main hub. There are also major airports in Fairbanks, Juneau, and Ketchikan. Sixteen other airports throughout the state also accommodate jet planes.

⛴ Boat/Ferry Travel

The ferries of the Alaska Marine Highway System will take you through some the state's most beautiful regions. These are meant for longer-haul trips, so you can reserve cabins in advance, or even camp out with tents and sleeping bags. The Inside Passage route, the most popular, stretches from Bellingham, Washington, all the way to Skagway and Haines (taking roughly 36 hours).

🚌 Bus Travel

Traveling by bus in Alaska can be more economical than traveling by train or by air, but don't count on it being your main mode of travel. Greyhound Canada, Denali Overland Transportation, and Green Tortoise are some of the most popular bus companies. Keep in mind that buses aren't an option in most of Southeast Alaska.

🚗 Car Travel

The Alaska Highway begins in British Columbia and stretches 1,442 miles through Canadian Yukon. The two-lane highway is paved for its entire length and is open year-round. Highway services are available about every 50 to 100 miles, but there are stretches where gas stations are sparser or open at limited hours, and areas where cell phone service is nonexistent, so planning ahead is crucial. The rest of the state's roads are found almost exclusively in the South Central and Interior regions. They lie mainly between Anchorage, Fairbanks, and the Canadian border.

Rental cars are plentiful in Alaska, and renting a car can be a good way to see the Interior, but note that many destinations (including major cities and towns in the Inside Passage like Juneau) cannot be reached by a car from Anchorage and the Interior. Be advised that most rental outfits don't allow you to drive on some of the unpaved roads such as the Denali Highway, the Haul Road to Prudhoe Bay, and the McCarthy Road. If your plans include any sketchy routes, make sure your rental agreement covers those areas.

Gas prices in the Anchorage area are usually higher than those in the Lower 48, and you can expect to pay even more in Juneau and Ketchikan, and far more in remote villages off the road network, where fuel must be flown in. Driving in Alaska is much less rigorous than it used to be, although it still presents some unusual obstacles. Frost damage can create potholes that require slower driving. Moose often wander onto roads and highways. If you encounter one, pull off to the side and wait for the moose to cross. Flying gravel is a hazard along the Alaska and Dalton highways, especially in summer. A bug screen will help keep gravel and kamikaze insects off the windshield, and some travelers use clear, hard plastic guards to cover their headlights.

Cruise Travel

Cruising the Inside Passage has become one of the most popular ways to see the state (not to mention one of the most popular cruise ship routes in the world). Nearly all the major cruise ship lines run trips (ranging from 5 days to 2 weeks) from May through September that take travelers past glaciers in the Inside Passage, stopping in ports of call like Haines, Skagway, Juneau, and Ketchikan.

Ride-Sharing

Uber and Lyft were only legally allowed in Alaska in 2017. Since then, major cities like Anchorage and Fairbanks have seen ridership spike, but it's best to depend on taxis in smaller towns.

Taxi Travel

Taxis within cities and larger towns are relatively dependable, although it's still better to call ahead to call for a car rather than hailing one of the street. Except for in the Bush communities, cabs can be ordered in advance for most towns in Alaska. Some popular cab companies are Alaska Yellow Cabs based in Anchorage, Arctic Taxi in Fairbanks, Alaska Cab in Kenai, and Kodiak City Cab in Kodiak.

Train Travel

The state-owned Alaska Railroad has service connecting Seward, Anchorage, Talkeetna, Denali National Park, and Fairbanks, as well as additional service connecting Anchorage with Whittier, Portage Glacier, and Spencer Glacier. The Alaska Railroad offers one of the last flagstop trains in North America, which you can hop on and off at will as you travel through roadless backcountry between Talkeetna and Hurricane Turn. Traveling by train isn't as economical as traveling by bus, but it's a wonderful way to see the scenery.

Gray Line of Alaska offers two- to seven-day packages that include luxury train travel from Anchorage to Fairbanks or vice versa, with at least a day of exploring in Denali National Park. For a scenic and historic five-hour trip between Skagway and Fraser, British Columbia, take the White Pass and Yukon Route, which follows the treacherous path taken by prospectors during the Klondike gold rush of 1897–98.

Before You Go

🌐 Passport

American travelers never need a passport to travel domestically. Non-American travelers always need a valid passport to visit Alaska. Passengers on Alaska cruises that depart from and return to the same U.S. port aren't currently required to carry a passport, but it's always a good idea to bring one if your ship travels through Canadian waters in the unlikely event that you must fly out of a Canadian airport during your trip. Note that a passport is required for certain shore excursions that cross the nearby U.S.–Canadian border.

🔖 Visa

For international travelers, a tourism visa is required for traveling to Alaska and the rest of the United States. Canadian visas are not required for shore excursions that involve crossing the Canadian/American border.

🖊 Immunizations

No specific immunizations or vaccinations are required for visits to Alaska.

📅 When to Go

HIGH SEASON $$$$
June through August is the height of cruise season, and when all operators and businesses are open. Crowds (and mosquitos) are high, but so are the temperature and sunshine (thanks to that midnight sun).

LOW SEASON $
Not all of Alaska has the fierce winters that people expect (the southeast and south central regions are actually quite mild), but no matter where you go, expect that many, if not nearly all, operators and business will be closed for the season. And of course, during the winter some towns do experience frigid temperatures and nearly 24 hours of darkness (this is especially true the farther north you travel).

VALUE SEASON $$
Fall can be quite lovely in Alaska, with temperatures and sunshine still high in September and October. Most operators will start to close up shop sometime in September, with most closing for the season by late September. October is the most affordable time to go that still gives you pleasant weather, but you won't have as many options for restaurants and hotels. April and May can be an equally lovely and affordable time to visit, but most operators and seasonal shops don't re-open for the season until the end of May.

➕ Safety

Cities in Alaska are generally safe and welcoming; as always, be sure to use common sense. The biggest dangers in the state are in the great outdoors, so be smart, responsible, and travel with a guide if you are not prepared for the realities of camping and the wilderness. Female solo travelers should feel safe, especially when traveling in tour groups. Cities like Anchorage and Fairbanks are LGBTQ-friendly, although not quite as much as their Lower 48 counterparts. While travelers should have no reason to feel unsafe, most other towns do not have openly gay communities, and LGBTQ travelers should especially exercise discretion in rural communities.

What to Pack for Alaska

WATERPROOF OR WATER-RESISTANT FOOTWEAR

Wherever your Alaskan travels take you, it's a good bet you'll encounter plenty of moisture. Even if most of your trip is spent on concrete, you'll still need to avoid wet feet. A cursory glance at any local and their brown-booted uniform (called the *xtratuf*) serves as a reminder of the importance of dry feet here. If you don't feel like purchasing and packing a big pair of boots, at least make sure your hiking shoes are water resistant.

SUNSCREEN AND HAT

While locals may wear their sunburned arms and ears like badges of honor, a nasty burn can torpedo the best-laid plans. You'll probably be wearing long sleeves so you won't need too much, but bring along a small container of sunscreen to protect the most sensitive areas. This is especially true if you plan on spending time on the water. Water will reflect the sun and can burn twice as fast.

BUG NET AND BUG SPRAY

The scourges of the Alaskan wilderness are the mosquitoes, no-see-ums, horseflies, white sox, and other six-legged pests that populate the state. For those who plan on backpacking or camping, a bug net is essential. Bug nets and spray take up very little space, but could very well be the most important items you bring.

WOOL OR SIMILAR CLOTHING

Packing clothes for Alaska can be difficult. More times than not, it's necessary to pack for all four seasons. You can mitigate this by leaving your cotton clothing at home and instead packing wool, polyester, or similar materials that wick away water and retain heat when wet. Layering these items along with a waterproof outer shell will make you as prepared as possible for any weather.

RAIN JACKETS, RAIN PANTS, AND WATERPROOF CASES

Wool and similar materials are all well and good, but they don't do much in a driving rainstorm. Don't scrimp on your raingear. Bring battle-tested gear that has either stitched seams and nylon fabric or is rubberized. Rubberized gear doesn't breathe as well as lighter shells, but you'll be glad you have it if the rain starts pouring. Also consider bringing an Otter Box or similar item to protect your phone and other electronics.

BINOCULARS

For most visitors, a trip to Alaska isn't complete without wildlife sightings. But these encounters aren't always right outside your window or along the trail. Whether you're scanning the tundra for grizzlies or the water for whales, a quality, sturdy, and waterproof pair of binoculars are worth their weight in gold. If you'll be on the water, consider attaching a small flotation device to the straps just in case.

BEAR SPRAY AND BEAR-PROOF CONTAINERS

This is a tricky one, as airplane companies are understandably hesitant to allow cans of concentrated mace in an enclosed environment traveling at 30,000 feet. Bear spray is also a semi-expensive purchase (expect to pay around $50). But think of it as traveler's insurance. Whether you plan on backpacking or just doing some hiking, the entire state is bear country. And while bear attacks are relatively rare, bear spray is statistically the safest deterrent. If nothing else, you can always purchase some when you arrive. If you're planning on camping, you will definitely need bear-proof containers for your food.

Essentials

🛏 Lodging

Alaskan hotels and motels are similar in quality to those in the Lower 48; you'll find many well-known chains in Anchorage and Fairbanks. Nearly every town (with the exception of Bush villages) has at least one B&B, and dozens of choices are available in larger cities. Westmark Hotels is a regional chain, owned by cruise-tour operator Holland America, with hotels in Anchorage, Fairbanks, Juneau, Sitka, Skagway, and near the entrance to Denali National Park, plus Dawson City and Whitehorse in Canada's Yukon Territory. Princess Tours owns a luxury hotel in Fairbanks and lodges outside Denali National Park, in Denali State Park, near Wrangell–St. Elias National Park, and on the Kenai Peninsula. The most unique way to stay in Alaska is at a wilderness lodge; most stays include all meals and a variety of outings (and can be quite expensive).

Off-season hotel rates are often much lower, but most travelers prefer to visit Alaska in summer, when days are long and temperatures are mild. During the shoulder season (early May and late September) travelers may find slightly lower rates, but some businesses and attractions may be closed.

🍴 Dining

Alaska is best known for its seafood, particularly king salmon, halibut, king crab, and shrimp. At the open-air (and often all-you-can-eat) salmon bakes in Juneau, Tok, Denali National Park, and Fairbanks, you can expect excellent grilled salmon and halibut. Anchorage has the greatest diversity of restaurants, including sophisticated fine dining, noisy brewpubs, fresh sushi, and a wide variety of international cuisines.

PAYING
Credit cards are widely accepted in resort restaurants and in many restaurants in major towns like Anchorage. Many small towns have only one or two eateries; some do not take credit cards.

RESERVATIONS AND DRESS
During summer high season, make reservations as soon as and wherever possible, especially in the Southeast. For popular restaurants, books as far ahead as you can (often 30 days). In terms of dress codes, Alaska is a casual place. Cruise ships are probably the only places you'll encounter formal wear, though some of the pricier lodges have dress codes for dinner.

🍸 Nightlife

Even in its major cities, nightlife in Alaska is mostly just bars and pubs, but the state has become known for some excellent microbrewies, including Denali Brewing, Skagway Brewing, and Moose's Tooth Brewing Co. You'll find some great popular brewpubs in Anchorage, Fairbanks, Haines, and Skagway, among others.

🛍 Shopping

Alaska is not quite the place for Fifth Avenue–level shopping, but you will find some gorgeous Native crafts. Everything from intricate Aleut baskets and Athabascan birch-bark statues to Inupiaq ivory carvings and Tlingit totems are for sale. Cruise ship ports like Juneau and Skagway are well-known for jewelry and souvenir stores that cater to cruise ship passengers. Locally owned boutiques can also be found throughout the state.

▶ Performing and Visual Arts

Anchorage and Fairbanks have some decent performing arts selections, with everything from theater to opera available. Juneau also has a blossoming contemporary art scene, but the best art scene in the state comes from the rich Native culture, reflected in the abundance of craft traditions.

▶ Activities

Nature is Alaska's greatest tourism draw, with eight national parks and multiple state parks and reserves for visitors to explore. Throughout the state you'll find plenty of opportunities for hiking, biking, mountain-climbing, bird-watching, kayaking, fishing, whitewater rafting, boating, glacier-trekking, and flightseeing.

Sadly, no major league sports team calls Alaska home just yet. Basketball is the most popular sport in the state, with ice hockey following close behind (college ice hockey gets the most attention). The biggest sport event of the state is the Iditarod Trail Sled Dog Race, a 1,149-mile-long trek that sees over 100 racers and their packs of canines race from Anchorage to Nome.

▶ Tipping

Tour-bus drivers who offer a particularly informative trip generally receive a tip from passengers at the end of the tour. Fishing guides are commonly tipped 10 percent, and gratuities may also be given to pilots following a particularly good flightseeing trip.

Tipping Guidelines

Bartender	$1–$5 per round of drinks, depending on the number of drinks
Bellhop	$1–$5 per bag, depending on the level of the hotel
Coat Check	$1–$2 per item checked unless there is a fee, then nothing
Hotel Concierge	$5 or more, if he or she performs a service for you
Hotel Doorman	$1–$2 if he helps you get a cab
Hotel Maid	$1–$3 a day (either daily or at the end of your stay, in cash)
Hotel Room-Service Waiter	$1–$2 per delivery, even if a service charge has been added
Porter at Airport or Train Station	$1 per bag
Restroom Attendants	Small change or $1 in more expensive restaurants
Skycap at Airport	$1–$3 per bag checked
Taxi Driver	15%–20%, but round up the fare to the next dollar amount
Tour Guide	10% of the cost of the tour
Valet Parking Attendant	$1–$2, but only when you get your car
Waiter	15%–20%, with 20% being the norm at high-end restaurants; nothing additional if a service charge is added to the bill

Great Itineraries

The Best of the Inside Passage, 7 Days

The Inside Passage is the second-longest and-deepest fjord in the world, and a ride on the ferry up the Passage during summer months offers fantastic views of waterfalls and sharp peaks cascading into the ocean; it can be a great way to spot orcas and humpback whales.

DAY 1: JUNEAU

Kick off your journey in Juneau, where you'll have to arrive by plane or boat, as there aren't any roads to it. Stay at Alaska's Capital Inn, a bed-and-breakfast far away from the cruise-ship traffic. Be sure to book in advance, as this place is popular with returning visitors.

Once you're settled into your quarters, take a ride on the Mt. Roberts Tramway, which takes you on a beautiful six-minute ride up the side of Mt. Roberts. Once you reach the top, you can spend a few hours hiking on the nearby trails, learning about the history of the Tlingit people, and spotting bald eagles. Afterward, head into downtown Juneau and peruse the shops and galleries, many of which specialize in original local art.

Finish the day with dinner at Tracy's King Crab Shack by enjoying some—what else—Alaskan king crab. An after-dinner drink at the touristy but famed Red Dog Saloon (one of Juneau's most historic bars since its opening in 1890) is another must.

DAY 2: MENDENHALL GLACIER
(Excursion takes approximately 5 hours)

One of Juneau's most popular attractions, Mendenhall Glacier, is nestled right up against the town. Whether you arrive by boat or plane, you can't miss it as you approach the capital city. The glacier sits at the back of the icy blue Mendenhall Lake. Several companies lead bus tours to the glacier, but Alaska Boat & Kayak Shop offers shuttle service from downtown Juneau as well as kayak rentals. Kayak across the lake and up close to icebergs that have calved off the glacier, or hit the trails and hike up to the waterfalls.

Grab lunch before checking out of the inn. Board an afternoon or early-evening flight to Gustavus on Wings of Alaska.

DAYS 3 AND 4: GLACIER BAY NATIONAL PARK
(25 minutes by plane from Juneau; 4½ hours by ferry)

Located at the northern tip of the Inside Passage, Glacier Bay National Park is one of the country's most awe-inspiring national treasures. Stay at the Glacier Bay Lodge, the only accommodation located inside the park. The lodge can arrange a daylong boat excursion that will take you past hundreds of lush green islands and straight up to the calving glaciers. Some excursions allow you to disembark and kayak around the glaciers for a couple of hours.

Or take a kayaking adventure like none you've ever had before. Experienced guides can be hired for multiday excursions that paddle all the way to the calving glaciers. Regardless of how far you paddle, the experience is incredibly rewarding. Though the lodge does rent solo kayaks, unless you are a very experienced sea kayaker, we recommend taking a tour.

Whichever way you decide to explore the park, you'll find great comfort in the hot meals and comfy beds at the end of the day.

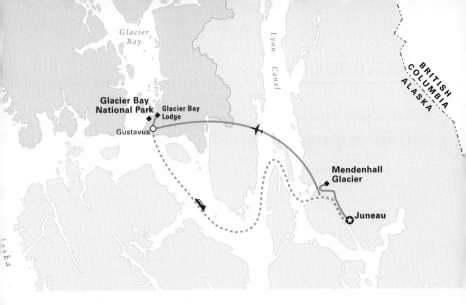

If you're only spending one night at the park, get up early on the day of your departure and set out on any of a number of great hikes that begin at the lodge. If you have time, consider tacking on a few extra days.

DAY 5: RETURN TO JUNEAU
(4½ hours by ferry from Glacier Bay)

The ferry departs Gustavus at different times depending on the day of the week, but it's usually before 3 pm.

Stay at the Silverbow Inn, in the heart of downtown. The location offers quick access to nature trails, the beach, and to the Douglas Island walkway. If you get back from Gustavus in time, drive or take the bus to Douglas Island. If you're visiting between September and May, try to catch a show at Perseverance Theatre, renowned for its great set designs and talented casts.

DAY 6: HIKING AROUND JUNEAU
On your last day in Juneau, get out and see some of the countryside. One of the locals' favorite hikes is Perseverance Trail. To get here, follow Gold Street until it turns into 8th Street. Follow 8th until it dead-ends at Basin Road. Take a left and keep walking until you get to the trail.

This 3-mile trail (one way) takes about three to four hours to hike.

After your hike, grab lunch at any of the many eateries around downtown Juneau, like Twisted Fish Company. Then immerse yourself in history at the Alaska State Museum, sample some of the locally brewed beer at Hangar on the Wharf, or take one last stroll along the waterfront.

DAY 7: TAKE OFF FOR HOME
Head to the airport for your flight back.

Great Itineraries

Ketchikan and the Inside Passage, 7 Days

Hands down, the best way to experience the Inside Passage is by boat. For visitors and locals, the ferry is the number one choice for traversing the fjord; it's economical, relaxing, and offers tremendous views. To optimize your time and cover more distance, fly some legs of the trip. Don't worry, this won't compromise your sightseeing: a bird's-eye view from your plane window is breathtaking, and not to be missed.

DAYS 1 AND 2: KETCHIKAN

Fly directly into Ketchikan and stay at the Black Bear Inn, an elegant, affordable waterfront B&B. It's highly regarded, so be sure to book well in advance.

Get settled in and take a day trip on a catamaran by Alaska Travel Adventures to the awe-inspiring Misty Fiords National Monument. The Ketchikan area is known for its salmon fishing, so if you're interested in catching your own dinner, book a day trip that includes fishing.

On your second day, acquaint yourself with the beautiful town of Ketchikan. This charming community is known for its contemporary and traditional Native art. Spend a few hours walking through the town's two famous totem pole parks, Totem Bight and Saxman Totem Pole Park. Stop in at the Soho Coho Gallery, owned by well-known Alaskan artist Ray Troll, where you'll find an array of locally made collectibles. And don't miss the Ketchikan Arts and Humanities Council's Main Street Gallery.

DAY 3: WRANGELL
(6 hours by ferry from Ketchikan)

Wrangell is less touristy than many of the towns along the Inside Passage. It's an excellent place to get away from the hectic cruise-ship foot traffic and the T-shirt and knickknack shops that go along with it. Check in at the Stikine Inn downtown and try to get one of the rooms with views of the water.

After you've unloaded at your hotel, take a stroll through the galleries and shops featuring wares by local artists and artisans. Grab lunch and walk down to the Petroglyph Beach State Historic Park and see ancient art chiseled on the rocks. No one knows who created these carvings or how long ago; they're curious, original, and intriguing.

For the latter part of the afternoon, take a jet-boat ride with Breakaway Adventures and soak in the nearby Chief Shakes Hot Springs.

DAY 4: PETERSBURG
(3-hour ferry ride from Wrangell)

Petersburg's Scandinavian heritage is evident from the moment you arrive. The Norwegian-style homes and boat docks set it apart from other Alaskan towns. Book a room in Scandia House and then spend the day glacier viewing and whale-watching with Tongass Kayak Adventures. Just 25 miles outside of town is LeConte Glacier, the continent's southernmost tidewater glacier and Petersburg's biggest draw.

DAY 5: JUNEAU
(8-hour ferry ride from Petersburg)

Most of the ferries from Petersburg to Juneau depart in the wee hours. You can book a cabin, or do as most Alaskans do and just curl up with your blanket on a deck chair under the heat lamps.

Once you're in Juneau, check into your room at Alaska's Capital Inn. Grab breakfast at Heritage Coffee Company and then take a helicopter ride on Temsco Helicopters to the Juneau Icefields. Spend an exciting afternoon dogsledding across the ice like the great Iditarod mushers do.

Once you're back in town, grab the bus to the Gold Creek Salmon Bake for dinner. If you'd like to walk off the meal, hike up to the remains of the old Wagner Gold Mine and do a little gold panning of your own.

DAY 6: HAINES
(4½-hour ferry ride from Juneau)

Check into Hotel Halsingland, the old Victorian officers' bunkers of Ft. Seward, then head over to the Mountain Market. This popular hangout is a health-food market–deli–coffee shop. Grab some things for a packed lunch, then rent a bike from Sockeye Cycle and spend an afternoon on the well-groomed trails that meander through the rain forest.

Get back to your hotel in time to take the Twilight Bear Viewing Trip or Valley of the Eagles Nature Tour (3–4 hours) with Alaska Nature Tours. Afterward, have a libation at the Fogcutter Bar and rub elbows with the locals. Don't lose track of time, though: Southeast bars stay open until the wee hours of morning, and you'll need to catch the ferry or flight back to Juneau the next day for your trip home.

DAY 7: HEAD HOME
Travel back to Juneau and depart for home.

Great Itineraries

Anchorage and Denali, 8 Days

Like all of Alaska, the Southcentral region is very spread out and the topography is diverse. But unlike in other regions, there are loads of ways to get around, and each mode of transport offers a different kind of experience.

DAY 1: ARRIVE IN ANCHORAGE

As soon as you land in Anchorage, you'll probably want to rent a car in preparation for an early departure the next day. Decompress after your flight at the tasteful Copper Whale Inn; it's a stone's throw from the Tony Knowles Coastal Trail and its great eateries and shops. For a leisurely stroll, walk along the Coastal Trail to Westchester Lagoon, or hike the entire 9 miles past Earthquake Park to Kincaid Park.

For dinner, Simon & Seafort's is within walking distance of the inn and has great food and a fantastic view across the water to Mt. Susitna (the "Sleeping Lady"). Humpy's Great Alaskan Ale House is a fun bar with live music and surprisingly good pub grub.

DAY 2: KAYAKING IN WHITTIER
(1½-hour drive from Anchorage)

Fuel up with an early breakfast at the inn, and then go pick up some picnic fixings for your day trip. Drive down the scenic Seward Highway and turn off toward Whittier. Before reaching Whittier, pull over at the Portage Glacier turnoff, where you can see the glacier and the iceberg-filled lake right from your car. Continue on to the Anton Anderson Memorial Tunnel, the longest highway tunnel in North America that's shared with trains.

Kayaking on the Prince William Sound is wonderful, and the knowledgeable guides at Alaska Sea Kayakers provide the gear and know-how to make it an experience of a lifetime.

At the end of the day, head back to Anchorage and return the car. Have dinner at the Glacier BrewHouse; be sure to sample a pint or two of the local craft beer. If you're not too tired, check out the nightlife at Crush Wine Bistro and Cellar and Bernie's Bungalow Lounge.

DAY 3: TALKEETNA
(7-hour train trip from Anchorage)

Board the morning train with the Alaska Railroad and enjoy the seven-hour scenic ride to Talkeetna, a small Alaska town where artists, pilots, and mountaineers congregate. It's where climbers preparing to ascend Denali hang out before they're flown to base camp. Book a room at the Susitna River Lodge and take a chartered flight over the summit (weather permitting) with Talkeetna Air Taxi. Spend the rest of the afternoon walking on a glacier.

Take a before- or after-dinner stroll through this tiny town, and check out the artwork that residents create during the quiet, cold winter months. Denali Brewing Company and Twister Creek Restaurant is a nice dinner option and a good place to soak in the bustling summer scene.

DAYS 4–6: DENALI NATIONAL PARK
(5-hour train trip from Talkeetna)

For more than 25 years, North Face Lodge has been family-owned and-operated. It offers three-, four-, or seven-night stays. A shuttle will pick you up at the train station and deliver you to a rustic wilderness lodge deep within Denali National Park. Knowledgeable naturalists offer daily guided outings; evening programs focus on the natural and cultural history of Denali.

Denali National Park is a 6 million-acre Arctic wonderland that teems with wildlife. On any given day you may see grizzlies, wolves, caribou, and moose. The weather around Denali is fickle, so there's never a guarantee of seeing the mountain's peaks, though that hardly matters as you explore the glaciers, forests, and vividly colored tundra. On day two in the park, take advantage of the lodge's outstanding off-trail wildlife-watching expedition. Fill the rest of your time here with canoeing on Wonder Lake, biking, or a flightseeing tour around the mountain.

DAY 7: ANCHORAGE
(8-hour train trip from Denali)

Take the afternoon train back to Anchorage and arrive in time for a late dinner. Check into one of our recommended hotels, and get ready for your flight the next day.

DAY 8: FLY HOME
Pack your bags and check out of the hotel. It's time to go to the airport and fly home.

MIGHTY DENALI

Denali has the highest peak in North America and it is an awesome sight—if you can see it. In the summer, the 20,310-foot peak has its own weather system. It can be sunny and warm down below, but it might be shrouded in cloud at the summit. It's often easier to see it from Anchorage, 140 miles away. Though the views may be blocked, it's still worth trying to catch a glimpse up close.

If you're not going to climb it or fly over it, a ride on the Denali Park Shuttle is the closest you will get to the High One. When you get to the Eielson Visitors Center at Mile 66, if the sky is clear and the mountain is out, continue on to Wonder Lake (approximately 88 more miles). It's a fantastic treat to catch Denali's peak reflecting in the water.

Great Itineraries

Wrangell–St. Elias, 9 days

This itinerary is a great way to see an impressive amount of Southcentral Alaska, but it needs to be well planned and executed with relative precision, as much of this trip depends on the departure times for trains and ferries. One mistake and your itinerary can change dramatically—which doesn't mean a ruined vacation, just not the one you'd planned on.

DAY 1: ANCHORAGE

For this trip, you'll overnight in Anchorage and catch the train out early the next morning. Make the most of your time here by booking a room at the Hotel Captain Cook. Put on your hiking shoes and grab the Flattop Mountain Shuttle. This popular trailhead is at the edge of the city, where the Chugach Mountain Range begins. The hour-long hike to the top can be strenuous, but from the summit you can see the entire city of Anchorage, the bay, and, on a clear day, the Alaska Mountain Range and even Denali. Should you opt to explore only the easier portion of the trail, you'll still enjoy excellent views. If you still have energy after Flattop, explore the Powerline Trail; it's the left-hand path at the trailhead. These trails are used year-round for hiking in the summer and snowshoeing, skiing, and snowmobiling in the winter. You'll understand why Anchoragites refer to their city as a great base camp.

After an afternoon of hiking in Anchorage's backyard, 49th State Brewery is a nice option for dinner.

DAY 2: SEWARD

(4-hour train ride from Anchorage)

The train ride to Seward offers stunning views that motorists miss. Once here, get situated at Hotel Edgewater.

Seward is renowned for its tremendous sea kayaking. Book a day trip with Sunny Cove Sea Kayaking. The experienced guides here can take you past pods of orcas, sea otters, and groups of seals. Afterward, dine at the locals' favorite hangout, Seward Brewing Company, for some excellent pub grub and locally brewed libations.

DAY 3: VALDEZ

(3-hour bus ride from Seward; 6-hour ferry trip from Whittier)

Book an early-morning bus to Whittier, where you'll connect immediately with the ferry for a six-hour trip to Valdez. Know that as the weather gets colder, ferries run less frequently, so be sure to plan ahead.

Arrange a room in Valdez's Mountain Sky Hotel and Suites and rent a car with Valdez U Drive; be sure to request an SUV or a high-clearance vehicle for the drive to McCarthy, just outside of Wrangell–St. Elias National Park. If you arrived late and want to linger in Valdez, spend the next day with H2O guides on a day trip to Worthington Glacier State Park. Dine at MacMurray's Alaska Halibut House, and be sure to try the fresh catch.

DAYS 4–7: WRANGELL–ST. ELIAS NATIONAL PARK AND PRESERVE

(5-hour drive from Valdez)

You've got some driving to do and one of the most gorgeous mountains in the state to see, so you'll want to get an early start. On the road, take care to fill the gas tank at every opportunity; gas stations here are few and far between. Summer is the only time that road construction can get done, so be prepared for delays.

Arrange your accommodations with Kennicott Glacier Lodge. After you've arrived, and if you still have energy, the lodge can help you book a tour of the mining ghost towns of Kennicott and McCarthy to explore the abandoned mines. The menu at the lodge is terrific, but there is also fine dining and a good-time saloon a few miles down the road at the McCarthy Lodge.

In the days to follow, get out and enjoy the park. Contact Wrangell Outfitters for a horseback-riding adventure into the heart of the preserve. The front desk at the lodge can also arrange glacier trekking, flightseeing, rafting, and alpine hiking. And the kitchen will pack you a picnic lunch.

DAY 8: WHITTIER AND ANCHORAGE CONNECTIONS

(6 hours by ferry from Valdez to Whittier; 2-hour train ride from Whittier to Anchorage)

It's another early-morning departure. Take your car back and catch the 7 am ferry to Whittier. There are snacks available on the ferry, but once you get to Whittier, try the halibut fish-and-chips at Varly's Swiftwater Seafood Cafe. You'll only have a couple of hours to spare before you catch the train to Anchorage, but Whittier is small and easy to explore.

AN ICY KENNICOTT HIKE

Kennicott Glacier extends 27 miles from where it originates at Mt. Blackburn to its terminus at the Kennicott River—just a short scenic hike from the Kennicott Glacier Lodge. You can walk right out onto the glacier, but using crampons on the ice is always a good idea, and a guide can ensure you don't get lost or make a wrong turn into a deep crevasse.

Once you're in Anchorage, if you're flying out the next day, book your stay at the Lakefront Anchorage, near the airport and right on the shore of Lake Spenard. Take a cab to Moose's Tooth Pub & Pizzeria; it's the best pizza in the state. If you're up for it, check out Kinley's Restaurant & Bar afterwards for dessert and some wine.

DAY 9: HEAD HOME

Say goodbye to Alaska and head for home.

54

Contacts

✈ Air Travel

AIRPORTS
Fairbanks International Airport. ☎ 907/474–2500 ⊕ www.dot.state.ak.us/faiiap. **Juneau International Airport.** ☎ 907/789–7821 ⊕ www.juneau.org/airport. **Ketchikan Airport.** ☎ 907/225–6800 ⊕ www.borough.ketchikan.ak.us/130/Airport. **Ted Stevens Anchorage International Airport.** ☎ 907/206–2525 ⊕ www.dot.alaska.gov/anc

AIR TAXI AND SMALL PLANE COMPANIES
Alaska Seaplanes. ☎ 907/789–3331 ⊕ www.fly-alaskaseaplanes.com. **Bering Air.** ☎ 800/478–5422 Nome reservations ☎ 800/478–3943 Kotzebue reservations ⊕ www.beringair.com. **Grant Aviation.** ☎ 888/359–4726 ⊕ www.flygrant.com. **PenAir.** ☎ 907/771–2640 ⊕ www.penair.com. **Ravn Alaska.** ☎ 907/266–8394 ⊕ www.flyravn.com. **Warbelow's Air Ventures.** ☎ 907/474–0518 ⊕ www.warbelows.com.

⛴ Boat/Ferry Travel

Alaska Marine Highway. ☎ 907/465–3941 ⊕ www.dot.state.ak.us/amhs. **Inter-Island Ferry Authority.** ☎ 907/225–4848 Ketchikan Terminal ☎ 907/530–4848 Hollis Terminal ⊕ www.interislandferry.com.

🚌 Bus Travel

Alaska Park Connection. ☎ 800/266–8625 ⊕ www.alaskacoach.com. **Alaska/Yukon Trails.** ☎ 907/479–2277 ⊕ www.alaskashuttle.com. **Denali Overland Transportation.** ☎ 907/733–2384 ⊕ www.denalioverland.com. **Green Tortoise.** ☎ 415/956–7500 ⊕ www.greentortoise.com. **Greyhound Canada Transportation Corp.** ☎ 800/661–8747 ⊕ www.greyhound.ca. **Interior Alaska Bus Line.** ☎ 800/770–6652 ⊕ www.interioralaskabusline.com. **Quick Shuttle.** ☎ 604/940–4428 ⊕ www.quickcoach.com. **Stage Line.** ☎ 907/235-2252 ⊕ www.stagelineinhomer.com.

🚗 Car and Taxi Travel

Alaska Department of Transportation. ☎ 511 in Alaska ☎ 866/282–7577 outside ⊕ Alaska 511.alaska.gov. **Alaska Yellow Cabs.** ☎ 907/222–2222 ⊕ www.alaskayellowdispatch.com. **Arctic Taxi.** ☎ 907/455–0000 ⊕ www.arctictaxi.com. **Alaska Cab.** ☎ 907/283–6000 ⊕ www.akcab.com. **Kodiak City Cab.** ☎ 907/486–5555 ⊕ www.kodiakcitytaxi.com.

⚓ Cruise Travel

Celebrity Cruises. ☎ 800/647–2251 ⊕ www.celebritycruises.com. **Holland America.** ☎ 877/932–4259 ⊕ www.hollandamerica.com. **Princess Cruises.** ☎ 800/774–6237 ⊕ www.princess.com. **Norwegian Cruise Line.** ☎ 866/234–0292 ⊕ www.ncl.com. **Royal Caribbean.** ☎ 866/562–7625 ⊕ www.royalcaribbean.com

🚆 Train Travel

Alaska Railroad. ☎ 907/265–2494 ⊕ www.alaskarailroad.com. **Gray Line Alaska.** ☎ 907/264–7983 ⊕ www.graylinealaska.com. **White Pass & Yukon Route.** ☎ 800/343–7373 ⊕ www.wpry.com.

📍 Visitor Information

Alaska Department of Fish and Game. ☎ 907/465–4100 ⊕ www.state.ak.us/adfg. **Alaska Division of Parks.** ☎ 907/269–8400 ⊕ www.alaskastateparks.org. **Alaska Public Lands Information Centers.** ⊕ www.alaskacenters.gov.

ANCHORAGE

3

Updated by
Joey Besl

⊙ Sights	🍴 Restaurants	🛏 Hotels	🛍 Shopping	🍸 Nightlife
★★★☆☆	★★★★☆	★★★★☆	★★★☆☆	★★★☆☆

WELCOME TO ANCHORAGE

TOP REASONS TO GO

★ **Fishing:** Anglers can cast for huge king salmon or feisty silvers while wading among reflections of skyscrapers at Ship Creek.

★ **Winter celebrations:** Beginning in late February, locals celebrate the two-week Fur Rendezvous. Events, from the blanket toss to the Running of the Reindeer—Alaska's spin on the classic Pamplona tradition—lead up to the start of the Iditarod Trail Sled Dog Race in early March.

★ **Shopping:** Shops and vendors at the Saturday and Sunday markets sell everything from kid-friendly tchotchkes to elegant Alaska Native crafts and locally produced foods.

★ **Seafood:** Dining out in Anchorage means feasting on local halibut, salmon, king-crab legs, scallops, and oysters. Many fine restaurants hide in not-so-pretty strip malls.

★ **Hiking and biking:** Laced with more than 120 miles of paved urban trails, Anchorage is a paradise for hikers and bicyclists.

1 **Downtown.** The city's cultural center has a festive atmosphere on summer afternoons, with flowers hung from street lamps and the smell of grilled onions and reindeer hot dogs in the air along 4th Avenue.

2 **Midtown.** Some 3 miles east of the airport, Midtown is a newer neighborhood with an assortment of restaurants, shopping centers, and large hotels.

3 **Spenard.** Sandwiched between the airport and Midtown, Spenard is one of Anchorage's oldest neighborhoods, yet also one of its up-and-comers.

4 **Greater Anchorage.** This is a massive city—nearly the size of Delaware—and gems are tucked into all its corners. You can rent a bike Downtown and head west along the 11-mile Tony Knowles Coastal Trail past tidal marshes and inlet views to 1,400-acre Kincaid Park.

By far Alaska's largest and most sophisticated city, Anchorage is situated in a truly spectacular location, and is the state's medical, financial, and banking center, as well as the home to the executive offices of most of the Alaska Native corporations.

The city has nearly 300,000 people, accounting for roughly 40% of the state's population. The relative affluence of this white-collar city—with a sprinkling of olive drab from nearby military bases—fosters an ever-growing range of restaurants, shops, and first-rate entertainment. The permanently snow-covered peaks and volcanoes of the Alaska Range lie to the west of the city while part of the craggy Chugach Range is within the eastern edge of the municipality; the Talkeetna and Kenai ranges are visible to the north and south. Two arms of Cook Inlet embrace the town's western and southern borders, and on clear days Denali looms on the northern horizon

Dena'ina Athabascan people have lived in this area for more than 1,000 years. Their fish camps once dotted the shores of Cook Inlet, only a short distance from Downtown Anchorage. And yet Anchorage is a young city, incorporated in only 1915. Nearly everything has been built since the 1970s—an Anchorage home dating from the 1950s basically merits historic status. The city got its start with the construction of the federally built Alaska Railroad, completed in 1917, and traces of its railroad heritage remain today. The city's architecture is far from memorable—though it has its quirky and charming moments—but the surrounding mountains make up for it.

Boom and bust periods followed major events: an influx of military bases during World War II; a massive buildup of Arctic missile-warning stations during the Cold War; reconstruction following the devastating Good Friday earthquake of 1964; and in the late 1960s the biggest jackpot of all—the discovery of oil at Prudhoe Bay and the construction of the Trans-Alaska Pipeline. It is no surprise that Anchorage then positioned itself as the perfect home for the pipeline administrators and support industries, and it continues to attract a large share of the state's oil-tax dollars.

Planning

WHEN TO GO
You'll find plenty to do year-round in Anchorage, though most visitors (particularly first-timers) might be happiest from late May through early September when the days are longer—up to 19 hours, 21 minutes during the summer solstice—and the temperatures warmer. If you choose one of the shoulder seasons, go with fall. There's less chance of rain, the snow has not yet arrived on trails except in the highest mountain passes, and there's an excellent chance for warm, sunny days, cool nights, and dazzling color changes in the trees and tundra.

But if you choose fall, pack a few extra layers as a just-in-case for early snow (or be prepared to visit one of Anchorage's many gear shops): the city's earliest measurable dose of snow fell on September 20, 1947.

Of the snow-free months, May is typically the driest, while August and September are the wettest. July is the warmest month, with an average temperature of 58.4°F; May is the coolest at 46.6°F. But don't be fooled by statistics. Late-May temperatures can exceed 70°F, and "hot" July and August days sometimes break 80°F. Of course, rainy low-pressure systems from the Gulf of Alaska can skulk in at any time, bringing wet and cool weather.

With such vagaries, do as the locals do: come prepared to go with the flow. That means packing light rain jackets and layers as well as tank tops and sunblock, and allowing for some flexibility with your plans.

GETTING HERE AND AROUND
AIR TRAVEL
Ted Stevens Anchorage International Airport is 6 miles from Downtown Anchorage on International Airport Road. Several carriers, including Ravn Alaska and PenAir, connect Anchorage with smaller Alaskan communities. Floatplane operators and helicopters serve the area from Lake Hood, which is adjacent to and part of Anchorage International Airport. A number of smaller air taxis and air-charter operations are at Merrill Field, 2 miles east of Downtown on 5th Avenue.

Taxis queue up at the lower level of the airport terminals outside the baggage-claim areas. They are on a meter system; it costs about $20, not including tip, for a ride Downtown. Most of the larger hotels provide free airport shuttle services.

AIRPORT Ted Stevens Anchorage International Airport ⊠ 5000 W. International Airport Rd., West Anchorage

☎ 907/266–2526 ⊕ www.anchorageairport.com.

BUS TRAVEL
The municipal People Mover bus system covers the high-traffic areas of Anchorage, with most routes originating Downtown. A one-way fare is $2 for rides anywhere in the city; day passes good for unlimited rides are $5. Route 40 connects Downtown and the airport and runs late on weeknights. ■ TIP→ **Get schedules and information from the central bus depot at 6th Avenue and G Street.**

CONTACT People Mover ☎ 907/343–6543 ⊕ www.peoplemover.org.

CAR TRAVEL
The Glenn Highway enters Anchorage from the north and becomes 5th Avenue near Merrill Field; this route will lead you directly into Downtown. Gambell Street leads out of town to the south, becoming New Seward Highway at about 20th Avenue. South of town, it becomes the Seward Highway. Yes, that means there's only one road in and one road out of Anchorage. If you bring your RV or rent one on arrival, know that parking an RV Downtown on weekdays is challenging. There's a big parking lot on 3rd Avenue between C and E streets, but on summer weekends from 10 am to 6 pm it's reserved for the outdoor Anchorage Market. Parking is usually not a problem in other parts of town. You can find an up-to-date parking map from Anchorage Downtown Partnership at ⊕ www.anchoragedowntown.org (click on "Parking" under the "About ADP" tab).

TAXI TRAVEL
If you need a taxi, call one of the cab companies for a pickup; it's not common to hail one. Prices are $2.75 for a pickup, plus an additional $2.50 for each mile. Allow 20 minutes for arrival of the cab during morning and evening rush hours. Alaska Yellow Cab has taxis with wheelchair lifts.

CONTACTS Alaska Yellow Cab ☎ *907/222–2222.* **Checker Cab** ☎ *907/644–4444* ⊕ *www.akcheckercab.com.*

TRAIN TRAVEL

From mid-May through mid-September, the Alaska Railroad runs daily between Anchorage and Seward; daily between Anchorage and Fairbanks via Talkeetna and Denali National Park and Preserve; and daily between Anchorage and Whittier, Portage, Spencer, and Grandview. Winter service is available once each month from Anchorage to Talkeetna and, weekly, a round-trip from Anchorage to Fairbanks and back. Call for schedule and fare information.

If you choose to travel by rail independently, the Alaska Railroad cars have glass-dome observation cars in summer and onboard guides year-round, and they make the trip between Anchorage and Fairbanks and Anchorage and Seward while hooked up to the same engines as the cruise-line cars. Alaska Railroad's website has details.

CONTACT Alaska Railroad ☎ *907/265–2494, 800/544–0552* ⊕ *www.akrr.com.*

RESTAURANTS

Anchorage's dining scene has, to the relief of repeat visitors and, even more so, locals, been on the rise for the past several years. Established (and still highly recommended) restaurants like Jens' and Marx Bros. Café have been joined by the likes of the small-plate and wine-focused Crush Wine Bistro and Cellar and the Pacific Rim cuisine–focused Ginger. No matter the restaurant, the local catch is a frequent star. Beware: eating salmon or halibut in-state may ruin you for fish served in the Lower 48. Anchorage also offers up plenty of worldly flavors thanks to the city's ethnic diversity. And nobody should leave Anchorage without trying the local fast-food specialty: a reindeer sausage from the carts along 4th Avenue in summer.

HOTELS

Most of the major chains are represented in Anchorage, and there are some strong independent hotels as well. Anchorage is also home to many bed-and-breakfasts. New chain hotels have clustered in Midtown in recent years, but consider staying Downtown if you're traveling without a car. Reservations at least a week ahead are a must for the major hotels, especially during the summer months.

Hotel and restaurant reviews have been shortened. For full information, visit Fodors.com. Restaurant prices are per person for a main course at dinner or if dinner is not served, at lunch. Hotel prices are for two people in a standard double room in high season.

What It Costs			
$	$$	$$$	$$$$
RESTAURANTS			
under $14	$14–$22	$23–$30	over $30
HOTELS			
under $100	$100–$175	$176–$250	over $250

TOURS

Tour Anchorage and the surrounding mountains and glaciers of Southcentral Alaska by land or by air with one of the many sightseeing companies in the region. The Log Cabin and Visitor Information centers have brochures for Anchorage bus tours.

Any air-taxi company can arrange for a flightseeing trip over Anchorage and environs. The fee is determined by the length of time you are airborne, the number of passengers, and the size of the plane.

Anchorage Trolley Tours

BUS TOURS | This one-hour city tour starts and ends at the Log Cabin Visitor's Center, taking guests on a 15-mile loop through Anchorage's original neighborhoods and past landmarks like the Alaska Railroad terminal and Lake Hood, the busiest floatplane base in the world. ✉ *Downtown* ☎ *907/276–5603, 888/917–8687* ⊕ *www.alaskatrolley.com* ✉ *From $20.*

Gray Line Alaska

BUS TOURS | Part of the international Gray Line brand, this company arranges Alaska tours by road or rail. Guests can add a host of options to their vacation packages, including city tours, float trips, jetboat excursions, and dog sled demonstrations across the state. ☎ *907/264–7983, 888/425–1737* ⊕ *www.graylinealaska.com* ✉ *From $399.*

Rust's Flying Service

AIR EXCURSIONS | If you want to land on a glacier in full view of Denali, check with Rust's. Among the city's most established flightseeing operations, Rust's regularly flies guests from its Anchorage base to backcountry lodges and bear-viewing platforms. There are also flightseeing tours of Prince William Sound and Denali National Park and Preserve. ✉ *Anchorage* ☎ *907/243–1595, 800/544–2299* ⊕ *www.flyrusts.com* ✉ *From $110.*

HEALTH AND SAFETY

Though most areas populated by tourists are safe to wander, Anchorage is a city, so it's best just to stay aware as you walk around town. That definitely holds true if you choose to hike any local trails—even those within the city limits. Before Anchorage was a paved city, it was wild. Many locals have stories of surprise visits by a moose or bear during a morning bathrobe run to get the newspaper. Moose and other animals walk the trails, too. If traveling into the Chugach Mountains, be sure to purchase bear spray at any outdoor retailer in advance. As you walk along, make some noise, either by singing or talking to a friend to help ward off the animals. The award for the biggest pest of all goes to the mosquito. Bring repellent with you for all hiking excursions.

VISITOR INFORMATION

Alaska sees nearly 2 million visitors each summer and, of that total, more than 40% spend at least one night in Anchorage. The tourist-friendly city offers a wealth of information and services to help visitors along the way. In addition to the Log Cabin and Visitor Information Center Downtown, there are two visitor information centers in Ted Stevens Anchorage International Airport: one in the north terminal (open mid-May through September) and one in the south terminal in the C Concourse baggage claim area (open year-round).

Alaska Department of Fish and Game

Visit this state website to purchase permits and licenses, plus find helpful information like hunting seasons and fishing lakes across the state. ✉ *333 Raspberry Rd., Midtown* ☎ *907/267–2218* ⊕ *www.adfg.alaska.gov.*

Alaska Public Lands Information Center

INFO CENTER | **FAMILY** | Stop here for information on all of Alaska's public lands, including national and state parks, national forests, and wildlife refuges. You can plan a hiking, sea-kayaking, bear-viewing, or fishing trip; purchase state and national park passes; find out about public-use cabins; learn about Alaska's plants and animals; or head to the theater for films highlighting different parts of the state. The bookstore also sells maps and nature books. Guided walks to historic Downtown sights depart daily throughout the summer at 11 am and 3:15 pm. The center is housed in a federal facility, meaning a security screening is required to enter. ✉ *605 W. 4th Ave., at F St., Suite 105, Downtown* ☎ *907/644–3661, 866/869–6887* ⊕ *www.alaskacenters.gov/anchorage.cfm.*

Log Cabin and Visit Anchorage Information Center

Housed in a rustic log cabin, the center's sod roof is festooned with huge hanging baskets of flowers, and a giant jade boulder—Alaska's state gemstone—stands outside. After a stop in the cabin, step out the back door to the more spacious visitor center stocked with brochures. Ask advice from the friendly and incredibly erudite volunteers: if they don't know something, it's not worth knowing. There are also two visitor information centers in Ted Stevens Anchorage International Airport, one in the north terminal and one in the south terminal in the C Concourse baggage claim area. ⊠ *546 W. 4th Ave., Downtown* ☎ *907/276–4118, 800/478–1255 to order visitor guides* ⊕ *www. anchorage.net.*

Downtown

Anchorage's main hub holds the majority of its hotels and restaurants, as well as the city's main sights. The streets are lined with art galleries and shops; the weekend markets promise good shopping for those seeking souvenirs.

Anchorage is a pedestrian- and bike-friendly city. Downtown Anchorage's flower-lined streets are easily explored on foot, and several businesses rent out bicycles. The area is confined to the south by the Delaney Park Strip, Anchorage's 15-block backyard, where you'll find kite-flying, pickup soccer games, and free yoga every Wednesday in the summer (check ⊕ *www.thealaskaclub. com* for times). Fourth Avenue remains the beating heart of the city, lined with steaming–reindeer sausage carts by day and crowded bars by night, and Downtown thrives all year long (especially during First Friday Art Walks). The grid plan was laid out by the Army Corps of Engineers, and streets and avenues run exactly east–west and north–south, with numbers in the first direction and letters of the alphabet or Alaska place-names (Barrow, Cordova, Denali, etc.) in the other. The only aberration is the absence of a J Street—a concession, some say, to the city's early Swedish settlers, who had difficulty pronouncing the letter. You'll

need a car for longer stays, expeditions, and to reach some of the city's better restaurants without relying on taxis. In the snow-free months a network of paved trails provides good avenues for in-city travel for bicyclists and walkers.

Outside Downtown, Anchorage is composed of widely scattered neighborhoods largely hidden by busy thoroughfares. And although there's no shortage of excellent restaurants Downtown, many of the town's best places are found in bland strip malls. Also, you're never more than a block or two from a good espresso stand or coffeehouse.

◉ Sights

Alaska Railroad Historic Depot

TRANSPORTATION | Totem poles and a locomotive built in 1907 are outside this station, the headquarters of the Alaska Railroad since 1915. Photographs and plaques inside explain the history of the railroad, which brought an influx of people into the city during the early 1900s. During February's Fur Rendezvous Festival, model-train buffs set up their displays here. ⊠ *411 W. 1st Ave., Downtown* ☎ *907/265–2494, 800/544–0552* ⊕ *www.alaskarailroad.com* ☉ *Closed Sun. mid-Sept.–mid-May.*

★ Anchorage Museum

MUSEUM | **FAMILY** | This striking, contemporary building with first-rate exhibits is an essential stop for visitors who want to celebrate the history of the North. The star of the museum is the Smithsonian Arctic Studies Center, which features more than 600 objects from Alaska Native cultures and short films that teach visitors about modern-day Native life. Wander the Art of the North galleries filled with works that showcase Alaska landscape, history, and beauty. The Alaska Exhibition shares Alaska's diversity and history with a knock-out eye for design. Cap the visit in the 9,000-square-foot, kid-focused Discovery Center, which includes a planetarium. Curated exhibitions rotate regularly and frequently spotlight Arctic issues, Northern design, and the unique perspective of life at these latitudes. The bright and modern Muse restaurant serves delicious lunches and dinners, and the gift shop is one of Anchorage's best places to buy Alaska Native art and other souvenirs. ✉ *625 C St., Downtown* 🕾 *907/929–9200* ⊕ *www. anchoragemuseum.org* 🎟 *$18* 🕙 *Closed Mon. in winter.*

Historic City Hall
GOVERNMENT BUILDING | Offices of Visit Anchorage now occupy this 1936 building. A few exhibits and historic photos are right inside the lobby. Out front, take a look at the marble sculpture dedicated to William Seward, the secretary of state who engineered the purchase of Alaska from Russia. ✉ *524 W. 4th Ave., Downtown* 🕙 *Closed weekends.*

Oscar Anderson House Museum
MUSEUM | City butcher Oscar Anderson built Anchorage's first permanent frame house in 1915, at a time when most of Anchorage consisted of tents. Visits are by guided 45-minute tours only. ✉ *420 M St., in Elderberry Park, Downtown* 🕾 *907/274–2336* 🎟 *$10* 🕙 *Closed Sept.–May.*

★ Point Woronzof
CITY PARK | FAMILY | Perched between the airport and the coast, this city park provides an entertaining hodgepodge of nature and noise—you can enjoy beautiful views of Mt. Susitna while trans-Pacific cargo jets periodically roar overhead. Walk down to the beach and head east for a picture-perfect view of the city skyline framed against the Chugach Mountains. Just off the Tony Knowles Coastal Trail, expect food carts and ice cream trucks as your reward if you make the 5-mile bike ride from Downtown. ✉ *9700 Point Woronzoff Rd., near end of Northern Lights Blvd., Anchorage.*

Resolution Park
CITY PARK | This tiny park has a cantilevered viewing platform dominated by

a monument to Captain Cook, whose explorations in 1778 led to the naming of Cook Inlet and many other geographic features in Alaska. Mt. Susitna, known as Sleeping Lady, is the prominent low mountain to the northwest, and Mts. Spurr and Redoubt, active volcanoes, are just south of Mt. Susitna. Denali, Mt. Foraker, and other peaks of the Alaska Range are often visible from more than 100 miles away. ✉ *3rd Ave. at L St., Downtown.*

Ship Creek
DAM | FAMILY | The creek is dammed right Downtown, with a footbridge across the dam and access from either bank. There's a waterfall; salmon running upstream from June through August; anglers; and, above it all, Downtown Anchorage. Farther upstream (follow Whitney Road and turn left on Post Road) is the William Jack Hernandez Sport Fish Hatchery—during the runs you can see salmon in the clear shallow water as they try to leap up the falls. Look for the wheelchair-accessible fishing platform on the trail directly north of the Comfort Inn. ✉ *Ship Creek Ave., Downtown.*

★ Tony Knowles Coastal Trail
TRAIL | Strollers, runners, bikers, dog walkers, and in-line skaters cram this recreation trail on sunny summer evenings, particularly around Westchester Lagoon. In winter, cross-country skiers take to it by storm. The trail begins off 2nd Avenue, west of Christensen Drive, and curls along Cook Inlet for approximately 11 miles to Kincaid Park, beyond the airport. In summer you might spot beluga whales offshore in Cook Inlet. Access points are on the waterfront at the ends of 2nd and 5th avenues and at Westchester Lagoon near the end of 15th Avenue. When you get to the high points in the trail, look north; Denali is visible on clear days. ✉ *Anchorage.*

One of Alaska's best museums, the Anchorage Museum focuses on the history of the state, including several essential exhibits on Alaska Native cultures.

🍴 Restaurants

The Bubbly Mermaid Oyster Bar

$$ | SEAFOOD | This tiny seafood joint easily offers the quirkiest dining experience in Downtown: almost the entire room is taken up by a boat-prow bar. At the helm, owner Apollo Naff has created a convivial environment where fellow diners become fast friends over plates of Alaska oysters and other briny bites such as crab cake po'boys, seafood chowder, and seared scallops in umami sauce. **Known for:** Alaska oysters; nautical ambience; menu items inspired by chef's Tijuana roots. ⑤ *Average main: $15* ✉ *417 D St., Downtown* ☎ *619/665–2852.*

Club Paris

$$$$ | STEAKHOUSE | Alaska's oldest steak house has barely changed since opening in 1957. The restaurant, with its dark wood and old-fashioned feel, serves tender, flavorful steaks of all kinds, along with a large seafood selection. **Known for:** four-inch thick filet mignon; homemade desserts; classic martinis. ⑤ *Average main: $32* ✉ *417 W. 5th Ave., Downtown* ☎ *907/277–6332* ⊕ *www.clubparisrestaurant.com* ⊗ *No lunch Sun.*

★ Crow's Nest Restaurant

$$$$ | EUROPEAN | An absolute must for epicures and adventurous eaters, Crow's Nest uses inspired combinations to highlight, but never overpower, the freshest ingredients Alaska has to offer. Located on the top floor of the Hotel Captain Cook, this is also the best restaurant view in Anchorage, spanning the Chugach Mountains to the east, the Alaska Range to the north and west, and the city 20 stories below. **Known for:** unforgettable views and atmosphere; excellent steaks and seafood; 10,000-bottle wine cellar. ⑤ *Average main: $44* ✉ *Hotel Captain Cook, 939 W. 5th Ave., 20th fl., Downtown* ☎ *907/343–2217* ⊕ *www.captaincook.com* ⊗ *Closed Sun. No lunch.*

★ Crush Wine Bistro and Cellar

$$ | ECLECTIC | The combination of shared small plates and an international wine list makes this Anchorage's most conversation-friendly dining venue. The menu—ranging from crab tartine to pork empanadas—is both inventive and budget-friendly. **Known for:** daily brunch; charcuterie plates; expansive next-door bottle shop. $ *Average main: $17* ✉ *328 G St., Downtown* ☎ *907/865–9198* ⊕ *www.crushak.com* ⊗ *No dinner Sun.*

Fire Island Rustic Bakeshop

$ | **BAKERY** | **FAMILY** | Led by head baker, local musician, and James Beard semifinalist Carlyle Watt, the scones and sandwiches at Fire Island draw bustling morning crowds. The original location is embedded in a cozy neighborhood just blocks from Downtown, and makes a perfect destination for a leisurely morning muffin run. **Known for:** busy open kitchen; hearty handcrafted breads; a different menu every day. $ *Average main: $7* ✉ *1343 G St., at 14th Ave., Downtown* ☎ *907/569–0001* ⊕ *www.fireislandbread. com* ⊗ *Closed Mon., Tues., and Jan. No dinner.*

Ginger

$$$ | **ASIAN** | Beautifully crafted Pacific Rim dishes like mu shu tacos and curry-crusted ahi tuna are a mainstay at Ginger, where the menu offers food that will please both adventurous and more traditional diners. Decorated in beautiful woods and warm tones, the interior perfectly complements the menu. **Known for:** hip happy hour; plenty of vegetarian options; artful plates in an artful setting. $ *Average main: $26* ✉ *425 W. 5th Ave., Downtown* ☎ *907/929–3680* ⊕ *www. gingeralaska.com.*

Glacier BrewHouse

$$$ | **AMERICAN** | The scent of hops permeates the cavernous, wood-beam BrewHouse, where at least a dozen beers are brewed on the premises. Locals mingle with visitors in this noisy, always-busy heart-of-town restaurant, and dinner selections range from chili-lime shrimp to fettuccine jambalaya and fresh seafood (in season). **Known for:** brick-oven pizzas;

can't-miss dessert menu; great home-brewed beer. $ *Average main: $25* ✉ *737 W. 5th Ave., Downtown* ☎ *907/274–2739* ⊕ *www.glacierbrewhouse.com.*

★ Marx Bros. Cafe

$$$$ | **AMERICAN** | Inside a small frame house built in 1916, this nationally recognized 14-table restaurant opened in 1979 and is still going strong thanks to a daily-changing menu that highlights classic Alaskan ingredients. The wine list encompasses more than 700 international choices. **Known for:** exceptionally deep wine cellar; table-made Caesar salads; homemade butter pecan ice cream. $ *Average main: $47* ✉ *627 W. 3rd Ave., Downtown* ☎ *907/278–2133* ⊕ *www. marxcafe.com* ⊗ *Closed Sun. and Mon. No lunch.*

New Sagaya's City Market

$ | **ECLECTIC** | Stop at either the Downtown or Midtown New Sagaya's grocery stores for quick lunches, healthy to-go food (perfect for hiking or camping), and Kaladi Brothers coffee. The in-house bakery and deli, L'Aroma, makes specialty breads, sandwiches, California-style pizzas, and a wide range of snack-worthy pastries. **Known for:** fresh seafood counter; Asian ingredients galore; outdoor seating. $ *Average main: $9* ✉ *900 W. 13th Ave., Downtown* ☎ *907/274–6173* ⊕ *www. newsagaya.com.*

Orso

$$$ | **ITALIAN** | The menu at Orso ("bear" in Italian) has gradually shifted from its Mediterranean roots, adding Alaskan touches like baked seafood mac and cheese to the selection of traditional pastas, fresh seafood, and locally famous desserts. Be sure to ask about the daily specials. **Known for:** light bites at happy hour; fresh takes on Italian standards; gluten-free options. $ *Average main: $29* ✉ *737 W. 5th Ave., at G St., Downtown* ☎ *907/222–3232* ⊕ *www.orsoalaska.com* ⊗ *No lunch.*

Anchorage

Simon & Seafort's Saloon & Grill

$$$$ | SEAFOOD | Windows overlooking Cook Inlet vistas, along with the high ceilings and a classic brass-and-wood interior, have long made this an Anchorage favorite. The menu includes prime rib and other steak-house classics, but the main attraction is fresh Alaska seafood. **Known for:** king crab dishes; happy hour with an ocean view; enormous steaks. $ *Average main: $36* ⊠ *420 L St., Downtown* ☎ *907/274–3502* ⊕ *www.simonandseaforts.com.*

★ Snow City Cafe

$ | ECLECTIC | On summer days, Snow City attracts some serious crowds— and for good reason. This modern but unassuming café, convenient to many of the Downtown hotels, serves one of Anchorage's best (and reasonably priced) breakfasts all day long. **Known for:** inventive eggs Benedict; build-your-own omelets with snow crab and salmon; long waits unless you go early or make a reservation. $ *Average main: $13* ⊠ *1034 W. 4th Ave., Downtown* ☎ *907/272–2489* ⊕ *www.snowcitycafe.com* ☽ *No dinner.*

Wild Scoops

$ | ECLECTIC | FAMILY | Step inside this Downtown microcreamery for Alaska-inspired ice cream flavors like almond birch brittle and rhubarb crumble. The homemade, small-batch ice cream options rotate constantly, emphasizing local ingredients like honey, blueberries, sea salt, and even beer. **Known for:** the favorite ice cream of Alaskan locals; innovative ingredients; fresh and unique flavors. $ *Average main: $5* ⊠ *429 E St., Downtown* ☎ *907/744–7295* ⊕ *www.wildscoops.com.*

🛏 Hotels

Anchorage Marriott Downtown

$$$$ | HOTEL | One of Anchorage's biggest lodgings, the brightly decorated Marriott appeals to business travelers, tourists, and corporate clients. **Pros:** great views; modern, up-to-date facilities; near Downtown's best restaurants. **Cons:** extra charge for Wi-Fi; pricey valet parking; cruise-ship crowds at times in summer. $ *Rooms from: $359* ⊠ *820 W. 7th Ave., Downtown* ☎ *907/279–8000, 800/228–9290* ⊕ *www.marriott.com/ancdt* ⟿ *392 rooms* ❙⊙❙ *No meals.*

Comfort Inn Downtown Ship Creek

$$$ | HOTEL | FAMILY | The namesake Ship Creek gurgles past this popular family hotel, which is a short walk northeast of the Alaska Railroad Historic Depot and practically on top of the Creek's parallel paved walking trail. **Pros:** free parking; pet-friendly rooms; loaner poles for guests with fishing licenses. **Cons:** walk into Downtown is an uphill climb; train noise; close to an industrial part of town. $ *Rooms from: $249* ⊠ *111 Ship Creek Ave., Downtown* ☎ *907/277–6887, 800/424–6423* ⊕ *www.choicehotels.com* ⟿ *100 rooms* ❙⊙❙ *Breakfast.*

Copper Whale Inn

$$ | B&B/INN | This location offers the best of both worlds: it's walkable to everything worth seeing in Downtown, but it's on the quiet end of 5th Avenue, right next to a small park and the 11-mile Coastal Trail. **Pros:** bike rentals in the front yard; convenient Downtown location; beautiful private gardens. **Cons:** some rooms are small; not wheelchair-friendly; occasional city street noise. $ *Rooms from: $199* ⊠ *440 L St., Downtown* ☎ *907/258–7999, 866/258–7999* ⊕ *www.copperwhale.com* ⊟ *No credit cards* ⟿ *14 rooms* ❙⊙❙ *Breakfast.*

Historic Anchorage Hotel

$$$ | HOTEL | Part of the Anchorage landscape since 1916, experienced travelers call this little building the most charming hotel in town. **Pros:** excellent staff; on the National Register of Historic Places; complimentary breakfast in the hotel's former saloon. **Cons:** some rooms are small; no airport shuttle; street noise affects some rooms. $ *Rooms from: $219* ⊠ *330 E St., Downtown* ☎ *907/272–4553,*

800/544–0988 ⊕ www.historicanchorage-hotel.com ⇋ 26 rooms ⋅⃝⋅ Breakfast.

★ Hotel Captain Cook

$$$$ | HOTEL | Recalling Captain Cook's voyages to Alaska and the South Pacific, dark teak paneling lines the hotel's interior, and a nautical theme continues into the guest rooms. **Pros:** very well-trained and accommodating staff; excellent lobby bar and rooftop restaurant; destination hotel for visiting dignitaries, including President Obama in 2015. **Cons:** 24-hour parking passes cost $30; lots of lobby traffic; no airport shuttle. ⑤ *Rooms from: $300* ⊠ *939 W. 5th Ave., Downtown* ☎ *907/276–6000, 800/843–1950* ⊕ *www.captaincook.com* ⇋ *642 rooms* ⋅⃝⋅ *No meals.*

Oscar Gill House

$$ | B&B/INN | Originally built by Gill in the settlement of Knik (north of Anchorage) in 1913, this historic home has been transformed into a comfortable B&B in a quiet neighborhood along Delaney Park Strip, with Downtown attractions a short walk away. **Pros:** great breakfast; cozy home with some old Anchorage history; very hospitable owners. **Cons:** shared bath in two of the rooms; no king-size beds; no elevator to second floor. ⑤ *Rooms from: $135* ⊠ *1344 W. 10th Ave., Downtown* ☎ *907/279–1344* ⊕ *www.oscargill.com* ⇋ *3 rooms, 1 with bath* ⋅⃝⋅ *Breakfast.*

Sheraton Anchorage Hotel & Spa

$$$ | HOTEL | The 16-story Sheraton is one of the city's best hotels, with rooms that are sleek (but not sterile), and accented with comfy beds and postcard views. **Pros:** tasteful, modern rooms; great views from the upper floors; impressive amenities including on-site dining and spa. **Cons:** fees for parking; extra charge for Wi-Fi; several blocks from most Downtown businesses. ⑤ *Rooms from: $284* ⊠ *401 E. 6th Ave., Downtown* ☎ *907/276–8700, 800/325–3535* ⊕ *www.sheratonanchorage.com* ⇋ *370 rooms* ⋅⃝⋅ *No meals.*

Westmark Anchorage Hotel

$$$ | HOTEL | Reserve a room on the higher floors of this 13-story hotel for some of the city's best mountain views. **Pros:** central Downtown location; private balconies in every room; free Wi-Fi. **Cons:** between Downtown's busiest avenues; few frills; no airport shuttle. ⑤ *Rooms from: $209* ⊠ *720 W. 5th Ave., Downtown* ☎ *907/276–7676, 800/544–0970* ⊕ *www.westmarkhotels.com* ⇋ *200 rooms* ⋅⃝⋅ *No meals.*

ⓨ Nightlife

Anchorage does not shut down when it gets dark—well, that is when it actually does get dark (it's still light at 3 am in the summer!). Bars here—and throughout Alaska—open early (in the morning) and close as late as 3 am on weekends. The listings in the *Alaska Dispatch News* entertainment section, published on Friday, and in the free weekly *Anchorage Press* (⊕ *www.anchoragepress.com*) cover concerts, theater performances, movies, and a roundup of nightspots featuring live music.

BARS AND NIGHTCLUBS

Bernie's Bungalow Lounge

BARS/PUBS | This low-key lounge pulls in plenty of twentysomethings looking to dance, drink, and tackle the late-night menu served on the expansive outdoor patio. On weekends there is usually a good local DJ upstairs and a mediocre live band outside. ⊠ *626 D St., Downtown* ☎ *907/276–8808* ⊕ *www.bernies-lounge.com.*

49th State Brewing Company

BREWPUBS/BEER GARDENS | The rustic interior here is all stone, wood, and antlers, but the real attraction is the sun-soaked back deck and rooftop, where, on clear days, you can see Denali hovering over the northern horizon. The menu of pizzas and hearty bar bites emphasizes all things Alaska, including giant burgers appropriately named for noteworthy peaks. Beers are brewed on-site using local ingredients like Sitka spruce tips and Talkeetna birch syrup. The restaurant also hosts a range of events in its on-site theater, including improv comedy and trivia nights. ✉ *717 W. 3rd Ave., Downtown* ☎ *907/277–7727* ⊕ *www.49statebrewing.com.*

Club Paris

BARS/PUBS | Lots of old-timers favor the dark bar of Club Paris. This is your spot if you like a stiff, no-nonsense drink. ✉ *417 W. 5th Ave., Downtown* ☎ *907/277–6332* ⊕ *www.clubparisrestaurant.com.*

Simon & Seafort's Saloon & Grill

BARS/PUBS | A trendy place for the dressy crowd, the bar at Simon & Seafort's Saloon & Grill has stunning views of Cook Inlet, a special single-malt-Scotch menu, and tempting cocktails. The lavender martini is a highlight. Take advantage of the two happy hours each day, including a late-night stretch starting at 9 pm. ✉ *420 L St., Downtown* ☎ *907/274–3502* ⊕ *www.simonandseaforts.com.*

Williwaw

BARS/PUBS | This central three-story entertainment hub tries to be everything for everybody, and mostly succeeds. With a rooftop bar, coffee shop, acoustic lounge, sort-of-secret speakeasy, and concert venue, there's always something going on here. Check the online schedule for events like movie nights, trivia, dance parties, and even "yoga & beer". ✉ *601 F St., Downtown* ☎ *907/868–2000* ⊕ *www. williwawsocial.com.*

GAY AND LESBIAN BARS

Mad Myrna's

BARS/PUBS | Anchorage's premier gay bar offers dozens of LGBTQ community events as well as nightly karaoke and DJ performances on Friday and Saturday. It's best known for its Friday night Divas Variety Show; you haven't seen drag until you've seen it Alaska-style. ✉ *530 E. 5th Ave., Downtown* ☎ *907/276–9762.*

LIVE MUSIC

See the "Play" section in Friday editions of the *Alaska Dispatch News* for complete listings of upcoming concerts and other performances, or get the same entertainment information online at ⊕ *www.adn.com.*

Anchorage Market and Festival

FESTIVALS | A range of performers in nearly every genre are featured for free at the Anchorage Market and Festival every weekend from mid-May to mid-September. ✉ *3rd Ave. and E St., Downtown* ☎ *907/272–5634* ⊕ *www.anchoragemarkets.com.*

★ Humpy's Great Alaskan Alehouse

MUSIC CLUBS | One of Anchorage's best bars, Humpy's Great Alaskan Alehouse serves up rock, blues, and folk several nights a week, including an open mike on Sunday, along with dozens of microbrews (more than 40 beers are on tap) and surprisingly tasty pub grub. Trivia buffs should head to Humpy's on Tuesday night for the weekly pub quiz. You can grab one of Humpy's delicious halibut burgers on your way out of town—the company has a satellite restaurant in Terminal B of the Anchorage airport. ✉ *610 W. 6th Ave., Downtown* ☎ *907/276–2337* ⊕ *www.humpys.com.*

Music in the Park

MUSIC | **FAMILY** | On summertime Wednesdays, open-air concerts are presented at noon in Peratrovich Park (also known as Old City Hall Park). Come back with the family on Mondays at noon, when music is geared to the little ones. ✉ *500 W. 4th Ave., at E St., Downtown* ⊕ *www. anchoragedowntown.org.*

Performing Arts

Alaska Center for the Performing Arts

ARTS CENTERS | Four theaters make up the Alaska Center for the Performing Arts, which is home to 10 resident performing arts companies—including Alaska Dance Theatre, Anchorage Opera, and the Anchorage Symphony Orchestra. The center also showcases traveling production companies. The lobby box office sells tickets to the productions and is a good all-around source of cultural information. Take a look inside to learn more about upcoming events, or relax amid the blossoms in the adjacent flower-filled Town Square Park on a sunny afternoon. ⊠ *621 W. 6th Ave., at G St., Downtown* ☎ *907/263–2787* ⊕ *www.alaskapac.org.*

🛍 Shopping

ART

The Anchorage **First Friday Arts Walk** is a popular monthly (and year-round) event, with dozens of galleries, coffee shops, and restaurants offering a chance to sample hors d'oeuvres while looking over the latest works by regional artists. The *Anchorage Press* prints a "First Friday" guide the first Thursday of every month.

4th Avenue Market Place

ART GALLERIES | This drab building houses several shops selling Alaska Native art and crafts, including exquisite hand-woven baskets and delicately beaded jewelry. Don't miss Two Spirits Gallery: many artists work on-site, so it's a go-to place for anybody interested in meeting the people behind the crafts. ⊠ *411 W. 4th Ave., Downtown.*

International Gallery of Contemporary Art

ART GALLERIES | Anchorage's premier fine-arts gallery, the International Gallery of Contemporary Art has changing exhibits monthly and features some of Alaska's most forward-thinking work. ⊠ *427 D St., Downtown* ☎ *907/279–1116* ⊕ *www. igcaalaska.org.*

CLOTHING

Circular

CLOTHING | Score eco-conscious dresses, weekend wear, and accessories at this forward-thinking women's clothing boutique. ⊠ *320 W. 6th Ave., Downtown* ☎ *907/274–2472* ⊕ *www.circularboutique.com.*

David Green Master Furrier

CLOTHING | Although furs may not be to everyone's taste or ethics, a number of Alaska fur companies have stores and factories in Anchorage. One of the city's largest and best-known furriers is David Green Master Furrier, whose family has been in the fur business in Alaska since 1922. ⊠ *130 W. 4th Ave., Downtown* ☎ *907/277–9595* ⊕ *www.davidgreenfurs. com.*

Laura Wright Alaskan Parkys

CLOTHING | Started in 1947 in Fairbanks by Laura Wright, this family business is now owned by Wright's granddaughter, Sheila Ezelle. The store sells distinctive Alaskan Inupiaq "parkys" (parkas) for both summer and winter, and she will even custom sew one for you. ⊠ *411 W. 4th Ave., Downtown* ☎ *907/274–4215.*

Oomingmak

CLOTHING | The Alaska Native–owned cooperative Oomingmak sells items made of qiviut, the ubersoft and warm undercoat of musk ox, from inside one of the few small houses remaining in Downtown. Scarves, shawls, hats, and tunics are knitted in traditional patterns by women in villages across Alaska. ⊠ *604 H St., Downtown* ☎ *907/272–9225, 888/360–9665* ⊕ *www.qiviut.com.*

FOOD

★ Anchorage Market and Festival

OUTDOOR/FLEA/GREEN MARKETS | On weekends from mid-May to mid-September, the Anchorage Market and Festival opens for business in the parking lot at 3rd Avenue and E Street. Dozens of vendors offer Alaskan-made crafts, ethnic imports, and deliciously fattening food. Stock up on birch candy and salmon jerky to snack on while traveling or as perfect made-in-Alaska gifts for friends back home. ⊠ *3rd Ave. between E and C Sts., Downtown* ☎ *907/272–5634* ⊕ *www. anchoragemarkets.com.*

The Kobuk Tea Company

LOCAL SPECIALTIES | One of Alaska's most popular tea companies, Kobuk serves up a variety of classic and unique teas, including their signature Samovar tea (a samovar is a traditional Russian container used to brew tea). Pastries, coffee, fine china, and other gifts are also for sale. ⊠ *504 W. 5th Ave., Anchorage* ☎ *907/272–3626* ⊕ *www.kobukcoffee. com.*

Midtown

Once you're done wandering the shops and handful of notable attractions Downtown, consider heading south to Midtown. The neighborhood has some of Anchorage's best restaurants and plenty of gear stores to help prep your out-of-town adventures. Midtown is sandwiched between high-traffic thruways, but these are lined with diverse shops proffering everything from high-quality brews to artisan truffles to secondhand camp stoves. It's also a good neighborhood to stay in if you'd rather be slightly outside the main tourist fray. In this functional section of Anchorage, however, don't expect much in the way of sightseeing.

◉ Sights

Alaska Heritage Museum at Wells Fargo
MUSEUM | More than 900 Alaska Native artifacts are the main draw in the quiet unassuming lobby of a large Midtown bank—it's reputed to be one of the largest private collections of Native artworks in the country. Also here you'll find paintings by Alaskan artists, a library of rare books, and a 46-troy-ounce gold nugget. The gallery is free to stroll through; call ahead to arrange a guided tour. ⊠ *Wells Fargo Bank, 301 W. Northern Lights Blvd., at C St., Midtown* ☎ *907/265–2834* ⊕ *www.wellsfargohistory.com/museums* 🖾 *Free* ⊙ *Closed weekends.*

UAA Planetarium and Visualization Theater
SOUND/LIGHT SHOW | **FAMILY** | Kick back in this plush 60-seat auditorium as professors from the University of Alaska Anchorage add live commentary to Northern-focused science and education films, including several titles produced by the university itself in hard-to-reach Alaska destinations. The theater offers Friday night double features during the academic year. ⊠ *3101 Science Cir., Midtown* ☎ *907/786–1838* ⊕ *www.uaa. alaska.edu/planetarium* 🖾 *$10.*

🍴 Restaurants

CampoBello Bistro
$$$ | **ITALIAN** | Considering its strip mall location, CampoBello has surprisingly sophisticated Italian entrées and deliciously indulgent desserts. Step inside for a romantic lunch or dinner surrounded by splashes of modern art on the walls and candles on the tables. **Known for:** Alaska seafood with Italian flair; shrimp and scallops Florentine; homemade four-cheese ravioli. ⑤ *Average main: $26* ⊠ *601 W. 36th Ave., Midtown* ☎ *907/563–2040* ⊕ *www.campobello-bistro.com* ⊙ *Closed Sun. and Mon. No lunch Sat.*

Jens'
$$$$ | **EUROPEAN** | Don't let the Midtown strip mall that houses Jens' put you off: this is a true fine-dining establishment. Chef-owner Jens Haagen Hansen's culinary legacy has led to the frequently changing menu that includes Alaska salmon, halibut, and rockfish. **Known for:** Danish lunch specials; "almost world-famous" pepper steaks; light bites at the wine bar. ⑤ *Average main: $35* ⊠ *701 W. 36th Ave., at Arctic Blvd., Midtown* ☎ *907/561–5367* ⊕ *www.jensrestaurant. com* ▭ *No credit cards* ⊙ *Closed Sun. and Jan. No lunch Sat., no dinner Mon.*

Moose's Tooth Pub & Pizzeria
$$ | **PIZZA** | Always the top pick when local newspapers rate Anchorage pizzerias, Moose's Tooth is packed all week, despite the ample seating (it can hold up to 300 guests). The reason for the popularity is obvious: handcrafted beers

from the on-site brewery, and a seemingly endless roster of pizzas topped with inventive options like jalapeños, cream cheese, shrimp, and lime. **Known for:** energetic outdoor waiting area; house-made brews, root beer, and cream soda; Alaska's best pizza. $ *Average main: $19* ⊠ *3300 Old Seward Hwy., Midtown* ☎ *907/258–2537* ⊕ *www.moosestooth.net.*

🛏 Hotels

Embassy Suites Anchorage
$$$$ | HOTEL | California chic meets Alaska at this upscale Anchorage hotel where you will find a long list of amenities, including a hot cooked-to-order breakfast and an evening manager's reception featuring complimentary hors d'oeuvres and cocktails. **Pros:** top-of-the-line facilities; freebies at manager's reception; great breakfast. **Cons:** neighborhood is a high-traffic area; only some rooms have a (distant) mountain view; no sights within walking distance. $ *Rooms from: $299* ⊠ *600 E. Benson Blvd., Midtown* ☎ *907/332–7000, 800/362–2779* ⊕ *www.embassysuites.hilton.com* ➟ *169 suites* ⦿| *Breakfast.*

SpringHill Suites Anchorage Midtown
$$$ | HOTEL | Spacious one-room suites have separate living and sleeping areas with either a king bed or two double beds plus a pullout sofa, microwave, mini-refrigerator, and flat-screen TV. **Pros:** complimentary parking; 24-hour airport shuttle; nice pool. **Cons:** small laundry facilities for such a large hotel; most restaurants within easy walking distance are national chains; very cookie-cutter decor. $ *Rooms from: $229* ⊠ *3401 A St., Midtown* ☎ *907/562–3247* ⊕ *www.marriott.com/ancsh* ➟ *102 suites* ⦿| *Breakfast.*

🍸 Nightlife

★ Kinley's Restaurant & Bar
WINE BARS—NIGHTLIFE | The lounge side of Kinley's is one of those rare rooms that's equally suitable for a romantic date, entertaining clients, or a girls' night out. Anchorage has many spots that will happily sell you a good $100 bottle of wine; however, Kinley's has a special knack for finding wines that taste luxe, but don't break the bank. Pair with a happy hour appetizer special or one of their exquisite desserts, such as the mocha bourbon pecan torte. ⊠ *3230 Seward Hwy., Midtown* ☎ *907/644–8953* ⊕ *www.kinleysrestaurant.com.*

🛍 Shopping

Alaska Fur Exchange
CRAFTS | In a large Midtown store, Alaska Fur Exchange sells both furs and Alaska Native artwork. ⊠ *4417 Old Seward Hwy., Midtown* ☎ *907/563–3877* ⊕ *www.alaskafurexchange.com.*

Spenard

The spirit of Spenard is captured by its winding namesake road—an anomaly in this meticulously gridlike city. The quieter neighborhood lies just west of Midtown and is known for its artsy vibe, some of the city's most notable casual restaurants, a good farmers' market, and Anchorage's largest independent bookstore, Title Wave.

🍽 Restaurants

Gwennie's Old Alaska Restaurant
$ | AMERICAN | Historic Alaskan photos, mounted animals, and state memorabilia adorn this old family favorite near the airport. Lunch and dinners are available, but the restaurant is best known for its old-fashioned all-day breakfasts, which include menu items like reindeer sausage and crab omelets. **Known for:** sourdough pancakes; generous portions; endless entertainment from the wall decor. $ *Average main: $11* ⊠ *4333 Spenard Rd., Spenard* ☎ *907/243–2090* ⊕ *www.gwenniesrestaurant.com.*

Organic Oasis

$$ | CAFÉ | Part-eatery and part-community center and event space, this popular café offers plenty of healthy (or, at least, healthy-sounding) fare, including fresh-squeezed juices, smoothies, organic sandwiches, fresh vegan soups, and tempeh burgers. While vegans and vegetarian visitors to Anchorage should definitely make a beeline to Organic, omnivores are not left in the cold: the menu also includes burgers, chicken, salmon, and grilled Buffalo rib eyes. **Known for:** house-baked breads and buns; inventive juice bar; organic beer and wine. $ *Average main: $16* ✉ *2610 Spenard Rd., Spenard* ☎ *907/277–7882* ⊕ *www.organicoasis.com.*

Spenard Roadhouse

$$ | AMERICAN | The amusing assortment of wall art here pays homage to the roadhouses that dot the state, but Spenard Roadhouse is by no means just a place to grab a quick meal while traveling. The warm and inviting restaurant offers creative comfort food, plus an unforgettable weekend brunch menu; the "hair o' the dog" cocktails alone are worth the journey to Spenard. **Known for:** bacon of the month; tater tots the locals love; house-infused vodkas and bourbon flights. $ *Average main: $16* ✉ *1049 W. Northern Lights Blvd., Spenard* ☎ *907/770–7623* ⊕ *www.spenardroadhouse.com.*

Yak and Yeti Himalayan Restaurant

$ | INDIAN | Savor the flavors of India, Nepal, and Tibet in this cozy, homey restaurant owned by Lobsang Dorjee, a Tibetan who grew up in India, and his wife, lifelong Alaskan Suzanne Hull. Yak and Yeti delivers authenticity and depth, balancing the familiar—pork vindaloo, palak paneer, samosas—with the unexpected, such as *lhasa momos,* a type of Tibetan dumpling.**Known for:** hefty vegetarian options; cozy mugs of chai; cost-conscious entrées. $ *Average main: $12* ✉ *3301 Spenard Rd., Spenard* ☎ *907/743–8078* ⊕ *www.yakandyetialaska.com* ☉ *Closed Sun.*

Spenard Food Truck Carnival 🍴

Although the food truck trend was a little slow to catch on in Anchorage and is still fairly disorganized, avid food truckers can count on the Spenard Food Truck Carnival, which occurs 11 am to 2 pm on Thursday, late March through mid-September in the parking lot at Chilkoot Charlie's, 2435 Spenard Road. There are typically up to 10 food trucks featuring everything from fresh Alaska fish tacos to BBQ. A local favorite is Kastle's Kreations, whose owners have won on *Cupcake Wars* on the Food Network.

🛏 Hotels

Courtyard by Marriott Anchorage Airport

$$$ | HOTEL | Business travelers pack this modern hotel near the airport thanks to its well-designed lobby that includes comfortable media pods with cell phone chargers, TVs, and more. **Pros:** close to airport; free Wi-Fi; complimentary airport shuttle. **Cons:** fee for breakfast; business traveler focus; not close to attractions. $ *Rooms from: $229* ✉ *4901 Spenard Rd., Spenard* ☎ *907/245–0322* ⊕ *www.marriott.com/anccy* ⇱ *154 rooms* ❍| *No meals.*

Hampton Inn by Hilton

$$$ | HOTEL | Midway between the airport and Downtown, the Hampton has all the standard features of a good hotel, and a few that are better than average, such as designer furnishings, an indoor swimming pool, and a whirlpool. **Pros:** free Wi-Fi; great beds; excellent breakfast. **Cons:** some rooms near the pool can be noisy and smell of chlorine; basic chain-hotel ambience; surrounded by chain restaurants. $ *Rooms from:*

$229 ⊠ 4301 Credit Union Dr., Spenard 🕾 907/550–7000, 800/426–7866 ⊕ www.hamptoninn.com 🛏 101 rooms ⦿ Breakfast.

The Lakefront Anchorage
$$$$ | **HOTEL** | Perched on the shore of Lake Spenard, this Anchorage favorite is one of the city's best spots to watch planes come and go; guests can even arrange quick floatplane tours from the hotel's private dock. **Pros:** airport shuttle available; old Alaska hunting-lodge feel; pet-friendly (it's even home to the Iditarod mushers each February). **Cons:** noise from airplanes on Lake Hood; distant from Downtown attractions; no complimentary breakfast. ⑤ Rooms from: $289 ⊠ 4800 Spenard Rd., Spenard 🕾 907/243–2300, 800/544–0553 ⊕ www.millenniumhotels.com/anchorage 🛏 248 rooms ⦿ No meals.

🌙 Nightlife

Anchorage Brewing Company
BREWPUBS/BEER GARDENS | Arguably the most artistic brewery in the entire state, ABC's inventive beers skew toward the intensely sour. Grab a glass in the high-ceiling tasting room and wander freely among the brewery's towering wood casks, or carry your pint outside to the cozy patio with a firepit. ⊠ 148 W. 91st Ave., South Anchorage 🕾 907/677–2739 ⊕ www.anchoragebrewing.company.

★ Chilkoot Charlie's
BARS/PUBS | A rambling timber building with sawdust floors, loud music, weekend DJs, and rowdy customers, Chilkoot Charlie's is where young Alaskans go to get crazy. The legendary bar has many unusual nooks and crannies, including a room filled with Russian artifacts and a reconstructed version of Alaska's infamous Birdhouse Bar. ⊠ 2435 Spenard Rd., Spenard 🕾 907/272–1010 ⊕ www.koots.com.

🎭 Performing Arts

Bear Tooth Theatrepub
FILM | The popular Bear Tooth Theatrepub screens second-run films—from art house to blockbuster—for only $4 and also serves tasty pizzas, sandwiches, burritos, salads, and Broken Tooth beers while you watch. Once you purchase your ticket at the box office, you may need to wait in line outside while the previous movie lets out, so make sure you're in the right line—and dress for the weather. ⊠ 1230 W. 27th Ave., Spenard 🕾 907/276–4200 ⊕ www.beartooththeatre.net.

🛍 Shopping

BOOKS
Title Wave Books
BOOKS/STATIONERY | Easily the largest independent bookstore in Alaska, Title Wave Books fills a 24,000-square-foot space in the Northern Lights Center. The shelves are filled with nearly half a million used books, CDs, and DVDs across more than 1,600 categories, including a large section of Alaska-focused books. The staff is very knowledgeable, and the store hosts regular game nights and children's story times. Anyone can bring in used books and trade them for store credit. ⊠ 1360 W. Northern Lights Blvd., Spenard 🕾 907/278–9283, 888/598–9283 ⊕ www.wavebooks.com.

The Writer's Block
BOOKS/STATIONERY | Alaska authors line the shelves at this cozy literary café, a neighborhood gathering place that is a combination bookstore and coffee shop. The busy events calendar showcases local artists of all stripes, including spoken word performances, art openings, and book launches. ⊠ 3956 Spenard Rd., Spenard 🕾 907/929–2665 ⊕ www.writersblockak.com.

GIFTS

Dos Manos

GIFTS/SOUVENIRS | This laid-back gallery features individually screen-printed T-shirts, leather satchels, silver jewelry, and affordable wall art displayed along a sweeping three-story spiral staircase. Most items don't say "Alaska" on them, but everything here is handmade in the state by established and emerging artists. ✉ *1317 W. Northern Lights, Suite 3, Spenard* ☎ *907/569–6800*.

SPORTS AND OUTDOOR EQUIPMENT

Alaska Mountaineering & Hiking

SPORTING GOODS | This Alaskan-owned store is the go-to specialist for any gear having to do with, yep, mountaineering or hiking. Whether you're setting out on a series of day hikes or you're planning a serious climb, the knowledgeable staff can help you choose the right equipment for the task. Take the time to chat up the staff and you may hear some amazing Denali stories. ✉ *2633 Spenard Rd., Spenard* ☎ *907/272–1811* ⊕ *www.alaska-mountaineering.com*.

REI

SPORTING GOODS | If you get to Alaska and discover you've left some critical camping or outdoor recreation gear behind, REI rents camping, skiing, and paddling equipment. It also gives regular seminars on season-specific outdoor topics. The salespeople are very knowledgeable about local conditions and activities, and the gear required to get you out and back safely. ✉ *1200 W. Northern Lights Blvd., Spenard* ☎ *907/272–4565* ⊕ *www.rei.com/anchorage*.

Greater Anchorage

Anchorage has swelled since its start as a tent city just over a century ago. Although the hub of activity is still centered Downtown, some of the city's largest and best attractions as well as a number of newer and noteworthy restaurants are situated throughout Greater Anchorage, which can look a bit sprawly and prosaic in places but also extends into the scenic Chugach foothills to the east.

◉ Sights

Alaska Aviation Museum

MUSEUM | **FAMILY** | The state's unique aviation history is presented here with more than 25 vintage aircraft, a flight simulator, a theater, and an observation deck along the world's busiest seaplane base. Highlights include a Stearman C2B, the first plane to land on Denali back in the early 1930s, and a recently restored 1931 Fairchild Pilgrim aircraft. You may see volunteers busily restoring an aircraft, and docents eager to talk about their bush pilot experiences. A free shuttle to and from Anchorage Airport is available, as is luggage storage. ✉ *4721 Aircraft Dr., West Anchorage* ☎ *907/248–5325* ⊕ *www.alaskaairmuseum.org* 🎟 *$15*.

Alaska Botanical Garden

GARDEN | **FAMILY** | The garden showcases perennials hardy enough to make it in Southcentral Alaska in several large display gardens, a pergola-enclosed herb garden, and a rock garden amid 110 acres of mixed boreal forest. There's a 1-mile nature trail loop to Campbell Creek, with views of the Chugach Range and a wildflower trail between the display gardens. Interpretive signs guide visitors and identify plants along the trail. Docent tours are available upon request. ✉ *4601 Campbell Airstrip Rd., off Tudor Rd. (park at Benny Benson School), East Anchorage* ☎ *907/770–3692* ⊕ *www.alaskabg.org* 🎟 *$12*.

★ Alaska Native Heritage Center

NATIVE SITE | **FAMILY** | On a 26-acre site facing the Chugach Mountains, this facility provides an introduction to Alaska's Native peoples. The spacious Gathering Place has interpretive displays, artifacts, photographs, demonstrations, Native dances, storytelling, and films, along with a gift shop selling crafts and artwork. Step outside for a stroll around the adjacent lake, where seven village exhibits represent 11 Native cultural groups through traditional structures and exhibitions. As you enter the homes in these villages, you can visit with the hosts, hear their stories, and try some of the tools, games, and utensils used in the past. ✉ *8800 Heritage Center Dr., (Glenn Hwy. at Muldoon Rd.), East Anchorage* ☎ *907/330–8000, 800/315–6608* ⊕ *www.alaskanative.net* ✉ *$25* ⊙ *Closed mid-Sept.–mid-May.*

Alaska Zoo

ZOO | FAMILY | Roam the trails and visit with the polar bears, caribou, brown and black bears, seals, tigers, snow leopards, moose, wolves, lynx, and a large array of birds that call the Alaska Zoo home. The zoo provides a wide array of programs included with admission, such as zookeeper talks and toddler story times, that concentrate on promoting the conservation of arctic and subarctic animal species. Throughout the summer for an additional fee you can join daily two-hour tours that include two behind-the-scenes stops. ✉ *4731 O'Malley Rd., 2 miles east of New Seward Hwy., South Anchorage* ☎ *907/346–2133* ⊕ *www.alaskazoo.org* ✉ *$15.*

Potter Marsh

BODY OF WATER | FAMILY | Sandhill cranes, trumpeter swans, and other migratory birds, as well as the occasional moose or beaver, frequent this marsh about 10 miles south of Downtown on the Seward Highway. An elevated boardwalk makes viewing easy, and in summer there are salmon runs in the creek beneath the bridge. An old railroad service building just south of the marsh operates as a state park office. ✉ *Seward Hwy., South Anchorage* ☎ *907/269–8400.*

🍴 Restaurants

Kincaid Grill

$$$$ | AMERICAN | This out-of-the-way restaurant provides a respite after a summertime hike or wintertime ski in nearby Kincaid Park. Meals are artistically presented, and the diverse and creative menu, with a focus on Alaska regional cuisine, seafood, and game meats, changes seasonally. **Known for:** seafood gumbo; chocolate bourbon soufflé; long list at the wine bar. ⑤ *Average main: $33* ✉ *6700 Jewel Lake Rd., South Anchorage* ☎ *907/243–0507* ⊕ *kincaidgrill.com* ⊙ *Closed Sun. and Mon. No lunch.*

Peanut Farm Sports Bar and Grill

$$ | AMERICAN | This 70-screen sports bar has room for athletic fans of every stripe, from hockey (of course) to mushing and beyond. There's also an outdoor deck, pool tables, and a large and varied menu of tasty bar favorites. **Known for:** best wings in the city; patio on the bank of Campbell Creek; fireside seating in an original log cabin building. ⑤ *Average main: $18* ✉ *5227 Old Seward Hwy., South Anchorage* ☎ *907/563–3283* ⊕ *www.wemustbenuts.com* ▭ *No credit cards.*

🏨 Hotels

Camai Bed and Breakfast

$$ | B&B/INN | At this elegant B&B, Anchorage's oldest, two of the suites have private entries and plenty of space for families, and all suites have private baths and in-room satellite televisions. **Pros:** some suites have private exterior entrances; very experienced hosts; lovely deck and hot tub. **Cons:** relatively long way from Downtown restaurants; located in a neighborhood cul-de-sac; only continental breakfast in winter. ⑤ *Rooms from: $150* ✉ *3838 Westminster Way, East Anchorage* ☎ *907/333–2219,* ⊕ *www.camaibnb.com* ⬧ *3 suites* ⧦ *Breakfast.*

Just outside of the city center, Potter Marsh is a beautiful place to bird-watch and to catch the sunrise.

Dimond Center Hotel

$$ | HOTEL | FAMILY | For the price, the Dimond Center Hotel offers a shocking number of perks: every room has a 72-inch soaking tub, huge flat-screen television, microwave, and mini-refrigerator—not to mention the generous breakfast buffet, with waffles and biscuits and gravy. **Pros:** airport shuttle; free Wi-Fi; no fee for parking. **Cons:** 5 miles from Downtown; surrounded by national chain stores; shares a parking lot with the city's largest mall. $ *Rooms from: $199* ⊠ *700 E. Dimond Blvd., South Anchorage* ☎ *907/770–5000, 866/770–5002* ⊕ *www. dimondcenterhotel.com* ⤢ *109 rooms* ❖ *Breakfast.*

🛍 Shopping

Mountain View Sports Fly Shop

SPORTING GOODS | If you're looking for brand names like Abel, Simms, Filson, Patagonia, and Mountain Hardwear, this locally owned store is your place. It is pretty much fly-fishing central in Anchorage, and you can find expert advice and guidance for your prospective fishing and hunting adventures. There's also an excellent book section that covers all sorts of outdoor activities in Alaska. ⊠ *11124 Old Seward Hwy., Midtown* ☎ *907/222–6633* ⊕ *www.mtviewsports.com.*

🏃 Activities

Few American cities feel as connected to the outdoors as Anchorage. From the in-town Tony Knowles Coastal Trail to a nearly endless supply of trails and other outdoor adventures in the Chugach National Forest and on nearby waterways, Anchorage is an outdoor-lover's playground. And that doesn't just hold true for the warmer months; a nearby ski resort offers downhill delights, and there's plenty of dog mushing, ice-skating, and other wintry sports to try. Up for some spectator sports instead? Anchorage doesn't disappoint: summer-league baseball, the start of the Iditarod, and even shoulder-to-shoulder "combat" fishing await you.

BASEBALL

Mulcahy Stadium

BASEBALL/SOFTBALL | Two summer baseball teams made up of college students—the Bucs and the Glacier Pilots—play at Mulcahy Stadium, right off the Chester Creek Trail. With tickets only $5, it's an excellent option for a summer evening in town. The games can get intense—many athletes have gone on to play in the major leagues—but the setting is relaxed, with innings played under evening sunshine amid sweeping views of the Chugach Mountains. The short season lasts from June through July. ⊠ *E. 16th Ave. at Cordova St., Downtown* ⊕ *www.anchoragebucs.com/view/anchoragebucs/our-mission-15/mulcahy-stadium.*

BICYCLING

Anchorage has more than 120 miles of paved bicycle trails, and many streets have marked bike lanes. Although busy during the day, Downtown streets are uncrowded and safe for cyclists in the evening.

Alaskabike

BICYCLING | Serious gearheads can book multiday touring packages through this company to explore Southcentral, the Interior, the Yukon Territory, and nearby scenic highways. Another option is the all-inclusive multisport tour, which features biking, hiking, canoeing, sea kayaking, and a glacier cruise. ⊠ *Anchorage* ☎ *907/245–2175, 866/683–2453* ⊕ *www.alaskabike.com.*

Alaska Pablo's Bicycle Rentals

BICYCLING | Rates start at $10 at this shop perched just two blocks from the ocean and the Tony Knowles Coastal Trail. Treat yourself to a postride reward at the hot dog stand out front, run by the owner's twin brother. ⊠ *501 L St., Downtown* ☎ *907/250–2871* ⊕ *www.pablobicyclerentals.com.*

Downtown Bicycle Rental

BICYCLING | With an inventory of more than 140 bikes of all types, Downtown Bicycle Rental also rents trailers, clip-in pedals, and shoes. The minimum rental rate is $16 for three hours, which includes free lock, helmet, panniers, and trail map. In winter, fat bikes and studded-tire bikes are available for $25 per day. Owner Peter Roberts offers once-a-day shuttle van rides to the Flattop trailhead in summer for both hikers and bikers. ⊠ *333 W. 4th Ave., Downtown* ☎ *907/279–3334* ⊕ *www.alaska-bike-rentals.com.*

Lifetime Adventures

BICYCLING | Just 30 miles north of Anchorage, Lifetime Adventures operates out of the state park campground at Eklutna Lake, renting out bikes, trailers, and kayaks. You can choose the popular Paddle & Pedal package where you paddle in one direction and pedal your way back. Closer to town, the company also rents bikes outside Copper Whale Inn, just a block uphill from the Tony Knowles Coastal Trail. ⊠ *440 L St., at 5th Ave.* ☎ *907/746–4644* ⊕ *www.lifetimeadventures.net.*

BIRD-WATCHING

Popular bird-watching places include the Tony Knowles Coastal Trail, which provides access to Westchester Lagoon and nearby tide flats, along with Potter Marsh on the south end of Anchorage.

Anchorage Audubon Society

BIRD WATCHING | The Anchorage chapter of the National Audubon Society offers downloadable birding checklists on their website and can refer you to local birders who will advise you on the best bird-watching spots. The society also hosts bird-watching field trips and events, like the Potter Marsh-a-Thon Birding Smackdown every May. ⊠ *Anchorage* ⊕ *www.anchorageaudubon.org.*

Wilderness Birding Adventures

BIRD WATCHING | With nearly a dozen naturalist guides on staff, Homer-based Wilderness Birding Adventures offers backcountry birding, wildlife, and natural-history trips to remote parts of Alaska, as well as village-based, birding-focused trips to some of the state's birding hot spots. ⊠ *Anchorage* ☎ *907/299–3937* ⊕ *www.wildernessbirding.com.*

CANOEING, CRUISING, AND KAYAKING

Local lakes and lagoons, such as Westchester Lagoon, Goose Lake, and Jewel Lake, have favorable conditions for canoeing and kayaking. More adventurous paddlers should head to Whittier or Seward for sea kayaking.

Alaska Raft and Kayak

CANOEING/ROWING/SKULLING | Rent or buy from a flotilla's worth of small boats, including kayaks, canoes, pack rafts, and one-man fishing pontoons. And if your trip was wilder than expected, the store also repairs boats of all styles and sizes. ⊠ *401 W. Tudor Rd., Midtown* ☎ *907/561–7238, 800/606–5950* ⊕ *www.alaskaraftandkayak.com.*

Kenai Fjord Tours

TOUR—SPORTS | Give your arms a rest, soak up glacier views, and spot the abundant wildlife of Kenai Fjords National Park from a cruise boat. Kenai Fjord Tours offers day-trip packages to Kenai Fjords National Park late March through September, with transportation via coach and train between Anchorage and Seward. ⊠ *509 W. 4th Ave., Downtown* ☎ *888/478–3346, 907/777–2800* ⊕ *www.kenaifjords.com.*

DOG MUSHING

Fur Rondy Festival

LOCAL SPORTS | World-championship dog-mushing races are run in February, with three consecutive 25-mile heats through Downtown Anchorage, out into the foothills, and back. People line the route with cups of coffee in hand to cheer on their favorite mushers. The three-day races are part of the annual Fur Rendezvous Festival, one of the largest winter festivals in the United States. Other cabin fever–kicking attractions include the running of the reindeer (yes, just like Pamplona but with reindeer), a snow-sculpture competition, Alaska Native blanket toss (a holdover from earlier days when dozens of people would launch a hunter high into the air, trampoline-style, in an effort to spot distant seals, walrus, and whales), a carnival, and even snowshoe softball. Fur Rondy events start in late February, culminating ten days later with the ceremonial Iditarod start on 4th Avenue in early March. ⊠ *Anchorage* ⊕ *www.furrondy.net.*

Iditarod Trail Sled Dog Race

LOCAL SPORTS | The 1,049-mile Iditarod Trail Sled Dog Race commemorates the delivery of serum to Nome by dog mushers during the diphtheria epidemic of 1925. In early March, dog teams leave the mushing hub of Willow, about 70 miles northeast of Anchorage, and wind through the Alaska Range, across the Interior, out to the Bering Sea coast, and on to Nome. Depending on weather and trail conditions, winners can complete the race in less than nine days. ⊠ *Anchorage* ☎ *907/376–5155 Iditarod trail headquarters* ⊕ *www.iditarod.com.*

FISHING

Nearly 30 local lakes and streams are stocked with catchable game fish.

■ **TIP** → **You must have a valid Alaska sportfishing license to fish in the state. Fishing licenses may be purchased at any Fred Meyer or Carr's/Safeway grocery or local sporting goods store, or online at www.admin.adfg.state.ak.us/buyonline. Nonresidents can buy an annual license or a 1-, 3-, 7-, or 14-day permit. A separate king salmon stamp is required to fish for the big guys.** Rainbow trout, arctic char, landlocked salmon, Dolly Varden, grayling, and northern pike are among the species found in waters like Jewel Lake in South Anchorage and Mirror and Fire lakes near Eagle River. Coho salmon return to Ship Creek (Downtown) in mid-July, and king salmon are caught there between late May and early July. Campbell Creek and Bird Creek just south of town are also good spots for coho (silver) salmon. Anywhere in Alaska there are fish, it's possible there are also bears, so stay aware.

Alaska Department of Fish and Game

FISHING | Contact the Alaska Department of Fish and Game for licensing information. For information about Anchorage-area lakes, go to the website; click on "Sport" under the Fishing menu, the Southcentral portion of the "Information by Area" map, and then Anchorage. ⊠ *Anchorage* ☎ *907/267–2218* ⊕ *www. adfg.alaska.gov.*

The Bait Shack

FISHING | You don't have to leave Downtown to fish for salmon—they come right through Ship Creek. Dustin Slinker, the friendly owner of the Bait Shack, will tell you exactly where to fish so you're almost guaranteed to land a salmon; first timers are welcome. He'll also fillet and vacuum pack your catch. Daily rentals include a rod, reel, waders, tackle box, and landing net and cost $40; you can also purchase a fishing license here. Dustin rents gear for up to two weeks if your plans expand beyond the Bait Shack's backyard, but Ship Creek offers urban fishing among locals—a markedly different experience from pricey fishing charters. ⊠ *212 W. Whitney Rd., Downtown* ☎ *907/522–3474* ⊕ *www.thebaitshackak.com.*

Slam'n Salm'n Derby

FISHING | Each June, locals fish for king salmon on Ship Creek to raise money for the Downtown Soup Kitchen. If you're not into fishing, the crowded combat fishing is just as entertaining to observe from the bridge. ⊠ *211 W. Ship Creek Ave., Downtown* ⊕ *www.anchorage.net/events/salmon-derby.*

FLIGHTSEEING

This area is the state's air-travel hub. Plenty of flightseeing services operating out of city airports and floatplane bases can take you on spectacular tours of **Denali,** the **Chugach Range, Prince William Sound, Kenai Fjords National Park,** and the **Harding Icefield.** Anchorage hosts the greatest number and variety of services,

including companies operating fixed-wing aircraft, floatplanes, and helicopters.

★ Rust's Flying Service

TOUR—SPORTS | An Anchorage company in business since 1963, Rust's will take you on narrated flightseeing tours of Denali, Columbia Glacier, and Prince William Sound. Rust's also offers bear-viewing flights to Lake Clark National Park and Preserve and the Bristol Bay region, and can arrange multiday fishing and hiking trips to various backcountry locations. Rust's also owns Talkeetna-based K2 Aviation and offers skiplane glacier landings on Denali. ⊠ *4525 Enstrom Circle, West Anchorage* ☎ *907/243–1595, 800/544–2299* ⊕ *www.flyrusts.com.*

HIKING

Hiking is king in Anchorage all yearlong thanks to Chugach State Park, which provides nearly 500,000 acres of exploration right in the city's backyard. You'll find Alaskans from all walks of life hiking in summer, even at midnight. Winter and spring are easily tackled with snow spikes, and nearly every resident has their favorite berry patch on the mountains when fall arrives.

Crow Pass

HIKING/WALKING | This 23-mile trek—formerly part of the Iditarod Trail—is a popular overnight hiking trail for Anchorage residents (and yes, there's a trail marathon every July). Hikers can leave from the Crow Pass trailhead in Girdwood or the Eagle River Nature Center in Eagle River. There are marked campsites throughout, as well as rental yurts near Eagle River and a public-use cabin three miles uphill from Girdwood. Reservations are required for both. Prepare to get wet at river crossings, and plan your transport—it's a 70-mile drive between trailheads. ⊠ *Eagle River Trailhead, 32750 Eagle River Rd.* ⌕ *$5 daily parking fee.*

★ Flattop Mountain

HIKING/WALKING | Alaska's most popular peak, this manageable 3-mile round-trip escalates in difficulty, gaining nearly

Iditarod Trail History

Since 1973, mushers and their sled-dog teams have raced 1,000 miles across Alaska in the Iditarod Trail Sled Dog Race, one of the longest sled-dog races in the world.

After a ceremonial start in Downtown Anchorage on the first Saturday in March, dog teams wind through Alaska, battling almost every imaginable winter challenge. Iditarod mushers and dogs endure extreme cold, deep snow, gale-force winds, whiteouts, river overflow, and moose attacks, not to mention fraying tempers. Less than 10 days later, the front-runners in the "Last Great Race" cross under the burled-wood arch finish line in Nome, on the Bering Sea coast.

Race Revival

The Iditarod's origins can be traced to two events: an early-1900s long-distance race called the All-Alaska Sweepstakes, and the delivery of a lifesaving serum to Nome by dog mushers during a diphtheria outbreak in 1925.

Fascinated with the trail's history, Alaskan sled-dog enthusiasts Dorothy Page and Joe Redington Sr. staged the first race in 1967 to celebrate the role of mushing in Alaska's history. Only 50 miles long and with a purse of $25,000—no small amount at that time—it attracted the best of Alaska's competitive mushers. Enthusiasm waned in 1969, however, when the available winnings fell to $1,000. Instead of giving up, Redington expanded the race.

In 1973, after three years without a race, he organized a 1,000-mile race from Anchorage to Nome, with a then-outrageous purse of $50,000. Critics scoffed, but 34 racers entered. First place went to a little-known musher named Dick Wilmarth, who finished in 20 days. Redington then billed the Iditarod as a 1,049-mile race to symbolize Alaska, the 49th state.

The Race Begins

The race actually begins in Willow, a 70-mile drive north of Anchorage. The first few hundred miles take mushers and dogs through wooded lowlands and hills, including the aptly named Moose Alley.

Teams then cross the Alaska Range and enter Interior Alaska, with Athabascan villages and gold-rush ghost towns, including one called Iditarod. Next, the trail follows the frozen Yukon River, then cuts over to the Bering Sea coast for the final 220-mile "sprint" to Nome. It was here, in 1985, that Libby Riddles drove her team into a blinding blizzard en route to a victory that made her the first woman to win the race. After that, Susan Butcher won the race four times, but the all-time record holder is Rick Swenson, with five victories. Lance Mackey holds the record for most consecutive wins, with his back-to-backs from 2007 to 2010. Mitch Seavey and his son Dallas traded the title from 2012 to 2017, setting the speed record three times. Currently, Mitch has the fastest time ever, finishing in 8 days, 3 hours, and 40 minutes in 2017.

Sled dogs start the Iditarod in Willow and stop here, at the Finger Lake Checkpoint, 194 miles into the 1,150-mile trek.

1,500 feet from the parking lot. But whether you reach the flagpole at the summit or simply stroll the 0.3-mile wheelchair-accessible loop at the base, you'll be treated to astounding views of the Anchorage Bowl and Cook Inlet. Downtown Bicycle Rental runs a once-daily shuttle from mid-April to mid-October originating from its shop on 4th Avenue. ⊠ Glen Alps Trailhead, Glen Alps Rd. 🖅 $5 parking fee.

Thunderbird Falls

HIKING/WALKING | A reasonable 2-mile round-trip hike with easy road access, Thunderbird Falls is the simplest hike near Anchorage. The wide trail skirts the rim of Eklutna Canyon before culminating in a wooden viewing platform of Thunderbird Falls. Hikers can also scramble downhill to reach the pools below the 200-foot falls, which frequently freeze in winter. ⊠ Mile 25.2 of Glenn Hwy. 🖅 $5 daily parking fee.

SKIING

Cross-country skiing is extremely popular in Anchorage. Locals ski or skate-ski on trails in town at Kincaid Park or Hillside and farther away at Girdwood Valley, Turnagain Pass, and Chugach State Park. Downhill skiing is convenient to Downtown. A number of cross-country ski events are held annually in Anchorage.

Alaska Mountaineering & Hiking

SKIING/SNOWBOARDING | The locally owned outdoors shop Alaska Mountaineering & Hiking has a highly experienced staff and plenty of cross-country skis for sale or rent. ⊠ 2633 Spenard Rd., Spenard ☎ 907/272–1811 ⊕ www.alaskamountaineering.com.

Hilltop Ski Area

SKIING/SNOWBOARDING | Conveniently located on the eastern edge of town, Hilltop Ski Area is a beginner-friendly slope and a favorite for families. ⊠ Abbott Rd. near Hillside Dr., East Anchorage ☎ 907/346–2167 ski hotline ⊕ www.hilltopskiarea.org.

Kincaid Park

BICYCLING | On 1,400 acres of rolling, timbered hills and bordered on the west by Cook Inlet, Kincaid Park is a scenic treasure with maintained trails groomed for diagonal and skate-skiing. National cross-country skiing events (including U.S. Olympic team qualifying events) are sometimes held along the 60 km (37 miles) of interwoven trails—including 20 km (12 miles) that are lighted for night skiing. The park is open year-round: for skiing in winter; and for mountain biking, hiking, and other outdoor activities in summer. ⊠ *Main entrance at far west end of Raspberry Rd., 9401 W. Raspberry Rd., Southwest Anchorage.*

Side Trips from Anchorage

A ski resort, summer vacation spot, and home to an eclectic collection of locals, the town of Girdwood sits in a deep valley and is surrounded by tall mountains on three sides and, on the fourth, Turnagain Arm, one of the most photogenic sites in Southcentral Alaska.

Girdwood

40 miles southeast of Anchorage.

Originally called Glacier City, Girdwood got its start as a gold-mining town. The town was renamed for James Girdwood, an Irish linen merchant who had four gold claims. But the name wasn't the only thing that changed over the years; the town itself was moved 2½ miles from its original site after the 1964 earthquake.

Today Girdwood's main attraction is the Alyeska Ski Resort, the largest ski area in Alaska. Besides enjoying the obvious winter attractions, you can hike up the mountain, rent a bike, or visit several upscale restaurants and gift shops. Girdwood is wetter than Anchorage; it often

rains or snows here while the sun shines to the north.

GETTING HERE AND AROUND
Though it's only 40 miles from Ted Stevens Anchorage International Airport, consider allowing extra time if you make the drive to Girdwood. The drive down the New Seward Highway is stunning; look out for beluga whales and Dall sheep. Other options include a ride on the Alaska Railroad *Coastal Classic* or *Glacier Discovery* train (*907/265–2494, 800/544–0552 ⊕ www.alaskarailroad. com*). Once in Girdwood, you can get pretty much anywhere on the fare-free bus routes provided by Glacier Valley Transit (⊕ *www.glaciervalleytransit.com*).

WHEN TO GO
Though Girdwood is best known for its winter ski activities, there's plenty to do year-round. The town's restaurants remain popular with locals—snow or no snow—and the area offers some of Anchorage's best hiking trails, fishing, and much more.

◉ Sights

Girdwood Center for Visual Arts

ARTS VENUE | Though you'll go to Girdwood to ski or hike, you'll end up spending time perusing the crafts and artwork at this nonprofit co-op gallery. With pieces from more than 30 artists on display, there's plenty to look at—and you might end up taking care of any gift needs (from the trip or for the holidays) in one fell swoop. Opening days vary from fall through spring, so it's best to call ahead. ⊠ *194 Olympic Mountain Loop, Girdwood ☎ 907/783–3209 ⊕ www. gcvaonline.org.*

⚡ Activities

Alaska Backcountry Access

TOUR—SPORTS | This outfitter takes people out of town for jet-boat rides up Twentymile River, summertime snowmobiling near Godwin Glacier, and much more. Families with kids six and older might enjoy their slightly adventurous, naturalist-led day trip that includes a hike, panning for gold, and a cable hand-tram trip across Glacier Creek. Winter excursions includes snowmobile outings across Southcentral Alaska. ☒ *Girdwood* ☎ *907/783–3600* ⊕ *www.akback.com.*

Alyeska Resort

SKIING/SNOWBOARDING | Alaska's largest and best-known downhill ski resort encompasses more than 1,600 skiable acres of terrain for all skill levels, where snowfall averages nearly 670 inches annually. Alyeska features a day lodge, hotel, restaurants, six lifts, a tram, a vertical drop of 2,500 feet, and 76 named trails for all abilities—including North America's longest continuous double black run. The tram is also open in summer ($29), providing access to Seven Glaciers restaurant and ridgeline hiking trails. Brave the stout hike up the mountain, and you can ride the tram down for free. Ski and snowboard rentals are available, and local guides teach classes on the mountain. ☒ *1000 Arlberg Ave., Girdwood* ☎ *907/754–2111, 800/880–3880* ⊕ *www.alyeskaresort.com* ☞ *$85; $61 for night skiing.*

Chugach Powder Guides

SKIING/SNOWBOARDING | This helicopter and Sno-Cat skiing operation focuses on backcountry skiing and snowboarding in the interior Chugach Range, the Seward area, and the Talkeetna Mountains. Set itineraries and private charters are both available. ☒ *Girdwood* ☎ *907/783–4354* ⊕ *www.chugachpowderguides.com.*

Winner Creek

HIKING/WALKING | An excellent outdoor option in Girdwood, Winner Creek is 45 minutes south of Anchorage. Leaving from the Hotel Alyeska's backyard, this gradual, well-maintained trail cuts through the country's northernmost rain forest. The first 3 miles span boggy boardwalks and wooden bridges over bubbling creeks before ending at the hand tram, a man-powered cage that transports hikers two at a time over Glacier Creek. The trail continues another 9 miles to Crow Creek Road, but many hikers simply take the tram twice and head back to town for a celebratory meal. ☒ *Trailhead behind Hotel Alyeska, 1000 Arlberg Ave., Girdwood.*

🍴 Restaurants

The Bake Shop

$ | **AMERICAN** | Order at the counter at this old-time, family-owned Girdwood favorite. Skiers and snowboarders drop by for a quick lunch or garden-fresh pizzas in winter while summertime early birds enjoy cups of coffee and fluffy omelets on the flower-filled patio. **Known for:** sourdough pancakes; legendary sweet rolls; bottomless soups perfect for cold ski days. ⑤ *Average main: $10* ☒ *194 Olympic Mountain Loop, Girdwood* ☎ *907/783–2831* ⊕ *www.thebakeshop. com* ⊗ *Closer Tues. and Wed. in winter.*

Double Musky Inn

$$$$ | **SOUTHERN** | Anchorage residents say eating at this beloved spot is well worth the one-hour drive south to Girdwood and the inevitable wait for dinner. The interior is completely covered with tacky art and Mardi Gras souvenirs, but the windows frame views of huge Sitka spruce trees and the diverse menu mixes hearty Cajun-style meals with such favorites as garlic seafood pasta, rack of lamb, French pepper steak, and lobster kebabs. **Known for:** tasty Cajun creations; gooey, chocolate-rice pie; gorgeous views. ⑤ *Average main: $34* ☒ *Mile 0.3, Crow Creek Rd., Girdwood* ☎ *907/783–2822* ⊕ *www.doublemuskyinn.com* ⊗ *Closed Mon. and late Oct.–mid-Dec. No lunch.*

★ Seven Glaciers

$$$$ | **EUROPEAN** | This refined yet relaxing mountaintop restaurant is perched 2,300 feet up Mt. Alyeska, accessed by a 60-passenger aerial tram (free with dinner reservations, otherwise $29 round-trip). The forward-thinking menu capitalizes on local produce and seafood, highlighted in dishes such as scallop bisque with smoked salmon mousse. **Known for:** Alaska-grown ingredients and top-tier seafood; 32-page wine menu; unforgettable panoramic mountain views. ⑤ *Average main: $47* ✉ *Hotel Alyeska, 1000 Arlberg Rd., Girdwood* ☎ *907/754–2237* ⊕ *www.alyeskaresort.com/dining* ⊘ *No lunch.*

🛏 Hotels

Carriage House Accomodations

$$ | B&B/INN | This Girdwood inn is across from the Double Musky restaurant and close to Alyeska Resort's downhill ski slopes. **Pros:** elegant furnishings; gazebo-enclosed hot tub; very nice breakfast spread. **Cons:** location a bit remote for some; restaurant traffic may be bothersome; shared kitchen and dining room in the inn. ⑤ *Rooms from: $150* ✉ *388 Crow Creek Rd., Girdwood* ☎ *907/783–9464* ⊕ *www.thecarriagehousebandb. com* ⤢ *4 rooms, 3 chalets* ⑩ *Breakfast.*

★ The Hotel Alyeska

$$$$ | HOTEL | Most rooms have stunning views of the Chugach Mountains and the lush forests surrounding this large and luxurious hotel at the base of Alyeska Ski Resort. **Pros:** great views; top-notch service; frequent ski-and-stay packages in winter. **Cons:** some rooms are on the small side; public traffic in lobby; car needed from Anchorage. ⑤ *Rooms from: $309* ✉ *1000 Arlberg Ave., Girdwood* ☎ *907/754–2111, 800/880–3880* ⊕ *www. alyeskaresort.com/hotel* ⤢ *327 rooms* ⑩ *No meals.*

◉ Nightlife

Girdwood Brewing Company

BREWPUBS/BEER GARDENS | Tall windows frame the Chugach Mountains and old skis fence the patio at this airy brewery, opened by twin brothers, head brewers, and noted powder hounds Rory and Brett Marenco. Like all Anchorage breweries, Girdwood Brewing Company closes by 8 pm, so make sure to end your adventures on the nearby tides, trails, and mountaintops early enough to grab a pint. ✉ *2700 Alyeska Hwy., Girdwood* ☎ *907/783–2739* ⊕ *www.girdwoodbrewing.com.*

The Sitzmark

MUSIC CLUBS | Guests can ski straight to the back patio and firepit at this rollicking bar and grill. The Sitz hosts an event nearly every winter night under its spiral-painted ceiling, from game nights and trivia to nationally touring music acts. The bar closes each spring and fall as the Hotel Alyeska shifts between mountain bike and ski seasons; call to confirm hours before visiting. ✉ *100 Olympic Cir., Anchorage* ☎ *907/754–2275* ⊕ *www. thesitzmark.com.*

Chapter 4

JUNEAU, THE INSIDE PASSAGE, AND SOUTHEAST ALASKA

4

Updated by
Amy Fletcher

👁 Sights   🍴 Restaurants   🛏 Hotels   🛍 Shopping   🍸 Nightlife

★★★★★   ★★★★☆   ★★★★☆   ★★★★☆   ★★★☆☆

WELCOME TO JUNEAU, THE INSIDE PASSAGE, AND SOUTHEAST ALASKA

TOP REASONS TO GO

★ **Native art and culture:** Home of the Tlingit, Haida, and Tsimshian, Southeast is passionate about preserving and perpetuating Native cultures. Native art forms include totem poles, weavings, and masks.

★ **Rivers of ice:** Visitors relish the opportunity to walk on Southeast's accessible glaciers or to admire them on flightseeing or kayak trips.

★ **Tongass National Forest:** America's largest national forest is home to bears, bald eagles, Sitka black-tailed deer, wolves, and marine mammals.

★ **Fishing nirvana:** Southeast is an angler's paradise. The region's healthy populations of salmon and halibut—as well as the wealth of charter boats and fishing lodges—make this a premier fishing destination.

★ **Taking the ferry:** The Alaska Marine Highway is the primary means of transportation here. It's a low-cost, high-adventure alternative to cruising, and an easy way to spend time talking to Alaskans.

As remote as it is, Southeast Alaska shares a few traits with heavily populated regions. It has skyscrapers (the towering peaks of the Coast Range), traffic jams (try to swim through a salmon creek midsummer), and sprawl (the rain forests cover hundreds of thousands of acres).

1 Ketchikan. A town famous for its colorful totem poles, rainy skies, steep streets, and lush island setting.

2 Misty Fiords National Monument. A wilderness area filled with gorgeous fjords and coastal scenery.

3 Metlakatla. A quiet Inside Passage Native community.

4 Price of Wales Island. The largest island in southeast Alaska.

5 Wrangell. A fishing and timber community on North America's largest undammed river.

6 Petersburg. A hard-to-acess town that will reward you with fishing and Nordic influence.

7 Sitka. A vibrant arts community with excellent parks and kayaking.

8 Juneau. Alaska's charming capital and home to the famed Mendenhall Glacier.

9 Juneau's Nearby Villages. Native communities that offer insight into the area's indigenous cultures.

10 Admiralty Island. The home of the Southeast's largest population of brown bears.

11 Tracy Arm. A narrow fjord that leads to Sawyer Glacier.

12 Glacier Bay National Park and Preserve. The continent's largest (and most stunning) collection of tidewater glaciers.

13 Gustavus. The gateway to Glacier Bay National Park.

14 Haines. A small town known for fishing and an eagle preserve.

15 Skagway. A famed Gold Rush town with gorgeous scenery and an incredible railway.

The communities of Southeast Alaska occupy a small fraction of this dramatic landscape, dotting mountainsides and natural harbors every hundred miles like far-flung pebbles. Ketchikan in the south, Sitka in the middle, and Juneau in the north are among the most visited locales.

In between, layers of mist-covered mountains and stretches of quiet forest remind visitors of what Southeast residents know and respect: this is nature's domain. West of Haines in the far northern reaches lies Glacier Bay National Park and Preserve, with its soaring glaciers, and the entire region provides habitats for bears, mountain goats, wolves, whales, and eagles. This is a world of steep-shouldered islands, cliff-rimmed fjords, snowcapped peaks, and majestic glaciers. Even in the biggest population centers, such as Juneau, man-made structures seem to sit lightly on the land, invariably dwarfed by their surroundings. Lush stands of spruce, hemlock, and cedar blanket thousands of islands. The region's myriad bays, coves, lakes, and swift, icy rivers provide some of the continent's best fishing grounds. Many of Southeast's wildest and most pristine landscapes are within Tongass National Forest, which comprises nearly 17 million acres—almost three-quarters of the Panhandle's land.

Southeast lacks only one thing: connecting roads. The lack of pavement between the area's communities presents obvious challenges to four-wheeled transport. The isolation and the wet weather discourage people from moving in. To help remedy the transportation question, the state created the Alaska Marine Highway System, a network of passenger and vehicle ferries, some of which have staterooms, observation decks, video theaters, arcades, cafeterias, and heated, glass-enclosed solariums.

Southeast's natural beauty and abundance of wildlife have made it a popular cruise destination. About 25 big ships ply the Inside Passage—once the traditional route to the Klondike goldfields and today the centerpiece of many Alaska cruises—during the height of summer. Smaller ships (some locally owned) also cruise through. Regular air service to Southeast is available from Seattle and other parts of Alaska, primarily Anchorage.

Three groups of Native peoples inhabit Southeast's coastal region: the Tlingit (*klink*-it), Haida, and Tsimshian (*sim-shee-ann*). Because their cultures were once in danger of being lost, there's an ever-growing focus on preserving and perpetuating Native traditions and teaching visitors about their ways of life. Efforts are under way in many towns to teach the often tricky-to-master Native languages in schools and through other programs. These efforts received a boost in 2014, when Alaska's legislature voted to recognize 20 indigenous languages as official state tongues, including Lingít (Tlingit language), Xaad Kil (Haida language), and Sm'algyax (Tsimshian language).

Southeast Natives, like their coastal neighbors in British Columbia, have rich traditions of Northwest Coast art, including carved poles, masks, baskets, and ceremonial objects. These traditions continue to evolve through the work of contemporary artists. In most villages and towns there's been a push to help residents learn these art forms and keep them alive for generations to come.

Residents—some from other states, some who can trace their ancestors back to the gold-rush days, and some whose ancestors came over the Bering Land Bridge from Asia thousands of years ago—are an adventurous bunch. The rough-and-tumble spirit of Southeast often combines with a worldly sophistication: those who fish for a living might also be artists, Forest Service workers may run a B&B on the side, and homemakers may be Native dance performers.

The Southeast Panhandle stretches some 500 miles from Yakutat at its northernmost point to Ketchikan and Metlakatla at its southern end. At its widest point, the region measures only 140 miles, and in the upper Panhandle just south of Yakutat, at 30 miles across, it is downright skinny by Alaska standards. Most of the Panhandle consists of a sliver of mainland buffered on the west by islands and on the east by the imposing peaks of the Coast Mountains.

Those numerous coastal islands—more than 1,000 throughout the Inside Passage—collectively constitute the Alexander Archipelago. Most of them present mountainous terrain with lush covers of timber, though large clear-cuts are also common. Most communities are on islands rather than on the mainland. The principal exceptions are Juneau, Haines, and Skagway, plus the hamlets of Gustavus and Hyder. Island outposts include Ketchikan, Wrangell, Petersburg, Sitka, and the villages of Craig, Pelican, Metlakatla, Kake, Angoon, and Hoonah. Bordering Alaska just east of the Panhandle lies the Canadian province of British Columbia.

MAJOR TOWNS AND REGIONS

Ketchikan and Around. The self-proclaimed "Salmon Capital of the World," Ketchikan is the doorway to Southeast. Be sure to check out the area's charter-fishing opportunities and wealth of local art. Ketchikan is a jumping-off point for Misty Fiords National Monument and visits to the Tsimshian community of Metlakatla.

Wrangell and Petersburg. These towns provide access to the magnificent Stikine River. Wrangell, which welcomes some of the smaller cruise ships, is the primary hub for those who want to travel to the Anan Wildlife Observatory to see both brown and black bears fishing for salmon. Petersburg has a vibrant fishing community and stellar access to fishing, whale-watching, and hiking.

Sitka. With its mixed history of Tlingit, Russian, and American rule, Sitka is known for its vibrant art community, excellent parks (including Sitka National Historical Park), and many outdoor activities. It's a must-see for anyone traveling in Southeast and a must-paddle for kayakers of all experience levels.

Juneau and Around. Cruise passengers flock by the hundreds of thousands to take in the state capital's historic charm, artsy community, and natural beauty, including world-famous Mendenhall Glacier. But with a number of hotels and bed-and-breakfasts, Juneau also welcomes independent travelers. The city is the access point for surrounding attractions, including Admiralty Island National Monument, home to Southeast's largest population of brown bears.

Glacier Bay National Park and Preserve. Southeast's signature attraction, Glacier Bay is home to the continent's largest collection of tidewater glaciers, which are incredible to see. The park's remote, undeveloped location—Gustavus, the closest town, isn't really a town at

4

Juneau, the Inside Passage, and Southeast Alaska

all—ensures that travelers in search of quiet repose will not be disappointed.

Haines and Skagway. The northern outposts of the Inside Passage, these two towns seem to have it all. Haines, on stunning Chilkat Peninsula, is home to fishermen, helicopter-skiing guides, and eagle aficionados who flock to the nearby Chilkat Bald Eagle Preserve. Just down the road from Klukwan, a village 22 miles outside Haines, visitors can learn more about Tlingit culture. Skagway has gorgeous scenery, an incredible railway, and a boisterous gold-rush history.

Planning

WHEN TO GO

The best time to visit is May through August, when weather is mildest, rain is less frequent, daylight hours are longest, wildlife is most abundant, and festivals and visitor-oriented activities are in full swing. But remember: Southeast sits in a rain forest, so rain can rule the day. There's a reason why XtraTuf waterproof boots are nicknamed "Southeast sneakers." Summertime high temperatures hover around the low to mid-60s, with far warmer days interspersed throughout. Shoulder-season temperatures are cooler, and the region is less crowded. Bring rain gear, layered clothing, sturdy footwear, a hat, and binoculars.

Allow yourself at least a week here. Plenty of adventures await ambitious independent travelers who plan ahead and ride state ferries.

If strolling through downtown shopping districts and museum-hopping is your idea of a perfect afternoon, journey to Ketchikan, Juneau, Skagway, Sitka, or Petersburg. For a wilderness experience in a peaceful, remote location, consider booking a multiple-night stay at one of Southeast's remote fly-in lodges.

FESTIVALS
Alaska Folk Festival
MUSIC FESTIVALS | FAMILY | The magic of this free, weeklong music festival is its inclusivity: every performer, regardless of his or her level of professionalism, is given 15 minutes on stage, with the exception of the featured guest artists, who play two one-hour sets. Held each April, Folk Fest draws singers, banjo masters, and fiddlers from all over the state and beyond. Past guest artists have included folk singer Nanci Griffith and western swing band Hot Club of Cowtown. Almost as fun as the festival itself is the after-hours bar scene that blossoms around it. Most local bars host performances and jam sessions; on the weekend the music continues into the wee hours. ⊠ *Centennial Hall, 101 Egan Dr., Juneau* ☎ *907/463–3316* ⊕ *www. akfolkfest.org.*

★ Celebration
CULTURAL FESTIVALS | FAMILY | More than 2,000 Native dancers gather in Juneau every even-numbered year in June to celebrate their heritage and the continued vitality of Alaska Native cultures. First held in 1982, this four-day cultural festival brings together tribal groups from all over the state, and includes a parade through the streets of Juneau for which participants don traditional, often very elaborate, handmade regalia. There's also a juried art show, Native fashion show, toddler regalia review, food contests, and a Native artist market. All events are open to the public, but the dance performances require a purchased ticket. ⊠ *1 Sealaska Plaza, Juneau* ☎ *907/463–4844* ⊕ *www.sealaskaheritage.org/institute/ celebration* 🎟 *$18 one-day pass.*

Great Alaska Craft Beer and Homebrew Festival
FESTIVALS | This wildly popular festival in Haines, known locally as Beerfest, offers a five-course gourmet brewers' dinner, beer-tasting sessions, a home-brew competition, and live music. Tickets, which sell out quickly, go on sale in early

February. ⊠ *296 Fair Dr., Haines* ☏ *907/766–2476* ⊕ *www.seakfair.org/events/beer-fest.*

Juneau Jazz & Classics

MUSIC FESTIVALS | FAMILY | Performers from all over the world head to Juneau each May to celebrate music from Bach to Brubeck. Taj Mahal, Arlo Guthrie, Booker T. Jones, and the Manhattan Transfer are among past guests. First held in 1987, the festival runs for more than two weeks, showcasing jazz and classics along with blues, rock, and soul. Many events require tickets but others—such as lunch-hour concerts at the State Office Building and jazz jams at a local bar called the Lucky Lady—are free. In this spirit of accessibility, visiting musicians also perform in Juneau schools. ⊠ *350 Whittier St., Suite 105, Juneau* ☏ *907/463–3378* ⊕ *www.jazzandclassics.org.*

Little Norway Festival

CULTURAL FESTIVALS | FAMILY | Enthusiasm for Petersburg's Norwegian heritage, expressed by rowdy locals dressed in horned helmets and fur vests, make this event one to catch. The festival has been held annually since 1958 on the weekend closest to May 17, *Syttende Mai,* or Norwegian Constitution Day. You won't find better Norwegian folk dancing or beer-batter halibut outside Norway. ⊠ *Petersburg* ☏ *907/772–4636* ⊕ *www.petersburg.org.*

Sitka Summer Music Festival

MUSIC FESTIVALS | FAMILY | Now under the artistic direction of world-renowned cellist Zuill Bailey, this monthlong celebration in June attracts musicians from as far away as Europe and Asia for concerts and special events. Most performances are held in the Sitka Historical Society and Museum. ⊠ *104 Jeff Davis St., Sitka* ☏ *907/747–6774* ⊕ *www.sitkamusicfestival.org.*

Sitka WhaleFest

FESTIVALS | FAMILY | Hosted by the Sitka Sound Science Center, this four-day festival and scientific symposium is held around town in early November, when the whales are plentiful (as many as 80) and tourists are not. Events include lectures, concerts, races, and cruises. ⊠ *834 Lincoln St., Suite 22, Sitka* ☏ *907/747–8878* ⊕ *www.sitkawhalefest.org.*

Southeast Alaska State Fair

FESTIVALS | From a logging show to a fiddle contest, the Southeast Alaska State Fair provides a slice-of-life introduction to the state's eclectic pastimes. Music is a highlight, and there are also kids' activities, tons of food options, and impressive crafts. ⊠ *296 Fair Dr., Haines* ☏ *907/766–2476* ⊕ *www.seakfair.org* 🎫 *From $10 per day.*

GETTING HERE AND AROUND

AIR TRAVEL

Alaska Airlines and Delta Airlines operate several flights daily from Seattle to Juneau, Ketchikan, and Sitka (Alaska's flights are year-round, Delta's are seasonal); connections are also available to Wrangell, Petersburg, Sitka, and Glacier Bay. Alaska Airlines also flies from Juneau to Anchorage, from which connections are available to much of the rest of state.

CONTACTS Alaska Airlines ☏ *800/252–7522* ⊕ *www.alaskaair.com.* **Delta Airlines** ☏ *800/221–1212* ⊕ *www.delta.com.*

FLIGHTSEEING

There's no better way to view Southeast's twisting channels, towering mountains, and gleaming glaciers than from one of the region's many small-aircraft flights.

Several services offer daily flights between Southeast's larger towns—Juneau, Haines, Skagway, Ketchikan, Sitka, Petersburg, and Wrangell—in addition to the bevy of helicopter flightseeing services that specialize in short, scenic flights.

Flying between destinations in Southeast—while significantly more expensive—is an experience you won't forget. If your itinerary includes an extra day or two in Southeast (particularly in Juneau), consider flying to and from a neighboring community. Round-trip tickets from Juneau to Skagway, for instance, start at around $250, as compared to approximately $170 for a one-hour flightseeing trip in and around Juneau. **Alaska Seaplanes** offers wheeled plane and floatplane access to 11 destinations around Juneau, as well as charter services (☎ 907/789–3331 ⊕ www.flyalaska-seaplanes.com).

Another floatplane service offering access to remote cabins and freshwater fishing destinations, **Southeast Aviation**, is Ketchikan-based (☎ 888/359–6478 ⊕ www.southeastaviation.com).

FERRY TRAVEL
The Alaska Marine Highway System operates stateroom-equipped vehicle and passenger ferries from Bellingham, Washington, and from Prince Rupert, British Columbia. Popular among budget-minded travelers and those seeking an alternative to cruise-ship travel, the ferry system allows passengers to create their own itineraries. In Southeast the vessels call at Metlakatla, Ketchikan, Wrangell, Petersburg, Kake, Sitka, Angoon, Tenakee, Hoonah, Juneau, Gustavus, Pelican, Haines, Skagway, and Yakutat—and it's possible to take the ferry all the way to Southcentral and Southwest Alaska.

■ TIP→ In summer, ferry staterooms sell out before sailing time; reserve months ahead. There are common areas on the ferries where you can throw a sleeping bag or sit in a recliner seat.

If you are planning to take a car on the ferry, early reservations for vehicle space are also highly recommended. This is particularly true for recreational vehicles. Ferry travel is also an ideal way for bicyclists to hop from town to town. There is a fee of $15 to $50 (depending on your route) to bring a bicycle aboard. A separate ferry, operated by the Inter-Island

Ferry Authority, runs between Ketchikan and Hollis (on Prince of Wales Island).

CONTACTS Alaska Marine Highway ☎ 907/465–3941, 800/642–0066 ⊕ www.dot.state.ak.us/amhs. **B.C. Ferries** ☎ 888/223–3779 ⊕ www.bcferries.com. **Inter-Island Ferry Authority** ☎ 907/225–4848, 866/308–4848 ⊕ www.interislandferry.com.

HEALTH AND SAFETY
Southeast Alaska is, as we've mentioned, wet. Make sure you bring rain gear. No sense catching cold on vacation. Also, if you're new to catching seafood, consider hiring a guide to help you find the safest spots—Alaska's waters are powerful. Don't rent a boat and go out solo—even in a skiff—if you don't have boating experience. Shifts in weather and tides, along with other factors, can turn a pleasant kayaking experience into something far less fun.

MONEY MATTERS
Most towns—especially ones frequented by cruise ships—have plenty of ATMs, but it doesn't hurt to have some cash in your wallet, especially if you're visiting some of the smaller places on Prince of Wales Island.

RESTAURANTS
From scallops to king salmon, fresh seafood dominates menus in Southeast. Juneau, Sitka, Skagway, and Ketchikan have all variety of ethnic eateries, along with some notable restaurants serving more sophisticated, contemporary fare. Many towns also have good greasy spoons or roadhouses where you can get a serving of local gossip along with your breakfast or slice of pie.

HOTELS
Lodging choices along the Inside Passage include high-end hotels and B&Bs both fancy and simple. Ketchikan and Juneau contain fine hotels, and luxurious fishing lodges attract anglers on Prince of Wales Island and in other locales.

These accommodations can be pricey, but rates drop from mid-September to mid-May. Excellent alternatives to local hotels, the many regional B&Bs provide the opportunity to meet fellow travelers, enjoy a homemade breakfast such as smoked-salmon omelets or authentic sourdough pancakes, and learn about the area from local business owners. Budget travelers will find hostels and even the occasional no-frills motel in many of the larger towns.

CONTACTS Alaska Travelers Accommodations ☎ 907/247–7117 ⊕ www.alaskatravelers.com.

CABINS
The Alaska State Parks and the U.S. Forest Service have cabins for rent.

Alaska State Parks
$ | RENTAL | Near Ketchikan and Juneau, the park system has a small number of cabins for which reservations can be made up to six months in advance. **Pros:** scenic locations; wildlife viewing; private. **Cons:** no electricity or running water; preparation time can be extensive; often remote. ⑤ *Rooms from: $45* ⊕ *www.dnr. alaska.gov/parks* ⌕ *From $45 a night.*

U.S. Forest Service Cabins
$ | RENTAL | At up to $45 per night, Forest Service cabins make for a cheap and charming escape, but they're popular; reserve in person, by mail, or online—up to six months in advance of your planned arrival date—with the National Recreation Reservation System ⊕ *www.reserveamerica.com.* **Pros:** scenic location; wildlife viewing; private. **Cons:** no electricity or running water; preparation time can be extensive; often remote. ⑤ *Rooms from: $45* ☎ 877/444–6777 ⊕ *www.recreation. gov.*

EQUIPMENT RENTALS
A few local outfitters rent cabin supplies. Alaska Wilderness Outfitting, part of Experience One Charters in Ketchikan, rents supplies such as cooking utensils, Coleman stoves, coolers, knives, and hot pads. Sitka Alaska Outfitters in Sitka can outfit you with a complete camping package that includes everything from sleeping pads to bear spray.

CONTACTS Experience One Charters ⊠ *3857 Fairview Ave., Ketchikan* ☎ *907/225–2343* ⊕ *www.latitude56.com.* **Sitka Alaska Outfitters** ⊠ *105 B Monastery St., Sitka* ☎ *907/966–2301* ⊕ *www. sitkaalaskaoutfitters.com.*

Restaurant and hotel reviews have been shortened. For full information, visit Fodors.com. Restaurant prices are the average cost of a main course at dinner or, if dinner is not served, at lunch. Hotel prices are the lowest cost of a standard double room in high season.

What It Costs			
$	$$	$$$	$$$$
RESTAURANTS			
under $14	$14–$22	$22–$30	over $30
HOTELS			
under $100	$100–$200	$201–$300	over $300

TOURS
Alaska Tour & Travel
NATIONAL/STATE PARK | This operator offers shore excursions in Juneau, Ketchikan, and Skagway, as well as customized tour packages through Southcentral Alaska and to most of the major national parks. ⊠ *9170 Jewel Lake Rd., Suite 202, Anchorage* ☎ *907/245–0200, 800/208–0200* ⊕ *www.alaskatravel.com* ⌕ *From $29.*

Alaska Tours
NATURE PRESERVE | This organization helps individuals and groups plan trips from Southeast to the Northwest and everything in between. ⊠ *600 Barrow St., Suite 200, Anchorage* ☎ *907/277–3000, 866/317–3325* ⊕ *www.alaskatours.com* ⌕ *Call for pricing.*

Mountain Travel Sobek

NATURE PRESERVE | Alaska Discovery, one of the oldest outfits in the state and a subsidiary of Mountain Travel Sobek, organizes adventure tours throughout Southeast. ⊠ *Ketchikan* ☎ *888/831–7526* ⊕ *www.mtsobek.com* ✉ *From $1195.*

Viking Travel, Inc.

NATURE PRESERVE | This reservations service can help you with your Alaska Marine Highway trip or other Alaska vacation plans. The agency has special airfares that are booked in conjunction with ferry itineraries. ⊠ *101 N. Nordic Dr., Petersburg* ☎ *907/772–3818, 800/327–2571* ⊕ *www.alaskaferry.com* ✉ *From $1700.*

VISITOR INFORMATION

Visitor information centers are generally open mid-May through August, daily from 8 to 5, with additional hours when cruise ships are in port; between September and mid-May they're typically open weekdays from 8 to 5.

Ketchikan

Ketchikan is famous for its colorful totem poles, rainy skies, steep–as–San Francisco streets, and lush island setting. Some 13,500 people call the town home, and, in the summer, cruise ships crowd the shoreline, floatplanes depart noisily for Misty Fiords National Monument, and salmon-laden commercial fishing boats motor through Tongass Narrows. In the last decade Ketchikan's rowdy, blue-collar heritage of logging and fishing has been softened by the loss of many timber-industry jobs and the dramatic rise of cruise-ship tourism, but visitors can still glimpse the rugged frontier spirit that once permeated this hardscrabble cannery town. Art lovers should make a beeline for Ketchikan: the arts community here is very active.

The town is at the foot of 3,000-foot Deer Mountain, near the southeastern corner of Revillagigedo (locals shorten it to Revilla) Island. Prior to the arrival of white miners and fishermen in 1885, the Tlingit used the site at the mouth of Ketchikan Creek as a summer fish camp. Gold discoveries just before the turn of the 20th century brought more immigrants, and valuable timber and commercial fishing resources spurred new industries. By the 1930s the town bragged that it was the "salmon-canning capital of the world." You will still find some of Southeast's best salmon fishing around here.

Ketchikan is the first bite of Alaska that many travelers taste. Despite its imposing backdrop, hillside homes, and many staircases, the town is relatively easy to walk through. Favorite downtown stops include Creek Street, a narrow boardwalk filled with locally owned shops, and the Southeast Alaska Discovery Center, where you can learn about the Tongass National Forest from local rangers. A bit farther away you'll find the Totem Heritage Center. Out of town (but included on most bus tours) are two longtime favorites: Totem Bight State Historical Park to the north and Saxman Totem Park to the south.

GETTING HERE AND AROUND

Ketchikan is a regular cruise-ship and ferry stop, and Alaska Airlines serves the town from Seattle. A three-minute ride on the Gateway Borough Ferry ($5) will get you from the airport to town, and there's a water taxi (cost varies) that serves waterfront marinas and piers.

If you're traveling out of town on the highway in either direction, you won't go far before you run out of road. The North Tongass Highway ends about 18 miles from downtown, at Settler's Cove Campground. The South Tongass Highway terminates about 13 miles from town. Side roads soon end at campgrounds and at trailheads, viewing points, lakes, boat-launching ramps, and private property.

Buses serve Ketchikan and outlying areas, and during the cruise-ship season (from May to September) a free shuttle bus travels a circular route from Berth 4. Notable stops include the Southeast Alaska Discovery Center, Creek Street, and the Totem Heritage Center.

ESSENTIALS

VISITOR INFORMATION Ketchikan Visitors Bureau ✉ *131 Front St.* ☎ *907/225–6166, 800/770–3300* ⊕ *www.visit-ketchikan. com.* **U.S. Forest Service** ✉ *648 Mission St.* ☎ *907/225–3101* ⊕ *www.fs.fed.us/ r10/tongass.*

Sights

Creek Street

HISTORIC SITE | This was once Ketchikan's red-light district. During Prohibition, Creek Street was home to numerous speakeasies, and in the early 1900s more than 30 houses of prostitution operated here. Today the small, colorful houses, built on stilts over the creek waters, have been restored as interesting shops. When the fish are running the Creek Street footbridge makes a stellar viewing platform for salmon and trout, as well as the sea lions and other animals that eat them. ✉ *Ketchikan* ⊕ *creekstreetketchikan.com.*

The Rock

PUBLIC ART | Ketchikan is known for its public art, and this bronze monument by local artist Dave Rubin provides a striking introduction. *The Rock* (2010) depicts seven life-size figures representative of Ketchikan's history: a Tlingit drummer, a logger, a miner, a fisherman, an aviator, a pioneer woman and Tlingit Chief George Johnson (the sculpture's only specific portrayal). The piece is located on the waterfront next to the Ketchikan Visitors Bureau. For a complete listing of Ketchikan's public art, galleries, museums, and cultural organizations, pick up a copy of *Art Lives Here*, the bureau's free guide. ✉ *Front and Mill Sts., on boardwalk.*

St. John's Episcopal Church

RELIGIOUS SITE | Completed in 1904 and Ketchikan's oldest house of worship, St. John's has an interior constructed of red cedar cut in the Native-operated sawmill in nearby Saxman. When cruise ships are in town, a docent is on hand to answer questions. ✉ *503 Mission St.* ☎ *907/225–3680.*

Salmon Ladder

VIEWPOINT | Get out your camera and set it for high speed at the fish ladder, a series of pools arranged like steps that allow fish to travel upstream around a dam or falls. When the salmon start running, from June onward, thousands of fish leap the falls or take the easier fish-ladder route. They spawn in Ketchikan Creek's waters farther upstream. Many can also be seen in the creek's eddies above and below the falls. The falls, fish ladder, and a large carving of a jumping salmon are just off Park Avenue on Married Man's Trail. The trail was once used by married men for discreet access to the red-light district on Creek Street. ✉ *Married Man's Trail, off Park Ave.*

Saxman Totem Park

NATIVE SITE | A 2½-mile paved walking path–bike trail parallels the road from Ketchikan to Saxman Native Village, named for a missionary who helped Native Alaskans settle here before 1900. A totem park dominates the center of Saxman, with poles representing human- and animal-inspired figures, including bears, ravens, whales, and eagles. Saxman's Beaver Clan tribal house is said to be the largest in Alaska. Carvers create totem poles and totemic art objects in the adjacent carver's shed. You can get to the park on foot or by taxi, bicycle, or city bus. You can visit the totem park on your own, but to visit the tribal house and theater you must take a tour. ✉ *S. Tongass Hwy., 2 miles south of town* ⊕ *www.capefoxtours.com/alaskan-native-dancers* 🎫 *$5.*

Ketchikan

Schoenbar Rd.

Forest Ave.

Schoenbar Rd.

Schoenbar Trail

Ketchikan Creek

City Park

Deermount St.

Water St.

TO
ALASKA
STATE FERRY
& AIRPORT

Main St.

Cedar St.

Pine St.

Grant St.

Bawden St.

Edmonds St.

Seaman's
Park

Married Man's
Trail

Park Ave.

Venetia Way

Park Ave.

Woodland Ave.

Funicular

Creek St.

Stedman St.

Main St.

Front St.

Dock St.

Mission St.

Mill St.

Spruce Mill St.

Thomas
Basin

Thomas St.

Deermount St.

Cruise Ship
Docks

Tongass Narrows

GRAVINA
ISLAND

0   1/4 mile
0   1/4 kilometer

KEY
- ① Exploring Sights
- ① Restaurants
- ① Hotels

Sights ▼
1 Creek Street............ **D4**
2 *The Rock*.................**C5**
3 St. John's Episcopal
  Church **C4**
4 Salmon Ladder...........**C3**
5 Saxman Totem Park **E6**
6 Southeast Alaska
  Discovery Center **C4**
7 Tongass Historical
  Museum **C4**
8 Totem Bight
  State Historical Park .. **A3**
9 Totem Heritage Center .. **E3**
10 Whale Park..............**C4**

Restaurants ▼
1 Annabelle's Famous
  Keg and Chowder
  House **B4**
2 Bar Harbor Restaurant.. **A3**
3 Diaz Café **D4**
4 New York Café **D4**
5 Ocean View
  Restaurant...............**A3**
6 Sweet Mermaids **B4**

Hotels ▼
1 Best Western Plus
  Landing **A3**
2 Black Bear Inn...........**A3**
3 Cape Fox Lodge..........**C4**
4 Gilmore Hotel **B4**
5 Inn at Creek Street
  & New York Hotel........**D4**
6 Rodeway Inn
  Edgewater...............**A3**

Southeast Alaska Discovery Center

INFO CENTER | **FAMILY** | This impressive public lands interpretive center contains exhibits—including one on the rain forest—that focus on the resources, Native cultures, and ecosystems of Southeast. The U.S. Forest Service and other federal agencies provide information on Alaska's public lands, and a large gift shop sells natural-history books, maps, and videos about the region's sights. America the Beautiful–National Park and Federal Recreational Land Passes are accepted and sold. ⊠ *50 Main St.* ☎ *907/228–6220* ⊕ *www.alaskacenters.gov/ketchikan. cfm* ☒ *$5 May–Sept., free Oct.–Apr.* ☉ *Closed Sat.–Thurs. in Oct.–Apr.*

Tongass Historical Museum

MUSEUM | Native artifacts and pioneer relics revisit the mining and fishing eras at this museum in the same building as the library. Exhibits include a big, brilliantly polished lens from Tree Point Lighthouse, well-presented Native tools and artwork, and photography collections. Other exhibits are temporary, but always include Tlingit items. ⊠ *629 Dock St.* ☎ *907/225–5600* ⊕ *www.ktn-ak. us/tongass-historical-museum* ☒ *$6* ☉ *Closed Oct.–Apr.*

★ Totem Bight State Historical Park

NATIVE SITE | About a quarter of the Ketchikan bus tours include this park that contains many totem poles and has a hand-hewn Native clan house. Totem Bight sits on a scenic spit of land facing the waters of Tongass Narrows. Master Native carvers crafted the first replica poles here as part of a U.S. Forest Services program that began in the late 1930s. The tools the carvers used were handmade in the Native style, and modern paints were used to re-create colors originally made using natural substances from clamshells to lichen. The clan house, open daily in summer, was built to resemble a type that might have held several related families. Note the raven painting on the front: each eye contains a small face. ⊠ *N. Tongass Hwy., about*

10 miles north of town ☎ *907/247–8574 Ketchikan Ranger Station* ⊕ *dnr.alaska. gov/parks/units/totembgh.htm* ☒ *Free.*

Totem Heritage Center

NATIVE SITE | Gathered from Tlingit and Haida village sites, many of the Native totems in the center's collection are well over a century old—a rare age for cedar carvings, which are eventually lost to decay in Southeast's exceedingly wet climate. Crafts of the Tlingit, Haida, and Tsimshian cultures are also on display inside the facility, and outside stand several more poles carved in the three decades since it opened. The center offers guided tours and hosts classes, workshops, and seminars related to Northwest Coast Native art and culture. ⊠ *601 Deermount St.* ☎ *907/225–5900* ⊕ *www.ktn-ak.us/totem-heritage-center* ☒ *$6* ☉ *Closed weekends in Oct.–Apr.*

Whale Park

CITY PARK | This small park on a traffic island across from St. John's Episcopal Church is the site of the Chief Kyan Totem Pole, now in its third incarnation. The current replica was erected in 1993, and was restored and re-raised in 2005. The original was carved in the 1890s, but over the decades it deteriorated and it was replaced in the 1960s. The 1960s edition is housed in the Totem Heritage Center. ⊠ *Mission and Bawden Sts.*

🏃 Activities

CANOPY TOURS
Alaska Canopy Adventures

TOUR—SPORTS | Featuring a series of zip lines, aerial boardwalks, and suspension bridges, canopy tours provide an up-close view of the coastal forests. At Alaska Canopy Adventures—a course at the Alaska Rainforest Sanctuary, 8.4 miles south of town—the longest of the tour's eight zip lines stretches more than 800 feet, and whisks you along some 130 feet off the ground. Ketchikan's version of this fast-growing outdoor activity often includes Alaskan wildlife viewing—black

The Aquaculture Debate

Life Cycle of an Alaskan Salmon

Five species of wild Pacific salmon are found in Alaska waters. All are anadromous (they spend part or all of their adult lives in saltwater but depart to freshwater streams and rivers to spawn), and all five species have at least two common names: pink (humpback) salmon, chum (dog) salmon, coho (silver) salmon, sockeye (red) salmon, and chinook (king) salmon. The smallest of these five, the pink salmon, has an average weight of only about 3 or 4 pounds, while king salmon can often tip the scales at more than 25 pounds. King salmon is generally considered the most flavorful, but sockeye and coho are also very highly regarded. Pink and chum salmon are the mainstay of canneries.

After spending a year or more in the ocean (the length of time varies among the species), Pacific salmon return to their native streams to spawn and die. The annual summertime return of adult salmon is a major event in Alaska, both for the animals (including bears) that depend on this bounty, and for thousands of commercial fishers and sport anglers.

Farmed or Wild?

Alaska has long been famous for its seafood, and one of the first acts following statehood in 1959 was to protect fisheries from overharvesting. Today the stocks of salmon and other fish remain healthy, and careful management ensures that they will remain so in the future. In the 1980s and 1990s, aquaculture—fish farming—grew into an enormous international business, particularly in Norway, Chile, the United Kingdom, and British Columbia. Leery of the consequences to wild salmon, Alaska has never allowed any salmon aquaculture.

Pen-raised fish are affordable, available year-round, and of a consistent quality, but controversy surrounds the practice of fish farming. Many people believe it has a disastrous impact on the environment, citing such issues as disease; pollution from the waste of huge concentrations of fish; and the harvesting of nonnative species, such as Atlantic salmon.

The Employment Question

On the other side of the debate, there are those who believe that fish farming is helping to protect Earth's valuable—and decreasing—populations of salmon. Proponents of fish farms point out that the practice also offers revenue and more jobs. Offshore fish farming in the United States is a highly incendiary topic of debate; those supporting it believe that if the farms are placed in deep ocean pockets, the pollution from and medication given to the pen-raised fish will be scattered better by strong currents. Many environmentalists beg to differ, hoping to establish stringent guidelines before opening the ocean to fish-farming corporations.

One Alaska bumper sticker says: "Friends don't let friends eat farmed salmon." Just across the border, in British Columbia, many people find employment as fish-farm workers. No matter which side you agree with in the aquaculture debate, be sure to enjoy a plate of delicious wild salmon during your visit to Alaska—perhaps one you've hooked yourself.

bears and eagles are frequently spotted from on high. Book online (discounts available) or through your cruise line. ✉ *116 Wood Rd.* ☎ *907/225–5503* ⊕ *www.alaskacanopy.com* ✉ *From $189.*

Southeast Exposure

TOUR—SPORTS | A rain-forest zip line and ropes course is offered through Southeast Exposure, a well-known kayaking outfit in the area. ✉ *37 Potter Rd.* ☎ *907/225–8829* ⊕ *www.southeastexposure.com* ✉ *From $90 (kayaking) and $125 (zip-lining).*

DRIVING TOURS
Adventure Kart Expedition

TOUR—SPORTS | **FAMILY** | There's no faster route to feeling like a kid on a first go-kart outing than spending a few hours in one of Adventure Kart Expedition's cool little off-road vehicles. After choosing a helmet, you'll get a quick lesson in the how-tos of driving one of the vehicles. Then you, and the people in the lineup of ATVs you'll race along with, will put pedal to metal (literally) as you zip down old backcountry timber trails. Wear old clothes: there's no way you're coming back from this one clean. Depending on the weather, the trails will either be dusty or mud-filled; but they're always fun. Kids can ride along if they meet the height and weight requirements (50 inches and 40 pounds) and have an adult participating with them. ✉ *Whipple Creek* ☎ *907/225–8400* ⊕ *www.adventurekarts.com* ✉ *From $209.*

FISHING
Bering Sea Crab Fishermen's Tour

BOATING | **FAMILY** | This popular tour builds on the success of the Discovery Channel program *Deadliest Catch*, allowing visitors to ride on a Bering Sea crab boat featured on the show, the *Aleutian Ballad*, in the company of experienced commercial fishermen. The three-hour trip includes wildlife viewing, a live touch tank with sea creatures (released unharmed at the end of the tour), eagle feeding, details about Alaskan fish, and plenty of stories

about life on the water. The tour takes place in protected waters and is suitable for kids. ✉ *Ketchikan* ☎ *888/ 239–3816, 907/821–2722* ⊕ *www.alaskacrabtour. com* ✉ *From $179.*

Ketchikan Visitors Bureau

FISHING | Sportfishing for salmon and trout is excellent in the Ketchikan area, in both saltwater and freshwater lakes and streams. The visitor bureau has information about the many local boat owners who offer charter and guide services. ✉ *50 Front St.* ☎ *907/225–6166, 800/770–3300* ⊕ *www.visit-ketchikan. com.*

HARBOR AND AIR TOURS
Alaska Travel Adventures

TOUR—SPORTS | This company's backcountry Jeep trips are fun, as are the 20-person canoe outings perfect for people just dipping their toes into (very) soft adventure travel. ✉ *Ketchikan* ☎ *800/323–5757, 907/247–5295* ⊕ *www. bestofalaskatravel.com* ✉ *$99 (canoe outings), $159 (Jeep trips).*

Allen Marine Tours

TOUR—SPORTS | One of Southeast's best-known tour operators, Allen Marine conducts Misty Fiords National Monument catamaran tours throughout the summer. The company also offers half-day wildlife viewing tours. ✉ *5 Salmon Landing* ☎ *907/225–8100, 877/686–8100* ⊕ *www. allenmarinetours.com.*

Southeast Aviation

TOUR—SPORTS | Head out on a floatplane to tour the glaciers and mountains of Misty Fiords National Monument. Charters are available. ✉ *1249 Tongass Ave.* ☎ *907/225–2900, 888/359–6478* ⊕ *www. southeastaviation.com* ✉ *From $249.*

HIKING

Get details on hiking around Ketchikan from the Southeast Alaska Discovery Center and Ketchikan Visitors Bureau (⇨ *Exploring, above*).

Deer Mountain

HIKING/WALKING | The 3-mile trail from downtown to the 3,000-foot summit of Deer Mountain will repay your efforts with a spectacular panorama of the city below and the wilderness behind. The trail officially begins at the corner of Nordstrom Drive and Ketchikan Lake Road, but consider starting on the paved, 1½-mile scenic walk on the corner of Fair and Deermount streets. Pass through dense forests before emerging into the alpine country. A shelter cabin near the summit provides a place to warm up. ⊠ *Fair and Deermount Sts.* ⊕ *www. seatrails.org/com_ketchikan/trl-deer-mountain.htm.*

Ward Lake Recreation Area

HIKING/WALKING | About 6 miles north of town, this recreation area has hikes next to lakes and streams and beneath towering spruce and hemlock trees; it also has several covered picnic spots and a pleasant campground. An easy 1.3-mile nature trail circles the lake, which is popular for steelhead and salmon fishing. ⊠ *Ward Lake* 🕿 *907/225–2148 Ketchikan Ranger District.*

LOCAL INTEREST

Cape Fox Tours

LOCAL SPORTS | A Native-owned company, Cape Fox Tours leads tours of Saxman Totem Park. Visitors can also book a Saxman Native Village and Great Alaskan Lumberjack Show combination tour. Book tours in advance or at the Ketchikan Visitors Bureau. ⊠ *300 Spruce Mill Way* 🕿 *907/225–4846* ⊕ *www.capefoxtours. com.*

Great Alaskan Lumberjack Show

LOCAL SPORTS | FAMILY | The show consists of a 60-minute lumberjack competition providing a Disneyesque taste of old-time woodsman skills, including ax throwing, bucksawing, springboard chopping, log-rolling duels, and a 50-foot speed climb. It's a little hokey, but it's good fun (and kids will love it). Shows take place in a covered, heated grandstand directly behind the Salmon Landing Marketplace and are presented rain or shine all summer. ⊠ *420 Spruce Mill Way* 🕿 *907/225–9050, 888/320–9049* ⊕ *www. alaskanlumberjackshow.com* 🖃 *$37.*

SEA KAYAKING

Southeast Exposure

KAYAKING | This outfit conducts a 3½-hour guided Eagle Islands sea-kayak tour and a 4½-hour Tatoosh Islands sea-kayak tour in Behm Canal. ⊠ *37 Potter Rd.* 🕿 *907/225–8829* ⊕ *www.southeastexposure.com* 🖃 *From $90.*

★ Southeast Sea Kayaks

KAYAKING | Paddle across the Tongass Narrows in this company's 2½-hour introductory tour or venture farther afield on one of its guided multinight trips to Misty Fiords. Travelers with just one day to spend on a Ketchikan adventure should consider the five-hour combination tour of kayaking through Orcas Cove and flightseeing Misty Fiords National Monument. It's hard to beat a day that includes a transfer from a boat to a floatplane. ⊠ *3 Salmon Landing* 🕿 *907/225–1258, 800/287–1607* ⊕ *www.kayakketchikan. com* 🖃 *From $93.*

SNORKELING

★ Snorkel Alaska

SNORKELING | While signing up to go snorkeling in Alaska may seem like little more than a novelty, it takes just a few seconds in the waters off Ketchikan to understand that you're about to have an incredibly special experience. (Don't worry, you'll be given a wet suit to keep you warm.) Experienced guides provide both novice and experienced snorkelers the necessary information to quickly become comfortable and begin underwater gazing at giant sunflower stars, bright blood stars, sea cucumbers, and more. ⊠ *S. Tongass Hwy. and Roosevelt Dr.* 🕿 *907/247–7782* ⊕ *www.snorkelalaska. com* 🖃 *$117.*

Walking Around Ketchikan

The **Ketchikan Visitors Bureau,** on the docks that parallel Front Street, is a good starting point for a stroll through town. Next to the bureau you can't miss local artist Dave Rubin's The Rock, a bronze sculpture depicting seven figures associated with Ketchikan's past. With the water on your right, walk down Front Street and pass through the Salmon Landing Marketplace; at the **Southeast Alaska Discovery Center** you can learn about the region's wild places. Up Mill Street is minuscule **Whale Park,** whose centerpiece, Israel Shotridge's Chief Kyan totem pole, commemorates the Tlingit leader who sold the land that evolved into Ketchikan. From here you can follow Stedman Street across the bridge to **Thomas Street,** which overlooks one of Ketchikan's four harbors. Following Deermount Street uphill for several blocks, you'll come across the **Totem Heritage Center** and its collection of ancient totem poles. From here, Park Avenue runs parallel to Ketchikan Creek, heading downhill

to the fish ladder and the salmon carving next to the Falls at Salmon Falls Resort. Glance uphill from the falls to see historic **Grant Street Trestle,** where the road becomes a steep plank bridge supported by pilings. It's about a 10-minute walk down Park Avenue from the hatchery.

From the fish ladder, a boardwalk path follows Ketchikan Creek and leads to trendy **Creek Street.** For a good side trip, take the short funicular ($2) to **Cape Fox Lodge** to get a great view of the harbor. Back on the Creek Street boardwalk is **Dolly's House,** a brothel in days gone by. Retrace your steps up the boardwalk and cross the **Creek Street Footbridge;** you may see salmon during summertime runs. Just in front of you is the Chief Johnson Totem Pole (Johnson, the chief depicted in *The Rock,* was a Tlingit leader). Nearby is the **Tongass Historical Museum,** with relics of the early days of mining and fishing. A left turn onto Bawden Street will take you past **St. John's Church.**

🍴 Restaurants

Annabelle's Famous Keg and Chowder House

$$ | SEAFOOD | An unpretentious Victorian-style restaurant on the Gilmore Hotel's ground floor, Annabelle's serves pastas, steamer clams and other seafood dishes, and several kinds of chowder. Prime rib on Friday and Saturday evenings is a favorite, and the lounge, which has a jukebox, has a friendly vibe. **Known for:** seafood chowder; Alaskan crab; relaxed atmosphere. ⑤ *Average main: $20* ✉ *326 Front St.* ☎ *907/225–6009* ⊕ *www.annabellesketchikan.com.*

★ Bar Harbor Restaurant

$$$ | SEAFOOD | Martin Smith, one of Southeast's, if not Alaska's, most inventive chefs, owns this restaurant in a tiny, blue-and-white waterfront house about 1½ miles outside town. The interior is a cozy spot to dine, but try to get a seat on the back deck. **Known for:** fish tacos; pesto and crab gnocchi; waterfront dining. ⑤ *Average main: $24* ✉ *2813 Tongass Ave.* ☎ *907/225–2813.*

Diaz Café

$ | ASIAN | Take a break from salmon saturation at this Old Town Ketchikan spot on historic Stedman Street. The café serves hearty Filipino cuisine beloved both of locals and cruise-ship staffers hungry for

Ketchikan's beautiful waterfront is decked out with multicolor homes and shops.

a taste of home, and the linoleum-and-tile 1950s interior is a wonderful time warp. **Known for:** lumpia; chicken adobo; retro decor. ⑤ *Average main: $10* ✉ *335 Stedman St.* ☎ *907/225–2257* ⊕ *diazcafe. business.site* ⊘ *Closed Mon.*

New York Café

$$ | **AMERICAN** | The 1920s-era roots of this space adjacent to the New York Hotel come through in the antique bar and fixtures, creating a casual yet elegant place to enjoy a meal while staring out the plate-glass windows at life on busy Stedman Street, or admiring the mural by local artist Ray Troll that spans one wall. The menu includes reasonably priced seafood, salads, and burgers, along with Mediterranean-influenced fare. **Known for:** old-fashioned charm; local beer on tap; fish-and-chips. ⑤ *Average main: $18* ✉ *211 Stedman St.* ☎ *907/247–2326* ⊕ *newyorkcafe.net.*

Ocean View Restaurant

$$ | **MEXICAN** | A favorite with locals, the Ocean View serves decent burgers, steaks, pasta, pizzas, and seafood, but the main draws are the authentic and very filling Mexican dishes. Three tables in the back look out to the Tongass Narrows. **Known for:** gigantic menu; fajitas; chicken marsala. ⑤ *Average main: $15* ✉ *1831 Tongass Ave.* ☎ *907/225–7566* ⊕ *oceanviewmexx.com.*

Sweet Mermaids

$ | **BAKERY** | A tiny coffee shop and bakery, Sweet Mermaids is a great choice for breakfast. If you're here for lunch, try the salmon chowder—the perfect antidote for a rainy afternoon. **Known for:** bagels with cream cheese and lox; homemade cinnamon rolls; sunny, enthusiastic staff. ⑤ *Average main: $8* ✉ *340 Front St.* ☎ *907/225–3287* ▭ *No credit cards* ⊘ *No dinner.*

Hotels

Best Western Plus Landing

$$ | **HOTEL** | Named for the state ferry landing directly across the road, this Best Western property has large, comfortable rooms decorated with mission-style furniture, and although the hotel is more than a mile from downtown, there's no need for a car; a free shuttle provides transport around town. **Pros:** near ferry; underground parking; free shuttle around town. **Cons:** pricey given the location and amenities; bland room decor; some road noise. $ *Rooms from: $195* ✉ *3434 Tongass Ave.* ☎ *907/225–5166, 800/428–8304* ⊕ *www.landinghotel.com* ⇆ *107 rooms* ⊠ *No meals.*

Black Bear Inn

$$$ | **B&B/INN** | The views of the Tongass Narrows from inside this waterfront B&B are remarkable, and the four rooms all have plush furniture, comfortable beds, and porches or balconies. **Pros:** free parking; a phenomenal backyard space; gracious local hosts. **Cons:** outside downtown; some road noise; rental car recommended. $ *Rooms from: $225* ✉ *5528 N. Tongass Hwy.* ☎ *907/225–4343* ⊕ *www.stayinalaska.com* ▭ *No credit cards* ⇆ *6 rooms* ⊠ *Free Breakfast.*

Cape Fox Lodge

$$$ | **HOTEL** | With scenic views of the town and Thomas Basin from 135 feet above Creek Street, Cape Fox Lodge is cozy yet luxurious, and offers spacious rooms with traditional tribal colors and watercolors of Alaska birds. **Pros:** all rooms have views; on-site artwork by master carvers; beautiful site overlooking town. **Cons:** rooms are rather plain; hotel has a bit of a conference-property feel; few amenities. $ *Rooms from: $235* ✉ *800 Venetia Way* ☎ *907/225–8001, 866/225–8001 reservations* ⊕ *www.capefoxlodge.com* ⇆ *72 rooms* ⊠ *No meals.*

Gilmore Hotel

$$ | **HOTEL** | Crammed between the large buildings along Front Street, the Gilmore is a rustic historic property best suited for travelers who value character over modern amenities. **Pros:** handy location; has plenty of historic character; some rooms view marina. **Cons:** not handicapped accessible; bar and street noise can be annoying; rooms could use renovation. $ *Rooms from: $119* ✉ *326 Front St.*

☎ *907/225–9423, 800/275–9423* ⊕ *www.gilmorehotel.com* ▭ *No credit cards* ⇆ *38 rooms* ⊠ *Breakfast.*

Inn at Creek Street & New York Hotel

$$ | **HOTEL** | More than a century old, this quaint hotel's delightfully old-school hotel rooms are on the small side, but they have character in spades: one-of-a-kind antique furnishings, cozy quilts on the queen beds, and tile floors with pedestal sinks in the bathrooms. **Pros:** loft suites have jetted tubs; adjacent to the New York Café; standard rooms are reasonably priced. **Cons:** fills up quickly; small rooms; steep staircase and no elevator. $ *Rooms from: $159* ✉ *207 Stedman St.* ☎ *907/225–0246, 866/225–0246* ⊕ *www.thenewyorkhotel.com* ⇆ *8 rooms* ⊠ *No meals.*

Rodeway Inn Edgewater

$$ | **HOTEL** | A modern lodge 3 miles from the center of town, the Rodeway Inn Edgewater's waterside rooms, including three spacious suites, are decorated with simple furniture and have balconies overlooking Tongass Narrows—a good place to watch seals, otters, and eagles. **Pros:** great views of Tongass in selected rooms; courtesy van service anywhere in town; freezer available for fish storage. **Cons:** inconvenient location; not all rooms have good views; some rooms are small. $ *Rooms from: $170* ✉ *4871 N. Tongass Hwy.* ☎ *907/247–2600, 888/686–2600* ⊕ *www.rodewayinnedgewater.com* ▭ *No credit cards* ⇆ *44 rooms* ⊠ *Free Breakfast.*

ⓨ Nightlife

Ketchikan is a bit of a party town, especially when crews stumble off fishing boats with cash in hand. You won't have trouble finding something going on at several downtown bars.

The Asylum Bar

BARS/PUBS | With 22 beers on tap, including many regional varieties, this downtown favorite has four indoor and outdoor spaces and free Wi-Fi. Hungry patrons can order food from the Burger Queen and have it delivered to their table. ✉ *522 Water St.* ☎ *907/220–0809* ⊕ *www.theasylumbar.com.*

Fat Stan's Lounge

BARS/PUBS | Young locals pack into lively, informal Fat Stan's, a cute spot with a decent selection of beers, wines, and spirits. You can snack on pizza as you sip. ✉ *Salmon Landing Marketplace, 5 Salmon Landing* ☎ *907/247–9463.*

🛍 Shopping

Crazy Wolf Studio

ART GALLERIES | Authentic Northwest Coast art is the specialty of this crowded gallery run by local Tsimshian artist Ken Decker and his wife. Well-known Southeast artists such as Haida basket weaver Holly Churchill and Tlingit carver Gene Chilton exhibit their work here. ✉ *633 Mission St.* ☎ *907/225–9653* ⊕ *www.crazywolfstudio.com.*

Main Street Gallery

ART GALLERIES | The gallery, a light and cheery space run by the Ketchikan Area Arts and Humanities Council, showcases established artists and rising stars. It's well worth a visit. ✉ *330 Main St.* ☎ *907/225–2211* ⊕ *ketchikanarts.org/main-street-gallery.*

Parnassus Books

BOOKS/STATIONERY | A book lover's bookstore with creaky floors and cozy quarters, Parnassus stocks many Alaskan titles. ✉ *105 Stedman St.* ☎ *907/225–7690.*

Scanlon Gallery

ART GALLERIES | In business since 1972, Scanlon carries the prints of well-known Alaska artists, including Byron Birdsall, John Fehringer, Barbara Lavallee, Rie Muñoz, and Jon Van Zyle. The gallery also exhibits jewelry, glasswork, and pottery. ✉ *318 Mission St.* ☎ *907/247–4730, 888/228–4730* ⊕ *www.scanlongallery.com.*

Soho Coho Art Gallery

ART GALLERIES | Design, art, clothing, and collectibles can all be found at stylish Soho Coho. Also here are T-shirts featuring the work of owner Ray Troll—best known for his wacky fish art—and works by other Southeast artists. ✉ *5 Creek St.* ☎ *907/225–5954, 800/888–4070* ⊕ *www.trollart.com.*

Misty Fiords National Monument

40 miles east of Ketchikan by air.

Pristine wilderness areas can be accessed from Ketchikan, most notably Misty Fiords National Monument and Prince of Wales Island. Both are somewhat remote, but tour companies abound to guide you to them.

👁 Sights

Ketchikan Visitors Bureau

INFO CENTER | Most visitors to Misty Fiords arrive on day trips via floatplane from Ketchikan or on board catamarans. The bureau can provide a list of local providers. ✉ *Ketchikan* ☎ *800/770–3300* ⊕ *www.visit-ketchikan.com.*

★ Misty Fiords National Monument

NATIONAL/STATE PARK | Cliff-faced fjords (or fiords, if you follow the attraction's spelling), tall mountains, waterfalls, and islands with spectacular coastal scenery draw visitors to this wilderness area just east of Ketchikan. Most arrive on day trips via floatplane or aboard a catamaran. Both methods have their advantages: air travel reveals Misty Fiord's enormous scope, while trips by sea afford more intimate vistas. You can also kayak here, but it's a long paddle from Ketchikan. For a more manageable trip, consider having a boat drop you off within the monument. Traveling on these waters can be an almost mystical experience, with the green forests reflected in the many fjords' waters. You may find yourself in the company of a whale, see a bear along the shore fishing for salmon, or even pull in your own salmon. The 15 cabins the Forest Service manages here can be booked through the Recreation.gov website. ⊠ *Ketchikan* ☎ *907/225–2148 Ketchikan-Misty Fiords Ranger District* ⊕ *www.recreation.gov.*

★ **Salmon Glacier**

NATURE SITE | A spectacular unpaved road from Hyder into Canada winds 17 miles to remote Salmon Glacier, one of the few glaciers accessible by road in Southeast Alaska and the fifth biggest glacier in North America. In summer, take Granduc Mine Road (also referred to as Salmon Glacier Road), which climbs several thousand feet to a viewing area. Be prepared for potholes, steep drop-offs, and incredible vistas along the way.

Metlakatla

12 miles south of Ketchikan.

The village of Metlakatla—the name translates roughly as "saltwater passage"—is on Annette Island, a dozen miles by sea from busy Ketchikan but a world away culturally. A visit to this quiet community offers the chance to learn about life in a small Inside Passage Native community.

In most Southeast Native villages the people are of Tlingit or Haida heritage, but most residents of Metlakatla are Tsimshian. They moved to the island from British Columbia in 1887 with William Duncan, an Anglican missionary from England. The town grew rapidly and soon contained dozens of buildings, including a cannery, a sawmill, and a church that could seat 1,000 people. Congress declared Annette Island a federal Indian reservation in 1891, and it remains the only reservation in Alaska today. Every year on August 7, locals celebrate Metlakatla's founding with a parade, foot races, food stands, and fireworks.

During World War II the U.S. Army built a major air base 7 miles from Metlakatla that included observation towers to spy on Japanese subs, as well as airplane hangars, gun emplacements, and housing for 10,000 soldiers. After the war it served as Ketchikan's airport for many years, but today the long runways are virtually abandoned save for a few private flights.

GETTING HERE AND AROUND

Alaska Marine Highway System ferries connect Ketchikan and Metlakatla by sea, and Pacific Airways and Taquan Air provide flights. Tours operated by Metlakatla Tours include visits to Duncan Cottage, the cannery, and the longhouse, along with a Tsimshian dance performance. Local taxis can take you to other Annette Island sights, including Yellow Hill and the old Air Force base.

ESSENTIALS

AIRPLANE CONTACT Pacific Airways
☎ *907/225–3500, 877/360–3500* ⊕ *www. flypacificairways.com.* **Taquan Air** ⊠ *4085 Tongass Ave., Ketchikan* ☎ *907/225–8800* ⊕ *www.taquanair.com.*

FERRY CONTACT Alaska Marine Highway System ☎ *907/465–3941, 800/642–0066* ⊕ *www.dot.state.ak.us/amhs.*

TOUR INFORMATION Metlakatla Tours
☎ *907/886–8687* ⊕ *www.visitmetlakatla. com.*

 Sights

Longhouse

NATIVE SITE | Father William Duncan, an Anglican missionary, strove to eliminate some aspects of Tsimshian culture and Christianize the people of Metlakatla, but they have resurrected their past and perform old and new dances in traditional regalia. The best place to catch these performances is at the longhouse that faces Metlakatla's boat harbor. Three

BARANOF ISLAND

Frederick Sound

Kake

Petersburg
see detail map

ALEXANDER

Chatham Strait

KUIU ISLAND

BRITISH COLUMBIA

Stikine River

ARCHIPELAGO

Point Baker
El Capitan Cave

Coffman Cove

Prince of Wales Island

Klawock
Craig
Hollis

Thorne Bay

Hydaburg

Wrangell
see detail map

Misty Fiords National Monument

REVILLAGIGEDO ISLAND

Salmon Glacier

Hyder
Stewa

Ketchikan
see detail map

Metlakatla

ANNETTE ISLAND

Gulf of Alaska

0 ———— 50 miles
0 ———— 50 kilometers

ALASKA
BRITISH COLUMBIA

Alaska Marine Hwy.

Side Trips from Ketchikan

QUEEN CHARLOTTE ISLAND

TO BELLINGHAM, WA

Prince Rupert

---

totem poles stand in back of the building, and a Tsimshian design covers the front. Inside are displays of Native crafts and a model of fish traps once common throughout the Inside Passage. Next to the longhouse are booths displaying locally made arts and crafts. ⊠ *Metlakatla* ☎ *907/886–4441* ⊕ *www.metlakatla.com.*

William Duncan Memorial Church
RELIGIOUS SITE | This clapboard church is one of tiny Metlakatla's nine churches. The original burned in 1948. The current version, topped with two steeples, was rebuilt several years later. Nearby, **Father Duncan's Cottage,** maintained to appear exactly as it would have in 1891, contains original furnishings, personal items, and a collection of turn-of-the-20th-century music boxes. ⊠ *4th Ave. and Church St.* ☎ *907/886–4441* ⊕ *www.metlakatla.com* ☞ *$2.*

Yellow Hill
VIEWPOINT | A boardwalk 2 miles from town leads up the 540-foot Yellow Hill. Distinctive yellow sandstone rocks and panoramic vistas make this a worthwhile detour on clear days. ⊠ *West of Airport Rd., 2 miles south of town.*

🛏 **Hotels**

Metlakatla Inn
$$ | B&B/INN | Decorated with local Native art, this two-story inn offers standard motel accommodations with private decks off the upstairs rooms. **Pros:** cozy atmosphere; private decks on upstairs rooms; helpful owners. **Cons:** nothing fancy here; tends to book up well in advance; restaurant closed on Sunday. ⑤ *Rooms from: $109* ⊠ *3rd Ave. and Lower Milton St.* ☎ *907/886–3456* ⊕ *www.metlakatlainn.com* ⤶ *9 rooms* ⑩ *No meals.*

Prince of Wales Island

43 miles northwest of Ketchikan.

Prince of Wales Island stretches more than 130 miles from north to south, making it the largest island in Southeast Alaska. Only two other American islands—Kodiak in Alaska and Hawaii in the Hawaiian chain—are larger. Prince of Wales (or "P.O.W." as locals call it) has a multitude of landforms, a plethora of wildlife, and exceptional sportfishing, especially for steelhead, salmon, and trout anglers, with the Karta and Thorne rivers among the favorite fishing areas.

The island has long been a major source of timber, both from Tongass National Forest lands and those owned by Native corporations. While much of the Native land has been cut over, environmental restrictions on public lands have greatly reduced logging activity. The island's economy is now supported by small-scale logging operations, tourism, and commercial fishing.

About 5,800 people live full-time on Prince of Wales Island, scattered in small villages and towns. A network of 1,500 miles of roads—nearly all built to access clear-cuts—crisscrosses the island, providing connections to even the smallest settlements.

GETTING HERE AND AROUND

The Inter-Island Ferry Authority operates a daily vehicle and passenger ferry between Ketchikan and Prince of Wales Island. The ferry terminal is in the settlement of Hollis, 31 miles from Craig on a paved road. The relative abundance of roads, combined with ferry and air access from Ketchikan, makes it easy to explore the island.

ESSENTIALS

FERRY INFORMATION Inter-Island Ferry Authority ☎ *907/530–4848*, *866/308–4848* ⊕ *www.interislandferry.com.*

VISITOR INFORMATION Prince of Wales Chamber of Commerce ☎ *907/775–2626* ⊕ *www.princeofwalescoc.org.*

Sights

Craig

TOWN | The primary commercial center for Prince of Wales is Craig, on the island's western shore. This town of 1,200 retains a hard-edged aura fast disappearing in the many Inside Passage towns where tourism now holds sway. Although sightseeing attractions are slim, the town exudes a frontier spirit, and its small-boat harbors buzz with activity. ⊠ *Craig* ⊕ *www.craigak.com.*

El Capitan Cave

CAVE | The best known of the large natural caverns that pockmark northern Prince of Wales Island has one of the deepest pits in the United States. Paleontologists have found a wealth of black bear, brown bear, and other mammal fossils in the cave's 13,000 feet of passageways, including some that date back more than 12,000 years. The Forest Service leads free, two-hour tours of El Capitan Cave several times a week in summer. It takes some work to get to the cave's mouth, but if you're up for a 1,100-foot hike up a 367-step stairway, it's well worth the effort. The rangers pause along the way to give visitors time to catch their breath. Reservations are required at least two days ahead, and no children under age seven are permitted. Bring a flashlight and wear hiking or rubber boots. A light jacket is also helpful, as the cave gets quite cool. ⊠ *Mile 51, N. Prince of Wales Rd.* ☎ *907/828–3304 Ranger station.*

Hydaburg

TOWN | The Haida village of Hydaburg, approximately 40 miles south of Klawock (via chip-sealed road), lies along scenic Sukkwan Strait. A small collection of totem poles occupies the center of this Haida settlement, the only one in Alaska. Originally from what was formerly known as the British Columbia's Queen

Charlotte Islands (they were renamed Haida Gwaii, meaning "Islands of the Haida People," in 2010 by the Canadian government), the Haida settled on Prince of Wales around 1700. ⊠ *Hydaburg* ⊕ *www.princeofwalescoc.org.*

Klawock

TOWN | A half dozen miles from Craig is the Tlingit village of Klawock, with a sawmill, cannery, hatchery, and the island's only airport. The town is best known for its striking totem poles in **Totem Park.** Several of these colorful poles were moved here in the 1930s; others are more recent carvings. You can watch carvers restoring old totems at the carving shed, across the road from the grocery store.

Along the bay you'll find **St. John's by the Sea Catholic Church,** with stained-glass windows picturing Native Alaskans. ⊠ *Klawock* ☎ *907/755–2345 church* ⊕ *www.princeofwalescoc.org.*

Prince of Wales Hatchery

FISH HATCHERY | Klawock is also home to Prince of Wales Hatchery, one of the state's most effective hatcheries. Though the hatchery isn't open to the public, visitors can watch the coho and sockeye salmon in the Klawock River (but keep an eye out for bears). ⊠ *Mile 9 along Craig-Hollis Hwy., Craig* ☎ *907/755–2231* ⊕ *www.adfg.alaska.gov.*

🍴 Restaurants

Zat's Pizza

$ | **PIZZA** | With its bright red tables and tall wooden booths, this informal pizza spot serves beer on tap and is a fun place to come with a group. As is typical in this part of the world, your experience will be vastly improved if you're not in a hurry—Zat's is known for its friendly service, but not necessarily its speed. **Known for:** meatball subs; build-your-own pizza; lively local crowd. ⑤ *Average main: $10* ⊠ *420 Port Bagial Blvd., Craig* ☎ *907/826–2345* ◷ *Closed Sun. and Mon.*

🛏 Hotels

Dreamcatcher Bed & Breakfast

$$ | **B&B/INN** | Within walking distance of downtown Craig, the Dreamcatcher has three rooms with outside entrances and private baths. **Pros:** close to shops and restaurants; beautiful water views; rooms have patios. **Cons:** often booked up; bathrooms can be small; basic breakfast. ⑤ *Rooms from: $139* ⊠ *1405 E. Hamilton Dr., Craig* ☎ *907/826–2238* ⊕ *www.dreamcatcherbedandbreakfast. com* ⇥ *3 rooms* ⊙| *Breakfast.*

Shelter Cove Lodge

$$$$ | **RENTAL** | Tall windows front the water at this modern lodge along Craig's South Boat Harbor that offers all-inclusive fishing packages starting at $2,850 per person for four nights at the lodge, with three full days out fishing. **Pros:** all-inclusive; harbor-view rooms; good wildlife viewing opportunities. **Cons:** expensive; no elevator; food can be heavy. ⑤ *Rooms from: $1424* ⊠ *703 Hamilton Dr., Craig* ☎ *907/826–2939, 888/826–3474* ⊕ *www. sheltercovefishinglodge.com* ◷ *Restaurant closed Sept.–May* ⇥ *10 rooms* ⊙| *All-inclusive.*

★ Waterfall Resort

$$$$ | **RESORT** | Guests at this upscale fishing lodge a 45-minute floatplane ride from Ketchikan can choose from several accommodation styles, eat bountiful meals with all the trimmings, and fish from custom-built 25-foot cabin cruisers under the care of expert fishing guides. **Pros:** plenty of saltwater fishing; good views; opportunity to spot wildlife. **Cons:** most kitchens in the condos aren't used, since meals are provided by the resort; remote location; uninteresting room decor. ⑤ *Rooms from: $1735* ⊠ *West coast of Prince of Wales* ☎ *907/225–9461, 800/544–5125* ⊕ *www.waterfallresort.com* ◷ *Closed Sept.–late May* ⇥ *44 rooms* ⊙| *All-inclusive.*

Wrangell

87 miles north of Ketchikan.

An unassuming timber and fishing community, Wrangell sits on the northern tip of Wrangell Island, near the mouth of the fast-flowing Stikine River—North America's largest undammed river. The Stikine plays a large role in the lives of many Wrangell residents, including those who grew up homesteading on the islands that pepper the area. Trips on the river with local guides are highly recommended for the insight they provide into the Stikine and a very Alaskan way of life. Like much of Southeast, Wrangell has suffered in recent years from a declining resource-based economy. But locals are working to build tourism. Bearfest celebrates Wrangell's proximity to the Anan Wildlife Observatory, where you can get a close-up view of brown and black bears.

Part of the ancestral homelands of the Stikine Tlingit, Wrangell has also flown three national flags in its time. Russia established Redoubt St. Dionysius here in 1834. Five years later Great Britain's Hudson's Bay Company leased the southern Alaska coastline, renaming the settlement Ft. Stikine. It was rechristened Wrangell when the Americans took over in 1867; the name came from Baron Ferdinand Petrovich von Wrangel, governor of the Russian-American Company.

Rough-around-the-edges Wrangell is off the track of the larger cruise ships, so it doesn't get the same seasonal traffic that Ketchikan and Juneau do. Its downtown is nearly devoid of the souvenir shops that dominate so many of its counterparts elsewhere, and the gift shops and art galleries that are here sell locally created work. Wrangell is very welcoming to visitors; independent travelers would do well to add a stop here during their Southeast wanderings.

GETTING HERE AND AROUND

Alaska Marine Highway System ferries connect Wrangell and other Southeast ports, and some small cruise ships stop here. Alaska Airlines operates daily flights from Seattle and Juneau. The town is fairly compact, and most sights are within walking distance of the city dock or ferry terminal.

FERRY CONTACT Alaska Marine Highway System ☎ *907/465–3941, 800/642–0066* ⊕ *www.dot.state.ak.us/amhs.*

ESSENTIALS
VISITOR INFORMATION Tongass National Forest Wrangell Ranger District ✉ *525 Bennett St.* ☎ *907/874–2323* ⊕ *www.fs.usda. gov/tongass.* **Wrangell Visitor Center** ✉ *296 Campbell Dr., in Nolan Center* ☎ *907/874–2829, 800/367–9745* ⊕ *www.wrangellalaska.org.*

◉ Sights

★ Anan Wildlife Observatory
NATURE PRESERVE | A prime spot to view brown and black bears, Anan lies within the Tongass National Forest. Each summer as many as 30 or 40 bears gather at Anan Creek to feed on huge runs of pink salmon. On an average visit of about three hours you might spot bears while strolling the ½-mile viewing boardwalk. Once on the platform, you will likely see many bears. For 30-minute intervals, five people at a time can slip into a photo blind, accessible from the platform, that provides opportunities to shoot close-up, stream-level images of bears catching salmon. Anan is accessible only by boat or floatplane. Passes are required from July 5 to August 25 for the limited number of visits the Forest Service permits each day. Unless you have experience navigating the Stikine by boat and in walking through bear country, it's best to visit Anan with a local guide. Most guide companies provide passes ✉ *Wrangell* ✛ *About 30 miles southeast of Wrangell* ☎ *907/874–2323 Wrangell Ranger District*

Wrangell

TO STIKINE RIVER ↑

A B C D E

1
2
3
4
5
6
7

Zimovia Strait

Wrangell Airport

Airport Rd.

Airstrip

Mt Dewey
400 ft

Mt Dewey Trail

Evergreen Ave.

Alaska Ferry Terminal

St. Michael St.

2nd Ave.

1st Ave.

3rd St.

Mission St.

2nd St.

Stikine Ave.

Reid St.

Church

Front St.

Bennett Street

Outer Dr.

Cruise Ship Dock

Wrangell Harbor

Wrangell Ave.

Loop Trail

Point Shekesti

Case Ave.

Zimovia Hwy.

Inner Harbor

Peninsula St.

Case Ave.

Harbor

Zimovia Hwy.

KEY

- 1 *Exploring Sights*
- 1 *Restaurants*
- 1 *Hotels*
- 7 *Tourist Information*
- *Bike Path*

0 ——— 1/4 mi
0 ——— 1/4 km

Sights ▼

1 Anan Wildlife
  Observatory **D7**
2 Chief Shakes Island
  and Tribal House **D5**
3 Chief Shakes's
  Grave Site **D5**
4 Irene Ingle
  Public Library **C4**
5 Kiks.ádi Totem Park **D5**

6 Mt. Dewey **C3**
7 Nolan Center **C5**
8 Petroglyph Beach
  State Historic Park **B2**
9 Rainbow Falls **D7**

Restaurants ▼

1 Diamond C Cafe **D4**
2 Stikine Inn Restaurant .. **C4**
3 Zak's Café **D4**

Hotels ▼

1 Grand View
  Bed & Breakfast **D7**
2 Rooney's Roost
  Bed & Breakfast **C4**
3 Shakes Slough Cabins .. **E4**
4 Stikine Inn **C4**

Walking Around Wrangell

Start on Campbell Drive at the **Nolan Center**, where the informative and entertaining exhibits at the town museum will help you bone up on local history and biology. Head away from the water on Outer Drive and turn right on Front Street to check out **Kiks.ádi Totem Park.** Continue on Front Street to Shakes Street, following it to the footbridge that leads to the town's prize attraction, **Chief Shakes Island and Tribal House.** Soak in the harbor view from here and examine the old totem poles. For a more elevated harbor view, reverse course and turn right on Case Avenue, which leads up a hill to **Chief Shakes's Grave Site.** From the grave site, head up Church Street to the **Irene Ingle Public Library**, where you'll find ancient petroglyphs out front. About 0.6 mile north of the ferry terminal along Evergreen Avenue lies **Petroglyph Beach.** Most of the beach's noteworthy ancient etchings are scattered along the rocky shore.

Petroglyph Beach and Chief Shakes Island are about a mile and a half apart. Plan on taking three hours to complete this walk and sightsee a little.

If you're game for more walking, climb **Mt. Dewey,** the woodsy hill right behind town. Five miles south of town lies **Rainbow Falls,** another fun hike.

⊕ www.wrangell.com/visitorservices/anan-bear-and-wildlife-observatory.

Chief Shakes Island and Tribal House

NATURE PRESERVE | A footbridge from the bottom of Shakes Street provides access to this small island in the center of Wrangell's protected harbor. The Tribal House, constructed in 1940 as a replica of the original 19th-century structure, was completely restored by local carvers in 2012 and 2013, as were the surrounding totem poles. The interior of the building can be viewed for a fee; arrangements should be made through Wrangell Cooperative Association ⊕ wca-t.com. ⊠ Off Shakes St. ☎ 907/874–4304 ⊕ www.wrangell.com/visitorservices/chief-shakes-tribal-house 🎫 $4.

Chief Shakes's Grave Site

NATIVE SITE | Buried here is Shakes V, who led the local Tlingit during the first half of the 19th century. A white picket fence surrounds the grave, and two killer-whale totem poles mark his resting spot, which overlooks the harbor. ⊠ Case Ave.

Irene Ingle Public Library

LIBRARY | The library, behind the post office, has two ancient petroglyphs out front and is home to a large collection of Alaskan books and computers with free Internet access. ⊠ 124 2nd St. ☎ 907/874–3535 ⊕ www.wrangell.com/library ⊗ Closed Sun.

Kiks.ádi Totem Park

NATIVE SITE | The Kiks.ádi Totem, one of several in the park, bears crests owned by the clan and other animal figures, including a frog, a beaver, and a raven. The totem is a replica carved in 1987. ⊠ Front St.

Mt. Dewey

VIEWPOINT | Despite the name, this landmark is more a hill than a peak. Still, it's a steep 15-minute climb up the John Muir Trail from town to the top. The observation platform there provides views of waterways and islands whose names—among them Zarembo, Vank, and Woronkofski—recall the area's Russian history. The trail is named for naturalist John Muir, who, in 1879, made his way up the trail and built a campfire.

Locals didn't realize there was anybody up on Mt. Dewey and the light from the fire caused a commotion below. Access the trail, which passes through a second-growth forest, on 3rd Street behind the high school. ⊠ *Wrangell.*

Nolan Center

MUSEUM | The nexus of cultural life in Wrangell, the center houses the town's museum, a 200-seat combination movie theater, performance space, and convention facility, and a visitor center. Exhibits at the **Wrangell Museum** chronicle the region's rich history. On display here are the oldest known Tlingit house posts (dating from the late 18th century), decorative posts from Chief Shakes's clan house, petroglyphs, century-old spruce-root and cedar-bark baskets, masks, gold-rush memorabilia, and fascinating photographs. If you're spending any time in town, don't pass this up. The **Wrangell Visitor Center,** staffed when the museum is open, has information about local touring options. ⊠ *296 Campbell Dr.* ☎ *907/874–3699* ⊕ *www.wrangell.com/ cc/welcome-nolan-center.*

Petroglyph Beach State Historic Park

NATIONAL/STATE PARK | Scattered among other rocks at this public beach are three-dozen-or-more large stones bearing designs and pictures chiseled by unknown ancient artists. No one knows why the rocks at this curious site were etched the way they were, or even exactly how old the etchings are. You can access the beach via a boardwalk, where you'll find signs describing the site, along with carved replicas of the petroglyphs. Most of the petroglyphs are to the right between the viewing deck and a large outcropping of rock in the tidal beach area. Because the original petroglyphs can be damaged by physical contact, only photographs are permitted. But you are welcome to use the replicas to make a rubbing from rice paper and charcoal or crayons (available in local stores). ⊠ *½ mile north of ferry terminal, off Evergreen Ave.* ⊕ *dnr.alaska.gov/parks/aspunits/ southeast/wrangpetroshs.*

Rainbow Falls

TRAIL | The trail to this scenic waterfall starts across the road from Shoemaker Bay, 5 miles south of Wrangell. A ¾-mile trail climbs uphill through the rain forest, with long stretches of boardwalk steps, ending at an overlook just below the falls. Hikers with more stamina can continue another 3 miles and 1,500 vertical feet to Shoemaker Bay Overlook. ⊠ *Wrangell.*

🏃 Activities

AIR CHARTERS

Sunrise Aviation

TOUR—SPORTS | This charter-only air carrier flies to the Anan Wildlife Observatory, LeConte Glacier, and Forest Service cabins. ⊠ *Wrangell Airport, Airport Rd.* ☎ *907/874–2319, 800/874–2311* ⊕ *www.wrangell.com/organization/ sunrise-aviation.*

BICYCLING

A waterfront trail connects Wrangell with Shoemaker Bay Recreation Area, 4½ miles south of town. The trail is mainly flat; more adventurous souls can brave the dozens of miles of logging roads that crisscross the island.

BOATING

★ Breakaway Adventures

BOATING | This well-established outfitter, in business for nearly three decades, leads a variety of jet-boat trips, including a tour to Chief Shakes Glacier and the nearby hot springs. Tours can be arranged for groups of up to 50 people. You can catch one of its water taxis to Petersburg or Prince of Wales Island, as well as to one of the area's U.S. Forest Service cabins. ⊠ *City dock* ☎ *907/874–2488, 888/385–2488* ⊕ *www.breakawayadventures.com* ☕ *From $140.*

FISHING
Wrangell Visitor Center
FISHING | Numerous companies schedule salmon- and trout-fishing excursions ranging in length from an afternoon to a week. Contact the visitor center for information on guide services and locations. ⊠ *Nolan Center, 296 Campbell Dr.* ☎ *800/367–9745* ⊕ *www.wrangellalaska. org.*

WILDLIFE VIEWING
The following Wrangell-based guide companies are authorized to run trips to Anan.

Alaska Charters and Adventures
TOUR—SIGHT | This outfit leads small group tours (six guests or fewer) to Anan for day trips of seven or eight hours. Most of the time is spent above Anan Creek on an observation deck reached via a half-mile trail. Reservations are recommended well in advance. The same company also offers whale-watching tours, kayak adventures, and fishing trips. ⊠ *Wrangell* ☎ *888/993–2750* ⊕ *www.alaskaupclose. com* 🍽 *From $328.*

Alaska Vistas
TOUR—SIGHT | Watch bears feeding on salmon at a small waterfall from an observatory deck with this reliable outfitter. Like other Anan tours, this one includes an hour-long boat ride from Wrangell. Alaska Vistas also leads rafting trips down the Stikine River along with jet-boat tours and sea-kayaking adventures. ⊠ *Box 2245* ☎ *907/874–3006, 888/874–3006* ⊕ *www.alaskavistas.com* 🍽 *From $270.*

Alaska Waters
TOUR—SIGHT | This family-owned business leads six-hour tours from late June to August. Cofounder Wilma Stokes-Leslie, who is of Tlingit and Haida descent, was born and raised in Wrangell, as were many of the other members of her team. ⊠ *7 Stikine Ave.* ☎ *907/874–2378, 800/347–4462* ⊕ *www.alaskawaters.com* 🍽 *From $290.*

🍴 Restaurants

Diamond C Cafe
$ | CAFÉ | The breakfasts at the Diamond C are just part of the attraction; the café also serves as the gathering place for locals and, really, it's fun to just sit back and listen. As you dig into the breakfast hash and other goodies, though, there's a chance you'll only have eyes for your plate. **Known for:** biscuits and gravy; casual diner vibe; generous portions. ⑤ *Average main: $10* ⊠ *223 Front St.* ☎ *907/874–3677* 🕐 *No dinner.*

Stikine Inn Restaurant
$$ | AMERICAN | With views overlooking the water, the Stikine Inn's restaurant (often called the Stik) is easily the prettiest place to dine in Wrangell. Given the town's scarcity of options, the place could just assemble a get-by menu, but the salads, pizzas, burgers, and hearty soups here are seriously tasty. **Known for:** burgers; oversized desserts; views. ⑤ *Average main: $15* ⊠ *107 Stikine Ave.* ☎ *907/874–3388* ⊕ *www.stikineinn.com/ dining* 🕐 *Closed Nov.–Mar.*

Zak's Cafe
$$ | AMERICAN | The café has a no-frills look, but it serves good food at reasonable prices. Check out the dinner specials or try the steaks, seafood, and salads. **Known for:** low-key, local atmosphere; seafood chowder; steak. ⑤ *Average main: $16* ⊠ *316 Front St.* ☎ *907/874– 3355* 🕐 *No dinner weekends.*

🛏 Hotels

Grand View Bed & Breakfast
$$ | B&B/INN | An unassuming beachfront home 2 miles from town, the Grand View has spectacular views across Zimovia Strait. **Pros:** amazing location and views; visitors get the inside scoop from a true local; free Wi-Fi. **Cons:** outside of town; transaction fees for credit cards; options for evening activities limited. ⑤ *Rooms from: $165* ⊠ *Mile 2, Zimovia Hwy.*

☎ 907/874–3225 ⊕ www.grandviewbnb.com ➬ 3 rooms ¦◎¦ Breakfast.

Rooney's Roost Bed & Breakfast

$$ | B&B/INN | This century-old home—easily Wrangell's most charming digs—is just a block from downtown and each of its four rooms has been decorated with a different theme. **Pros:** large, delicious breakfast; owned by a local who grew up in Wrangell; located in town. **Cons:** rooms book up quickly; a bit hard to find; some street noise. $ Rooms from: $115 ✉ 206 McKinnon St. ☎ 907/874–2026 ⊕ www.rooneysroost.com ➬ 4 rooms ¦◎¦ Breakfast.

Shakes Slough Cabins

$ | RENTAL | In addition to offering stunning views of the Popof Glacier and Mt. Basargin, these remote and very rustic Forest Service cabins are a 4-mile boat ride from Shakes Slough Hot Springs, where you can soak in open-air and enclosed hot tubs. **Pros:** open-air hot tub; stunning, remote location; wildlife viewing. **Cons:** cabins have no electricity or water; hard to get to except with a local boat guide; tend to book up fast. $ Rooms from: $40 ✉ Wrangell Ranger District, 525 Bennett St. ☎ 907/874–2323, 877/444–6777 National Recreation Reservation Service ⊕ www.recreation.gov ➬ 2 rooms ¦◎¦ No meals.

Stikine Inn

$$ | B&B/INN | Half the rooms at Wrangell's largest inn have excellent ocean views, and others look out on Mt. Dewey and downtown. **Pros:** scenic waterfront location; good restaurant; smoke-free. **Cons:** uninspired decor; no elevator; nighttime activities limited. $ Rooms from: $180 ✉ 107 Stikine Ave. ☎ 907/874–3388, 888/874–3388 ⊕ www.stikineinn.com ▤ No credit cards ➬ 34 rooms ¦◎¦ No meals.

🛍 Shopping

Angerman's Sporting Goods

GIFTS/SOUVENIRS | This is primarily a place for locals to stock up on practical outdoor clothing and fishing gear, but Angerman's also sells souvenir T-shirts, jewelry, gifts, and other tourist items. ✉ 2 Front St. ☎ 907/874–3640.

Petersburg

22 miles north of Wrangell.

Getting to Petersburg is an experience, whether you take the "high road" by air or the "low road" by sea. Alaska Airlines claims one of the shortest jet flights in the world, from takeoff at Wrangell to landing at Petersburg. The schedule calls for 20 minutes of flying, but it's usually more like 15. At sea level only ferries and smaller cruisers can squeak through Wrangell Narrows with the aid of more than 50 buoys and range markers along the 22-mile waterway, which takes almost four hours to negotiate. But the inaccessibility of Petersburg is also part of its charm: you'll never be overwhelmed here by hordes of cruise passengers. The Scandinavian heritage is gradually being submerged by the larger American culture, but you can occasionally hear Norwegian spoken, especially during the Little Norway Festival, held annually on the weekend closest to May 17th (⇨ *see When to Go in the Planning section, above*). If you're in town during the festival, take part in one of the fish feeds that highlight the celebration.

One of the most pleasant things to do in Petersburg is to roam among the fishing vessels tied up dockside in the harbor. This is one of Alaska's busiest, most prosperous fishing communities, with an enormous variety of seacraft. You'll see small trollers, big halibut vessels, and sleek pleasure craft. By watching shrimp, salmon, or halibut catches being brought ashore (though be prepared for the pungent aroma), you can get a real appreciation for this industry.

GETTING HERE AND AROUND

Once you arrive in Petersburg by ferry on the Alaska Marine Highway or by airplane, a host of activities await. For help finding tours of the area, contact travel agency Viking Travel or the Petersburg Visitor Information Center.

ESSENTIALS

FERRY CONTACT Alaska Marine Highway System ☎ *907/465–3941, 800/642–0066* ⊕ *www.dot.state.ak.us/amhs.*

TOUR INFORMATION Viking Travel ☎ *907/772–3818, 800/327–2571* ⊕ *www.alaskaferry.com.*

VISITOR INFORMATION Petersburg Visitor Information Center ⊠ *1st and Fram Sts.* ☎ *907/772–4636, 866/484–4700* ⊕ *www. petersburg.org.*

◉ Sights

Blind Slough Recreation Area

NATIONAL/STATE PARK | This recreation area includes a number of sites scattered along the Mitkof Highway from 15 to 20 miles south of Petersburg. Blind River Rapids Trail is a wheelchair-accessible 1-mile boardwalk that leads to a three-sided shelter overlooking the river—one of Southeast's most popular fishing spots—before looping back through the muskeg. Not far away is a bird-viewing area where several dozen trumpeter swans spend the winter. In summer you're likely to see many ducks and other waterfowl. At Mile 18 the state-run hatchery releases thousands of king and coho salmon each year. The kings return in June and July, the coho in August and September. Nearby is a popular picnic area. Four miles south of the hatchery is a Forest Service campground. ⊠ *Petersburg* ☎ *907/772–3871 USFS Petersburg Ranger District* ⊕ *www.fs.usda.gov/detail/r10/ specialplaces/?cid=fsbdev2_038848.*

Clausen Memorial Museum

MUSEUM | The exhibits here explore commercial fishing and the cannery industry, the era of fish traps, the social life of Petersburg, and Tlingit culture. Don't miss the 126½-pound king salmon—the largest ever caught commercially—as well as the Tlingit dugout canoe; the Cape Decision lighthouse station lens; and *Earth, Sea and Sky,* a 3-D wall mural outside. ⊠ *203 Fram St.* ☎ *907/772–3598* 🖂 *$3.*

Eagle's Roost Park

CITY PARK | Just north of the Petersburg Fisheries cannery, this small roadside park is a great place to spot eagles, especially at low tide. On a clear day you will also discover dramatic views of the sharp-edged Coast Range, including the 9,077-foot summit of Devil's Thumb. ⊠ *617 N. Nordic Dr.*

Hammer Slough

BODY OF WATER | Houses on high stilts and the historic Sons of Norway Hall border this creek that floods with each high tide, creating a photogenic reflecting pool. ⊠ *Hammer Slough Trail.*

★ LeConte Glacier

NATURE SITE | Petersburg's biggest draw lies at the foot of the Stikine Ice Cap. Accessible only by air or water, LeConte Glacier is the continent's southernmost tidewater glacier and one of its most active, often calving off so many icebergs that the tidewater bay at its face is carpeted shore to shore with them. ⊠ *25 miles northeast of Petersburg* ☎ *907/772–4636 Petersburg visitor information* ⊕ *www.petersburgak.org.*

Sons of Norway Hall

LOCAL INTEREST | Built in 1912, this large, white, barnlike structure just south of the Hammer Slough is the headquarters of an organization devoted to keeping alive the traditions and culture of Norway. Petersburg's Norwegian roots date back to 1897, when Peter Buschmann arrived and founded the Icy Strait Packing Company cannery. As his business and family

Petersburg

A **B** **C** **D** **E**

SASBY ISLAND

KUPREANOF ISLAND

Narrows

Wrangell

3 *Nordic Dr.*

Wrangell St.
Valkyrie St.
Lake St.

1 **3**

1st St.

4 *Dolphin*

Excel St.
Petersburg Visitor Information Center **i**

2 *5th St.*
Fram St.

2 *Gjoa St.*

3 *Haugen Dr.*
Ira II

6 *3rd St.*
Kisena

Sing Lee Alley **4** *2nd St.*

Floatplane Base

Ferry Terminal **1**

S. Nordic Dr.

Odin St.

Lumber St.

Mort Freyer Sports Park

Sandy Beach Rd.

Haugen Dr.

Petersburg Airport ✈

Haugen Dr.

Sandy Beach

Mitkof Highway

Mill Rd.
Cornelius
Lyon

MITKOF ISLAND

1

| 0 | | 1/2 mile |
| 0 | | 1/2 kilometer |

KEY
1 *Exploring Sights*
1 *Restaurants*
1 *Hotels*

Sights ▼

1 Blind Slough
   Recreation Area **B7**
2 Clausen Memorial
   Museum **C3**
3 Eagle's Roost Park **B2**
4 Hammer Slough **B3**

5 LeConte Glacier **E2**
6 Sons of Norway Hall ... **B3**

Restaurants ▼

1 Coastal Cold Storage ... **C3**
2 Helse Restaurant **B3**
3 Inga's Gallery **B3**
4 Papa Bear's Pizza **B3**

Hotels ▼

1 Nordic House
   Bed & Breakfast **B4**
2 Scandia House **C3**
3 Tides Inn **C3**

flourished, others arrived to join them, many of Norwegian descent. By 1920, they and the area's Tlingit residents had established a year-round community of 600 residents. The hall, its red shutters decorated with colorful Norwegian rosemaling designs, is listed on the National Register of Historic Places. Outside sits a replica of a Viking ship that is a featured attraction in the annual Little Norway Festival each May. On the building's south side is a bronze tribute to deceased local fishermen. ⊠ *23 S. Sing Lee Alley* ☎ *907/772–4575* ⊕ *www. petersburgsons.org.*

🏃 Activities

BOATING

Jensen's Boat Rentals

BOATING | This outfit's fleet of skiffs range from 18 to 22 feet and include safety items, coolers, and fish dip nets and crab pots. Other fishing equipment is available for rental. ⊠ *Petersburg* ☎ *907/772–4635* ⊕ *www.jensensboatrentals.com.*

Whale Song Cruises

TOUR—SPORTS | A great way to experience the Petersburg area from the water, these cruises take place aboard a custom-built, 29-foot aluminum boat suitable for 14 passengers. Choose from a half-day sightseeing trip to LeConte Bay to view the southernmost tidewater glacier in North America or a full-day whale-watching trip into Frederick Sound. Hot beverages and snacks are included. The captain, longtime local Ron Loesch, also runs the *Petersburg Pilot,* the town's weekly newspaper. ⊠ *207 N. Nordic Dr.* ☎ *907/772–9393* ⊕ *www.whalesong-cruises.com* ✉ *Call for pricing.*

HIKING

Raven's Roost Cabin Hike

HIKING/WALKING | A 4.2-mile trail begins at the southern edge of the Petersburg airport's runway and winds 1,800 feet in elevation to Raven's Roost Cabin. Along the way you take in a panorama that reaches from the ice-bound Coast Range

to the protected waters and forested islands of the Inside Passage far below. Get details on these and other hikes from the Petersburg Visitor Information Center or the Petersburg Ranger District. The two-story Forest Service cabin is available for rent ($40 per night). ⊠ *Petersburg Ranger District, 12 N. Nordic Dr.* ☎ *907/772–3871* ⊕ *www.fs.usda.gov/recarea/tongass/recarea/?recid=79036.*

FLIGHTSEEING

Pacific Wings

TOUR—SPORTS | You can see the Stikine River and LeConte Glacier from above on a flightseeing tour with the locally popular air-taxi operator Pacific Wings. ⊠ *1500 Haugen Dr.* ☎ *907/772–9258* ⊕ *www. pacwing.com.*

KAYAKING

★ Tongass Kayak Adventures

TOUR—SPORTS | The day and overnight kayaking trips conducted by Tongass Kayak Adventures include ones to the icebergs in LeConte Glacier Bay and to see the whales of Frederick Sound. They also offer half-day trips around Petersburg Harbor and across Wrangell Narrows. ⊠ *Petersburg* ☎ *907/772–4600* ⊕ *www. tongasskayak.com* ✉ *From $95.*

🍴 Restaurants

Coastal Cold Storage

$ | **SEAFOOD** | This busy little seafood deli in the heart of Petersburg is a great place for a quick bite en route to your next adventure. Live or cooked crab is available for takeout, and the shop can process your sport-caught fish. **Known for:** beer-battered halibut bits; outdoor seating; full-service fish processing. **⑤** *Average main: $10* ⊠ *306 N. Nordic Dr.* ☎ *907/772–4177.*

Helse Restaurant

$ | **AMERICAN** | Locals flock to this cheery spot for lunch; it's the closest thing to home cooking Petersburg has to offer, and most days it's open from 8:30 to 4, even in winter. Helse also doubles as an ice cream and espresso stand. **Known for:** halibut chowder; mom-and-pop atmosphere; ice cream. $ *Average main: $7* ✉ *13 Sing Lee Alley* ☎ *907/772–3444* ⊘ *Closed Sun.*

Inga's Galley

$ | **PACIFIC NORTHWEST** | Locally sourced ingredients—including Southeast seafood and organic produce—are at the heart of casual Inga's menu. The dishes at this local favorite, a glorified food cart with picnic tables, change "with season, availability, and mood," and most go superbly well with the Baranof Island Brewery beers poured here (there's also wine). **Known for:** outdoor, picnic-style dining; smoked salmon chowder; vegetarian options. $ *Average main: $12* ✉ *104 N. Nordic Dr.* ☎ *907/772–2090* ⊘ *Closed mid-Sept.–mid-Apr.*

Papa Bear's Pizza

$ | **PIZZA** | This oft-crowded restaurant specializes in pizza, Italian sandwiches, tortilla wraps, and ice cream. Traditional pizzas are on the menu but also ones with fanciful add-ons, such as barbecued chicken. **Known for:** chubby chicken pizza; thin crust; local following. $ *Average main: $12* ✉ *219 S. Nordic Dr.* ☎ *907/772–3727* ⊕ *www.papabearspizza. com* ⊘ *Closed Sun.*

🛏 Hotels

Nordic House Bed & Breakfast

$$ | **B&B/INN** | Just three blocks from the ferry terminal and within easy walking distance of town, Nordic House is a great home base from which to explore Petersburg. **Pros:** central waterfront location; kitchen comes stocked with supplies; great views. **Cons:** uninspired decor; not much to do at night; deck can be noisy. $ *Rooms from: $107* ✉ *806 S. Nordic Dr.* ☎ *907/772–3620* ⊕ *www.nordichouse. net* ⊷ *4 rooms* ⊘| *Breakfast.*

Scandia House

$$ | **HOTEL** | On Petersburg's main drag, Scandia House offers some rooms with kitchenettes and king-size beds, and others with in-room hot tubs and harbor views. **Pros:** some pets allowed; airport and ferry shuttle; central location. **Cons:** fourth-floor rooms (including the three suites) are not accessible by elevator; small rooms; dated decor. $ *Rooms from: $130* ✉ *110 Nordic Dr.* ☎ *907/772–4281, 800/722–5006* ⊕ *www. scandiahousehotel.com* ⊷ *33 rooms* ⊘| *Breakfast.*

Tides Inn

$$ | **HOTEL** | Petersburg's largest hotel is a block uphill from the town's main thoroughfare, and its rooms, some with kitchenettes, have comfortable but timeworn furnishings. **Pros:** central location; harbor views from the newer rooms; friendly staff. **Cons:** rooms in the old wing are dark and dated; no frills; limited breakfast options. $ *Rooms from: $125* ✉ *307 N. 1st St.* ☎ *907/772–4288, 800/665–8433* ⊕ *www.tidesinnalaska.net* ⊷ *45 rooms* ⊘| *Free Breakfast.*

🍸 Nightlife

Harbor Bar

BARS/PUBS | With ships' wheels, nautical pictures, and a mounted red snapper, the Harbor Bar's decor stays true to Petersburg's seafaring spirit. The bar's liquor store has a separate entrance. ✉ *310 N. Nordic Dr.* ☎ *907/772–4526.*

🛍 Shopping

FireLight Gallery

ART GALLERIES | This gallery sells jewelry, gifts, and art, including paintings, prints, and handmade pottery, by local and Alaskan artists. ✉ *211 N. Nordic Dr.* ☎ *907/772–2161* ⊕ *firelightgallery.com.*

Northern Lights Smokeries

FOOD/CANDY | Owner Thomas Cumps has made a name for himself with his hot-smoked white king, red king, and sockeye salmon, along with a local favorite, cold-smoked black cod. It's best to call ahead to make sure Cumps will be around before you stop by. You can take your fish with you or have it shipped. ⌧ *501 Noseeum St.* ☎ *907/518–1616* ⊕ *www.nlsmokeries.com.*

Sing Lee Alley Books

BOOKS/STATIONERY | Off an alley in a big, beautiful white house that served as a boardinghouse to fishermen and schoolteachers, this shop stocks books on Alaska, best sellers, cards, and gifts. ⌧ *11 Sing Lee Alley* ☎ *907/772–4440.*

Tonka Seafoods

FOOD/CANDY | Sample smoked or canned halibut and salmon at Tonka Seafoods, located in the old Mitkof Cannery building. Be sure to taste the white king salmon—an especially flavorful type of chinook that the locals swear by. Tonka will also ship. ⌧ *1200 S. Nordic Dr.* ☎ *888/560–3662* ⊕ *www.tonkaseafoods. com.*

Sitka

110 miles west of Petersburg.

It's hard not to like Sitka, with its eclectic blend of Alaska Native, Russian, and American history and its dramatic and beautiful open-ocean setting. This is one of the best Inside Passage towns to explore on foot, with St. Michael's Cathedral, Sheldon Jackson Museum, Castle Hill, Sitka National Historical Park, and the Alaska Raptor Center topping the must-see list.

Sitka was home to the Kiks.ádi clan of the Tlingit people for centuries prior to the 18th-century arrival of the Russians under the direction of territorial governor Alexander Baranof, who believed the region was ideal for the fur trade. The governor also coveted the Sitka site for its beauty, mild climate, and economic potential; in the island's massive timber forests he saw raw materials for shipbuilding. Its location offered trading routes as far west as Asia and as far south as California and Hawaii. In 1799

Baranof built St. Michael Archangel—a wooden fort and trading post 6 miles north of the present town.

Strong disagreements arose shortly after the settlement. The Tlingits attacked the settlers and burned their buildings in 1802. Baranof, however, was away in Kodiak at the time. He returned in 1804 with a formidable force—including shipboard cannons—and attacked the Tlingits at their fort near Indian River, site of the present-day 105-acre Sitka National Historical Park, forcing many of them north to Chichagof Island.

By 1821 the Tlingits had reached an accord with the Russians, who were happy to benefit from the tribe's hunting skills. Under Baranof and succeeding managers, the Russian-American Company and the town prospered, becoming known as the Paris of the Pacific. The community built a major shipbuilding and repair facility, sawmills, and forges, and even initiated an ice industry, shipping blocks of ice from nearby Swan Lake to the booming San Francisco market. The settlement that was the site of the 1802 conflict is now called Old Sitka. It is a state park and listed as a National Historic Landmark.

The town declined after its 1867 transfer from Russia to the United States, but it became prosperous again during World War II, when it served as a base for the U.S. effort to drive the Japanese from the Aleutian Islands. Today its most important industries are fishing, government, and tourism.

GETTING HERE AND AROUND

Sitka is a common stop on cruise routes for smaller ships and a regular stop along the Alaska Marine Highway System. Alaska Airlines also operates flights from Seattle and other Alaskan cities to Sitka. The best way to see the town's sights is on foot.

Sitka

TO STARRIGAVAN RECREATION AREA
& SITKA FERRY TERMINAL

Halibut Point Rd.

Edgecombe Dr.

Peterson Ave.

Thomsen Harbor

Halibut Point Rd.

Verstovia St.

Lake St.

Monastery St.

Lakeview St.

Sitka Channel

Katlian St.

Marine St.

Swan Lake

DeGroff St.

Baranof St.

Biorka St.

Oja St.

Etolin St.

Sitka National Cemetery 1867

Indian River Rd.

Airport

JAPONSKI ISLAND

Airport Rd.

Sealing Cove

O'Connell Bridge

Lake St.

Seward St.

Lincoln St.

Jeff Davis St.

College Dr.

Kelly St.

Maksoutoff

Sawmill Creek Rd.

Crescent Harbor

Eastern Anchorage

Sitka National Historical Park

| 0 | 400 yrds |
| 0 | 400 meters |

ALEUTSKI ISLAND

Cruise Ship Anchorage

TURNING ISLAND

Sitka Sound

KUTKAN ISLAND

KEY

- Exploring Sights
- Restaurants
- Hotels

Sights ▼

1. Alaska Raptor Center ... **E4**
2. Castle Hill **C5**
3. Fortress of the Bear **A1**
4. Harbor Mountain **E6**
5. Russian Bishop's House **D4**
6. Sheldon Jackson Museum **E5**
7. Sitka Historical Society and Museum... **D5**
8. Sitka National Historical Park **E5**
9. Sitka Sound Science Center **D5**
10. St. Michael's Cathedral **D5**
11. Totem Square **C5**
12. Whale Park **E6**

Restaurants ▼

1. Highliner Coffee **D4**
2. Ludvigs Bistro............ **C4**
3. Mean Queen **C5**
4. Nugget Restaurant....... **A4**

Hotels ▼

1. Baranof Wilderness Lodge.................... **E6**
2. Totem Square Hotel & Marina.......... **C5**
3. Wild Strawberry Lodge.................... **C3**
4. Westmark Sitka.......... **D4**
5. White Sulphur Springs Cabin **A1**

ESSENTIALS

AIRLINE CONTACT Alaska Airlines
☎ 800/252–7522 ⊕ www.alaskaair.com.

FERRY CONTACTS Alaska Marine Highway System ☎ 907/465–3941, 800/642–0066 ⊕ www.dot.state.ak.us/amhs. **Sitka Ferry Terminal** ✉ 5307 Halibut Point Rd. ☎ 907/747–8737.

VISITOR INFORMATION Sitka Convention and Visitors Bureau ✉ 104 Lake St. ☎ 907/747–8604 ⊕ www.sitka.org.

◉ Sights

Alaska Raptor Center
ZOO | FAMILY | Above Indian Creek, a 20-minute walk from downtown, Alaska's only full-service avian hospital rehabilitates from 100 to 200 birds each year. Well-versed guides provide an introduction to the center (there's also a short video), and guests can visit with one of these majestic birds. The primary attraction is an enclosed 20,000-square-foot flight-training center, built to replicate the rain forest, where injured eagles relearn survival skills, including flying and catching salmon. Visitors watch through one-way glass windows. A large deck out back faces an open-air enclosure for eagles and other raptors whose injuries prevent them from returning to the wild. Additional mews with hawks, owls, and other birds lie along a rain-forest path. The gift shop sells all sorts of eagle paraphernalia, the proceeds from which fund the center's programs. ✉ 1000 Raptor Way, off Sawmill Creek Rd. ☎ 907/747–3662, 800/643–9425 ⊕ www.alaskarap-tor.org ⊠ $13 ⊙ No tours Oct.-Apr.

Castle Hill
MEMORIAL | On this hill, Alaska was formally handed over to the United States on October 18, 1867, and the first 49-star U.S. flag was flown on January 3, 1959, signifying Alaska's statehood. To reach the hill, take the first right off Harbor Drive just before O'Connell Bridge; then enter the paved path switchbacks to the top, where you can read the interpretive signs on the area's Tlingit and Russian history and take in the views of Crescent Harbor and downtown Sitka. On a clear day, look for the volcanic flanks of Mt. Edgecumbe on the horizon. ✉ Harbor Rd. ☎ 907/747–6249 DNR Sitka Ranger Station ⊕ www.dnr.alaska.gov/parks/aspunits/southeast/baranofcastle.htm.

Fortress of the Bear
NATURE PRESERVE | FAMILY | An independently operated animal rescue center, Fortress of the Bear offers the chance to see bears up close without worry for safety. The center, 5 miles east of Sitka, shelters a handful of brown and black bears, both adults and cubs, in large enclosures that allow them to interact and play. In addition to creating a hospitable environment for bears that might otherwise be euthanized, the center educates visitors about human–animal interaction. Catch a shuttle (907/747–3550) to the facility from downtown Sitka, or contact Sitka Tours (907/747–5800, www.sitkatoursalaska.com). ✉ 4639 Sawmill Creek Rd. ☎ 907/747–3032 ⊕ www.fortressofthebear.org ⊠ $10.

Harbor Mountain
VIEWPOINT | During World War II the U.S. Army constructed a road to the 2,000-foot level of Harbor Mountain, a perfect spot from which to watch for invading Japanese subs or ships (none were seen). This road has been improved over the years, and it is possible to drive 5 miles to a spectacular summit viewpoint across Sitka Sound. A trail climbs uphill from the parking lot, then follows the ridge 2½ miles to a Forest Service shelter. From there, ambitious hikers can continue downhill another 3½ miles to Sitka via the **Gavan Hill Trail.** ✉ Harbor Mountain Rd.

Russian Bishop's House
HOUSE | The Russian–American Company built this registered historic landmark for Bishop Innocent Veniaminov. Completed in 1843 and one of Alaska's few

remaining Russian-built log structures, the house, which faces the harbor, contains exhibits on the history of Russian America. In several places, portions of the structure are peeled away to expose Russian building techniques. The ground level is a free museum. The National Park Service operates the house and rangers lead guided tours of the second floor, which holds the residential quarters and a chapel. ⊠ *501 Lincoln St.* ☎ *907/747–0110* ⊕ *www.nps.gov/sitk* ⧠ *Tours $4.*

Sheldon Jackson Museum

MUSEUM | This octagonal museum that dates from 1895 contains priceless Alaska Native items collected by Dr. Sheldon Jackson (1834–1909), who traveled the remote regions of Alaska as an educator and missionary. The collection represents every Alaska Native culture. On display are carved masks, Chilkat blankets, dogsleds, kayaks, and even the impressive helmet worn by Chief Katlian during an 1804 battle against the Russians. The museum's small but well-stocked gift shop carries books, paper goods, and handicrafts created by Alaska Native artists. ⊠ *104 College Dr.* ☎ *907/747–8981* ⊕ *www.museums.state.ak.us* ⧠ *$7 mid-May–mid-Sept., $5 mid-Sept.–mid-May* ⊙ *Closed Sun. and Mon.*

Sitka Historical Society and Museum

MUSEUM | A Tlingit war canoe sits beside this brick building, formally named Harrigan Centennial Hall. Check out the museum's collection of Tlingit, Victorian-era, and Alaska-purchase historical artifacts; there's an auditorium for New Archangel Dancers performances, which take place when cruise ships are in port. ⊠ *330 Harbor Dr.* ☎ *907/747–6455 museum, 907/747–5516 for New Archangel Dancers schedule* ⊕ *www.sitkahistory. org* ⧠ *Free.*

★ Sitka National Historical Park

MUSEUM | The main building at this 113-acre park houses a small museum with fascinating historical exhibits and photos of Tlingit Native culture. Highlights include a brass peace hat given to the Sitka Kiksádi by Russian traders in the early 1800s and Chilkat robes. Head to the theater to watch a 12-minute video about Russian–Tlingit conflict in the 19th century. Ask a ranger to point you toward the Centennial Totem Pole, installed in 2011 to honor the park's 100th anniversary. Also here is where Native artisans demonstrate silversmithing, weaving, wood carving, and basketry. Make an effort to strike up a conversation with the artists; they're on-site to showcase and discuss their work and Tlingit cultural traditions. At the far end of the building are seven totems (some more than a century old) that have been brought indoors to protect them from decay. Behind the center a wide, 2-mile path winds through the forest and along the shore of Sitka Sound. Scattered along the way are some of the most skillfully carved Native totem poles in Alaska. Keep going on the trail to see spawning salmon from the footbridge over Indian River. In summer, Park Service rangers lead themed walks that focus on the Russian–Tlingit conflict, the area's natural history, and the park's totem poles. ⊠ *106 Metlakatla St.* ☎ *907/747–0110 visitor center* ⊕ *www. nps.gov/sitk* ⧠ *Free.*

Sitka Sound Science Center

MUSEUM | FAMILY | The exhibits and activities at this waterfront facility highlight Sitka's role as a regional hub for whale biologists, fisheries-management experts, and other specialists. Attractions include a touch tank, five wall-mounted aquariums, a killer-whale skeleton, and a fish hatchery. Well-placed signs throughout this working science center describe what's going on, providing a great introduction for kids to hands-on environmental science. ⊠ *834 Lincoln St.* ☎ *907/747–8878* ⊕ *www.sitkascience.or* ⧠ *$7* ⊙ *Closed Sun.*

St. Michael's Cathedral

RELIGIOUS SITE | One of Southeast's best-known landmarks, the onion-dome cathedral is so treasured by locals that in 1966

Walking Around Sitka

Many visitors begin tours of Sitka under the distinctive onion dome of **St. Michael's Cathedral,** right in the town center. A block behind the cathedral along Harbor Drive is **Harrigan Centennial Hall,** a low-slung convention hall that houses the smallish **Sitka Historical Society and Museum** and an information desk that opens when cruise ships are in port. A block east, along Lincoln Street, you'll find the **Russian Bishop's House,** one of the symbols of Russian rule. Continue out on Lincoln Street along the bustling boat harbor to Sheldon Jackson College, where the worthwhile **Sheldon Jackson Museum** is packed with Native cultural artifacts. Close by is the **Sitka Sound Science Center,** which has an aquarium touch tank, a killer-whale skeleton, and other marine-related items of interest. Another ½ mile out along gently curving Metlakatla Street is the **Sitka National Historical Park,** where you can chat with Native artisans as they craft carvings and silver jewelry. Behind the main building a network of well-signed paths takes you through the rain forest past more than a dozen totem poles and to the site of a Tlingit fort from the battle of 1804. A signed trail crosses the Indian River (watch for spawning salmon in late summer) and heads across busy Sawmill Creek Road to the **Alaska Raptor Center,** for an up-close look at bald eagles.

Return to town along Sawmill Creek Road. On your right, you'll see the white headstones of the small Sitka National Cemetery. Back downtown, you can browse the many shops or walk along Harbor Drive and take the path to the summit of **Castle Hill,** where Russia transferred Alaska to American hands—these are the best views in town. If you follow the path down the other side of the hill, check out the impressive **Sitka State Pioneers Home,** with the statue of pioneer "Skagway Bill" Fonda. Across the street is **Totem Square,** with its tall totem pole and three ancient anchors. Adjacent to the Pioneers Home is the **Sheet'ka Kwaan Naa Kahidi** community house. Traditional Tlingit dance performances take place here in summer.

Sitka has many attractions, and you can easily spend a full day exploring this culturally rich area. You can accomplish the walk in two to three hours if you do not spend much time at each stop.

as a fire engulfed the building, townspeople risked their lives and rushed inside to rescue precious Russian icons, religious objects, and vestments. An almost exact replica of St. Michael's was completed in 1976. Today you can view what may well be the largest collection of Russian icons in the United States, among them *Our Lady of Sitka* (also known as the *Sitka Madonna*) and the *Christ Pantocrator* (*Christ the World Judge*), displayed on the altar screen. ⊠ *240 Lincoln St.*

☎ *907/747–8120* ⊕ *stmichaelcathedral. org.*

Totem Square

PLAZA | On this grassy square across the street from the Sitka Pioneer Home are three anchors discovered in local waters and believed to be of 19th-century British origin. Look for the double-headed eagle of czarist Russia carved into the cedar of the park's totem pole. ⊠ *200 Katlian St.*

Whale Park

CITY PARK | FAMILY | This small waterside park sits in the trees 4 miles east of Sitka right off Sawmill Creek Road. Boardwalk paths lead to five viewing platforms and steps lead down to the rocky shoreline. A gazebo next to the parking area contains signs describing the whales that visit Silver Bay, and you can listen to their sounds from recordings and an offshore hydrophone. ⊠ *Sawmill Creek Rd.*

 Activities

BICYCLING
Yellow Jersey Cycle Shop

BICYCLING | If it isn't raining, rent a high-quality mountain bike from Yellow Jersey Cycle Shop and head out on the nearby dirt roads and trails. Staffers know Sitka's many mountain- and road-bike routes well. ⊠ *329 Harbor Dr.* ☎ *907/747–6317* ⊕ *www.yellowjerseycycles.com* ⊠ *From $20.*

BOAT AND KAYAK TOURS
Alaska Travel Adventures

BOATING | Alaska Travel Adventures leads a three-hour kayaking tour in protected waters south of Sitka. The tour includes friendly guides, basic kayak instruction, and snacks at a remote cabin on the water. ⊠ *Sitka* ☎ *800/323–5757* ⊕ *www.bestofalaskatravel.com* ⊠ *$149.*

Allen Marine Tours

BOATING | One of Southeast's largest and best-known tour operators leads several boat-based Sitka Sound tours throughout the summer. The Wildlife Quest tours provide a fine opportunity to view humpback whales, sea otters, puffins, eagles, and brown bears in a spectacular setting. When seas are calm enough, Allen Marine conducts a tour to the bird sanctuary at St. Lazaria Islands National Wildlife Refuge. Private catamaran tours for up to six guests can also be arranged. ⊠ *1512 Sawmill Creek Rd.* ☎ *907/747–8100, 888/747–8101* ⊕ *www.allenmarine-tours.com* ⊠ *Call for rates.*

Sitka Sound Ocean Adventures

BOATING | The guide company's waterfront operation is easy to find: just look for the big blue bus at Crescent Harbor next to Sitka Historical Society. Sitka Sound runs various guided kayak trips through the mysterious and beautiful outer islands off the coast of Sitka. Guides help new-to-the-area paddlers understand Sitka Sound's wonders, and for day trips the company packs a great picnic. Experienced paddlers who want to go it alone can rent gear. ⊠ *Harbor Dr., at Centennial Hall* ☎ *907/752–0660* ⊕ *www.kayaksitka.com* ⊠ *From $79.*

BUS TOURS AND HISTORICAL WALKS
Sitka Tours

TOUR—SPORTS | Longtime local business Sitka Tours meets ferries and cruise ships and leads both bus tours and historical walks. ⊠ *Sitka* ☎ *907/747–5800* ⊕ *www.sitkatoursalaska.com.*

Tribal Tours

TOUR—SPORTS | This company conducts bus and walking tours that emphasize Sitka's rich Tlingit culture and include Naa Kahídi dance performances at the Tribal Community House. ⊠ *Sitka* ☎ *907/747–7137* ⊕ *www.sitkatours.com.*

FISHING

Sitka is home to a fleet of charter boats. The Sitka Convention and Visitors Bureau website ⊕ *visitsitka.org* has descriptions of and links to several dozen sportfishing operators.

The Boat Company

FISHING | This outfitter offers multiday wildlife-watching and fishing trips departing from Sitka and Juneau. ⊠ *Sitka* ☎ *360/697–4242, 877/647–8268* ⊕ *www.theboatcompany.org.*

HIKING AND WILDLIFE VIEWING
Sitka Trail Works

HIKING/WALKING | You can pick up a good map of local trails from this nonprofit organization that helps maintain them and also leads group hikes on Saturdays in the summer; check the website for details. ⊠ *801 Halibut Point Rd.* ☎ *907/747–7244* ⊕ *www.sitkatrailworks. org.*

Starrigavan Recreation Area

BIRD WATCHING | This recreation area 7 miles north of Sitka is a peaceful place to explore the rain forest. The state ferry terminal is less than a mile from Starrigavan, and a popular Forest Service campground is also here. Several easy trails pass through the area. ⊠ *Halibut Point Rd.* ☎ *907/747–6671.*

Restaurants

Highliner Coffee

$ | **AMERICAN** | Sitkans' favorite spot for coffee, Highliner also serves great bagels for breakfast and sandwiches at lunch. **Known for:** house brew; free Wi-Fi; breakfast burritos. $ *Average main: $8* ⊠ *327 Seward St.* ☎ *907/747–4924* ⊕ *stores. highlinercoffee.com.*

★ Ludvig's Bistro

$$$ | **MEDITERRANEAN** | Food lovers pack into Ludvig's to sample chef-owner Colette Nelson's remarkably creative cuisine, which means there's often a wait, but rest assured that your meal will be worth it. The interior evokes an Italian bistro, with rich yellow walls and copper-topped tables. **Known for:** king salmon and scallops; great reputation throughout the region; wine list. $ *Average main: $26* ⊠ *256 Katlian St.* ☎ *907/966–3663* ⊕ *www.ludvigsbistro.com* ⊗ *Closed Sun., mid-Sept.–Apr.*

Mean Queen

$ | **PIZZA** | Carefully crafted pizza and generously sized salads are the draw at the Mean Queen, a casual, friendly pub near the bridge. The views of Sitka Harbor make it a great spot to linger. **Known for:** creative pizzas; $3 beer on tap; views. $ *Average main: $20* ⊠ *205 Harbor Dr., upstairs* ☎ *907/747–0616* ⊕ *www.meanqueensitka.com.*

Nugget Restaurant

$ | **AMERICAN** | Travelers flying out of Sitka's airport repair to the Nugget while hoping their jet will arrive through the pea-soup fog outside. The Nugget serves American classics for breakfast, lunch, and dinner, but the homemade pies are the real attraction. **Known for:** homemade pie; better-than-usual airport dining; Friday night prime rib. $ *Average main: $12* ⊠ *Sitka Airport Terminal, 600 Airport Dr.* ☎ *907/966–2480.*

🛏 Hotels

Baranof Wilderness Lodge

$$$$ | **B&B/INN** | A quick floatplane ride from Sitka, this cozy fishing lodge is on Baranof Island, a remote and magnificent location from which to explore the surrounding landscape and view wildlife that includes bears, whales, and eagles. **Pros:** rate is all-inclusive from Sitka; beautiful surroundings; spacious rooms. **Cons:** expensive; remote; five-day stay. $ *Rooms from: $2340* ⊠ *Warm Springs Bay* ☎ *907/738–3597, 800/613–6551* ⊕ *www.flyfishalaska.com* ⊗ *Closed Oct.–May* ⇥ *8 rooms* ⦿ *All-inclusive.*

Totem Square Hotel & Marina

$$$ | **HOTEL** | In downtown Sitka and one of the town's better-run outfits, the inn's rooms are clean and well furnished, and some have town or harbor views (harbor are $10 extra). **Pros:** within walking distance of most attractions; some rooms have nice views; comfortable beds. **Cons:** rooms without harbor view overlook a parking lot; dated decor; a bit pricey. $ *Rooms from: $229* ⊠ *201 Katlian St.* ☎ *907/747–3693, 866/300–1353* ⊕ *www. totemsquarehotel.com* ⇥ *68 rooms* ⦿ *No meals.*

Westmark Sitka

$$$ | **HOTEL** | The Westmark has large rooms, many overlooking Crescent Harbor; the best are the corner suites. **Pros:** nice views; big rooms; restaurant on-site. **Cons:** lacks charm; service can be slow; high rates. $ *Rooms from: $245* ⊠ *330*

Seward St. ☎ 907/747–6241, 800/544–0970 in U.S., 800/999–2570 in Canada ⊕ www.westmarkhotels.com/sitka.php ⇢ 105 rooms ⏐○⏐ No meals.

White Sulphur Springs Cabin

$ | RENTAL | With incredible views and proximity to a hot-springs bathhouse, this isolated retreat 65 miles northwest of Sitka is one of Southeast's most prized public-use cabins. **Pros:** hot springs; Pacific Ocean views; completely private. **Cons:** guests must bring own bedding and cooking utensils; requires boat ride to location; no good water source nearby. ⑤ Rooms from: $60 ✉ West Chichagof–Yakobi Wilderness Area ☎ 907/747–6671 information, 877/444–6777 reservations ⊕ www.recreation.gov ⇢ 1 cabin ⏐○⏐ No meals.

★ Wild Strawberry Lodge

$$$$ | B&B/INN | At this fishing lodge with waterfront cabins, you'll gather for home-cooked meals after a long day of fishing to socialize and scheme for the next day's adventure; all-inclusive packages start at $2,075 per person. **Pros:** friendly hosts; lots of accommodation options; great food. **Cons:** can be noisy; expensive; arrival-night dinner not included. ⑤ Rooms from: $1383 ✉ 724 Siginaka Way ☎ 800/770–2628 ⊕ www.wildstrawberrylodge.com ⇢ 13 rooms ⏐○⏐ All-inclusive.

▼ Nightlife

Baranof Island Brewing Company

BREWPUBS/BEER GARDENS | Beer lovers will want to check out the brewery's taproom, open daily from 2 to 8 pm. Under state law, patrons can only consume up to 36 ounces in one visit. ✉ 1209 A Sawmill Creek Rd. ☎ 907/747–2739 ⊕ www.baranofislandbrewing.com.

Bayview Pub

BARS/PUBS | In addition to its selection of Alaskan and Pacific Northwest craft beers, "The Pub" is known for handcrafted classic cocktails made with freshly squeezed juices. Dinner is served nightly (lunch daily), and there's a late-night menu on Friday and Saturday nights. The pub has a stage for live music; nonmusical diversions include two pool tables, a dart area, and plenty of wide-screen TVs. ✉ 407 Lincoln St. ☎ 907/747–5300 ⊕ www.sitkabayview-pub.com.

Pioneer Bar

BARS/PUBS | As far as the locals are concerned, the few green-and-white-vinyl booths at this bar across from the harbor make a fine destination. The Pioneer is vintage Alaska, with pool tables, rough-hewn locals clad in Carhartts and XtraTuf boots, hundreds of pictures of local fishing boats, and occasional live music. Regulars, mostly local fishermen, swear by the submarine sandwiches and hot dogs. One downside: the Pioneer allows smoking, so you're likely to leave smelling like an ashtray. ✉ 212 Katlian St. ☎ 907/747–3456.

⚙ Performing Arts

New Archangel Dancers of Sitka

DANCE | Dedicated to preserving Alaska's Russian history, this all-female troupe has performed in Sitka since 1969. The 30-minute performances showcase authentic dances from the surrounding regions and Russia. Tickets are sold a half hour before performances, which take place at three venues, most often at Sitka Historical Society and Museum. ✉ Sitka ☎ 907/747–5516 ⊕ www.newarchangeldancers.com ⌑ $10.

Sheet'ka Kwaan Naa Kahidi Dancers

DANCE | Tlingit dancers in full regalia perform at the Sheet'ka Kwaan Naa Kahidi community house on Katlian Street. The schedule is listed on the board at Sitka Historical Society and Museum—common performance days are Wednesday, Thursday, and Saturday. Tickets are sold at the door 30 minutes

Continued on page 13

AMAZING WHALES
OF ALASKA

It's unforgettable: a massive, barnacle-encrusted humpback breaches skyward from the placid waters of an Alaskan inlet, shattering the silence with a thundering display of grace, power, and beauty. Welcome to Alaska's coastline.

Alaska's cold, nutrient-rich waters offer a bounty of marine life that's matched by few regions on earth. Eight species of whales frequent the state's near-shore waters, some migrating thousands of miles each year to partake of Alaska's marine buffet. The state's most famous cetaceans (the scientific classification of marine mammals that includes whales, dolphins, and porpoises) are the humpback whale, the gray whale, and the orca (a.k.a. the killer whale).

BEST REGIONS TO VIEW WHALES

Whales can be viewed throughout the world; after all, they are migratory animals. But thanks to its pristine environment, diversity of cetacean species, and jaw-dropping beauty, Alaska is perhaps the planet's best whale-watching locale.

From April through October, humpbacks visit many of Alaska's coastal regions, including the Bering Sea, the Aleutian Islands, and Prince William Sound. The **Inside Passage,** though, is the best place to see them: it's home to a migratory population of up to 600 humpbacks. Good bets for whale-viewing include taking a trip on the **Alaska Marine Highway,** spending time in **Glacier Bay National Park,** or taking a day cruise out of any of Southeast's main towns. While most humpbacks return to Hawaiian waters in

A gray whale greets whale-watchers

the winter, some spend the whole year in Southeast Alaska.

Gray whales favor the coastal waters of the Pacific, which terminate in the Bering Sea. Their healthy population—some studies estimate that 30,000 gray whales populate the west coast of North America—make them relatively

THE HUMPBACK: Musical, Breaching Giant

Humpbacks' flukes allow them to breach so effectively that they can propel two-thirds of their massive bodies out of the water.

Known for their spectacular breaching and unique whale songs, humpbacks are captivating. Most spend their winters in the balmy waters off the Hawaiian Islands, where females, or sows, give birth. Come springtime, humpbacks set off on a 3,000-mile swim to their Alaskan feeding grounds.

Southeast Alaska is home to one of the world's only groups of bubble-net feeding humpbacks. Bubble-netting is a cooperative hunting technique in which one humpback circles below a school of baitfish while exhaling a "net" of bubbles, causing the fish to gather. Other humpbacks then feed at will from the deliciously dense group of fish.

The Song of the Humpback

All whale species communicate sonically, but the humpback is the most musical. During mating season, males emit haunting, songlike calls that can last for up to 30 minutes at a time. Most scientists attribute the songs to flirtatious, territorial, or competitive behaviors.

QUICK FACTS:

Scientific name: *Megaptera novaeangliae*

Length: Up to 50 ft.

Weight: Up to 90,000 pounds (45 tons)

Coloring: Dark blue to black, with barnacles and knobby, lighter-colored flippers

Life span: 30 to 40 years

Reproduction: One calf every 2 to 3 years; calves are generally 12 feet long at birth, weighing up to 2,000 pounds (1 ton)

easy to spot in the spring and early summer months, especially around **Sitka** and **Kodiak Island** and south of the **Kenai Peninsula,** where numerous whale-watching cruises depart from Seward into **Resurrection Bay**.

Orcas populate nearly all of Alaska's coastal regions. They're most commonly viewed in the **Inside Passage** and **Prince William Sound,** where they reside year-round. A jaunt on the Alaska Marine Highway is one option, but so is a kayaking or day-cruising trip out of **Whittier** to Prince William Sound.

When embarking on a whale-watching excursion, don't forget rain gear, a camera, and binoculars!

Whale Size Chart

The Humpback
50 ft long / 45 tons

The Orca
30 ft long / 9 tons

The Gray
50 ft long / 45 tons

Human
6 ft tall / 0.085 tons

* 1 meter per square

THE GRAY WHALE: Migrating Leviathan

Though the average lifespan of a gray whale is 50 years, one individual was reported to reach 77 years of age—a real old-timer.

While frequenting Alaska during the long days of summer, gray whales tend to stay close to the coastline. They endure the longest migration of any mammal on earth—some travel 14,000 miles each way between Alaska's Bering Sea and their mating grounds in sunny Baja California.

Gray whales are bottom-feeders that stir up sediment on the sea floor, then use their baleen—a comblike collection of long, stiff hairs inside their mouths—to filter out sediment and trap small crustaceans and tube worms.

Their predilection for near-shore regions, coupled with their easygoing demeanor—some "friendly" gray whales have even been known to approach small tour boats—cements their spot on the short list of Alaska's favorite cetacean celebrities. (Gray whales aren't always in such amicable spirits: whalers dubbed mother gray whales "devilfish" for the fierce manner in which they protected their young.)

QUICK FACTS:

Scientific name: *Eschrichtius robustus*

Length: Up to 50 ft.

Weight: Up to 90,000 pounds (45 tons)

Coloring: Gray and white, usually splotched with lighter growths and barnacles

Life span: 50 years

Reproduction: One calf every 2 years; calves are generally 15 feet long at birth, weighing up to 1,500 pounds (3/4 ton)

AN AGE-OLD CONNECTION

Nearly every major Native group in Alaska has relied on whales for some portion of its diet. The Inupiaq and Yup'ik counted on whales for blubber, oil, meat, and intestines to survive. Aleuts used whale bones to build their semisubterranean homes. Even the Tlingit, for whom food was perennially abundant, considered a beached whale a bounty.

Subsistence whaling lives on in Alaska: although gray-whale hunting was banned in 1996, the Eskimo Whaling Commission permits the state's Native populations to harvest 50 bowhead whales every year.

Other Alaskan whale species:
Bowhead, northern right, minke, fin, and beluga whales also inhabit Alaskan waters.

barnacles

BARNACLES These ragged squatters of the sea live on several species of whales, including humpbacks and gray whales. They're conspicuously absent from smaller marine mammals, such as orcas, dolphins, and porpoises. The reason? Speed. Scientists theorize that barnacles are only able to colonize the slowest-swimming cetacean species, leaving the faster swimmers free from their unwanted drag.

THE ORCA: Conspicuous, Curious Cetacean

Why the name killer whale? Perhaps for this animal's skilled and fearsome hunting techniques, which are sometimes used on other, often larger, cetaceans.

Perhaps the most recognizable of all the region's marine mammals, orcas (also called killer whales) are playful, inquisitive, and intelligent whales that reside in Alaskan waters year-round. Orcas travel in multigenerational family groups known as pods, which practice cooperative hunting techniques.

Orcas are smaller than grays and humpbacks, and their 17-month gestation period is the longest of any cetacean. They are identified by their white-and-black markings, as well as by the knifelike shape of their dorsal fins, which, in the case of mature males, can reach 6 feet in height.

Pods generally adhere to one of three common classifications: residents, which occupy inshore waters and feed primarily on fish; transients, which occupy larger ranges and hunt sea lions, squid, sharks, fish, and whales; and offshores, about which little is known.

QUICK FACTS:

Scientific name:
Orcinus orca

Length: Up to 30 ft.

Weight: Up to 18,000 pounds (9 tons)

Coloring: Smooth, shiny black skin with white eye patches and chin and white belly markings

Life span: 30 to 50 years

Reproduction: One calf every 3 to 5 years; calves are generally 6 feet long at birth, weighing up to 400 pounds (0.2 ton)

before performances. ✉ *204 Katlian St.* ☎ *907/747–7137* ⊕ *www.sitkatours.com/pages/Dancers.html.*

🛍 Shopping

ART GALLERIES
Artist Cove Gallery

ART GALLERIES | Works by Alaska Native artists from Sitka and remote villages are the focus at this gallery that carries basketry, jewelry, and dolls. ✉ *241 Lincoln St.* ☎ *907/747–6990.*

Island Artists Gallery

ART GALLERIES | A co-op of local artists, this storefront gallery sells their jewelry, pottery, fine-art prints, and other works. ✉ *205 Lincoln St.* ☎ *907/747–6536* ⊕ *www.islandartistsgallery.com.*

Sitka Rose Gallery

ART GALLERIES | In an 1895 Victorian next to the Bishop's House, the gallery, Sitka's most charming shop, sells Alaskan paintings, sculptures, Native art, and jewelry. ✉ *419 Lincoln St.* ☎ *907/747–3030, 888/236–1536* ⊕ *www.sitkarosegallery.com.*

BOOKSTORES
Old Harbor Books

BOOKS/STATIONERY | The knowledgeable staff and impressive collection of Alaska titles make a visit to Old Harbor a pleasure. **The Backdoor Café** (⊕ *sitkabackdoor.com*), a cozy politically progressive hangout behind the bookstore, serves excellent espresso and fresh-baked pastries. ✉ *201 Lincoln St.* ☎ *907/747–8808* ⊕ *www.oldharborbooks.net.*

GIFTS
WinterSong Soap Company

GIFTS/SOUVENIRS | The colorful and scented soaps sold at this shop near St. Michael's Cathedral are handcrafted on the premises. ✉ *321 Lincoln St.* ☎ *907/747–8949, 888/819–8949* ⊕ *www.wintersongsoap.com.*

Juneau

100 miles northeast of Sitka.

Juneau, Alaska's capital and third-largest city, is on the North American mainland but can't be reached by road. Bounded by steep mountains and water, the city's geographic isolation and compact size make it much more akin to an island community such as Sitka than to other Alaskan urban centers, such as Fairbanks or Anchorage. Juneau is full of contrasts. Its dramatic hillside location and historic downtown buildings provide a frontier feeling, but the city's cosmopolitan nature comes through in fine museums, noteworthy restaurants, and a literate and outdoorsy populace. The finest of the museums, the Alaska State Museum, was completely rebuilt in 2016 following several years of planning and exhibit research. Another new facility, the Walter Soboleff Building, offers visitors a chance to learn about the indigenous cultures of Southeast Alaska–Tlingit, Haida, and Tsimshian. Other highlights include the Mt. Roberts Tramway, plenty of densely forested wilderness areas, quiet bays for sea kayaking, and even a famous drive-up glacier, Mendenhall Glacier. For goings-on, pick up the *Juneau Empire* (⊕ *www.juneauempire.com*), which keeps tabs on state politics, business, sports, and local news.

GETTING HERE AND AROUND
Juneau is an obligatory stop on the Inside Passage cruise and ferry circuit. Hence, the town has an overabundance of visitors in midsummer. **Alaska Airlines** also flies here. Downtown Juneau is compact enough that most of its main attractions are within walking distance of one another. Note, however, that the city is very hilly, so your legs will get a real workout. Look for the 20 signs around downtown that detail Juneau's fascinating history.

ESSENTIALS
AIRLINE CONTACT Alaska Airlines
☎ *800/252–7522* ⊕ *www.alaskaair.com.*

VISITOR INFORMATION Alaska Department of Fish & Game ☎ *907/465–4180 sportfishing seasons and regulations, 907/465–2376 license information* ⊕ *www.adfg.alaska.gov.* **Alaska Division of Parks** ✉ *400 Willoughby Ave.* ☎ *907/465–4563* ⊕ *dnr.alaska.gov/parks.* **Juneau Convention and Visitors Bureau** ✉ *800 Glacier Ave., Suite 201* ☎ *907/586–2201, 888/581–2201* ⊕ *www.traveljuneau.com.*

◉ Sights

Alaska State Capitol
GOVERNMENT BUILDING | Completed in 1931, this unassuming building houses the governor's office and hosts state legislature meetings in winter, placing it at the epicenter of Alaska's animated political discourse. Historical photos line the upstairs walls. Feel free to stroll right in. You can pick up a self-guided tour brochure as you enter. ✉ *Seward and 4th Sts.* ☎ *907/465–4648* ⊕ *www.akleg.gov* 🖵 *Free.*

★ Alaska State Library, Archives, and Museum
MUSEUM | FAMILY | The Andrew P. Kashevaroff State Library, Archives, and Museum, which opened in 2016 on the site of the old state museum, is among the most impressive cultural attractions in Alaska. In the permanent gallery, visitors weave through interconnected spaces that present Alaska's unique stories through carefully selected objects and culturally diverse narratives. Kids will love the pirate ship (built for them to climb on) and the eagle tree in the lobby, viewable from multiple levels. The new state-of-the-art building also houses Alaska's most important books, photographs, and documents, offering increased opportunities for researchers as well as more casual visitors. ✉ *395 Whittier St.* ☎ *907/465–2901* ⊕ *museums.alaska.gov* 🖵 *$12 summer, $7 winter* ⊘ *Closed Sun. and Mon. Oct.–Apr.*

DIPAC Macaulay Salmon Hatchery
FISH HATCHERY | FAMILY | Salmon are integral to life in Southeast Alaska, and Alaskans are proud of their healthy fisheries. A visit to the hatchery is a great introduction to the complex considerations involved in maintaining the continued vitality of this crucial resource. Watch through an underwater window as salmon fight their way up a fish ladder from mid-June to mid-October. Inside the busy hatchery, which produces almost 125 million young salmon annually, you will learn about the environmental considerations of commercial fishermen and the lives of salmon. A retail shop sells gifts and salmon products. The salmon hatchery is part of a larger nonprofit, Douglas Island Pink & Chum, Inc., and is usually referred to locally by its acronym, DIPAC. ✉ *2697 Channel Dr.* ✚ *3 miles northwest of downtown Juneau* ☎ *907/463–5114, 877/463–2486* ⊕ *www.dipac.net* 🖵 *$4, including short tour* ⊘ *Closed Oct.–Apr.*

Glacier Gardens Rainforest Adventure
FOREST | One of the upsides to living in a rain forest is the lush proliferation of plants and trees. At Glacier Gardens, they've turned local flora into an art form. Spread over 50 acres of rain forest, the family-owned Glacier Gardens has ponds, waterfalls, hiking paths, a large atrium, and gardens. The roots of fallen trees, turned upside down and buried in the ground, act as bowls to hold planters that overflow with begonias, fuchsias, and petunias. Guided tours in covered golf carts lead you along the 4 miles of paved paths, and a 580-foot-high overlook provides dramatic views of the Mendenhall wetlands wildlife refuge, Chilkat Mountains, and downtown Juneau. A café and gift shop are here, and the conservatory is a popular wedding spot. Admission includes a guided tour. The Juneau city bus, which departs from multiple locations downtown, stops in front of Glacier Gardens. ✉ *7600 Glacier Hwy.* ✚ *6½ miles northwest of downtown Juneau*

Juneau's History

Tlingit residents of the area originally made their home in nearby Auke Bay, where the rain is less oppressive and the vistas are more open, but in summers they frequently moved down the channel to what is now the Willoughby District of Juneau. Miners began arriving in the 1880s, including two colorful sourdoughs, Joe Juneau and Richard Harris. Led by a Tlingit chief named Kowee, Juneau and Harris discovered rich reserves of gold at Snow Slide Gulch, the drainage of Gold Creek around which the town was eventually built. Shortly thereafter a modest stampede resulted in the formation of a mining camp, which quickly grew to become the Alaska district government capital in 1906. The city may well have continued under its original appellation—Harrisburg, after Richard Harris—were it not for Joe Juneau's political jockeying at a miner's meeting in 1881.

For some 60 years after Juneau's founding, gold was the mainstay of the economy. In its heyday the AJ (for Alaska Juneau) Gold Mine was the biggest low-grade ore mine in the world. It was not until World War II, when the government decided it needed Juneau's manpower for the war effort, that the AJ and other mines in the area ceased operations. After the war, mining failed to start up again and government became the city's principal employer. Juneau's mines leave a rich legacy, though: before it closed, the AJ Gold Mine alone produced more than $80 million in gold.

☎ 907/790–3377 ⊕ www.glaciergardens. com ☞ $27 ⊙ Closed Oct.–Apr.

Governor's Mansion

HOUSE | This stately colonial-style home completed in 1912 overlooks downtown Juneau. With 14,400 square feet, 6 bedrooms, and 10 bathrooms, it's no miner's cabin. Out front is a totem pole that tells three tales: the history of man, the cause of ocean tides, and the origin of Alaska's ubiquitous mosquitoes. Unfortunately, tours of the residence are not permitted. ✉ 716 Calhoun Ave.

Juneau-Douglas City Museum

MUSEUM | **FAMILY** | Exhibits at this city-run museum interpret pioneer, mining, and Tlingit history. A diorama of a fire assay lab shows how the Bureau of Mines measured the gold content of rock samples, and there's a reconstructed Tlingit fish trap. Pioneer artifacts include a century-old store and kitchen. Digital story kiosks shed light on Alaska's quest for statehood, how government works here, civil rights in Alaska, and the cultures of Juneau. In the hands-on room, youngsters can try on clothes similar to ones worn by the miners and look at gold-rush stereoscopes. Engaging historic walking tours of downtown ($25) take place from May through September. ✉ 114 4th St. ☎ 907/586–3572 ⊕ www.juneau.org/library/museum/index.php ☞ $6 May–Sept., free Oct.–Apr.; $25 walking tour (includes museum admission) ⊙ Closed Sun. and Mon. Oct.–Apr.

Juneau Visitor Center

INFO CENTER | In a nod to the area's maritime history—and the nearly one million cruise-ship passengers who flock to the Capital City every summer—Juneau's colorful visitor center was designed by local architects to resemble a ship's transom. The building, which sits next to the cruise-ship dock at the southern end of the waterfront Seawalk, is clad in iridescent stainless-steel shingles.

Juneau

Sights ▼

1 Alaska State Capitol.... **D3**
2 Alaska State Library, Archives, and Museum . **C3**
3 DIPAC Macaulay Salmon Hatchery **B1**
4 Glacier Gardens Rainforest Adventure .. **B1**
5 Governor's Mansion.... **D2**
6 Juneau-Douglas City Museum **D3**
7 Juneau Visitor Center ... **E5**
8 Last Chance Mining Museum **E1**
9 Mendenhall Glacier **B1**
10 Mt. Roberts Tramway .. **D5**
11 Red Dog Saloon......... **D5**
12 St. Nicholas Russian Orthodox Church......... **E3**
13 Seawalk.................. **E5**
14 Shrine of St. Therese... **B1**
15 South Franklin St........ **E5**
16 Walter Soboleff Building **D4**
17 Wickersham State Historical Site **E3**

Restaurants ▼

1 Douglas Café............. **A2**
2 Gold Creek Salmon Bake **B2**
3 The Hangar on the Wharf **D4**
4 Heritage Coffee Company.................. **D4**
5 Island Pub **A2**
6 Rainbow Foods........... **E3**
7 The Rookery Café........ **E4**
8 Salt **D4**
9 The Sandpiper Café **C3**
10 Tracy's King Crab Shack **D5**
11 Twisted Fish Company .. **E5**

Hotels ▼

1 Alaska's Capital Inn **D3**
2 Aspen Suites Hotel **B1**
3 Auke Lake Bed & Breakfast **B1**
4 Driftwood Lodge **C3**
5 Four Points by Sheraton Juneau.... **D4**
6 Grandma's Feather Bed **B1**
7 Pearson's Pond Luxury Inn and Adventure Spa **B1**
8 Prospector Hotel......... **C3**
9 Silverbow Inn **D3**
10 U.S. Forest Service Cabins................... **B1**
11 Westmark Baranof Hotel **E4**

KEY

1 Exploring Sights
1 Restaurants
1 Hotels

Walking Around Juneau

The most common starting spot is **Marine Park**, right along the cruise-ship dock. From there, head up to Front Street to the **Walter Soboleff Building**, an Alaska Native arts and cultural center, one of the few modern buildings in this part of town. From there, walk up Main Street to the **State Office Building**, where you'll find an observation deck with vistas across the Gastineau Channel. The snug but cheery **Juneau–Douglas City Museum**, a local treasure, sits a short distance away at 4th and Main streets. The looming, banklike building across Main Street is the **Alaska State Capitol**. For a far more attractive example of governmental architecture, continue southwest on 4th Street until it becomes Calhoun Street and then head north to the **Governor's Mansion**. On your way back toward town, head down the public stairs on Calhoun and follow the signs to the new **Alaska State Library, Archives, and Museum**.

After viewing the museum, head back downtown to peruse the historic

buildings and busy shops, particularly those along **South Franklin Street.** Check out the Alaskan Hotel, the Alaska Steam Laundry Building, and the Senate Building before dipping inside the terminally crowded **Red Dog Saloon** at the intersection of South Franklin Street and Admiralty Way. Try a microbrew, and then continue down the street to the **Mt. Roberts Tramway,** a popular way to reach alpine country for a hike overlooking Juneau and the Gastineau Channel. Next door is the colorful new **Juneau Visitor Center.** From here you can stroll down the recently constructed **Seawalk,** which parallels South Franklin.

To cover downtown Juneau's many interesting sights, you should allow at least three or four hours for exploring. Add at least another hour if you're a museum fan, or if you plan to ride the **Mt. Roberts Tramway.** Don't miss drive-up **Mendenhall Glacier**; it's a few miles out of town so you'll need to take a car, taxi, or bus to get there.

Reminiscent of the scales of a fish, they change color depending on your angle of view. The center has complete details on Juneau sights and activities, plus walking-tour maps and a guide to local trails. Visitor information is also available at kiosks at Marine Park downtown and at the ferry terminal in Auke Bay. ⊠ *S. Franklin St.* ☎ *907/586–2201* ⊕ *www. traveljuneau.com* ⊗ *Closed Oct.–Apr.*

Last Chance Mining Museum
A 1½-mile hike or taxi ride behind town, this small museum is housed in the former compressor building of Juneau's historic AJ Gold Mine. The collection includes old mining tools, railcars, minerals, and a 3-D map of the ore body. If

you have time, and didn't arrive on foot, meander down back toward town. Unlike most of Juneau, Basin Road is flat and relatively quiet. The surrounding country is steep and wooded, with trails leading in all directions, including one to the summit of Mt. Juneau. At the base of the Perseverance Trail, not far from the museum, you can see the boarded-up opening to an old mining tunnel; even from a safe distance you can feel a chilly breeze wafting through the cracks. ⊠ *1001 Basin Rd.* ☎ *907/586–5338* ⊠ *$4.*

★ Mendenhall Glacier
NATURE SITE | FAMILY | Glaciers are abundant in Southeast Alaska, but only a very few are as accessible as the Mendenhall

Glacier. Alaska's most-visited drive-up glacier spans 12 miles and is fed by the massive Juneau Icefield. Like many other Alaska glaciers, it is retreating, losing more than 100 feet a year as huge chunks of ice calve into the small lake separating the glacier from the **Mendenhall Visitor Center**. The center has interactive and traditional exhibits, a theater and bookstore, and panoramic views. Nature trails lead along Mendenhall Lake, to Nugget Falls, and into the mountains overlooking Mendenhall Glacier; the trails are marked by posts and paint stripes delineating the historic location of the glacier, providing a sharp reminder of the Mendenhall's hasty retreat. An elevated viewing platform allows visitors to look for spawning sockeye and coho salmon—and the bears that eat them—at Steep Creek, ½ mile south of the visitor center along the Moraine Ecology Trail. Several companies lead bus tours to the glacier. A glacier express bus leaves from the cruise-ship terminal and heads right out to Mendenhall Glacier; ask at the visitor information center there. You can also get within a mile and a half of the glacier on the city bus, which is $2 one-way. For a different perspective, you can travel by helicopter to the surface of the glacier, or hire a guide to take you to one of the amazing, electric blue ice caves. Note that because the caves are inherently unstable, the Forest Service doesn't recommend self-guided tours. ⊠ *End of Glacier Spur Rd. off Mendenhall Loop Rd.* ✛ *13 miles north of downtown Juneau* ☎ *907/789–0097* ⊕ *www.fs.usda.gov/ detail/tongass/about-forest/offices* ☞ *Visitor center $5 May–Sept., free Oct.–Apr.* ◔ *Closed Mon.–Thurs. Oct.–Apr.*

★ Mt. Roberts Tramway

VIEWPOINT | FAMILY | One of Southeast's most popular tourist attractions whisks you from the cruise terminal 1,800 feet up the side of Mt. Roberts. After the six-minute ride you can take in a film on the history and legends of the Tlingits, visit the nature center, go for an alpine walk on hiking trails (including the 5-mile round-trip hike to Mt. Roberts's 3,819-foot summit), purchase Native arts and peruse the on-site gallery, or enjoy a meal while savoring mountain views. You can also get an up-close view of an "education" eagle in her mew. A local company leads guided wilderness hikes from the summit, and the bar serves locally brewed beers. Plan to spend one to two hours at the top. For a workout, hike up the mountain from town or hike up to Father Brown's Cross from the top; each takes about an hour. ⊠ *490 S. Franklin St.* ☎ *907/463–3412, 888/461–8726* ⊕ *www. mountrobertstramway.com* ☞ *$34* ◔ *Closed Oct.–Apr.*

Red Dog Saloon

RESTAURANT—SIGHT | The frontierish quarters of the Red Dog have housed an infamous Juneau watering hole since 1890. Nearly every conceivable surface in this two-story bar is cluttered with graffiti, business cards, and memorabilia, including a pistol that reputedly belonged to Wyatt Earp, who failed to reclaim the piece after checking it in at the U.S. Marshall's office on June 27, 1900. The saloon's food menu includes halibut, reindeer sausage, potato skins, burgers, and locally brewed Alaskan beers. A little atmospheric sawdust covers the floor, and musicians pump out ragtime piano tunes when cruise ships are docked. ⊠ *278 S. Franklin St.* ☎ *907/463–3658* ⊕ *www.reddogsaloon.com.*

St. Nicholas Russian Orthodox Church

RELIGIOUS SITE | Newly baptized Orthodox Natives and Siberian gold miners built what's now Southeast's oldest Russian church in 1894. Refurbished in the late 1970s, the onion-dome white-and-blue structure is a national historic landmark. Services sung in Slavonic, English, and Tlingit take place on weekends. ⊠ *326 5th St.* ☎ *907/586–1023* ⊕ *www.stnicholasjuneau.org.*

Seawalk

MARINA | Constructed as part of a long-range waterfront improvement plan, Juneau's Seawalk currently runs from Marine Park down to the end of South Franklin Street. Plans call for it to extend farther north to the Juneau–Douglas Bridge. The Seawalk provides a calmer pedestrian alternative to the narrow, crowded sidewalks of South Franklin Street; its rewards include beautiful views of Gastineau Channel and Douglas Island. Cruise ships and local boats operate in this area, so be prepared to sidestep disembarking passengers. One section passes between the Taku Smokeries fish-processing plant and an offloading dock for fishermen, allowing an occasional glimpse of an industry that remains an important part of Alaskan life. ⊠ *S. Franklin St.*

Shrine of St. Therese

RELIGIOUS SITE | If the crowds become overwhelming, and you have access to a vehicle, consider a visit to the Shrine of St. Therese, "out the road"—it's a peaceful site that's perfect for quiet contemplation. Built in the 1930s, this beautiful stone church and its 15 stations of the cross are the only structures on a serene tiny island accessible via a 400-foot-long pedestrian causeway. Visitors enjoy the Merciful Love Labyrinth, the black-granite Shrine Columbarium, and the floral gardens along the Good Shepherd Rosary Trail. Sunday services are held at 1:30 pm from June through August. For those wishing to explore the area for more than a few hours, the shrine offers a lodge and four rental cabins that run the gamut from rustic to resplendent. A round-trip taxi ride may cost $60 or more. ⊠ *Mile 23 Glacier Hwy.* ✛ *23 miles northwest of downtown* ☎ *907/586–2227* ⊕ *www. shrineofsainttherese.org.*

South Franklin Street

NEIGHBORHOOD | The buildings on South Franklin Street and neighboring Front Street, among the oldest and most inviting structures in the city, house curio and crafts shops, snack shops, and a salmon shop. Many reflect the architecture of the 1920s and '30s. When the small Alaskan Hotel opened in 1913, Juneau was home to 30 saloons; the Alaskan gives today's visitors the most authentic glimpse of the town's whiskey-rich history. The barroom's massive, mirrored oak back bar is accented by Tiffany lights and panels. Topped by a wood-shingled turret, the 1901 Alaska Steam Laundry Building now houses a toy store and other shops. The Senate Building, another of South Franklin's landmarks, is across the street. ⊠ *S. Franklin St.*

★ Walter Soboleff Building

MUSEUM | This center devoted to Alaska Native art, culture, and language opened is operated by Sealaska Heritage Institute and named for a local Tlingit elder who died at age 102 in 2011. It includes a gallery, a traditional clan house, a living-history center, research areas, and a shop selling work by Northwest Coast artists. The building's three major public art pieces—exterior red metal panels, a carved cedar house facade, and a modern glass screen in the clan house itself—were created by three of the top Northwest Coast artists in the world (Robert Davidson, David Boxley, and Preston Singletary), and represent the three indigenous tribes of Southeast Alaska—Haida, Tsimshian, and Tlingit, respectively. The art pieces also highlight the center's dual role in honoring tradition while remaining forward-facing and contemporary. Among the goals of this downtown historical district facility are promoting Juneau's role as a hub of Northwest Coast art and fostering cross-cultural understanding between Native and non-Native populations. ⊠ *105 Seward St.* ☎ *907/463–4844* ⊕ *www.sealaskaheritage.org* ☞ *$5* ☉ *Store closed Sun. and Mon. Oct.–Apr.*

Wickersham State Historical Site

HISTORIC SITE | At the top of the hill behind the capitol, on a rise sometimes known as "Chicken Ridge," stands the former residence of James Wickersham,

pioneer judge, delegate to Congress, prolific author, and gutsy outdoorsman. The white New England–style home, constructed in 1898, contains memorabilia from the judge's travels throughout Alaska—from rare Native basketry and ivory carvings to historic photos and a Chickering grand piano that came "'round the Horn" to Alaska in the 1870s. The tour provides a glimpse into the life of this dynamic man. ⌧ *213 7th St.* ☏ *907/586–9001* ⊕ *dnr.alaska.gov/parks/ units/wickrshm.htm* ⌑ *Free* ☺ *Closed Oct.–Apr.*

Activities

BIKING
Cycle Alaska
BICYCLING | Rentals from Cycle Alaska include everything from a helmet and minipump to a bottle of water and a granola bar. You can reserve a bike online at their website and also check out Juneau's free new bike map at *juneau-rides.org/juneau-bike-map*. ⌧ *1107 W. 8th St.* ☏ *907/780–2253* ⊕ *www.cycleak.com* ⌑ *From $37.*

BOATING, CANOEING, AND KAYAKING
Above & Beyond Alaska
BOATING | Juneau-based Above & Beyond conducts day and overnight camping trips, ice-climbing adventures, and Mendenhall Glacier and sea-kayaking trips. The owners also run the Alaska Boat & Kayak Shop, which offers kayak and canoe rentals. Both are located in Auke Bay. ⌧ *Auke Bay Harbor, 11521 Glacier Hwy., Auke Bay* ☏ *907/364–2333* ⊕ *www.beyondak. com* ⌑ *Tours from $240.*

★ Adventure Bound Alaska
BOATING | All-day trips to Sawyer Glacier within Tracy Arm in summer are available from Adventure Bound Alaska. ⌧ *76 Egan Dr.* ☏ *907/463–2509, 800/228–3875* ⊕ *www.adventureboundalaska.com* ⌑ *$160.*

Alaska Discovery
BOATING | Operated by Mountain Travel Sobek, Alaska Discovery leads 10- and 16-day trips down the Tatshenshini and Alsek rivers, 8-day kayaking trips in Glacier Bay, and 3-day camping trips in Point Adolphus, among other adventures. ⌧ *Juneau* ☏ *888/831–7526* ⊕ *www. mtsobek.com/trips/alaska-north-america/ alaska* ⌑ *From $2195.*

Alaska Travel Adventures
BOATING | Mendenhall River floats, lake kayaking, and lake canoeing are among the Juneau-area tours this outfit offers; lunch at a creek-side salmon bake is a popular add-on. ⌧ *9085 Glacier Hwy.* ☏ *800/323–5757, 907/789–0052* ⊕ *www. alaskatraveladventures.com* ⌑ *From $139.*

Allen Marine Tours
BOATING | Family-owned Allen Marine Tours conducts catamaran trips to Tracy Arm fjord, whale-watching adventures out of Auke Bay, and several land-and-water combination tours. Book through your cruise line, or call for prices. ⌧ *Juneau* ☏ *907/789–0081, 888/289–0081* ⊕ *www. allenmarinetours.com.*

CROSS-COUNTRY SKIING
Foggy Mountain Shop
SKIING/SNOWBOARDING | Find groomed cross-country ski trails near the Eaglecrest Ski Area and at Mendenhall Campground in the winter. You can rent skis and get advice about touring the trails and ridges around town from Foggy Mountain Shop. The shop also outfits hikers and climbers in summer. ⌧ *134 N. Franklin St.* ☏ *907/586–6780* ⊕ *www. foggymountainshop.com.*

Parks and Recreation Department
SKIING/SNOWBOARDING | In the winter, the department sponsors a group ski and snowshoe outing each Wednesday and Saturday when there's sufficient snow. Hikes are also offered in the summer. ⌧ *155 S. Seward St.* ☏ *907/586–5226, 907/586–0428 24-hr information* ⊕ *www. juneau.org/parkrec/hike.*

DOWNHILL SKIING AND ZIPLINING

Alaska Zipline Adventures

ZIP LINING | FAMILY | Each summer, Eaglecrest Ski Area serves as the home base for Alaska Zipline Adventures. Their exhilarating three-hour tour includes brief stopovers on enclosed tree-house platforms, allowing zipliners to catch their breath and snap photos of the surrounding Tongass National Forest. ⊠ *Juneau* ☎ *907/ 523–2920* ⊕ *www.alaskazip.com* ⊡ *From $159.*

Eaglecrest

SKIING/SNOWBOARDING | Southeast's only downhill ski area is on Douglas Island, 30 minutes from downtown Juneau. The resort typically offers skiing and snowboarding from late-November to mid-April on 620 acres of well-groomed and off-piste terrain. Amenities include four double chairlifts, cross-country trails, a beginner's slope, a ski school, a ski-rental shop, a cafeteria, and a tri-level day lodge. In the summer, hikers and bikers can explore the mountain via the service road that runs from the bottom of Eaglecrest to the top of the chairlift, a 2-mile trek with a heart-pumping 1,400-foot elevation gain. The road is usually snow-free by June. ⊠ *3000 Fish Creek Rd.* ☎ *907/790–2000* ⊕ *skijuneau.com.*

FISHING

Juneau Convention and Visitors Bureau

FISHING | The website and office for the Juneau Convention and Visitors Bureau has a complete list of operators and several companies that lead sportfishing trips from Juneau. ☎ *907/586–2201, 888/581–2201* ⊕ *www.traveljuneau.com.*

FLIGHTSEEING

Several local companies operate helicopter flightseeing trips to the spectacular glaciers flowing from Juneau Icefield. Most have booths along the downtown cruise-ship dock. All include a touchdown on a glacier, providing the opportunity to romp on these rivers of ice. Some also lead trips that include a dogsled ride on the glacier. Note that although we recommend the best companies, even some of the most experienced pilots have had accidents; always ask a carrier about its recent safety record before booking a trip.

★ Alaska Seaplanes

TOUR—SPORTS | Besides daily scheduled air service to 14 Southeast communities, Alaska Seaplanes also offers flightseeing tours and charters to other Southeast destinations. ⊠ *1873 Shell Simmons Dr.* ☎ *907/789–3331* ⊕ *www.flyalaskaseaplanes.com.*

Coastal Helicopters

TOUR—SPORTS | These helicopters land on several glaciers within the Juneau Icefield during a 1-hour tour; 1.5-hour dog-sled adventures are another popular option. ⊠ *8995 Yandukin Dr.* ☎ *907/789–5600, 800/789–5610* ⊕ *www.coastalhelicopters.com* ⊡ *$299 for ice field tour, $529 for dogsled.*

NorthStar Trekking

TOUR—SPORTS | No experience is necessary at NorthStar, which has three levels of excellent glacier hikes. The lowest level includes a one-hour interpretive walk while the highest consists of a three-hour hike that includes the chance to practice basic climbing and rope techniques. Dog-sled adventures are also available. Book through your cruise line, or call for prices. ⊠ *Juneau* ☎ *907/790–4530* ⊕ *www. northstartrekking.com.*

Temsco Helicopters

TOUR—SPORTS | The self-proclaimed pioneers of Alaska glacier helicopter touring, Temsco Helicopters offers glacier tours, dogsled adventures, and year-round flightseeing. Book through your cruise line or contact the company for pricing. ⊠ *1650 Maplesden Way* ☎ *907/789–9501, 877/789–9501* ⊕ *www. temscoair.com.*

Ward Air

TOUR—SPORTS | Take flightseeing trips to Glacier Bay, the Juneau Icefield,

4

Juneau, the Inside Passage, and Southeast Alaska JUNEAU

Elfin Cove, Tracy Arm, and Pack Creek with Ward Air, or charter a floatplane to access one of the area's remote U.S. Forest Service cabins. ⊠ *8991 Yandukin Dr.* ☎ *907/789–9150, 800/478–9150* ⊕ *www. wardair.com.*

★ Wings Airways and Taku Glacier Lodge

TOUR—SPORTS | This Juneau-based company specializes in glacier sightseeing followed by a salmon feast at a remote, historic Alaskan lodge, complete with glacier views in their Taku Lodge Feast & 5 Glacier Discovery Tour—one of the best day trips out of the state capital. The 5 Glacier Discovery Tour is also available as a stand-alone flightseeing trip. ⊠ *2 Marine Way, Suite 175* ☎ *907/586–6275* ⊕ *www.wingsairways.com* 🖃 *$225 for glacier tour, $320 for tour/lodge combo.*

GOLD-PANNING

Alaska Travel Adventures

LOCAL SPORTS | FAMILY | Gold panning is fun, especially for children, and Juneau is one of Southeast's best-known gold-panning towns. Sometimes you actually discover a few flecks of the precious metal in the bottom of your pan. You can buy a pan at almost any Alaska hardware or sporting-goods store. Alaska Travel Adventures has gold-panning tours near the famous Alaska-Juneau Mine. ⊠ *Juneau* ☎ *800/323–5757, 907/789–0052* ⊕ *www.alaskatraveladventures.com* 🖃 *From $69.*

HIKING

★ Gastineau Guiding

HIKING/WALKING | This company leads a variety of hikes in the Juneau area. Especially popular are the "Town, Tram, and Timberline Trek" tours, which include a shuttle ride through the historic district in downtown Juneau, a tram ride up Mt. Roberts, a short hike at the top, and a stop at the Alpine Tea house to sample Alaska-made tea. ⊠ *1330 Eastaugh Way, Suite 2* ☎ *907/586–8231* ⊕ *www.stepintoalaska.com* 🖃 *From $49.*

Parks and Recreation Department

HIKING/WALKING | The department sponsors a group hike every Wednesday morning and an additional hike on Saturday in the summer. ⊠ *155 S. Seward St.* ☎ *907/586–5226, 907/586–0428 24-hr information* ⊕ *www.juneau.org/parkrec/ hike.*

U.S. Forest Service

HIKING/WALKING | Hikers can contact the U.S. Forest Service for trail books and maps; some are available online for easy downloading. ⊠ *Juneau Ranger District office, 8510 Mendenhall Loop Rd.* ☎ *907/586–8800* ⊕ *www.fs.usda.gov/ detail/tongass/maps-pubs.*

SIGHTSEEING AND GLACIERS

AJ Mine Gastineau Mill Tour

TOUR—SPORTS | Former miners lead two-hour tours of the historic AJ Gold Mine south of Juneau. The tours, which depart from downtown by bus, include a gold-panning demonstration and time in the old tunnels that lace the mountains. ⊠ *Sheep Creek Mine Rd.* ☎ *907/463–5017* ⊕ *www.ajgastineauminetour.com* 🖃 *Call for prices.*

Juneau Convention and Visitors Bureau

TOUR—SPORTS | The bureau maintains a list of companies that conduct tours of Mendenhall Glacier, and others that provide boat trips to Tracy Arm's Sawyer Glacier, about 50 miles southeast of Juneau. The recently opened Juneau Visitors Center, next to the Mt. Roberts Tramway building on South Franklin Street, is the bureau's most convenient location for summertime visitors, and a fun example of local architecture. ⊠ *800 Glacier Ave., Suite 201* ☎ *907/586–2201, 888/581–2201* ⊕ *www.traveljuneau.com.*

WHALE-WATCHING

Alaska Galore Tours

WHALE-WATCHING | This company offers small-group whale-watching excursions of up to 20 guests aboard a luxury yacht with an onboard naturalist, as well as a combination whale-watch-and-flightseeing tour over the Juneau Icefield.

✉ *Juneau* ☎ *907/321–5859, 888/432–6722* ⊕ *alaska-whale-watching-juneau.com* 🖙 *From $149.*

Harv & Marv's Outback Alaska

WHALE-WATCHING | Experienced local captains lead these whale-watching excursions for groups of up to 6 or up to 18 passengers. Private tours can also be arranged. ✉ *Juneau* ☎ *907/209–7288, 866/909–7288* ⊕ *www.harvandmar-vs-alaska-whale-watching.com* 🖙 *From $145.*

★ Weather Permitting Alaska

WHALE-WATCHING | The small-boat luxury whale-watching trips of Weather Permitting last four hours, including van travel. Visitors get plenty of time to view whales, bears, sea lions, eagles, porpoises, and other animals, all the while enjoying dramatic scenery. With only 10 customers on a trip (excepting single groups of up to 12), this is among the most intimate and comprehensive whale watches anywhere. For a truly unique experience, schedule a customized trip with an "Alaskan celebrity" such as the famous whale photographer and marine biologist Flip Nicklin (if he's available). ✉ *19400 Beardsley Way* ☎ *907/789–5843* ⊕ *www.weatherpermittingalaska.com* 🖙 *From $189.*

🍴 Restaurants

Douglas Café

$ | **AMERICAN** | In the heart of quiet Douglas, across the bridge and a couple of miles from downtown Juneau, this family diner has Formica tables and a menu that includes omelets, sandwiches, kids' favorites, and burgers that are often cited as the best in the city. This is a good choice for those seeking an alternative to downtown Juneau's midsummer crowds. **Known for:** burgers and fries; hearty breakfasts; local crowd. ⑤ *Average main: $11* ✉ *916 3rd St., Douglas* ☎ *907/364–3307* ◷ *Closed Mon.*

Gold Creek Salmon Bake

$$$$ | **SEAFOOD** | Trees, mountains, and the rushing water of Salmon Creek surround the comfortable, canopy-covered benches and tables at this authentic, all-you-can-eat salmon bake operated through Alaska Travel Adventures. After dinner you can pan for gold in the stream, wander up a hill to explore the remains of a gold mine, or roast marshmallows over a fire. **Known for:** fresh-caught salmon cooked over fire; forest experience; picnic-style eating. ⑤ *Average main: $55* ✉ *1061 Salmon Lane Rd.* ☎ *907/789–0052, 800/323–5757* ⊕ *www.besto-falaskatravel.com/alaska_day_tours/pag-es/j_gold_creek_salmon.htm* ◷ *Closed Oct.–Apr.*

The Hangar on the Wharf

$$ | **ECLECTIC** | Crowded with locals and travelers, the Hangar occupies the building where Alaska Airlines started business, and though flight-theme puns (e.g., "Pre-flight Snacks" and the "Plane Caesar") dominate the menu, the comfortably worn wood and the vintage airplane photos create a casual experience that trumps the kitsch. Every seat has views of the Gastineau Channel and Douglas Island, and on warm days you can sit outdoors. **Known for:** prime rib; views; wide selection of beers on tap, including local options. ⑤ *Average main: $18* ✉ *Merchants Wharf Mall, 2 Marine Way* ☎ *907/586–5018* ⊕ *www.hanga-ronthewharf.com.*

Heritage Coffee Company

$ | **CAFÉ** | Established in 1974, Heritage Coffee serves locally roasted coffees, along with gelato, fresh pastries, and a variety of sandwiches. The flagship store sits on the corner of Front and Seward streets, while other locations include a smaller café with limited outdoor seating at 230 South Franklin Street, a branch inside Foodland IGA market, and a kiosk at the University of Alaska Southeast. **Known for:** espresso; lively atmosphere; baked goods. ⑤ *Average main: $9* ✉ *130*

Front St. ☎ *907/586–1088* ⊕ *www.herit-agecoffee.com.*

Island Pub

$ | **PIZZA** | Fast service, a full bar, views of the Gastineau Channel, and occasional live music have turned this Douglas pub into an area hot spot, but the real draw is pizza: thin, 13-inch focaccia crusts prepared fresh daily, topped with creative ingredients, and baked in a copper wood-fired oven. If you don't get too full, try a dessert pizza—bizarre, but surprisingly good. **Known for:** inventive topping combinations; thin focaccia crusts; local gathering spot. ⑤ *Average main: $10* ✉ *1102 2nd St., Douglas* ☎ *907/364–1595* ⊕ *www.theislandpub.com.*

Rainbow Foods

$ | **VEGETARIAN** | This crunchy natural foods market with a weekday buffet offers an ever-changing selection of hot entrées, salads, soups, and pizza, along with self-serve coffee and freshly baked breads. Check their website for a daily menu, and arrive before 11 am for the best choices; a few tables are available inside. **Known for:** organic, healthy snacks; lunch buffet; vegetarian options. ⑤ *Average main: $8* ✉ *224 4th St.* ☎ *907/586–6476* ⊕ *www.rainbow-foods.org.*

The Rookery Café

$$ | **ECLECTIC** | This lively café fills up quickly at noon with locals on lunch break, making it a great place for people-watching while munching on a salad. You can also grab a great breakfast here, including fresh-baked *pain au chocolat*, buttermilk corn cakes, and Stumptown coffee. **Known for:** baked goods; creative lunch options; popularity with locals. ⑤ *Average main: $14* ✉ *111 Seward St.* ☎ *907/463–3013* ⊕ *www.therookerycafe.com.*

Salt

$$$ | **MEDITERRANEAN** | Upscale American and Mediterranean fare is served at Salt, one of Juneau's nicest dining options, and though it's a bit pricey, the ambience

and service make it worth the extra expense. About a block away, on Franklin Street, is **Saffron,** an Indian restaurant run by the same owners, that serves naan, dahl, curry, and other tasty offerings. **Known for:** upscale dining; craft cocktails; filet mignon. ⑤ *Average main: $28* ✉ *200 Seward St.* ☎ *907/780–2221* ⊕ *www.saltalaska.com* ☻ *Closed Sun.*

The Sandpiper Café

$ | **AMERICAN** | This busy and bright café in the Willoughby District, about a five-minute walk from the center of town, is a popular destination for brunch on weekends. It's also a good choice for lunch if you're visiting the state museum, as it's less than a block away. **Known for:** French toast; Reuben sandwiches; weekend brunch. ⑤ *Average main: $12* ✉ *429 W. Willoughby Ave.* ☎ *907/586–3150* ☻ *No dinner.*

★ Tracy's King Crab Shack

$$ | **SEAFOOD** | Alaskan king crab—a not-to-be-missed Alaskan delicacy—is the specialty of popular Tracy's. There's often a line to place your order, but the wait is entirely worth it. **Known for:** crab bisque; Bristol Bay king crab legs with butter; casual, fun vibe. ⑤ *Average main: $15* ✉ *432 S. Franklin St.* ☎ *907/723–1811* ⊕ *www.kingcrabshack.com* ☻ *Closed Oct.–Apr.*

Twisted Fish Company

$$$ | **SEAFOOD** | Downtown Juneau's liveliest eatery, housed in a log-frame waterfront building adjacent to the base of the Mt. Roberts Tramway, serves fish as fresh as you'll find. Grab a seat on the deck and enjoy prime-time Gastineau Channel gazing over a glass of wine or locally brewed beer. **Known for:** Captain Ron's chowder; waterfront dining; halibut. ⑤ *Average main: $24* ✉ *550 S. Franklin St.* ☎ *907/463–5033* ⊕ *www.twistedfishcompany.com* ☻ *Closed Oct.–Apr.*

🛏 Hotels

★ Alaska's Capital Inn

$$$$ | B&B/INN | Gold-rush pioneer John Olds built this American foursquare home in 1906, and a major restoration transformed it into downtown Juneau's most elegant B&B. **Pros:** beautiful restoration of 1906 mansion; antiques; gourmet breakfasts. **Cons:** the inn sits atop a steep incline from the main section of downtown; room rates are a little high; less privacy than some other properties. ⓢ *Rooms from: $300* ✉ *113 W. 5th St.* ☎ *907/586–6507, 888/588–6507* ⊕ *www.alaskacapitalinn.com* ➹ *7 rooms* ⏹ *Breakfast.*

Aspen Suites Hotel

$$ | HOTEL | A standard all-suites hotel near the airport, the Aspen is well suited for business travelers and travelers with children. **Pros:** walking distance to Mendenhall Wetlands Trail; complimentary Wi-Fi; close to the airport. **Cons:** not near downtown attractions; housekeeping is weekly, not daily; basic hotel decor. ⓢ *Rooms from: $189* ✉ *8400 Airport Blvd.* ☎ *907/500–7700* ⊕ *www.aspenhotelsak.com/juneau* ➹ *78 rooms* ⏹ *No meals.*

Auke Lake Bed & Breakfast

$$ | B&B/INN | A stay at this lakeside B&B about 4½ miles northwest of Juneau's airport provides a glimpse into local living–you can explore small, quiet Auke Lake by paddleboat, canoe, or kayak; enjoy it from the shoreside hot tub; or walk the 3-mile trail that circles it. **Pros:** secluded residential area; lakefront location; walking distance to bus stop. **Cons:** outside town; few restaurant options nearby; no laundry facilities. ⓢ *Rooms from: $140* ✉ *11595 Mendenhall Loop Rd.* ☎ *907/790–3253, 800/790–3253* ⊕ *www.aukelakebb.com* ➹ *5 rooms* ⏹ *Breakfast.*

Driftwood Lodge

$$ | HOTEL | This workaday downtown motel is a good option for guests interested in preparing their own meals and exploring downtown Juneau on foot. **Pros:** well-equipped kitchenettes in many rooms; easy walking distance to downtown sights; ferry and airport shuttle service. **Cons:** not handicapped-accessible; spare and dated decor; parking lot out front. ⓢ *Rooms from: $112* ✉ *435 W. Willoughby Ave.* ☎ *907/586–2280, 800/544–2239* ⊕ *www.dhalaska.com* ➹ *62 rooms* ⏹ *No meals.*

Four Points by Sheraton Juneau

$$$ | HOTEL | A high-rise by Juneau standards, the seven-story Four Points by Sheraton (formerly the Goldbelt) is one of the city's better lodgings, with decent, if somewhat overpriced, rooms. **Pros:** walking distance to downtown sights; restaurant on-site; great views from many rooms. **Cons:** street-side rooms are noisy; a little pricey; no room service. ⓢ *Rooms from: $209* ✉ *51 W. Egan Dr.* ☎ *907/586–6900* ⊕ *www.fourpointsjuneau.com* ➹ *106 rooms* ⏹ *No meals.*

Grandma's Feather Bed

$$$ | B&B/INN | This charming Victorian-style hotel—the smallest property in the Best Western chain—is less than a mile from the airport in Mendenhall Valley and has spacious and homey rooms. **Pros:** delicious breakfast; deluxe suites with in-room whirlpool baths; beds topped with feather comforters. **Cons:** outside downtown; books up quickly; not set up for children. ⓢ *Rooms from: $210* ✉ *2358 Mendenhall Loop Rd.* ☎ *907/789–5566, 800/780–7234* ⊕ *www.grandmasfeatherbed.com* ➹ *14 rooms* ⏹ *Breakfast.*

★ Pearson's Pond Luxury Inn and Adventure Spa

$$$$ | B&B/INN | On a small pond near Mendenhall Glacier, this large, jaw-droppingly landscaped home may be Alaska's finest B&B. **Pros:** private balconies with excellent views; kayaks and bicycles for guest use; close to the glacier and hiking trails. **Cons:** two-night minimum during summer; limited public transportation;

not handicaped-accessible. $ *Rooms from: $399* ✉ *4541 Sawa Circle* ☎ *907/789–3772* ⊕ *www.pearsonspond. com* ⤶ *5 rooms* ⦿ *Breakfast.*

Prospector Hotel

$$ | HOTEL | A short walk west of downtown, this nicely appointed but visually unremarkable hotel is a favorite with business travelers year-round and lawmakers during the winter legislative session. **Pros:** convenient location; most pets accepted; restaurant on-site. **Cons:** lackluster exterior and lobby; rooms could use updating; street noise on the water side. $ *Rooms from: $149* ✉ *375 Whittier St.* ☎ *907/586–3737, 800/331–2711 outside Alaska, 800/478–5866 in Alaska* ⊕ *www.prospectorhotel.com* ⤶ *56 rooms* ⦿ *No meals.*

Silverbow Inn

$$$ | B&B/INN | Conveniently located in Juneau's historic downtown, the Silverbow has contemporary, charming hotel rooms on two upper levels. **Pros:** central location; easy walk to the sights; rooftop hot tub. **Cons:** no laundry facilities; limited parking; small rooms. $ *Rooms from: $209* ✉ *120 2nd St.* ☎ *907/586–4146, 800/586–4146* ⊕ *www.silverbowinn.com* ⤶ *11 rooms* ⦿ *Free Breakfast.*

★ U.S. Forest Service Cabins

$ | RENTAL | Scattered throughout Tongass National Forest, these rustic cabins–most of which are reached by floatplane or boat–offer a cheap and charming escape. **Pros:** a unique experience; affordable; amazing views. **Cons:** remote; no electricity or water; outdoor bathroom. $ *Rooms from: $35* ✉ *Juneau Ranger District, 8510 Mendenhall Loop Rd.* ☎ *907/586–8800, 877/444–6777 reservations* ⊕ *www. recreation.gov* ⤶ *150 cabins.*

Westmark Baranof Hotel

$$ | HOTEL | The Baranof has long been Juneau's most prestigious address; it's as close to a big-city boutique hotel as you're going to find in Southeast Alaska. **Pros:** elegant public areas; central location; 1930s flavor. **Cons:** lower floors are noisy; some rooms are small; dated room decor. $ *Rooms from: $159* ✉ *127 N. Franklin St.* ☎ *907/586–2660, 800/544–0970* ⊕ *www.westmarkhotels. com/juneau.php* ⤶ *200 rooms* ⦿ *No meals.*

ⓨ Nightlife

Alaskan Brewing Company

BARS/PUBS | The company's tasty, award-winning beers—including Alaskan Amber, Icy Bay IPA, White, Stout, Imperial Red, and Freeride APA—are brewed and bottled in Juneau. This is no designer brewery—it's in Juneau's industrial area, and there is no upscale café-bar attached—but the gift shop sells T-shirts and beer paraphernalia. You can also visit the brewery's Downtown Depot, on Franklin Street; though you can't sample the beer here, you can find out more about the brewing process and purchase Alaskan Brewing Company gear. From the Depot you can also take a shuttle to the brewery; $25 includes round-trip shuttle, brewery tour, and six beer samples. Shuttles run hourly in the summer. ✉ *Brewery: 5429 Shaune Dr.; Downtown Depot: 219 S. Franklin St.* ☎ *907/780–5866* ⊕ *www.alaskanbeer.com.*

Alaskan Hotel Bar

BARS/PUBS | A sign frequently placed outside this historic bar reads: "Have an Alaskan with an Alaskan at the Alaskan," referring to the locally made beer, the clientele, and the bar itself. And it's true that this triple convergence can be found here any night of the week—the bar always has at least one type of Alaskan Brewing Company beer on tap, and the crowd is primarily local, even in summer. On the ground floor of the Alaskan Hotel, this is Juneau's most historically authentic watering hole, with flocked-velvet walls, antique chandeliers, and vintage frontier-brothel decor. The atmosphere, however, is anything but dated, and the bar's live music and Thursday open-mike nights draw high-spirited, bordering on rowdy, crowds. ✉ *167 S. Franklin St.* ☎ *907/586–1000* ⊕ *www.thealaskanhotel.com.*

Amalga Distillery

BARS/PUBS | In the tasting room at the Amalga Distillery, you can sample Amalga's small-batch gin (up to two drinks per visit) while seated next to the brass and copper still in which the gin was made. The well-designed space also includes high ceilings and huge windows perfect for people-watching. ✉ *134 N. Franklin St.* ☎ *907/209–2015* ⊕ *www.amalgadistillery.com.*

Imperial Saloon

BARS/PUBS | A remodeled former dive where locals like to drink, shoot pool, and meet singles, the Imperial retains mounted moose and bison heads and other vestiges of its divey decor. Other noteworthy features include the original pressed-tin ceiling and what is reputed to be the longest bar in Alaska. The Front Street Cafe, located within the Imperial, serves food until 2:30 am on weekends. ✉ *241 Front St.* ☎ *907/586–1960.*

The Narrows

BARS/PUBS | An upscale alternative to Juneau's somewhat rowdy bar scene, The Narrows is the best place in the city to enjoy a classy, carefully prepared cocktail. The bar gets its name from the shape of the space—long and skinny—and its exposed brick walls, fireplace, and leather couches in back add to the intimate vibe. ✉ *148 S. Franklin St.* ☎ *415/205–3704* ⊕ *the-narrows.business.site.*

🎭 Performing Arts

Perseverance Theatre

THEATER | Alaska's only professional theater company performs classics and new productions from September through May. The company also stages plays in Anchorage each season, and some shows have toured more extensively, among them the all-Tlingit version of Shakespeare's *Macbeth*, which traveled

to the Smithsonian's National Museum of the American Indian in Washington, D.C. Perseverance is Juneau's most high-profile troupe, but also worth checking out are **Theatre in the Rough,** a fantastic all-volunteer theater troupe that's been staging Shakespearian works and other classics twice a year since 1991, and two opera companies, **Juneau Lyric Opera** and **The Orpheus Project.** ✉ *914 3rd St., Douglas* ☎ *907/364–2421* ⊕ *www.ptalaska.org.*

🛍 Shopping

ART GALLERIES
Annie Kaill's Gallery

ART GALLERIES | This gallery displays a mix of playful and whimsical original prints, pottery, jewelry, and other arts and crafts from Alaska artists. If you're in town on the first Friday of any month, ask the staff for a map of the First Friday Art Walk; more than a dozen downtown galleries participate in this monthly event by hosting evening exhibit openings, most of which feature the works of local artists. ✉ *244 Front St.* ☎ *907/586–2880* ⊕ *www.anniekaills.com.*

Caribou Crossings

ART GALLERIES | Locally owned and operated, this gallery sells artworks, craft items, and other creations—from sculptures to fossilized ivory bracelets to children's books—created by Alaskans. ✉ *497 S. Franklin St.* ☎ *877/586–5008, 907/586–5008* ⊕ *www.cariboucrossings.com.*

Juneau Artists Gallery

ART GALLERIES | The cooperatively run gallery, on the first floor of the old Senate Building, sells a mix of watercolors, jewelry, oil and acrylic paintings, etchings, photographs, art glass, ceramics, fiber arts, and pottery from more than 20 local artists. ✉ *175 S. Franklin St.* ☎ *907/586–9891* ⊕ *www.juneauartistsgallery.com.*

Kindred Post

ART GALLERIES | Kindred Post is more than the downtown area's sole post office.

The local owner, a poet and artist, has transformed the space into an elegant gallery that features locally made jewelry, ceramics, prints, and other works of art. ⊠ *145 S. Franklin St.* ☎ *907/523–5053* ⊕ *www.kindredpost.com* ⊙ *Closed Sun.*

Mt. Juneau Trading Post

ART GALLERIES | An Alaska Native family owns this crowded shop that specializes in traditional Northwest Coast artworks, from carved silver bracelets to high-end masks. ⊠ *151 S. Franklin St.* ☎ *907/586–3426* ⊕ *mtjuneautradingpost.com.*

Rie Muñoz Gallery

ART GALLERIES | Rie Muñoz, one of Alaska's best-known artists, was the creator of a stylized, simple, and colorful design technique that is much copied but rarely equaled. This gallery run by her son is located in the Mendenhall Valley, a 10-minute walk from the airport. ⊠ *2101 N. Jordan Ave.* ☎ *907/789–7449, 800/247–3151* ⊕ *www.riemunoz.com* ⊙ *Closed Sun. and Mon.*

Sealaska Heritage Store

ART GALLERIES | On the Front Street side of the Walter Soboleff Building, Juneau's regional Alaska Native arts and cultural center, this shop and gallery sells work by Northwest Coast and Alaska Native artists from Seattle to Yakutat and further north. Here you'll find a wide range of items, from moderately priced earrings and T-shirts to high-end, one-of-a-kind pieces. ⊠ *105 Front St.* ☎ *907/463–4844* ⊕ *www.sealaskaheritage.org.*

Trickster

ART GALLERIES | Owned and operated by a brother-and-sister team of young local artists, this small gallery offers visitors an introduction to finely crafted, contemporary Northwest Coast art in multiple mediums, including silver jewelry, art prints, children's books, and apparel. ⊠ *224 Front St.* ☎ *907/780–4000* ⊕ *trickstercompany.com.*

GIFTS

Wm. Spear Design

ART GALLERIES | Lawyer-turned-artist Wm. Spear produces fun and colorful enameled pins and zipper pulls. His quirky shop is above the local toy store, through a separate entrance. ⊠ *174 S. Franklin St.* ☎ *907/586–2209* ⊕ *www.wmspear.com.*

SEAFOOD

Taku Store

FOOD/CANDY | At the south end of town near the cruise-ship docks and Mt. Roberts Tramway, Taku Store processes nearly 6 million pounds of fish a year, mostly salmon. The smoked sockeye fillets make excellent gifts. You can view the smoking procedure through large windows, and then purchase the packaged fish in the deli-style gift shop or have some shipped back home. ⊠ *550 S. Franklin St.* ☎ *907/463–5319, 800/582–5122* ⊕ *www.takustore.com.*

Juneau's Nearby Villages

Though Juneau has a vibrant and active Native community, a visit to one of the surrounding villages can be a great way to increase your understanding of Southeast's indigenous cultures. Life is slower here than in Juneau, people are generally friendlier, and there's less competition for visitors' attention. From Juneau, you can fly or take one of the Alaska Marine Highway's ferries (*907/465–3941, 800/642–0066*) to **Kake, Angoon, Klukwan,** or **Hoonah.** All four are predominantly Tlingit. (For information on visiting a Haida or Tsimshian village in Southeast, see *Side Trips from Ketchikan.*) Kake's attractions include one of the world's tallest totem poles (132 feet), a historic salmon cannery, and the beautiful beaches of Kupreanof Island (⊕ *www.visitkake.com*). Angoon, on Admiralty Island, is a popular departure point for kayaking and sportfishing trips. Klukwan (⊕ *chilkatindianvillage.org*), located 22 miles outside of Haines, is home to the

Side Trips from Juneau

recently opened Jilkaat Kwaan Cultural Heritage and Bald Eagle Preserve Visitor Center. (See the entry in Haines for more information.) Hoonah's cannery building has been beautifully restored, and serves as part of Huna Totem Corporation's **Icy Strait Point** (⊕ www.icystraitpoint.com) cruise port. Highlights at Icy Strait Point include one of the world's longest zip lines, Native dance performances, and whale-watching trips to nearby Point Adolphus. Icy Strait Point is only open when cruise ships are in port, so book well in advance whether you're coming via cruise or not.

Independent travelers won't find much organized touring in Kake or Angoon, but you will find hotels (reservations strongly suggested), and guided fishing and natural-history trips can be arranged by asking around.

🛏 Hotels

★ Favorite Bay Lodge

$$$$ | B&B/INN | This high-end sportfishing lodge—often cited among the top three luxury lodges in Alaska—offers guests an opportunity to fish in both the saltwater and freshwater areas of Admiralty Island with local guides. **Pros:** pristine wilderness setting; local fishing expertise; rate includes transportation, meals, activities, and fish processing. **Cons:** remote location; pricey; three-day minimum stay. ⑤ Rooms from: $3740 ⊠ 917 Killisnoo Rd., Angoon ☎ 866/788–3344, 907/788–3344 ⊕ www.favoritebay.com ⇆ 12 rooms ¶⊙¶ All-inclusive.

Icy Strait Lodge

$$ | B&B/INN | One of Hoonah's few lodging options, Icy Strait Lodge is a great base from which to explore this small, friendly Native community. **Pros:** on-site restaurant; boat and car rentals available; beautiful views. **Cons:** rooms a bit dated; can be noisy at night; nighttime activities limited. $ *Rooms from: $140* ✉ *435 Airport Rd., Hoonah* ☎ *907/945–3636* ⊕ *www.icystraitlodge.com* ⊐ *14 rooms* ꭅ *No meals.*

Keex' Kwaan Lodge
$$ | **B&B/INN** | In Kake, the Keex' Kwaan Lodge offers a serene setting, views of the water, and helpful hosts who can give you inside tips on their community. **Pros:** waterfront views; washer and dryer on premises; near the beach and local store. **Cons:** limited breakfast options; basic decor; no restaurant on-site. $ *Rooms from: $149* ✉ *538 Keku Rd., Kake* ☎ *907/723–8386* ⊕ *www.kakealaska.com* ⊐ *12 rooms* ꭅ *Free Breakfast.*

Admiralty Island

40 miles south of Juneau.

There's only one year-round community—Angoon—on this huge island; the rest is wilderness, home to healthy populations of bears, eagles, deer, birds, salmon, and whales. A visit to Admiralty offers an unparalleled introduction to the nonhuman inhabitants of this area, and their unspoiled habitat.

◉ Sights

Admiralty Island
ISLAND | The island is famous for its lush old-growth rain forest and abundant wildlife, including one of the largest concentrations of brown bears anywhere on the planet. The Tlingit name for the island is Kootznoowoo (Xootsnoowú), meaning "fortress of the bears." Ninety miles long, with 678 miles of coastline, Admiralty—the second-largest island in Southeast Alaska—is home to an estimated 1,600 bears, almost one per square mile. ✉ *Admiralty Island, Juneau*

⊕ *www.nps.gov/glba/learn/nature/admiralty-island-province.htm.*

Admiralty Island National Monument
NATURE PRESERVE | The Forest Service's Admiralty Island National Monument has a canoe route that crosses the island via a chain of lakes and trails, and some of the region's best sea kayaking and sportfishing happens here. The area is said to have the world's highest density of nesting bald eagles, and there are large concentrations of humpback whales. Fourteen public-use cabins are available for overnight stays. ✉ *Admiralty Island, Juneau* ⊕ *www.fs.usda.gov/recmain/tongass/recreation.*

★ Pack Creek
NATURE PRESERVE | More than 90% of Admiralty Island is preserved within the Kootznoowoo Wilderness. Its chief attraction is Pack Creek, where you can watch brown bears feeding on salmon. One of Alaska's premier bear-viewing sites, Pack Creek is comanaged by the U.S. Forest Service and the Alaska Department of Fish and Game. Permits are required during the main viewing season, from June 1 through September 10. If you're headed to Pack Creek without a guide or an experienced visitor, be sure to cover the basics of bear safety before your trip. Permits for Pack Creek can be processed through *www.recreation.gov.* ✉ *Admiralty Island, Juneau* ☎ *907/586–8800* ⊕ *www.fs.usda.gov/recarea/tongass/recreation* ▦ *From $20.*

Tracy Arm

45 miles south of Juneau.

One of the most popular and rewarding day trips out of Juneau is a boat trip to Tracy Arm. The narrow fjord south of the city offers access to the two-part Sawyer Glacier. En route the boats pass through twisting passageways between nearly vertical rock walls, dodging vibrant blue icebergs and stopping to let passengers catch glimpses of passing wildlife, including whales, dolphins, eagles, seals, sea lions, and bears. Calving—when pieces of the glacier break off and fall into the water—is common here and a breathtaking thing to see, even for the locals. Companies offering service to Tracy Arm include Allen Marine and Adventure Bound Alaska.

Glacier Bay National Park and Preserve

60 miles northwest of Juneau.

Near the northern end of the Inside Passage, Glacier Bay National Park and Preserve is one of America's most magnificent national parks. Visiting Glacier Bay is like stepping back into the Little Ice Age—it's one of the few places in the world where you can approach such a variety of massive tidewater glaciers. Sounding like cannon fire, bergs the size of 10-story office buildings come crashing from the "snout" of a glacier, each cannon blast signifying another step in the glacier's steady retreat. The calving iceberg sends tons of water and spray skyward, propelling mini–tidal waves outward from the point of impact. Johns Hopkins Glacier calves so often and with such volume that large cruise ships can seldom come within 2 miles of its face.

GETTING HERE AND AROUND
Fly into nearby Gustavus (a 30-minute flight from Juneau) or take the Alaska Marine Highway ferry into Gustavus and take a 9-mile shuttle ride to the park or arrive via cruise ship.

PLANNING YOUR TIME
Despite its name, Glacier Bay National Park is not a frigid, icy place year-round. In the summer, the weather can be temperate and the forest turns lush and green—you won't see glaciers from the visitor center on Bartlett Cove. The best weather is in May and June, the driest

two months of the year in Southeast. Fly in from Juneau in the afteroon, then go out for a kayaking trip in Bartlett Cove. The next morning, rise early for the 8-hour day boat tour to get up close and personal with glaciers.

◉ Sights

★ **Glacier Bay National Park and Preserve**
NATIONAL/STATE PARK | Tidewater glaciers in Glacier Bay National Park calve icebergs into the sea with loud blasts. Humpback whales breach, spout, and slap their tails against the water. Coastal brown bears feed on sedge, salmon, and berries. Bald eagles soar overhead, and mountains in the Fairweather Range come in and out of view. This magical place rewards those who get out on the water—whether it be in a cruise, a day boat, or a kayak. Glacier Bay is a marvelous laboratory for naturalists of all persuasions. Glaciologists, of course, can have a field day. Animal lovers can hope to see the rare glacial "blue" bears of the area, a variation of the black bear, which is here along with the brown bear; mountain goats in late spring and early summer; and seals on floating icebergs. Humpback whales are also abundant in these waters; the best time to see them is June through early August. Birders can look for the more than 200 species that have already been spotted in the park, and you are assured bald eagle sightings. The bay is a still-forming body of water fed by the runoff of the icefields, glaciers, and mountains that surround it. Today many glaciers in the park, including the namesake glacier of naturalist John Muir, who was one of the region's earliest proponents, continue to retreat: the Muir Glacier's terminus is now scores of miles farther up the bay from the small cabin he built there. However, some of the glaciers are still healthy, such as the Johns Hopkins Glacier and the Marjorie Glacier, which receive enough snow to maintain their size or even grow. **Bartlett**

Cove, an area that's been ice-free for more than 200 years, has a lush spruce-and-hemlock rain forest as well as the 2,500-square-foot **Huna Tribal House** (Xunaa Shuká Hít), a space for tribal members and for visitors to learn about Tlingit history and culture. ⊠ *Gustavus* ☎ *907/697–2230, 907/697–2627 boating information* ⊕ *www.nps.gov/glba.*

Activities

National Park Service naturalists come aboard cruise ships to explain the great glaciers and to help spot bears, mountain goats, whales, porpoises, and birds. Several experienced operators can also guide you or set you up to explore on your own.

BOATING AND LOCAL INTEREST

Glacier Bay Day Boat Tour

BOATING | Daily summertime boat tours, operated by Glacier Bay Lodge and Tours, leave from the dock at Bartlett Cove, near Glacier Bay Lodge, at 7:30 am and return at 3:30 pm. These eight-hour trips into Glacier Bay have a Park Service naturalist aboard a high-speed 155-passenger catamaran. A light lunch is included. Campers and sea kayakers heading up the bay ride the same boat. ⊠ *179 Bartlett Cove, Gustavus* ☎ *888/229–8687* ⊕ *www.visitglacierbay.com* ✉ *$225.*

HIKING

Glacier Bay's steep and heavily forested slopes aren't the most conducive to hiking, but several short hikes begin at the Glacier Bay Lodge. The popular **Forest Loop Trail,** a pleasant 1-mile jaunt, begins in a forest of spruce and hemlock and finishes on the beach. Also beginning at the lodge is the **Bartlett River Trail**—a 5-mile round-trip path that borders an intertidal lagoon, culminating at the Bartlett River estuary. The **Bartlett Lake Trail,** part of a 6-mile walk that meanders through rain forest, ends at the quiet lakeshore.

SEA KAYAKING

The most adventurous way to explore Glacier Bay is by paddling your own kayak through the bay's icy waters and inlets. But unless you're an expert, you're better off joining a guided tour.

Alaska Discovery

KAYAKING | You can book a six-day or an eight-day guided expedition through Alaska Discovery. Operated by Mountain Travel Sobek, the company provides safe, seaworthy kayaks and tents, gear, and food. Its guides are tough, knowledgeable Alaskans, and they've spent enough time in Glacier Bay's wild country to know what's safe and what's not. Private and custom-designed tours for small groups can also be organized through this company. ⊠ *Gustavus* ☎ *888/831–7526* ⊕ *www.mtsobek.com/trips/br/region-north-america* ✉ *From $4195.*

Alaska Mountain Guides

KAYAKING | Take day kayaking trips for whale-watching at Point Adolphus, a premier humpback gathering spot, as well as multiday sea-kayaking expeditions next to tidewater glaciers in Glacier Bay National Park, with Alaska Mountain Guides. ⊠ *Gustavus* ☎ *907/313–4422, 800/766–3396* ⊕ *www.alaskamountain-guides.com* ✉ *From $460.*

Glacier Bay Sea Kayaks

KAYAKING | Kayak rentals for Glacier Bay exploring and camping can be arranged through Glacier Bay Sea Kayaks. You will be given instructions on handling the craft plus camping and routing suggestions for unescorted trips. Guided day trips with knowledgeable guides are available in Bartlett Cove. The company is an official NPS concession for guided day kayak trips. ⊠ *Bartlett Cove, Gustavus* ☎ *907/697–2257* ⊕ *www.glacierbay-seakayaks.com* ✉ *Trips from $95.*

Spirit Walker Expeditions

KAYAKING | Take one- to seven-day sea-kayaking trips from Gustavus to various parts of Icy Strait with Spirit Walker Expeditions. Trips to Glacier Bay

Kayaking through Glacier Bay is one of the best and most popular ways to get up-close and personal with the region's glaciers.

and other remote areas of Southeast Alaska, including Fords Terror and West Chichagof, are also offered on a limited basis. ✉ *Gustavus* ☎ *800/529–2537* ⊕ *www.seakayakalaska.com.*

WHALE-WATCHING
TAZ
WHALE-WATCHING | Step aboard the M/V *TAZ* and check out Icy Strait and Point Adolphus, near the entrance to Glacier Bay, for awesome views of humpback whales and many other marine mammals. All tours out of Gustavus include binoculars, snacks, and hot beverages. Half-day tours and custom charters accommodating up to 28 passengers are offered, as well as "Weddings with the Whales," where you can get married while surrounded by humpbacks. ✉ *Gustavus* ☎ *907/321–2302, 888/698–2726* ⊕ *www.taz.gustavus.com* ✉ *From $123.*

 Hotels

Glacier Bay Lodge
$$$ | HOTEL | The only accommodation within the national park, this lodge is

constructed of massive timbers and blends well into the thick rain forest surrounding it on three sides. **Pros:** ample hiking trails nearby; good local seafood at restaurant; packages include meal, transfers, and boat tour of Glacier Bay. **Cons:** dining options within the park are all on the property; location is somewhat remote; dated decor. ⑤ *Rooms from: $225* ✉ *179 Bartlett Cove Rd., Gustavus* ☎ *888/229–8687* ⊕ *www.visitglacierbay. com* ⊙ *Closed mid-Sept.–mid-May* ⌾ *49 rooms* ⦿ *Breakfast.*

Gustavus

50 miles west of Juneau, 75 miles south of Skagway.

For airborne visitors, Gustavus is the gateway to Glacier Bay National Park and Preserve. The long, paved jet airport, built as a refueling strip during World War II, is all the more impressive because of the limited facilities at the field. Gustavus itself is less of a town than a scattering of homes, farmsteads, a craft studio, fishing and guiding charter companies, an art gallery, and other tiny enterprises run by hospitable individualists. Visitors enjoy the unstructured outdoor activities in the area, including beach and trail hiking in the Nature Conservancy's Forelands Preserve.

GETTING HERE AND AROUND
Alaska Airlines serves Gustavus daily in the summer from Juneau. Smaller, light-aircraft companies also serve the community out of Juneau. The Alaska Marine Highway System stops in Gustavus twice a week ⊕ *www.dot.state. ak.us/amhs*. Glacier Bay is best experienced from the water, whether from the deck of a cruise ship, on a tour boat, or from the level of a sea kayak.

Activities

HIKING
The entire Gustavus beachfront was set aside by the Nature Conservancy, enabling visitors to hike the shoreline for miles. The beachfront is part of the **Alaska Coastal Wildlife Viewing Trail** (⊕ *wildlife. alaska.gov*). The spring and fall bird migrations are exceptional on Gustavus estuaries, including Dude Creek Critical Habitat Area, which provides a stopover before crossing the ice fields for sandhill cranes. Maps and wildlife-viewing information are available from the **Alaska Division of Wildlife Conservation** (⊕ *wildlife. alaska.gov*).

Restaurants

Barring a personal invitation from a local who has just been out fishing, most of the good places to dine in Gustavus are inside lodgings—notably the Gustavus Inn and the Bear Track Inn's Excursion Restaurant.

Clove Hitch Cafe
$ | AMERICAN | Located near the town's main intersection, known as Four Corners, the Clove Hitch Cafe is a favorite with locals. The lively, unfussy eatery

serves eclectic American fare. **Known for:** pizza; fish-and-chips; small-town vibes. ⑤ *Average main: $12 ⊠ 1250 Gustavus Rd.* ☎ *907/697–2800.*

Fireweed Gallery Coffee and Tea House
$ | AMERICAN | Inside a gallery that features work by local and regional artists, this café at Four Corners offers light fare such as crepes, pastries, and cookies, as well as milk shakes and specialty espresso drinks and teas. The café's drive-up window is groundbreaking for Gustavus (but if you're a visitor, you'll want to go in to see the art and crafts). **Known for:** espresso and sweet treats; local art; drive-through. ⑤ *Average main: $8 ⊠ 1250 Gustavus Rd.* ☎ *907/697–3013* ⊕ *www.fireweedcoffee.com.*

Hotels

Annie Mae Lodge
$$ | B&B/INN | This quiet two-story lodge, one of the few Gustavus places open year-round, faces the Good River, has beautiful grounds, and is a five-minute walk from the beach. **Pros:** good views; some rooms open to wraparound veranda; amazing food with meal plan. **Cons:** property is not on the beach; two of the rooms share a bathroom; spotty Internet reception. ⑤ *Rooms from: $200 ⊠ 2 Grandpas Farm Rd.* ☎ *907/697–2346, 800/478–2346* ⊕ *www.anniemae.com* ⌑ *11 rooms* ⑩ *Breakfast; All meals.*

Bear Track Inn
$$$$ | B&B/INN | Built of spruce logs on a 97-acre property facing Icy Strait, this inn's strengths include an inviting lobby with a central fireplace and moose antler chandeliers, and spacious and luxuriously furnished guest rooms. **Pros:** views; rate includes meals and air from Juneau; great restaurant. **Cons:** high room rate; no room TVs; spotty Internet reception. ⑤ *Rooms from: $625 ⊠ 255 Rink Creek Rd.* ☎ *907/697–3017* ⊕ *www.beartrackinn.com* ☾ *Closed Oct.–Apr.* ⌑ *14 rooms* ⑩ *All-inclusive; All meals.*

Haines

75 miles north of Gustavus, 80 miles northwest of Juneau.

Haines encompasses an area that has been occupied by Tlingit peoples for centuries on the collar of the Chilkat Peninsula, a narrow strip of land that divides the Chilkat and Chilkoot inlets. It's hard to imagine a more beautiful setting—a heavily wooded peninsula with magnificent views of Portage Cove and the snowy Coast Range. Unlike most other towns in Southeast Alaska, Haines can be reached by the 152-mile Haines Highway, which connects at Haines Junction with the Alaska Highway. It's also accessible by the state ferry (☎ 907/465–3941, 800/642–0066) and by planes on scheduled service from Juneau. The Haines ferry terminal is 4½ miles northwest of downtown, and the airport is 4 miles west.

Haines is an interesting community, its history the product of equal parts Tlingit homeland, enterprising gold-rush boom-town and regimented military outpost. A new cultural center in Klukwan, 20 miles up the road, is a good place to learn about the area's Native roots and ongoing traditions. The region's gold-rush history is evidenced by Jack Dalton, who in the 1890s maintained a toll route from the settlement of Haines into the Yukon, charging $1 for foot passengers and $2.50 per horse. His Dalton Trail later provided access for miners during the 1897 gold rush to the Klondike.

The downtown area is small, and the town exudes a down-home friendliness. Perhaps this is because Haines sees fewer cruise ships, or maybe it's the grand landscape and ease of access to the mountains and sea. Whatever the cause, visitors should be prepared for a relative lack of souvenir and T-shirt shops compared to other ports. Local weather is drier than in much of Southeast Alaska.

Smoking is banned in all businesses, including bars, restaurants, and shops. Accommodations are allowed to have smoking rooms; be sure to reserve one if needed.

GETTING HERE AND AROUND

Haines is connected to other towns in Southeast Alaska by the Alaska Marine Highway, and from here you can connect with smaller vessels serving Bush communities. The Haines–Skagway Fast Ferry, a catamaran, connects its two namesake cities in 45 minutes, with several trips weekly in summer. Special rates are available for guests who also book a ride on Skagway's White Pass Summit Train. Alaska Fjordlines offers express service to Juneau.

Haines is among Southeast Alaska's few towns accessible by road; be aware that the weather and wildlife in this area present hazards on the highway. Take the Alaska Highway to Haines Junction and then drive southwest on the Haines Highway to the Alaska Panhandle. The town is a delightful place to explore on foot. Alaska Seaplanes serves Haines from Juneau and Skagway.

ESSENTIALS

AIRLINE CONTACT Alaska Seaplanes
☎ 907/789–3331 ⊕ www.flyalaskasea-planes.com.

FERRY CONTACTS Alaska Fjordlines
✉ *Small boat harbor, 295 Congress Way, Skagway* ☎ 800/320-0146 ⊕ alaskafjord-lines.com. **Haines–Skagway Fast Ferry**
✉ *39 Beach Rd.* ☎ 907/766–2100, 888/766–2103 ⊕ www.hainesskagway-fastferry.com.

VISITOR INFORMATION Haines Convention and Visitors Bureau ✉ *122 2nd Ave. S* ☎ 907/766–6418, 800/458–3579 ⊕ www.haines.ak.us.

◎ Sights

Alaska Chilkat Bald Eagle Preserve

NATURE PRESERVE | In winter, the section of the preserve between Mile 19 and Mile 21 of the Haines Highway harbors the largest concentration of bald eagles in the world. In November and December, more eagles gather outside Haines than live in the continental United States. Thousands come to feast on the late run of salmon in the clear, ice-free waters of the Chilkat River, which is heated by underground warm springs. ⊠ *Haines Hwy.* ☎ *907/766–2292* ⊕ *www.dnr.alaska.gov/parks/units/eagleprv.htm.*

Alaska Indian Arts

NATIVE SITE | FAMILY | Dedicated to the preservation and continuation of Alaska Native art, this nonprofit organization occupies what was Ft. Seward's hospital. You can watch artisans doing everything from carving totem poles to creating delicate silver jewelry. ⊠ *Ft. Seward, south side of parade ground* ☎ *907/766–2160* ⊕ *www.alaskaindianarts.com* ☞ *Free.*

American Bald Eagle Foundation

MUSEUM | FAMILY | The main focuses at this natural history museum are bald eagles and associated fauna of the Chilkat Preserve. Lectures, displays, videos, and a taxidermy-heavy diorama help tell their stories, and there's a raptor center that has live presentations and an aviary displaying live eagles. ⊠ *113 Haines Hwy., Box 49* ☎ *907/766–3094* ⊕ *www.baldeagles.org* ☞ *$12* ⊗ *Closed Sun.*

Chilkat State Park

NATIONAL/STATE PARK | This park on the Chilkat Inlet has beautiful and accessible viewing of both the Davidson and Rainbow glaciers. The Seduction Point Trail, about 7 miles one way, takes hikers to the very tip of the peninsula upon which Haines sits. ⊠ *Mile 7, Mud Bay Rd.* ☎ *907/766–2292 Haines Ranger Station* ⊕ *www.dnr.alaska.gov/parks/aspunits/southeast/chilkatsp.htm.*

Ft. William H. Seward National Historic Landmark

INFO CENTER | Stately clapboard homes stand against a mountain backdrop on the sloping parade grounds of Alaska's first U.S. Army post. As you enter you'll soon see the gallant, white-columned former commanding officer's quarters, now part of the **Hotel Halsingland**. Circle the parade ground if you like, passing the other homes along Officers Row. On the parade ground's south side at **Alaska Indian Arts**, you can watch artists at work. The Haines Convention and Visitors Bureau has a walking-tour brochure of the fort. ⊠ *Ft. Seward Dr.* ⊕ *www.nps.gov/places/fort-william-h-seward.htm.*

Haines Brewing Company

WINERY/DISTILLERY | This downtown microbrewery sells beer by the sample glass, pint glass, or liter growlers to go. Captain Cook's Spruce Tip Ale is a good choice, best enjoyed on the back deck if the weather complies. In recent years Haines has become known as a hub for the craft beer movement; in May, the town hosts the Great Alaska Craft Beer & Home Brew Festival, a wildly popular event. ⊠ *4th and Main Sts.* ☎ *907/766–3823* ⊕ *www.hainesbrewing.com* ⊗ *Closed Sun.* ☞ *Cash only.*

★ Haines Highway

SCENIC DRIVE | The breathtaking Haines Highway, a National Scenic Byway, starts at Mile 0 in Haines and continues 152 miles to Haines Junction. You don't have to drive the entire length to experience its beauty, as worthwhile stops are all along the route. At about Mile 6 a delightful picnic spot is near the Chilkat River. At Mile 9.5 the view of Cathedral Peaks, part of the Chilkat Range, is magnificent. At Mile 9 begins the **Alaska Chilkat Bald Eagle Preserve**. In winter the stretch between Mile 19 and Mile 21 harbors the largest concentration of bald eagles in the world. At Mile 33 is a roadside restaurant called, aptly, **33-Mile Roadhouse** (*www.33mileroadhouse.com*), where you fill your tank and coffee mug, grab a

Haines

TO MT. RIPINSKY

TO CHILKOOT LAKE, FERRY TERMINAL

TO AIRPORT, MOSQUITO LAKE, GOLDEN CIRCLE ROUTE,

Haines Convention and Visitors Bureau

Haines Highway

5th Ave.
4th Ave.
3rd Ave.
2nd Ave.
Union St.
Dalton St.
Main St.
Willard St.
Mission St.
Front St.
Small Boat Harbor
Tlingit Park
Lookout Park
Portage Cove
Port Chilkat Dock
Mud Bay Rd.
Parade Ground
Fort Seward
Totem St.
Portage Dr.
Soapsuds Alley
Haines HWY.

0   200 yrds
0   200 meters

KEY

1 Exploring Sights
1 Restaurants
1 Hotels

Sights ▼

1 Alaska Chilkat Bald Eagle Preserve.......... **B1**
2 Alaska Indian Arts...... **B5**
3 American Bald Eagle Foundation................ **C3**
4 Chilkat State Park....... **A5**
5 Ft. William H. Seward National Historic Landmark **B5**
6 Haines Brewing Company................. **B1**
7 Haines Highway **B2**
8 Hammer Museum **D2**
9 Jilkaat Kwaan Heritage Center......... **B1**
10 Kroschel Wildlife Center.................... **B1**
11 Port Chilkoot Distillery... **C5**
12 Sheldon Museum and Cultural Center.......... **D3**

Restaurants ▼

1 Bamboo Room **D2**
2 Fireweed Restaurant....**C5**
3 Mountain Market........**C2**
4 The Pilotlight **C5**

Hotels ▼

1 Beach Road House......**C5**
2 Captain's Choice Motelight **D2**
3 The Cliffhanger...........**C3**
4 Hotel Halsingland........**B4**

Walking Around Haines

A stroll through downtown Haines is best started at the **Haines Convention and Visitors Bureau**, at 2nd and Willard streets, where you can pick up a walking-tour brochure. To learn a bit about the area's natural and cultural history, head to the **Sheldon Museum and Cultural Center**, on Main Street. From here, you can see the busy docks of Portage Cove, filled with commercial fishing boats and pleasure craft. Head down the hill (turning right on Front Street) to follow the shoreline a quarter mile to Lookout Park, a fine place to take in the view on a sunny day—which, in Haines, occurs more often than you might guess. Just up the hill from here is a small cemetery with graves dating from the 1880s. From the cemetery, steps emerge on Mission Street; follow it to 2nd Avenue, where a left turn will bring you to **American Bald Eagle Foundation**, a museum and research center for these majestic birds. Another nearly third of a mile out 2nd Avenue is perhaps the most interesting sight in Haines: **Ft. William H. Seward National Historic Landmark.** Nearby is **Alaska Indian Arts,** inside the old fort hospital.

burger and, most important, a piece of pie—do not leave without trying the pie. The United States–Canada border lies at Mile 42; stop at Canadian customs and set your clock ahead one hour. ⊠ *Haines Hwy.* ☎ *907/766–2234 HCVB* ⊕ *www.haines.ak.us/highway.*

Hammer Museum

MUSEUM | The owner started his impressive collection of 1,800 hammers decades ago and founded the museum—the world's first—in 2001. Noteworthy specimens include a Roman battle hammer and 6-foot-long posting hammers used to secure advertisements to exterior walls. ⊠ *108 Main St.* ☎ *907/766–2374* ⊕ *www.hammermuseum.org* ☑ *$5* ☉ *Closed Oct.–Apr.; Sun.*

Jilkaat Kwaan Heritage Center

Built near Klukwan, a Native village 23 miles up the road from Haines, this site offers visitors the chance to learn more about Tlingit culture, language, and traditions. Visit the site's Long House, built using traditional methods; find out about traditional Native crafts, including wood carving, beading, and the distinctive Chilkat blanket; see the process for smoking salmon; and much more. ⊠ *32 Chilkat Ave., Klukwan* ☎ *907/767–5485* ⊕ *jilkaatkwaanheritagecenter.org* ☑ *$15* ☉ *Closed mid-Sept.–mid-May; Sun.*

Kroschel Wildlife Center

NATURE PRESERVE | A must for animal lovers, this privately run operation 28 miles north of Haines provides an up-close look at Alaskan wildlife, including bears, caribou, moose, wolverines, porcupines, foxes, and wolves. More sanctuary than zoo, the center hosts small group tours, usually booked through cruise lines or other tourist outlets, but with notice may be able to arrange a visit for independent travelers. ⊠ *Mile 1.8 Mosquito Lake Rd.* ☎ *907/767–5464* ⊕ *www.kroschelfilms.com* ☑ *Rates vary depending on tour; expect to pay about $50.*

Port Chilkoot Distillery

WINERY/DISTILLERY | Located in Ft. Seward in a renovated old bakery, the Port Chilkoot Distillery offers craft cocktails and samples of its locally made spirits such as vodka, gin, and bourbon. As in other distilleries around the state, patrons are limited to two drinks on the premises. ✉ *34 Blacksmith St.* ☎ *907/766-3434* ⊕ *www.portchilkootdistillery.com* ☽ *Closed Sun.–Tues. in Sept.– mid-May; Sun. in mid-May–Aug.*

Sheldon Museum and Cultural Center

MUSEUM | In the 1880s, Steve Sheldon began assembling Native artifacts, items from historic Ft. Seward, and gold-rush memorabilia, such as Jack Dalton's sawed-off shotgun, and started an exhibit of his finds in 1925. Today his collection is the core of this museum's impressive array of artifacts, including Chilkat blankets, a model of a Tlingit tribal house, and the original lens from the Eldred Rock lighthouse just south of Haines on the Lynn Canal. Repatriated Bear Clan items such as an 18th-century carved ceremonial Murrelet hat are also on display. ✉ *11 Main St.* ☎ *907/766–2366* ⊕ *www.sheldonmuseum.org* ✇ *$10* ☽ *Closed Sun.*

🏃 Activities

AIR TOURS

Fly Drake

TOUR—SPORTS | The company offers Glacier Bay flightseeing tours from Haines and Skagway—including a single-passenger tour aboard a Super Cub—and operates an awe-inspiring custom tour of the Outer Coast that takes in mountain and sea. ☎ *907/303–0675* ⊕ *www.flydrake. com* ✇ *From $220.*

Mountain Flying Service

TOUR—SPORTS | A few doors up the street from the visitor center, this company leads flightseeing trips to nearby Glacier Bay National Park in a 1956 rebuilt propeller plane that seats up to seven passengers. Its Grand Flight package also includes a spin by a few mountains before heading out to the Gulf of Alaska. In late spring and early summer, glacier landings and snowfield takeoffs are offered for an additional $75. ☎ *907/766– 3007, 800/954–8747* ⊕ *www.mountainflyingservice.com* ✇ *From $200.*

BICYCLING

Sockeye Cycle Company

BICYCLING | Guided mountain- and road-bike tours along the roads and trails of Haines, including the breathtaking 360-mile Golden Circle route that connects Haines and Skagway via the Yukon Territory, are Sockeye's specialty. The outfit also rents, services, and sells bikes. ✉ *24 Portage St.* ☎ *907/766–2869, 877/292–4154* ⊕ *www.cyclealaska.com* ✇ *Rentals from $10.*

BOATING AND FISHING

Haines Convention and Visitors Bureau

BOATING | For information on numerous sportfishing charter boats in town, contact the Haines Convention and Visitors Bureau. ✉ *122 2nd Ave. S* ☎ *907/766– 6418, 800/458–3579* ⊕ *www.visithaines. com/activities.*

HIKING

Alaska Mountain Guides

HIKING/WALKING | The very experienced hands at this guide-service and rock-climbing school lead hiking and mountaineering excursions from Haines, from half-day trips to 24-day expeditionary courses for hiking, sea kayaking, fly-fishing, ice climbing, rock climbing, skiing, and mountaineering. Sea-kayak rentals are also available. ✉ *Haines* ☎ *907/313–4422, 800/766–3396* ⊕ *www. alaskamountainguides.com* ✇ *From $86.*

Battery Point Trail

HIKING/WALKING | A fairly level path that hugs the shoreline for 1.2 miles, Battery Point provides fine views across Lynn Canal. The trail begins a mile east of town, and a campsite can be found at Kelgaya Point near the end. For other hikes, pick up a copy of "Haines Is for Hikers" at the Haines Convention and Visitors Bureau. ✉ *Beach Rd., east end* ⊕ *www.seatrails.org/com_haines/trl-battery.htm.*

NATURE AND WILDLIFE VIEWING

★ Alaska Fjordlines

TOUR—SPORTS | The company operates a high-speed catamaran from Skagway and

Haines to Juneau and back throughout the summer, stopping along the way to watch sea lions, humpbacks, and other marine mammals. One-way service is also available. ✉ *Haines* ☎ *907/766–3395, 800/320–0146* ⊕ *www.alaskafjordlines. com* 🚢 *$169 round-trip; $130 one-way.*

Alaska Nature Tours

TOUR—SPORTS | This company conducts bird-watching and natural-history tours through the Alaska Chilkat Bald Eagle Preserve, operates brown bear–watching excursions in July and August, and leads hiking treks in summer. ✉ *109 2nd Ave.* ☎ *907/766–2876* ⊕ *www.alaskanature-tours.net* 🚢 *From $80.*

Chilkat River Adventures

TOUR—SPORTS | The flat-bottom jet-boat tours offered by Chilkat River Adventures are a great way to experience the bald eagle preserve in majestic Chilkat River Valley. ✉ *Haines* ☎ *907/766–2050, 800/478–9827* ⊕ *www.jetboatalaska.com* 🚢 *From $139.*

Restaurants

Bamboo Room

$ | **AMERICAN** | Pop culture meets greasy spoon in this unassuming coffee shop with red-vinyl booths that has been in the same family for more than 50 years. The menu doesn't cater to light appetites—it includes sandwiches, burgers, fried chicken, chili, and halibut fish-and-chips—but the place really is at its best for an all-American breakfast (available until 2 pm). **Known for:** diner-style breakfast; burgers; retro, relaxed atmosphere. ⑤ *Average main: $10* ✉ *11 2nd Ave., near Main St.* ☎ *907/766–2800* ⊕ *www.bamboopioneer.net.*

Fireweed Restaurant

$$ | **AMERICAN** | A local favorite, the Fireweed serves unusual pizza, pasta, and fish dishes you can wash down with beer on tap from the Haines Brewing Company. The casual restaurant is so popular that you may have to wait a bit

for your food—a perfect opportunity to try the Spruce Tip Ale and gaze out at the water. **Known for:** historic Ft. Seward building; seafood specials; local beer on tap. ⑤ *Average main: $18* ✉ *Bldg. No. 37, Blacksmith Rd.* ☎ *907/766–3838* ⊗ *Closed Sun. and Mon.*

Mountain Market

$ | **AMERICAN** | Meet the locals over espresso, brewed from fresh-roasted beans, and a fresh-baked pastry at this busy corner natural-foods store, deli, café, wine-and-spirits shop, de facto meeting hall, and hitching post. Mountain Market is great for lunchtime sandwiches, wraps, soups, and salads. **Known for:** coffee (roasted on the premises); pizza; one-stop shop. ⑤ *Average main: $8* ✉ *151 3rd Ave.* ☎ *907/766–3340* ⊕ *www.mountain-market.com.*

The Pilotlight

$$ | **ECLECTIC** | Locally sourced ingredients and a low-fuss, cozy atmosphere make the Pilotlight a great option for dinner in Haines. Beer and wine are available. **Known for:** homemade sourdough bread; local ingredients; beautiful presentation. ⑤ *Average main: $18* ✉ *31 Tower Rd.* ☎ *907/766–2962* ⊗ *Closed Tues.*

🏨 Hotels

Beach Road House

$ | **B&B/INN** | This property 1½ miles southeast of town has three cozy cabins with views of the Lynn Canal and two rooms in the main house, all with easy access to nearby nature trails. **Pros:** full kitchens in cabins; nice views; high-speed Wi-Fi. **Cons:** somewhat hard to find; basic decor; outside of town. ⑤ *Rooms from: $115* ✉ *Beach Rd., 1½ miles southeast of cruise dock* ☎ *907/766–3060, 866/741–3060* ⊕ *www.beachroadhouse.com* ⊗ *Rooms closed in winter; cabins open year-round* 🛏 *5 rooms* ❍ *No meals.*

Skagway

10th Ave.

TO GOLDEN CIRCLE ROUTE, WHITE PASS SUMMIT, GOLD RUSH CEMETERY, AND YUKON TERRITORY

9th Ave.

8th Ave.

7th Ave.

6th Ave.

5th Ave.

4th Ave.

3rd Ave.

2nd Ave.

1st Ave.

Klondike Gold Rush National Historic Park

Alaska Street

Main Street

State Street

Broadway

Spring Street

Dyea Road

Airstrip

White Pass & Yukon Route

Dewey Lakes Trails

Congress Way

Skagway Airport Terminal

Skagway Ferry Terminal

City Harbor

0 ——— 100 yds
0 ——— 100 m

KEY

1 *Exploring Sights*

1 *Restaurants*

1 *Hotels*

KEY

Tourist Information

Cruise Ship

Sights ▼

1 Arctic Brotherhood Hall **D4**
2 Corrington's Museum of Alaskan History **D3**
3 Golden North Hotel **D4**
4 Jewell Gardens **C1**
5 Klondike Gold Rush National Historical Park Museum **D4**
6 Moore Cabin **D3**
7 Skagway Museum **E2**

Restaurants ▼

1 Bites on Broadway **D2**
2 Bonanza Bar & Grill **D4**
3 Glacial Smoothies & Espresso **D4**
4 Skagway Brewing Company **D2**
5 Starfire **D3**
6 The Station **C3**

Hotels ▼

1 Chilkoot Trail Outpost ... **A5**
2 Mile Zero Bed & Breakfast **C1**
3 Sgt. Preston's Lodge **C2**
4 Skagway Inn Bed & Breakfast **D2**
5 White House **C2**

Captain's Choice Motelight

$$ | HOTEL | In the summer, overflowing flower boxes surround this Haines motel, where the accommodations are plain and somewhat dated, but most rooms have great views. **Pros:** beautiful grounds; easy walk to town; pet-friendly. **Cons:** some rooms are dark; amenities are limited; dated decor. ⑤ *Rooms from: $165* ✉ *108 2nd Ave. N, Box 392* ☎ *907/766–3111, 800/478–2345* ⊕ *www.capchoice.com* ⤵ *40 rooms* ⦿ *Free Breakfast.*

The Cliffhanger

$$$$ | B&B/INN | On the outskirts of Haines, straddling Mt. Ripinski, the Cliffhanger makes the most of its spectacular surroundings, providing unrestricted views of the Chilkat Range and Lynn Canal from the wraparound deck and from the giant windows of the two suites. **Pros:** mountainside views; private setting; dog-friendly. **Cons:** remote location; somewhat difficult to access; not good for travelers with young children. ⑤ *Rooms from: $199* ✉ *Mile 2, Haines Hwy.* ☎ *907/314–0099* ⊕ *www.cliffhangerbnb.com* ⤵ *2 rooms* ⦿ *Breakfast.*

Hotel Halsingland

$$ | HOTEL | On the National Register of Historic Places, this gracious hotel housed in former officers' quarters has original claw-foot bathtubs, nonworking fireplaces decorated with Belgian tiles, and charming and nicely maintained rooms. **Pros:** elegant, historic property; rental cars on-site; unique and quirky. **Cons:** small showers; small rooms; some rooms share a bath. ⑤ *Rooms from: $119* ✉ *13 Ft. Seward Dr.* ☎ *907/766–2000, 800/542–6363* ⊕ *www.hotelhalsingland.com* ⦿ *Closed mid-Nov.–Mar.* ⤵ *35 rooms* ⦿ *No meals.*

Nightlife

Fogcutter Bar

BARS/PUBS | A friendly spot to grab a beer and a snack while checking email—or visiting with the locals—the Fogcutter epitomizes the laid-back, unpretentious vibe for which Alaskans are known. ✉ *122 Main St.* ☎ *907/766–2555.*

🛍 Shopping

Magpie Gallery

ART GALLERIES | Locally owned and operated, Magpie has a selection of local arts and crafts including handmade jewelry, mugs, clothing, soaps, and prints. ✉ *144 2nd St.* ☎ *907/766–3400* ⦿ *Closed Sun.–Tues.*

Wild Iris Gallery

ART GALLERIES | Haines's most charming gallery displays attractive jewelry, prints, and fashion wear created by owner Fred Shields and his daughter Melina. Other local artists are also represented. The gallery is just up from the cruise-ship dock, and its summer gardens alone are worth the visit. ✉ *Portage St.* ☎ *907/766–2300.*

Skagway

14 miles northeast of Haines.

Located at the northern terminus of the Inside Passage, Skagway is a one-hour ferry ride from Haines. By road, however, the distance is 359 miles, as you have to take the Haines Highway up to Haines Junction, Yukon, then take the Alaska Highway 100 miles south to Whitehorse, and then drive a final 100 miles south on the Klondike Highway to Skagway. North-country folk call this sightseeing route the Golden Horseshoe or Golden Circle tour, because it passes a lot of gold-rush country in addition to spectacular lake, forest, and mountain scenery.

The town is an amazingly preserved artifact from North America's biggest, most-storied gold rush. Most of the downtown district forms part of the Klondike Gold Rush National Historical Park, a unit of the National Park System dedicated to commemorating and interpreting the frenzied stampede of

1897 that extended to Dawson City in Canada's Yukon.

Nearly all the historic sights are within a few blocks of the cruise-ship and ferry dock, allowing visitors to meander through the town's attractions at whatever pace they choose. Whether you're disembarking from a cruise ship, a ferry, or a dusty automobile fresh from the Golden Circle, you'll quickly discover that tourism is the lifeblood of this town. Unless you're visiting in winter or hiking into the backcountry on the Chilkoot Trail, you aren't likely to find a quiet Alaska experience around Skagway.

GETTING HERE AND AROUND

Skagway offers one of the few opportunities in the region to arrive by car. Take the Alaska Highway to the Canadian Yukon's Whitehorse and then drive on Klondike Highway to the Alaska Panhandle. Southeast Alaska's only railroad, the **White Pass and Yukon Route,** operates several different tours departing from Skagway, Fraser, British Columbia, and on some days, Carcross, Yukon. The tracks follow the historic path over the White Pass summit—a mountain-climbing, cliff-hanging route of as far as 67½ miles each way. Bus connections are available at Fraser to Whitehorse, Yukon. While the route is primarily for visitors, some locals use the service for transportation between Skagway and Whitehorse. The Haines–Skagway Fast Ferry, a passenger catamaran, makes several runs weekly (45 minutes each way) in summer between Skagway and Haines. Special rates are available for guests who book a ride on the White Pass Summit Train. A catamaran to Juneau is operated seasonally by Alaska Fjordlines (3 hours, with a stop in Haines), and the Alaska Marine Highway serves Skagway five days a week in the summer, three in winter.

ESSENTIALS

FERRY CONTACT Haines–Skagway Fast Ferry ⊠ *Skagway Small Boat Harbor, past southern end of Congress Way, Congress Way* ☎ *907/766–2100, 888/766–2103* ⊕ *www.hainesskagwayfastferry.com.*

VISITOR AND TOUR INFORMATION

Klondike Gold Rush National Historical Park ⊠ *Visitor center, 291 Broadway, at 2nd Ave.* ☎ *907/983–9200* ⊕ *www.nps. gov/klgo.* **Skagway Convention and Visitors Bureau** ☎ *907/983–2854, 888/762–1898* ⊕ *www.skagway.com.* **White Pass and Yukon Route** ☎ *907/983–2217, 800/343–7373* ⊕ *www.wpyr.com.*

◉ Sights

Arctic Brotherhood Hall

BUILDING | The local members of the Arctic Brotherhood, a fraternal organization of Alaska and Yukon pioneers, built their hall's (now renovated) false front out of 8,833 pieces of driftwood and flotsam from local beaches. The result: one of the most unusual buildings in all of Alaska. The AB Hall now houses the **Skagway Convention and Visitors Bureau,** along with public restrooms. ⊠ *Broadway between 2nd and 3rd Aves.* ☎ *907/983–2854, 888/762–1898 message only* ⊕ *www. skagway.com.*

Corrington's Museum of Alaskan History

MUSEUM | Inside a gift shop, this impressive (and free) scrimshaw museum highlights more than 40 exquisitely carved walrus tusks and other exhibits that detail Alaska's history. Dennis Corrington, a onetime Iditarod Race runner, and the founder of the museum, is often present. A bright flower garden decorates the exterior. ⊠ *5th Ave. and Broadway* ☎ *907/983–2579* 🎫 *Free.*

Golden North Hotel

HOTEL—SIGHT | Built during the 1898 gold rush, the Golden North Hotel was—until closing in 2002—Alaska's oldest hotel. Despite the closure, the building has been lovingly maintained and still retains its gold rush–era appearance; a golden dome tops the corner cupola. Today the downstairs houses shops. ⊠ *3rd Ave. and Broadway.*

Continued on page 172

THE KLONDIKE GOLD RUSH

At the end of the 19th Century, scoundrels and starry-eyed gold seekers alike made their way from Alaska's Inside Passage to Canada's Yukon Territory, with high hopes for heavy returns.

> "There are strange things done in the midnight sun
> By the men who moil for gold. . . ."
>
> —Robert Service, "The Cremation of Sam McGee"

Miners have moiled for gold in the Yukon for many centuries, but the Klondike Gold Rush was a particularly strange and intense period of history. Within a decade, the towns of Skagway, Dyea, and Dawson City appeared out of nowhere, mushroomed to accommodate tens of thousands of people, and just about disappeared again. At the peak of the rush, Dawson City was the largest metropolis north of San Francisco. Although only a few people found enough gold even to pay for their trip, the rush left an indelible mark on the nation's imagination.

A 1898 engraving shows a typical gold miner camp in the Klondike

A GREAT STAMPEDE

Historians squabble over who first saw the glint of Yukon gold. All agree that it was a member of a family including "Skookum" Jim Mason (of the Tagish tribe), Kate and George Carmack, and Dawson Charlie, who were prospecting off the Klondike River in 1896. Over the following months, word spread and claims were quickly staked. When the first boatload of gold reached Seattle in July 1897, gold fever ignited with the *Seattle Post-Intelligencer's* headline: "GOLD! GOLD! GOLD! Sixty-Eight Rich Men On the Steamer Portland." Within six months, 100,000 people had arrived in Southeast Alaska, intent upon making their way to the untold riches.

Skagway had only a single cabin standing when the gold rush began. Three months after the first boat landed, 20,000 people swarmed its raucous hotels, saloons, gambling houses, and dance halls. By spring 1898, the town was labeled "little better than a hell on earth." When gold was discovered in Nome the next year and in Fairbanks in the early 1900s, Skagway's population dwindled to 700 souls.

(above) Buildings in Skagway today still reflect what life was like during the Gold Rush

A GRITTY REALITY

To reach the mining hub of Dawson City, prospectors had to choose between two risky routes from the Inside Passage. From Dyea, the Chilkoot Trail was steep and bitterly cold. The longer, bandit-ridden White Pass Trail from Skagway killed so many pack animals that it earned the nickname Dead Horse Trail. After the mountains, there were still over 500 miles to travel. For those who arrived, dreams were quickly washed away, as most promising claims had already been staked by the Klondike Kings. Many ended up working as laborers. The disappointment was unbearable.

KLONDIKE KATE

The gold rush was profitable for clever entrepreneurs. Stragglers, outfitters, and outlaws took advantage of every opportunity to make a buck. Klondike Kate, a brothel keeper and dance-hall gal, had an elaborate song-and-dance routine that involved 200 yards of bright red chiffon.

TWO ENEMIES DIE IN A SKAGWAY SHOWDOWN

CON ARTIST "SOAPY" SMITH

Claim to Fame: Skagway's best-known gold-rush criminal, Soapy was the de facto leader of the town's loosely organized network of criminals and spies.

Cold-Hearted Snake: Euphemistically referred to as "colorful," he ruthlessly capitalized on the naïveté of prospectors.

Famous Scheme: Soapy charged home-sick miners $5 to wire a message home in his counterfeit Telegraph Office (the wires ended in a tangled pile behind a shed).

Shot Through the Heart: In 1898, just days after he served as grand marshal of Skagway's 4th of July parade, Soapy barged in on a meeting set up by his rival, Frank Reid. There was a scuffle, and they shot each other.

Famous Last Words: When he saw Reid draw his gun, Soapy shouted, "My God, don't shoot!"

R.I.P.: Soapy's tombstone was continually stolen by vandals and souvenir seekers; today's grave marker is a simple wooden plank in Skagway's Gold Rush Cemetery.

GOOD GUY FRANK REID

Claim to Fame: Skagway surveyor and all-around good fellow, Frank Reid was known for defending the town against bad guys.

The Grid Man: A civil engineer, Reid helped to make Skagway's streets wide and gridlike.

Thorn in My Side: Reid set up a secret vigilante meeting to discuss one very thorny topic: Soapy Smith.

In Skagway's Honor: Reid killed Soapy during the shootout on the city docks, breaking up Soapy's gang and freeing the town from its grip.

Dyin' Tryin': Reid's heroics cost him his life—he died some days later from the injuries he sustained.

R.I.P.: The town built a substantial monument in Reid's memory in the Gold Rush Cemetery, which you can visit to this day; the inscription reads: "He gave his life for the honor of Skagway."

(above) Soapy Smith (front), so named for his first con, which involved selling "lucky soap," stands with five friends at his infamous saloon.

FOLLOWING THE GOLD TRAIL TODAY

KEY

2.2 mi — Cumulative distance in miles from Dyea

Bennett — 33.0 mi — TO WHITEHORSE, YUKON

Log Cabin

Lindeman City — 26.0 mi — Warden Station

BRITISH COLUMBIA

20.5 mi — Happy Camp — Fraser

16.5 mi

CANADA
US — Chilkoot Pass/Warden Station — The Scales

16.0 mi

Ranger Station — Sheep Camp — White Pass

11.75 mi

10.5 mi — Pleasant Camp — White Pass City

7.8 mi — Canyon City

4.8 mi — Finnegan's Point

ALASKA

White Pass & Yukon RR

White Pass Trail

Klondike Hwy

Chilkoot Trail

Ranger Station — 0.0 mi
Dyea — Dyea Rd.

0 — 4 mi
0 — 4 km

Skagway — Taiya Inlet

Alaska Hwy.
Haines Junction — Whitehorse
Carcross
Yukon
British Columbia
CANADA US
GOLDEN CIRCLE — Klondike Hwy.
Alaska Haines Hwy.
Fraser
98
Haines — Skagway

Golden Circle Route

THE HISTORIC CHILKOOT TRAIL

If you're an experienced backpacker, consider hiking the highly scenic Chilkoot Trail, the 33-mile route of the 1897–98 prospectors from Skagway into Canada. Most hikers will need four to five days. The trail is generally in good condition, with primitive campsites strategically located along the way. Expect steep slopes and wet weather, along with exhilarating vistas at the summit. Deep snow often covers the pass until late summer. The trail stretches from Dyea (just outside of Skagway) to Lake Bennett. The National Park Service maintains the American side of the pass as part of **Klondike Gold Rush National Historical Park;** the Canadian side is part of the **Chilkoot Trail National Historic Site**. A backcountry permit is required.

■ TIP→ **To return to Skagway, hikers usually catch the White Pass & Yukon Route train from Lake Bennett. The fare is $97. For more information, visit www.wpyr.com/chilkoottrail.html.**

For more details, including backcountry permits (C$61.30), contact the summeronly **Chilkoot Trail Center** ☎ 907/983–9234 ⊕ www.nps.gov/klgo. Or you can call Parks Canada ☎ 800/661–0486 ⊕ www.pc.gc.ca/chilkoot.

GOLDEN DRIVES

The Golden Circle Route starts in Skagway on the Klondike Highway, then travels to Whitehorse. The route continues to Haines Junction, and then south to Haines. On the much longer Klondike Loop, you'll take Klondike Highway past Whitehorse, all the way to Dawson City, where the Klondike Highway meets the Alaska Highway. From start to finish, this segment covers 435 miles. From there, you can continue west and then south on the Alaska Highway, past Kluane National Park, and back down to Haines, a total distance of 890 miles. If you're

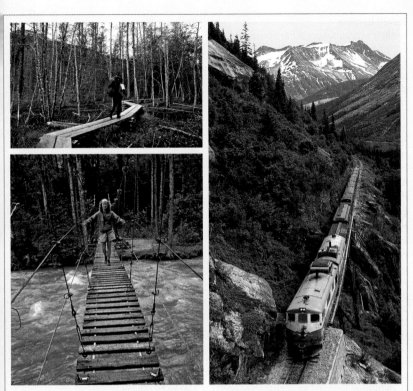

(top left) Trekking the Chilkoot Trail (right) White Pass & Yukon Route (bottom left) A bridge on Chilkoot Trail

taking the Klondike Highway north from Skagway, you must stop at Canadian customs, Mile 22. If you're traveling south to Skagway, check in at U.S. Customs, Mile 6.

WHITE PASS & YUKON ROUTE

You can travel the gold-rush route aboard the historic White Pass & Yukon Route (WP & YR) narrow-gauge railroad. The diesel locomotives tow vintage-style viewing cars up steep inclines, hugging the walls of precipitous cliffs with views of craggy peaks, forests, and plummeting waterfalls. It's open mid-May to late September only, and reservations are highly recommended.

■ TIP→ **Most of the commentary is during the first half of the trip and relates to sights out of the left side of the train, so sit on this side. A "seat exchange" at the summit allows all guests a canyonside view.**

Several options are available, including a fully narrated 3-hour round-trip excursion to White Pass summit (fare: $125). Sights along the way include Bridal Veil Falls, Inspiration Point, and Dead Horse Gulch. Through service to Whitehorse, Yukon (4 hours), is offered daily as well—in the form of a train trip to Fraser, where bus connections are possible on to Whitehorse (entire one-way fare to Whitehorse: $129). Also offered are the Chilkoot Trail hikers' service and a 4-hour roundtrip to Fraser Meadows on Thursday and Monday (fare: $159).

Call ahead or check online for details and schedules. ☎ 907/983–2217 or 800/343–7373 ⊕ www.wpyr.com.

Jewell Gardens

GARDEN | This unusual attraction incorporates two of Southeast Alaska's strengths: art and nature. Visitors can take a guided walk through the lush gardens while admiring the glass sculptures on display, and then watch glassblowing in action in the art studio—or even try it themselves under the watchful eye of local artisans. Tea or lunch can also be arranged. ⊠ *Klondike Hwy., just northwest of Alaska St.* ☎ *907/ 983–2111* ⊕ *www.jewellgardens.com* ✉ *Tour packages from $39.*

Klondike Gold Rush National Historical Park Museum

MUSEUM | Housed in the former White Pass and Yukon Route Depot, this wonderful museum contains exhibits, photos, and artifacts from the White Pass and Chilkoot trails. It's a must-see for anyone planning on taking a White Pass train ride, driving the nearby Klondike Highway, or hiking the Chilkoot Trail. Films, ranger talks, and walking tours are offered. Special free Robert Service poetry performances by Buckwheat Donahue—a beloved local character and head of the Skagway Convention and Visitors Bureau—occasionally take place at the visitor center next door. ⊠ *2nd Ave., south of Broadway* ☎ *907/983–2921, 907/983–9224* ⊕ *www.nps.gov/klgo* ✉ *Free.*

Moore Cabin

BUILDING | Built in 1887 by Captain William Moore and his son Ben Moore, the tiny cabin was the first structure built in Skagway. An early homesteader, Captain Moore prospered from the flood of miners, constructing a dock, warehouse, and sawmill to supply them, and selling land for other ventures. Next door, the larger **Moore House** (1897–98) contains interesting exhibits on the Moore family. Both structures are maintained by the Park Service, and the main house is open daily in summer. ⊠ *5th Ave. between Broadway and Spring St.* ☎ *907/983–2921.*

Skagway Museum

MUSEUM | This nicely designed museum—also known as the Trail of '98 Museum—occupies the ground floor of the beautiful building that also houses Skagway City Hall. Inside, you'll find a 19th-century Tlingit canoe (one of only two like it on the West Coast), historic photos, a red-and-black sleigh, and other gold rush–era artifacts, along with a healthy collection of contemporary local art and post–gold rush history exhibits. ⊠ *7th Ave. and Spring St.* ☎ *907/983–2420* ✉ *$2.*

🏃 Activities

BIKING
Sockeye Cycle Company

BICYCLING | Based in Haines, Sockeye also does business in Skagway during summer. The company specializes in guided bike tours, including a train–bike ride combo, and from May through September rents bikes. ⊠ *381 5th Ave.* ☎ *907/983–2851* ⊕ *www.cyclealaska. com* ✉ *From $10.*

BOATING
Alaska Fjordlines

TOUR—SPORTS | Passengers board a high-speed catamaran at 8 am and stop along the way to watch sea lions, humpbacks, and other marine mammals on this popular day tour from Skagway and Haines to Juneau and back. The boat gets to Juneau at 11 am, where a bus transports visitors into town and to Mendenhall Glacier, returning to the boat at 4:30 pm for the ride back to Skagway, where the boat returns at 8 pm. Call or check website for the schedule—up to six trips a week in the summer is common. ⊠ *Skagway* ☎ *907/766–3395, 800/320–0146* ⊕ *www. alaskafjordlines.com* ✉ *$169 round-trip; $130 one-way.*

BUS TOURS
Skagway Street Car Company

TOUR—SPORTS | Revisit the gold-rush days in modern restorations of the bright-yellow 1920s sightseeing buses with Skagway Street Car Company. Costumed

Walking Around Skagway

Skagway's rowdy history is memorialized at the corner of 1st Avenue and Main Street, where a marker notes the infamous 1898 gun battle between Soapy Smith and Frank Reid. From the marker, head two blocks east along 1st Avenue and turn left on Broadway into the heart of the town. Inside the old White Pass and Yukon Railroad Depot at 2nd Avenue and Broadway, you'll find the **Klondike Gold Rush National Historical Park** visitor center, one of Southeast's best museums.

The next block north on Broadway—the heart of historical Skagway—contains several of the town's best-known buildings. The two-centuries-old Red Onion Saloon remains a favorite place to imbibe under the watchful eyes of "working girl" mannequins. Next door is the **Arctic Brotherhood Hall,** the facade of which is constructed entirely of driftwood. Inside, you'll find the helpful **Skagway Convention and Visitors Bureau,** which is full of friendly faces and useful local information. The golden dome of the **Golden North Hotel,** built in 1898, sits across the street from the old Mascot Saloon. ■ TIP→ There are also public restrooms here. Keep going up Broadway for **Corrington's Museum of Alaskan History,** with its large collection of scrimshaw (carved ivory) art. A right turn on 5th Avenue

brings you to the Park Service's **Moore Cabin,** Skagway's oldest structure. The beautifully restored Skagway City Hall is housed in the same granite-front building as the **Skagway Museum.** Return to Broadway and follow it to 6th Avenue, where you can see *The Days of '98 with Soapy Smith* show inside historic Eagles Hall.

If you are up for a longer walk, continue 2 miles out of town along Alaska Street to the Gold Rush Cemetery, where you'll find the graves of combatants Soapy Smith and Frank Reid. The cemetery is also the trailhead for the short walk to Lower Reid Falls, an enjoyable jaunt through the valley's lush forest. (A city bus takes you most of the way to the cemetery for $2 each direction.) No tour of Skagway is complete without a train ride on the famed **White Pass and Yukon Route.** Trains depart from the corner of 2nd Street and Broadway several times a day in summer.

The six blocks that compose the heart of downtown Skagway can be explored in a half hour, but budget two hours to see the Park Service's historic buildings and the Skagway Museum. (If you include the 4-mile round-trip walk to the Gold Rush Cemetery, plan on three to four hours.) Leave some time to explore Skagway's many shops, restaurants, and other attractions.

conductors lead these popular 90-minute tours, but advance reservations are recommended for independent travelers, since most seats are sold aboard cruise ships. Call a week ahead in peak season to reserve a space. ⊠ *270 2nd Ave.* ☎ *907/983–2908* ⊕ *www.skagwaystreetcar.com.*

OUTDOOR ADVENTURES
Alaska Excursions

TOUR—SPORTS | Booking independently with Alaska Excursions, which leads wheeled (no snow) sled-dog tours, horseback-riding tours, and zip-line adventures, can be difficult, as cruise-ship groups reserve the bulk of available slots. Plan well ahead to join these tours. ⊠ *5th Ave.*

☎ 907/983–4444 ⊕ www.alaskaexcursions.com ☎ From $169.

★ Beyond Skagway Tours

TOUR—SPORTS | This family-operated tour company's customizable private tours include trips to Dyea, gold panning in Emerald Lake, a visit to a dog mushing camp, and train rides over the White Pass. Passports are required for some tours. ✉ 796 Alaska St. ☎ 907/612–0499 ⊕ www.beyondskagwaytours.com.

Packer Expeditions

TOUR—SPORTS | This company offers guided hikes on wilderness trails not accessible by road. One trip includes a helicopter flight, a 2-mile hike toward the Laughton Glacier, and a one-hour ride back to town on the White Pass Railroad. A longer hike on the same trail uses the train for access in both directions and includes time hiking on the glacier. They also guide kayaking trips on Lake Bernard, part of the waterways utilized by the gold stampeders in the 1890s. ✉ 4th Ave. and State St. ☎ 907/983–3005 ⊕ www.packerexpeditions.com ☎ Check with your cruise line or call for prices.

Temsco Helicopters

TOUR—SPORTS | This company flies passengers to Denver Glacier for an hour of learning about mushing and riding on a dogsled. Guided tours of other area glaciers are also conducted. ✉ 901 Terminal Way ☎ 907/983–2900, 866/683–2900 ⊕ www.temscoair.com ☎ Check with your cruise line or call for prices.

🍽 Restaurants

Bites on Broadway

$ | **BAKERY** | A quick walk from the cruise-ship docks, this tiny eatery is a good stop for a cheese biscuit and coffee in the morning or soup and a sandwich in the afternoon. You'll also find sweet treats such as muffins, tortes, and cakes. **Known for:** breakfast sandwiches; cheese biscuits; espresso. ⑤ Average main: $6

Dyea

Seven and a half miles outside Skagway, the town of Dyea was once a busy hub for miners-to-be preparing to head up the Chilkoot Trail. Today, it's the starting place for hikers braving the 33-mile Chilkoot Trail, and a few people still live in the area, but for the most part Dyea functions as both a fascinating historic site and a stunning place of beauty. Dyea is part of Klondike Gold Rush National Historical Park, and the National Park Service offers tours of the area. Or, for those who really want to experience Dyea's quiet, consider camping here.

✉ 648 Broadway Ave. ☎ 907/983–2166 ⊕ www.bitesonbroadway.com.

Bonanza Bar & Grill

$ | **AMERICAN** | Expect a lively crowd at the Bonanza, and possibly live music or bingo if you're here in the evening. The pub serves well-prepared American food with no surprises; if you're a sports fan, this is a good place to watch a game. **Known for:** halibut and chips; seafood chowder; upbeat atmosphere. ⑤ Average main: $15 ✉ 320 W. Broadway ☎ 907/983–6214.

Glacial Smoothies and Espresso

$ | **CAFÉ** | Prices are steeper at this local hangout than at some coffee shops, but the ingredients are fresh and local, and nearly everything on the menu is made on-site. Customers can cool down with a Mango Madness or Blueberry Blues smoothie, and soft-serve ice cream in summer. **Known for:** fresh fruit smoothies; locally sourced ingredients; soup and sandwich combo. ⑤ Average main: $7 ✉ 336 3rd Ave. ☎ 907/983–3223 ⊕ www.glacialsmoothies.com ⊗ No dinner.

Skagway Brewing Company

$$ | AMERICAN | Though beer is the primary business of Skagway Brewing, this local pub has a diverse dinner menu that includes burgers, halibut and chips, pasta dishes, hearty salads, and vegetarian options such as falafel. Whatever you order, sampling the locally made ale is a must; Skagway's five staples are Prospector Pale, Chilkoot Trail IPA, Boom Town Brown, Blue Top Porter, and Spruce Tip Blonde Ale. **Known for:** beer samplers; burger night; crowded with locals. $ *Average main: $17* ⊠ *730 Broadway* ☎ *907/983-2739* ⊕ *www.skagwaybrewing.com* ⊘ *No lunch in winter.*

★ Starfire

$$ | THAI | A popular spot with the locals, and known to attract repeat customers from as far away as Juneau, this Thai restaurant fills up very quickly in the summer around dinner hour; it's best to call ahead. One reason for the crowds is the authenticity of the traditional Thai cuisine; Starfire's American chef learned his recipes during visits to Thailand, where he watched local friends and their grandmothers at work in their kitchens. **Known for:** gang dang red curry; fresh herbs grown on-site; outdoor dining. $ *Average main: $17* ⊠ *4th Ave. and Spring St.* ☎ *907/983-3663* ⊕ *www.starfirealaska.com* ⊘ *Closed in winter.*

The Station

$ | AMERICAN | Housed in a former gas station, this year-round restaurant is known for its comfort-food specials. The huge calzones are stuffed and served piping hot with sides of house marinara and ranch dressing—build your own or choose one of the chef's creations. **Known for:** build-your-own calzones; cheesy bread; friendly local staff. $ *Average main: $10* ⊠ *444 4th St.* ☎ *907/983-2200* ⊕ *skagwayhotelandrestaurant.com/station.*

🛏 Hotels

Chilkoot Trail Outpost

$$ | B&B/INN | A great choice for visitors planning to make the famous 33-mile Chilkoot Trail hike, this lodging is a half mile from the trailhead and offers special packages for hikers that include pre- and posttrail lodging, train transportation from the trail's end at Lake Bennett, and several meals. **Pros:** quiet setting; flexible cabin layouts; friendly hosts. **Cons:** 7 miles from town; few amenities; unreliable Internet. $ *Rooms from: $165* ⊠ *Dyea Rd., 7 miles northwest of Skagway* ☎ *907/983-3799* ⊕ *www.chilkoottrailoutpost.com* ⇨ *8 cabins* ⦿ *Free Breakfast.*

Mile Zero Bed & Breakfast

$$ | B&B/INN | In a quiet residential area a few blocks from downtown, this comfortable B&B has spacious and well-insulated guest rooms, all with private entrances, phones, and baths. **Pros:** large rooms; communal areas are comfortable and clean; close to town. **Cons:** limited room amenities; not much of a view; no kitchen access. $ *Rooms from: $148* ⊠ *901 Main St.* ☎ *907/983-3045* ⊕ *www.mile-zero.com* ⇨ *7 rooms* ⦿ *Free Breakfast.*

Sgt. Preston's Lodge

$$ | HOTEL | A good choice for budget-conscious travelers and hikers, this motel-like lodge occupies a former army barracks where the rooms range from spacious and revamped to cramped and oddly shaped. **Pros:** convenient downtown location; handicapped-accessible room; pets allowed for a small fee. **Cons:** some rooms shaped oddly; some rooms are small; basic decor. $ *Rooms from: $105* ⊠ *370 6th Ave.* ☎ *907/983-2521, 866/983-2521* ⊕ *www.sgtprestonslodge.com* ⇨ *40 rooms* ⦿ *No meals.*

Skagway Inn Bed & Breakfast

$$ | B&B/INN | Each room in this family-friendly downtown Victorian inn (once a not-so-family-friendly bordello) is named after a different gold-rush gal. **Pros:** large breakfast served; nicely remodeled; antique furnishings. **Cons:** floors are creaky; walls are thin; some rooms without private bathrooms. ⑤ *Rooms from: $129* ✉ *655 Broadway* ☎ *907/983–2289, 888/752–4929* ⊕ *www.skagwayinn.com* ⊘ *Closed Oct.–Apr.* ⤴ *10 rooms* ⦿ *Free Breakfast.*

White House

$$ | B&B/INN | Built in 1902 by Lee Guthrie, a gambler and owner of one of the town's most profitable gold-rush saloons, the white-clapboard two-story B&B—about two blocks from downtown Skagway—is furnished with original Skagway antiques and handcrafted quilts. **Pros:** conveniently located; open year-round; one room is wheelchair accessible. **Cons:** most rooms require climbing stairs; no shuttle service; basic breakfast. ⑤ *Rooms from: $149* ✉ *475 8th Ave.* ☎ *907/983–9000* ⊕ *www.atthewhitehouse.com* ⤴ *10 rooms* ⦿ *Breakfast.*

ⓨ Nightlife

Red Onion Saloon

BARS/PUBS | Skagway was once host to dozens upon dozens of watering holes in its gold rush days, but the Red Onion is pretty much the sole survivor. The upstairs was Skagway's first bordello, and you'll find a convivial crowd of Skagway locals and visitors among the scantily clad mannequins who represent the building's former illustrious tenants. A ragtime pianist tickles the keys in the afternoons, and local musicians strut their stuff on Thursday night. Food is available in the bar. The saloon closes up shop for winter. ✉ *205 Broadway* ☎ *907/983–2222* ⊕ *www.redonion1898.com.*

🎭 Performing Arts

The Days of '98 with Soapy Smith

THEATER | Since 1927 locals and visiting actors have performed a show at Eagles Hall called *The Days of '98 with Soapy Smith.* You'll see cancan dancers (including Molly Fewclothes, Belle Davenport, and Squirrel Tooth Alice), learn a little local history, and watch desperado Soapy Smith being sent to his reward. At the evening show you can enjoy a few warm-up rounds of mock gambling with Soapy's money. Performances of Robert Service poetry start a half hour before showtime. Shows take place from one to four times daily, from mid-May through mid-September. ✉ *590 Broadway* ☎ *907/983–2545 mid-May–mid-Sept.* ⊕ *www.thedaysof98show.com* 🎟 *From $25.*

🛍 Shopping

Alaska Artworks

CRAFTS | For those in search of locally produced silver jewelry, watercolor prints, and other handmade crafts, this artist-owned shop is a good place to start. ✉ *510 Broadway* ☎ *907/983–3443* ⊕ *alaskaartworks.com* ⊘ *Closed Sept.–Apr.*

Skaguay News Depot & Books

BOOKS/STATIONERY | This small but quaint bookstore carries Alaska titles, children's books, magazines, maps, and gifts. Its moniker is a throwback to the town name's former spelling. The owner, Jeff Brady, ran the local newspaper, the *Skagway News,* for more than 30 years. ✉ *264 Broadway* ☎ *907/983–3354* ⊕ *www.skagwaybooks.com.*

THE KENAI PENINSULA AND SOUTHCENTRAL ALASKA

Updated by
Teeka Ballas

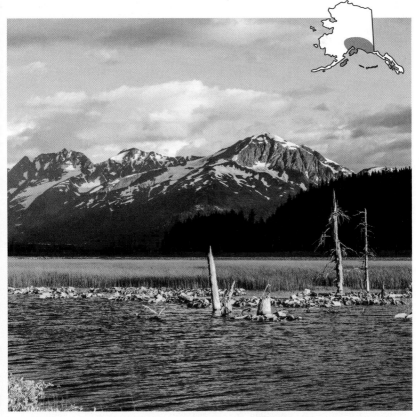

◉ Sights	🍴 Restaurants	🛏 Hotels	🛍 Shopping	🍸 Nightlife
★★★★★	★★☆☆☆	★★★☆☆	★★★☆☆	★★☆☆☆

WELCOME TO THE KENAI PENINSULA AND SOUTHCENTRAL ALASKA

TOP REASONS TO GO

★ **Fishing:** In summer, salmon fill the rivers, which you can fish on the bank or from your own boat with a guide. Fishing for halibut and rockfish is also possible from charter boats out of Homer or Seward.

★ **Wildlife:** Urban moose, black and brown bears, sea lions, Dall sheep, gray whales, and bald eagles are all common in the region.

★ **Scenery:** Boasting views of volcanoes and mountains that fall right into the water, the Kenai Peninsula is a buffet for the eyes.

★ **Glaciers:** Get up close and personal with glaciers on a tour to ski, dogsled, or hike a glacier's surface, or paddle out to one.

Southcentral Alaska is the epicenter of the state's population and commerce.

1 Chugach State Park. One of the four largest state parks in the United States.

2 Portage Glacier. A shrinking glacier that was once the most visited site in Alaska.

3 Whittier. A former Army base, now a major cruise port.

4 Chugach National Forest. A national forest filled with diverse geography.

5 Valdez. Prince William Sound's largest port.

6 Cordova. The gateway to the Copper River delta.

7 Hope. A gold-mining community with small town charm.

8 Seward. A railroad town in the middle of incredible scenery.

9 Kenai Fjords National Park. A rare opportunity to see glaciers up-close.

10 Cooper Landing. One of Alaska's most popular fishing locations.

11 Kenai National Wildlife Refuge. The best moose habitat in the region.

12 Kenai, Sterling, and Soldotna. Three towns offering fishing and moose sightings.

13 Homer. A unique town that blends art, fishing, and tourism.

14 Kachemak Bay State Park and State Wilderness Park. Alaska's first state park.

15 Seldovia. A small town with a strong Russian heritage.

16 Kodiak. One of the busiest fishing ports in the country.

17 Kodiak National Wildlife Refuge. The bear-viewing capital of Alaska.

18 Lake Clark National Park and Preserve. Home to two volcanoes and a salmon-filled lake.

19 Palmer. The state's major agricultural hub.

20 Wasilla. A pioneer town home to Sarah Palin and scenic vistas.

21 Talkeetna. A quirky town that serves as the base for climbing Denali.

22 Denali State Park. The national park's quieter and less crowded sibling.

23 Glennallen. A good base for Wrangell-St. Elias.

24 Wrangell-St. Elias National Park and Preserve. A national park encompassing one of the tallest peaks in North America and plenty of outdoor adventures.

Few places in the United States offer as diverse an array of natural beauty as Southcentral Alaska. From grizzly bears to migrating whales, and moose to spawning salmon, from icy peaks to calving glaciers, and ocean bays to rain forests, there is something to satiate every nature-lover.

The wonders of this area are traversable or viewable by car. Unlike other regions in Alaska, roads connect most towns, villages, and cities here. Most visitors to the Kenai Peninsula and Southcentral tend to begin and end their journey in Anchorage, the region's transportation hub. During summer, planes, trains, buses, and automobiles depart from here on a daily basis. RV rentals are also popular in Anchorage, and recreational vehicles can be seen in droves on the Seward Highway along Cook Inlet. Most highways have two lanes and are paved, but summertime traffic can be frustrating. Be wary of impatient drivers trying to get around slow-moving RVs. Stay aware of wildlife as well. Every year motorists kill hundreds of moose, and in turn there are many driver fatalities.

Southcentral Alaska is bordered on the south and the west by ocean waters: the Gulf of Alaska, Prince William Sound, and Cook Inlet. This region is lined with a smattering of quaint port towns. From Kodiak, a commercial-fishing port, to Homer, a funky artists' colony, each town has its own personality. Inland, the remnants of mining towns continue to grow and prosper in different ways. Talkeetna, a small village on the region's northern edge at the base of Denali, is

a starting point for many mountaineers. In the center of Southcentral is Alaska's farmland, the Matanuska-Susitna Valley, generally referred to as the "Mat-Su Valley," the "Matsu," or just "The Valley." The region boasts 75-pound cabbages and gigantic award-winning rhubarb.

All of Southcentral is wrapped in the embrace of several mountain ranges. In a crescent shape south and east of Anchorage lies the 300-mile-long Chugach Mountain Range, which bends all the way around the gulf to Valdez, where it meets the Wrangell–St. Elias National Park. The Chugach, St. Elias, and Wrangell mountain ranges are so immense that they are often referred to, collectively, as the "mountain kingdom of North America."

The mountain peaks don't end there, however. Across Cook Inlet, easily viewed from Anchorage, is the Alaska Range, which, on clear days, offers impressive views of a distant but looming Denali. The Alaska Range's southwest tip meets the 600-mile Aleutian Range, which spreads out across the Gulf of Alaska atop the Aleutian Islands. These islands are riddled with both dormant and active volcanoes and are part of the Pacific Ocean's great Ring of Fire.

Whether you're hoping to explore mountains or ocean, tundra, taiga, or forest—from the coastal rain forests around Seward and Kodiak to the rough Arctic chill of glaciers flowing off the Harding Icefield—each climate zone and ecosystem is available in this region.

MAJOR REGIONS

Prince William Sound. Tucked into the east side of the Kenai Peninsula, the sound is a peaceful escape from the throngs of people congesting the towns and highways. Enhanced with steep fjords, green enshrouded waterfalls, and calving tidewater glaciers, Prince William Sound is a stunning arena. It has a convoluted coastline, in that it is riddled with islands, which makes it hard to discern just how vast the area is. The sound covers almost 15,000 square miles—more than 12 times the size of Rhode Island—and is home to more than 150 glaciers. The sound is vibrantly alive with all manner of marine life, including salmon, halibut, humpback whales, orcas, sea otters, sea lions, and porpoises. Bald eagles are easily seen soaring above, and often brown and black bears, Sitka black-tailed deer, and gray wolves can be spotted on the shore. On the west side of the sound, Chugach State Park is just outside Anchorage, with access to the once impressive Portage Glacier while Whittier serves as a major port for the Sound. Chugach National Forest is found east of the sound, along with Valdez and Cordova.

Kenai Peninsula. The Kenai Peninsula, thrusting into the Gulf of Alaska south of Anchorage, is Southcentral's playground, offering salmon and halibut fishing, spectacular scenery, and wildlife viewing. Commercial fishing is important to the area's economy; five species of Pacific salmon run up the aqua-color Kenai River every summer. Campgrounds and trailheads for backwoods hiking are strung along the roads. Along the way you can explore three major federal holdings on the peninsula—the western end of

the sprawling Chugach National Forest, Kenai National Wildlife Refuge, and Kenai Fjords National Park. Towns like Hope, Seward, Cooper Landing, Kenai, Sterling, and Soldotna make good bases for your stay.

Homer. Literally the end of the road, Homer is an alluring blend of commercial fishermen, artists, bohemians, and tourists. With bluffs sloping down to Kachemak Bay, it's hard to find a spot in town without a view of the ocean or mountains. Be sure to try the excellent restaurants and sip a locally brewed beer. Nearby Kachemak Bay State Park and State Wilderness Park and the settlement of Seldovia make for good side trips from Homer.

Kodiak Island. The second-largest island in the United States, Kodiak Island is part of a 177-mile-long archipelago. Kodiak City, in the northeastern part of the island, is the way station for supplies to the six neighboring island villages and those visiting the 1.6-million-acre Kodiak National Wildlife Refuge, where tourists hope to spot the enormous Kodiak brown bears. Russian explorers discovered Kodiak Island in 1763, and the city of Kodiak served as the original headquarters of the Russian-America Company, which was managed by Alexander Baranov with the intent of colonization for exploitation of resources. Because it was the original headquarters of the company, Kodiak is often referred to as the "first capital of Russian America." Situated as it is in the northwestern Gulf of Alaska, Kodiak has been subjected to several natural disasters. In 1912 a volcanic eruption on the nearby Alaska Peninsula covered the town site in knee-deep drifts of ash and pumice. The 1964 earthquake and resulting tsunami destroyed the island's large fishing fleet and smashed Kodiak's low-lying downtown area

Mat-Su Valley and Beyond. Giant homegrown vegetables and the headquarters of the best-known dogsled race in the world are among the most prominent attractions of the Matanuska-Susitna (Mat-Su) Valley. The Valley, an hour north of Anchorage by road, draws its name from its two largest rivers, the Matanuska and the Susitna, and is bisected by the Parks and Glenn highways. Southwest of Anchorage, Lake Clark National Park and Preserve is only accessible via small plane, but is one of the hidden gems of the area. The region has two small but prominent cities, Wasilla (on the George Parks Highway) and Palmer (on the Glenn Highway). To the east, the Glenn Highway connects to the Richardson Highway by way of several high mountain passes sandwiched between the Chugach Mountains to the south and the Talkeetnas to the north. The town of Talkeetna serves as the gateway to Denali State Park while Glennallen is a good base for those visiting Wrangell-St. Elias National Park and Preserve.

Planning

WHEN TO GO

Summer is the peak season all over the state. In the Kenai Peninsula and Southcentral this means it is rarely too hot or too cold, particularly along the coast, although rainfall occurs often and without warning. Long daylight hours make it possible to enjoy the beauty and the bounty of Alaska around the clock. However, if you're hoping to catch more hours of darkness, there are always the shoulder seasons. Unfortunately, the weather in spring and fall tends to be more unpredictable than in summer, with random appearances of snow and dramatic drops in temperature. Autumn starts early, with the deciduous trees beginning to show color in mid-August. Visitor services generally close by the end of September. Numerous festivals take place throughout the year.

FESTIVALS
Alaska State Fair
FESTIVALS | FAMILY | Giant vegetables are big attractions at Palmer's Alaska State Fair. Shop for Alaskan-made gifts and crafts, and whoop it up with midway rides, livestock and 4-H shows, bake-offs, home-preserved produce contests, food, and live music. The fair runs for 12 days, starting in late August and ending on Labor Day. ⊠ *Mile 40.2, Glenn Hwy., Palmer* ☎ *907/745–4827* ⊕ *www. alaskastatefair.org.*

Copper River Delta Shorebird Festival
FESTIVALS | FAMILY | The arrival of as many as 5 million birds in the Copper River Delta each May is cause for three to five days of festivities during the first week of the month that include workshops and guided field trips. The birds, mostly western sandpipers and dunlins, feed and rest here on their long migration to their northern nesting grounds. Alaska Airlines often offers discounted fares to festivalgoers—check the chamber website for details. ⊠ *Cordova* ☎ *907/424–7260* ⊕ *www.cordovachamber.com.*

Copper River Salmon Jam!
FESTIVALS | FAMILY | In mid-July, this small-town festival draws an impressive number of artists, musicians, and athletes for the celebration of salmon (of course!) and the Salmon Runs Marathon. ⊠ *Cordova* ☎ *907/424–7260* ⊕ *www. salmonjam.org.*

Ice Worm Festival
FESTIVALS | FAMILY | To shake off the winter blues, the residents of tiny Cordova gather for a weeklong celebration in early February. The festivities include a parade and numerous other entertaining activities, including the Ice Worm Variety Show and the Miss Ice Worm Coronation. ⊠ *Cordova* ☎ *907/424–7260* ⊕ *www. icewormfestival.com.*

Kachemak Bay Shorebird Festival
FESTIVALS | FAMILY | Early-summer visitors to Homer join thousands of migrating shorebirds for the Kachemak Bay

Shorebird Festival on the second weekend in May. Experts offer bird-watching trips and photography demonstrations, and the simultaneous Wooden Boat Festival provides a chance to meet some of Alaska's finest boatbuilders. Various kids' events add to the fun. ⊠ *Homer* ⊕ *www. kachemakshorebird.org.*

Mt. Marathon Race

FESTIVALS | FAMILY | An event held every July 4 since 1915, this race attracts runners and spectators from near and far while the entire town celebrates. The whole affair takes less than an hour, but the route is arduous: straight up the mountain (3,022 feet) and back down to the center of town. Racers are chosen on a lottery basis; enter before April for a chance, and be sure to book a hotel room well in advance. ⊠ *Seward* ☎ *907/224–8051* ⊕ *www.mmr.seward. com.*

Salmonfest

FESTIVALS | Every August, thousands of people from all over the state and country converge on the tiny town of Ninilchik, on the Kenai Peninsula 37 miles outside of Homer, to celebrate music, food, and fish. Over the course of a three-day weekend, countless vendors of arts and crafts set up shop while approximately 50 musical acts take to the four stages, drawing awareness and bolstering support for the protection of Bristol Bay waters and fishing habitat. ⊠ *Kenai Peninsula* ☎ *907/435–0525* ⊕ *www.salmonfestalaska.org.*

Seward Halibut Tournament

FESTIVALS | FAMILY | For the whole month of June, locals and visitors set out to catch the largest halibut of the season. There are daily winners and end-of-tournament winners. The current record holder is a 337-pound catch. ⊠ *Seward* ☎ *907/224–8051* ⊕ *halibut.seward.com.*

Seward Music and Arts Festival

ARTS FESTIVALS | FAMILY | The Seward Arts Council hosts this family-friendly indoor festival the first weekend of October. The three-day festival draws some of Alaska's finest musicians. Many arts activities take place, and artists and craftspeople sell their works in booths. ⊠ *913 Port Ave., Seward* ⊕ *www.sewardfestival. com.*

Silver Salmon Derby

FESTIVALS | FAMILY | For more than 60 years, anglers from near and far have been gathering every mid-August for the state's oldest and most popular fishing derby. Vying for the largest tagged coho (silver salmon), they can win up to $50,000. ⊠ *Seward* ☎ *907/224–8051* ⊕ *www.seward.com.*

Talkeetna Winterfest

FESTIVALS | FAMILY | The monthlong celebration known as Winterfest encourages visitors to visit Talkeetna during the very snowy and very cold month of December, offering plenty of activities, events, and live music. Part of this is the tongue-in-cheek Wilderness Woman Contest, where women compete in a variety of events like fishing, sawing wood, and yes, sandwich prep (that's the tongue-in-cheek part, don't worry). Afterward, women are invited to the annual Bachelor Auction & Ball where they can purchase a dance from any of Talkeetna's eligible bachelors. Proceeds from both events go to funding local domestic violence programs. ⊠ *Talkeetna* ⊕ *www. alaska.org/detail/talkeetna-winterfest.*

GETTING HERE AND AROUND
BOAT AND FERRY TRAVEL

With its glaciers, mountains, fjords, and sea mammals, the coast is great to experience by ferry. The ferries between Valdez and Whittier run by way of Columbia Glacier in summer, where it is not unusual to witness giant fragments of ice calving from the face of the glacier into Prince William Sound.

The Alaska Marine Highway, the state-run ferry operator, has scheduled service to Valdez, Cordova, Whittier, Homer, and Seldovia on the mainland; to Kodiak and Port Lions on Kodiak Island; and to the port of Dutch Harbor in the Aleutian Islands. These connect to the ferries that operate in Southeast Alaska, but the two systems connect only on once-a-month sailings. Ferries operate on two schedules; summer (May through September) sailings are considerably more frequent than winter (October through April) service. Check your schedules carefully: ferries do not stop at all ports every day. Reservations are required on all routes and should be made as far in advance as possible.

Many major cruise lines also use Whittier as a port of embarkation/disembarkation for cruises through Alaska's Southeastern Peninsula.

CONTACTS Alaska Marine Highway ☎ 800/642–0066 ⊕ www.ferryalaska. com.

BUS TRAVEL

For bus service in the region, contact Interior Alaska Bus Line, Stage Line, Park Connection Motor Coach, or Seward Bus Line.

CONTACTS Interior Alaska Bus Lines ☎ 800/770–6652 ⊕ www.interioralaskabusline.com. **Park Connection Motor Coach** ☎ 800/266–8625 ⊕ alaskacoach. com. **Seward Bus Line** ☎ 907/563–0800, 888/420–7788 ⊕ www.sewardbuslines. net. **Stage Line** ☎ 907/868–3914 Anchorage, 907/235–2252 Homer ⊕ www. stagelineinhomer.com.

CAR TRAVEL

Car is definitely the way to go when exploring the Kenai Peninsula and Southcentral Alaska; the road system is more developed than in most other regions, and is mostly paved. It also has some great driving routes that involve putting your car on a ferry. If you're renting, know that not all rental companies will let you do this (start with the larger chains, which are more likely to have a seaworthy rental policy available), so aim to get your ducks in a row about two or three months in advance before

the ferry-friendly rental agencies are all booked for your dates.

TRAIN TRAVEL

Anchorage is the region's hub, connected by rail and road to major ports in Southcentral. To the east, you can reach McCarthy and Valdez by an indirect but scenic drive on the Glenn and Richardson highways. The Seward and Sterling highways connect to nearly every town on the Kenai Peninsula. The Alaska Railroad Corporation operates the Alaska Railroad, which runs 470 miles between Seward and Fairbanks via Anchorage. There's daily service between Anchorage and Fairbanks in summer, and in winter there's one round-trip per week. Service to Seward from Anchorage runs every weekend from mid-May to September.

CONTACTS Alaska Railroad ☎ 800/544–0552 ⊕ www.akrr.com.

HEALTH AND SAFETY

In Southcentral, it's important to stick to basic principles of Alaska safety: hiring a guide for anything outside your comfort zone might just prove to be the most important investment you've ever made. Follow bear safety rules; especially down the Kenai Peninsula, know that moose can be the more dangerous encounter, so use extreme respect and caution.

MONEY MATTERS

Nothing is too surprising on the financial front here: try to bring cash if you're traveling to a small town, and even if you've prepaid for a guide's services, remember to bring a little something to tip with at the end of the day or trip. Food, lodging, and sundries are going to be significantly higher in Alaska than the rest of the country, especially the more remote you go—remember, almost everything gets to Alaska via barge or approximately 2,000 miles of highway.

RESTAURANTS

The best way to describe the hospitality industry in Alaska is "informal," and this applies all over the state—even in

Prince William Sound

Anchorage. Don't worry if you still have your hiking clothes on when you go out to eat. Every kind of food is available, especially in larger towns, but options decline considerably from mid-September through April.

HOTELS

Accommodations in Alaska, particularly in the sparsely populated areas, can be quite rugged. You will find a lot of establishments have only shared bathrooms, and amenities such as a coffeepot, television, and Internet access are scant, although the latter is beginning to find its way even into remote villages. In the most rural of places it is not entirely unheard of to find no bathrooms in the establishment, but rather an outhouse or "honey bucket" out back. If such things are important to you, it's wise to inquire in advance.

Restaurant and hotel reviews have been shortened. For full information, visit Fodors.com. Restaurant prices are the average cost of a main course at dinner or, if dinner is not served, at lunch. Hotel prices are the lowest cost of a standard double room in high season.

What It Costs			
$	$$	$$$	$$$$
RESTAURANTS			
under $14	$14–$22	$23–$32	over $32
HOTELS			
under $100	$100–$200	$201–$300	over $300

Chugach State Park

Bordering Anchorage to the east.

One of the four largest state parks in the United States, Chugach State Park covers approximately 495,000 acres. Located entirely in Southcentral, it lies mostly within the Municipality of Anchorage—just 7 miles from Downtown.

GETTING HERE AND AROUND

The Chugach forms the backdrop of Anchorage, and trailheads are accessible at the top of O'Malley, Huffman, and DeArmoun roads; south of Anchorage at Potter Valley, McHugh Creek, and Bird Ridge on the Seward Highway; and to the north of town at Arctic Valley Road (6 miles out) and Eagle River Road (13 miles out).

ESSENTIALS

VISITOR INFORMATION Chugach State Park Headquarters ✉ *18620 Seward Hwy., Anchorage* ☎ *907/345–5014* ⊕ *www.dnr. alaska.gov/parks/units/chugach.*

 Sights

Chugach State Park

NATIONAL/STATE PARK | Comprising nearly a half million acres, Chugach State Park is the third-largest state park in the United States. On the edge of Anchorage, the park is Alaska's most accessible wilderness, with nearly 30 trails for hikers of all abilities. Totaling more than 150 miles, the hiking trails range in length from 2 miles to 30 miles. Although Chugach, connected as it is to Alaska's largest city, is technically an urban park, this is far from being a typical urban setting. Hardly tame, this is real wilderness, home to Dall sheep, mountain goats, brown bears, moose, and several packs of wolves. Miners who sought the easiest means of traversing the mountain peaks and passes initially blazed most of the park's trails. Today they are restored every spring and maintained by park rangers and various volunteer

groups. Hiking in the park is free whether you're here for an afternoon or a week, though a $5 daily parking fee is charged at several popular trailheads. The park serves up some truly intoxicating views, and, depending on what perch you're looking down from, you can see across the bay to the looming white mountains of the Alaska Range, the great tides of Cook Inlet, and, on clear days, Denali in all its glory. One of the best and most easily accessible places to seek out such a view is from Flattop Mountain, on the park's western edge. The peak is the most popular destination within Chugach Park. A 1-mile hike leads to the top, and hikers of all abilities make the trek, but be aware it is strenuous. ⊕ *www.dnr. alaska.gov/parks/units/chugach* ✉ *Free; $5 parking fee at some trailheads.*

Eagle River Nature Center

INFO CENTER | Eagle River Road leads 12 miles into the mountains from the bedroom community of Eagle River. The nature center, at the end of the road, has wildlife displays, telescopes for wildlife spotting, and 9 miles of hiking trails. Volunteers are on hand to answer questions, lead hikes, and host naturalist programs. A cabin that sleeps eight and a pair of yurts (round insulated tents) that sleep four and six are available to rent ($65 per night). A 1½-mile hike in is required. Amenities include woodstoves, firewood, and outdoor latrines. The center is also the trail end for the Crow Pass Trail, a 26-mile section of the Historic Iditarod Trail. ✉ *32750 Eagle River Rd., Eagle River* ☎ *907/694–2108* ⊕ *www. ernc.org* ✉ *Parking $5.*

Activities

The **Little Rodak Trail** is less than 1 mile long and has a viewing platform that overlooks the Eagle River valley. **Albert Loop Trail** behind the nature center has markers that coordinate with a self-guided hike along its 3-mile route; pick up a brochure at the Eagle River Nature Center.

HIKING

Several trailheads along the edge of Anchorage lead into the park and its 3,000- to 5,000-foot-tall peaks. The park's most popular day climb is **Flattop Mountain,** which towers 3,500 feet above sea level. It's reached via the Glen Alps Trailhead off Upper Huffman Road on Anchorage's Hillside. A 1-mile trail climbs 1,300 feet from the Glen Alps parking area to the top. On a bright summer day you'll encounter plenty of company. Bring along a daypack with plenty of water and energy bars, a rainproof jacket, good hiking boots, and trekking poles.

Every summer solstice, locals climb to the top of Flattop Mountain to celebrate the longest day of the year. If you're in town for this event, it's great fun; there's even an impromptu concert by musicians who lug their instruments to the top of the mountain. Parking spots are at a premium, so arrive early.

MOUNTAIN BIKING

Mountain biking has become very popular in the park, and most, but not all, trails are open to bikes; check the signs and symbols at the trailheads if in doubt. The Powerline Pass trail from the Glen Alps parking lot is wide and well maintained for bikes and offers a great view from the pass, as well as opportunities to spot moose, Dall sheep, bears, and maybe even wolves.

Pablo's Bicycle Rentals

BICYCLING | You can rent mountain and road bikes from Pablo's. ⊠ *501 L St., Anchorage* ☎ *907/277–2453* ⊕ *www. pablobicyclerentals.com.*

Portage Glacier

54 miles southeast of Anchorage.

Until recently Portage Glacier was the most visited site in Alaska. The glacier

has receded dramatically in the past decade, and these days it is easier to see where it used to be. The road to the glacier follows Portage Lake, where icebergs calved from the glacier still lazily float, impressing visitors with their aqua blue colors.

GETTING HERE AND AROUND

Accessible by car from Anchorage, Portage Glacier lies within Chugach National Forest just west of the tunnel to Whittier. In summer, Gray Line of Alaska leads boat tours along the face of Portage Glacier aboard the 200-passenger *Ptarmigan.*

ESSENTIALS

VISITOR AND TOUR INFORMATION
Begich-Boggs Visitor Center ⊠ *Portage Lake Loop, Girdwood* ☎ *907/783–2326 summer, 907/783–3242 winter* ⊕ *www. fs.usda.gov/detail/chugach.*

◉ Sights

Alaska Wildlife Conservation Center
NATURE PRESERVE | FAMILY | The center is a 144-acre, 2-mile drive-through loop with places where you can see up close the many animals the park has adopted and rescued. For more than a decade the center has been raising wood bison, which have been extinct in Alaska since the 1800s and were endangered in Canada. In 2015, the center reintroduced 100 wood bison to the wild, 340 miles west of Anchorage; a small herd remains at the center. Visitors can see moose, elk, eagles, musk ox, porcupine, and the elusive lynx. An elevated walkway at the center also allows visitors the thrilling experience of seeing bears at eye level. ⊠ *Mile 79, 43640 Seward Hwy., Anchorage* ☎ *907/783–2025* ⊕ *www.alaskawildlife.org* ☚ *$15.*

Byron Glacier
NATURE SITE | The mountains surrounding Portage Glacier are covered with smaller glaciers. A 1-mile hike off Byron Glacier Road—the trail begins about a mile south

of the Begich-Boggs Visitor Center—leads to the Byron Glacier overlook. The glacier is notable for its accessibility—this is one of the few places where you can hike onto a glacier from the road system. In summer, naturalists lead free weekly treks in search of microscopic ice worms. ⊠ *Byron Glacier Rd., off Portage Glacier Rd.* ⊕ *www.alaska.org/detail/byron-glacier-trail.*

Indian Valley Meats

STORE/MALL | A popular place where for almost 40 years Alaskans have had their game processed, Indian Valley Meats has a shop that sells smoked salmon and reindeer, along with buffalo sausage made on the premises. The folks here will smoke, can, and package any fish you've caught, and they'll arrange for shipping. ⊠ *200 Huot Circle, off Seward Hwy. at Mile 104 (follow Indian Rd. northeast to Poppy La.), Indian* ☎ *907/653–7511* ⊕ *www.indianvalleymeats.com.*

Portage

ARCHAEOLOGICAL SITE | The 1964 earthquake destroyed the town of Portage. The ghost forest of dead spruce in the area was created when the land subsided by 6 to 10 feet after the quake and saltwater penetrated inland from Turnagain Arm, killing the trees. ⊕ *www.alaska.org/guide/portage-valley.*

Portage Glacier

NATURE SITE | The glacier is one of Alaska's most frequently visited tourist destinations. A 6-mile side road off the Seward Highway leads to the Begich-Boggs Visitor Center, on the shore of Portage Lake and named after two U.S. congressmen who disappeared on a small-plane journey out of Anchorage in 1972. The center is staffed by Forest Service personnel, who can help plan your trip and explain the natural history of the area. A film on glaciers is shown hourly, and icebergs sometimes drift down to the center from Portage Glacier. Due to global climate change, Portage, like most of the glaciers in Alaska, has receded from view in recent years. ⊠ *Portage Lake Loop, Girdwood* ⊕ *www.fs.fed.us/r10/chugach.*

Turnagain Arm

BODY OF WATER | Several hiking trails are accessible from the Seward Highway, including the steep paths up Falls Creek and Bird Ridge. Both offer spectacular views of Turnagain Arm, where explorer Captain Cook searched for the Northwest Passage. The arm has impressive tides, and notably, the second-largest bore tide in North America. These bore tides can reach up to 40 feet, and move at an impressive 30 miles per hour (an average tide flows at 10 to 15 miles an hour). An increasingly popular, yet somewhat dangerous, sport is windsurfing the tidal bore. To view the bore tide, station yourself at one of the turnoffs along the arm about 2½ hours after low tide in Anchorage.

During the summer, beluga whales are frequent visitors to the arm as they patrol the muddy waters in search of salmon and hooligan, a variety of smelt. During high tide from July to August, when the surface of the water is calm, belugas are often spotted from the highway, frequently causing traffic jams as tourists and residents pull off the road for a chance to take in this increasingly rare sight. For reasons that are still unclear to scientists, Southcentral's beluga population has declined from 1,300 in 1980 to fewer than 290 today; they are currently listed as critically endangered, making a sighting of them even more exciting.

🔵 Activities

COMBINATION TRIPS
★ NOVA

TOUR—SPORTS | In business since 1975, this company conducts river rafting, glacier hiking, and backcountry combo trips from its office near Matanuska Glacier. ⊠ *38100 Glenn Hwy., Glacier View* ☎ *800/746–5753* ⊕ *www.novalaska.com* 🎫 *From $90.*

PORTAGE GLACIER TOURS

Gray Line of Alaska

TOUR—SPORTS | Gray Line leads boat tours along the face of Portage Glacier aboard the 200-passenger *Ptarmigan*. The view of Portage Lake and the surrounding peaks and hanging glaciers (the high-up glaciers that terminate at the tops of cliffs) is awe-inspiring, especially on a sunny day when the icy-blue hues of the glaciers shine through. ☎ *888/425–1737* ⊕ *www.graylinealaska.com* ✉ *$90.*

ROCK AND ICE CLIMBING

Alaska Rock Gym

CLIMBING/MOUNTAINEERING | For information about rock- and ice-climbing activities, stop by Alaska Rock Gym. There's a great indoor gym here, and staffers can point you to the routes local climbers have set along the Seward Highway just south of town. ✉ *665 E. 33rd Ave., Anchorage* ☎ *907/562–7265* ⊕ *www. alaskarockgym.com.*

Whittier

60 miles southeast of Anchorage.

The entryway to Whittier is unlike any other: a 2½-mile drive atop railroad tracks through the Anton Anderson Memorial Tunnel, cut through the Chugach Mountain Range. Once on the other side of the tunnel, you enter the mysterious world of Whittier, the remnants of a military town developed during World War II. The only way to get to Whittier was by boat or train until the tunnel opened to traffic in 2000.

This quaint hamlet, nestled at the base of snow-covered peaks at the head of Passage Canal on the Kenai Peninsula, has an intriguing history. In the 1940s the U.S. Army constructed a port in Whittier and built the Hodge and Buckner buildings to house soldiers. These enormous monoliths are eerily reminiscent of Soviet-era communal apartment buildings. The Hodge Building (now called Begich Towers) houses almost all of Whittier's 215 year-round residents. The town averages 30 feet of snow in the winter, and in summer gets a considerable amount of rainfall. Whittier's draw is primarily fishing, but there are a number of activities to be had on Prince William Sound, including kayaking and glacier tours with some of the best glacier viewing in Southcentral Alaska.

Whittier is very small, and there is not much to look at in town, but the location is unbeatable. Surrounding peaks cradle alpine glaciers, and when the summer weather melts the huge winter snow load you can catch glimpses of the brilliant blue ice underneath. Sheer cliffs drop into Passage Canal and provide nesting places for flocks of black-legged kittiwakes, while sea otters and harbor seals cavort in the small-boat harbor and salmon return to spawn in nearby streams. A short boat ride out into the sound reveals tidewater glaciers, and an alert wildlife watcher can catch sight of mountain goats clinging to the mountainsides and black bears patrolling the beaches and hillsides in their constant search for food.

■**TIP**➜ **Many companies' phones in Whittier are disconnected from October through April. If you can't get through to a number with prefix 472, check the company's website for an alternate number.**

GETTING HERE AND AROUND

Unless you come in on a cruise ship, ferry, or other boat, your only way in and out of Whittier is through the tunnel. Its access, however, is limited by the railroad schedule, so it's not always possible to breeze in and out of town. ■**TIP**➜ **For current tunnel information and schedules, check the tunnel's website.** Tolls are $13 for passenger vehicles and $22 to $38 for RVs and trailers; waits of up to an hour are possible, and summer hours are from 5:30 am until 11 pm.

ESSENTIALS
TUNNEL INFORMATION Anton Anderson Memorial Tunnel ⊠ *Portage Glacier Rd.* ☎ *877/611–2586* ⊕ *dot.alaska.gov/creg/ whittiertunnel.*

Sights

Portage Pass
TRAIL | Historically a route used by Alaska Natives, Russian fur traders, and early settlers, this 1-mile hike (one-way) offers tremendous views of Portage Glacier. To access the hike, drive through the Anton Anderson Memorial Tunnel to Whittier and take the first right after the railroad tracks, onto a gravel road marked "Forest Access." The trail will be just a short way up from there on the right. There's a 750-foot elevation gain, so bring your hiking poles. ⊠ *Whittier.*

Activities

BOATING AND WILDLIFE VIEWING
★ 26 Glacier Cruise
BOATING | Phillips Cruises & Tours has been running the 26 Glacier Cruise through Prince William Sound for many years. The high-speed catamaran covers 135 miles of territory in 4½ hours, leaving Whittier and visiting Port Wells, Barry Arm, and College and Harriman fjords. The boat is a very stable platform, and even visitors prone to seasickness take this cruise with no ill effects. The heated cabin has large windows, upholstered booths, and wide aisles, and a snack bar and a saloon are on board. Potential wildlife sightings include humpback whales, orcas, sea otters, harbor seals, sea lions, bears, mountain goats, and eagles. You can drive to Whittier and catch the boat at the dock, or you can arrange with the company to travel from Anchorage by rail or bus. The tour rate includes a hot lunch of cod or chicken. ⊠ *Cliffside Marina, 100 W. Camp Rd.* ☎ *907/276–8023* ⊕ *www. phillipscruises.com* ☞ *$159.*

Alaska Sea Kayakers
BOATING | This outfit supplies sea kayaks and gear for exploring Prince William Sound and conducts guided day trips, multiday tours, instruction, and boat-assisted and boat live-aboard kayaking trips. The company practices a leave-no-trace camping ethos, and is very conscientious about avoiding bear problems. All guides are experienced Alaska paddlers, and group sizes are kept small. ⊠ *Whittier* ☎ *907/472–2534, 877/472–2534* ⊕ *www. alaskaseakayakers.com* ☞ *Day trips from $89.*

Lazy Otter Charters
BOATING | With three boats and two landing craft, Lazy Otter runs sightseeing trips, operates a water taxi to Forest Service cabins, drops off sea kayakers at scenic points, and has ride-along and share-a-ride programs, a way to see Prince William Sound on a smaller budget. Customized sightseeing trips last from four to nine hours. Day trips include lunch from the Lazy Otter Café. ⊠ *Whittier* ☎ *800/587–6887, 907/694–6887* ⊕ *www.lazyotter.com* ☞ *Custom sightseeing trips from $255 per person (minimum of four).*

Major Marine Tours
BOATING | Major Marine Tours runs a five-hour cruise from Whittier that visits two tidewater glaciers. The waters of Prince William Sound are well protected and relatively calm, making this a good option if you tend to get seasick. Seabirds, waterfowl, and bald eagles are always present, and the chance to get close to the enormous walls of glacier ice is not to be missed. A number of different cruises are available from mid-March to mid-September, ranging from $119 to $150 per person. ⊠ *Whittier* ☎ *907/274–7300* ⊕ *www.majormarine.com.*

On many tours in Prince William Sound, you'll spot sea lions sunning themselves on rocks.

🍴 Restaurants

China Sea
$$ | CHINESE | This MSG-free Chinese restaurant features local seafood and amazingly fresh vegetables. The grilled halibut is fantastic, and for nonfish lovers, the Mongolian beef and kung pao chicken are excellent choices. **Known for:** one of the best Chinese restaurants in Southcentral Alaska; fresh fish and vegetables (a rarity in these parts); location right near the ferry terminal. $ *Average main: $15* ✉ *6 Harbor Rd.* ☎ *907/472–3663* ⊗ *Closed mid-Sept.–late May.*

Lazy Otter Café & Gifts
$ | CAFÉ | Amid the summer shops and docks, this little café offers warm drinks and soups, sandwiches, and fresh-baked pastries, along with an Alaskan favorite, soft-serve ice cream. The busy shop only has a couple of indoor seats, but there's outdoor seating overlooking the harbor, which is quite pleasant on sunny days. **Known for:** excellent seafood chowder and salmon spread; outdoor seating with views of harbor; only good coffee in town. $ *Average main: $9* ✉ *Lot 2, Whittier Harbor* ☎ *907/472–6887.*

Varly's Ice Cream & Pizza Parlor
$ | PIZZA | On a hot summer day and even on not-so-hot days, locals yearn for some Varly's ice cream or if the weather's cold and rainy, for some decent pizza. The owners (who also manage Varly's Swiftwater Seafood Café) take great pride in what they do, and it shows: the homemade pizza here is certainly something to write home about. **Known for:** homemade pizza dough and breads; outdoor seating; authentic frontier-feel. $ *Average main: $9* ✉ *Lot 1A Triangle Lease Area, Whittier Harbor* ☎ *907/472–2547* ⊕ *www.swiftwaterseafoodcafe.com* ⊗ *Closed Oct.–Apr.*

Varly's Swiftwater Seafood Café
$$ | SEAFOOD | The epicurean heart of Whittier for more than two decades, Varly's offers delightful surprises like its famed calamari burger—squid tenderized and fried in a secret batter. Other menu items include burgers, homemade chowders, rockfish, halibut, and salmon. **Known for:** best fried fish in the state; fresh seafood

straight out of the water; true fishermen's wharf atmosphere. ⑤ *Average main: $20* ✉ *Harbor Loop* ☎ 907/472–2550 ⊕ *www. swiftwaterseafoodcafe.com* ⊗ *Closed mid-Sept.–May.*

Hotels

Inn at Whittier

$$ | **HOTEL** | With its lighthouse-tower design and its weathered-looking gray slats, this hotel set among shanties and harbor boats blends in well with its surroundings. **Pros:** comfortable beds; great views; nice restaurant and bar. **Cons:** no kitchen amenities; some downstairs rooms have only parking lot views; some rooms don't have working televisions. ⑤ *Rooms from: $180* ✉ *5a Harbor Rd.* ☎ *907/472–3200* ⊕ *www.innatwhittier. com* ⊗ *Closed Oct.–Mar.* ⇆ *25 rooms* ⦿ *Breakfast.*

June's Whittier Condo Suites

$$ | **HOTEL** | A former military housing tower that is now home to most of the town's residents, June's also offers bed-and-breakfast condos, half with million-dollar bay views and half with gorgeous mountain and glacier views. **Pros:** full amenities including Wi-Fi; lovely views; quirky decor. **Cons:** unattractive exterior; rooms with the best views cost more; some rooms could use updating. ⑤ *Rooms from: $165* ✉ *Begich Towers, 100 Kenai St.* ☎ *907/472–6001 office, 907/841–5102 cell* ⊕ *www.juneswhittiercondosuites.com* ⇆ *10 rooms* ⦿ *No meals.*

Chugach National Forest

40 miles east of Anchorage.

The 6,908,540 acres of national forest—a little larger than New Hampshire—stretch across the Kenai Peninsula and Southcentral region, from southeast of Cordova to northwest of Seward. The diverse geography here includes the shorelines, glaciers, forests, and rivers of the Copper River delta, the Eastern Kenai Peninsula, and Prince William Sound.

GETTING HERE AND AROUND

Your best bet for getting around the area is by rental car. The Seward Highway between Anchorage and Seward has a number of trail access points. (Check the highway for mile markers, with the distance measured from Seward.) At Mile 64, just south of Turnagain Pass, is the turnoff to the Johnson Pass Trail, a relatively flat trail to walk. Seven miles farther south, take the Hope Highway 18 miles to its end and find the Porcupine Campground. From there the Gull Rock Trail follows the shore of Turnagain Arm for 5 miles, offering scenic views across the arm and the chance to spot beluga whales foraging for salmon. Farther south on the Seward Highway, at Mile 23, the Ptarmigan Creek Trail starts at the campground and climbs 3½ miles into the mountains, ending next to a lake surrounded by snowy peaks.

ESSENTIALS

VISITOR INFORMATION Alaska Public Lands Information Center ✉ *605 W. 4th Ave., Suite 105, Anchorage* ☎ *907/644–3661, 866/869–6887* ⊕ *www.alaska-centers.gov.* **Forest Headquarters** ✉ *161 E. 1st Ave., Anchorage* ☎ *907/743–9500 Anchorage* ⊕ *www.fs.usda.gov/chugach.*

◉ Sights

Chugach National Forest

FOREST | Sprawling east of Chugach State Park, Chugach National Forest encompasses nearly 6 million acres. The forest covers most of the Kenai Peninsula and parts of Prince William Sound, and is the second-largest national forest in the United States, exceeded in size only by the Tongass in Southeast Alaska. The forest has abundant recreational opportunities: hiking, camping, backpacking, fishing, boating, mountain biking, horseback riding, hunting, and flightseeing.

Southcentral Alaska is not the best terrain for rock climbing (aside from Denali), as the rock is predominantly composed of hardened ocean sediments that are weak and crumbly. There are, however, some places for great bouldering, and in the wintertime ice climbing is quite popular, as are snowshoeing, skiing, snowmachining, and dog mushing. Hiking trails offer easy access into the heart of the forest. You can spend a day hiking or looking for wildlife, or you can embark on a multiday backpacking excursion. At all but the most popular trailheads a five-minute stroll down a wooded trail can introduce you to the sights, smells, and tranquility of backcountry Alaska. Be prepared to be self-sufficient when entering Chugach Forest. Trailheads typically offer nothing more than a place to park and perhaps an outhouse. Running water, trail maps, and other amenities are not available. Also, be "bear aware" whenever you travel in bear country—and all of Alaska is bear country. ⊕ *www. fs.usda.gov/chugach.*

🏃 Activities

Crow Pass Trail
HIKING/WALKING | This 26-mile backpacking trail begins outside Girdwood and ends at the Eagle River Nature Center. Part of the Historic Iditarod Trail, Crow Pass is a truly great hike. The first 3 miles are the most strenuous—after that the worst things hikers have to contend with are snow above the tree line and icy-cold river crossings. During summer in Alaska it's wise to cross through rivers only in the morning to avoid the rising waters throughout the day as snow and glaciers melt under the many hours of sunshine. In addition to offering splendid views, Crow Pass Trail winds around the front of the amazing Raven Glacier terminus. The glacier is ½ mile wide and more than 2 miles long, with many deep crevasses. You can camp anywhere along the trail, though it's important to know that

camping near the glacier, even at the peak of summer, is a chilly endeavor. The one cabin along the trail sits above the tree line at 3,500 feet, just across from rich crystalline-blue Crystal Lake. The cabin is almost always booked at least six months in advance. ☎ *877/444–6777 cabin reservations* ⊕ *www.fs.usda.gov/ chugach.*

Resurrection Pass Trail
HIKING/WALKING | Its colorful summer wildflowers are the big draw of this 39-mile backpacking trail through the Chugach National Forest. There's also a chance to spot wildlife: moose, caribou, Dall sheep, mountain goats, black and brown bears, wolves, coyotes, and lynx all traverse the forest. The trail's northern leg starts south of the town of Hope, following an old mining trail through the Kenai Mountains to its end near Cooper Landing. The trail branches off at one point to the Devil's Pass trailhead along the Seward Highway. Besides cabins, the U.S. Forest Service has provided several "official" campsites along the trail, where you'll find a cleared patch of ground and a fire ring. You are free, however, to pitch your tent wherever you'd like to. ✉ *Resurrection Creek Rd* ⊹ *At Mile 15 Hope Highway in Hope, turn south onto Resurrection Creek Road, then drive 4 miles to trailhead parking* ⊕ *www.fs.usda.gov/ chugach* 🖾 *Free.*

🏨 Hotels

U.S. Forest Service Cabins
$ | **RENTAL** | Along trails, near wilderness alpine lakes, in coastal forests, and on saltwater beaches, these rustic cabins offer retreats for solo hikers or groups. **Pros:** remote locations; cheap prices; beautiful surroundings. **Cons:** extremely basic; often booked months in advance for summer; mice often inhabit them. $ *Rooms from: $65* ☎ *877/444–6777 reservations* ⊕ *www.recreation.gov* 🛏 *41 cabins* ⏺️ *No meals.*

Valdez

6 hours northeast of Whittier by water, 304 miles east of Anchorage.

Valdez (pronounced val- *deez*) is the largest of the Prince William Sound communities. This year-round ice-free port was the entry point for people and goods going to the Interior during the gold rush. Today that flow has been reversed, as Valdez Harbor is the southern terminus of the Trans-Alaska Pipeline, which carries crude oil from Prudhoe Bay and surrounding oil fields nearly 800 miles to the north. This region, with its dependence on commercial fishing, is still feeling the aftereffects of the 1989 massive oil spill that released 11 million gallons of oil into Prince William Sound. Much of Valdez looks modern, because the business area was relocated and rebuilt after its destruction by the 1964 Good Friday earthquake. Even though the town is younger than the rest of developed Alaska, it's quickly acquiring a lived-in look especially due to its extreme annual snowfall.

Many Alaskan communities have summer fishing derbies, but Valdez may hold the record for the number of such contests, stretching from late May into September for halibut and various runs of salmon. If you go fishing, by all means enter the appropriate derby. Every summer the newspapers run sob stories about tourists who landed possible prizewinners but couldn't share in the glory (or sizable cash rewards) because they hadn't forked over the five bucks to officially enter the contest. The **Valdez Silver Salmon Derby** is held the entire month of August. Fishing charters abound in this area of Prince William Sound, and for good reason: these fertile waters provide some of the best saltwater sportfishing in all of Alaska.

GETTING HERE AND AROUND

Valdez is road-accessible, and the 304-mile drive from Anchorage is stunning if a bit long to do in one day. The Richardson Highway portion of the drive takes you through Thompson Pass, high alpine country with 360-degree views. As you approach the town, the road descends into a steep canyon with rushing waterfalls—a popular ice-climbing destination in winter. Valdez's port is a stop on the Alaska Marine Highway, from which you can also sail to Cordova and Whittier. There's also a commercial airport.

The downtown is above the harbor, and two main avenues—Hazelet and Meals—run north–south with smaller streets branching off.

ESSENTIALS

RENTAL CARS Valdez U-Drive ✉ *300 Airport Rd.* ☎ *907/835–4402* ⊕ *www. valdezudrive.com.*

VISITOR AND TOUR INFORMATION
Valdez Visitor's Center ✉ *309 Fairbanks Dr.* ☎ *907/835–2984* ⊕ *www.valdezalaska. org.*

◉ Sights

Columbia Glacier

NATURE SITE | A visit to Columbia Glacier, which flows from the surrounding Chugach Mountains, should definitely be on your Valdez agenda. Its deep aquamarine face is 5 miles across, and it calves icebergs with resounding cannonades. This glacier is one of the largest and most readily accessible of Alaska's coastal glaciers. The state ferry travels past its face, and scheduled tours of the glaciers and the rest of the sound are available by boat and aircraft from Valdez, Cordova, and Whittier. ✉ *Valdez* ⊕ *www.alaska.org/ detail/columbia-glacier.*

Maxine & Jesse Whitney Museum

MUSEUM | This museum contains one of the largest collections of Alaska Native artifacts. Over the course of several decades, Maxine Whitney, a gift-shop owner,

195

The Kenai Peninsula and Southcentral Alaska VALDEZ

5

amassed the ivory and baleen pieces, masks, dolls, fur garments, and other objects on display. Whitney donated her collection to Prince William Sound Community College in 1998; the museum is adjacent to the college. ⊠ *Prince William Community College, 303 Lowe St.* ☎ *907/834–1690* ⊕ *mjwhitneymuseum. org* ✉ *Free* ◷ *Closed Oct.–Apr.*

Valdez Museum & Historical Archive

MUSEUM | FAMILY | The museum has two sections, the Egan and the Hazelet, named after their respective streets. The highlights of the Hazelet include a 35- by 40-foot model of what Old Town looked like before the 1964 earthquake and artifacts of the historic event that registered 9.5 on the Richter scale. An award-winning film that screens often describes the quake. Two blocks away, the Egan explores the lives, livelihoods, and events significant to Valdez and surrounding regions. On display are a restored 1880s Gleason & Baily hand-pump fire engine, a 1907 Ahrens steam fire engine, and a 19th-century saloon, and there are exhibits about local Alaska Native culture, early explorers, bush pilots, and the 1989 oil spill. Every summer the museum hosts an exhibit of quilts and fiber arts made by local and regional artisans, and other exhibits are presented seasonally. ⊠ *217 Egan Dr.* ☎ *907/835–2764 Egan Dr., 907/835–407 S. Hazelet Ave.* ⊕ *www. valdezmuseum.org* ✉ *$9.*

🏃 Activities

ADVENTURE EXCURSIONS
Alaska Backcountry Adventure Tours

TOUR—SPORTS | This company can create any number of adventure tours that will take you just about anywhere an ATV or snowmachine can go just outside of Valdez. With single or multiday trips, you can explore mile after mile of untouched wilderness and snow. The trips are tailored to all levels of experience. ⊠ *Palmer* ☎ *800/478–2506, 907/745–2505* ⊕ *www. snowmobile-alaska.com* ✉ *From $155.*

Alaska River Wrangellers

FISHING | An hour outside of Wrangell St. Elias, the Wrangellers offers a variety of sportfishing excursions. This is an excellent way to explore the scenic waterways of the Copper and Tonsina rivers, and a chance to catch the various types of salmon and rainbow trout that call these waterways home. This outfit holds a special permit that allows catching king salmons into August. ⊠ *McCarthy* ☎ *888/822–3967* ⊕ *www. riverwrangellers.com* ✉ *From $225 per person.*

Anadyr Adventures

TOUR—SPORTS | For more than a quarter century this company has led sea-kayak trips into Alaska's most spectacular wilderness, Prince William Sound. Guides will escort you on day trips, multiday camping trips, "mother ship" adventures based in a remote anchorage, or lodge-based trips for the ultimate combination of adventure by day and comfort by night. If you're already an experienced kayaker, Anadyr will outfit you and you can travel on your own. Also available are guided hiking and glacier trips, ice caving at Valdez Glacier, soft-adventure charter-boat trips in the sound, and water-taxi service to or from anywhere on the eastern side of the sound. ⊠ *225 N. Harbor Dr.* ☎ *907/835–2814, 800/865–2925* ⊕ *www.anadyradventures.com* ✉ *Day trips from $79.*

Dean Cummings' H2O Guides

TOUR—SPORTS | Top-notch heli-skiing and snowboarding experiences are H2O's specialty. For more than two decades, this company has been providing access to an amazing 150-square-mile playground. ⊠ *Valdez* ☎ *907/835–8418* ⊕ *www.alaskahelicopterskiing.com.*

Pangaea Adventures

KAYAKING | Since 1996, Pangaea has been navigating the aquatic world surrounding Valdez with guided trips via kayak, raft, sailboat, and water taxi. They also offer multiday hiking and camping adventure trips. ⊠ *Valdez* ☎ *907/835–8442, 800/660–9637* ⊕ *www.alaskasummer. com* 🍽 *From $109.*

Vertical Solutions Helicopter Flightseeing
FLYING/SKYDIVING/SOARING | These copters deliver a bird's-eye view of Prince William Sound, Valdez, and the Columbia Glacier. They also provide heli-taxi services and glacier landings—an exciting way to experience this amazing place. All the helicopters have big bubble windows, maximizing the viewing pleasure. ⊠ *290 Airport Rd.* ☎ *907/831–0643* ⊕ *www. vshelicopters.com* 🍽 *$250.*

BOATING AND WILDLIFE VIEWING
Lu-Lu Belle Glacier Wildlife Tours
BOATING | The "Limousine of the Prince William Sound," Valdez-based *Lu-Lu Belle* sets sail on small-group whale-watching and wildlife-viewing cruises that also goes up close to the massive Columbia Glacier. Cruises last about seven hours. There's a snack bar on board, but it's good to pack a lunch, too. ⊠ *Valdez* ☎ *800/411–0090* ⊕ *www.lulubelletours. com* 🍽 *$140.*

Sound Eco Adventures
AIR EXCURSIONS | Woman-owned and -operated, Sound Eco can guide you through Prince William Sound almost any way possible. From helicopter to kayak, whale watching to hiking adventures, the company employs a team of expert navigators well versed in the history, flora, and fauna of the region. The boat is fitted with an eco-friendly outboard engine, and trips are limited to six to minimize the environmental impact. ⊠ *Valdez* ☎ *907/835–8687* ⊕ *www.soundecoad-ventures.com* 🍽 *From $75.*

Stan Stephens Glacier & Wildlife Cruises
BOATING | This outfit conducts two different Prince William Sound glacier and wildlife-viewing tours. The nine-hour Meares Glacier Excursion takes in the glacier but also detours to spots where orcas, harbor seals, and other sea creatures are often sighted. Lunch and late-afternoon soup are provided. A light snack is served on the seven-hour Columbia Glacier Cruise, which also makes wildlife-viewing stops. Both tours include commentary about local commercial-fishing operations, the Alyeska Pipeline terminal, the 1964 earthquake, and defunct gold mines. ⊠ *Valdez* ☎ *866/867–1297* ⊕ *www.stanstephen-scruises.com* 🍽 *$165 Meares tour, $132 Columbia tour.*

🍴 Restaurants

A Rogue's Garden
$ | CAFÉ | For a quarter century, this downtown natural foods store has been serving Valdez and its visitors espresso and organic coffees, delicious fresh-baked goods, and fruit smoothies. There's also a sandwich bar for paninis and soups made from scratch. **Known for:** best lunch destination in town; fresh rustic bread; great selection of natural foods and kitchen items. ⑤ *Average main: $10* ⊠ *354 Fairbanks St.* ☎ *907/835–5880* ⊕ *www. roguesgarden.com* ⊗ *Closed Sun.*

Fat Mermaid
$$ | SEAFOOD | This funky waterfront eatery delivers tasty breakfast, lunch, and dinner dining year-round indoors as well as outside on a smoke-free patio on warm summer days. The menu includes gourmet pizzas, Alaskan seafood, burgers, and several healthy options. **Known for:** 15 craft beers on tap; great specialty cocktails; outside harbor-view seating. ⑤ *Average main: $20* ⊠ *143 N. Harbor Dr.* ☎ *907/835–3000* ⊕ *www.thefatmermaid. com.*

MacMurray's Alaska Halibut House
$$ | SEAFOOD | At this very casual family-owned establishment you order at the counter, sit at the Formica-covered tables, and check out the photos of local fishing boats. The battered halibut is excellent—light and not greasy. **Known for:** old-school fish-and-chips; relaxed atmosphere; amazing fried halibut. ⑤ *Average main: $15* ⊠ *208 Meals Ave.* ☎ *907/835–2788* ⊗ *Closed Sun.*

Old Town Burgers

$$ | BURGER | Not every burger is created equal, and the cooks at Old Town are dead set to prove it with its collection of Hawaiian burgers, mushroom burgers, and cheeseburgers. This restaurant favored by locals also serves up food for those seeking Alaska-specific fare such as halibut sandwiches, halibut and chips, and fried salmon (perhaps the only place in the state where you can find that). **Known for:** enormous portions of breakfast plates; best burgers in town; delicious curly fries. ⑤ *Average main: $15* ✉ *139 E. Pioneer Dr.* ☎ *907/461–8335.*

Roadside Potatohead Valdez

$$ | AMERICAN | This cozy little converted house overlooks the harbor and is the go-to place for locals in the summer. Whether it's for breakfast, lunch, or dinner, they're all about the potato—be sure to try the potatohead burrito or the spuds with gravy. **Known for:** excellent breakfast burritos; tastiest fries for hundreds of miles; all things potatoes. ⑤ *Average main: $10* ✉ *225 North Harbor Dr.* ☎ *907/835–3058* ⊕ *www.theroadside-potatohead.com* ⊙ *Closed Oct.–Apr.*

🛏 Hotels

If you roll into town without reservations, especially if it's after hours, stop at the Valdez Convention and Visitors Bureau on the corner of Fairbanks. It posts vacancies in bed-and-breakfasts on the window when it closes for the day.

Best Western Valdez Harbor Inn

$$$ | HOTEL | Near the harbor, this hotel comes complete with views of mountains, sea otters, seals, and waterfowl. **Pros:** lovely location on an inlet; great views; very clean. **Cons:** standard-issue decor; some rooms are cramped; hot water is inconsistent. ⑤ *Rooms from: $198* ✉ *100 Harbor Dr.* ☎ *907/835–3434, 888/222–3440* ⊕ *www.valdezharborinn.com* ⇥ *88 rooms* ❏ *Breakfast.*

Mountain Sky Hotel and Suites

$$$ | HOTEL | This hotel is within easy walking distance of shops, restaurants, and the small boat harbor, the center of summertime activity in Valdez. **Pros:** decent amenities; quiet; convenient location. **Cons:** not much personality; on-site eatery is inconsistent; rooms don't have air-conditioning. ⑤ *Rooms from: $189* ✉ *100 Meals Ave.* ☎ *800/478–4445* ⊕ *www.mountainskyhotel.com* ⇥ *101 rooms* ❏ *No meals.*

★ Prince William Sound Lodge

$$$$ | B&B/INN | This fly-in lodge on a remote shore of northeastern Prince William Sound offers a range of vacation activities, including hiking, kayaking, bird-watching, wildlife viewing, and great silver salmon fishing (August 20–September 15). **Pros:** gourmet meals; incredible location; excellent hospitality. **Cons:** remote, fly-in location; cash or check only; no light-blocking shades on cabin windows. ⑤ *Rooms from: $325* ✉ *Valdez* ☎ *907/440–0909* ⊕ *www.princewilliamsound.us* ⊟ *No credit cards* ⊙ *Closed late Sept. 15–Apr.* ⇥ *5 rooms* ❏ *All meals.*

Tsaina Lodge

$$$$ | RESORT | This is no ordinary Alaska lodge—it's more like a sleek, modern, adventure base camp. **Pros:** very clean; excellent views; good on-site dining. **Cons:** expensive; rooms a bit small; shared balconies. ⑤ *Rooms from: $279* ✉ *Mile 35 Richardson Hwy.* ☎ *907/835–3535* ⊕ *www.tsainalodge.com* ⇥ *24 rooms.*

Cordova

6 hours southeast of Valdez by water, 150 miles east of Anchorage by air.

A small town with the spectacular backdrop of snowy Mt. Eccles, Cordova is the gateway to the Copper River delta—one of the great birding areas of North America. Originally named Puerto

Cordova by Spanish explorer Salvador Fidalgo in 1790, this peaceful fishing town of approximately 2,300 inhabitants is perched at the head of the Orca Inlet in eastern Prince William Sound. Early in the 20th century, Cordova became the port city for the Copper River and Northwestern Railway, which was built to serve the Kennicott Copper mines 191 miles away in the Wrangell Mountains. Since the mines and the railroad shut down in 1938, Cordova's economy has depended heavily on fishing. Attempts to develop a road along the abandoned railroad line connecting to the state highway system were dashed by the 1964 earthquake, so Cordova remains isolated, accessible only by plane or ferry.

GETTING HERE AND AROUND

Take the scenic ferry or a water taxi from either Whittier or Valdez along the Alaska Marine Highway, or catch a commercial flight from Anchorage (on Ravn Alaska or Alaska Air) or Juneau via Yakutat (Alaska Air). If taking the ferry from Valdez, be sure your operator points out Bligh Reef—it's where the *Exxon Valdez* oil spill occurred, along with numerous other shipwrecks.

Once in Cordova, the center of town is foot-friendly. But you'll want some wheels for heading down the Copper River Highway, a scenic drive to the Copper River delta, the largest contiguous wetlands along the Pacific Coast in North America, and a temporary refueling station for 5 million migrating shorebirds every May.

ESSENTIALS

FERRY INFORMATION Alaska Marine Highway ✉ *6858 Glacier Hwy., Juneau* ☎ *800/642–0066* ⊕ *www.ferryalaska. com.*

RENTAL CARS Chinook Auto Rentals ✉ *Cordova Airport, Mile 13, Copper River Hwy.* ☎ *877/424–5279* ⊕ *www.chinookautorentals.com.*

VISITOR INFORMATION Cordova Chamber of Commerce ✉ *404 1st St.* ☎ *907/424–7260* ⊕ *www.cordovachamber.com.*

◉ Sights

Copper River Delta

NATURE PRESERVE | This 35-mile-wide wetlands complex east of Cordova, a crucial habitat for millions of migratory birds on the Pacific Flyway, is one of North America's most spectacular vistas. The delta's nearly 700,000 acres are thick with marshes, forests, streams, lakes, and ponds. Numerous terrestrial mammals including moose, wolves, lynx, mink, and beavers live here, and the Copper River salmon runs are world-famous. When the red and king salmon hit the river in spring, there's a frantic rush to net the tasty fish and rush them off to markets and restaurants all over the country. The delta is connected by the Million Dollar Bridge, an impressive feat of engineering notable for its latticework. The Forest Service built an impressive viewing pavilion across the Copper River from **Childs Glacier**—famous for the spectacle of its calving icebergs and tidal waves—but in 2011 a natural change in the river's flow compromised a bridge at Mile 36. There had been plans for reconstruction at one time, but due to budgetary constraints and lack of political interest, efforts to rebuild the bridge have been swept off the table indefinitely. The only way to see the glacier now is to book a boat tour out of Cordova or float 100 miles or so from upriver. The difficulty of getting here has not been a deterrent, however, as visitors from all over the world still come just to see the awe-inspiring glacier. However, in recent years, the glacier no longer calves with much frequency due to receding and the lowering of river waters. ✉ *Copper River Hwy.*

Cordova Museum

MUSEUM | Exhibits at the Cordova Museum document early explorers to the area, Alaska Native culture, the Kennicott Mine and Copper River and Northwestern Railway era, and the growth of the commercial fishing industry. An informative brochure outlines a self-guided walking tour of the town's historic buildings. The gift shop sells local postcards, Cordova and Alaskan gifts, and regional history books. ⊠ *622 1st St.* ☎ *907/424–6665* ⊕ *www.cordovamuseum.org* ✉ *$1* ☉ *Closed Mon. and Tues.*

Activities

Alaganik Slough

BIRD WATCHING | A dedicated bird-watcher can spend hours at Alaganik Slough peering into the vegetation, seeking out interesting avian species. A 5-mile road off the Copper River Highway leads to a wheelchair-accessible boardwalk as well as covered viewing shelters, restrooms, and picnic areas. ⊠ *Turnoff at Mile 17, Copper River Hwy.*

Alaskan Wilderness Outfitting Company

TOUR—SPORTS | This outfit operates an air-taxi service out of Cordova and arranges fresh- and saltwater fly-out fishing experiences. Services range from drop-offs to guided tours with lodge accommodations. Alaskan Wilderness also provides access to floating cabins in Prince William Sound, a private fly-in cabin in Wrangell–St. Elias, and a full-service lodge for silver salmon fishing on the Tsiu River. ⊠ *Cordova* ☎ *907/424–5552* ⊕ *www.alaskawilderness.com* ✉ *Call for prices.*

Copper River Delta

BIRD WATCHING | Spring migration to the Copper River Delta provides some of the finest avian spectacles in the world. Species include the western sandpiper, American dipper, orange-crowned warbler, and short-billed dowitcher. Trumpeter swans and dusky Canada geese can also be viewed. ⊠ *Cordova.*

Cordova Air Services

TOUR—SPORTS | The service conducts aerial tours of Prince William Sound on planes with wheels or floats. ⊠ *Cordova* ☎ *907/424–3289.*

★ Riverside Inn & Airboat Tours

TOUR—SPORTS | Lifelong Alaskans Jack and Cherrie Stevenson own one of the only permitted Cordova outfitters currently taking visitors to Childs Glacier. You have to get yourself to Mile 36, where the road comes to a halt at the river. From there, the first part of the trip takes place aboard a large airboat (if the water is high enough) that crosses the raging Copper River. You are then driven the rest of the way to the glacier, where you can spend a day hiking the area's many trails or just staring at ice that soars to heights of 300 feet. ⊠ *Cordova* ☎ *907/424–7135* ⊕ *www.riversideinncordova.com* ✉ *Tours $150 per person, 4-person minimum.*

🍴 Restaurants

Anchor Bar & Grill

$$ | **BURGER** | A fisherman's bar, the Anchor is built for appetites and not ambience. There's a great deck outside overlooking the water, though, and the burgers and sandwiches—enormous, delicious, and made with fresh bread—are all the rage in Cordova. **Known for:** fresh-made bread and hamburger buns; genuine local hangout; beautiful outdoor seating with lake views. ⑤ *Average main: $15* ⊠ *207 Breakwater Ave.* ☎ *907/424–3262.*

Baja Taco

$ | **MEXICAN** | A funky bus turned food stand with an attached dining room, Baja Taco serves creative Tex-Mex dishes. Some come with a little added Alaskan pizzazz like the halibut-cheek tacos or the fish of the day. **Known for:** super groovy school bus kitchen; best salsas and tacos in the region; location right next to the water. ⑤ *Average main: $12* ⊠ *1 Harbor Loop Rd.* ☎ *907/424–5599* ⊕ *www.bajatacoak.com* ☉ *Closed Sept.–May.*

Did You Know?

Real glacier drama happens in Prince William Sound. The area has the highest concentration of calving tidewater glaciers in the state, and so it's your best chance to see glaciers calving (that's when pieces of the glacier break off into the water, creating a thunderous sound).

OK Restaurant

$$ | **CHINESE** | This Asian food dining destination specializing in Chinese and Korean cuisine is a favorite with locals who want a little diversity in their palate. OK is particularly known for its outstanding Mongolian beef and fresh sushi in summer. **Known for:** only Asian eatery that doesn't require a boat ride; fantastic interiors; delicious homemade kimchi. $ *Average main: $19* ⊠ *616 1st St.* ☎ *907/424–3433.*

Powder House Bar and Grill

$$$ | **SEAFOOD** | On clear summer evenings, you can relax on this roadside bar's deck overlooking Eyak Lake and enjoy whatever the cook's in the mood to make. Located inside a former storage shed for railroad explosives, this place serves homemade soups, burgers, and sushi (on Fridays); seasonal seafood including shrimp, scallops, razor clams, and whatever else is fresh, is also available every night. **Known for:** rustic charm; scenic mountain views from the back porch; fantastic burger specials. $ *Average main: $25* ⊠ *Mile 2.1, Copper River Hwy.* ☎ *907/424–3529.*

Reluctant Fisherman Restaurant

$$$ | **SEAFOOD** | This restaurant is about the closest thing to fine dining in Cordova, and it's generally packed with tourists, fishermen, and locals who appreciate both the food and the drinks. Each summer, the chef blows the menu up with something new and fabulous, but you're guaranteed to find a number of excellent fish dishes always fresh and right off the fishing boats. **Known for:** great outdoor seating; location next to the boat docks; ceviche and grilled salmon. $ *Average main: $25* ⊠ *407 Railroad Ave.* ☎ *907/424–3272* ⊕ *www.reluctant-fisherman.com.*

 Hotels

Northern Nights Inn

$$ | **B&B/INN** | Commanding a dramatic view of Orca Inlet a few blocks from downtown Cordova, this turn-of-the-20th-century inn has three roomy suites and one "sleeping room" furnished with antiques. **Pros:** great location; big bright rooms; suites have full kitchens. **Cons:** three rooms accessible only by stairs; no Wi-Fi; views aren't great. $ *Rooms from: $125* ⊠ *500 3rd St.* ☎ *907/424–5356* ⊕ *www.northernnightsinn.com* ⇆ *4 rooms.*

★ Orca Adventure Lodge

$$ | **B&B/INN** | This converted cannery at the end of the road offers a peek into what life in the region must have been like in the 1880s. **Pros:** full slate of amenities, including outdoor activities; views include sea otters congregating outside; great food. **Cons:** 3 miles outside of town; no television; dim lighting in rooms. $ *Rooms from: $165* ⊠ *301 Orca Rd.* ☎ *907/424–7249, 866/424–6722* ⊕ *www.orcaadventurelodge.com* ⊗ *Restaurant closed Oct.–May* ⇆ *38 rooms.*

Reluctant Fisherman Inn

$$ | **HOTEL** | At this waterfront fisherman's hotel you can watch the commercial-fishing fleet and other maritime traffic sail by. **Pros:** perfect location in the heart of Cordova; great view of the marina or the mountains; clean and comfortable rooms. **Cons:** rooms on north side can be noisy with nightlife activity; no kitchen amenities; only harbor-view rooms have balconies. $ *Rooms from: $174* ⊠ *407 Railroad Ave.* ☎ *907/424–3272* ⊕ *www.reluctantfisherman.com* ⇆ *41 rooms* ❍l *Breakfast.*

U.S. Forest Service Cabins

$ | **RENTAL** | The Cordova Ranger District of the Chugach National Forest maintains a series of simple backcountry cabins for rent. **Pros:** beautiful and remote; affordable; perfect for experiencing true wilderness. **Cons:** you must be self-sufficient and comfortable in the wilderness; zero amenities (including running water); must be booked six months in advance. $ *Rooms from: $75* ⊠ *Cordova* ☎ *877/444–6777* ⊕ *www.recreation.gov* ⇆ *17 cabins.*

Shopping

Copper River Fleece

CLOTHING | All over Southcentral you'll find locals sporting American-made fleece hoodies, jackets, vests, and hats with decorative trim featuring Tglingit and Haida designs. Cordova resident Jennifer Park designed the clothing and commissioned Alaska Native artist Michael Webber to create the trim. Found in many souvenir shops around the state, they can also be purchased online—but the only outlet store for these nifty articles of clothing is in Cordova. ⊠ *504 1st St.* ☎ *800/882–1707* ⊕ *www.copperriver-fleece.com.*

Hope

88 miles south of Anchorage, 74 miles north of Seward.

The little gold-mining community of Hope sits just across Turnagain Arm from Anchorage. To visit, however, you must drive the 88 miles all the way around the arm. Your reward is a quiet little community that is accessible to but not overrun by tourists. Miners founded Hope in 1896, and the old log cabins and weathered frame buildings in the town center are favorite photography subjects. In its peak, Hope had a population of 3,000. Now, according to the 2010 census, there are just 192 residents. You'll find gold-panning, fishing, and hiking opportunities here, and the northern trailhead for the 39-mile-long Resurrection Pass Trail is nearby. Contact the U.S. Forest Service for information on campgrounds, cabin rentals, and hikes in the area.

GETTING HERE AND AROUND

The only way to get to Hope is by car. Head south on the Seward Highway out of Anchorage. About 40 miles past the Girdwood turnoff look for the Hope exit. From there a two-lane road meanders through the forest for 16 miles before ending in the town center.

Activities

MOUNTAIN BIKING

The Kenai Peninsula offers outstanding opportunities for mountain bikers seeking thigh-busting challenges amid extraordinary scenery. **Crescent Creek Trail** (at Mile 44.9 of Sterling Highway; drive 3 miles to the trailhead at end of gravel road); **Devil's Pass** (at Mile 39½ of Seward Highway); **Johnson Pass** (at Miles 32.6 and 63.7 of Seward Highway); and the **Resurrection Pass trail systems** offer miles of riding for a wide range of expertise. Cyclists here are subject to highly fickle mountain weather patterns. But remember that you're never really alone in wild Alaska: be sure to bring along bear spray and bug dope (repellent). For maps and descriptions of trails, visit the website of the state's Department of Natural Resources. ⊕ *www.dnr.alaska.gov.*

Restaurants

Creekbend Cafe

$$ | **AMERICAN** | This locally beloved roadhouse diner, formerly known as Tito's Discovery Café, serves remarkably fresh salads, delicious sandwiches, and is, notably, the only place in town open for breakfast. They are also known for extraordinary homemade pies. **Known for:** roadside stop perfect for breakfast; incredible homemade pies and pastries; fantastic outdoor concert venue. Ⓢ *Average main: $15* ⊠ *Mile 16½, 19842 Hope Hwy.* ☎ *907/782–3274* ☉ *Closed Oct.–mid-May.*

Hotels

Bowman's Bear Creek Lodge

$$ | **B&B/INN** | This lodge is comprised of seven cabins either situated around a pond or creekside. **Pros:** excellent food at restaurant; nightly campfire around the pond; very peaceful. **Cons:** some cabins have shared bathhouse; 16 miles off the main highway; no cable or television. Ⓢ *Rooms from: $200* ⊠ *Mile 15.9, Hope*

Hwy. ☎ 907/782–3141 ⊕ www.bow-mansbearcreeklodge.com ↪ 5 cabins.

Seaview Cafe & Bar

$ | RENTAL | True to its name, this rustic little establishment in the original Hope town site offers great views of the Arm and the Chugach. **Pros:** charming historic location; scenic surroundings; true Alaskan lodging experience. **Cons:** cabins are rustic; no running water; outhouses only. ⑤ Rooms from: $60 ✉ Main St., Box 110 ☎ 907/782–3300 ⊕ www.seaviewcafe-alaska.com ▭ No credit cards ☽ Closed mid-Sept.–mid-May ↪ 50 tent sites, 16 RV sites, 2 cabins.

🛍 Shopping

Sherritt Fine Art Gallery

ART GALLERIES | This cozy gallery space exhibits Scott Sherritt's Alaska-influenced paintings, as well as those of other Alaska artists. ✉ 2nd and B. Sts. ☎ 907/782–3436 ☽ Closed Oct.–Apr. and Sun.

Seward

74 miles south of Hope, 127 miles south of Anchorage.

It is hard to believe that a place as beautiful as Seward exists. Surrounded on all sides by Kenai Fjords National Park, Chugach National Forest, and Resurrection Bay, Seward offers all the quaint realities of a small railroad town with the bonus of jaw-dropping scenery. This little town of about 2,750 citizens was founded in 1903, when survey crews arrived at the ice-free port and began planning a railroad to the Interior. Since its inception, Seward has relied heavily on tourism and commercial fishing. It is also the launching point for excursions into Kenai Fjords National Park, where it is quite common to see marine life and calving glaciers.

GETTING HERE AND AROUND

As a cruise-ship port, Seward has several routes in and out. Arrive by boat via the Alaska Marine Highway, or from Anchorage take a luxury Ultradome railcar, or drive the 127 miles from Anchorage. Although there's a small airport, only private planes use it. It's possible to walk around town or from the harbor to downtown, or hop onto the free shuttle that runs during summer.

ESSENTIALS

VISITOR AND TOUR INFORMATION
Seward Chamber of Commerce ✉ 2001 Seward Hwy. ☎ 907/224–8051 ⊕ www.seward.com.

👁 Sights

★ Alaska SeaLife Center

ZOO | FAMILY | A research center as well as visitor center, Alaska SeaLife rehabilitates injured marine wildlife and provides educational experiences for the general public. The facility includes massive cold-water tanks and outdoor viewing decks as well as interactive displays of cold-water fish, seabirds, and marine mammals, including harbor seals and a 2,000-pound sea lion. The center was partially funded with reparations money from the Exxon Valdez oil spill. Films, hands-on activities, a gift shop, and behind-the-scenes tours where you can interract with different animals ($74.95) complete the offerings. ✉ 301 Railway Ave. ☎ 907/224–6300, 800/224–2525 ⊕ www.alaskasealife.org ▭ $25.

Iditarod Trail

TRAIL | The first mile of the historic original trail—at first called the Seward-to-Nome Mail Trail—runs along the beach and makes for a nice, easy stroll. ✉ Seward.

Lowell Point

LOCAL INTEREST | If you drive south from the Alaska SeaLife Center, after about 10 minutes you'll reach Lowell Point, a wooded stretch of land along the bay with access to beach walking, hiking, and

Kenai Peninsula and Kodiak Island

kayaking. This is a great day-trip destination, and camping is an option. ✉ *Lowell Point Rd.*

Nash Road

VIEWPOINT | For a different view of the town, drive out Nash Road, around Resurrection Bay, and look down at Seward, nestled at the base of the surrounding mountains like a young bird in its nest. ✉ *Seward* ⊕ *www.alaska.org/detail/nash-road.*

Seward Community Library & Museum

LIBRARY | Seward's museum, community center, and library is a one-stop attraction, with the museum just downstairs from the library. The museum displays art by prominent Alaskan artists as well as relics from the past that weave together the stories of the gold rush, Russian settlements, and the upheaval created by the 1964 earthquake. A movie illustrating the disaster and one about the Iditarod Trail are played back-to-back daily ($4 suggested donation). ✉ *239 6th Ave.* ☎ *907/224–3902* ⊕ *www.cityofseward.us/libmus* 🎬 *Movie $5.*

 Activities

For more details on Kenai Fjords, see Kenai Fjords National Park.

ADVENTURE AND WILDLIFE VIEWING

Exit Glacier Guides

TOUR—SPORTS | This highly regarded outfit conducts tours of Exit Glacier, and not just to the moraine, where most tourists stop; the guides also lead travelers right onto the glacier. The company also offers guided hikes on the Harding Icefield, remote camping trips, and, for experienced climbers, backcountry heli- and fly-ins to remote peaks. ✉ *Seward* ☎ *907/224–5569* ⊕ *www.exitglacier-guides.com* 🎫 *From $80 (Exit Glacier and Harding Glacier Hike).*

BOATING

The Fish House

FISHING | This booking agency has a fleet of more than 40 Resurrection Bay and Kenai Peninsula fishing charters specializing in silver salmon and halibut fishing. You can book a half- or full-day charter (full-day only for halibut). The Fish House is also a supplier of tackle, gear, and clothing. ✉ *1303 4th Ave.* ☎ *907/224–3674, 800/257–7760* ⊕ *www.thefishhouse.net* 🎫 *From $199.*

Major Marine Tours

TOUR—SPORTS | This family-run operation has been offering aquatic tours of the fjords for more than 25 years. On board, a National Park Service ranger narrates the half- and full-day cruises of Resurrection Bay and Kenai Fjords National Park. For an additional price ($24), meals of salmon, prime rib, or vegetarian chili are available on the five- and six-hour cruises; all other trips include a deli-style lunch. Whether whale watching or glacier gazing, you're sure to have extraordinary wildlife sightings and awe-inspiring views. Major Marine can arrange transportation between Anchorage and Seward. ✉ *Seward* ☎ *907/274–7300, 800/764–7300* ⊕ *www.majormarine.com* 🎫 *From $84.*

DEEP-SEA FISHING

Crackerjack Sportfishing

FISHING | Crackerjack runs half-day salmon and full-day halibut fishing charters as well as two- to five-day fishing expeditions in Kenai Fjords National Park and beyond. The local captains have been guiding in Seward for years and offer trips year-round. ✉ *Seward* ☎ *800/566–3912* ⊕ *www.crackerjackcharters.com* 🎫 *From $235.*

HIKING

For a comprehensive listing of all the trails, cabins, and campgrounds in the Seward Ranger District of Chugach National Forest, check the website of the U.S. Forest Service (⊕ *www.fs.fed.us*).

Caines Head Trail

HIKING/WALKING | This 4½-mile trail that starts at Lowell Point allows easy, flat hiking south along the coast, but with a hitch. Much of the hike is over tidal mudflats, so care must be taken to time it correctly: with tides here running in the 10- to 20-foot range, bad planning isn't just a case of getting your feet wet. It's officially advised that the trail be hiked only when there's a "plus 4-foot tide or greater" in summer. Two cabins can be rented (call ahead to book) at Derby Cove and Callisto Canyon. ✉ *Seward* ☎ *877/444–6777.*

Lost Lake/Primrose Trail

HIKING/WALKING | A 16-mile end-to-end loop, the trail winds through spruce forests and up into the high alpine area. The Lost Lake trailhead is near Mile 5 of the Seward Highway, and the other end is at the Primrose campground, at Mile 17. The trails are steep and usually snow-covered through late June, but the views along the Lost Lake valley are worth the climb. Above the tree line you're in mountain-goat country—look for white, blocky figures perched precariously on the cliffs. The lake is a prime spot for rainbow trout fishing. As usual, be bear-aware. The Dale Clemens cabin, at Mile 4½ from the Lost Lake trailhead, has propane heat and a captivating view of Resurrection Bay. Cabins must be booked in advance. ✉ *Seward* ☎ *877/444–6777.*

KAYAKING

Kayak Adventures Worldwide

CANOEING/ROWING/SKULLING | Take a guided trip in sea kayaks from Kayak Adventures Worldwide, an outfit comprising a staff passionate about kayaking and the aquatic world. They offer half-day and full-day trips to Resurrection Bay and Aialik Bay. This Seward-based outfitter also runs multiday trips in Kenai Fjords, offers customized booking dates, teaches sea kayaking and safety skills, and is a great resource for weather updates and travel insurance. ✉ *328 3rd Ave.* ☎ *907/224–3960* ⊕ *www.kayakak.com* ✉ *From $75.*

Sunny Cove Sea Kayaking

KAYAKING | In the bay, around the islands or on a glacial lake, this outfitter offers multiday ($450) and single day ($70) excursions in the region known for its exemplary kayaking opportunities. ✉ *1304 4th Ave.* ☎ *907/224–4426* ⊕ *www.sunnycove.com* ✉ *From $75.*

🍴 Restaurants

Chinooks Bar

$$$ | SEAFOOD | Just about everything at this restaurant in the small-boat harbor is made on-site, from the salad dressings to the infused liquors in the inventive libations. The award-winning chef prepares only sustainable Alaskan seafood, and information is provided about where it comes from and when it's in season. **Known for:** fantastic cocktail menu; inventive fresh seafood dishes; upstairs seating with views of the harbor and mountains. $ *Average main: $25* ✉ *1404 4th Ave.* ☎ *907/224–2207* ⊕ *www.chinooksak.com* 🕐 *Closed Jan. and Feb.*

The Cookery

$$$ | AMERICAN | Featuring local oysters harvested daily along with locally sourced meats and vegetables, this eating and drinking establishment is a favorite. In addition to freshly shucked and broiled oysters, the Cookery is also known for its melding of flavors to make scrumptious and wildly popular dishes like the wild and tame mushroom toast. **Known for:** freshest oysters in town; beautiful food presentation; exceptional food for a small fishing town. $ *Average main: $25* ✉ *209 5th Ave.* ☎ *907/422–7459* ⊕ *www.cookeryseward.com.*

★ Le Barn Appétit

$$ | FRENCH FUSION | This little restaurant and inn serves some of the finest crepes in Alaska with options that range from savory like creamed beef and spinach to sweet like strawberries, Nutella, and whipped cream. The delightful proprietor is known to throw together fantastic French dinners for parties that call ahead, and if you're lucky, you'll also taste his quiche lorraine or chicken cordon bleu. **Known for:** best French crepes in Alaska; great hospitality; good for groups. ⓢ *Average main: $18* ✉ *11786 Old Exit Glacier Rd.* ☎ *907/224–8706* ⊕ *www.lebarnappetit.com* ☾ *No dinner (except by special advance reservation).*

Ms. Gene's Place

$$$ | **AMERICAN** | A charming, wood-paneled restaurant and Victorian lounge inside the 1905 Hotel Seward, Ms. Gene's serves breakfast and dinner year-round. The dinner menu changes weekly, though dishes such as seared ahi tuna, bacon-wrapped scallops, and grilled rib-eye steak appear frequently. **Known for:** romantic dining; historic hotel location; fantastic halibut cheeks dishes. ⓢ *Average main: $30* ✉ *221 5th Ave.* ☎ *907/224–6447* ⊕ *www.hotelsewardalaska.com* ☾ *Closed Mon. and Tues. No lunch and no dinner Sun.–Thurs.*

Railway Cantina

$$ | **MEXICAN** | Serving burritos and beer, this harbor-area hole-in-the-wall is locally renowned for its flavorful burritos, quesadillas, and great halibut and rockfish tacos. Various hot sauces, some contributed by customers who brought them from their travels, complement the fare. **Known for:** fantastic blackened halibut burrito; grab-and-go hot food; excellent hot sauce collection. ⓢ *Average main: $14* ✉ *1401 4th Ave.* ☎ *907/224–8226* ⊕ *www.railwaycantina.com* ▭ *No credit cards.*

Resurrection Roadhouse

$$$ | **AMERICAN** | Part of the Seward Windsong Lodge, the Roadhouse offers great food and a deck that overlooks the Resurrection River and the surrounding mountains. Standard Alaska seafood fare fills the menu, along with multiple Alaska-brewed beers on tap. **Known for:** quiet and away from town; outdoor seating with views of the mountains and Resurrection River; Alaskan microbrews. ⓢ *Average main: $25* ✉ *31772 Herman*

Leirer Rd., Mile ½, Exit Glacier Rd. ☎ *800/808–8068* ⊕ *www.sewardwindsong.com* ☾ *Closed mid-Sept.–mid-May.*

The Sea Bean Cafe

$ | **DELI** | Duck into this splendid café for a cup of tea or organic coffee, to stay or to go, and fine soups, wraps, and panini. The Sea Bean also has smoothies. **Known for:** vegetarian, vegan, and gluten-free options; great place to eat and read or work on your computer; grab-and-go options for those heading off on tours. ⓢ *Average main: $10* ✉ *225 4th Ave.* ☎ *907/224–6623* ⊕ *www.seabeancafe.com.*

Seward Brewing Company

$$ | **AMERICAN** | This two-story microbrewery serves up diverse and wildly unusual pub grub prepared with locally sourced ingredients. The restaurant's interior and exterior design blends rustic-chic, modern deco, and industrial elements, with two highlights being the high ceilings and enormous copper fish welded by a local artist. **Known for:** only locally brewed craft beer in town; mostly locally sourced ingredients; salted watermelon salad. ⓢ *Average main: $16* ✉ *139 4th Ave.* ☎ *907/422–0337* ⊕ *www.sewardbrewery.com.*

🛏 Hotels

Alaska Paddle Inn

$$ | **B&B/INN** | Located in the small community of Lowell Point, this inn has two rooms, a Main House, and a Spruce House, all of which have gorgeous water and mountain views. **Pros:** Resurrection Bay views; kitchenettes in inn rooms; waffle irons and mix in rooms. **Cons:** getting to the upstairs room requires climbing 20 steps; the inn fills up quickly so book well in advance; Main House does not have a private bedroom. ⓢ *Rooms from: $199* ✉ *13745 Beach Dr.* ☎ *907/362–2628* ⊕ *www.alaskapaddleinn.com* ⇄ *2 rooms, 1 cabin* ◉ *Breakfast.*

Breeze Inn

$$ | **HOTEL** | Across the street from the small-boat harbor, this modern 100-room hotel is very convenient if you're planning an early-morning fishing trip. **Pros:** walking distance to downtown; Wi-Fi available; free shuttle to nearby attractions and shopping. **Cons:** rooms are bland and chain motel–like; one section of the inn is older and a little more dated; can be busy. $ *Rooms from: $179* ✉ *1306 Seward Hwy.* ☎ *907/224–5237, 888/224–5237* ⊕ *www.breezeinn.com* ⇦ *100 rooms* ¶ *No meals.*

Hotel Edgewater

$$$ | **HOTEL** | The rooms at this hotel overlook Resurrection Bay, and on clear days the panorama of mountains, glaciers, and the bay is breathtaking. **Pros:** convenient to attractions, restaurants, and shops; breakfast included; comfortable rooms. **Cons:** more expensive than other waterfront lodgings in town; lacks local flare; not all rooms have balconies or views. $ *Rooms from: $280* ✉ *202 5th Ave.* ☎ *907/224–2700, 800/780–7234* ⊕ *www.hoteledgewater.com* ⊙ *Closed Oct.–Apr.* ⇦ *76 rooms* ¶ *Breakfast.*

Hotel Seward

$$ | **HOTEL** | Conveniently located downtown, the Seward is near restaurants, shopping, and the Alaska SeaLife Center. **Pros:** cool historic building; excellent downtown location; free access to gym next door. **Cons:** no elevator in one wing; shared bathrooms in older rooms; no free breakfast. $ *Rooms from: $159* ✉ *221 5th Ave.* ☎ *907/224–8001, 800/440–2444* ⊕ *www.hotelsewardalaska.com* ⇦ *62 rooms* ¶ *No meals.*

Kenai Fjords Wilderness Lodge

$$$$ | **RENTAL** | On a private parcel of land on Resurrection Bay's Fox Island, this beautiful retreat is only a 45-minute boat ride from Seward. **Pros:** tranquil setting; tremendous views; very comfortable beds. **Cons:** limited adventuring to be found on the island; no urban amenities; not the best food. $ *Rooms from: $520* ✉ *Fox Island* ☎ *800/808–8068* ⊕ *www.kenaifjordslodge.com* ⊙ *Closed Sept.–May* ⇦ *8 cabins* ¶ *All meals.*

Seward Windsong Lodge

$$ | **HOTEL** | In a thickly forested setting near the bank of the Resurrection River, this lodging 2 miles north of Seward has the feel of a mountain time-share cabin. **Pros:** incredible river valley views; on-site Resurrection Roadhouse is convenient for dining; away from the bustle of cruise ship pedestrians. **Cons:** outside town, so guests must rent a car or rely on the lodge's shuttle; has a corporate feel; many of the staff are uninformed of in-town destinations. $ *Rooms from: $172* ✉ *31772 Herman Leirer Rd., Mile ½, Exit Glacier Rd.* ☎ *907/265–4501, 800/808–8068* ⊕ *www.sewardwindsong.com* ⇦ *196 rooms* ¶ *No meals.*

Stoney Creek Inn

$$ | **B&B/INN** | Sandwiched between two streams—one glacial, the other salmon-on-spawning—this B&B about 6 miles outside Seward offers respite from the summer buzz. **Pros:** quiet location; not too far from town; has sauna and Jacuzzi. **Cons:** car might be necessary to get here; far from urban conveniences; decor a bit dated. $ *Rooms from: $150* ✉ *33422 Stoney Creek Ave.* ☎ *907/224–3940* ⊕ *www.stoneycreekinn.net* ⇦ *5 rooms* ¶ *Breakfast.*

★ Teddy's Inn the Woods

$$ | **B&B/INN** | A sole, beautifully decorated cabin nestled in the woods across from Kenai Lake, Teddy's is surrounded by mountains and hiking trails. **Pros:** fantastic setting; charming and hospitable owners; very clean and comfortable. **Cons:** nearest restaurant and grocery store are a bit of a drive away; lacks some urban amenities; so quiet at night it might be difficult for urban dwellers to sleep. $ *Rooms from: $120* ✉ *Mile 23, 29792 Seward Hwy.* ☎ *907/288–3126* ⊕ *www.seward.net/teddys* ⇦ *1 cabin* ¶ *Breakfast.*

Van Gilder Hotel

$$ | HOTEL | Built in 1916 and listed on the National Register of Historic Places, the Van Gilder is steeped in local history. **Pros:** historic site; entertaining decor; central location. **Cons:** shared kitchen; a little on the rustic side; shared bathrooms. ⑤ *Rooms from: $139* ✉ *308 Adams St.* ☎ *800/478–0400* ⊕ *www.vangilderseward.com* ⇗ *24 rooms* ⑩ *Breakfast.*

🖐 Shopping

Ranting Raven

GIFTS/SOUVENIRS | FAMILY | The shelves at this gallery and art shop are packed with local artwork, Alaska Native crafts and jewelry, and ravens—lots of them, including a couple of murals that adorn the side exterior. ✉ *238 4th Ave.* ☎ *907/224–2228.*

Resurrect Art Coffeehouse

FOOD/CANDY | A darling coffeehouse and gallery-gift shop, Resurrect is located inside a 1932 church—the ambience and the views from the old choir loft are reason enough to stop by. This a good place to find Alaskan gifts, many of them by local artists and craftspeople, that aren't mass-produced. ✉ *320 3rd Ave.* ☎ *907/224–7161* ⊕ *www.resurrectart.com.*

Kenai Fjords National Park

125 miles south of Anchorage.

On the southeast side of the Kenai Peninsula, along the Gulf of Alaska, nearly 670,000 acres were designated as the Kenai Fjords National Park in 1980 as part of the Alaska National Interest Lands Conservation Act. Abundant wildlife thrives in these icy waters and dense forests. Evidence of the Ice Age can be seen everywhere; though, as the glaciers rapidly shrink, this is also where the effects of changing climates is also readily evident.

GETTING HERE AND AROUND

The only land route to the park is via Herman Leirer (Exit Glacier) Road, which ends at Exit Glacier. Boats leaving Seward for half-day tours and longer trips are ample. Beyond that, access is limited, unless you charter a boat or airplane, or arrange for a tour with one of the local companies.

ESSENTIALS

VISITOR INFORMATION Kenai Fjords National Park Visitor Center ✉ *1212 4th Ave., Seward* ☎ *907/224–7500* ⊕ *www.nps.gov/kefj.*

Sights

Exit Glacier

NATURE SITE | A mass of ice that caps the Kenai Mountains, the Harding Icefield covers more than 1,100 square miles, and oozes more than 40 glaciers from its edges and down the mountainsides; Exit Glacier is the most accessible part of the ice field. Just outside Seward, if you hike a mile up the paved trail that starts at the parking lot, you'll find yourself at the terminal moraine of Exit Glacier. Look for the marked turnoff at Mile 3.7 as you enter town, or you can take the hourly shuttle from downtown ($15 round-trip). There's a small walk-in campground here, a ranger station, and access to the glacier. The hike to the ice field from the parking lot is a 9-mile round-trip that gains 3,000 feet in elevation, so it's not for the timid or out of shape. But if you're feeling up to the task, the hike and views are breathtaking. Local wildlife includes mountain goats and bears both black and brown, so keep a sharp eye out for them. Due to recent ice fall at the toe of the glacier, the entire toe is currently off-limits. ✉ *Herman Leirer Rd., Seward* ⊕ *www.nps.gov/kefj/planyourvisit/exit-glacier-area.htm.*

★ Kenai Fjords National Park

NATIONAL/STATE PARK | Seward is the gateway to the 669,984-acre Kenai Fjords National Park. This is spectacular coastal parkland incised with sheer, dark, slate cliffs rising from the sea, ribboned with white waterfalls, and tufted with deep-green spruce. Kenai Fjords presents a rare opportunity for an up-close view of blue tidewater glaciers as well as some remarkable ocean wildlife. If you take a day trip on a tour boat out of Seward, it's highly likely you'll see frolicking sea otters, crowds of Steller sea lions lazing on the rocky shelves along the shore, a porpoise or two, bald eagles, and tens of thousands of seabirds. Humpback whales and orcas are sighted occasionally, and mountain goats wander the seaside cliffs. The park's coastal fjords are a favorite of sea kayakers, who can camp or stay in reserved public-use cabins. One of the park's chief attractions is Exit Glacier, which can be reached only by the one road that passes into Kenai Fjords. Trails inside the park lead to an overlook of the vast Harding Icefield. Named for President Warren G. Harding, this area has more than three-dozen glaciers flowing from it. Backcountry travelers should also be aware that some of the park's coastline has been claimed by local Native organizations and is now private property. Check with park headquarters to avoid trespassing on Native land. ☎ 907/224–7500 ⊕ www.nps.gov/kefj.

🏃 Activities

BOATING

Major Marine Tours

BOATING | This outfit runs ranger-led boat tours through the park, with both half- and full-day excursions available. ☎ 907/274–7300 ⊕ www.majormarine. com ⛴ From $84.

COMBO TOURS

Exit Glacier Guides

TOUR—SPORTS | You can ride this company's $15 shuttle from town to the glacier, and there are guided hikes to it and Harding Icefield. ✉ 405 4th Ave., Seward ☎ 907/224–5569 ⊕ www.exitglacier-guides.com ⛴ From $85.

Kenai Fjords Tours

TOUR—SPORTS | FAMILY | From May to September, this outfit offers five different Resurrection Bay wildlife tours. Cruise options include visits to Fox Island, interpretive programs by National Park Service rangers, up-close viewing of calving glaciers, and opportunities to see orcas, puffins, otters, harbor seals, porpoises, and sea lions. Lunch or dinner of prime rib and salmon on Fox Island is included in some tours. ✉ Seward ☎ 888/478–3346 ⊕ www.kenaifjords.com ⛴ From $80.

🛏 Hotels

National Park Service Cabins

$ | RENTAL | The Kenai Fjords National Park manages three cabins, including two along the coast, favored by sea kayakers and for summer use only, and one at Exit Glacier. **Pros:** you'll get all the nature you want; secluded and quiet; affordable. **Cons:** coastal cabins are accessible by boat or floatplane only; zero frills or amenities (including running water); very remote. ⑤ Rooms from: $75 ☎ 907/644–3661, 866/869–6887 ⊕ www.nps.gov/kefj ⇌ 3 cabins.

Cooper Landing

100 miles south of Anchorage.

Centrally located on the Kenai Peninsula, Cooper Landing is within striking distance of some of Alaska's most popular fishing locations. Here the Russian River flows into the Kenai River, and fishing opportunities abound. Solid lines of traffic head south from Anchorage every summer weekend, and the confluence of the two rivers gets so crowded with enthusiastic anglers that the pursuit of salmon is often referred to as "combat fishing." However, a short walk upstream will separate you from the crowds and afford a chance to enjoy these gorgeous blue rivers.

The Russian River supports two runs of red (sockeye) salmon every summer, and it's the most popular fishery in the state. The Kenai River is famous for its runs of king (chinook), red, pink, and silver (coho) salmon, as well as large rainbow trout and Dolly Varden char. A number of nearby freshwater lakes, accessible only by hiking trail, also provide excellent fishing for rainbow trout and Dolly Varden.

Don't let the presence of dozens if not hundreds of fellow anglers lull you into a sense of complacency: in recent years the amount of brown bear activity at the Russian River has increased noticeably. This needn't deter you from enjoying yourself, though. Be aware of the posted signs warning of recent bear sightings, observe the local "rules of the road" about fishing and disposing of carcasses, and keep your senses tuned.

Cooper Landing serves as a trailhead for the 39-mile-long Resurrection Pass Trail, which connects to the village of Hope and the Russian Lakes/Resurrection River trails, which run south to Exit Glacier near Seward. The town's central location also affords easy access to saltwater recreation in Seward and Homer.

GETTING HERE AND AROUND

Follow the line of traffic flowing south out of Anchorage on the Seward Highway; take a right at the "Y" onto the Sterling Highway and soon you'll be there—just don't blink or you'll miss it. Look for the lodges and tackle shops that spring up from the wilderness, dotting either side of the highway. Cooper Landing does not have a commercial airport.

Activities

FISHING

Most lodges in Cooper Landing cater to the fishing crowd; ask when you make your reservation.

Alaska Troutfitters

FISHING | Guided trout and salmon fly-fishing on the Kenai River is the specialty of this outfit that also offers classes that cover everything from casting technique to fishing entomology. Alaska Troutfitters conducts hike-in, drift-boat, and fly-in trips. Package deals include instruction, fishing, transportation, and lodgings that resemble camp cabins. ⊠ *Cooper Landing* ☎ *907/595–1212* ⊕ *www.aktroutfitters.com* ☎ *From $175.*

Alaska Wildland Adventures

FISHING | From the lodge in Cooper Landing, south of Anchorage, these folks provide fishing adventures on the upper and lower Kenai River, some of which may include a stay at either their Riverside, Glacier, or Backcountry Lodge. ⊠ *Cooper Landing* ☎ *907/783–2928, 800/334–8730* ⊕ *www.alaskawildland. com* ☎ *From $525.*

HORSEBACK RIDING

Alaska Horsemen Trail Adventures

HORSEBACK RIDING | This Cooper Landing–based company offers single- and multiday horseback trips into the Kenai Mountains via Crescent Lake, Resurrection, and other area trail systems. ⊠ *Cooper Landing* ⊕ *www.alaskahorsemen.com* ☎ *From $109.*

MULTISPORT OUTFITTERS

Alaska River Adventures

FISHING | These Cooper Landing–based guides take small groups fishing throughout the region, with self-professed "well-seasoned old pros." Alaska River Adventures is only one of two operators permitted to offer trips on the Goodnews River. Horseback riding, river rafting, hiking, gold panning, and lodging are also available. Book early for the Goodnews

Continued on page 216

ALASKA'S GLACIERS
NOTORIOUS LANDSCAPE ARCHITECTS

(opposite and above) Facing the Taku Glacier challenge outside Juneau.

Glaciers—those massive, blue-hued tongues of ice that issue forth from Alaska's mountain ranges—perfectly embody the harsh climate, unforgiving terrain, and haunting beauty that make this state one of the world's wildest places. Alaska is home to roughly 100,000 glaciers, which cover almost 5% of the state's land.

FROZEN GIANTS

A glacier occurs where annual snowfall exceeds annual snowmelt. Snow accumulates over thousands of years, forming massive sheets of compacted ice. (Southeast Alaska's **Taku Glacier**, popular with flightseeing devotees, is one of Earth's meatiest: some sections measure over 4,500 feet thick.) Under the pressure of its own weight, the glacier succumbs to gravity and begins to flow downhill. This movement results in sprawling masses of rippled ice (Alaska's **Bering Glacier**, at 127 miles, is North America's longest). When glaciers reach the tidewaters of the coast, icebergs calve, or break off from the glacier's face, plunging dramatically into the sea.

THE RAPIDLY RETREATING GLACIERS IN KENAI FJORDS NATIONAL PARK

Harding Icefield

Exit Glacier

Harding Icefield Trail

Interpretive shelter

Exit Creek

Nature Trail

Ranger Station

KENAI NATIONAL WILDLIFE REFUGE

Lowell Glacier

Exit Glacier
see detail
map at left

Exit Glacier Rd

Seward Highway

Phoenix Peak
5,155ft

6

Seward

Killey Glacier

Icefield

Resurrection Bay

KENAI FJORDS NATIONAL PARK

Skee Glacier

Bear Glacier

Callisto Peak
3,223ft

Harding

Aialik Glacier 2006

Addison Glacier

Pedersen Glacier

AIALIK PENINSULA

Bulldog Cove

Fox Island

Hive Island

Trauli Glacier

Chernof Glacier

Northwestern Glacier

Holgate Glacier 2006

2006

Harding
Gateway

Rugged Island

KENAI MOUNTAINS

Chernof Glacier

McCarty Glacier

(Highest point in park)
6,450ft

Holgate Arm

HARRIS PENINSULA

Aialik Bay

Cheval Island

Northwestern Lagoon

1900

Dora Passage

Dinglestadt Glacier

2006

Pasqua Arm

Granite Passage

Harbor Island

Chat Island
Alaska Maritime National Wildlife Refuge

Kachemak Glacier

Glacier

McCarty Fjord

Sandy Bay

Granite Island

Harris Bay

Natoa Island

1942

Matushka Island

1926

Cloudy Mountain
1,810ft

Gulf   of   Alaska

1905

Thunder Bay

Black Mountain
2,028ft

West Arm

Black Bay

Nuka Bay

McArthur Pass

Pye Islands

Alaska Maritime National Wildlife Refuge

0 ____ 5 mi

0 ____ 5 km

An overwhelming majority of the world's glaciers are melting at a startling clip. Alaska's climate has steadily warmed over the past three decades, dramatically increasing glacial retreat. One fact is clear: many of the state's icy icons will soon melt away. For now, though, Alaska's glaciers remain as captivating as ever. Our favorite spots for glacier viewing include **Glacier Bay National Park** in Southeast and **Portage**, **Columbia**, **Aialik** and **Exit** glaciers in South Central.

KEY

1926 *Historical extent of glaciation*

ICY BLUE HIKES & THUNDEROUS BOATING EXCURSIONS

Glaciers enchant us with their size and astonishing power to shape the landscape. But let's face it: nothing rivals the sheer excitement of watching a bus-size block of ice burst from a glacier's face, creating an unholy thunderclap that resounds across an isolated Alaskan bay.

Most frequently undertaken with a seasoned guide, **glacier trekking** is becoming increasingly popular. Many guides transport visitors to and from glaciers (in some cases by helicopter or small plane), and provide ski excursions, dogsled tours, or guided hikes on the glacier's surface. Striding through the surreal landscape of a glacier, ice crunching underfoot, can be an otherworldly experience. Whether you're whooping it up on a dogsled tour, learning the fundamentals of glacier travel, or simply poking about on a massive field of ice, you're sure to gain an acute appreciation for the massive scale of the state's natural environment.

You can also experience glaciers via boat, such as the Alaska Marine Highway, a cruise ship, a small chartered boat, or even your own bobbing kayak. Our favorite out of Seward is the ride with Kenai Fjords Tours. Don't be discouraged by rainy weather. Glaciers often appear even bluer on overcast days. When piloting your own vessel, be sure to keep your distance from the glacier's face.

Taking in the sights at Mendenhall Glacier

DID YOU KNOW?

What do glaciers and cows have in common? They both *calve*. While bovine calving refers to actual calf-birth, the word is also used to describe a tidewater glacier's stunning habit of rupturing icebergs from its terminus. When glacier ice meets the sea, steady tidal movement and warmer temperatures cause these frequent, booming deposits.

GLACIER-VIEWING TIPS

■ The most important rule of thumb is never to venture onto a glacier without proper training or the help of a guide.

■ Not surprisingly, glaciers have a cooling effect on their surroundings, so wear layers and bring gloves and rain gear.

■ Glaciers can powerfully reflect sunlight, even on cloudy days. Sunscreen, sunglasses, and a brimmed hat are essential.

■ Warm, thick-soled waterproof footwear is a must. Crampons are highly recommended.

■ Don't forget to bring a camera and binoculars (preferably waterproof).

River: only six trips are allowed each year. ⊠ *Cooper Landing* ☎ *907/595–2000* ⊕ *www.alaskariveradventures.com* ⊠ *From $175.*

🍴 Restaurants

Kingfisher Roadhouse

$$ | **AMERICAN** | With a back side that faces Kenai Lake and offers splendid views, and food equally worth your attention, this unassuming roadhouse is *the* place to stop in Cooper Landing. The halibut crab cakes with an excellent homemade tartar sauce come highly recommended, and there are always great fish options at the peak of the season.**Known for:** extraordinary views of Kenai Lake; live music venue in the evenings; great seafood options. $ *Average main: $20* ⊠ *Mile 47.3, 19503 Sterling Hwy.* ☎ *907/595–2861* ⊕ *www. letseat.at/kingfisherak* ⊘ *Closed Mon. and Tues. in Sept.–mid-June. No dinner Sept.–mid-June. No lunch Mon. and Tues. mid-June–Sept.*

Sunrise Inn

$$ | **AMERICAN** | The owners of this cheerful little restaurant on the shore of Kenai Lake call it a "backwoods bistro." The very reasonably priced menu includes excellent breakfast foods, homemade soups and chowders, wraps and vegetarian items, and hand-grated french fries. **Known for:** late-night food stop; amazing interior woodwork and a fish stream floor; live music in summer. $ *Average main: $15* ⊠ *Mile 45, Sterling Hwy.* ☎ *907/595–1222* ⊕ *www.sunriseinncooperlandingalaska.com.*

🛏 Hotels

Eagle Landing Resort

$$ | **B&B/INN** | Cabins here come in three variations—regular, deluxe, and riverfront, all with private baths, heat, and kitchens. **Pros:** accommodations that fit any budget; great views; fantastic kitchens. **Cons:** some staircases are steep; certain upstairs rooms are only semiprivate; lacks many urban amenities. $ *Rooms from: $165* ⊠ *Mile 48.1, Sterling Hwy., Box 748* ☎ *907/595–1213, 866/595–1213* ⊕ *www.eaglelandingresort.net* ⊠ *12 cabins* ☉ *No meals.*

Great Alaska Adventure Lodge

$$$$ | **B&B/INN** | Midway between Seward and Homer, this lodge lives up to its name with activities that include natural-history and other soft-adventure options, and a remote bear-viewing camp. **Pros:** all-inclusive; right along the Sterling Highway; perfect for fishing lovers. **Cons:** highway location can get noisy; expensive rates; not for people who dislike tours. $ *Rooms from: $1597* ⊠ *Mile 82½, 33881 Sterling Hwy., Sterling* ☎ *866/411–2327* ⊕ *www.greatalaska. com* ⊘ *Closed Oct.–mid-May* ⊠ *25 rooms* ☉ *All meals.*

Gwin's Lodge

$$ | **B&B/INN** | One of Alaska's oldest roadhouses, Gwin's is the epicenter of much activity on the peninsula and a one-stop shop providing food, lodging, and fishing tackle. **Pros:** everything you need in one place; pretty decent food; very quaint and historic. **Cons:** lofts have very low ceilings; can sometimes have rowdy patrons in the evenings; restaurant closed in off-season. $ *Rooms from: $100* ⊠ *Mile 52, 14865 Sterling Hwy.* ☎ *907/595–1266* ⊕ *www.gwinslodge.com* ⊠ *15 rooms* ☉ *No meals.*

★ The Inn at Tern Lake

$$ | **B&B/INN** | In a valley of spruce trees between the jagged peaks of the Kenai Mountains, this B&B inn offers a stunning backdrop—and bounty of experiences—in every season. **Pros:** babbling springs and terns on the lake complete the Alaska experience; stunning views; comfortable and inviting. **Cons:** isolated location far from amenities; mosquitoes can be a nuisance; far from the big city. $ *Rooms from: $175* ⊠ *Mile 36, Seward Hwy.* ☎ *907/288–3667* ⊕ *www.ternlakeinn.com* ⊠ *4 rooms* ☉ *Breakfast.*

Kenai Princess Wilderness Lodge

$$$ | **HOTEL** | "Elegantly rustic" might best describe this sprawling complex approximately 45 miles from Seward. **Pros:** cozy rooms have fireplaces; beautiful location; quiet atmosphere. **Cons:** rooms don't have views of the river; caters mainly to cruise passengers and those on tours; food is cruise-ship quality. $ *Rooms from: $229* ✉ *Mile 47.7, Sterling Hwy.* ☎ *907/595–1425, 800/426–0500* ⊕ *www.princesslodges.com/kenai_lodge.cfm* ⊘ *Closed mid-Sept.–May* ⇨ *86 rooms* ⦿ *No meals.*

Kenai Riverside Lodge

$$$ | **RENTAL** | Run by Alaska Wildland Adventures, this collection of buildings on the bank of the Kenai River offers a "roughing it in authentic comfort" all-inclusive package with cabins that have private baths. **Pros:** beautiful wooded location; great adventure and expedition packages; relaxing sauna. **Cons:** cabins are a bit small; packages can get expensive; very fishing focused. $ *Rooms from: $295* ✉ *Mile 50.1, 16520 Sterling Hwy.* ☎ *800/478–4100* ⊕ *www.kenairiversidelodge.com* ⊘ *Closed Oct.–mid-May* ⇨ *8 cabins* ⦿ *Free Breakfast.*

Kenai National Wildlife Refuge

95 miles northwest of Kenai Fjords National Park, 150 miles southwest of Anchorage.

The refuge, which encompasses nearly 2 million acres, was originally established to protect the Kenai moose, and it remains the finest moose habitat in the region. Wildlife viewing is popular, of course, and the canoeing and kayaking opportunities attract many visitors each summer.

Moose are the most commonly seen large animals in the refuge—it was originally named the Kenai National Moose Range.

GETTING HERE AND AROUND

There are several roads in the refuge, and the Sterling Highway bisects it, but the best access is by canoe. ■**TIP**➡ **Road access to the canoe trailheads is off the Swanson River Road at Mile 83.4 of the Sterling Highway.** Other than canoeing, the only way to get into the far reaches of the refuge is by airplane. Floatplane services in Soldotna, where the refuge is headquartered, can fly you into the backcountry. The refuge office maintains lists of transporters, air taxis, canoe rentals, and big-game guides that are permitted to operate on refuge lands. To reach the main visitor center–refuge office on Ski Hill Road, turn south on Funny River Road in Soldotna just west of the Kenai River Bridge, and follow the signs.

ESSENTIALS

VISITOR INFORMATION Kenai National Wildlife Refuge Visitor Center ✉ *1 Ski Hill Rd., Soldotna* ☎ *907/260–2820* ⊕ *kenai.fws.gov.*

⊙ Sights

Kenai National Wildlife Refuge

NATURE PRESERVE | The refuge's nearly 2 million acres include a portion of the Harding Icefield as well as two large and scenic lakes, Skilak and Tustumena. This is the area's premier moose habitat, and the waterways are great for canoeing and kayaking. The refuge maintains two visitor centers. The main center, in Soldotna, has wildlife dioramas, free films and information, and a bookstore and gift shop. There's also a seasonal "contact" center at Mile 58 of the Sterling Highway, open from mid-June to mid-August. Wildlife is plentiful even by Alaskan standards. Although caribou seldom appear near the road, Dall sheep and mountain goats live on the peaks near Cooper Landing, and black and brown bears, wolves, coyotes, lynx, beavers, and lots of birds reside here, along with many moose. The refuge's canoe trail system runs through the Swan Lake and Swanson River areas. Covering more than 140 miles on 100 lakes and the Swanson River, this route escapes the notice of most visitors and residents. It's a shame because this series of lakes linked by overland portages offers fantastic access to the remote backcountry, well away from what passes for civilization in the subarctic. The fishing improves exponentially with distance from the road system.

⚽ Activities

CANOEING

The best way to experience the refuge's backcountry is by canoe. The **Swan Lake Canoe System** and the **Swanson River Canoe System** are accessed from the road system at the turnoff at Mile 83.4 of the Sterling Highway. Several loop trips enable visitors to fish, hike, and camp away from the road system and motorized boat traffic. Fishing for trout, salmon, and Dolly Varden is excellent, and the lakes and portages offer access to more than 100 miles of waterways. The Kenai National Wildlife Refuge Visitor Center has a thorough list of canoeing outfitters.

Alaska Canoe & Campground

CAMPING—SPORTS-OUTDOORS | Whether you're looking for a canoe, kayak, raft, or drift boat—or tackle or camping gear—this company comes highly recommended by locals and travelers alike. They'll properly outfit you and send you on your Refuge adventure, on your own or with a guide. ✉ *25292 Sterling Hwy., Sterling* ☎ *907/262–2331* ⊕ *www.alaskacanoetrips.com* ⌖ *From $35 per day.*

HIKING

Hiking trails branch off from the Sterling Highway and the Skilak Lake Loop. The degree of difficulty ranges from easy half-mile walks to strenuous climbs to mountain lakes. Bring topographic maps, water, food, insect repellent, and bear awareness. You won't find toilets, water fountains, or signposts. Remember:

brown and black bears are numerous on the Kenai Peninsula.

Hotels

Kenai Backcountry Lodge

$$$$ | RENTAL | Getting off the road, and beaten track, is the most authentic way to experience Alaska, and the Kenai Backcountry Lodge is about as true as it gets, with access only by boat across Skilak Lake. **Pros:** backcountry experience without roughing it too much; gorgeous remote location; experienced and knowledgeable guides. **Cons:** only two cabins have private bathrooms; no major amenities; can be pricey. ⑤ *Rooms from: $1950* ✉ *Kenai Peninsula* ☎ *800/334–8730* ⊕ *www.alaskawildland.com/kenaibackcountrylodge.htm* ☉ *Closed Sept.–May* ⌖ *4 log cabins, 5 tent cabins* ⍾ *All-inclusive.*

USFWS Cabins

$ | RENTAL | These cabins are in remote areas of the Kenai National Wildlife Refuge accessible only by air or boat. **Pros:** the true experience of being off the grid; beautiful surroundings; peace and quiet. **Cons:** making a reservation is not easy; no amenities; comfort depends on what you bring with you. ⑤ *Rooms from: $75* ✉ *Soldotna* ☎ *877/444–6777* ⊕ *www.fws.gov/refuge/Kenai/cabin.html* ⌖ *16 cabins* ⍾ *No meals.*

Kenai, Sterling, and Soldotna

116 miles northwest of Seward, 148 miles southwest of Anchorage.

Because of their proximity to each other, the towns of Kenai, Sterling, and Soldotna are often mentioned together, and all three are within the Kenai Peninsula Borough. Soldotna and Sterling, with their strategic location on the peninsula's northwest coast, serve as the Kenai Peninsula's commercial and sportfishing hub.

Along with Kenai, whose onion-dome Holy Assumption Russian Orthodox Church is a highlight of the old town, they are home to Cook Inlet oil-field workers and their families. Sterling and Soldotna's commercial center stretches along the Sterling Highway, making this a good stopping point for those traveling up and down the peninsula. The town of Kenai lies near the end of a road that branches off the Sterling Highway in Soldotna. Near Kenai is Captain Cook State Recreation Area, one of the least-visited state parks on the road system. This portion of the peninsula is level and forested, with numerous lakes and streams pocking and crisscrossing the area. Trumpeter swans return here in spring, and sightings of moose are common.

GETTING HERE AND AROUND

As you're driving either north or south on the Sterling Highway from Cooper Landing or Homer, you'll know you've hit Soldotna when you're suddenly stuck in traffic in between strip malls. From the north the slowdown is gradual, but from Homer, it's quite sudden. Kenai is 11 miles up the Kenai Spur Highway, which originates in central Soldotna. Commercial flights are available to Kenai from Anchorage.

ESSENTIALS

VISITOR INFORMATION Kenai Visitor and Convention Bureau ⊠ *11471 Kenai Spur Hwy., Kenai* ☎ *907/283–1991* ⊕ *kenai-chamber.org.*

 Sights

Clam Gulch

VIEWPOINT | FAMILY | In addition to fishing, clam digging is also popular at Clam Gulch, 24 miles south of Soldotna on the Sterling Highway. This is a favorite of local children, who love any excuse to dig in the muddy, sloppy goo. Ask locals on the beach how to find the giant razor clams (recognized by their dimples in the sand). Ask also for advice on how

to clean the clams—cleaning is pretty labor-intensive, and it's easy to get into a clam-digging frenzy when the conditions are favorable, only to regret your efforts when cleaning time arrives. The clam digging is best when tides are minus 4 or 5 feet. A sportfishing license, available at grocery stores, sporting-goods shops, and drugstores, is required for clam diggers 16 years old and over. ⊠ *Soldotna.*

Activities

FISHING

Anglers from around the world come for the salmon-choked streams and rivers, most notably the Kenai River and its companion, the Russian River. Knowledgeable fishery professionals figure it's only a matter of time before someone with sportfishing gear catches a 100-pounder (the record is currently a 97-pound, 4-ounce fish caught in 1985). There are two runs of kings up the Kenai every summer. The first run starts in mid-May and tapers off in early July, and the second run is from early July until the season ends on July 31. Generally speaking, the first run has more fish, but they tend to be smaller than second-run fish. "Smaller," of course, has a whole different meaning when it comes to these fish. Fifty- and 60-pounders are unremarkable here, and 40-pound fish are routinely tossed back as being "too small." The limit is one king kept per day, five per season, no more than two of which can be from the Kenai—unless an emergency order states otherwise. In addition to a fishing license, you must obtain a special Alaska king salmon license stamp and a harvest record. These can be purchased on the Alaska Department of Fish and Game website (⊕ *www.adfg.alaska.gov*), or check with your guide, as most guides sell them. The river also supports two runs of red (sockeye) salmon every year, as well as runs of silver (coho) and pink (humpback) salmon. Rainbow trout of near-mythic proportions inhabit the river, as do Dolly

Varden char. Limits vary from place to place, so be sure to check your fishing booklet.

Farther up the river, between Kenai Lake in Cooper Landing and Skilak Lake, motorboats are banned, so a more idyllic experience can be had. Scores of guide services ply the river, and if you're inexperienced at the game, consider hiring a guide for a half-day or full-day trip. Deep-sea fishing for salmon and halibut out of Deep Creek is challenging Homer's position as the preeminent fishing destination on the southern Kenai Peninsula. This fishery is unusual in that tractors launch boats off the beach and into the Cook Inlet surf. The local campground and RV lot is packed on summer weekends.

Some 300 fishing charters and guides operate here, and all of them stay busy during the summer fishing season.

Kenai River Trips

TOUR—SPORTS | Head down the Kenai River and learn about the surroundings and wildlife with these guides. One of the oldest and largest outfitters on the peninsula, the company has trips to suit just about everyone, from scenic floating to overnight cabin stays and fishing excursions. ✉ *Soldotna* ☎ *800/478–4100* ⊕ *www.alaskarivertrips.com* 🍴 *From $65 (float), $295 (fish), $209 (cabins).*

MULTISPORT OUTFITTERS

Alaska Canoe & Campground

CANOEING/ROWING/SKULLING | This company operates fishing, kayaking, and canoeing trips. It also has cabins, offers instruction, and operates shuttles to put-in and take-out points. ✉ *35292 Sterling Hwy., Soldotna* ☎ *907/262–2331* ⊕ *www. alaskacanoetrips.com* 🍴 *From $150 for guided kayaking trip.*

🍴 Restaurants

Burger Bus

$ | BURGER | A great spot to hit after a day of fishing, the Burger Bus is just as it sounds: an old school bus converted into a kitchen, with a shack built around it, and delicious burgers on offer. The portions are big and the flavors are great. **Known for:** excellent halibut burger; great grub-on-the-go stop before or after a fishing excursion; unique school bus kitchen setup. 🆂 *Average main: $11* ✉ *409 Overland Ave., Kenai* ☎ *907/283–9611.*

The Duck Inn Cafe

$$$ | AMERICAN | With pizzas, burgers, chicken, steaks, and seafood on the Duck Inn's menu, there's something for everyone. Portions are generous, and the prices are reasonable. **Known for:** unique and varied halibut dishes; greatly accommodating menu for diverse eaters; duck-themed artwork. 🆂 *Average main: $25* ✉ *Mile 19½, 43187 Kalifornsky Beach Rd., Soldotna* ☎ *907/262–2656* ⊕ *www. duckinnalaska.net.*

The Moose Is Loose

$ | CAFÉ | This place is known all over Southcentral Alaska for its amazing doughnuts. You can also pick up cinnamon rolls, scones, cookies, cakes, and other pastries. **Known for:** fresh doughnuts like the Moose Snack; kitsch moose gifts; amazing staff. 🆂 *Average main: $3* ✉ *44278 Sterling Hwy., Sterling* ☎ *907/260–3036* 🕙 *Closed Mon.*

St. Elias Brewing Company

$$ | AMERICAN | Everything at St. Elias is homemade: the ever-changing beers, the stone-fired rustic pizza, the sandwiches, and even the desserts. The calzones are to die for and the Mt. Redoubt chocolate cake with a molten center is simply divine. **Known for:** fantastic rustic pizzas; locally brewed beer; great live music concerts in the summer. 🆂 *Average main: $15* ✉ *434 Sharkathmi Ave., Sterling* ☎ *907/260–7837* ⊕ *www.steliasbrewing-co.com.*

Hotels

Aspen Hotel Soldotna

$$ | HOTEL | This Soldotna hotel sits on a bluff overlooking the Kenai River, and if you get a river-view room you'll have a front-row seat for the fishing action during salmon runs. **Pros:** hot tub for all guests; great swimming pool; riverfront location. **Cons:** bland corporate feel; urban setting, despite being along the river; no air-conditioning for the rare hot days. ⑤ *Rooms from: $174 ⊠ 326 Binkley Cir., Soldotna ☎ 907/260–7736, 888/308– 7848 ⊕ www.aspenhotelsak.com ⇆ 63 rooms* ⑩ *Breakfast.*

Best Western King Salmon Motel

$$ | HOTEL | Large rooms, including some with kitchenettes, make this motel a great option for families. **Pros:** meticulously cleaned; coffee and food in walking distance; food voucher for the café next door. **Cons:** surrounded by strip malls; beds are hard; pillows are lumpy. ⑤ *Rooms from: $159 ⊠ 35546–A Kenai Spur Hwy., Soldotna ☎ 907/262–5857, 888/262–5857 ⊕ bestwesternalaska.com/ hotels ⇆ 49 rooms* ⑩ *Breakfast.*

Salmon Catcher Lodge

$$$ | B&B/INN | For a break from hotel mayhem or to immerse yourself in the world of angling, this upscale lodge delivers both tranquil beauty and a flurry of fishing activity. **Pros:** plenty of tranquillity; great angling opportunities; rates include processing of up to 50 pounds of caught fish. **Cons:** setting may be too remote for some; there are a lot of cabins for being a remote location; not many amenities. ⑤ *Rooms from: $269 ⊠ 32911 Ralph La., Kenai ☎ 907/335–2001 ⊕ www. salmoncatcherlodge.com ⇆ 46 rooms* ⑩ *Breakfast.*

Homer

77 miles south of Soldotna, 226 miles southwest of Anchorage.

At the southern end of the Sterling Highway lies the city of Homer, at the base of a narrow spit that juts 4 miles into beautiful Kachemak Bay. Glaciers and snowcapped mountains form a dramatic backdrop across the water.

Founded in the late 1800s as a gold-prospecting camp, this community was later used as coal-mining headquarters. Chunks of coal are still common along local beaches; they wash into the bay from nearby slopes where the coal seams are exposed. Today the town of Homer is an eclectic community with most of the tacky tourist paraphernalia relegated to the Spit (though the Spit has plenty else to recommend it, not the least of which is the 360-degree view of the surrounding mountains); the rest of the town is full of local merchants and artisans. The community is an interesting mix of fishermen, actors, artists, and writers. Much of the commercial fishing centers on halibut, and the popular Homer Jackpot Halibut Derby is often won by fish weighing more than 300 pounds. The local architecture includes everything from dwellings that are little more than assemblages of driftwood to steel commercial buildings and magnificent homes on the hillside overlooking the surrounding bay, mountains, forests, and glaciers.

GETTING HERE AND AROUND

The Sterling Highway ends in Homer, and the drive in is beautiful. Once there, you'll see signs on your left for Pioneer Avenue, Homer's commercial district. On the right is the historic town center, and if you keep to the road you'll hit the Spit. Homer also has a commercial airport, with flights daily to and from Anchorage, Seldovia, and elsewhere. If you're traveling on the Marine Highway system, ferries to Kodiak and beyond dock several times a week in summer.

ESSENTIALS

VISITOR INFORMATION Visit Homer ✉ *201 Sterling Hwy.* ☎ *907/235–8766* ⊕ *www. homeralaska.org.*

Sights

★ Homer Spit

BODY OF WATER | FAMILY | Protruding into Kachemak Bay, Homer Spit provides a sandy focal point for visitors and locals. A 4½-mile paved road runs the length of the Spit, making it the world's longest road into the ocean. A commercial-fishing-boat harbor at the end of the path has restaurants, hotels, charter-fishing businesses, sea-kayaking outfitters, art galleries, and on-the-beach camping spots. Fly a kite, walk the beaches, drop a line in the Fishing Hole, or just wander through the shops looking for something interesting; this is one of Alaska's favorite summertime destinations. ✉ *Homer.*

★ Islands and Ocean Visitors Center

MUSEUM | FAMILY | This center provides a wonderful introduction to the Alaska Maritime National Wildlife Refuge. The refuge covers some 3½ million acres spread across some 2,500 Alaskan islands, from Prince of Wales Island in the south to Barrow in the north. The 37,000-square-foot eco-friendly facility with towering windows facing Kachemak Bay is a must-see for anyone interested in wild places. A film takes visitors along on a voyage of the Fish and Wildlife Service's research ship, the MV *Tiglax.* Interactive exhibits detail the birds and marine mammals of the refuge (the largest seabird refuge in America), and one room even re-creates the noisy sounds and pungent smells of a bird rookery. In summer, guided bird-watching treks and beach walks are offered, and you can take a stroll on your own on the walkways in the Beluga Slough, where Alaskan poet Wendy Erd's commissioned work lines the way. ✉ *95*

Sterling Hwy. ☎ *907/235–6961* ⊕ *www. islandsandocean.org* ✎ *Free.*

Kachemak Bay

BODY OF WATER | The bay abounds with wildlife, including a large population of puffins and eagles. Tour operators take visitors past bird rookeries or across the bay to gravel beaches for clam digging. Most fishing charters include an opportunity to view whales, seals, porpoises, and birds close-up. At the end of the day, walk along the docks on one of the largest coastal parks in America. ✉ *Homer.*

Pratt Museum

MUSEUM | FAMILY | The Pratt is an art gallery and a cultural and natural-history museum rolled into one. In addition to monthly exhibits showcasing some of Alaska's finest artists, the museum has an exhibit on the 1989 *Exxon Valdez* oil spill; botanical gardens; nature trails; a gift shop; and pioneer, Russian, and Alaska Native displays. You can spy on wildlife with robotic video cameras set up on a seabird rookery and at the McNeil River Bear Sanctuary. A refurbished homestead cabin and outdoor summer exhibits are along the trail out back. ✉ *Bartlett St., off Pioneer Ave.* ☎ *907/235–8635* ⊕ *www. prattmuseum.org* ✎ *$10* ⊗ *Closed Jan.*

⚡ Activities

BEAR WATCHING

Emerald Air Service

WILDLIFE-WATCHING | Homer is a favorite departure point for viewing Alaska's famous brown bears in Katmai National Park. Emerald Air is one of several companies offering daylong and custom photography trips. ✉ *Homer* ☎ *907/235–4160, 877/235–9600* ⊕ *www.emeraldair-service.com* ✎ *From $650.*

Hallo Bay Wilderness

WILDLIFE-WATCHING | This outfit delivers guided close-range viewing without the crowds. The day trips are eventful, but the overnight stays at Hallo Bay's eco-friendly coastal lodging provide the ultimate in world-class bear and wildlife viewing. ⊠ *Homer* ☎ *907/235–2237, 888/535–2237* ⊕ *www.hallobay.com* 🖃 *Day trip $625, overnight trips from $1299.*

Smokey Bay Air

WILDLIFE-WATCHING | This outfitter supplies the surrounding area with air taxi services, but also provides excellent bear-viewing trips at Katmai and Lake Clark national parks. On the way you'll have a chance to view volcanos and glaciers, then land and peruse the terrain while carefully spying on bears. ⊠ *2100 Kachemak Bay Dr.* ☎ *907/235–1511, 888/281–2635* ⊕ *www.smokeybayair.com.*

BOATING AND FISHING

Homer is a major commercial fishing port (especially for halibut) and a popular destination for sport anglers in search of giant halibut or feisty king and silver salmon. Quite a few companies offer charter fishing in summer, from about $250 to $350 per person per day, including bait and tackle. The pricing is usually based on how many different types of fish you're going after.

Central Charters & Tours

TOUR—SPORTS | Central can arrange fishing trips in outer Kachemak Bay and Lower Cook Inlet—areas known for excellent halibut fishing. Boat sizes vary considerably; some have a six-person limit, whereas others can take up to 16 passengers. The company also conducts non-fishing boat tours and bear viewing. ⊠ *4241 Homer Spit Rd.* ☎ *907/235–7847* ⊕ *www.centralcharter.com* 🖃 *Boat tours from $59, fishing trips from $295, bear viewing from $675.*

Fishing Hole

BOATING | Near the end of the Spit, Homer's famous Fishing Hole, aka the Nick Dudiak Fishing Lagoon, is a small bight stocked with king and silver salmon smolt (baby fish) by the Alaska Department of Fish and Game. The salmon then head out to sea, returning several years later to the Fishing Hole, where they are easy targets for wall-to-wall bankside anglers throughout summer. The Fishing Hole isn't anything like casting for salmon along a remote stream, but your chances are good and you don't need to drop $800 for a flight into the wilderness. Fishing licenses and rental poles are available from fishing-supply stores on the Spit. ⊠ *Homer.*

Homer Jackpot Halibut Derby

FISHING | Anyone heading out on a halibut charter is advised to buy a $10 ticket for the derby, which ends with the season in September. First prize for the largest halibut is $10,000, plus 50¢ per ticket sold. In addition, more than 100 fish are tagged; anglers who catch them win cash or other prizes worth up to $50,000. Food for thought: in 2013, the angler who caught the fish bearing the $50K tag hadn't bought a derby ticket. ⊠ *Homer* ☎ *907/235–7740* ⊕ *www.homerhalibut-derby.com.*

Homer Ocean Charters

TOUR—SPORTS | Locally owned and operated, Homer Ocean Charters has been in business since 1979, setting up fishing, sea-kayaking, and sightseeing trips. It also offers water-taxi services and bare-bones cabin rentals on Otter Cove. ⊠ *4287 Homer Spit Rd.* ☎ *800/426–6212* ⊕ *www.homerocean.com* 🖃 *From $250.*

Inlet Charters

TOUR—SPORTS | Try Inlet Charters for fishing charters (halibut and salmon), fish processing, water-taxi services, lodging, sea kayaking, and wildlife cruises. ⊠ *Homer* ☎ *800/770–6126* ⊕ *www. halibutcharters.com* 🖃 *From $250.*

SEA KAYAKING

True North Kayak Adventures

KAYAKING | Several local companies offer guided sea-kayaking trips to protected coves within Kachemak Bay State Park and nearby islands. True North has a range of such adventures, including a three-day trip and a boat and kayak day trip to Yukon Island (both trips include round-trip water taxi to the island base camp, guide, all kayak equipment, and meals). ✉ *Homer* ☎ *907/235–0708* ⊕ *www.truenorthkayak.com* ✉ *Day trips from $115; overnight from $375.*

 Restaurants

Café Cups

$$$ | ECLECTIC | It's hard to miss this place as you drive down Pioneer Avenue—look for the huge namesake cups on the building's facade. The café serves dinners that incorporate the locally abundant seafood; vegetarian options are also offered. **Known for:** unique Alice in Wonderland-like cup architecture; romantic dining; fantastic dinner specials. Ⓢ *Average main: $25* ✉ *162 W. Pioneer Ave.* ☎ *907/235–8330* ⊕ *www.cafecupsofhomer.com* ⊙ *Closed Sun. and Mon. No lunch.*

Fat Olives Restaurant

$$ | MEDITERRANEAN | Pumpkin-color walls, light streaming through tall front windows, and a playful collection of Italian posters add to the appeal of this fine Tuscany-inspired bistro. The menu encompasses enticing appetizers, salads, sandwiches, calzones, and pizzas throughout the day, along with oven-roasted chicken, fresh seafood, pork loin, and other fare in the evening. **Known for:** classic Italian cuisine; good wine selection; excellent pizza options. Ⓢ *Average main: $15* ✉ *276 Olson La.* ☎ *907/235–8488* ⊕ *www. fatoliveshomer.com.*

Fritz Creek General Store

$ | ECLECTIC | Be sure to check out this old-fashioned country store, gas station, liquor store, post office, video-rental shop, and deli. The latter is the primary reason for stopping at Fritz's: the food is amazingly good—brisket smoked right out back, homemade bread, pastries, and pizza by the slice. **Known for:** best sandwiches in town; great place to mingle with locals; off-the-beaten path vibe. Ⓢ *Average main: $10* ✉ *Mile 8.2, 55770 E. End Rd.* ☎ *907/235–6753.*

⭐ La Baleine

$ | AMERICAN | One of the few places on the Spit open at 5 am, this is a perfect stop before a day of fishing, but lunch is an equally fulfilling experience. La Baleine serves fantastic breakfast sandwiches on fresh ciabatta rolls—complimentary cup of locally roasted coffee included. **Known for:** best breakfast sandwiches in town; fantastic homemade ramen bowls; locally sourced ingredients. Ⓢ *Average main: $12* ✉ *4450 Homer Spit Rd.* ☎ *907/299–6672* ⊕ *www.labaleinecafe. com* ⊙ *Closed Mon. No dinner.*

⭐ Little Mermaid

$$$ | AMERICAN | This hot spot draws crowds from all over the world, despite the fact it's too small to fit them all. Its size makes Little Mermaid feel cozy and the staff seem familial—with the emphasis on local ingredients, each bite makes Homer feel a little more like home. **Known for:** cozy ambience; best seafood destination in town; famed Hot Stone Bowl with local fish and veggies. Ⓢ *Average main: $25* ✉ *Harborview Boardwalk, 4246 Homer Spit Rd.* ☎ *907/399–9900* ⊕ *www.littlemermaidhomer.com* ⊙ *Closed Tues.*

Two Sisters Bakery

$ | CAFÉ | This very popular café is a short walk from Bishops Beach, Beluga Slough, and the Islands and Ocean Visitors Center. In addition to fresh breads and pastries, Two Sisters specializes in deliciously healthy lunches, such as vegetarian focaccia sandwiches, homemade soups, quiche, and salads. **Known for:** fantastic fresh bread; best place to drink coffee and read the morning paper; wraparound porch perfect for summer. Ⓢ *Average main: $10* ✉ *233 E. Bunnell Ave.* ☎ *907/235–2280* ⊕ *www.twosistersbakery.net* ⊙ *Closed Sun. No dinner.*

Hotels

Alaskan Suites

$$$ | HOTEL | With five modern log cabins and a two-bedroom house (it sleeps six), Alaskan Suites offers million-dollar views from a hilltop on the west side of Homer. **Pros:** crow's-nest views; highway location with no highway noise; quaint but classy. **Cons:** not within walking distance of anything; views so beautiful you may never want to go home; not as remote as it could be. $ *Rooms from: $295* ✉ *3255 Sterling Hwy.* ☎ *907/235–1972, 888/239–1972* ⊕ *www.alaskansuites.com* ↪ *5 cabins* ⦿ *No meals.*

Driftwood Inn

$$ | B&B/INN | With an RV park, two deluxe lodges, a cottage, and a historic inn, the Driftwood accommodates a range of travelers. **Pros:** accommodations for every budget; relaxed, cozy atmosphere; close to Bishop's Beach. **Cons:** some of the inn's rooms are small; not much variety or selection of food; decor a little old-fashioned. $ *Rooms from: $129* ✉ *135 W. Bunnell Ave.* ☎ *907/235–8019* ⊕ *www.thedriftwoodinn.com* ↪ *22 rooms, 1 cottage* ⦿ *Breakfast.*

Homer Inn & Spa

$$$ | B&B/INN | As well as a fabulous view of the ocean, this beachfront boutique inn offers three minisuites and a villa, all decorated with local art and character. **Pros:** incredible views of the bay, glaciers, and volcanoes; all rooms are ocean-facing; spa services on-site. **Cons:** Old Town and main commerce area are not in close walking distance; no restaurant on-site; no beach access. $ *Rooms from: $239* ✉ *895 Ocean Dr. Loop* ☎ *907/235–1000, 800/294–7823* ⊕ *www.homerinnandspa. com* ↪ *3 suites, 1 villa* ⦿ *No meals.*

Land's End Resort and Lodges

$$ | HOTEL | Spread across the best real estate on the Spit, Land's End offers splendid bay views from variously styled rooms and suites. **Pros:** the Spit-end location puts you well into the bay; great views of the bay and mountains; great dining on-site. **Cons:** you might be disappointed if you get a room without a view; large, corporate feel; location makes it a bit of a drive to Old Town. $ *Rooms from: $185* ✉ *4786 Homer Spit Rd.* ☎ *907/235–0400, 800/478–0400* ⊕ *www.lands-end-resort.com* ↪ *166 rooms.*

Old Town Bed & Breakfast

$$ | B&B/INN | In the oldest commercial building in Homer, this bright and cozy B&B offers peace, convenience, and sweeping views of the bay and mountains. **Pros:** warm and inviting; good location; great views. **Cons:** some rooms have shared baths; have to climb a set of stairs; the stairs are at an angle so it feels as though you're inebriated. $ *Rooms from: $130* ✉ *106 W. Bunnell Ave., in Old Inlet Trading Post* ☎ *907/235–7558* ⊕ *www.oldtownbedandbreakfast.com* ↪ *3 rooms* ⦿ *Breakfast.*

▼ Nightlife

Alice's Champagne Palace

MUSIC CLUBS | Dance to lively bands on weekends at Alice's, which attracts nationally known singer-songwriters. ✉ *195 E. Pioneer Ave.* ☎ *907/235–6909.*

Pier One Theater

THEATER | For more than four decades, this community theater has presented locally written and outside plays. Recent seasons have seen a Molière comedy and narratives of people in the fishing industry. The theater is in an old barnlike building on the Homer Spit. ✉ *3858 Homer Spit Rd.* ☎ *907/235–7333* ⊕ *www. pieronetheatre.org.*

Salty Dawg Saloon

BARS/PUBS | The Spit's infamous Salty Dawg is a tumbledown lighthouse of sorts, sure to be frequented by a carousing fisherman or 20, along with half the tourists in town. ✉ *4380 Homer Spit Rd.* ☎ *907/235–6718* ⊕ *www.saltydogsaloon. com.*

🛍 Shopping

ART AND GIFTS

Bunnell Street Arts Center

ART GALLERIES | The gallery, which occupies the first floor of a historic trading post, showcases and sells innovative Alaskan-made contemporary art. It also hosts workshops, lectures, musical performances, and other community events. ✉ *106 W. Bunnell Ave., at Main St.* ☎ *907/235–2662* ⊕ *www.bunnellarts.org.*

Ptarmigan Arts

ART GALLERIES | A cooperative gallery, Ptarmigan shows photographs, paintings, pottery, jewelry, woodworking, and other pieces by local fine and craft artists. ✉ *471 E. Pioneer Ave.* ☎ *907/235–5345* ⊕ *www.ptarmiganarts.com.*

CLOTHING

The Fringe

CLOTHING | Located in the belly of the Bunnell Art Gallery, Fringe is a used and new clothing boutique. Its biggest draw are the locally made wearable art pieces that range from groovy hats to clever, funky dresses and linens. ✉ *106 W. Bunnell St.* ☎ *907/235–4999.*

Nomar

CLOTHING | The company manufactures equipment and clothing for commercial fishermen. Its Homer shop sells Polarfleece garments and other rugged outerwear, plus duffels, rain gear, and children's clothing. ✉ *104 E. Pioneer Ave.* ☎ *907/235–8363, 800/478–8364* ⊕ *www.nomaralaska.com.*

FOOD

Coal Point Seafood Company

FOOD/CANDY | Homer is famous for its halibut, salmon, and Kachemak Bay oysters. For fresh fish, head to Coal Point Seafood Company, which can also package and ship fish that you catch. ✉ *4306 Homer Spit Rd.* ☎ *907/235–3877, 800/325–3877* ⊕ *www.welovefish.com.*

Kachemak Bay State Park and State Wilderness Park

10 miles southeast of Homer.

Kachemak Bay is Alaska's first state park and only wilderness park. It protects roughly 400,000 acres of coast, mountains, glaciers, forests, and wildlife on the lower Kenai Peninsula. The park encompasses a line of snowcapped mountains and several large glaciers. The prominent one visible from Homer Spit is Grewingk Glacier. One of the most popular trails in the park is a 2-mile hike that ends at the lake in front of the glacier.

GETTING HERE AND AROUND

There are more than 80 hiking trails and a number of lodges and campsites in Kachemak Bay State Park and State Wilderness Park. They are only accessible by boat, except for a few that are also accessible by floatplane. Mako's Water Taxi and Danny J Ferry provide boat service to the park.

ESSENTIALS

WATER TAXI CONTACTS Danny J Ferry ☎ *907/399–2683* ⊕ *www.halibut-cove-alaska.com/ferry.htm.* **Mako's Water Taxi** ✉ *Homer Spit Rd., Homer* ☎ *907/235–9055* ⊕ *www.makoswatertaxi.com.*

👁 Sights

Halibut Cove

TOWN | A small artists' community directly across from the tip of Homer Spit, Halibut Cove is a fine place to spend time meandering along the boardwalk and visiting galleries. The cove is lovely, especially during salmon runs, when fish leap and splash in the clear water. The *Danny J* ferries people across from Homer Spit, with a stop at the rookery at Gull Island and two or three hours to walk around Halibut Cove. The ferry makes two trips daily: the first ($58) leaves Homer at noon and returns at 5 pm, and the second ($35) leaves at 5 pm and returns at 10 pm. Central Charters and the Saltry Restaurant handle all bookings. Several lodges are on this side of the bay, on pristine coves away from summer crowds. Mako's Taxi provides service to most of the lodging destinations in the area. ✉ Homer ☎ 907/399–2683 ⊕ www.halibut-cove-alaska.com/ferry.htm ⊗ Closed Oct.–Apr.

Kachemak Bay State Park and State Wilderness Park

NATIONAL/STATE PARK | Recreational opportunities in this beautiful park, which encompasses about 400,000 acres, include boating, sea kayaking, fishing, hiking, and beachcombing. Among the attractions here are Grewingk Glacier, Poot Peak, China Poot Bay, Halibut Cove Lagoon, Tutka Bay, Humpy Creek, and China Poot (Leisure) Lake—trails accessible from Kachemak Bay lead to all of them. Facilities are minimal, but include 20 primitive campsites and five public-use cabins. Most Homer water taxi operators can drop you off and pick you up at specific points and can provide advice about hiking, camping, and kayaking trips. ✉ Access to park by boat or plane only ☎ 907/262–5581 ⊕ www.dnr.alaska.gov/parks/units/kbay/kbayl.htm.

🍴 Restaurants

Halibut Cove Live

$$$$ | SEAFOOD | Set on a superb floating stage on Halibut Cove, HCL hosts dinner several times a summer, each featuring a renowned guest chef from somewhere in the state, locally grown produce, and fresh seafood. There's also live jazz music. **Known for:** unique (and expensive) dining and music experience; fantastic fresh seafood dishes; very romantic ambience. ⑤ Average main: $250 ☎ 907/235–0541 ⊕ www.halibutcovelive.com.

Camping on Kachemak Bay

Twenty primitive, free campsites with pit toilets and fire rings are scattered along the shores of Kachemak Bay across from Homer and are accessible by boat (water taxis operate here daily in summer). The sites are available on a first-come, first-served basis, and camping is allowed nearly everywhere in the park (not restricted to developed sites). Large groups can reserve sites, which are listed on the park's website. ☎ 907/235–7024 or ☎ 907/262–5581 ⊕ www.dnr.alaska.gov/parks/units/kbay/kbayl.htm.

★ The Saltry Restaurant

$$$ | SEAFOOD | At the top of the dock overlooking Halibut Cove, this is one of Southcentral's most beautiful places to sit and soak up the pleasures of a summer afternoon. Locally caught seafood, the restaurant's specialty, is prepared with finesse, and the dish for vegetarians is always a mouthwatering delight. **Known for:** one of the best Alaskan culinary experiences; romantic dining; location on art-filled boardwalk. ⑤ Average main: $28 ✉ 9 W. Ismilof Rd., Halibut Cove ☎ 907/399–2683 ⊕ www.thesaltry.com ⊗ Closed late Sept.–early May.

🛏 Hotels

Alaska State Parks Cabins

$ | RENTAL | Three public-use cabins are within Kachemak Bay's Halibut Cove lagoon area, another is near Tutka Bay lagoon, and a fifth is at China Poot Lake. **Pros:** total solitude; great views; true wilderness. **Cons:** remote locations with no amenities; all cabins except one accessible only by boat; no running water or electricity. ⑤ Rooms from: $75 ✉ Homer

☎ *907/262–5581* ⊕ *www.dnr.alaska.gov/ parks/cabins/kenai.htm* ➾ *5 cabins.*

Kachemak Bay Wilderness Lodge

$$$$ | RESORT | Across Kachemak Bay from Homer, this lodge provides wildlife-viewing opportunities and panoramic mountain and bay vistas in an intimate setting for up to 14 guests. **Pros:** extraordinary facility; sauna and outdoor hot tub; stunning location. **Cons:** pricey; might be too remote for some; few standard hotel amenities. ⑤ *Rooms from: $2100* ✉ *Homer* ☎ *907/235–8910* ⊕ *www.alaskawildernesslodge.com* ◐ *Closed Oct.–Apr.* ➾ *4 cabins, 1 room in lodge* ❖ *All meals.*

★ Tutka Bay Lodge

$$$$ | RESORT | In a small cove 9 nautical miles from Homer Spit (boat ride included in the room rates), this resort offers luxury and relaxation. **Pros:** experienced guide on all trips; amazing location; incredible food. **Cons:** expensive; cell phone service may be dodgy; three-night minimum stay. ⑤ *Rooms from: $5035* ✉ *Homer* ☎ *907/235–3905, 907/274–2710* ⊕ *withinthewild.com/lodges/tutka-bay* ➾ *5 cabins* ❖ *All meals.*

Seldovia

16 miles south of Homer.

The town of Seldovia is another off-the-road-system settlement on the south side of Kachemak Bay that retains the charm of an earlier Alaska. The town's Russian bloodline shows in its onion-dome church and its name, which means "herring bay." For many years this was the primary fishing town on the bay, but today the focus is on tourism. The town was heavily damaged in the 1964 earthquake, but a few stretches of old boardwalk survive and houses stand on stilts along Seldovia Slough. Seldovia has several restaurants and lodging places, plus a small museum and a hilltop Russian Orthodox church. The area abounds with hiking, mountain-biking, and sea-kayaking

options, and is a favorite performance destination for many Alaskan musicians during the summer months.

GETTING HERE AND AROUND

Seldovia's not an island, but it is only accessible by the Alaska Marine Highway ferry, water taxi, or by air from Homer.

🍴 Restaurants

Linwood Bar & Grill

$$ | AMERICAN | With a great outdoor deck and a heap of local company, the Linwood emphasizes its "bar" side at night and serves up hearty grilled burgers, pizzas, and seafood by day and into the early evening. Musicians from all over the state take the boat over to perform for Seldovians here. **Known for:** excellent outdoor deck; live music from around the state; great pub food. ⑤ *Average main: $15* ✉ *257 Main St.* ☎ *907/234–7674* ⊕ *www.linwoodbar.com.*

🏨 Hotels

Sea Parrot Inn

$$ | B&B/INN | In view of the harbor and just a short walk away, the Sea Parrot Inn is hard to miss. **Pros:** convenient harbor location; welcoming hosts; robust breakfast included in rate. **Cons:** setting may be too cozy for some guests; boat ride required to get there; can get loud on live music nights. ⑤ *Rooms from: $135* ✉ *226 Main St.* ☎ *907/234–7829* ⊕ *www.seaparrotinn.com* ➾ *4 rooms* ❖ *Breakfast.*

Seldovia Boardwalk Hotel

$$ | HOTEL | With fabulous views of the harbor and tastefully decorated rooms, the Boardwalk has many of the simple amenities found in an urban hotel, but with a cozy B&B feel. **Pros:** in-town location; great waterfront views; beautiful sundeck overlooking the water. **Cons:** some rooms primarily have street views; takes a boat to get here; small rooms. ⑤ *Rooms from: $149* ✉ *239 Main St.* ☎ *907/234–7816* ⊕ *www.seldoviahotel.com* ➾ *12 rooms* ❖ *Breakfast.*

Kodiak

248 miles southwest of Anchorage by air.

Today, commercial fishing is king in Kodiak. Despite its small population—about 6,475 people scattered among the several islands in the Kodiak group—the city is among the busiest fishing ports in the United States. The harbor is also an important supply point for small communities on the Aleutian Islands and the Alaska Peninsula.

Visitors to the island tend to follow one of two agendas: either immediately fly out to a remote lodge for fishing, kayaking, or bear viewing; or stay in town and access whatever pursuits they can reach from the limited road system. If the former is too pricey an option, consider combining the two: drive the road system to see what can be seen inexpensively, then add a fly-out or charter-boat excursion to a remote lodge or wilderness access point.

Floatplane and boat charters are available from Kodiak to many remote attractions, chief among them the Kodiak National Wildlife Refuge, which covers four islands in the Gulf of Alaska: Kodiak, Afognak, Ban, and Uganik.

GETTING HERE AND AROUND

Access to the island is via the Alaska Marine Highway ferry (which makes several stops a week) or by plane. A few roads stretch out of town, perfect for a day of sightseeing. The action, however, is in town. Your first exploring stop should be the Kodiak Island Convention & Visitors Bureau. Here you can pick up brochures, pamphlets, and lists of all the visitor services on Kodiak and the surrounding islands, and get help with planning your adventures. If you want to strike out and hike the local trails, there's an informative *Hiking and Birding Guide* published by the Kodiak Audubon Society.

ESSENTIALS

VISITOR INFORMATION Kodiak Island Convention & Visitors Bureau ✉ *100 Marine Way, Suite 200* ☎ *907/486–4782, 800/789–4782* ⊕ *www.kodiak.org.*

👁 Sights

Alutiiq Museum and Archaeological Repository

MUSEUM | Home to one of the largest collections of Alaska Native materials in the world, the Alutiiq Museum contains archaeological and ethnographic items dating back 7,500 years. The more than 150,000 artifacts include harpoons, masks, dolls, stone tools, seal-gut parkas, grass baskets, and pottery fragments. The museum store sells Alaska Native arts and educational materials. ✉ *215 Mission Rd., Suite 101* ☎ *844/425– 8844* ⊕ *www.alutiiqmuseum.org* 💲 *$7* ⊘ *Closed Sun. and Mon.*

Baranov Museum

MUSEUM | The museum presents artifacts from the area's Russian past in an 1808 structure built to warehouse sea-otter pelts. On display are samovars, intricate Native basketry, and other relics from the early Native Koniags and the later Russian settlers. Albums of archival photography portray various aspects of the island's history. In the early 1800s, the museum's namesake, Alexander Baranov, was the chief manager for the fur-trading Russian-American Company. Baranov commissioned the building that now houses the museum, which W.J. Erskine, who owned a big cod fishery, made his home in 1911. ✉ *101 Marine Way* ☎ *907/486–5920* ⊕ *www.baranovmuseum.org* 💲 *$5* ⊘ *Closed Sun. and Mon.*

Fort Abercrombie State Historical Park

HISTORIC SITE | **FAMILY** | As part of America's North Pacific defense during World War II, Kodiak was the site of an important naval station, now occupied by the Coast Guard fleet that patrols the surrounding fishing grounds. Part of the old military installation has been incorporated into this park north of town. Self-guided tours take you past concrete bunkers and gun emplacements, and trails wind through moss-draped spruce forest. There's a highly scenic overlook, great for bird- and whale watching, and inside a bunker a volunteer group runs the **Kodiak Military History Museum.** ✉ *Mile 3.7, E. Rezanof Dr.* ☎ *907/486–6339* ⊕ *www. dnr.alaska.gov/parks/units/kodiak/ftaber. htm* ✎ *$5.*

Holy Resurrection Russian Orthodox Church
RELIGIOUS SITE | The ornate Russian Orthodox church is a visual feast, both inside and out. The cross-shaped building is topped by two onion-shaped blue domes, and the interior contains brass candelabra, distinctive chandeliers, and numerous icons representing Ortho-dox saints. Three different churches have stood on this site since 1794. The present structure, built in 1945, is on the National Register of Historic Places. ✉ *385 Kashevaroff Ave.* ☎ *907/486–5532 parish priest* ⊕ *www.oca.org/parishes/ oca-ak-kodhrc* ✎ *Free.*

Kodiak National Wildlife Refuge Visitor Center
INFO CENTER | **FAMILY** | Indispensable for those exploring the wildlife refuge, this center a block from the downtown ferry dock is an interesting stop on its own. Wander through exhibits about the refuge's flora and fauna, attend an inter-pretive talk, and marvel at the complete 36-foot hanging skeleton of a male gray whale on the second floor. ✉ *402 Center Ave.* ☎ *907/487–2626* ⊕ *www.fws.gov/ refuge/kodiak.*

🏃 Activities

Kodiak Adventures Unlimited
TOUR—SPORTS | This outfit with a summer kiosk in St. Paul Harbor (across from Wells Fargo) books charter and tour oper-ators for all of Kodiak. ✉ *105 W. Marine Way* ☎ *907/486–8766* ⊕ *www.kodiakad-venturesunlimited.com.*

Memory Makers Tour and Guide Service
TOUR—SPORTS | Guide Dake Schmidt is knowledgeable and passionate about fishing local rivers; his angling half- and full-day trips are a boon for those not flying off to remote lodges. Fishing gear, lunch (on full-day excursions), and a ride in a comfortable van are provided. Mem-ory Makers also conducts sightseeing, wildlife-viewing, and photography tours. ✉ *1523B Mission Rd.* ☎ *907/486–7000* ⊕ *www.memorymakersinak.com* ✎ *From $150 half-day, $300 full-day.*

🍴 Restaurants

Henry's Great Alaskan Restaurant
$$ | **AMERICAN** | A big, boisterous, friendly place near the small-boat harbor, Henry's has a menu that's equally big. There's fresh local seafood, of course, but also everything from barbecue and rack of lamb to gourmet salads, pastas, and even some Cajun dishes. **Known for:** great post-fishing dining destination; tasty seafood bowls; very relaxed environ-ment. ⑤ *Average main: $20* ✉ *512 W. Marine Way* ☎ *907/486–8844* ⊕ *www. henrysgreatalaskan.com* ⊙ *Closed Sun. Oct.–Apr.*

Java Flats
$ | **CAFÉ** | This great coffee shop repre-sents the true essence of Kodiak life. Fantastic breakfast burritos, vegetarian sandwiches, and excellent coffee make this the perfect place to stock up on provisions before embarking on exciting bear-watching and salmon-fishing adven-tures. **Known for:** tasty vegetarian sand-wiches; grab-n-go options; best coffee in town. ⑤ *Average main: $12* ✉ *11206 W. Rezanof Dr.* ☎ *907/487–2622* ⊕ *www. javaflats.com* ⊙ *Closed Mon. and Tues.*

Kodiak Hana Restaurant
$$ | **SEAFOOD** | This converted powerhouse facility allows a close-up view of Near Island and the channel connecting the boat harbors with the Gulf of Alaska. Enjoy fine steaks and classic seafood dishes, or fresh sushi and sashimi while

watching the procession of fishing boats gliding past on their way to catch or deliver your next meal. **Known for:** excellent sushi; great views of marine wildlife; diverse fresh fish dishes. $ *Average main: $20* ✉ *516 E. Marine Way* ☎ *907/481–1088* ⊕ *www.powerhousekodiak.com* ⊘ *Closed Mon. No lunch Sun.*

Rendezvous Bar & Grill

$$ | **AMERICAN** | A shanty roadhouse of sorts, Rendezvous serves drinks all night and caters to locals. Every afternoon (except Monday), however, the locals and tourists show up in droves to fill their bellies with the tastiest eats on the island. **Known for:** amazing fish tacos; laid-back ambience; no food (just drinks) after 7:30 pm. $ *Average main: $15* ✉ *11652 Chiniak Hwy.* ☎ *907/487–2233* ⊘ *No lunch or dinner Mon.*

 ## Hotels

A Channel View Bed & Breakfast

$$ | **B&B/INN** | Owned and operated by a fifth-generation Kodiak Alaskan, this emerald-isle favorite has sea views and is conveniently located less than 1 mile from downtown Kodiak. **Pros:** channel views; very hospitable owners; nicely furnished. **Cons:** slightly inconvenient if you don't have a car and aren't keen on a 20-minute walk into town; must take stairs to get to some rooms; two-night minimum. $ *Rooms from: $149* ✉ *1010 Stellar Way* ☎ *907/486–2470* ⊕ *www.kodiakchannelview.com* ⇌ *4 rooms* ⦿| *Breakfast.*

Best Western Kodiak Inn

$$$ | **HOTEL** | Rooms here have soothing floral decor, and some overlook the harbor. **Pros:** downtown location; local seafood at restaurant; free Wi-Fi. **Cons:** harbor-view rooms are on the street; quiet rooms don't have great views; despite location, it's still a corporate chain. $ *Rooms from: $205* ✉ *236 W. Rezanof Dr.* ☎ *907/486–5712* ⊕ *www.bestwestern.com* ⇌ *82 rooms* ⦿| *Breakfast.*

Cliff House B&B

$$ | **B&B/INN** | Perched on Kodiak's rocky coastline, this house contains a suite of three rooms with a common sitting area, private entrance, shared bath, and kitchen facilities, complete with homemade granola and a "bottomless cookie jar." **Pros:** excellent views; cozy library for rainy-day relaxation; cliffside deck. **Cons:** some rooms share a bathroom; decor a bit dated; cookie jar might be too tempting for some. $ *Rooms from: $190* ✉ *1223 W. Kouskov St.* ☎ *907/486–5079* ⊕ *www.galleygourmet.biz* ⦿| *Breakfast.*

Comfort Inn Kodiak

$$ | **HOTEL** | This chain property is a five-minute walk from the main terminal at the airport, about 4½ miles from downtown (free airport transportation is provided). **Pros:** can fish for salmon in the river out back; comfortable and clean rooms; friendly staff. **Cons:** a bit out of town, so you might need a vehicle; no air-conditioning for the hot days; not very attractive from the outside. $ *Rooms from: $180* ✉ *1395 Airport Way* ☎ *907/487–2700, 800/544–2202* ⊕ *www.comfortinn.com* ⇌ *50 rooms* ⦿| *Breakfast.*

Nightlife

Kodiak Island Brewing Co.

WINERY/DISTILLERY | Freshly brewed, unfiltered beer is the specialty here, sold in liters, growlers, pigs, and kegs, so you can stock up for your wilderness expedition and avoid beer withdrawal. Drop on by for a couple of pints in the tasting room. Brewer Ben Millstein will give you a tour of the facility on request. ✉ *117 Lower Mill Bay Rd.* ☎ *907/486–2537* ⊕ *www.kodiakbrewery.com.*

Kodiak brown bears are often spotted by rivers and streams, fishing for salmon.

Kodiak National Wildlife Refuge

50 miles south of Katmai National Park, 300 miles southwest of Anchorage.

Many visitors to Kodiak National Wildlife Refuge come here to view Kodiak bears. Seeing these beautiful animals, which weigh a pound at birth but up to 1,500 pounds when fully grown, is worth the trip to this rugged country. The bears are spotted easily in July and August, feeding along salmon-spawning streams. Chartered flightseeing trips go to the area, and exaggerated tales of encounters with these impressive beasts are frequently heard.

GETTING HERE AND AROUND

The refuge is accessible only by boat or plane. The Alaska Marine Highway ferry stops at the town of Kodiak several times a week in summer. The visitor bureau there has lists of the numerous guides, outfitters, and air taxis that service the refuge.

◉ Sights

★ Kodiak National Wildlife Refuge

NATURE PRESERVE | The opportunity to view Kodiak brown bears alone is worth the trip to this rugged country. Approximately 3,000 Kodiak brown bears, the biggest brown bears anywhere—sometimes topping out at more than 1,500 pounds—share the refuge with a few other land mammals: red foxes, river otters, short-tailed weasels, and tundra voles. Additionally, several additional mammals have been introduced to the archipelago: Sitka black-tailed deer, snowshoe hare, beaver, muskrat, Roosevelt elk, and mountain goat. The 1.9-million-acre Kodiak National Wildlife Refuge lies mostly on Kodiak Island and neighboring Afognak and Uganik islands, in the Gulf of Alaska. All are part of the Kodiak Archipelago, separated from Alaska's mainland by the stormy Shelikof Strait. Within the refuge are rugged mountains, tundra meadows and lowlands, thickly forested hills, plus lakes, marshes, and hundreds of miles of pristine coastland. No place in the refuge is more than 15 miles from the ocean. The weather here is generally wet and cool, and storms born in the North Pacific often bring heavy rains. Dozens of species of birds flock to the refuge each spring and summer, including Aleutian terns, horned puffins, black oystercatchers, ravens, ptarmigan, and chickadees. At least 600 pairs of bald eagles live on the islands, building the world's largest bird nests on shoreline cliffs and in tall trees. Six species of Pacific salmon—chums, kings, pinks, silvers, sockeyes, and steelhead—return to Kodiak's waters from May to October. Other resident species include rainbow trout, Dolly Varden (an anadromous trout waiting for promotion to salmon), and arctic char. The abundance of fish and bears makes the refuge popular with anglers, hunters, and wildlife watchers. ⊠ *Kodiak.*

🏃 Activities

Kodiak Brown Bear Center
WILDLIFE-WATCHING | Part of the Kodiak Regional Native Corporation, this outfit has exclusive access to 112,000 acres that are free of motorized distractions. KBBC limits its tours to groups of six, ensuring an extraordinary bear-viewing experience. Lodging is within a series of modern cabins with porches facing Karluk Lake. Gourmet meals are prepared every day, and a traditional Alutiiq steam bath is on the premises. ⊠ *Kodiak* ☎ *877/335–2327* ⊕ *www.kodiakbearcenter.com.*

🛏 Hotels

Kodiak Refuge Public-Use Cabins
$ | **RENTAL** | One of the Kodiak National Wildlife Refuge's lesser-known wonders is its collection of eight fantastic cabins scattered throughout the refuge. Set along the coast and on inland lakes, the cabins are bare-bones but do

include bunks (which do not come with mattresses), kerosene heaters (you bring in your own kerosene), tables, and benches. **Pros:** true Alaska wilderness; plenty of solitude; affordable. **Cons:** zero amenities; roughing it is not for everyone; the chance of getting weathered in for a couple of days requires a loose schedule. ⑤ *Rooms from: $75* ⊠ *1390 Buskin River Rd., Kodiak* ☎ *907/487–2600* ⊕ *www. recreation.gov* ⌕ *Reservations essential* ⇥ *8 cabins.*

Lake Clark National Park and Preserve

100 miles southwest of Anchorage by air.

When the weather is good, an idyllic choice beyond the Mat-Su Valley is the huge Lake Clark National Park and Preserve, on the Alaska Peninsula and a short flight from Anchorage or Kenai and Soldotna.

GETTING HERE AND AROUND
There's no road access to the park, so all visits are via small plane. There are no roads within the park, nor are any groceries or camping supplies available. Most people fly into Port Alsworth, where lodging and supplies are available; while you're there sign in at the visitor center.

ESSENTIALS
VISITOR INFORMATION Lake Clark Administrative Headquarters ☎ *907/644–3626.*

👁 Sights

Lake Clark National Park and Preserve
NATURE PRESERVE | The 3.4 million acres on the Alaska Peninsula that comprise Lake Clark National Park and Preserve stretch from the coast to the heights of two grand volcanoes: Mt. Iliamna and Mt. Redoubt. The latter made headlines in 2009 when it erupted, sending ash floating over the region. Both volcanoes top out above 10,000 feet. The country in

Mat-Su Valley and Beyond

KEY

⚓ Ferry Lines

0 — 50 miles
0 — 75 km

YUKON

Beaver Creek

CANADA
U.S.A.

Mt. Logan ▲

Malaspina Glacier

Mt. St. Elias ▲

Yakutat

Northway

Nabesna

Wrangell Mountains ◆

Kennicott Mine
Kennicott
McCarthy

Wrangell–St. Elias National Park and Preserve ◆

Tok

Slana

Chistochina

Gakona
Glennallen

Copper Center

Chitina

Chitina River

Copper River

CHUGACH MOUNTAINS

Cape St. Elias

Gulf of Alaska

Paxson

Richardson Hwy.

4

Delta Junction

4

Richardson Hwy.

Glenn Hwy.

1

Matanuska R.

4

Cordova

Copper River Hwy.

Valdez

Chugach National Forest

Prince William Sound

8

Denali State Park

Denali Hwy.
(closed in winter)

Independence Mine State Historical Park

Sutton

Palmer
Pyrah's Pioneer Peak Farm

COLUMBIA GLACIER

Whittier

Portage

MONTAGUE ISLAND

Resurrection Bay

Cantwell

Denali National Park and Preserve

Denali ▲

3

George Parks Hwy.

Talkeetna

Alaska RR

Hatcher Pass Rd.

Musk-Ox Farm

Wasilla

Chugach State Park

Girdwood

Chenega Bay

Seward

ALASKA RANGE

Petersville

Trapper Creek

Finger Lake

Willow

Eagle River

Anchorage

Hope

Cooper Landing

9

Kenai Fjords National Park

Cook Inlet

Kenai National Wildlife Refuge

Sterling

Seward Hwy.

Sterling Hwy.

KENAI PENINSULA

Lake Clark National Park and Preserve ◆

Kenai

Soldotna

Clam Gulch

Ninilchik

Anchor Point

Homer

Kachemak Bay

Nondalton

Newhalen

Iliamna Lake

between holds glaciers, waterfalls, and turquoise-tinted lakes. The 50-mile-long Lake Clark, filled by runoff waters from the mountains that surround it, is an important spawning ground for thousands of red (sockeye) salmon.

The river-running is superb here. You can make your way through dark forests of spruce and balsam poplars or hike over the high, easy-to-travel tundra. The animal life is profuse: look for bears, moose, Dall sheep, wolves, wolverines, foxes, beavers, and mink on land; seals, sea otters, and white (aka beluga) whales offshore. Wildflowers embroider the meadows and tundra in spring, and wild roses bloom in the shadows of the forests. Plan your trip to Lake Clark for the end of June or early July, when the insects may be less plentiful. Or consider late August or early September, when the tundra glows with fall colors.

Activities

★ Alaska Alpine Adventures

TOUR—SPORTS | Founded by two adventure enthusiasts, Alaska Alpine offers kayaking, climbing, and hiking packages—from 7 to 12 days—in Lake Clark National Park and Preserve (and all over the state). Their guides, among the best in the state, are extremely experienced and are certified as Wilderness First Responders. ☎ 877/525–2577 ⊕ www.alaskaalpineadventures.com ✉ From $3150.

Hotels

Silver Salmon Creek Lodge

$$$$ | **RESORT** | This comfortable family-run lodge hugs the coast of Lake Clark National Park and is an ideal base for brown bear viewing without platforms—visitors may spot a mother and cubs, bears digging for clams on the beach, eating sedge grass, or fishing for salmon. **Pros:** phenomenal coastal brown bear viewing; rates include flight, meals, and guides; excellent professional photo

ops. **Cons:** only accessible by floatplane from Anchorage or Soldotna/Homer; very pricey; bear sighting not guaranteed. ⑤ Rooms from: $2150 ⊠ West Side of Cook Inlet, Lake Clark National Park ☎ 888/872–5666, 907/252–5504 ⊕ www.silversalmoncreek.com ➬ 14 rooms ⦿ All-inclusive.

★ Winterlake Lodge

$$$$ | **RESORT** | A rest stop and checkpoint for the Iditarod dogsled race and Iditarod Invitational winter bike race, this lodge in the North Tordrillo Mountains along the shore of Finger Lake is as luxurious as it is remote. **Pros:** pristine location; high-end dining at every meal; plenty of outdoor adventures included in rate. **Cons:** very remote; pricey; not for those who just want to relax or explore on own. ⑤ Rooms from: $1300 ☎ 907/274–2710 ⊕ www.withinthewild.com/lodges/winterlake ➬ 5 cabins ⦿ All-inclusive; All meals.

Palmer

40 miles northeast of Anchorage.

With mountain-ringed farms, Palmer is charming and photogenic. This is the place to search for 100-pound cabbages and fresh farm cheese. Historic buildings are scattered throughout the Mat-Su Valley; in 1935 the federal government relocated about 200 farm families here from the Depression-ridden Midwest. Now it has developed into the state's major agricultural region. Good growing conditions of rich soil and long hours of summer sunlight result in some huge vegetables.

GETTING HERE AND AROUND

The Glenn Highway heads north out of Anchorage and right through Palmer. The Chugach Range lines both sides of Palmer's valley, and if you continue past the town you'll find yourself smack in the middle of the mountains.

ESSENTIALS

VISITOR INFORMATION **Mat-Su Convention & Visitors Bureau** ⊠ *7744 E. Visitors View Ct.* ☎ *907/746–5000* ⊕ *www.alaskavisit.com.* **Palmer Chamber of Commerce** ⊠ *723 S. Valley Way* ☎ *907/745–2880* ⊕ *www.palmerchamber.org.*

Sights

Independence Mine State Historical Park

HISTORIC SITE | Gold mining was an early mainstay of the Mat-Su Valley's economy. You can tour the long-dormant Independence Mine on the Hatcher Pass Road, a loop that in summer connects the Parks Highway just north of Willow to the Glenn Highway near Palmer. The stunningly scenic drive travels past forested streams and alpine meadows and winds high above the tree line. The road to Independence Mine from the Palmer side is paved; the section between the mine and Willow is gravel. In the 1940s the mine employed as many as 200 workers. Today it is a 271-acre state park that has good cross-country skiing in winter. Only the wooden buildings remain; one of them, the red-roof manager's house, is now used as a visitor center. ⊠ *Hatcher Pass Rd., 19 miles northwest of Glenn Hwy.* ☎ *907/745–2827 visitors center, 907/745–3975 Mat-Su park office* ⊕ *www.dnr.alaska.gov/parks/units/indmine.htm* ⌿ *$5 day-use parking.*

Musk Ox Farm

FARM/RANCH | **FAMILY** | Fifty or so animals roam at the Musk Ox Farm, which conducts 30-minute guided tours. There's a hands-on museum and a gift shop featuring hand-knitted items made from the cashmere-like underfur (qiviut) combed from the musk ox. The scarves, caps, and more are made by Oomingmak, an Alaska Native collective. ⊠ *Mile 50.1, Glenn Hwy.* ☎ *907/745–4151* ⊕ *www.muskoxfarm.org* ⌿ *$11.*

Pyrah's Pioneer Peak Farm

FARM/RANCH | **FAMILY** | On a sunny day the town of Palmer looks like a Swiss calendar photo, with its old barns and log houses silhouetted against craggy Pioneer Peak. On nearby farms on the Bodenburg Loop off the old Palmer Highway you can pay to pick your own raspberries and other fruits and vegetables. The peak picking time at Pyrah's Pioneer Peak Farm, which cultivates 35 kinds of fruits and vegetables, occurs around mid-July. ⊠ *Mile 2.6, Bodenburg Loop* ☎ *907/745–4511* ⊕ *www.pppfarm.net* ⊘ *Closed Sept.–June.*

🍴 Restaurants

Palmer City Alehouse

$$ | **AMERICAN** | A hot meeting place in the old train depot, Palmer City echoes with the sound of local chatter. Though it doesn't provide much of a romantic dining experience, it has a great ambience, and the standard pub fare—salads, pizzas made in a fire-brick oven, and handmade burgers—are better than average. **Known for:** historic location; wide beer selection; good pub food. Ⓢ *Average main: $15* ⊠ *320 E. Dahlia Ave.* ☎ *907/746–2537* ⊕ *www.alaskaalehouse.com.*

Vagabond Blues

$ | **CAFÉ** | The folks at this aroma-filled spot serve up fresh and tasty pastries, quiches, wraps, salads, panini and other sandwiches, and espresso drinks. A convivial setting for meetings, board games, and pleasant conversation by day, Vagabond is a popular venue for touring musical acts several times a month. **Known for:** best coffee in town; healthy food options; grab-and-go meals. Ⓢ *Average main: $12* ⊠ *642 S. Alaska St.* ☎ *907/745–2233.*

🛏 Hotels

Alaska's Harvest B&B

$$ | **B&B/INN** | Two miles outside Palmer on 15 acres of wooded land, the Hand family's peaceful inn has tremendous views of snowcapped mountains from across a sheep pasture. **Pros:** beautiful views; hospitable hosts; kitchens stocked with breakfast food. **Cons:** only three rooms have private bathrooms; alcohol not allowed; could use some updating. ⑤ *Rooms from: $149* ✉ *2252 N. Love Dr.* ☎ *907/745–4263* ⊕ *www.alaskasharvest. com* ⇆ *6 rooms* ⦿ *Breakfast.*

Colony Inn

$ | B&B/INN | All guest rooms in this lovingly restored historic building are tastefully decorated with antiques and quilts. **Pros:** quiet; charming; centrally located. **Cons:** front desk a five-minute walk away at Valley Hotel; rooms are small; no air-conditioning for the abnormally warm days. ⑤ *Rooms from: $100* ✉ *325 E. Elmwood Ave.* ☎ *907/745–3330* ⊕ *www.akcolonyinn.com* ⇆ *12 rooms* ⦿ *No meals.*

Hatcher Pass Lodge

$$ | B&B/INN | This lodge has spectacular views and can serve as a base camp for hiking, berry picking, and—in fall and winter—skiing. **Pros:** views and nature right outside your door; food is quite tasty; comfortable beds. **Cons:** no kitchens and a bit far from town, so dining options are limited; not all rooms have private baths; decor a bit dated. ⑤ *Rooms from: $150* ✉ *Mile 17, Hatcher Pass Rd., Box 763* ☎ *907/745–5897, 907/745–1200* ⊕ *www. hatcherpasslodge.com* ⇆ *3 rooms, 9 cabins* ⦿ *No meals.*

Nightlife

Arkose Brewery

WINERY/DISTILLERY | This microbrewery has a flavor portfolio inspired by both Germany and the Pacific Northwest. Expect to find seven fresh-brewed staples as well as one seasonal beer. Have a pint at the bar or fill a growler and head off on an adventure. Due to strict Alaska laws, food can be purchased to accompany your beverage at a food truck parked outside—always sure to be a delicious treat. ✉ *650 E. Steel Loop* ☎ *907/746–2337* ⊕ *www.arkosebrewery.com* ☾ *Closed Mon.*

Wasilla

42 miles north of Anchorage, 10 miles west of Palmer.

Wasilla made national news in 2008 when Sarah Palin, the former governor of the state and former mayor of the town, was picked to be the Republican vice-presidential candidate. Wasilla is one of the valley's original pioneer communities, and over time has served as a supply center for farmers, gold miners, and mushers. Today fast-food restaurants and strip malls line the Parks Highway. Rolling hills and more scenic vistas can be found by wandering the area's back roads. ∎**TIP→ Wasilla is the best place for stocking up if you're heading north to Talkeetna or Denali.**

GETTING HERE AND AROUND

Wasilla is accessible by car. Going north along the Glenn Highway, turn off just before Palmer and head west. You'll soon be in Wasilla. With its abundant strip malls, the town is not known for glamour or beauty, but take a side road or cruise past one of the many lakes in the region and you're sure to grab some great pictures.

ESSENTIALS

VISITOR INFORMATION Wasilla Chamber of Commerce ✉ *415 E. Railroad Ave.* ☎ *907/376–1299* ⊕ *www.wasillachamber. org.*

⊙ Sights

Iditarod Trail Headquarters

MUSEUM | FAMILY | The famous competition's headquarters displays dogsleds, mushers' clothing, and trail gear, and you can watch video highlights of past races. The gift shop sells Iditarod items. Dogsled rides take place year-round; in summer rides on wheels are available for $10. ✉ *2100 S. Knik–Goose Bay Rd.* ☎ *907/376–5155* ⊕ *www.iditarod.com* ⛂ *Free.*

Museum of Alaska Transportation and Industry

MUSEUM | FAMILY | On a 20-acre site the museum exhibits some of the machines that helped develop Alaska, from dogsleds to jet aircraft and everything in between. The Don Sheldon Building houses aviation artifacts as well as antique autos, trains, and photographic displays. There is also a snowmachine (Alaskan for snowmobile) exhibit. ✉ *3800 W. Museum Dr., off Mile 47 Parks Hwy.* ☎ *907/376–1211* ⊕ *www.museumofalaska.org* ✑ *$8.*

Restaurants

Cadillac Cafe

$$ | CAFÉ | Hearty fare fills the menu at this diner-style café, including homemade pies, juicy burgers, burritos, pasta dishes, and pizzas turned out of a wood-fired oven. The owner describes the decor as "Alaska minimalist," but the booths are plush and comfortable, and hand-rubbed wood is evident. **Known for:** best pies in town; diverse menu; family dining destination. ⑤ *Average main: $15* ✉ *Pittman Rd. and Parks Hwy., at Mile 49* ☎ *907/357–5533.*

The Grape Tap

$$$ | AMERICAN | With a menu that ebbs and flows with the seasons yet consistently delivers fantastic dishes, try The Grape Tap. This 60-seat restaurant and European wine cellar is set in a 1930s pioneer home that's been renovated with contemporary colors and style. **Known for:** excellent fine dining; fantastic wine selection; romantic ambience. ⑤ *Average main: $30* ✉ *322 N. Boundary St.* ☎ *907/376–8466* ⊕ *www.thegrapetap. com* ☾ *Closed Sun. and Mon. No lunch.*

Hotels

Best Western Lake Lucille Inn

$$ | HOTEL | This well-maintained resort on Lake Lucille provides easy access to several recreational activities, including boating in summer and ice-skating and snowmobiling in winter. **Pros:** beautiful lakefront property; very clean; comfortable rooms. **Cons:** sound of nearby powerboats can get annoying; not all rooms have a lake view; rooms do not have microwaves. ⑤ *Rooms from: $180* ✉ *1300 W. Lake Lucille Dr., Mile 43½, Parks Hwy.* ☎ *907/373–1776, 800/528–1234* ⊕ *www.bestwesternlakelucilleinn. com* ➲ *54 rooms* ❍| *Breakfast.*

★ Pioneer Ridge Bed and Breakfast Inn

$$ | B&B/INN | Each of the spacious, log-partitioned rooms in the converted old Fairview Dairy barn and award-winning inn is decorated according to a theme. **Pros:** cozy and warm; gorgeous views; excellent breakfast. **Cons:** not handicapped-friendly; walls are thin; not every room has a private bath. ⑤ *Rooms from: $139* ✉ *2221 Yukon Circle, HC31, Box 5083K* ☎ *907/376–7472, 800/478–7472* ⊕ *www.pioneerridge.com* ➲ *6 rooms, 1 cabin* ❍| *Breakfast.*

Talkeetna

56 miles north of Wasilla, 112 miles north of Anchorage.

Talkeetna lies at the end of a spur road near Mile 99 of the Parks Highway. The town maintains a Wild West vibe with a small, unpaved downtown area surrounding a central green. Lucky is the traveler who gets a few sunny days—Denali looms distantly over the town. Mountaineers congregate here to begin their assaults on Denali in Denali National Park; those just off the mountain are recognizable by their tanned faces with white "raccoon eyes" resulting from their sunglasses. The Denali mountain rangers have their climbing headquarters here, as do most glacier pilots who fly climbing parties to the mountain. A carved pole at the town cemetery honors deceased mountaineers.

Talkeetna is a must-visit if you're driving between Anchorage and Denali or Fairbanks. Talkeetna has quirky locals and a pebbly shore along the Susitna with fantastic views of Denali on a clear day. Be sure to visit the **West Rib Pub and Grill** (☎ 907/733–3354 ⊕ www.westribpub. info), on Main Street in the back of Nagley's Store (in business since 1921 and a minimuseum of sorts). You're likely to hear tales of the former mayor of Talkeetna, Stubbs, an affable orange cat who served as the town's leader for 19 years before he died in 2017. Grab a seat out back and wash down the delicious chili, burgers, and fries with a local microbrew.

◉ Sights

Talkeetna Historical Society Museum
MUSEUM | Exhibits at this downtown museum explore the history of Talkeetna and Denali climbs, and the town's colorful history. The Talkeetna Historical Society publishes a walking-tour map, available at the museum, that points out sites of historical interest. ⊠ Mile 14½, Talkeetna Spur and D St. ☎ 907/733–2487 ⊕ www. talkeetnahistoricalsociety.org ⊠ $3.

🏃 Activities

BOATING, FLOATING, AND FISHING
Mahay's Riverboat Service
BOATING | With the immense peaks of Denali as its backdrop, Mahay's operates jet-boat sightseeing and adventure tours on the Susitna and Talkeetna rivers. The company also conducts a Devil's Canyon Tour, a 130-mile round-trip river excursion through Denali State Park and into Devil's Gorge. ⊠ Talkeetna ☎ 907/733–2223 ⊕ www.mahaysriverboat.com ⊠ From $75.

Phantom Tri-River Charters
BOATING | Phantom operates fishing trips out of Talkeetna and on the nearby Deshka River, can provide all the necessary tackle and gear, and uses covered and

heated boats. ☎ 907/733–2400 ⊕ phantomsalmoncharters.com ⊠ Contact company for prices.

FLIGHTSEEING
★ K2 Aviation
FLYING/SKYDIVING/SOARING | Adventures in the sky is the name of the game at K2, which has a long and solid history of Alaska flights. Among your options: get a bird's-eye view of Denali Park's famous peaks, land on one of its many surrounding glacier, or land at Kahiltna Base Camp and actually attempt to climb the Great One. A sister company provides standard air-taxi and flightseeing services. ⊠ 14052 E. 2nd St. ☎ 907/733–2291, 800/764–2291 ⊕ www.flyk2.com ⊠ From $220.

Talkeetna Air Taxi
TOUR—SPORTS | Check out Denali from the air, then swoop down to a glacier to test your boots. Maybe even land on one. Talkeetna Air is known in the region as the glacier-landing company. Spending the extra dollars to land on a glacier is highly recommended—standing on a glacier next to the greatest vertical relief on the planet compares to nothing else. ⊠ Talkeetna ☎ 907/733–2218, 800/533–2219 ⊕ www.talkeetnaair.com ⊠ From $220.

HIKING
Alaska Mountaineering School
HIKING/WALKING | Whether it's on mountaineering expeditions to Denali or less extreme treks into the Alaska Range, this Talkeetna company takes the time to train you before heading out to glacier trek or hit the pristine backcountry, and it teaches excellent mountaineering courses and workshops. ⊠ 13765 3rd St. ☎ 907/733–1016 ⊕ www.climbalaska.org.

🍴 Restaurants

Denali Brewing Company Twister Creek Restaurant
$$ | AMERICAN | Like every good brewery, Denali Brewing Company has a large outdoor porch for sunny days, and a menu of savory items to soak up the

The First to Summit Denali

Between 1903 and 1912 eight expeditions walked the slopes of 20,310-foot Denali. But none had reached the absolute top of North America's highest peak. Thus the stage was set for Hudson Stuck, a self-described American amateur mountaineer.

Missionary Man

Stuck came to Alaska in 1904, drawn not by mountains but by a missionary calling. As the Episcopal Church's archdeacon for the Yukon River region, he visited Alaska Native villages year-round. His passion for climbing was unexpectedly rekindled in 1906, when he saw from afar the "glorious, broad, massive uplift" of Denali, the "father of mountains."

The Team

Five years after that wondrous view, Stuck pledged to reach Denali's summit—or at least try. For his climbing party he picked three Alaskans experienced in snow and ice travel, though not in mountaineering: Harry Karstens, a well-known explorer and backcountry guide who would later become the first superintendent of Mt. McKinley National Park; Robert Tatum, Stuck's missionary assistant; and Walter Harper, a part Alaska Native who served as Stuck's interpreter.

The Climb

Assisted by two sled-dog teams, the group began its expedition on St. Patrick's Day, 1913, at Nenana, a village 90 miles northeast of Denali. A month later they began their actual ascent of the great peak's northern side, via the Muldrow Glacier. The glacier's surface proved to be a maze of crevasses, some of them wide chasms with no apparent bottom. Carefully working their way up-glacier, the climbers established a camp at 11,500 feet. From there the team chopped a staircase up several miles—and 3,000 vertical feet—of rock, snow, and ice. Their progress was delayed several times by high winds, heavy snow, and near-zero visibility.

By May 30 the climbers had reached the top of the ridge (later named in Karstens's honor) and moved into a high glacial basin. Despite temperatures ranging from subzero to 21°F, they kept warm at night by sleeping on sheep and caribou skins and covering themselves with down quilts, camel-hair blankets, and a wolf robe.

The Summit

On June 6 the team established its high camp at 18,000 feet. The following morning was bright, cloudless, and windy. Three of the climbers suffered headaches and stomach pains, but given the clear weather everyone agreed to make an attempt. They left camp at 5 am and by 1:30 pm stood within a few yards of Denali's summit. Harper, who had been leading all day, was the first to reach the top, soon followed by the others. After catching their breath, the teammates shook hands, said a prayer of thanks, made some scientific measurements, and reveled in their magnificent surroundings.

In his classic book *The Ascent of Denali*, Hudson Stuck later reflected, "There was no pride of conquest, no trace of that exultation of victory. ... Rather, was the feeling that a privileged communion with the high places of the earth had been granted."

beer. Burgers, fish-and-chips, and a host of appetizers pack their menu, but we highly recommend the reindeer meat loaf. **Known for:** award-winning microbrews; great pub food; locally produced cider, mead, and spirits also available. $ *Average main: $20* ✉ *13605 N. Main St.* ☎ *907/733–2537* ⊕ *www.denalibrewingcompany.com.*

Mountain High Pizza Pie
$$ | PIZZA | Homemade flatbreads, pizzas, calzones, and an excellent array of salads and garlic-filled dishes are the reasons locals congregate at this laidback downtown eatery all year long. The calzones are true works of art. **Known for:** great pizzas and calzones; family-friendly atmosphere; favorite hangout for locals. $ *Average main: $15* ✉ *22165 S. C St.* ☎ *907/733–1234* ⊕ *www.pizzapietalkeetna.com.*

Wildflower Cafe
$$$ | SEAFOOD | Off the lobby of an inn, the Wildflower has one menu that specializes in Alaskan seafood and one that features pub food like sandwiches, burgers and appetizers. There's also a good wine menu and 40 beers on tap. **Known for:** excellent seafood; best wine menu in town; quiet and sophisticated ambience. $ *Average main: $25* ✉ *13578 N. Main St.* ☎ *907/733–2695* ⊕ *www.talkeetnasuites.com.*

🛏 Hotels

★ Susitna River Lodging
$$ | B&B/INN | On the bank of the Susitna River and an easy ½-mile walk from downtown Talkeetna, this year-round lodge is idyllic. **Pros:** comfortable beds and pillows; gorgeous river and mountain views; great gathering space outside with firepits. **Cons:** no breakfast served; a short walk to town; no television in the cabins. $ *Rooms from: $199* ✉ *23094 S. Talkeetna Spur* ☎ *907/733–0505* ⊕ *www.susitnariverlodge.com* ⊷ *4 suites, 4 cabins* ⦿ *No meals.*

Swiss-Alaska Inn
$$ | B&B/INN | Family-run since 1976, this rustic-style property is well-known among those who come to fish in the Talkeetna, Susitna, and Chulitna rivers. **Pros:** very quiet; restaurant on premises; friendly staff. **Cons:** about ½ mile from town; a little off-the-beaten path; no air-conditioning for rare hot days. $ *Rooms from: $155* ✉ *East Talkeetna, by boat launch, 22056 S. F St.* ☎ *907/733–2424* ⊕ *www.swissalaska.com* ⊷ *20 rooms* ⦿ *No meals.*

Talkeetna Alaskan Lodge
$$$ | HOTEL | This lodge that occupies some of Talkeetna's best real estate has great hiking trails and splendid views of Denali. **Pros:** tremendous views of Denali on clear days, and of forests on rainy ones; comfortable rooms; dining on-site. **Cons:** 2 miles from Talkeetna's town center; none of Talkeetna's charm; no air-conditioning. $ *Rooms from: $205* ✉ *Mile 12½, Talkeetna Spur Rd.* ☎ *877/777–4067* ⊕ *www.talkeetnalodge.com* ⊷ *212 rooms* ⦿ *No meals.*

Talkeetna Roadhouse
$ | B&B/INN | This circa-1917 log roadhouse has a common sitting area and rooms of varying sizes. **Pros:** down-home Alaska at its best; perfectly situated location; delicious food. **Cons:** shared bathrooms; walls are thin; rooms are very basic. $ *Rooms from: $66* ✉ *13550 E. Main St.* ☎ *907/733–1351* ⊕ *www.talkeetnaroadhouse.com* ⊷ *5 rooms, 2 cabins, 1 apartment* ⦿ *No meals.*

🛍 Shopping

Dancing Leaf Gallery
ART GALLERIES | Featuring contemporary art and crafts all made by Alaskans, this is the go-to stop for gifts, a touch of Alaska, and an education. The high-ceiling, spacious gallery was constructed out of repurposed historic railroad timber. Be sure to give yourself enough time to browse as there is a lot to see. ✉ *13618*

Main St. ☎ 907/733–5323 ⊕ www.danc-ingleafgallery.com.

Nagley's General Store

CONVENIENCE/GENERAL STORES | First opened around 1900, this is the only grocery store in town, and where most locals go to get caught up on the gossip. Nagley's is also where you can go to get a great cup of hot coffee, a scoop of ice cream, adult libations, and other standard trading post items. This was also the former home of Stubbs the Cat Mayor, and workers are happy to tell you about the many store cats who came before and after him. ⊠ *13650 Main St. ☎ 907/733–3663 ⊕ www.nagleysstore.com.*

Denali State Park

34 miles north of Talkeetna, 132 miles north of Anchorage.

Between the Talkeetna Mountains and the Alaska Range, Denali State Park combines wooded lowlands and forested foothills topped by alpine tundra.

GETTING HERE AND AROUND

The George Parks Highway bisects Denali State Park and offers not only a majestic view of year-round snow-covered mountaintops, but also a mad array of wildlife. The highway is paved, but after the breakup of winter ice it tends to be riddled with potholes. It's always wise when driving in Alaska to have at least one good spare tire.

ESSENTIALS

VISITOR INFORMATION **Alaska State Parks, Mat-Su Area Office** ☎ *907/745–3975.*

Sights

Denali State Park

NATIONAL/STATE PARK | Overshadowed by the larger and more charismatic Denali National Park and Preserve, the 325,240-acre "Little Denali," or Denali State Park, offers excellent road access, beautiful views of Denali, scenic campgrounds, and prime wilderness hiking and backpacking opportunities within a few miles of the road system. The terrain here varies from the verdant, low-lying banks of the Tokositna River to alpine tundra. Moose, wolves, and grizzly and black bears inhabit the park, along with lynx, red foxes, land otters, beavers, porcupines, and myriad other species.

 ## Activities

Adventure Denali

FISHING | This outfit offers year-round, combat-free, catch-and-release fishing on its private lakes and nearby rivers. Stay for a while at the company's lodge or just fish for an afternoon—choices include lake fishing, river fishing, ice fishing, and fly-fishing. The experts here will even teach you how to fish. Adventure Denali is one of the few angler outfitters that actively encourages women to participate. ⊠ *Mile 214½ George Parks Hwy. ☎ 907/768–2620 summer, 907/354–0016 winter ⊕ www.adventuredenali.com* ☛ *From $175.*

Curry-Kesugi Ridge

HIKING/WALKING | Denali State Park's chief attraction, other than views of Denali, is the 35-mile-long Curry-Kesugi Ridge, which forms a rugged spine through the heart of the park that is ideal backpacking terrain. The initial climb to get to the ridge is strenuous, but once you get up high, it's mostly gentle up-and-down terrain. The trail runs from the Troublesome Creek trailhead at Mile 137.3 to the Little Coal Creek trailhead at Mile 163.9. The Byers Lake campground at Mile 147 has a trailhead for a spur trail that intersects the Kesugi Ridge trail, offering an alternative to hiking the entire trail. Views of Denali and the Alaska Range from the ridge trail are stunning. This is a bear-intensive area, especially around Troublesome Creek in late summer when the salmon runs are in full force.

Denali Backcountry Lodge

BICYCLING | In Kantishna, 92 miles into Denali National Park, this all-inclusive lodge is operated by Pursuit, an international travel company that offers naturalist hikes, rafting, and flightseeing packages. ☎ 800/808–8068 ⊕ www.alaskacollection.com/denali-national-park-interior ⌦ From $545 nightly.

Peters Hills

BICYCLING | Another destination favored by backcountry travelers is Peters Hills, accessible from Petersville Road in Trapper Creek. Denali State Park borders the hills, and primitive trails and campgrounds are used year-round. It's especially popular with snowmachiners in winter and mountain bikers in summer. ⊕ www.trails.com/us/ak/petersville/peters-hills.

Hotels

Alaska State Parks Cabins

$ | RENTAL | Three public-use cabins are in Denali State Park, along the shores of Byers Lake. **Pros:** more accessible than most wilderness cabins; stunning surroundings; great way to experience Alaska. **Cons:** very basic; no running water or electricity; no indoor bathrooms. ⑤ Rooms from: $75 ⊠ Anchorage ☎ 907/269–8400 ⊕ www.dnr.alaska.gov/parks/cabins/matsu.htm ⇥ 3 cabins ⦿ No meals.

McKinley Princess Wilderness Lodge

$$ | HOTEL | When the sky is clear and Denali is visible, this lodge has excellent views of North America's highest peak, especially from the lobby, which has two-story windows. **Pros:** has everything you might need; great location; delicious food. **Cons:** too huge for some; somewhat bland decor; many large tour groups. ⑤ Rooms from: $189 ⊠ Mile 133, Parks Hwy., Trapper Creek ☎ 907/733–2900, 800/426–0500 ⊕ www.princess-lodges.com/mckinley-lodge.cfm ☉ Closed mid-Sept.–mid-May ⇥ 464 rooms.

Glennallen

187 miles northeast of Anchorage.

This community of a few more than 500 residents is a good spot to gas up before continuing on to Wrangell–St. Elias National Park and Preserve. It's 124 miles from Glennallen to McCarthy, the last 58 miles on unpaved gravel. It is also the service center for the Copper River basin and is a fly-in base for several wilderness outfitters.

GETTING HERE AND AROUND

The Glenn Highway from Anchorage to Glennallen is relatively well maintained all year-round. The town's main street, however, is sand and gravel.

ESSENTIALS

VISITOR INFORMATION Bureau of Land Management ☎ 907/271–5960 ⊕ www.blm.gov/ak.

Restaurants

Tahi Tok

$ | THAI | Originally a large purple bus parked next to the gas station at the town's crossroads, this window service eatery is by far the best place in town. It serves surprisingly fresh vegetables and delightfully spicy dishes. **Known for:** unique window service setting; great pad Thai; various spicy dishes. ⑤ Average main: $12 ⊠ 189 Glenn Hwy.

Hotels

Caribou Hotel

$$ | HOTEL | Mauve and sea-green rooms fill this modern hotel where two-bedroom suites offer a very chic contrast to the pair of rustic cabins that are also available; the latter are primarily for those who want to get a taste of living in the Bush. **Pros:** good restaurant next door; comfortable rooms; friendly owner. **Cons:** not very glamorous; some rooms share a bathroom; no views. ⑤ Rooms from:

$149 ⊠ Mile 187, Glenn Hwy. ☎ 907/822–3302 ⊕ www.caribouhotel.com ⤴ 86 rooms, 2 cabins ❑ No meals.

Wrangell–St. Elias National Park and Preserve

77 miles southeast of Glennallen, 264 miles east of Anchorage.

Encompassing 13.2 million acres (it's nearly the size of West Virginia), the Wrangell–St. Elias National Park and Preserve stretches from one of the tallest peaks in North America, Mt. St. Elias (elevation 18,009 feet), to the ocean. This region is filled with adventures waiting to happen, mountains to be explored. Far, far removed from the hustle of cruise ships and tourist attractions, this is the wild Alaska.

People here have been living off the land in this region for centuries, and they still do. The town of Kennicott, once a profitable copper-mining company town, went bust in 1930, and what remains are excellently preserved buildings and the mill used to extract the copper ore. Kennicott is a now a National Historic Landmark and includes the Kennicott Glacier Lodge, in a replica mine building. Just a few miles down the road is the good-time town of McCarthy where historically mine workers went to drink and gamble. It has some of the same character today—this is where locals and seasonal guides live and play. Limited services are available in McCarthy and Kennicott: there are two places to stay, one food truck, two restaurants, and one bar.

GETTING HERE AND AROUND

The park is accessible from Alaska's highway system via one of two gravel roads. The unpaved Nabesna Road leaves the Glenn Highway–Tok Cutoff at the village of Slana and takes you 45 miles into the park's northern foothills. The better-known route is McCarthy Road, which stretches for 60 miles as it follows an old railroad bed from Chitina to the Kennicott River. The drive from Chitina to McCarthy is unpaved, bumpy, and potholed and can take two and a half hours or more. At the end of the road you must park and cross the river via a footbridge.

Some car rental companies will not allow you to drive to Wrangell-St. Elias due to the wear and tear it puts on the car. ■ TIP→ **Before setting out on McCarthy Road, make sure your car has a working jack and a properly inflated spare tire, or else potholes, old railroad ties, and occasional railroad spikes may cause damage and leave you stranded.**

If you want to avoid the unpaved McCarthy Road, consider flying from the Chitina Airport. The flight takes about 30 minutes and you'll see glaciers along the way.

ESSENTIALS

AIR CONTACTS Wrangell Mountain Air ☎ 800/478–1160, 907/554–4411 ⊕ www.wrangellmountainair.com.

VISITOR INFORMATION Wrangell–St. Elias Visitors Center ⊠ Mile 106.8, Richardson Hwy., Copper Center ☎ 907/822–7250 ⊕ www.nps.gov/wrst.

◉ Sights

Kennecott Mine

MINE | In the early 1900s, prospectors found copper ore in the mountains above the Kennicott Glacier. A mine, railway (now the McCarthy Road), and company town were soon built. But, by 1930s the ore was gone, the company moved out, and the town became a ghost town. The abandoned Kennecott Mine is one of Wrangell–St. Elias National Park and Preserve's main attractions. The open-pit mine is reminiscent of ancient Greek amphitheaters, and the abandoned structures are as impressive as the mountains they stand against. Restorations of the mine have been a continuous and ongoing effort for over a decade.

The Kennecott Copper Corporation named the Kennecott Mine after the Kennicott Glacier—theories on the differing spellings range from accidental to intentional misspelling. Nowadays, though, the varied spellings help to differentiate the man-made landmarks from the natural features.

Malaspina Glacier

NATURE SITE | Wrangell–St. Elias's coastal mountains are frequently wreathed in snow-filled clouds, their massive height making a giant wall that contains the great storms brewed in the Gulf of Alaska. As a consequence, they bear some of the continent's largest ice fields, with more than 100 glaciers radiating from them. One of these, the Malaspina Glacier, is 1,500 square miles—larger than the state of Rhode Island. This tidewater glacier has an incredible pattern of black-and-white stripes made by the other glaciers that coalesced to form it. If you fly between Juneau and Anchorage, look for Malaspina Glacier on the coast north of Yakutat.

Mt. St. Elias

MOUNTAIN—SIGHT | The white-iced spire of Mt. St. Elias, in the St. Elias Range, reaches more than 18,000 feet. It's the second-highest mountain peak on the North American continent and the crown of the planet's highest coastal range. It also contains the world's longest ski descent.

Wrangell Mountains

MOUNTAIN—SIGHT | Covering a 100-mile-by-70-mile area, the Wrangells tower above the 2,500-foot-high Copper River plateau, and the peaks of Mts. Jarvis, Drum, Blackburn, Sanford, and Wrangell rise from 15,000 feet to 16,000 feet from sea level.

★ Wrangell–St. Elias National Park and Preserve

NATURE PRESERVE | In a land of many grand and spectacularly beautiful mountains, those in the 13.2-million-acre Wrangell–St. Elias National Park and Preserve are possibly the finest of them all. This extraordinarily compact cluster of immense peaks belongs to four different mountain ranges. Rising through many eco-zones, the Wrangell–St. Elias Park and Preserve is largely undeveloped wilderness parkland on a grand scale. The area is perfect mountain-biking and primitive-hiking terrain, and the rivers invite rafting for those with expedition experience. The mountains attract climbers from around the world—whereas Alaska's mountains have been summited many times over, there is the opportunity here to be the first or one of few to summit. Most climbers fly in from Glennallen or Yakutat. Although there are few facilities in Wrangell-St. Elias this is one of the few national parks in Alaska you can drive to. You don't have to be a backcountry camper to experience this park—it's possible to stay in comfortable lodgings in Kennicott or McCarthy and experience the massive glaciers that stand at the foot of Kennicott—Root Glacier and Kennicott Glacier or go on a multiday, guided rafting tour along the Nizina.

🏃 Activities

Alaska Vistas

KAYAKING | This Wrangell outfitter provides custom vacations specific to your interests. Opportunities include bear viewing, traveling the Stikine River by steamboat to see the largest flock of bald eagles in the country, and trips into the Tongass National Rain Forest. The company also offers kayaking, hiking, glacier trips, and unguided support to those who want to get out on their own. ✉ *103 Front St., Wrangell* ☎ *907/874–3006* ⊕ *www.alaska-vistas.com* ✉ *Call for prices.*

★ St. Elias Alpine Guides

TOUR—SPORTS | Based in the town of McCarthy and operating for more than three decades, this guide outfit gives introductory mountaineering lessons, leads excursions ranging from half-day hikes to monthlong backpacking trips, and is the only company contracted by the Park Service to conduct guided tours of historic Kennicott buildings. Don't miss hiking on Root Glacier—it's an incredible experience and accessible to anyone who can hike 5 miles. If you'd rather raft than hike, its Copper Oar rafting outfit (*www.copperoar.com*) has river trips into the heart of the wilderness. ☎ *907/554–4445, 888/933–5427* ⊕ *www.steliasguides.com* ⌘ *From $90.*

🍴 Restaurants

★ McCarthy Lodge

$$$$ | AMERICAN | A town with only 42 year-round residents, so far away from urban comforts, seems an unlikely place to secure a five-star meal, but that's exactly what the chefs here deliver. Because the restaurant is so remote, the chefs have to be creative to assemble meals from ingredients grown, caught, and raised in the region. **Known for:** unexpected fine dining where you least expect it; seared local duck; romantic ambience. ⑤ *Average main: $40* ⊠ *101 Kennicott Ave., McCarthy* ☎ *907/554–4402* ⊕ *www.mccarthylodge.com* ☉ *No lunch.*

Meatza Wagon

$$ | AMERICAN | With everything made from scratch, this food truck is like no other. Because the region is so far removed from the main road system, the chef heavily relies on locally sourced foods. **Known for:** fantastic pork tacos; grab-and-go meals; vegetarian and gluten-free options. ⑤ *Average main: $15* ⊠ *McCarthy* ⊕ *www.meatzawagon.com.*

The Potato

$ | AMERICAN | A semi-covered shack, The Potato is where the locals go when they don't feel up to cooking. It offers delicious flavors, live music, and a super laid-back vibe. **Known for:** fries, fries, and more fries; fun and relaxed ambience; live music venue. ⑤ *Average main: $10* ⊠ *McCarthy* ☎ *907/554–4405* ⊕ *www.theroadsidepotatohead.com* ☉ *Closed Oct.–Apr.*

🛏 Hotels

Copper River Princess Wilderness Lodge

$ | HOTEL | At the gateway to the park, this lodge has views of the Wrangell–St Elias mountain range and the Copper and Klutina rivers. **Pros:** luxurious lodge in the wilderness; dramatic views; plenty of activities offered. **Cons:** little else nearby in the way of amenities; frequently occupied by tour groups; no Wi-Fi in rooms. ⑤ *Rooms from: $150* ⊠ *1 Brenwick Craig Rd., Mile 102, Richardson Hwy., Copper Center* ☎ *800/426–0500 reservations* ⊕ *www.princesslodges.com/copper-river-lodge.cfm* ☉ *Closed mid-Sept.–mid-May* ⤴ *85 rooms.*

Kennicott Glacier Lodge

$$ | HOTEL | Perched at the top of a 10-mile dirt road originating in McCarthy, the lodge is an astounding site: its red and white panels and manicured lawns beside the aged and worn Kennecott Mine, the stunning backdrop of snow-crested mountain peaks, the receding glacier splayed out in front. **Pros:** lots of character; delicious food; great location. **Cons:** some rooms have shared bath; no air-conditioning; family-style dinner not for everyone. ⑤ *Rooms from: $189* ⊠ *15 Kennicott Millsite, 5 miles north of McCarthy, Kennicott* ☎ *800/582–5128* ⊕ *www.kennicottlodge.com* ☰ *No credit cards* ☉ *Closed mid-Sept.–mid-May* ⤴ *35 rooms* 🍴 *All meals.*

Chapter 6

DENALI NATIONAL PARK AND PRESERVE

Updated by David Cannamore

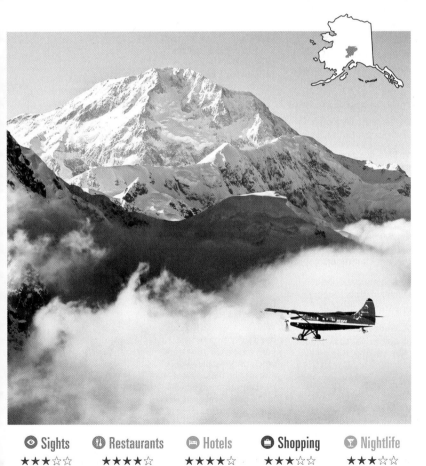

⊙ Sights	🍴 Restaurants	🛏 Hotels	🛍 Shopping	🍸 Nightlife
★★★☆☆	★★★★☆	★★★★☆	★★★☆☆	★★★☆☆

WELCOME TO DENALI NATIONAL PARK AND PRESERVE

TOP REASONS TO GO

★ **Backcountry hiking:** Getting off the road system and into the park's managed units allows for a true wilderness experience, limited only by time and the strength of your legs. For on-trail hiking try Savage River or Mt. Healy Overlook Trail.

★ **Denali flightseeing:** Soar over river valleys and up glaciers to the slopes of Denali to see the continent's wildest scenery. Some tours also offer landings on Ruth Glacier.

★ **Sled-dog demonstrations:** Watch half-hour demonstrations at the nation's oldest working dogsled kennel. Since the 1920s, sled dogs have been hauling rangers and workers to Denali's interior.

★ **Rafting:** Experience Denali in its wild rapids or serene flat water.

★ **Wonder Lake:** It takes all day to get to Wonder Lake via bus, but your chances of spotting wildlife are excellent. And from Wonder Lake the view of the massive slopes of Denali is something you'll never forget.

1 The Entrance. Just outside the park you'll find a strip of hotels, restaurants, and shops; just inside the park are the official visitor center, the least scenic campsites in Denali, and a level of chaos—at least in high season—that does not reflect the park's amazing beauty. Just put all this at your back as soon as you can.

2 Eielson Visitor Center. Deep in the heart of the park, near a favored caribou trail, Eielson offers great mountain views and sweeping vistas of the glaciated landscape. If you can't make it all the way to Wonder Lake, at least make it here.

3 The Mountain. Call it Denali or just "the Mountain." It's the highest spot on the continent, a double-edged peak that draws more than 1,000 climbers a year. Fewer than half make it to the top, but that's okay: it's easy enough to enjoy the view from below.

4 Wonder Lake. The end of the road for most vehicles, the lake is a full day's ride on one of the park buses. For your time, when the weather allows, you get the best view of the mountain anywhere in the park. And even when the mountain is hiding in the clouds, this is one of the prettiest stretches of landscape in the world.

DENALI
NATIONAL PARK

Wilderness
Access
Center
Healy

Sanctuary River
(mile 22)

Murie Science
and Learning
Center

Teklanika (mile 29)
Denali Park Road

Riley Creek
Campground

Savage
River
(mile 13)

Visitor Center
Park Entrance &
Headquarters

WYOMING
HILLS

Sable Mtn
6002ft

Igloo Creek
(mile 34)

Feng Mtn
6736ft

Kankone Peak
4987ft

Polychrome Mtn
5790ft

Sable Pass

Kantishna

Toklat (mile 53)

Polychrome Pass

Panorama
Mountain
5778ft

Thorofare
Pass

Highway Pass

Wonder Lake
(mile 85)

Stony Dome 4700ft

Mount Pendleton
7840ft

Cantwell

derness area boundary

Eielson Visitor Center
(mile 66)

Denali Highway

DENALI NATIONAL
PARK WILDERNESS

R A N G E

Red Mtn
7165ft

Wilderness area boundary

Mt Brooks
11940ft

Muldrow Gl

Mt Mather
12123ft

Mt Keven
12210 ft

North Peak
19470ft

DENALI

Mt Eldridge
10433ft

Eldridge Glacier

hiltna Dome
12525ft

South Peak
20310ft

Explorers Peak
8540ft

Mt Crosson
12800ft

Mt Hunter
14573ft

Mooses Tooth
10335ft

Denali
Viewpoint
North

Chulitna

Mt Foraker
12400ft

Tokositna Glacier

Ruth Gl

George Parks Highway

Avalanche Spire
10105ft

Mt Goldie
6315ft

DENALI
STATE
PARK

The Alaska Railroad

hitna Glacier

Denali
Viewpoint
South

DUTCH HILLS

PETERS   HILLS

nt Kliskon
3ft

view Mountain
6ft

Talkeetna

Trapper
Creek

KEY	
←·→	Rail Line
------	Trail
▲	Campground
🏠	Lodge
🅿	Picnic Area
👫	Ranger Station
🍴	Restaurant
🚌	Free shuttle bus

Denali National Park and Preserve is Alaska's most visited attraction for many reasons. The most accessible of Alaska's national parks and one of only three connected to the state's highway system, the 6-million-acre wilderness offers spectacular mountain views, a variety of wildlife, striking vegetation, and unforgettable landscapes.

Denali National Park lies 120 miles south of Fairbanks and 240 miles north of Anchorage on the George Parks Highway. The keystone of the park is Mt. Denali itself. The mountain was named Mt. McKinley from 1917 to 2015, but President Obama changed the name of this peak back to Denali, an Athabascan name meaning "the High One." It is often referred to by Alaskans simply as "the Mountain." The peak measures in at 20,310 feet, the highest point on the continent. Denali is also the tallest mountain in the world—yes, Mt. Everest is higher, but it sits on the Tibetan plateau, as if it was standing on a chair to rise above Denali, which starts barely above sea level.

Denali is part of the Alaska Range, harsh, rigid 600-mile backbone of snow, ice, and rock that cuts sharply through the center of the park. The 92-mile park road runs parallel to the north side of the range, winding along its foothills. Mt. Hunter (14,573 feet) and Mt. Foraker (17,400 feet) stand sentinel to the south of Denali with glaciers flowing across the entire range.

Another, smaller group of mountains— the Outer Range, north of Denali's park road—is a mix of volcanics and heavily metamorphosed sediments. Though not as breathtaking as the Alaska Range, the Outer Range is popular with hikers and backpackers because its summits and ridges are not as technically difficult to reach.

But despite its dizzying height, Denali is not always easy to see. Like most great mountains, it has a tendency to create its own weather, which for a majority of the time involves a large amount of clouds. The mountain is only visible from the park about a third of the time in summer. The deeper you travel into the park and the longer you linger in her shadow, the better the odds are that the cloudy veil will be lifted.

While you wait to catch a glimpse of Denali, there's plenty more to look for. Dozens of mammal species populate the park, including the "Big Five" of Alaskan animals: the moose, grizzly bear, wolf, Dall sheep, and caribou. Snowshoe hare and arctic ground squirrels watch with suspicious eyes from the roadside, and the sky is filled with the calls of willow ptarmigan and eagles. Tundra and spruce-laden Taiga forests lead to the rocky foothills of the Alaska Range, populated by lichens and small grasses favored by caribou. There are also the harsh glaciers and sharp peaks of the mountains themselves, but be aware that mountaineering in this region is not a casual endeavor. Only about half of those who attempt to summit North America's highest peak succeed and careful planning is required months in advance.

But for those that would prefer not to risk the thin air of Denali's summit, there are still several ways to experience the park, from half-day excursions to weeklong adventures. Hiking trails dot the area near the visitor center while the more bold might try a multiday backpacking trip through the tundra. Tour buses cover the length of the park road, with six campgrounds available along it. The buses feature informative and keen-eyed drivers, who are constantly looking to spot wildlife. Flightseeing tours are offered from the nearby community of Healy, which, barring bad weather, will get you up close to the mountains (Denali included), and many even include a glacier walk.

Several of Denali's most spectacular landforms are found deep in the park, but are still visible from the park road. The multicolor volcanic rocks at Cathedral Mountain and Polychrome Pass reflect the vivid hues of the American Southwest. The braided channels of glacially fed streams such as the Teklanika, Toklat, and McKinley rivers serve as highway routes for both animals and hikers. The debris- and tundra-covered ice of the Muldrow Glacier, one of the largest glaciers to flow out of Denali National Park's high mountains, is visible from Eielson Visitor Center, at Mile 66 of the park road. Wonder Lake, a narrow kettle pond that's a remnant from Alaska's ice ages, lies at Mile 85, just a few miles from the former gold-boom camp of Kantishna.

Planning

WHEN TO GO

Denali's main season runs mid-May through early September. About 90% of travelers come in these months, and with good reason: warmish weather, long days, and all the facilities are open. Shoulder seasons (early May and late September) can be incredibly beautiful in the park, with few people around; plus, you can often drive your own car a fair way down the park road, since the buses don't run. Exact opening and closing dates for seasonal properties tend to vary year to year, and when traveling close to shoulder season, it's best to inquire directly before your visit to ensure a place is open. In winter the only way into the park is on skis or snowshoes or by dogsled. You'll have the place almost entirely to yourself—most of the businesses at the park entrance are closed—and if you're comfortable in deep snow and freezing weather, there is no better time to see Denali.

TIMING

You can do a bus tour of the park in a single day. Allow for all day, and try to go at least as far as Eielson Visitor Center. If you can, go out to Wonder Lake. A few buses go a few miles farther to Kantishna, but the views from Wonder Lake are better; there's no reason to go those last miles unless you're staying at one of the inholding lodges.

If you have more than a single day, the best thing to do is camp in the park. The longer you stay deeper in the park, the better chance you'll have of seeing Denali, which, on average, is only visible one day out of three. Again, Wonder Lake is the spot of choice.

It's also easy to fill a day around the park entrance, taking rafting trips on the Nenana River or going on some of the short hikes near the visitor center.

No matter how much time you have, plan ahead. Bus and campsite reservations are available for the summer season beginning December 1. ■TIP➔ **Reserve tickets for buses ahead of time; call the numbers provided here or log on to www. reservedenali.com.** Although you can often just walk up and get on something, it may not be the experience you're after. Advance planning makes for the best trips.

GETTING HERE AND AROUND
BUS TRAVEL

Only one road penetrates Denali's expansive wilderness: the 92-mile Denali Park Road, which winds from the park entrance to Wonder Lake (as far as the regular buses go) and on the inholding of Kantishna, the historic mining district in the heart of the park, where there are a couple of private lodges. The first 15 miles of the road are paved and open to all vehicles. During the summer months, the road beyond the checkpoint at Savage River is limited to tour buses, special permit holders, and the community members of Kantishna. To get around the park, you need to get on one of the buses or start hiking.

CAR TRAVEL

The park is 120 miles south of Fairbanks, or 240 miles north of Anchorage, on the George Parks Highway, which is the most common access route.

There is a second, seldom-used road to the park: the Denali Highway leads from Paxon, which is accessible from the Richardson Highway (it connects Fairbanks and Valdez) to Cantwell, coming out just south of the park entrance. This 134-mile road is mostly unpaved, with few services. Only people with high-clearance cars should try it. The Denali Highway is closed in winter.

Personal vehicles are not allowed within Denali National Park, unless you are staying at the Teklanika Campground at Mile 29 (a three-day minimum stay is required). There is a road lottery for a day in September (the exact date varies every year) where you can drive your personal vehicle into the park, but these days are often crowded and traffic-filled even if you come sans-vehicle.

MOUNTAIN BIKE TRAVEL

Mountain bikes are allowed anywhere on the park road and can be transported for free on the park's shuttle buses. Before heading out, you should check with the park rangers at the visitor center; if there has been a wolf kill or a lot of bear sightings by the road, bike access might be limited.

TRAIN TRAVEL

For those who don't want to drive, Denali National Park is a regular stop on the Alaska Railroad's Anchorage–Fairbanks route. The railway sells packages that combine train travel with hotels and trips into the park. There are great views along the way, especially when crossing the Hurricane Gulch Bridge, and the train is a lovely, comfortable way to travel. The final approach to the park is much prettier by train than via car.

HEALTH AND SAFETY

Denali's weather is incredibly variable, so even if you're not hiking, carry durable rain gear made of a breathable material, and dress in layers. Good, sturdy, broken-in hiking boots, a hat, and warm gloves are a must, as are polypropylene long underwear and layers of wool or fleece for hikers. Avoid cotton, which is a poor insulator when wet. Bring insect repellent, binoculars, and a camera. Park water isn't safe to drink, and past the park entrance there's no food except what you bring in yourself. If camping or hiking, don't forget to bring a mandatory bear-proof food container or borrow one from the park headquarters. Potable water is available at the Riley Creek, Savage River, Teklanika, and Wonder Lake campgrounds.

PARK ESSENTIALS

Admission to Denali is $10 per person for a seven-day entrance permit. The park never closes. There may not be anybody around to accept the admission fee in deep winter, but the gates are always open. Don't count on cell-phone reception past the first mile or two beyond the visitor center.

RESTAURANTS

There's a small grill-style restaurant near the park's visitor center, but otherwise there are no traditional restaurants or grocery stores inside the park so you'll need to carry in your food. Just outside the park entrance, in the area known as Glitter Gulch, you'll find dozens of restaurants open during the summer only. Year-round grocery stores are found ten miles north of the entrance in the town of Healy.

HOTELS

There are plenty of options right outside the park entrance, but don't expect to find anything open in winter.

Restaurant and hotel reviews have been shortened. For full information, visit Fodors.com. Restaurant prices are the average cost of a main course at dinner or, if dinner is not served, at lunch. Hotel prices are the lowest cost of a standard double room in high season.

What It Costs			
$	$$	$$$	$$$$
RESTAURANTS			
under $14	$14–$22	$23–$32	over $32
HOTELS			
under $100	$100–$175	$176–$250	over $250

TOURS

Don't be alarmed by the crowded park entrance; that gets left behind very quickly. After the chaos of private businesses that line the George Parks Highway and the throngs at the visitor center, there's

pretty much nothing else in the park but wilderness. From the bus you'll have the opportunity to see Denali's wildlife in natural settings, as the animals are habituated to the road and vehicles, and go about their daily routine with little bother. In fact, the animals really like the road: it's easier for them to walk along it than to work through the tundra and tussocks.

Bus trips take time. The maximum speed limit is 35 mph, and the buses don't hit that very often. Add in rest stops, wildlife sightings, and slowdowns for passing, and it's an 8- to 11-hour day to reach the heart of the park and the best Denali views from Miles 62–85. Buses run from May 20 to September 13, although if you're running up close against one of those dates, call to make sure. ■**TIP→ If you decide to tour the park by bus, you have two choices: a sightseeing bus tour or a ride on the shuttle bus. The differences between the two are significant.**

BUSES AND SHUTTLES
Camper buses

NATIONAL/STATE PARK | These buses serve permitted backpackers and those staying in campgrounds along the road. Seats in the back of the bus are removed for gear storage and there is room for two bikes (the bike spaces must be reserved ahead of time). While there is no formal narration, bus drivers aren't likely to let you miss anything important. The $40 pass includes transportation anywhere down the road as far as Wonder Lake for the length of the backpacker's stay; kids under 16 are free. Tell the driver ahead of time where you'd like to get out. ✉ *Denali National Park* ☎ *800/622–7275* ⊕ *www.reservedenali.com* ✉ *$40* ⊙ *Closed mid-Sept.–mid-May.*

Shuttle buses

NATIONAL/STATE PARK | The park's shuttle and transit buses are a more informal, cheaper, and independent way to experience Denali. These buses are green-painted, converted school buses while the formally narrated tour buses are tan. While these trips are not formally narrated, the majority of bus drivers enjoy sharing information with riders, and the buses are equipped with speakers. Transit buses offer the freedom to disembark virtually anywhere along the road system and explore the park for yourself. Catching a ride back is as simple as returning to the road and waiting for the next transit bus to come by. Note that full buses will not stop so it's possible to wait for an hour or more for your ride back. Like the narrated tours, transit buses are operated by Doyon/Aramark and bookings are made through the concessionaire. Reservations are not required, and about a quarter of the seats are saved for walk-ons. But if you're visiting during peak season, it's best to make reservations ahead of time to ensure availability. Schedules can be found on the National Park Service's Denali website; departure times are relatively reliable although they can fluctuate during the summer. ⊠ *Denali National Park* ☎ *800/622–7275* ⊕ *www.reservedenali.com* 💰 *Free–$60* ⊘ *Closed mid-Sept.–mid-May.*

Tour buses

NATIONAL/STATE PARK | Guided bus tours offer the most informative introduction to the park. Each trip is led by a trained naturalist who drives the bus and gives a full narration. All tours include rest stops approximately every 90 minutes. Unlike the transit buses, you are not allowed to wander off on your own. The shortest is the five-hour Natural History Tour that travels to Teklanika at Mile 27. Besides moose and the occasional caribou, chances of seeing the park's large mammals are limited on this route, and glimpses of Denali are possible but not probable. The next longest option is the seven to eight-hour Tundra Wilderness Tour that reaches Stony Brook at Mile 62; this is the best choice for wildlife and photography enthusiasts. The longest narrated tour is the Kantishna Experience, a 12-hour extravaganza that runs

the full 92 miles of park road to the old mining town of Kantishna. Advance reservations are required for all bus tours, and they can be made starting on December 1, with exact departure times fluctuating depending on demand and time of year. It's best to consult Doyon/Aramark for an exact schedule as departure times are often not set until a few days before. ⊠ *Denali National Park* ☎ *800/622–7275* ⊕ *www.reservedenali.com* 💰 *From $80* ⊘ *Closed mid-Sept.–mid-May.*

VISITOR INFORMATION
PARK CONTACT INFORMATION
Denali National Park Headquarters

⊠ *Denali National Park* ☎ *907/683–2294 information* ⊕ *www.nps.gov/dena* ⊘ *All but Riley Creek (no visitor facilities) closed mid-Sept.–late May.*

VISITOR CENTERS
Denali Visitor Center

INFO CENTER | Open from mid-May through mid-September, the center is a mile-and-a half beyond the park's entrance, and includes two floors worth of displays detailing the park's natural and cultural history along with several life-size representations of the park's largest animals. A theater on the main floor plays the 20-minute film *The Heartbeats of Denali* twice an hour. The center is the starting point for most interpretive ranger hikes and several other trails you can explore independently. This is also the place to go for your backcountry camping permits (permits aren't necessary for day hikes). Nearby facilities include the railroad and bus depots, the Morino Grill, and the Alaska Geographic bookstore. ⊠ *Denali National Park Rd., Denali National Park* ☎ *907/683–9532* ⊕ *www.nps.gov/ dena* ⊘ *Closed mid-Sept.–mid-May.*

Eielson Visitor Center

INFO CENTER | Famous for its views of Denali, the Eielson Visitor Center is found at Mile 66 of the park road. Park rangers are present throughout the day either leading presentations or hikes such as

Continued on page 259

In the heart of mainland Alaska, within 6-million-acre Denali National Park & Preserve, the continent's most majestic peak rises into the heavens. Formerly known as Mount McKinley, this 20,310-foot massif of ice, snow, and rock has been renamed to honor its Alaska Native name Denali, or "the High One." Some simply call it "The Mountain." One thing is certain: It's a giant among giants, and the most dominant feature in a land of extremes and superlatives.

Those who have walked Denali's slopes know it to be a wild, desolate place. As the highest peak in North America, Denali is a target of mountaineers who aspire to ascend the "seven summits"—the tallest mountains on each continent. A foreboding and mysterious place, it was terra incognita—unclimbed and unknown to most people—as recently as the late 1890s. Among Athabascan tribes, however, the mountain was a revered landmark; many generations regarded it as a holy place and a point of reference.

NAMING TERRA INCOGNITA

Linguists have identified at least eight native Alaskan names for the mountain, including Deenaalee, Doleyka, Traleika, and Dghelay Ka'a. The essence of all the names is "the High One" or "Big Mountain." The first recorded sighting of Denali by a foreign explorer was in 1794, when Captain George Vancouver spotted it in the distance. More than a century later, after a summer of gold-seeking, Ivy Leaguer William Dickey reported his experiences in the *New York Sun*. His most significant news was of a massive peak, which he dubbed "Mt. McKinley," after Republican William McKinley of Ohio. Mountaineer Hudson Stuck, who led the first mountaineering team to "McKinley's" summit, was just one in a long line of Alaskans to protest this name. In Stuck's view, the moniker was an affront to both the mountain and Alaska's native people. For these very reasons, a vast majority of Alaskans called the continent's highest peak by its original name, Denali. On August 28, 2015 President Obama changed the name of the mountain back to Denali.

Denali Facts & Figures

■ The mountain's vertical rise is the highest in the world. This means that at 18,000 feet over the lowlands (which are some 2,000 feet above sea level), McKinley's vertical rise is even greater than Mt. Everest, at 29,035-feet (which rises 12,000 feet above the Tibetan plateau, some 17,000 feet above sea level).

Halfway to the summit, Denali's weather is equivalent to that of the North Pole in severity. In summer, night temperatures may reach -40° F.

11,000' Camp

Route proceeds behind ridge

Kahiltna Pass 10,320'

West Buttress Route

Kahiltna Glacier

Climbers begin expeditions by flying to the Kahiltna Glacier Base Camp at 7,200 ft.

■ The safest route to the summit is the West Buttress. Eighty to 90% of climbers attempting to ascend the peak take this route, with only about half reaching the top.

■ More than 30 people—including some world-class mountaineers—have been killed on the West Buttress.

■ From base camp to high camp, climbers must trek some 16 miles and 10,000

vertical feet—a trip that takes two to three weeks.

■ The most technically challenging stretch is the ascent to 18,200-foot Denali Pass; climbers must cross a steep snow-covered slope

■ In addition to coping with severe weather, climbers face avalanches, open crevasses, hypothermia, frostbite, and high-altitude illnesses. More than 120 people have died on the mountain and hundreds more have been seriously injured.

■ Denali's awesome height and its subarctic location make it one of the coldest mountains on Earth, if not the coldest.

■ Primarily made of granite, Denali undergoes continual shifting and uplift thanks to plate tectonics (the Pacific plate pushing against the North American Plate); it grows about 1 mm per year.

South Summit
20,310'

North Summit
19,470'

Denali Pass
18,200'

Denali

Northwest Buttress

High Camp
17,200'

South Buttress

Cassin Ridge

Ridge Camp
16,200'

West Buttress

West Rib

14,200' Camp

The high camp is at 17,200 feet; teams often find themselves stuck here waiting out storms and high winds. From high camp it takes another 8 to 12 hours of physically demanding climbing to reach the summit.

Windy Corner Camp
13,000'

This very steep and treacherous headwall is navigated with a fixed line (climbers are clipped to each other and to a line screwed into the mountain). Dangerous and exhilarating!

then a shallow bowl called the Football Field.

■ Then, still roped together, climbers ascend an 800-foot snow-and-ice wall to reach the "top of the continent" itself.

Fearless climbers facing the icy challenge at 16,400 feet on the West Buttress Route.

EARLY MILESTONES

Climbing Mt. McKinley in the early 1900s

■ In 1903, two different expeditions made the first attempts to climb Denali. The highest point reached? 11,000 feet. Over the next decade, other expeditions would try, and fail, to reach the top.

■ Finally, in 1913, a team led by Hudson Stuck reached the summit. The first person to the top was Walter Harper, a native Alaskan.

■ After the Stuck party's success in 1913, no attempts were made to climb the mountain until 1932. That year, for the first time, a pilot landed a small plane on one of the mountain's massive glaciers. Another first: a party climbed both the 20,320-foot South Peak and 19,470-foot North Peak. More tragically, the first deaths occurred on the mountain.

■ Alaskans Dave Johnston, Art Davidson, and Ray Genet completed the first winter ascent of Denali in February 1967. Japanese climber Naomi Uemura completed the first solo ascent in 1970.

A FLIGHT TO REMEMBER

Talkeetna is the home of the popular Denali Flyers. Pilots take you on a variety of air tours into the Alaska Range in small, ski-equipped planes. Flights usually include a passage through the Ruth Glacier's Great Gorge, which is bordered by breathtaking granite spires. Leaving the gorge, you'll enter immense glacial basins of the Don Sheldon Amphitheater (named in honor of the first Denali Flyer). Most trips also include flights past Denali's southern flanks and show glimpses of its climbing routes. Longer tours circle the mountain, passing among the perennially ice-capped upper slopes, saw-toothed ridges, and vertical rock faces. Flights generally range from 30 minutes to 3 hours and cost $200 to $400 per person.

FLOWER QUEST

Though most visitors to Denali have things quite large on their minds (grizzlies, moose, the mountain itself), it's often the little things that people remember long after their visits are over. Dozens and dozens of varieties of wildflowers bloom throughout the summer (though early July is the best time). In 2012, one of the park's rangers, Jake Frank, set out to photograph at least 120 species in the park. His final tally? 185. Over ten weeks, Frank photographed everything from the Alaska state flower, Alpine forget-me-nots to bright magenta Chukchi primroses, delicate arctic poppies, and much more. Along with counting flowers on a multi-mile hike, either just off the road or deep in Denali backcountry, consider going micro, too. Hike up above the treeline, grab a seat, and count the number of tiny alpine flowers (and fruit plants, including lowbush blueberries and cranberries) crowded into just a few inches of the tundra.

the leisurely Eielson Stroll. While there is a small gallery of Denali-inspired art here, this visitor center is all about the view, dominated, with a little luck, by the mountain itself. The center opens on June 1 and closes on the second Thursday after Labor Day. It's accessible by any of the shuttle buses that pass Mile 66, excluding the Kantishna Experience tour. ⊠ *Mile 66, Park Rd., Denali National Park* ⊕ *www.nps.gov/dena/planyourvisit/the-eielson-visitor-center.htm* ⊗ *Closed early Sept.–May.*

Murie Science and Learning Center

COLLEGE | Next to the Denali Visitor Center, Murie Science and Learning Center is the foundation of the park's science-based education programs, and also serves as the winter visitor center when the Denali Visitor Center is closed. Hours during the summer vary, and the center usually only opens for special presentations. During off-season camping at the Riley Campground, it's the go-to spot for ranger information and, yes, bathrooms with running water. ⊠ *Mile 1.5, Park Rd., Denali National Park* ☎ *907/683–6432* ⊕ *www.nps.gov/rlc/murie.*

Wilderness Access Center

INFO CENTER | Also known as the Bus Depot, this center just inside the park entrance is where you can reserve campgrounds and bus trips into the park. For those that arrive after 7 pm, campground reservations can be made at the Riley Creek Mercantile until 11 pm. There's also a coffee stand—your last chance for a cup of joe unless you bring the makings for campsite coffee with you. ⊠ *Mile 0.5, Park Rd., Denali National Park* ☎ *907/683–9532* ⊕ *www.nps.gov/dena/planyourvisit/wildernessaccesscenter.htm* ⊗ *Closed mid-Sept.–mid-May.*

◉ Sights

It's important to reserve tickets for narrated bus tours ahead of time; call the numbers provided here (⇨ *see the*

Denali's Dinosaurs ◉

On June 27, 2005, a geologist discovered the track of a theropod, or a three-toed carnivorous dinosaur, in 65- to 70-million-year-old Cretaceous sedimentary rock, just 35 miles west of the park entrance. This is the first hard evidence of dinosaurs in the Interior of Alaska. While the initial discoveries were made by geologists, subsequent finds were uncovered by participants in a teacher workshop with the Murie Science and Learning Center.

Denali Planner) or log on to ⊕ *www.reservedenali.com.*

With a landmass larger than Massachusetts, Denali National Park and Preserve has too much area for even the most dedicated vacationer to explore in one go. When planning your trip, consider whether you want to strike out on your own as a backcountry traveler or to stay at a lodge nearby and enjoy Denali as a day hiker with the help of a tour or shuttle bus. Both options require some advance planning, for bus tickets or backcountry permits. But both options also offer a magnificent experience.

★ Denali

MOUNTAIN—SIGHT | In the heart of mainland Alaska, within 6-million-acre Denali National Park and Preserve, the continent's most majestic peak rises into the heavens. Formerly known as Mt. McKinley, this 20,310-foot massif of ice, snow, and rock has been renamed to honor its Alaska Native name, Denali, or "the High One." Some simply call it "the Mountain." One thing is certain: it's a giant among giants, and the most dominant feature in a land of extremes and superlatives. Those who have walked Denali's slopes

Plants and Wildlife in Denali

Mammals

Thirty-seven species of mammals reside in the park, from wolves and bears to little brown bats and pygmy shrews that weigh a fraction of an ounce. The most sought-after species among visitors are the large mammals: grizzlies, wolves, Dall sheep, moose, and caribou. All inhabit the forest or tundra landscape that surrounds Denali Park Road. You can expect to see Dall sheep finding their way across high meadows and peppering distant mountaintops (look for the tiny white dots), grizzlies and caribou frequenting stream bottoms and tundra, moose in the forested areas both near the park entrance and deep in the park, and the occasional wolf or fox that may dart across the road.

Birds

The park also has a surprisingly large avian population in summer, with 167 identified species. Most of the birds migrate in fall, leaving only two-dozen year-round resident species, including ravens, boreal chickadees, and hawk owls. Some of the summer birds travel thousands of miles to nest and breed in subarctic valleys, hills, and ponds. The northern wheatear migrates from southern Asia, warblers arrive from Central and South America, and the arctic tern annually travels 24,000 miles while commuting between the Arctic and Antarctica.

Taiga

Vegetation in the park consists largely of taiga and tundra. Taiga is coniferous forest in moist areas below a tree line of 2,700 feet and consists mainly of white and black spruce trees. Due to the layer of permafrost that lies just under the surface of the land, the trees have shallow root systems. This means they are very susceptible to wind and weather conditions, and it's not at all unusual to see entire sections of forest, usually black spruce, leaning to one side, or leaning every which way like a bunch of jackstraws. Called a "drunken forest," the lean comes from trees trying to make their home in permafrost that thaws, freezes, and thaws again, shifting the soil right under the roots. Ground cover in the taiga forest includes dwarf birch, blueberry, and willow shrubs.

Tundra

The rest of the landmass not covered by ice and snow is carpeted by tundra, consisting of a variety of delicate plants such as lichens, berries, bright wildflowers, and woody plants. This complex carpet of low-lying vegetation generates brilliant color, especially in August, when the fall weather begins. Take a really close look at tundra: it's like being a giant and looking down on a forest, it's all so perfect and detailed and tiny. A single square foot of tundra can hold 40 or 50 different species. The park as a whole contains more than 650 species of flowering plants, plus who knows how many mosses, fungi, and lichen. While you're busy watching for moose and bears, don't forget to check out the plants.

know it to be a wild, desolate place. As the highest peak in North America, Denali is a target of mountaineers who aspire to ascend the "seven summits"—the tallest mountains on each continent. A foreboding and mysterious place, it was terra incognita—unclimbed and unknown to most people—as recently as the late 1890s. Among Athabascan tribes, however, the mountain was a revered landmark; many generations regarded it as a holy place and a point of reference. The mountain's vertical rise is the highest in the world. This means that at 18,000 feet over the lowlands (which are some 2,000 feet above sea level), Denali's vertical rise is even greater than that of Mt. Everest, at 29,035-feet (which sits 12,000 feet above the Tibetan plateau, some 17,000 feet above sea level). Denali's awesome height and its subarctic location make it one of the coldest mountains on Earth, if not *the* coldest. Primarily made of granite, Denali undergoes continual shifting and uplift thanks to plate tectonics (the Pacific Plate pushing against the North American Plate); it grows about 1 millimeter per year. ⊠ *Denali National Park.*

🏃 Activities

MULTISPORT OUTFITTERS
★ Denali Outdoor Center
TOUR—SPORTS | With two locations, one in Glitter Gulch and another close to Healy, Denali Outdoor Center can take you rafting on Class IV rapids, kayaking, put you on a mountain bike, and then get you a cabin so you can sack out and recover from your day. Prices for white-water rafting and inflatable kayak trips (which include instruction and all equipment) start at $94; bike rentals cost $25 for six hours, $40 for the day, and tours cost $57. Lakefront cabins on Otto Lake near Healy run $106 per night, or just stay at the campground for $12 per person. ⊠ *Mile 0.5, Otto Lake Rd., off Mile 247, Parks Hwy., Healy* ☎ *907/683–1925, 888/303–1925* ⊕ *www.denalioutdoorcenter.com* ⊗ *Mid-May–mid-Sept.*

FLIGHTSEEING
A flightseeing tour of the park is one of the best ways to get a sense of the Alaska Range's size and scope. Flightseeing is also the best way to get close-up views of Denali and its neighboring giants, and maybe even stand on a glacier, all without the hassle of days of hiking and lugging food and gear.

Most Denali flightseeing is done out of Talkeetna, a small end-of-the-road town between Anchorage and Denali, and the operators will offer several tours, including a quick fly-by, a summit tour, a glacier landing—something for everybody. But there are a few outfitters nearer to the park that fly either from McKinley Park airstrip or the small airfield in Healy, 20 miles north. It's best to take the longest, most detailed tour you can afford, so you don't go back home wishing you'd had a chance to see more.

Fly Denali
AIR EXCURSIONS | This is the only flightseeing company based in Healy with a permit to land on the glaciers of Denali. Prices are $549 for adults, and include more than 100 minutes of flight time and 20–30 minutes on the Ruth Glacier and its amphitheater. ⊠ *Healy Airport, Healy Rd., Healy* ⊕ *Turn right off George Parks Highway at Mile 238.7 and follow 2 miles* ☎ *907/683–2359, 877/770–2359* ⊕ *www.flydenali.com.*

HIKING
There are few places in the world wilder and more beautiful to hike than Denali's wilderness regions. It's easy to get lost in the beauty and the desire to climb just one more ridge, but know your limits and consult park staff before you head out. Also be sure to follow "Leave No Trace" etiquette, be prepared for bear encounters, and bring all necessary equipment.

With the exception of the trails near the entrance and at the Savage River checkpoint, the park is essentially trailless. Distances may look attainable from a distance, with foothills off the side of

In the fall, the mountains of Denali National Park are surrounded by brilliant orange and red foliage.

the road appearing no more than an hour away. Be wary of such predictions. Distances in the tundra are farther than they appear and while it may look smooth, bogs, willows, alder, and other obstacles can quickly hinder the best-laid plans. Be conservative with your goals, take your time, and leave a hike plan with someone that includes your intended destination and when to expect to hear from you. Once you finalize this plan, do not deviate from it.

A big draw for more experienced hikers and backpackers are the foothills and ridges accessible from the park road. As long as you don't go deep into the Alaska Range, it's possible to reach some summits and high ridges without technical climbing expertise. Stamina and physical fitness are required however. Once up high, hikers find easy walking and sweeping views of braided rivers, tundra benches and foothills, and ice-capped mountains.

NATURE TRAILS AND SHORT WALKS

The park offers plenty of options for those who prefer to stay on marked and groomed pathways. The entrance area has more than a half-dozen forest and tundra trails. These range from easy to challenging, so there's something suitable for all ages and hiking abilities. Some, like the **Taiga Loop Trail** and **McKinley Station Loop Trail,** are less than 1½ miles; others, like the **Rock Creek Trail** and **Triple Lakes Trail,** are several miles round-trip, with an altitude gain of hundreds of feet. Along these paths you may see beavers working on their lodges in Horseshoe Lake; red squirrels chattering in trees; red foxes hunting for rodents; sheep grazing on tundra; golden eagles gliding over alpine ridges; and moose feeding on willow.

The **Savage River Trail,** farthest from the park entrance and as far as private vehicles are allowed, offers a 1¾-mile round-trip hike along a raging river and under rocky cliffs. Be on the lookout for caribou, Dall sheep, foxes, and marmots.

Moose and Bear Safety

Moose

Commonly underestimated by visitors and locals alike, moose can pose a threat despite their lack of claws and sharp teeth. They may look gangly, but are fast moving and will charge when threatened. Per park guidelines, moose should be enjoyed from a respectable distance of at least 25 yards. If the animal's behavior changes, you're too close. Give mother moose and their calves extra distance as they can be especially unpredictable. If a moose charges, seek shelter in a thick stand of trees or behind any large object that it can't get through. Remember: moose can kick with either their front *or* back hooves.

Bears

Most visitors seek the Goldilocks bear encounter: not too far, not too close, but just right. But bears are capable of reaching speeds of 35 miles per hour, which can turn "just right" into "oh no!" in a heartbeat. The best method is to prevent bad bear encounters before they happen. This means giving bears lots of space, making plenty of noise while hiking, and keeping a clean camp with food stored properly in bear cans away from your tent. Park-issued, bear-proof containers come in two sizes that weigh three and seven pounds, respectively. Small containers hold 3–5 days worth of food for one person. Bigger ones can hold enough food for 7–10 days. Some personal bear containers are also accepted; check the park website for other approved containers. If you do come across a bear at close range, do not run as a bear perceives anything that runs as food. Speak calmly to the bear. Make yourself appear as big as possible (i.e., open up your jacket, spread your legs, or if in a group, stand together to form a "super creature") and back away slowly in the direction from which you came. Scan the surrounding area for cubs or a moose kill, both of which a bear will defend passionately.

Bears that choose to approach or stand on their hind legs are not necessarily aggressive. Most are simply curious and want a better look at you. A bear standing sideways to show its full profile, huffing, or jaw-popping are signs of potential aggression. Should a bear charge, stand your ground and deploy bear spray at a close distance. Most charges are simply bluffs. Play dead as a last resort by falling to the ground, curling in a ball, and wrapping your hands around your neck to protect it. Signs are peppered across the park with additional bear safety tips and park rangers are well-versed in bear safety.

The only relatively long, marked trail for hiking in the park, **Mt. Healy Overlook Trail,** is accessible from the entrance area; it gains 1,700 feet in 2½ miles and takes about four hours round-trip, with outstanding views of the Nenana River below and the Alaska Range, including the upper slopes of Denali.

GUIDED HIKES

In addition to exploring the park on your own, you can take free ranger-guided discovery hikes and learn more about the park's natural and human history. Rangers lead daily hikes throughout summer. Inquire at the visitor center. You can also tour with privately operated outfitters.

Rangers will talk about the area's plants, animals, and geological features. Before heading into the wilderness, even on a short hike, check in at the Backcountry Information Center located in the visitor center. Rangers will update you on conditions and make route suggestions. Because this is bear country, the Park Service provides backpackers with bear-proof food containers. These containers are mandatory if you're staying overnight in the backcountry.

KAYAKING AND RAFTING

Several privately owned raft and tour companies operate along the Parks Highway near the entrance to Denali, and they schedule daily rafting, both in the fairly placid areas on the Nenana and through the 10-mile-long Nenana River canyon, which has stretches of Class IV–V rapids—enough to make you think you're on a very wet roller coaster. The Nenana is Alaska's most accessible white water, and if you don't mind getting a little chilly, a river trip is not just a lot of fun, it's also a fantastic way to see a different side of the landscape. Most outfitters lend out dry suits for river trips; it takes a few minutes to get used to wearing one (they feel tight around the neck) but they're essential gear to keep you safe if you fall into the water.

★ Denali Outdoor Center

KAYAKING | This tour operator has a respected reputation among locals for its scenic rafting trips on the Nenana River and splash-filled trips down the Nenana River canyon's rapids where no river experience is necessary (tours start at $94). One of the most challenging trips is a two-hour paddle in inflatable kayaks. They are easy to get out of, stable, and self-bailing, but if you're not used to paddling yourself, you're going to have sore arms. The company also teaches white-water kayaking. All gear is provided, including full dry suits, something you'll appreciate in the splash. Budget travelers can rent canoes or kayaks on Otto Lake for $8 an hour. Camping sites ($12 by the lake), rental cabins ($106) with Wi-Fi in the laundry-shower room,

The Stampede Trail

One of Healy's greatest attractions is the **Stampede Trail,** perhaps most famous to today's traveler for being where Christopher McCandless of *Into the Wild* fame met his end. On the Stampede Trail you can enter Denali by snowmobile, dogsled, cross-country skis, or mountain bike. This wide, well-traveled path leads all the way to Kantishna, 90 miles inside the park. To get here, take the George Parks Highway 2 miles north of Healy to Mile 251.1, where Stampede Road intersects the highway.

and mountain-bike tours ($57) and rentals ($25 for six hours) are also available. Plus, there's a free local shuttle from hotels, lodges, the Alaska Railroad depot, the Denali visitor center, and Otto Lake. There are two locations, the Healy office on Otto Lake Road and the Canyon office on Parks Highway. ⊠ *Mile 238.9, Parks Hwy., Denali National Park* ☏ *907/683–1925, 888/303–1925* ⊕ *www.denalioutdoorcenter.com.*

Denali Raft Adventures

WHITE-WATER RAFTING | This outfitter launches its rafts several times daily on two- and four-hour scenic and white-water trips on the Nenana River. GORE-TEX dry suits are provided. Guests under the age of 18 must have a release waiver signed by a parent or guardian. Contact the company for copies before the trip. Courtesy pickup at hotels and the train depot is available within a 7-mile radius of their location. Two-hour, half-day, and full-day tours are available, starting at $97 per person. ⊠ *Mile 238.6, Parks Hwy., Denali National Park* ☏ *907/683–2234, 888/683–2234* ⊕ *www.denaliraft.com* ⊗ *June–mid-Sept.*

MOUNTAIN BIKING

Mountain biking is allowed along the entire park road, and no permit is required for day trips. The first 15 miles of the road are paved. Beyond the Savage River checkpoint the road is dirt and gravel, and during the day the road is busy with the park buses, which can leave bikers choking on dust. The road can get really sloppy in the rain, too. The best time to bike is late evening, when the midnight sun is shining and buses have stopped shuttling passengers for the day. When biking on the road, you need to be aware of your surroundings and observe park rules. Do not try to outride bears, moose, or wolves as it's a race you won't win. Off-road riding is forbidden, and some sensitive wildlife areas are closed to hiking and biking. The Sable Pass area is always closed to off-road excursions on foot or bike because of the high bear population, and other sites are closed due to denning activity or recent signs of carcass scavenging. Check current conditions at the visitor center before heading out. Denali Outdoor Center rents mountain bikes by the hour, half day, or full day. They also conduct guided 2- to 2½-hour tours on trails near the Otto Lake center, which come complete with bike, helmet, water bottle, and shuttle service.

To bike deep in the park, take a transit shuttle to Eielson Visitor Center at Mile 66, one of the highest points along the park road. From here you can ride downhill to Wonder Lake at Mile 85, and then catch another bus to the top of the hill. Private vehicles aren't allowed this far into the park, minimizing dust and traffic.

MOUNTAINEERING

Alaska Mountaineering School

CLIMBING/MOUNTAINEERING | This outfitter leads backpacking trips in wilderness areas near Talkeetna and elsewhere in the state, including the Brooks Range, and glacier treks that can include overnighting on the ice. It also conducts mountaineering courses that run from 6 to 12 days, expeditions to Denali (figure on at least three weeks; prices from $8,900) and other peaks in the Alaska Range, and climbs for all levels of expertise. A novice course, which should be enough to get you comfortable in the mountains, runs about $2,000. AMS also offers multisport treks, one of which includes packrafting, for $3,900. While you're in Talkeetna, check out the AMS mountain and gear shop on F Street. ✉ *13765 3rd St., Talkeetna* ☎ *907/733–1016* ⊕ *www. climbalaska.org.*

WINTER SPORTS

Snowshoers and skiers generally arrive with their own gear and park or camp at the Riley Creek Campground at the park entrance. The Park Service does keep some loaner snowshoes on hand; check at the Murie Science and Learning Center (which doubles as the winter visitor center). Dog mushing can also be done with your own team, or you can contact one of the park concessionaires that run single-day or multiday trips.

Denali Dog Sled Expeditions

LOCAL SPORTS | Owned by the couple behind Earthsong Lodge, Denali Dog Sled Expeditions is the only dogsledding company that has the National Park Service okay to run trips in Denali National Park. And, midwinter, the park will feel as if it's all yours. The company specializes in multiday trips of 3 to 10 days (from $2,685). Early in the season and between trips, they also offer day trips of one to four hours (from $140); call ahead to check availability. Denali Dog Sled Expeditions also offers cross-country skiers dogsled team support for multiday winter cabin and hut trips in the park. ✉ *Mile 4, Stampede Rd., Healy* ✛ *17 miles northwest of Denali National Park* ☎ *907/683–2863* ⊕ *www.earthsong-lodge.com* ✉ *From $140.*

🍴 Restaurants

IN THE PARK
The Denali Doghouse

$ | **AMERICAN** | It's all about the dog at this casual, dog-decorated and hot-dog-theme joint. The owners are locals and rely on made-in-Alaska products so all quarter-pound burger patties are hand-pressed while fries and onion rings are fresh. **Known for:** quick lunch and dinners; reindeer hot dogs; one of the cheaper (and most filling) options in Glitter Gulch. $ *Average main: $8 ⊠ Mile 238.6, Parks Hwy., Denali National Park ☎ 907/683–3647 ⊕ www.denalidoghouse.com ⊗ Closed mid-Sept.–mid-May.*

Denali Park Salmon Bake

$$ | **SEAFOOD** | Affectionately known as "The Bake," this upbeat and lively spot does everything it can to make every night a party: from frequent live music events, to karaoke, to cramming every holiday into the summer season, there's always something happening. While salmon and other Alaska seafood is on the menu, there is no traditional all-you-can-eat salmon buffet. **Known for:** live music (by local musicians) and dancing; Alaska-sourced elk burger; Alaska beers on tap. $ *Average main: $18 ⊠ Mile 238.5, Parks Hwy., Denali National Park ☎ 907/683–2733 ⊕ www.denaliparksalmonbake.com ⊗ Closed late Sept.–early May.*

Moose-AKa's

$$ | **EASTERN EUROPEAN** | Just as unique as its name, Moose-AKa's brings something different to the table for those in Glitter Gulch. Specializing in authentic European items, they offer crepes, stuffed peppers, and, of course, moussaka. **Known for:** fantastic European-inspired menu where you'd least expect it; Serbian-inspired tempura fried crepes; cozy atmosphere. $ *Average main: $17 ⊠ Mile 238.9, George Parks Hwy., Denali National Park ☎ 907/687–0003 ⊕ www.moose-akas.com ⊗ Closed mid-Sept.–mid-May.*

★ Prospector's Historic Pizzeria and Ale House

$$ | **AMERICAN** |**FAMILY** | Built to have an old-time-saloon feel, this restaurant serves a seemingly endless selection of handcrafted pizzas, as well as salad, soup, pastas, and brick-oven sandwiches. Farm-to-table ingredients are used whenever possible and include locally grown greens, Alaska raised meat, and seafood. **Known for:** Deadliest Catch pizza that comes with a pound of king crab legs; largest and most diverse beer selection around; wide-ranging menu that includes gluten-free, vegetarian, and vegan options. $ *Average main: $20 ⊠ Mile 238.9, Parks Hwy., Denali National Park ☎ 907/683–7437 ⊕ www.prospectorspizza.com ⊗ Closed late Sept.–early May.*

OUTSIDE THE PARK
ALONG THE GEORGE PARKS HIGHWAY
McKinley Creekside Cafe

$$ | **AMERICAN** | This is the place for hearty, delicious food, including breakfast, lunch, dinner, and weekend brunch. While the menu does offer some very good salads, the real treats include pork and hominy chili, grilled halibut tacos, and Alaskan salmon with a rotating cast of sides and marinades. **Known for:** fantastic desserts baked in-house; weekend brunch menu with rotating specials; generous boxed lunches. $ *Average main: $18 ⊠ Mile 224, Parks Hwy., Denali National Park ☎ 907/683–2277 ⊕ www.mckinleycabins.com ⊗ Closed mid-Sept.–mid-May.*

Panorama Pizza Pub

$$ | **PIZZA** | Situated in a cluster of restaurants and cabins along Carlo Creek, Panorama is one of the more lively and festive options. Hand-tossed pizzas include one with Alaskan microbrewed beer baked into the crust. **Known for:** live music venue including open mike nights; deck with views of Carlo Creek; wide array of pizzas and sandwiches. $ *Average main: $20 ⊠ Mile 224, Parks Hwy., in front of Perch Cabins, Carlo Creek*

☎ 907/683–2623 ⊕ www.panoramapiz-zapub.com ☺ Closed Oct.–Apr. No lunch.

The Perch Restaurant, Bar, and Cabins

$$$ | AMERICAN | Built on top of an old glacier moraine, the Perch offers dining in a more removed and relaxed setting than elsewhere in the area. Steak and seafood make up the menu although gluten-free and vegetarian options are also available. **Known for:** impressive wine selection; bay windows overlooking the mountains; working closely with local organic farmers. $ *Average main: $25* ⊠ *Mile 224, Carlo Creek* ☎ *888/322–2523, 907/683–2523* ⊕ *www.denaliperchresort.com* ☺ *Closed mid-Sept.–mid-Apr.*

★ 229 Parks Restaurant and Tavern

$$$ | AMERICAN | Led by a two-time James Beard Award–nominated chef, this hot spot is spoken of with reverential tones by locals. With its own veggie gardens and sourcing from nearby farms, this is as local as you can get. **Known for:** daily-changing menu with all items made in-house; wintertime-only brunches on Sundays and Mondays; rotating art shows throughout the summer. $ *Average main: $28* ⊠ *Mile 229.7, Parks Hwy., Denali National Park* ☎ *907/683–2567* ⊕ *www.229parks.com* ☺ *Closed May–mid-June and Tues.–Thurs. in Oct.–Apr. No lunch except Sun. and Mon. in Oct.–Apr. No dinner Sun. and Mon. in Oct.–Apr.*

HEALY
Black Diamond Grill

$$$ | AMERICAN | For a casual and fami-ly-oriented atmosphere, dine with a view in this lodge-style, off-the-beaten-path locals hangout. The menu features hand-pressed burgers, New York steaks, crab cakes, penne pasta, salads with local and organic greens, and fresh-baked desserts. **Known for:** mountain views; outdoor seating; large main dining room good for large groups. $ *Average main: $25* ⊠ *Mile 1, Otto Lake Rd., Healy* ⊕ *Off Mile 247, Parks Hwy.* ☎ *907/683–4653*

Ruth Glacier

Even the shortest flightseeing trips usually include a passage through the Great Gorge of **Ruth Glacier**, one of the major glaciers flowing off Denali's south side. Bordered by gray granite walls and gigantic spires, this spectacular chasm is North America's deepest gorge. Leaving the area, flightseers enter the immense, mountain-encircled glacial basins of Ruth Glacier's Don Sheldon Amphitheater. Among the enclosing peaks are some of the range's most rugged and descrip-tively named peaks, including Moose's Tooth and Rooster Comb. Truly, it's one of the most beautiful places on the planet.

⊕ *www.blackdiamondtourco.com* ☺ *Closed mid-Sept.–mid-May.*

★ 49th State Brewing Company

$$ | AMERICAN | Top-notch craft beer and plenty of food options makes 49th State Brewing Company a must when passing through Healy. Committed to using local ingredients whenever possible, they offer plenty of Alaska-grown dishes, the keystone being the Alaskan-raised, all-you-can-eat pig roast on Friday nights. **Known for:** Yak burger raised on a farm in southeast Alaska; live music throughout the summer; outdoor beer garden with beers brewed on-site. $ *Average main: $20* ⊠ *Mile 248.4, Parks Hwy., Healy* ☎ *907/683–2739* ⊕ *www.49statebrew-ing.com* ☺ *Closed early Oct.–early May.*

Rose's Café

$$ | AMERICAN | A local hangout with friendly service, good American cuisine, generous portions, and fair prices makes Rose's Café the quintessential roadside diner suitable for any meal. Located just far enough north from the park entrance to be overlooked by most visitors, you're

Tent and RV Camping in Denali

If you want to camp in the park, either in a tent or an RV, there are six campgrounds, with varying levels of access and facilities. Two of the campgrounds—Riley Creek (near the park entrance, essentially no scenery at all) and Savage River (Mile 13; on a very clear day, you might be able to see the mountain from here, but not much of it)—have spaces that accommodate tents, RVs, and campers. Visitors with private vehicles can also drive to the Teklanika campsite (Mile 29; a three-night minimum stay helps keep the traffic down), but they must first obtain park-road travel permits.

Sanctuary River (Mile 22, the smallest campground in the park, ideal if you want to be alone but can't backpack), Igloo Creek (Mile 43, comparable to Sanctuary River), and Wonder Lake (Mile 85, the cream of the crop in Denali camping—best views of the mountain and great easy hikes) have tent spaces only. The camper buses offer the only access to these sites. Riley Creek is the only campground open year-round, but does not have potable water during the winter and other amenities may not be available. Visit ⊕ *www.reservedenali.com* for details.

bound to be surrounded by Healy locals here. **Known for:** appropriately named one-pound Grizzly Burger; staying open year-round; to-go food options. Ⓢ *Average main: $15* ✉ *249 George Parks Hwy., Healy* ☎ *907/683–7673* ⊕ *www. rosescafealaska.com.*

🛏 Hotels

IN THE PARK

If you can afford it, stay at a wilderness lodge within Denali, like Camp Denali and North Face Lodge or the Kantishna Roadhouse.

★ Camp Denali and North Face Lodge

$$$$ | RESORT | The legendary, family-owned and-operated Camp Denali and North Face Lodge both offer stunning views of Denali and active learning experiences deep within Denali National Park, at Mile 89 on the park road. **Pros:** only in-park lodge with a view of Denali; knowledgeable and attentive staff; strong emphasis on learning. **Cons:** credit cards not accepted; steep rates and three-night minimum stay; alcohol is BYO. Ⓢ *Rooms*

from: $1280 ✉ *Mile 89, Denali Park Rd., Denali National Park* ☎ *907/683–2290* ⊕ *www.campdenali.com* ▭ *No credit cards* ☉ *Closed mid-Sept.–late May* ⌂ *18 cabins (Camp Denali), 15 rooms (North Face Lodge)* ⅋ *All-inclusive.*

Kantishna Roadhouse

$$$$ | RESORT | Run by the Athabascan Doyon Tourism, this establishment at Mile 95 on the park road offers an enriching wilderness getaway. **Pros:** guided hikes with naturalists; home to the only saloon in the Denali backcountry; transport from the train station is provided. **Cons:** no connection to the outside world besides a phone booth; lacks a direct view of Denali; two-night minimum stay. Ⓢ *Rooms from: $1080* ✉ *Mile 92, Denali Park Rd., Denali National Park* ☎ *800/942–7420, 907/374–3041* ⊕ *www. kantishnaroadhouse.com* ☉ *Closed mid-Sept.–early June* ⌂ *32 rooms* ⅋ *All-inclusive.*

OUTSIDE THE PARK

ALONG THE GEORGE PARKS HIGHWAY

Hotels, motels, RV parks, campgrounds, and some restaurants are clustered along the highway near the park entrance, which is at Mile 237.3. You can judge distance from the park by mileage markers; numbers increase northward and decrease southward.

Denali Cabins

$$ | RESORT | Cedar cabins built within the taiga forest have all the basic amenities (including TV and phone), private baths, and shared hot tubs at this complex along the highway 8 miles south of the park entrance. **Pros:** quiet location; offers National Park day trips; relaxing sauna and hot tub. **Cons:** not on the river; few extra amenities offered; cabins tucked close together. ⑤ *Rooms from: $169* ✉ *Mile 229, Parks Hwy., Denali National Park* ☎ *800/808–8068, 907/683–2643* ⊕ *www.alaskacollection.com* ⊘ *Closed mid-Sept.–mid–May* ⇒ *46 cabins* ❑ *No meals.*

Denali Crows Nest Log Cabins

$$$$ | HOTEL | Sitting above the restaurants and other accommodations of Glitter Gulch, the Crows Nest offers a more secluded atmosphere while still being close to the park entrance. **Pros:** beautiful cabins; hot tub and sauna with tremendous views; within walking distance of Glitter Gulch restaurants. **Cons:** standard cabins are on the small side; not very accessible for those with mobility problems; rough-cut wood on cabin exteriors catches clothing and skin easily. ⑤ *Rooms from: $310* ✉ *Mile 238.5, Parks Hwy., Denali National Park* ☎ *907/683–2723* ⊕ *www.denalicrowsnestcabins.com* ⊘ *Closed mid-Sept.–late May* ⇒ *38 cabins* ❑ *Free Breakfast.*

Denali Mountain Morning Hostel and Cabins

$ | RENTAL | For those who wish to spend a night along an Alaskan river without breaking the bank, Mountain Morning Hostel and Cabins is a good option. **Pros:** free shuttle service to and from Denali National Park; great riverside location; one of the cheaper options in the region that books some tours at a discount. **Cons:** shared bathrooms; some of the private cabins are small with steep stairs or ladders; Wi-Fi doesn't reach all the cabins. ⑤ *Rooms from: $99* ✉ *Mile 224.1 Parks Hwy., Denali National Park* ☎ *907/683–7503* ⊕ *www.denalihostel. com* ⊘ *Closed mid-Sept.–mid-May* ⇒ *14 cabins* ❑ *No meals.*

Denali Park Village

$$$$ | RESORT | This sprawling 20-acre resortlike property operated by one of the National Park Service's largest concessionaires, Aramark, sits just 7 miles south of the park entrance next to the Nenana River. **Pros:** shuttle service for all guests; transfers to railroad depot; close to both park and nearby dining. **Cons:** not the place for quiet or to meet many (or any) locals; draws lots of big tour groups; resort-style complex lacks local flavor. ⑤ *Rooms from: $379* ✉ *Mile 231, Parks Hwy., Denali National Park* ☎ *800/276–7234* ⊕ *www.denaliparkvillage.com* ⊘ *Closed mid-Sept.–mid-May* ⇒ *338 rooms, 50 cabins* ❑ *No meals.*

McKinley Creekside Cabins

$$$ | HOTEL | These accommodations sit on 10 acres and are bordered on the south side by Carlo Creek, with 14 cabins right along the Creek and 13 rooms in a hotel-style building. **Pros:** great location by the water; nice mountain views; barbecue and covered pavillion next to the creek available. **Cons:** no TVs in cabins; right off the side of the highway; cabins close together with little privacy. ⑤ *Rooms from: $239* ✉ *Mile 224, Parks Hwy., Carlo Creek* ☎ *907/683–2277* ⊕ *www.mckinleycabins.com* ⊘ *Closed mid-Sept.–mid-May* ⇒ *32 cabins, 13 rooms* ❑ *No meals.*

★ Tonglen Lake Lodge

$$$$ | B&B/INN | FAMILY | Tucked away from the bustling highway, Tonglen Lake Lodge provides a unique, community-oriented environment for those who desire a deeper and more intimate Alaskan experience. **Pros:** the hub for the surrounding community of 150 residents; large yard complete with badminton and other lawn games; Sunday night performances showcase everything from theater to live music. **Cons:** personal transportation required; no Wi-Fi in cabins; narrow, bumpy dirt road to property. $ *Rooms from: $425* ✉ *Mile 230, Parks Hwy., Denali National Park* ✛ *Heading north, take first turn after Mile 230 and follow handmade signs 0.8 miles* ☎ *907/683–2570* ⊕ *www.tonglenlake.com* ✆ *Closed mid-Sept.–mid-May except 4 "guide" rooms* ✍ *10 cabins, 4 rooms* ⦿ *Free Breakfast.*

HEALY
Aurora Denali Lodge

$$ | **HOTEL** | Formerly the Motel Nord Haven, this property has five wooded acres to minimize the presence of the nearby George Parks Highway. **Pros:** open year-round; reading area with comfy couches; one of the least expensive options in the area. **Cons:** lacks character; no stove tops in kitchenettes; not directly on the road but traffic is still audible. $ *Rooms from: $190* ✉ *Mile 249.5, Parks Hwy., Healy* ☎ *907/683–4500, 800/683–4500* ⊕ *www.auroradenalilodge.com* ✍ *28 rooms* ⦿ *Breakfast.*

Denali Dome Home

$$$ | **B&B/INN** | A 7,200-square-foot modified geodesic dome houses this year-round B&B, decorated with Alaskana and local art. **Pros:** thoughtful and knowledgeable owners; unique architecture; car-rental and tour-booking service. **Cons:** anyone with dog allergies should beware of two Scottish terriers; anyone squeamish about animal hides should be warned the house is decorated with a few prize trophies; close to main road. $ *Rooms from: $260* ✉ *137 Healy Spur Rd., Healy* ☎ *907/683–1239, 800/683–1239* ⊕ *www.denalidomehome.com* ✍ *8 rooms* ⦿ *Breakfast.*

★ EarthSong Lodge

$$$ | **B&B/INN** | Above the tree line at the edge of Denali National Park, EarthSong has 13 cabins with views of open tundra backed by peaks of the Alaska Range, along with a team of sled dogs that run winter tours into Denali Park. **Pros:** nightly slideshows on dogsledding or Denali; owners offer a wealth of knowledge; off the beaten path vibe with great views. **Cons:** 17-mile drive from the park entrance; individual cabins don't have kitchenettes, so must share one coffeemaker, fridge, and microwave; no pickup or transportation service so rental car or personal vehicle a must. $ *Rooms from: $185* ✉ *Mile 4, Stampede Rd., Healy* ☎ *907/683–2863* ⊕ *www.earthsonglodge.com* ✆ *Closed mid-Sept.–mid-May* ✍ *13 cabins* ⦿ *No meals.*

Chapter 7

FAIRBANKS, THE YUKON, AND THE INTERIOR

Updated by
Joey Besl

7

◉ Sights	🍽 Restaurants	🛏 Hotels	🛍 Shopping	🍸 Nightlife
★★★☆☆	★★★★☆	★★★★☆	★★★☆☆	★★★☆☆

WELCOME TO FAIRBANKS, THE YUKON, AND THE INTERIOR

TOP REASONS TO GO

★ **Gold-rush heritage:** The frontier spirit of the richest gold rush in Alaska remains alive in Fairbanks. From exploring dredges to panning for gold, chances to relive the past abound.

★ **Sternwheeler cruises:** The Riverboat Discovery is an authentic sternwheeler that cruises the Chena and Tanana rivers, which served as "highways" long before there were roads.

★ **The gateway to the Arctic:** Fairbanks is an essential point for connections to northern Alaska—a vast land of the midnight sun and the northern lights.

★ **Dog mushing:** The Interior is Alaska's prime mushing spot. Many enthusiasts live here just so they can spend every free winter moment running sled dogs.

★ **The University of Alaska:** Fairbanks is home to Alaska's main university campus. This means great museums, endless cultural events, and all the other perks of a college town, albeit one where winter temperatures can drop to −50°F.

1 Fairbanks. The main hub of northern Alaska.

2 Chena Hot Springs. Home to an impressive hot springs resort.

3 Central and Circle. Small communities filled with history and nature.

4 Steese and White Mountains. Easily accessible mountains with plenty of hiking.

5 Yukon-Charley Rivers National Preserve. A gorgeous landscape perfect for solitude.

6 Manley Hot Springs. A mining town with year-round access to hot springs.

7 The Dalton Highway. The road connecting Interior Alaska to the oil bays of the North.

8 North Pole and Salcha. Two small towns celebrating Christmas and handicrafts.

9 Delta Junction. The western terminus of the Alaska Highway.

10 Tok. A pit stop for those traveling the Alaska Highway.

11 Chicken. The heart of the Fortymile Mining District.

12 Eagle. The former center of government for Interior Alaska.

13 Dawson City. The perfect Gold Rush town.

14 Whitehorse. The capital of the Yukon.

Alaska's Interior remains the last frontier, even for the Last Frontier state. The northern lights sparkle above a vast, mostly uninhabited landscape that promises adventure for those who choose to traverse it.

Come here for wildlife-rich, pristine land and hardy locals, a rich and quirky history, gold panning, nonstop daylight in the summer, or ice-sculpting competitions under the northern lights in winter. Outdoors enthusiasts can enjoy outstanding hiking, rafting, fishing, skiing, and dogsledding. And don't forget to top off the experience with a soak in the hot springs. The geology of the Interior played a key role in history at the turn of the 20th century. The image of early-1900s Alaska, set to the harsh tunes of countless honky-tonk saloons and the clanging of pans, is rooted around the Interior's goldfields. Gold fever struck in Circle and Eagle in the 1890s, spread into Canada's Yukon Territory in the big Klondike gold rush of 1898, headed as far west as the beaches of Nome in 1900, then came back to Alaska's Interior when Fairbanks hit pay dirt in 1903. Through it all, the broad, swift Yukon River was the rush's main highway. Flowing almost 2,300 miles from Canada to the Bering Sea, just below the Arctic Circle, it carried prospectors across the north in search of instant fortune.

Although Fairbanks has grown into a bustling city with some serious attractions, many towns and communities in the Interior seem little changed from the gold-rush days. Visiting the galleries at the Morris Thompson Cultural and Visitors Center makes it clear how intertwined the Interior's past and present lifestyles remain. When early missionaries set up schools in the Bush, the Alaska Native peoples were sent to regional centers for schooling and "salvation," but that stopped long ago, and today Interior Alaska's Native villages are thriving, with their own schools and a particularly Alaskan blend of modern life and tradition. Ft. Yukon, 145 miles northeast of Fairbanks on the Arctic Circle, is the largest Athabascan village in the state, with just less than 600 residents.

Alaska's current gold rush—the pipeline carrying (a little less each year) "black gold" from the oil fields in Prudhoe Bay south to the port of Valdez—snakes its way through the Interior. The Richardson Highway, which started as a gold stampeders' trail, parallels the Trans-Alaska Pipeline on its route south of Fairbanks. And gold still glitters in the Interior: Fairbanks, the site of the largest gold production in Alaska in pre–World War II days, is home to the Ft. Knox Gold Mine, which has approximately doubled Alaska's gold production. Throughout the region, with the price of gold down from its highs of a few years ago but still quite lofty, hundreds of tiny mines—from one-man operations to full-scale works—have geared up again, proving that what the poet Robert Service wrote more than 100 years ago still holds true: "There are strange things done in the midnight sun / by the men who moil for gold."

MAJOR REGIONS

Fairbanks. With a regional population of about 100,000, Fairbanks is Alaska's northern hub, home to the main campus of the University of Alaska and an important point along the Trans-Alaska oil pipeline. This rough-edged town has a symphony orchestra, Alaska's largest library, and a vibrant local arts scene, including one of the best museums in the state.

North of Fairbanks. The Alaska wilderness is right at Fairbanks's door, with hundreds of miles of subarctic wilderness to explore. Follow the manageable **Chena Hot Springs Road** to its end and you'll find a natural hot spring that is a local favorite spot for aurora viewing. The **Steese Highway** connects to historic goldfields in Central and Circle, and the **Elliott Highway** leads northwest and, before shifting to the southwest, connects to the roughly north–south Dalton Highway (built to assist construction of the Trans-Alaska Pipeline System). All three roads provide access to countless starting points for hiking, skiing, camping, fishing, canoeing, and other outdoor-oriented adventures including the Yukon-Charley Rivers National Preserve and Manley Hot Springs. A few roads and isolated villages are the extent of civilization here.

Fortymile Country. A trip through the Fortymile Country up the Taylor Highway will take you back in time more than a century—when gold was the lure that drew travelers to Interior Alaska. It's one of the few places to see active mining without leaving the road system. In addition, remote wilderness experiences and float trips abound. If you're headed to Fortymile Country from Fairbanks, you'll drive along the historic Richardson Highway, once a pack-train trail (think mules with bags) and a dogsled route for mail carriers and gold miners in the Interior. As quirky places to turn off a highway go, North Pole, Salcha, Delta Junction, Tok, Chicken, and Eagle are up there with the best of them.

Yukon Territory, Canada. The happy, shining promise of gold is what called Canada's Yukon Territory to the world's attention with the Klondike gold rush of 1897–98. Maybe as many as 100,000 people set off for the confluence of the Yukon and Klondike rivers, on the promise of nuggets the size of basketballs just waiting to be picked up. In the end, roughly only a dozen of them actually went home rich in gold, but all who returned did so rich in memories and stories that are still being told. Though the international border divides Alaska from Yukon Territory, the Yukon River tends to unify the region. Early prospectors, miners, traders, and camp followers moved readily up and down the river with little regard to national boundaries. An earlier Alaska strike preceded the Klondike find by years, yet Circle was all but abandoned in the stampede to the creeks around Dawson City and Whitehorse. Later gold discoveries in the Alaskan Fortymile Country, Nome, and Fairbanks reversed that flow across the border into Alaska.

Planning

WHEN TO GO

June and July bring near-constant sun (there's nothing quite like walking out of a restaurant at 11 pm into broad daylight), sometimes punctuated by afternoon cloudbursts. In winter it gets so cold (−40°F or below) that boiling water flung out a window can land as ice particles.

Like most of Alaska, many of the Interior's main attractions are seasonal, open from mid-May to mid-September. A trip in May avoids the rush, but it can snow in Fairbanks in spring. Late August brings fall colors, ripe berries, active wildlife, and the start of northern lights season, with marvelous shows, if you hit the right night. Winter-sports fans should come in March, when the sun's back but there's still plenty of snow. Festivals are a big part of life in Fairbanks, with the months of February and March bringing the most revelry.

FESTIVALS

Fairbanks Summer Arts Festival

FESTIVALS | Alaska's premier cultural gathering takes place over two weeks in late July on the University of Alaska Fairbanks campus. The festivities, which began as a small jazz festival, now attract visitors worldwide for American roots and other music, dance, and literary, healing, visual, and culinary arts. Guests are encouraged to participate in one- or two-week classes and miniworkshops. ⊠ *Fairbanks* ☎ *907/474–8869* ⊕ *www.fsaf.org.*

Golden Days

FESTIVALS | A street fair and parade through the city cap several days of events at this July celebration of Fairbanks's gold-rush past. ⊠ *Fairbanks* ☎ *907/452–1105* ⊕ *www.fairbankschamber.org/golden-days.*

Tanana Valley State Fair

FESTIVALS | FAMILY | This weeklong event in early August is Interior Alaska's largest annual gathering. If you've ever wondered just what a 50-pound cabbage looks like, this fair might be your best chance to find out. You can also peruse the handiwork of local artisans. ⊠ *1800 College Rd., Aurora* ⊕ *www.tananavalleyfair.org* 🎟 *$10.*

World Ice Art Championships and U.S. National Championships

FESTIVALS | An ice-sculpting extravaganza, these competitive events that unfold from late February to late March draw ice artists from around the world. ⊠ *Fairbanks* ☎ *907/451–8250* ⊕ *www.icealaska.com* 🎟 *From $15.*

Yukon Quest

FESTIVALS | FAMILY | The early February Yukon Quest calls itself the "toughest sled dog race in the world," passing through historic early-gold-rush territory. In odd-numbered years the 1,000-mile race starts in Whitehorse, in even-numbered ones in Fairbanks. Both the start and finish are festive events, with huge crowds on hand even when the temperatures plunge. ⊠ *Fairbanks* ☎ *907/452–7954* ⊕ *www.yukonquest.com.*

GETTING HERE AND AROUND

AIR TRAVEL

Fairbanks is the regional air hub. From Fairbanks you can catch a ride on regularly scheduled mail planes to small, predominantly Athabascan villages along the Yukon River or to Iñupiat settlements on the Arctic coast. All of the smaller air services operate the mail runs on varying schedules. If you want to visit a particular village, or just have the desire to see a bit of Alaska Native village life, contact any one of the services. Do be aware that not all villages are interested in tourism; some are more prepared than others, and in a few, you're just going to be a nuisance. And what's happening where can change fast, with season, with hunting conditions, with weather. Ask advice from local air carriers before heading out.

With many scheduled flights to bush villages in northwestern Alaska, the Interior, and the North Slope of the Brooks Range, Ravn is a trusted bush-flight service. Warbelow's Air Ventures flies to 13 villages around Interior Alaska and offers charters and tours, including trips on mail runs to bush villages. From its Fairbanks base, Wright flies to Interior and Brooks Range villages.

AIRLINE CONTACTS Ravn Alaska

☎ *907/266–8394, 800/866–8394 outside Alaska* ⊕ *www.flyravn.com.* **Warbelow's Air Ventures** ☎ *907/474–0518, 888/459–6250* ⊕ *www.warbelows.com.* **Wright Air Service** ⊠ *3842 University Ave. S* ☎ *907/474–0502* ⊕ *www.wrightairservice.com.*

CAR TRAVEL

Interior Alaska is sandwiched between two monumental mountain ranges: the Brooks Range to the north and the Alaska Range to the south. In such a vast wilderness many of the region's residents define their area by a limited network of two-lane highways. You really need a car in the Interior, even if you're exploring primarily in and around Fairbanks.

The Steese Highway, the Dalton Highway, and the Taylor Highway (which is closed in winter) are well-maintained gravel roads. However, summer rain can make them slick and dangerous. ■ TIP➜ **Rental-car companies have varying policies about travel on gravel roads, so check in advance to see what's permitted.**

The George Parks Highway runs south to Denali National Park and Preserve and on to Anchorage, the state's largest city, 360 miles away on the coast. The Richardson Highway extends southeast to Delta Junction before turning south to Valdez, which is also 360 miles away.

Two major routes lead north. You can take the Elliott Highway to the Dalton Highway, following the Trans-Alaska Pipeline to its origins at Prudhoe Bay on Alaska's North Slope (you can't drive all the way to the end, but you can get close). Alternatively, explore the Steese Highway to its termination at the Yukon River and the town of Circle.

■ TIP➜ **Alaskans don't refer to highways by their route numbers; if you do, you'll most likely get blank stares.**

TOURS

If you're interested in getting out into the wilderness or out to one of the villages, tours are the way to go. They are a far less stressful way to see this area, particularly if you have limited experience driving remote unpaved roads or traveling the backcountry of Alaska.

CUSTOM SIGHTSEEING
Alaska/Yukon Trails

ADVENTURE TOURS | This outfitter offers small group shuttles and tours from Fairbanks to Denali as well as up into the Yukon. ✉ *Fairbanks* ☎ *907/479–2277, 800/770–7275* ⊕ *www.alaskashuttle.com* ✉ *From $55.*

RIVER TRIPS
Riverboat Discovery

BOAT TOURS | These popular three-hour tours in a traditional stern-wheeler include the opportunity to visit an Athabascan village and watch a bush pilot flight demonstration. ✉ *1975 Discovery Dr., Fairbanks* ☎ *907/479–6673, 866/479–6673* ⊕ *www.riverboatdiscovery.com* ✉ *From $65.*

Sternwheeler Tanana Chief

BOAT TOURS | This cruise along the Chena River is on a vintage stern-wheeler and includes brunch and dinner options. ✉ *1020 Hoselton Rd., Fairbanks* ☎ *907/205–4988, 888/647–2501* ⊕ *www.tananachiefalaska.com* ✉ *From $25.*

SEA AND LAND TOURS
GoNorth Alaska Travel Center

ADVENTURE TOURS | Summer and winter tours include fishing, aurora-viewing, dogsledding, and wildlife-watching. ✉ *Fairbanks* ☎ *907/479–7271, 855/236–7271* ⊕ *www.gonorth-alaska.com* ✉ *From $95.*

Northern Alaska Tour Company

ADVENTURE TOURS | This Fairbanks-based tour company specializes in Arctic adventures, including half- and full-day excursions to the Arctic Circle, Utqiaġvik, and the Brooks Range. Aurora-watching trips take place in winter. ✉ *Fairbanks* ☎ *907/474–8600, 800/474–1986* ⊕ *www.northernalaska.com* ✉ *From $159.*

Trans Arctic Circle Treks Ltd

AIR EXCURSIONS | Consider one of this trusted company's flight and driving tours, which range from a few hours to several days, into the Arctic Circle. ✉ *Fairbanks* ☎ *907/479–5451, 800/336–8735* ⊕ *www.transarctictreks.com* ✉ *From $189.*

RESTAURANTS

Most restaurants fly in fresh salmon and halibut from the coast. Meat-and-potatoes main courses, pastas, pizzas, and pub fare dominate most menus, but an increasing number of establishments serving healthier fare, as well as ethnic restaurants (including more than a dozen Thai restaurants) have opened in and around Fairbanks in recent years. The food isn't the only thing full of local flavor: Alaskan pride runs strong, so expect to see snowshoes, bear hides, the state flag, and historic photos incorporated into restaurant decor. As for attire, even in the most elegant establishments Alaskans sometimes wear sweats or Carhartts.

HOTELS

You won't find ultraluxury hotels in the Interior, but the region does have bed-and-breakfasts, rustic-chic lodges, and national chains, as well as homespun local spots. B&Bs are usually owned by locals eager to provide travel tips or an unforgettable story.

Restaurant and hotel reviews have been shortened. For full information, visit Fodors.com. Prices in the restaurant reviews are the average cost of a main course at dinner or, if dinner is not served, at lunch. Prices in the hotel reviews are the lowest cost of a standard double room in high season.

What It Costs			
$	$$	$$$	$$$$
RESTAURANTS			
under $14	$14–$22	$22–$32	over $32
HOTELS			
under $100	$100–$200	$200–$300	over $300

HEALTH AND SAFETY

The main health concerns for travelers to the Interior are high anxiety caused by mosquito attacks and, far more dangerous—and a year-round concern—hypothermia. To protect yourself mentally (and physically) when a cloud of mosquitoes descends, your best bet is to apply DEET, and lots of it.

Hypothermia, the lowering of the body's core temperature, is an ever-present threat in Alaska's wilderness. Wear layers of warm clothing when the weather is cool or wet; this includes a good wind- and waterproof parka or shell, warm hat and gloves, and waterproof or water-resistant boots. Heed the advice of locals who will tell you "cotton kills." It does nothing to move moisture away from your skin, and can speed the onset of hypothermia. Any time you're in the wilderness, eat regularly to maintain energy, and stay hydrated.

Early symptoms of hypothermia are shivering, accelerated heartbeat, and goose bumps; this may be followed by clumsiness, slurred speech, disorientation, and unconsciousness. In the extreme, hypothermia can result in death. If you notice any of these symptoms in yourself or anyone in your group, stop, add layers of clothing, light a fire or camp stove, and warm up; a cup of tea or any hot fluid also helps. Avoid alcohol, which speeds hypothermia and impairs judgment. If your clothes are wet, change immediately. Be sure to put on a warm hat (most of the body's heat is lost through the head) and gloves. If there are only two of you, stay together: a person with hypothermia should never be left alone. Keep an eye on your traveling companions; frequently people won't recognize the symptoms in themselves until it's too late.

MONEY MATTERS

ATMs are widely available in all the cities, and most of the towns; if you move out to the villages, though, take cash and don't expect to find much in the way of banking services.

Fairbanks

On a first drive around Fairbanks, the city appears to be a sprawling conglomeration of strip malls, chain stores, and other evidence of suburbia. But look beyond the obvious in the Interior's biggest town and you'll discover why thousands insist that this is the best place to live in

Alaska—most citing the incredibly tight and supportive community.

The hardy Alaskans who refuse to leave during the cold and dark winters share a strong camaraderie. The fight to stave off cabin fever leads to creative festivals, from winter solstice celebrations to midnight baseball in summer. Quirky is celebrated in Fairbanks. But so is the ability to take care of business, no matter the obstacles (including seriously cold temperatures). It takes a special kind of confidence to live here, and that adds to the town's attractiveness.

Many old homes and commercial buildings trace their history to the city's early days, especially in the downtown area, with its narrow, winding streets following the contours of the Chena River. Even if each year brings more chain stores, the beautiful hillsides and river valleys remain. And the farmers' market here is a stunner. Of course, there is Fairbanks's fall, winter, and spring bonus: being able to see the aurora, or northern lights, an average of 243 nights a year.

These magic lights were a common sight to the Alaska Natives who lived and traveled through Interior Alaska for thousands of years. But outsiders started coming to Fairbanks for the view all because of one guy's bad day: in 1901 E.T. Barnette, a merchant traveling upstream, was forced to leave the boat with all his trading goods at a wooded spot in the middle of nowhere along the Chena River because the water was too shallow to pass. While awaiting passage farther east, Barnette's luck took a turn for the wonderful when an Italian prospector discovered gold 12 miles north of Barnette's settlement the next summer. The resulting gold rush created customers for his stockpile of goods and led to the birth of Fairbanks, which for a brief time became the largest and wealthiest settlement in Alaska.

The city is making some real efforts to preserve what's left of its gold-rush past,

most notably in the 44-acre Pioneer Park, where dozens of cabins and many other relics were moved out of the path of progress. Downtown Fairbanks began to deteriorate in the 1970s, before and after the boom associated with the building of the Trans-Alaska Pipeline. But the downward spiral ended long ago and most of downtown has been rebuilt.

One symbol of downtown's renaissance and a good first stop is the Morris Thompson Cultural and Visitors Center. The pride of downtown, the center represents a very successful collaboration between Explore Fairbanks (run by the city's convention and visitors bureau), the Alaska Public Lands Information Center, and the Tanana Chiefs Conference, whose goals include preserving local languages, knowledge, and customs, and promoting pride among Alaska Native youth. In addition to an impressive museum that will introduce you to the region's wonders, you'll find everything you need to plan the rest of your touring. You should also check out the University of Alaska Museum of the North, whose building is full of soothing, swooping lines that evoke glaciers, mountains, and sea life. The museum's collection of material about Alaska is among the state's best.

GETTING HERE AND AROUND
AIR TRAVEL
Alaska Airlines and Delta offer seasonal nonstop service between Fairbanks and Seattle. Alaska Airlines and Ravn Alaska fly the Anchorage–Fairbanks route. Hotel shuttles, rental cars, and taxis are available at the Fairbanks airport.

BUS TRAVEL
Alaska/Yukon Trails connects Fairbanks, Denali, Anchorage, Talkeetna, Whitehorse, and Dawson City. Hotels run shuttle buses to and from the airport, but once in town you'll find getting around by public transportation can be cumbersome.

BUS CONTACTS Alaska/Yukon Trails
☎ *800/770–7275, 907/479–2277*
⊕ *www.alaskashuttle.com.*

CAR TRAVEL

Fairbanks is at the junction of three major highways, the Parks, Steese, and Richardson. The town is too spread out for walking, and though you can get around by taxi, the cost of cabs will add up fast. Save yourself frustration and rent a car.

TRAIN TRAVEL

Between late May and early September, Alaska Railroad's daily passenger service connects Fairbanks to Anchorage, with stops at Talkeetna, Wasilla, and Denali National Park and Preserve. The route runs weekly through the winter, stopping in Talkeetna and Wasilla on the way to Anchorage. Standard trains have dining, lounge, and dome cars, as well as an outdoor viewing platform. Holland America and Princess offer luxurious travel packages as well.

TRAIN CONTACTS Alaska Railroad
☎ *907/265–2494, 800/544–0552* ⊕ *www. alaskarailroad.com.* **Gray Line Alaska**
☎ *888/425–1737* ⊕ *www.graylinealaska. com.* **Princess Tours** ☎ *800/426–0500*
⊕ *www.princesslodges.com.*

ESSENTIALS

VISITOR INFORMATION Alaska Department of Fish and Game ✉ *1300 College Rd.*
☎ *907/459–7207 for sportfishing information, 907/459–7206 for hunting and wildlife-related information* ⊕ *www.adfg. alaska.gov.* **Alaska Public Lands Information Center** ✉ *101 Dunkel St.* ☎ *907/459–3730*
⊕ *www.alaskacenters.gov/fairbanks. cfm.* **Explore Fairbanks** ✉ *101 Dunkel St.*
☎ *907/456–5774* ⊕ *www.explorefairbanks.com.* **Morris Thompson Cultural and Visitors Center** ✉ *101 Dunkel St.*
☎ *907/459–3700* ⊕ *www.morristhompsoncenter.org.*

TOURS

Gray Line Alaska

TOUR—SIGHT | The company conducts scenic and informative tours of the Fairbanks area. An eight-hour sightseeing package includes a stern-wheeler cruise and tour of a historic goldfield operation. Other tours include visits to Iditarod kennels and ATV treks through the forest under the midnight sun. ✉ *Fairbanks* ☎ *888/425–1737* ⊕ *www.graylinealaska. com* ⌨ *From $56.*

◉ Sights

Alaska Range Overlook

VIEWPOINT | Much of the north side of the Alaska Range is visible from this overlook, a favorite spot for time-lapse photography of the midwinter sun just peeking over the southern horizon on a low arc. The three major peaks, called the Three Sisters, are nearly always distinguishable on a clear day. From your left are Mt. Hayes, 13,832 feet; Mt. Hess, 11,940 feet; and Mt. Deborah, 12,339 feet. Much farther to the right, toward the southwest, hulks Denali, the highest peak in North America. On some seemingly clear days it's not visible at all. At other times the base is easy to see but the peak is lost in cloud cover. Look for the parking area just east of the University of Alaska Museum. ✉ *West Ridge, University of Alaska Fairbanks campus, Yukon Dr.*

Creamer's Field Migratory Waterfowl Refuge

NATURE PRESERVE | **FAMILY** | Thousands of migrating ducks, geese, and sandhill cranes stop here in spring as they head north to nesting grounds, and in late summer as they head south before the cold hits. It's amazing to watch them gather in huge flocks, with constant takeoffs and landings. This is also a great place to view songbirds and moose. Five miles of nature trails, open year-round, lead through fields, forest, and wetlands. Now on the National Register of Historic Places, Creamer's Dairy was the northernmost dairy in North America from 1910 to 1966. ✉ *1300 College Rd.*
☎ *907/459–7307 visitor center* ⊕ *www.*

adfg.alaska.gov ⊗ Visitor center closed Sun.–Fri. in mid-Sept.–May.

Fairbanks Ice Museum
MUSEUM | Ice has never been so cool—this museum presents the works of local and international artists who turn giant blocks of ice into intricate sculptures. The Ice Showcase, a large glass-wall display, is kept a consistent 20°F, and there's something to dazzle just about everyone (including an ice slide and occasional live demonstrations). Housed inside the historic Lacey Street Theater, the museum screens hourly films about the Northern Lights and ice carving. ⊠ *500 2nd Ave.* ☎ *907/451–8222* ⊠ *$15* ⊗ *Closed mid-Sept.–mid-May.*

★ Fountainhead Antique Automobile Museum
MUSEUM | Among the world's finest auto museums, Fountainhead provides a fascinating survey of history, design, culture, and, of course, cars (specifically ones from 1898 to 1938). Obscure makes—Buckmobiles, Packards, and Hudsons among them—compete for attention with more familiar specimens from Ford, Cadillac, and Chrysler. The museum's holdings include the first car ever made in Alaska, built in Skagway out of sheet metal and old boat parts. Alongside the cars, all but three of them in running condition, are equally remarkable historical photographs and exhibits of vintage clothing that illustrate the era's evolution of style, especially for women. ⊠ *Wedgewood Resort, 212 Wedgewood Dr.* ☎ *907/450–2100* ⊕ *www.fountainheadmuseum.com* ⊠ *$10* ⊗ *Closed Mon., Tues., and Thurs.–Sat. mid-Sept.–mid-May.*

Georgeson Botanical Garden
GARDEN | When most people think of Alaska's vegetation, they conjure up images of flat, treeless tundra, so the variety of native and cultivated flowers on exhibit here is often unexpected. The garden, 4 miles west of downtown, is part of the University of Alaska Fairbanks. A major focus of research is Interior Alaska's unique, short but intense midnight-sun growing season, and the results are spectacular. The nonstop daylight brings out rich and vibrant colors and—to the delight of locals and visitors—amazing vegetable specimens that don't grow anywhere near as big in the Lower 48. ⊠ *University of Alaska Fairbanks, 117 W. Tanana Dr.* ☎ *907/474–7222* ⊕ *www.georgesonbotanicalgarden.org* ⊠ *$5 suggested donation* ⊗ *Closed early Sept.–late May.*

Golden Heart Plaza
CITY PARK | This riverside park is the hub of downtown celebrations, including free evening concerts. The plaza is dominated by the towering statue of the Unknown First Family, encircled by plaques containing the names of 4,500 local families who contributed to the building of the plaza. ⊠ *1st Ave., east of Cushman St.*

Large Animal Research Station
COLLEGE | **FAMILY** | On the fringes of the University of Alaska campus is a 134-acre home to dozens of musk ox and domestic reindeer. Resident and visiting scientists study these large ungulates to better understand their physiologies and how they adapt to Arctic conditions. The station also serves as a valuable outreach program. Once nearly eradicated from Alaska, the shaggy, prehistoric-looking beasts known as musk ox are marvels of adaptive physiques and behaviors. Their qiviut, the delicate undercoat of soft hair, is combed out (without harming the animals) and made into yarn for scarves, hats, and gloves. The station has this unprocessed wool and yarn for sale to help fund the care of the animals. On tours you visit the pens for a close-up look at the animals and their young, while learning about the biology and ecology of the animals from a naturalist. Call ahead to arrange tours from mid-September through mid-May; otherwise you can just stop by. ⊠ *2220 Yankovich Rd., off Ballaine Rd.* ☎ *907/474–5724* ⊕ *www.lars.uaf.edu* ⊠ *Grounds free, tours $10.*

Fairbanks

KEY
- ● Exploring Sights
- ● Restaurants
- ● Hotels

Sights ▼
1 Alaska Range Overlook **B1**
2 Creamer's Field Migratory Waterfowl Refuge **I1**
3 Fairbanks Ice Museum **J3**
4 Fountainhead Antique Automobile Museum **J1**
5 Georgeson Botanical Garden **B2**
6 Golden Heart Plaza ... **J3**
7 Large Animal Research Station **B1**
8 Morris Thompson Cultural and Visitors Center **J3**
9 Pioneer Park **G4**
10 Trans-Alaska Pipeline **J1**
11 University of Alaska Museum of the North **C1**

Restaurants ▼
1 Alaska Coffee Roasting Company... **D3**
2 Alaska Salmon Bake.................. **G4**
3 The Cookie Jar........ **H2**
4 East Ramp Wood-Fired Pizza **C7**

TO CHENA HOT SPRINGS

5 Gambardella's Pasta Bella **I3**	**11** Pump House Restaurant and Saloon **A5**	**Hotels** ▼
6 Geraldo's.............. **J1**	**12** Sam's Sourdough Cafe....... **E2**	**1** A Taste of Alaska Lodge.......... **J2**
7 Ivory Jack's........... **B1**	**13** Silver Gulch Brewing and Bottling Co........ **J2**	**2** Aurora Express **A5**
8 Lavelle's Bistro....... **J4**		**3** Bridgewater Hotel.... **J3**
9 Pike's Landing........ **C5**	**14** Thai House **J4**	**4** Minnie Street Inn **J3**
10 Pita Place.............. **E1**	**15** Turtle Club **J2**	**5** Pike's Waterfront Lodge..... **C5**

6 River's Edge Resort... **C4**	
7 Sophie Station Suites **E5**	
8 SpringHill Suites by Marriott............. **J4**	
9 Wedgewood Resort... **J1**	

★ Morris Thompson Cultural and Visitors Center

INFO CENTER | As with visitor centers elsewhere, you can get help with everything at this multifaceted facility, from taking in local attractions to negotiating a backcountry adventure. But the highlights here are the museum-quality displays about Interior Alaska. A walk-through exhibit re-creates a fish camp, and you can walk through a full-size public-use cabin similar to ones you can rent on your own. Be sure to peer out the cabin window: an artful rendition of the northern lights awaits. Alaska Native artists frequently sell jewelry and other wares at the center; in addition to making a unique purchase you can chat with them about growing up in the villages or, in some cases, at fish camps such as the one the exhibit depicts. Named for a Tanana leader who dedicated his life to building bridges between Native and non-Native cultures, the center hosts summer programs showcasing Alaska Native art, music, storytelling, and dance. On the edge of the center's parking lot is **Antler Arch.** Made from more than 100 moose and caribou antlers, it serves as a gateway to the bike and walking path along the Chena River. ⊠ *101 Dunkel St.* ☎ *907/459–3700* ⊕ *www.morristhompsoncenter.org* 🔲 *Free.*

Pioneer Park

CITY PARK | **FAMILY** | The 44-acre park is along the Chena River near downtown Fairbanks, and has several museums, an art gallery, theater, civic center, children's playground, antique merry-go-round, and multiple restaurants. Owned and operated by the borough, the park also has a re-created gold-rush town with historic buildings saved from urban renewal, log-cabin gift shops, and a narrow-gauge train that circles the park. No-frills (dry) RV camping is available in the parking lot for $12 a night. No reservation is necessary. ⊠ *2300 Airport Way, at Peger Rd.* ☎ *907/459–1087* ⊕ *www.co.fairbanks. ak.us/pioneerpark* 🔲 *Park free; fees for* *some attractions* ⊙ *Museums and shops closed early Sept.–late May.*

Trans-Alaska Pipeline Just north of Fairbanks you can see and touch the famous Trans-Alaska Pipeline. This 48-inch-diameter pipe travels 800 miles from the oil fields on the North Slope of the Brooks Range over three mountain ranges and over more than 500 rivers and streams to the terminal in Valdez. There the crude oil is pumped onto tanker ships and transported to oil refineries in the Lower 48 states. Since the pipeline began operations in 1977, more than 17 billion barrels of North Slope crude have been pumped. Currently the pipe is carrying about 527,000 barrels per day (only a quarter of its peak figures from 1988). ⊠ *Mile 8.4, Steese Hwy.* 🔲 *Free.*

★ University of Alaska Museum of the North

MUSEUM | With sweeping exterior curves and graceful lines that evoke glaciers, mountains, and the Northern Lights, this don't-miss museum has some of Alaska's most distinctive architecture. Inside, two-story viewing windows look out on the Alaska Range and the Tanana Valley while Otto, the 8-foot, 9-inch brown bear specimen, greets visitors to the entrance of the Gallery of Alaska. "Please touch" items include the molars of a mammoth and a mastodon, animal pelts, replica petroglyphs, and a massive quartz crystal found in Alaska's Brooks Range. The gallery also contains dioramas showing the state's animals and how they interact, and the fantastic collection of Alaska Native clothes, tools, and boats provide insights into the ways that different groups came to terms with climatic extremes.

Another highlight is the Rose Berry Alaska Art Gallery, representing 2,000 years of Alaska's art, from ancient to modern. ⊠ *University of Alaska Fairbanks, 1962 Yukon Dr.* ☎ *907/474–7505* ⊕ *www. uaf.edu/museum* 🔲 *$14* ⊙ *Closed Sun. Sept.–May.*

Did You Know?

The University of Alaska Museum of the North is pure Alaska inside and out: the exterior was inspired by the state's alpine ridges, glaciers, Yukon River, and the northern lights, while the interior houses thousands of years of Alaskan art, culture, and nature. Don't miss Blue Babe, the 36,000-year-old steppe bison. The museum also features one of the best gift shops in the city.

Winter in Fairbanks

The temperature gets down to −40°F every winter in Fairbanks, but school is almost never canceled, no matter how cold it gets. In recent years, in fact, the only times schools have closed were when rare winter warm spells created icy conditions on the roads that made it too hazardous for bus travel. Young Alaskans are so hardy that outdoor recess takes place down to −20°F.

The weather is a great unifying factor among Fairbanks residents. Winter conditions freeze the pipes of university presidents as well as laborers. After a night of 40 below it's common to see cars bumping along as if the tires were flat; the bottoms of the tires freeze flat, and it takes a quarter mile or so before they warm up and return to round. Almost every car in Fairbanks has an electric plug hanging out front between the headlights. This is for a heater that prevents the car's engine block from getting so cold the engine won't start.

Activities

BASEBALL

Alaska Goldpanners

BASEBALL/SOFTBALL | Scores of baseball stars, including Tom Seaver and Dave Winfield, have passed through Fairbanks on their way to the major leagues. With a roster of college players on summer break, the Alaska Goldpanners play national teams at Growden Memorial Field. The baseball park also hosts the W.G. & Eddie Stroecker Midnight Sun Baseball Game, a Fairbanks tradition for more than 110 years, in which the Goldpanners play baseball at midnight of the summer solstice without the benefit of artificial lights. ✉ *201 Wilbur St.* ☎ *907/451–0095* ⊕ *www.goldpanners. com* 🎟 *$7; $25 for Midnight Sun game.*

BICYCLING

Bicyclists in Fairbanks use the paved paths from the University of Alaska campus around Farmers Loop to the Steese Highway. Another path follows Geist and Chena Pump roads into downtown Fairbanks. A shorter, less strenuous route is the bike path between downtown and Pioneer Park along the south side of the Chena River. Maps showing all the bike paths are available at Explore Fairbanks. Mountain bikers can test their skills in summer on the ski trails of the University of Alaska Fairbanks and the Birch Hill Recreation Area or on many of the trails and dirt roads around Fairbanks.

CanoeAlaska

BICYCLING | In addition to canoes and paddleboards, this riverside shop near Pioneer Park also rents several styles of bikes, with rates starting at $20 for a half-day. Take advantage of the Bike and Boat package to paddle the Chena River one-way and pedal along the riverbank back. ✉ *1101 Peger Rd., Pioneer Park* ☎ *907/457–2453* ⊕ *www.canoealaska. com.*

Fairbikes

BICYCLING | FAMILY | Fairbanks's bike-share program operates 20 pay-as-you-go stations across the city. Download the Fairbikes app to find the nearest location. ✉ *410 2nd Ave, Suite 103* ☎ *907/687– 6884* ⊕ *fairbikes.com.*

BOATING

For relaxing boating in or near Fairbanks, use Chena River access points at Nordale Road east of the city, at the Cushman and Wendell Street bridges near downtown, in Pioneer Park above the Peger River Bridge, at the state campground, and at the University Avenue Bridge.

The Tanana River, with a current that is fast and often shallow, is ideally suited for riverboats. On this river and others in the Yukon River drainage, Alaskans use long, wide, flat-bottom boats powered by one or two large outboard engines. The boats include a lift to raise the engine a few inches, allowing passage through the shallows; lately, it's more common just to get a jet boat, which doesn't have a propeller, and so can go into much shallower waters. Arrangements for riverboat charters can be made in almost any river community. Ask at Explore Fairbanks, in the Morris Thompson Cultural and Visitors Center.

★ CanoeAlaska

TOUR—SPORTS | This outfit rents gear and arranges pickups and drop-offs for the Class I waters of the lower Chena River (the only real challenge for canoeists on the lower river is watching out for powerboats), as well as other local rivers. ⊠ *Pioneer Park Boat Dock, 1101 Peger Rd., along Chena River* ☎ *907/457–2453* ⊕ *www.canoealaska.com* ⊠ *From $55 for an 8-hr kayak, canoe, or paddleboard rental.*

★ Riverboat Discovery

TOUR—SPORTS | Relive the city's riverboat history and the Interior's cultural heritage each summer aboard the Riverboat *Discovery,* a three-hour narrated trip by stern-wheeler along the Chena and Tanana rivers to a rustic Alaska Native village on the Tanana. The cruise provides a glimpse of the lifestyle of the dog mushers, subsistence fishermen, traders, and Alaska Natives who populate the Yukon River drainage. Sights along the way include operating fish wheels, a bush airfield, floatplanes, a smokehouse and cache, log cabins, and dog kennels once tended by the late Susan Butcher, the first person to win the Iditarod four

times. The Binkley family, with four generations of river pilots, has traveled the great rivers of the north for more than a century. ⊠ *1975 Discovery Dr.* ☎ *907/479–6673, 866/479–6673* ⊕ *www. riverboatdiscovery.com* ⊠ *$65.*

Sternwheeler Tanana Chief

TOUR—SPORTS | Dinner cruises (6:45 pm) take place on the Chena River four nights a week aboard the stern-wheeler *Tanana Chief,* a replica of the riverboats that once plied Interior rivers. Daytime sightseeing and other cruises also take place regularly. ⊠ *1020 Hoselton Rd.* ☎ *907/205-4988* ⊕ *www.tananachiefalaska.com* ⊠ *Sightseeing cruise $25; dinner cruise $55.*

CURLING

Hundreds of Fairbanksans participate each year in curling, a game in which people with brooms play a giant version of shuffleboard on ice. Curlers have an almost fanatical devotion to their sport, and they're eager to explain its finer points to the uninitiated.

Fairbanks Curling Club

LOCAL SPORTS | The club hosts an annual Yukon Title *bonspiel* (match) in early November and an international bonspiel on the first weekend of April. The club season runs from October to early April. Admission is free for those who want to watch a curling match or practice from the heated viewing area of the curling club arena. ⊠ *1962 2nd Ave.* ☎ *907/452– 2875* ⊕ *www.curlfairbanks.org.*

DOG MUSHING

Throughout Alaska, sprint races, freight hauling, and long-distance endurance runs are held throughout the winter, with the majority running in late February and March, when longer days afford more enjoyment of the remaining winter snow. Men and women often compete in the same classes in the major races. For children, various racing classes are based on age, starting with the one-dog category for the youngest. The Interior sees a constant string of sled-dog races from November to March, culminating in the North American Open Sled-Dog Championship, which attracts international competitors.

Alaska Dog Mushers Association

LOCAL SPORTS | The association, one of the oldest organizations of its kind in Alaska, holds many races at its Jeff Studdert Sled Dog Racegrounds. ✉ *925 Farmers Loop Rd., Mile 4* ☎ *907/457–6874* ⊕ *www. alaskadogmushers.com.*

Paws for Adventure Sled Dog Tours

LOCAL SPORTS | Paws offers everything from a quick ride to mushing immersion courses. Experience the joys of mushing—and snap plenty of photos—on a one-hour ride, or learn how to drive a team at the three-hour mushing school. The multiday trips include mushing school plus overnight mushing, camping, and stays at Tolovana Roadhouse. ✉ *George Rd., at Herning Rd., on A Taste of Alaska Lodge property* ☎ *907/699– 3960* ⊕ *www.pawsforadventure.com* 🛏 *From $75.*

Yukon Quest International Sled-Dog Race

LOCAL SPORTS | **FAMILY** | This endurance race held in February covers more than 1,000 miles between Fairbanks and Whitehorse, Yukon Territory, via Dawson and the Yukon River. Considered much tougher and, among mushers, more prestigious than the more famous Iditarod, the Quest goes through more remote lands, with fewer checkpoints. The starting point alternates between the two cities each year (Fairbanks gets even-numbered years). ✉ *Fairbanks Yukon Quest office, 550 1st Ave.* ☎ *907/452– 7954* ⊕ *www.yukonquest.com.*

FISHING

Although a few fish can be caught right in town from the Chena River, the best thing for an avid fishermen to do is hop on a plane or riverboat to get to the best areas for angling. Fishing trips include air charters to Lake Minchumina (an hour's flight from Fairbanks), known for good pike fishing and a rare view of the north

sides of Denali and Mt. Foraker. Another charter trip by riverboat or floatplane will take you pike fishing in the Minto Flats, west of Fairbanks off the Tanana River, where the mouth of the Chatanika River spreads through miles of marsh and sloughs.

Salmon run up the Tanana River most of the summer, but they're not usually caught on hook-and-line gear. Residents take them from the river with gill nets and fish wheels, using special commercial and subsistence permits. Check the "Outdoors" section in the Friday *Fairbanks Daily News–Miner* (or online) for weekly updates on fishing in the Interior. ■**TIP**→ **You can purchase fishing licenses ($15 and up for nonresidents) good for one day or longer at many sporting-goods stores and online at www.admin.adfg.state.ak.us/ license.**

Arctic Grayling Guide Service

FISHING | From June to October, Arctic Grayling conducts guided and unguided fishing trips via jet boat to fishing spots around the Fairbanks area for grayling and salmon. The company, a good bet for the serious angler, has been around for more than 30 years. ✉ *Fairbanks* ☎ *907/479–0479, 907/322–8004* ⊕ *www. wildernessfishing.com* 🛏 *From $365.*

GOLD PANNING
Gold Dredge 8

LOCAL SPORTS | From the comfort of a narrow-gauge railroad, Gold Dredge 8 offers a two-hour tour of a seasonal mining operation. Miners demonstrate classic and modern techniques, after which visitors get to try their luck panning for gold. Many historic elements from the old El Dorado Gold Mine have been transported here, so a tour provides a fairly complete look at how Fairbanks got rich. ✉ *1803 Old Steese Hwy. N* ☎ *907/479–6673, 866/479–6673* ⊕ *www.golddredge8.com* 🛏 *$40.*

Aurora Borealis 101

The light show often begins simply, as a pale yellow-green luminous band that arches across Alaska's night sky. Sometimes the band will quickly fade and disappear. Other nights, however, it may begin to waver, flicker, and pulsate. Or the quiescent band may explode and fill the sky with curtains of celestial light that ripple wildly above the northern landscape. Growing more intense, these dancing lights take on other colors: pink, red, blue, or purple. At times they appear to be heavenly flames, leaping across the sky, or perhaps they're exploding fireworks, or cannon fire.

Where to See Them

The Fairbanks area is one of the best places in the world to see the aurora borealis—commonly called the northern lights. Here they may appear more than 200 nights per year; they're much less common in Anchorage, partly because of urban glare.

As you watch these dazzling lights swirling from horizon to horizon, it is easy to imagine why many Northern cultures, including Alaska's Native peoples, created myths to explain auroral displays. What start out as patches, arcs, or bands can be magically transformed into vaporous, humanlike figures. Some of Alaska's Native groups have traditionally believed the lights to be spirits of their ancestors. According to one belief, the spirits are celebrating with dance and drumming; another says they're playing games. Yet another tradition says the lights are torches, carried by spirits who lead the souls of recently deceased people to life in the afterworld.

Where Do They Come From?

During Alaska's gold-rush era some non-Native stampeders supposed the aurora to be reflections of ore deposits. Even renowned wilderness explorer John Muir allowed the northern lights to spark his imagination. In 1890, Muir once stayed up all night to watch a gigantic, glowing auroral bridge and bands of "restless electric auroral fairies" who danced to music "too fine for mortal ears."

Scientists have a more technical explanation for these heavenly apparitions. The aurora borealis is an atmospheric phenomenon that's tied to explosive events on the sun's surface, known as solar flares. Those flares produce a stream of charged particles, the "solar wind," which shoots off into space. When such a wind intersects with Earth's magnetic field, most of the particles are deflected; some, however, are sent into the upper atmosphere, where they collide with gas molecules such as nitrogen and oxygen. The resulting reactions produce glowing colors. The aurora is most commonly a pale green, but its borders are sometimes tinged with pink, purple, or blue. Especially rare is the all-red aurora, which appears when charged solar particles collide with oxygen molecules from 50 to 200 miles above Earth's surface.

■ TIP→ **Alaska's long hours of daylight hide the aurora in summer, so the best viewing is from September through March.** Scientists at the University of Alaska Geophysical Institute give a daily forecast from late fall to spring of when the lights will be the most intense at ⊕ *auroraforecast.gi.alaska. edu.*

HIKING

Creamer's Field Migratory Waterfowl Refuge has three nature trails within its 1,800 acres on the edge of Fairbanks. The longest trail is 2 miles, and one is wheelchair accessible.

WILDLIFE-WATCHING

★ Running Reindeer Ranch

WILDLIFE-WATCHING | After just a few minutes communing with the ranch's herd of reindeer, it's hard not to get a little giggly. Before long it seems like second nature being surrounded by the herd, and by the time you've exhausted your camera snapping photos, that's when the fun begins. You just settle into listening to owner Jane Atkinson, whose love for the natural world, the animals she cares for, and indeed all of Alaska's wildlife, is infectious. Reservations must be made in advance; the minimum tour size is four, but smaller groups can pay the difference. ✉ *1470 Ivans Alley* ☎ *907/455–4998* ⊕ *www.runningreindeer.com* 🍴 *$55 per guest.*

🍴 Restaurants

Alaska Coffee Roasting Company

$ | **CAFÉ** | With its tasty treats and eclectic artwork from around the world, this hangout is so popular that a line often curls out the door. It's a worthy stop either for a to-go lunch to bring on a hike or a well-made cup of joe and a cookie, a scone, or a muffin to savor inside. **Known for:** tasty cinnamon rolls and other pastries; wood-fired pizzas; coffee roasted in-house. ⑤ *Average main: $9* ✉ *4001 Geist Rd.* ☎ *907/457–5282* ⊕ *www. alaskacoffeeroasting.com.*

Alaska Salmon Bake

$$$$ | **SEAFOOD** | Salmon cooked over an open fire with a sauce of lemon and brown sugar is a favorite at this indoor-outdoor restaurant in Pioneer Park's Mining Valley. Bering Sea cod, prime rib, a salad bar, beverages, and dessert are also included at the all-you-can-eat dinner. **Known for:** sunny outdoor seating; wood-grilled salmon; cabin dedicated to just desserts. ⑤ *Average main: $36* ✉ *Airport Way and Peger Rd.* ☎ *907/452–7274, 800/354–7274* ⊕ *www.akvisit.com* ⊘ *Closed mid-Sept.–mid-May.*

The Cookie Jar

$$ | **AMERICAN** | It's hard to believe the forever-in-motion staffers at the Cookie Jar can squeeze in the time to provide such friendly service, but they do. Don't miss the French toast made from sliced cinnamon rolls, but if you're not in a breakfast mood, don't worry: the menu includes everything from salads to coq au vin. **Known for:** all-day breakfast options; homemade bread and biscuits; massive waits on weekends. ⑤ *Average main: $16* ✉ *1006 Cadillac Ct.* ☎ *907/479–8319* ⊕ *www.cookiejarfairbanks.com.*

East Ramp Wood-fired Pizza

$ | **PIZZA** | **FAMILY** | This place—located just north of the control tower of Fairbanks International Airport—combines both the Alaskan love of airplanes and the universal love of pizza. Grab a paper menu, circle your preferred toppings from the extensive list, and a made-to-order pizza will be ready in minutes from the 700-degree wood-fired pizza oven. **Known for:** spicy puttanesca sauce; large selection of toppings; nice view of the airport runways. ⑤ *Average main: $13* ✉ *3788 S. University Ave.* ☎ *907/451–7492* ⊕ *www. eastramppizza.com.*

Gambardella's Pasta Bella

$$$ | **ITALIAN** | Locals crowd into this family-run Italian restaurant that has earned a reputation as one of the best in town. The menu includes salads, pasta, pizza, vegetarian entrées, and submarine sandwiches on homemade bread. **Known for:** romantic balcony and patio seating; excellent tiramisu; heavenly lasagna. ⑤ *Average main: $25* ✉ *706 2nd Ave.* ☎ *907/457–4992* ⊕ *www.gambardellas. com* ⊘ *No lunch weekends.*

Geraldo's

$$ | ITALIAN | No one in Fairbanks puts fresh chopped garlic to better use than Geraldo's, which has gourmet pizza, seafood, pasta, and veal dishes. A painting of Don Corleone hangs on the wall, and Frank Sinatra and Dean Martin provide background music for this cozy and often crowded spot near Wedgewood Resort. **Known for:** tasty baked lasagna; famous mozzarella bread; plenty of pizza. ⑤ *Average main: $20* ✉ *701 College Rd.* ☎ *907/452–2299.*

Ivory Jack's

$$ | AMERICAN | Jack "Ivory" O'Brien used to deal Alaskan ivory and whalebone out of this open and airy bar-restaurant tucked into the gold-rich hills of the Goldstream Valley on the outskirts of Fairbanks. These days you can choose from a dozen-and-a-half appetizers, followed by sandwiches, burgers, pizza, or entrées such as chicken Dijon and Alaskan king crab. **Known for:** crab-stuffed mushrooms; weekend ribs specials; gluten-free options. ⑤ *Average main: $22* ✉ *2581 Goldstream Rd.* ☎ *907/455–6665* ⊕ *www.ivoryjacksrestaurant.com.*

Lavelle's Bistro

$$$$ | AMERICAN | With offerings ranging from rack of lamb and lobster cakes to halibut and New York steaks, this impressive restaurant has won a loyal local following. Lavelle's also serves more than 30 wines by the glass and holds regular wine tastings and other events, lending the restaurant an air of sophistication far removed from the frontier image cultivated elsewhere in Fairbanks. **Known for:** 3,000-bottle wine cellar; entrée-worthy salads; late night weekend menu. ⑤ *Average main: $33* ✉ *SpringHill Suites, 575 1st Ave.* ☎ *907/450–0555* ⊕ *www. lavellesbistro.com* ⊗ *No lunch.*

Pike's Landing

$$ | AMERICAN | The seats in the dining room of this extended log-cabin building are perfect for cooler weather, but the huge paddle-up deck dotted with firepits is the real draw here. The menu is mostly salads, sandwiches, burgers, and seafood, but the chance to enjoy the views over the Chena River and the landmark "Love Alaska" sign is what keeps diners coming. **Known for:** fried chicken and waffles; Sunday brunch; extensive waterfront deck. ⑤ *Average main: $23* ✉ *4438 Airport Way* ☎ *907/479–6305* ⊕ *www. pikes-landing.com.*

Pita Place

$ | MIDDLE EASTERN | Fairbanksans have been going mad for Nadav Weiss's falafel and hand-baked pitas ever since he started serving them at the Tanana Valley Farmer's Market, and now they're available year-round at this stand. In summer, enjoy the comfy outdoor seating, or pair lunch at the stand with a visit to the farmers' market just a few blocks away at 2600 College Road. **Known for:** great Middle Eastern classics; Turkish coffee; long lines that move quickly. ⑤ *Average main: $8* ✉ *3300 College Rd.* ☎ *907/687–2456* ⊕ *www.pitasite.com* ⊗ *Closed Sun. yr-round, Mon. in summer, and Sat. in winter. No dinner.*

Pump House Restaurant and Saloon

$$$$ | AMERICAN | Alongside the Chena River, this upscale 1930s mining pump station–turned–restaurant claims to be the northernmost oyster bar in the world. Listed on the National Register of Historic Places, a grizzly bear in a glass case stands sentry over a room full of Victorian-era antiques, and during the summer, be sure to enjoy the midnight sun on the deck out back by the river. **Known for:** wild game and seafood chowder; Wednesday night karaoke in the saloon; busy Sunday brunch. ⑤ *Average main: $28* ✉ *796 Chena Pump Rd.* ☎ *907/479–8452* ⊕ *pumphouse.com* ⊗ *Closed Jan. and Mon. mid-Sept.–mid-May. No lunch.*

Sam's Sourdough Cafe

$ | AMERICAN | Although Sam's serves meals all day, Fairbanksans know it as one of the best breakfast places in town. Sourdough recipes are a kind of minor religion in Alaska, and Sam's serves an extensive menu of sourdough specialties, including hotcakes, cheese steaks, and French toast, as well as standard meat-and-eggs options, all at reasonable prices. **Known for:** local flair on comfort food; reindeer sausage; long waits on weekends. ⑤ *Average main: $13* ✉ *3702 Cameron St., at University Ave.* ☎ *907/479–0523.*

★ Silver Gulch Brewing and Bottling Co.

$$$ | **AMERICAN** | Beer lovers should definitely make the 10-mile trip from town to North America's northernmost brewery. Several Silver Gulch brews can be found throughout the state, so be sure to check out the rotating specialty brews served only at the restaurant. **Known for:** reindeer sausage and beer cheese soup; inventive brick oven pizzas; summertime beer garden. ⑤ *Average main: $22* ✉ *2195 Old Steese Hwy.* ☎ *907/452–2739* ⊕ *www. silvergulch.com* ⊗ *No lunch weekdays.*

★ Thai House

$$ | **THAI** | Fairbanks isn't known for a varied selection of international cuisine, but Thai food is an exception, and many locals consider Thai House the best in town. The food itself is complex, flavorful, and exceedingly fresh. **Known for:** Fairbanks's first and most popular Thai restaurant; staff dressed in elegant silks; vegetarian options like green curry tofu. ⑤ *Average main: $16* ✉ *412 5th Ave., Downtown* ☎ *907/452–6123* ⊕ *www. thaihousefairbanks.com* ⊗ *Closed Sun.*

Turtle Club

$$$$ | **AMERICAN** | Don't go to this wood-walled dining room expecting great variety, but you should go if you have a big appetite, and are hungry for prime rib, lobster, prawns, or king crab. There's also a good salad bar, prompt service, and homemade bread that comes with every order. **Known for:** seafood dinners; dimly lit date nights; packed crowds on weekends. ⑤ *Average main: $32* ✉ *2098 Old Steese Hwy., Fox* ☎ *907/457–3883* ⊗ *No lunch.*

🏨 Hotels

A Taste of Alaska Lodge

$$$ | **B&B/INN** | Though just a 20-minute drive from Fairbanks, A Taste of Alaska is far enough outside town to make you feel as though you're at a wilderness retreat; the 280-acre property, graced with fields and forested woodlands, has great views of the Alaska Range to the south, and in winter you can see the northern lights. **Pros:** eclectic decor; quiet, on-site trails; interesting and unique history. **Cons:** 20 minutes to town; dated interior; lodge rooms have private entrances, but some also open directly into dining area. ⑤ *Rooms from: $185* ✉ *551 Eberhardt Rd.* ☎ *907/488–7855* ⊕ *www.atasteofalaska.com* ⤴ *11 rooms* ⦿| *Breakfast.*

Aurora Express

$$$ | **B&B/INN** | Rooms inside historic railcars make this off-the-beaten-path inn well worth the detour. **Pros:** area's most distinctive lodging; sweeping valley views; 1,500-square-foot open-air pavilion. **Cons:** far from town; phone in common area only; unique decor not for everyone. ⑤ *Rooms from: $165* ✉ *1550 Chena Ridge Rd.* ☎ *907/474–0949, 800/221–0073* ⊕ *fairbanksalaskabe-dandbreakfast.com* ⊟ *No credit cards* ⊗ *Closed early Sept.–late May* ⤴ *7 rooms* ⦿| *Breakfast* ☞ *No children under 12.*

Bridgewater Hotel

$$ | **HOTEL** | In the heart of downtown Fairbanks, just above the Chena River, the Bridgewater has gone through several incarnations, emerging most recently as a modern, European-style hotel. **Pros:** good location; free airport and train shuttle; the most character of any downtown Fairbanks hotel. **Cons:** small, modest rooms; no refrigerators; restaurant serves breakfast only. ⑤ *Rooms from: $159* ✉ *723 1st Ave., Downtown* ☎ *907/452–6661, 833/303–4760* ⊕ *www.bridgewaterhotel.net* ⊗ *Closed*

mid-Sept.–mid-May 🛏 *93 rooms* 🍴 *No meals.*

Minnie Street Inn

$$ | **B&B/INN** | A short walk from the river and downtown Fairbanks, this charming B&B is one of the most convenient—and comfortable—in Fairbanks. **Pros:** elegant decor; central location; views of Northern Lights from deck. **Cons:** no pets allowed; parking lot is cramped; two-night minimum stay is required. ⑤ *Rooms from: $119* ✉ *345 Minnie St., Downtown* ☎ *907/456–1802* ⊕ *www.minniestreetbandb.com* 🛏 *12 rooms* 🍴 *No meals.*

Pike's Waterfront Lodge

$$$$ | **HOTEL** | Log columns and beams support the high ceiling in the lobby of this hotel and conference center designed to remind guests of the city's gold rush past. **Pros:** location along the Chena River; Pike's Landing next door is a hot spot; close to the airport. **Cons:** small gym; restaurant in a separate building; historic signs everywhere can become information overload. ⑤ *Rooms from: $267* ✉ *1850 Hoselton Rd.* ☎ *907/456–4500, 877/774–2400* ⊕ *www.pikeslodge.com* 🛏 *180 rooms, 28 cabins* 🍴 *Breakfast.*

River's Edge Resort

$$$ | **HOTEL** | If you want the privacy of a cottage, a bit of elbow room, and the amenities of a luxury hotel, you'll find them all at this resort on the bank of the Chena River. **Pros:** prime Chena River location; private cabins; shuttle service to both the airport and railroad terminal. **Cons:** no kitchenettes; no pets; half-mile to nearest shop or bar. ⑤ *Rooms from: $190* ✉ *4200 Boat St., University West* ☎ *907/474–0286, 800/770–3343* ⊕ *www.riversedge.net* ⊘ *Closed mid-Sept.–mid-May* 🛏 *94 rooms* 🍴 *No meals.*

Sophie Station Suites

$$$ | **HOTEL** | Its quiet location and helpful staff make this spacious hotel near the airport one of Fairbanks's best. **Pros:** free Wi-Fi; full kitchens; free trolley to area attractions. **Cons:** average interior decor;

fitness center is small; edge-of-town airport location. ⑤ *Rooms from: $169* ✉ *1717 University Ave.* ☎ *907/479–3650, 800/528–4916* ⊕ *www.fountainheadhotels.com* 🛏 *149 suites* 🍴 *No meals.*

SpringHill Suites by Marriott

$$$ | **HOTEL** | At the center of the commercial district's former heart, the SpringHill Suites has 140 very comfortable suites, each with a microwave, a refrigerator, living-room furniture, and a well-lighted work area. **Pros:** comfortable in-room work areas; location in the heart of downtown; on-site restaurant is a Fairbanks favorite. **Cons:** small breakfast lounge; public traffic in lobby; moderate-sized gym. ⑤ *Rooms from: $199* ✉ *575 1st Ave., Downtown* ☎ *907/451–6552, 800/314–0858* ⊕ *www.marriott.com/faish* 🛏 *140 suites* 🍴 *Breakfast.*

★ Wedgewood Resort

$$$ | **RESORT** | Wild and cultivated flowers adorn the landscaped grounds of this 105-acre resort bordering the Creamer's Field Migratory Waterfowl Refuge. **Pros:** free shuttle downtown; trails through a wildlife sanctuary; antique automobile museum on-site. **Cons:** away from other Fairbanks attractions; one fitness center for seven buildings; apartment block appearance. ⑤ *Rooms from: $189* ✉ *212 Wedgewood Dr.* ☎ *907/452–1442, 800/528–4916* ⊕ *www.fountainheadhotels.com/wedgewood* ▭ *No credit cards* 🛏 *463 rooms.*

🅨 Nightlife

Check the *Fairbanks Daily News-Miner* website for current nightspots, plays, concerts, and art shows.

Blue Loon

BARS/PUBS | Between Ester and Fairbanks on the Parks Highway, the Blue Loon presents year-round entertainment and serves great grill food and pizzas. Movies screen twice a night, except when there's a special event. National bands and comedians perform here, and there are outdoor concerts in summer and a DJ spins until late on weekends. ✉ *2999 Parks Hwy., Mile 353.5* ☎ *907/457–5666* ⊕ *www.theblueloon.com* ⊗ *Closed Sun. and Mon.*

Fairbanks Distilling Company

BARS/PUBS | Housed in the former 1930s city hall, this family-staffed distillery is a labor of love for owner Patrick Levy. He provides tours by appointment; downstairs, the whiskey ages in a former Fairbanks Police Department holding cell. Visit any night and you'll likely find him behind the hand-built copper bar, radiating Fairbanks pride while pouring drinks made from local Fox spring water and Nenana potatoes. ✉ *410 Cushman St., Downtown* ☎ *907/452–5055* ⊕ *www. fairbanksdistilling.com.*

★ HooDoo Brewing Co

BARS/PUBS | The go-to spot for locals thirsting for well-crafted beer in Fairbanks is HooDoo. The company sells growlers to go, but its beer is best enjoyed outdoors on a sunny afternoon around the brewery's spool tables—or if the weather gets bad, inside the airy taproom. The beer line is often long, but it moves quickly and it's a good place to meet new friends. The only issue is that it closes at 8 pm. Free brewery tours take place on Saturday at 4 pm. ✉ *1951 Fox Ave.* ☎ *907/459–2337* ⊕ *www.hoodoobrew. com* ⊗ *Closed Sun. and Mon.*

Howling Dog Saloon

BARS/PUBS | A local institution, the Howling Dog specializes in live blues and rock and roll. A party crowd of college students, airline pilots, tourists, miners, and bikers assembles for the cocktails, bar food, and music. Shows are played on a red-carpet stage acquired after Ronald Reagan and Pope John Paul II's visit to Fairbanks in 1984. ✉ *2160 Old Steese Hwy. N, Mile 11.5, Fox* ☎ *907/456–4695* ⊕ *www.howlingdogsaloonak.com.*

Lavelle's Taphouse

BARS/PUBS | This downtown bar boasts 36 taps that highlight a range of Alaska breweries while the walls feature black-and-white images of Fairbanks history. The small space attracts a younger crowd and fills up quickly. ✉ *414 2nd Ave., Downtown* ☎ *907/888–2220* ⊕ *www. lavellestaphouse.com.*

Senator's Saloon

BARS/PUBS | On a warm summer evening, the saloon at the Pump House Restaurant is a fine place to listen to music alongside the Chena River. You can also peruse the wine list at the mahogany bar or shoot pool on the billiards table dating from 1898. ✉ *796 Chena Pump Rd.* ☎ *907/479–8452* ⊕ *www.pumphouse. com* ⊗ *Closed Jan. and Mon. in Sept.– late May.*

🎭 Performing Arts

Palace Theatre

THEATER | The theater hosts the *Golden Heart Revue,* a musical-comedy show about the founding and building of Fairbanks. ✉ *Pioneer Park, Airport Way and Peger Rd.* ☎ *907/452–7274, 800/354–7274* ⊕ *www.akvisit.com/the-palace-theatre* 🎟 *$24.*

🛍 Shopping

ART GALLERIES

The Alaska House Art Gallery

ART GALLERIES | Owners Yolande Fejes and Ron Veliz takes the "Alaska" in their gallery's name seriously; almost everything here is made in the state (with a few Canadian artists represented). Visit this hand-built log house for fine art and souvenirs made with regional pride. The gallery is also a worthy stop during the monthly First Friday showcase of local artists and their works. ✉ *1003 Cushman St., Downtown* ☎ *907/456–6449* ⊕ *www. thealaskahouse.com.*

CRAFTS

A Weaver's Yarn

CRAFTS | Artists Susan and Martin Miller own this shop that will delight knitters both new and experienced. It's the perfect place to buy a gift for that knitter back home or to pick up some qiviut, the pricey but exquisite undercoat wool of the musk ox that is some of the world's softest material. ⊠ *1810 Alaska Way, College* ☎ *907/374–1995* ⊕ *www.aweaversyarn.com.*

Beads and Things

CRAFTS | This shop sells Alaska Native handicrafts from around the state, along with a world's worth of beads for those who want to design their own pieces. ⊠ *537 2nd Ave., Downtown* ☎ *907/456–2323.*

Great Alaskan Bowl Company

CRAFTS | The big one-stop shop for Alaskan-made gifts and souvenirs, Great Alaskan specializes in lathe-turned bowls made out of Alaskan birch. ⊠ *4630 Old Airport Rd.* ☎ *907/474–9663, 800/770–4222* ⊕ *www.woodbowl.com.*

JEWELRY
Judie Gumm Designs

JEWELRY/ACCESSORIES | In her small shop, owner Judie Gumm fashions stunning and moderately priced silver and gold designs best described as sculptural interpretations of Northern images. Gumm, a longtime Ester resident, is a fun person to chat up about life in this small and quirky community tucked just off the highway west of Fairbanks. ⊠ *3600 Main St., Ester* ☎ *907/479–4568, 800/478–4568* ⊕ *www.judiegumm.com.*

Taylor's Gold-N-Stones

JEWELRY/ACCESSORIES | Taylor's uses gemstones mined in Alaska and creates unique gold designs. ⊠ *3578 Airport Way, University Avenue* ☎ *907/456–8369, 800/306–3589* ⊕ *www.taylorsgold.com.*

OUTERWEAR AND OUTDOOR GEAR
Apocalypse Design

SPORTING GOODS | In business since 1983, Apocalypse makes its own specialized cold-weather clothing for dog mushers and other winter adventurers. Travelers from colder areas of the Lower 48 will appreciate the double-layer fleece mittens, among other items. ⊠ *201 Minnie St.* ☎ *907/451–7555, 877/521–7555* ⊕ *www.akgear.com.*

Beaver Sports

SPORTING GOODS | This store that facilitates midnight-sun runs stocks quality backpacking, biking, paddling, and skiing gear. ⊠ *3480 College Rd., College* ☎ *907/479–2494* ⊕ *www.beaversports.com.*

Nenana

56 miles southwest of Fairbanks, 75 miles north of Denali National Park.

For a break from the buzz of the George Parks Highway, take a detour in Nenana (rhymes with "banana"), a town of approximately 380 people, on the banks of the Tanana River and under the shadow of Toghotthele Hill or, in Athabascan, the "mountain that parallels the river." The downtown avenue seems stuck in time, a relic of the early Alaska Railroad construction heyday from 1915 to 1923.

Nenana has several claims to fame: home to the world's second-largest single-span bridge, 700 feet long; the site where President Warren Harding drove the golden spike into Alaska's railroad to commemorate its completion (and possibly where he caught the case of pneumonia that contributed to his death a few weeks later); and the start of the 1925 serum run to Nome. It's also home to the Nenana Ice classic, where Alaskans annually bet on the date and time of the river's spring breakup. Ongoing since 1917, the jackpot sometimes climbs over $300,000.

🍴 Restaurants

Rough Woods Inn & Cafe

$$ | DINER | At first glance, the Rough Woods looks like a typical Alaska lodge, all burled wood and carved bears, but it's much more thanks to owner Ruth Coy. In this town with few dining alternatives, Coy could get away with a so-so menu,

but instead she challenges herself, making her own herb bread for her popular breakfast sandwich (served all day). **Known for:** small-batch microbrews; pie of the day; Nenana's only year-round eatery. ⑤ *Average main: $19* ⊠ *2nd and A Sts.* ☎ *907/832–5299* ⊘ *Closed Tues.*

Chena Hot Springs

62 miles northeast of Fairbanks.

Nature is the star all along the road from Fairbanks that leads to the **Chena Hot Springs Resort,** and even there it remains center stage thanks to the area's relaxing hot springs. The resort uses 165°F spring water to power three turbines, a feat that initially shocked geothermal experts who believed that water temperatures must be at least 220°F. This free source of power allows the resort to run

greenhouses through the –40°F winters. The daily 2 pm and 4 pm free Renewable Energy tours end at these productive greenhouses, where row upon row of lettuce—up to 25 heads a day—and five varieties of tomatoes thrive off a hydroponic, or soil-free, system. Order a salad at the resort's restaurant and taste the special flavor of local, fresh-picked greens.

◉ Sights

Chena Hot Springs Road
SCENIC DRIVE | The 57-mile paved road, which starts 5 miles northeast of Fairbanks, leads to Chena Hot Springs Resort, a favorite playground of Fairbanks residents. From Mile 26 to Mile 51 the road passes through the Chena River State Recreation Area, a diverse nearly 400-square-mile wilderness. You can stop

for a picnic, take a hike for an hour or an extended backpacking trip, fish for the beautiful yet gullible arctic grayling, or rent a rustic backcountry cabin to savor a truly wild Alaskan adventure. Grayling fishing in the Chena River is catch-and-release, single-hook, artificial lure only. Several stocked lakes along the road allow catch-and-keep fishing for rainbow trout, well suited for the frying pan. Keep a sharp eye out for moose along the roadside. ✉ *Fairbanks*.

🏃 Activities

DOG MUSHING
Chena Dog Sled Adventures
LOCAL SPORTS | This outfit provides winter visitors a chance to drive a dog team or ride in a sled. Popular options include two- and three-day trips that include mushing, ice fishing, and a visit to Chena Hot Springs. Call ahead for reservations, directions, and accommodations (on-site cabin rental is available). Don't follow Google Maps for this location—you'll be led astray. ✉ *40 miles east of Fairbanks near Mile 24, Chena Hot Springs Rd., Two Rivers* ☎ *907/488–5845* ⊕ *www. ptialaska.net/~sleddogs*.

HIKING
Granite Tors Trail
HIKING/WALKING | A 15-mile loop that can be done in a day, this trail provides an opportunity to see dramatic "tors"—fingers of rock protruding through grassy meadow—reminiscent of the *moai* monuments of Easter Island. The trail gains nearly 3,000 feet in elevation, but the views at the top make the climb worthwhile. Although the Interior landscapes lack the impressive mountain views of other parts of the state, the enormous expanse of rolling hills and seemingly endless tracts of forest are every bit as awe-inspiring. Come with adequate clothing, including rain gear, no matter how promising the skies look when you start. A shorter hike is the 3½-mile

Angel Rocks Trail, near the area's eastern boundary.

PADDLING
Alaska Wilderness Enterprises
BOATING | This company, in addition to multiday hunting expeditions, leads guided fishing tours and scenic float trips on the Chena River. Half-day and full-day options are available. When the temperatures drop, try your hand at ice fishing. ✉ *7445 Chena Hot Springs Rd., Fairbanks* ☎ *907/488–7517* ⊕ *www.wildernessenterprises.com* 🍴 *From $150*.

Chena River State Recreation Area
CANOEING/ROWING/SKULLING | The recreation area has numerous well-marked river-access points. The area's lower sections are placid, but the section above the third bridge, at Mile 44.1, can be hazardous for inexperienced boaters. The Chena Hot Springs Road parallels the Chena River, and canoeists use several put-in points along the way. ✉ *Fairbanks*.

🍴 Restaurants

Two Rivers Lodge
$$$$ | SEAFOOD | Fairbanksans are known to make the 40-mile round-trip for the delicious dinners here, including prime rib, steaks, and Alaskan seafood dishes. Don't be discouraged by the lakeside building's outward appearance—rustic logs belie the menu's elegance. **Known for:** great prime rib; seafood selections; extensive burger menu in the smoky side bar. ⑤ *Average main: $30* ✉ *Mile 16, Chena Hot Springs Rd., Fairbanks* ☎ *907/488–6815* ⊕ *www.tworiverslodge. com* ☺ *Closed Mon. No lunch*.

🛏 Hotels

Chena Hot Springs Resort
$$$ | RESORT | Soaking in the resort's hot springs has long been a popular experience for tourists and locals, especially in winter, when a soak is often paired with overhead aurora sightings. **Pros:** 100% powered by geothermal energy;

Thanks to the long hours of darkness this region sees every winter, Northern Lights viewing is particularly brilliant here.

an activity for every interest; some of the state's best hot springs. **Cons:** fee for Wi-Fi; rooms could use some updating; long access road gets icy in winter. ⑤ *Rooms from: $209* ✉ *Mile 56.5, Chena Hot Springs Rd.* ☎ *907/451–8104* ⊕ *www.chenahotsprings.com* ⊅ *86 rooms* ❑ *No meals.*

Public-Use Cabins

$ | **RENTAL** | Usually reserved by locals and adventurers with extensive backcountry experience, these cabins have woodstoves, bunks, and tools for cutting wood; you have to supply everything else—food, bedding, water, cooking utensils, and, at some, firewood. **Pros:** a uniquely northern Alaska experience; wilderness is at your doorstep; three cabins are road-accessible. **Cons:** only amenities are the ones you bring along; farthest cabin is 10 miles down the trail; extremely popular and often booked. ⑤ *Rooms from: $35* ✉ *Chena River State Recreation Area, Miles 32 to 50, Chena Hot Springs Rd.* ☎ *907/451–2705* ⊕ *www.dnr.alaska.gov/parks/cabins/north* ⌂ *Reservations essential* ⊅ *9 cabins.*

Central and Circle

Central is 128 miles northeast of Fairbanks; Circle is 162 miles northeast of Fairbanks.

Though small, both of these communities on the Steese Highway loom large for those interested in history and nature. Central got its start in 1894 as a roadhouse called Central House. Mining remains a way of life here, with small private operations peppering the landscape. Claim jumpers definitely are not welcome. The Yukon River town of Circle is one of two entry points into the Yukon–Charley Rivers National Preserve.

◉ Sights

Steese Highway

SCENIC DRIVE | The 161-mile Steese Highway follows the Chatanika River and several other creeks along the southern part of the White Mountains. The highway eventually climbs into weatherworn alpine mountains, peaking at Eagle

Summit (3,624 feet), about 100 miles from Fairbanks, before dropping back down into forested creek beds en route to the town of Central. From Central you can drive the 30-plus miles on a winding gravel road to Circle, a small town on the Yukon River. The highway is paved to Mile 81 and is usually in good shape. A possible exception is in winter, when Eagle Summit is sometimes closed due to drifting snow.

Hotels

Chatanika Lodge

$ | B&B/INN | Rocket scientists from the nearby Poker Flat Research Range gather at this cedar lodge, as do mushers, snowmachiners, and local families (including the owners, who expanded the bar so much it consumed their cabin). **Pros:** a local favorite; decor is full of Alaskan character; friendly, longtime owners. **Cons:** long drive from Fairbanks; shared bathrooms; dated interiors. ⑤ *Rooms from: $80 ⊠ Mile 28.5, 5760 Steese Hwy., Chatanika* ☏ *907/389–2164* ⊕ *www.chatanikalodge.com* ⌁ *11 rooms* ⍥ *No meals.*

Steese and White Mountains

30 miles north of Fairbanks via Elliott Hwy.

The Steese and White Mountains are readily accessible, just a quick jaunt up the Elliott Highway. Once you're here, you'll have a few hundred thousand acres pretty much to yourself, with opportunities for everything from a short hike to a monthlong expedition.

◉ Sights

Beaver Creek

SPORTS—SIGHT | Rising out of the White Mountains National Recreation Area, Beaver Creek makes its easy way north. If you have enough time, it's possible to run its entire length to the Yukon, totaling 360 river miles if done from road to road. If you make a shorter run, you will have to arrange a takeout via small plane. A lot of people make the trip in five or six days, starting from Nome Creek and taking out at Victoria Creek. Contact CanoeAlaska to schedule a trip. Don't try this on your own unless you're an expert in a canoe.

Birch Creek

SPORTS—SIGHT | In the Steese National Conservation Area you can take a four- to five-day or 126-mile float trip on the lively, clear-water Birch Creek, a challenge with its several rapids; Mile 94 of the Steese Highway is the access point. Along the way you should see plenty of moose, caribou, and dozens of species of birds. This stream winds its way north through the historic mining country of the Circle District. The first takeout point is the Steese Highway Bridge, 25 miles from Circle. Most people exit here to avoid the increasingly winding river and low water. From there Birch Creek meanders on to the Yukon River well below the town. Fairbanks outfitter CanoeAlaska can arrange shuttles for these trips.

Steese National Conservation Area and the White Mountains National Recreation Area

NATURE PRESERVE | For those who want to immerse themselves in nature for several days at a time, the Steese National Conservation Area and the White Mountains National Recreation Area have opportunities for backcountry hiking and paddling. Both areas have road-accessible entry points, but you cannot drive into the Steese Conservation Area. The White Mountains Recreation Area has limited camping facilities from June to November; reservations are not accepted. Winter adventurers can snowmachine or snowshoe out to 12 public-use cabins and two shelters; none are accessible by car. ☏ *907/474–2200 Bureau of Land Management (BLM)* ⊕ *www.blm.gov/ visit/white-mountains.*

⚙ Activities

Tour companies are scarce in the area. Outdoor activities are generally do-it-yourself.

Chatanika River

CANOEING/ROWING/SKULLING | A choice spot for canoeists and kayakers, the Chatanika River is still fairly close to Fairbanks. The most northerly access point is at Cripple Creek campground, near Mile 60, Steese Highway. Other commonly used access points are at Long Creek (Mile 45, Steese Highway); at the state campground, where the Chatanika River crosses the Steese Highway at Mile 39; and at the state's Whitefish Campground, where the river crosses the Elliott Highway at Mile 11. The stream flows into the Minto Flats below this point, and river access is more difficult.

Water in the Chatanika River may or may not be clear, depending on mining activities along its upper tributaries. In times of very low water, the upper Chatanika River is shallow and difficult to navigate. Avoid the river in times of high water, especially after heavy rains, because of the danger of sweepers, floating debris, and hidden gravel bars. Contact the Alaska Public Lands Information Center for the status of river conditions before heading out on any of the area's waterways. ☎ 907/459–3730 river conditions information.

Summit Trail

HIKING/WALKING | The Bureau of Land Management maintains the moderately difficult 20-mile Summit Trail, from the Elliott Highway, near Wickersham Dome, north into the White Mountains National Recreation Area. This nonmotorized trail can be explored as a day hike or in an overnight backpacking trip. It quickly rises into alpine country with 360-degree vistas that include abundant wildflowers and bird-watching in summer, blueberry picking in fall. This is not a loop trail, but ends at Beaver Creek—so you'll need to leave vehicles at both ends or arrange a ride back. Bring water, as sometimes the sources are scarce, and take advantage of the rest shelter at Mile 8. ✉ Wickersham Dome Trailhead, Mile 28, Elliott Highway ☎ 907/474–2200 Fairbanks BLM office ⊕ www.blm.gov/visit/summit-trail.

🛏 Hotels

Public-Use Cabins

$ | RENTAL | The Bureau of Land Management runs 12 public-use cabins in the White Mountains National Recreation Area and one road-accessible cabin on the Elliot Highway, with 300 miles of interconnecting trails. **Pros:** remote locations allow for an intimate experience with the land; may be reserved up to 30 days in advance; a true Alaskan experience. **Cons:** permits required; most are inaccessible during summer; three-night maximum stay. ⑤ Rooms from: $25 ✉ Fairbanks District Office of BLM, 222 University Ave., Fairbanks ☎ 907/474–2200 ⊕ www.blm.gov/visit/white-mountains-cabins ⇆ 12 cabins.

Yukon–Charley Rivers National Preserve

20 miles north of Eagle, 100 miles east of Fairbanks.

A dream landscape for adventurers who crave solitude, the preserve sits on the border of Canada and Alaska. The only ways in are by driving long gravel roads or taking a float trip or charter flight. Once here, miles of camping, hiking, canoeing, and fishing a-plenty await—often with no one else in sight for days. Those who prefer their solitude dressed up with snow should schedule a winter mushing or snowmachining trip.

■ TIP➜ **Novices should refrain from exploring the preserve solo; consider hiring** a guide familiar with the area or have an experienced outdoors person accompany you.

GETTING HERE AND AROUND

Byroads from the towns of Circle and Eagle lead into the preserve. You can also arrive by boat or floatplane.

◉ Sights

Yukon–Charley Rivers National Preserve

NATURE PRESERVE | The stretch of the Yukon River between the former gold-rush towns of Eagle and Circle is protected in the 2.5-million-acre Yukon–Charley Rivers National Preserve. In the Charley River watershed, a crystalline white-water stream flows out of the Yukon-Tanana uplands, allowing for excellent river running for expert rafters. The field office in Eagle and the NPS office in Fairbanks provide guidance to boaters.

In great contrast to the Charley, the Yukon River is a powerful waterway, dark with mud and glacial silt. The only bridge built across it in Alaska carries the Trans-Alaska Pipeline. The river surges deep, slow, and through this stretch, generally pretty flat, and to travel on it in a small boat is a humbling and magnificent experience. You can drive from Fairbanks to Eagle (via the Taylor Highway off the Alaska Highway) and to Circle (via the Steese Highway), and from either of these arrange for a ground-transportation shuttle back to your starting city at the end of your Yukon River trip. Weeklong float trips down the river from Eagle to Circle, 156 miles away, are also possible. There are no developed campgrounds or other visitor facilities within the preserve, but low-impact backcountry camping is permitted. ⊠ *National Park Service, 4175 Geist Rd., Fairbanks* ☎ *907/457–5752, 907/547–2233 camping information* ⊕ *www.nps.gov/yuch.*

⛹ Activities

HIKING

Alaska Public Lands Information Center

HIKING/WALKING | The center has detailed information about the trails in the Yukon–Charley Rivers National Preserve. ⊠ *101 Dunkel St., Fairbanks* ☎ *907/459–3730* ⊕ *www.alaskacenters.gov/fairbanks.cfm.*

Circle-Fairbanks Historic Trail

HIKING/WALKING | The trail stretches 58 miles from the vicinity of Cleary Summit to Twelve-Mile Summit. This route, which is not for novices, follows the old summer trail used by gold miners; in winter they generally used the frozen Chatanika River to make this journey. The trail has been cleared and roughly marked with mileposts and rock cairns, but there are no facilities and water is often scarce. Most of the trail is on state land, but it does cross valid mining claims that must be respected. It's easy to become disoriented; the State Department of Natural Resources strongly recommends that backpackers on this trail equip themselves with the following USGS topographical maps: Livengood A-1, Circle A-6, Circle A-5, and Circle B-4. ☎ *907/451–2705 Fairbanks DNR Office.*

Pinnell Mountain National Recreation Trail

HIKING/WALKING | The Bureau of Land Management maintains the Pinnell Mountain National Recreation Trail, connecting Twelve-Mile Summit and Eagle Summit on the Steese Highway. This 27-mile-long trail passes through alpine meadows and along mountain ridges, all above the tree line. It has two emergency shelters with water catchment systems, although no dependable water supply is available in the immediate vicinity. This is not a trip for novice hikers; most hikers spend three days making the traverse. ☎ *907/474–2200 Fairbanks BLM office* ⊕ *www.blm.gov/ak.*

RAFTING

Rafting trips on the Charley River are for experts only. With access via a small plane, you can put in a raft at the headwaters of the river and travel 88 miles down this exhilarating, bouncing waterway. Contact the National Park Service for more information. The river here is too rough for open canoes.

WINTER SPORTS

Once past Mile 20 of the Steese Highway you enter a countryside that seems to have changed little in 100 years, even though you're only an hour from downtown Fairbanks. Mountains loom in the distance, and in winter a solid snowpack of 4 to 5 feet makes the area great for snowshoeing, backcountry skiing, and snowmachine riding.

Manley Hot Springs

152 miles northwest of Fairbanks.

A colorful, close-knit, end-of-the-road type place, this town was a trading center for placer miners who worked the nearby creeks. Most of the community joins in the fun of events like the Spring Carnival and the Crafter's Guild Bazaar. If you travel here over land, take a moment to reflect that year-round access to Manley Hot Springs only became available in 1982, when the state began plowing the Elliott Highway in winter.

GETTING HERE AND AROUND

To get to Manley, pick up the Elliott Highway just north of Fairbanks in Fox, heading north to Livengood and then west. It's a long, winding drive of four to five hours.

👁 Sights

Manley Hot Springs

HOT SPRINGS | The Elliott Highway, which starts 10 miles north of Fairbanks in Fox, takes you to the Tanana River and the small community of Manley Hot

Springs. Residents maintain a small public campground across from the Manley Roadhouse. Northern pike are caught in the nearby slough, and a dirt road leads to the Tanana River, with its summer runs of salmon. The Manley Hot Springs Resort has closed, but the hot springs are only a short walk from the campground. The highway is paved for the first 73 miles from Fairbanks, until the junction with the Dalton Highway. ✉ *Manley Hot Springs.*

🛏 Hotels

Manley Roadhouse

$ | B&B/INN | Built in 1903 during the gold rush into the Interior, Alaska's oldest functioning roadhouse caters to a diverse crowd of vacationers, miners, and road-maintenance crews. **Pros:** authentically historic building; location near hot springs; free Wi-Fi. **Cons:** no phones; seven rooms share bathrooms; rooms located above the noisy bar. 💲 *Rooms from: $100* ✉ *Mile 152, Elliott Hwy., 100 Front St.* ☎ *907/672–3161* ⊕ *www.manleylodge.com* 🚫 *No credit cards* 🕙 *Closed Oct.–May* ⤴ *13 rooms, 3 cabins* 🍽 *No meals.*

The Dalton Highway

Plenty of hardy, adventurous visitors "do the Dalton," a 414-mile gravel highway that connects Interior Alaska to the oil fields at Prudhoe Bay on the Beaufort Sea. Alaska's northernmost highway, the Dalton was built in the mid-1970s so that trucks could haul supplies to Prudhoe and Trans-Alaska Pipeline construction camps in Alaska's northern reaches. The Dalton is both an engineering marvel and a reminder of the state's economic dependence on oil production. It carries crude oil across three mountain ranges, 34 major rivers—including the Yukon—and hundreds of smaller creeks. It crosses permafrost regions and three

Continued on page 308

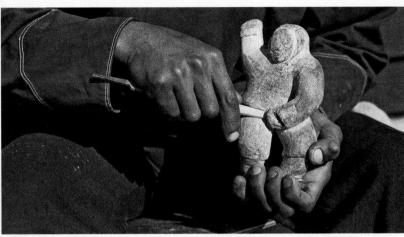

NATIVE ARTS AND CRAFTS

Intricate Aleut baskets, Athabascan birch-bark wonders, Inupiaq ivory carvings, and towering Tlingit totems are just some of the eye-opening crafts you'll encounter as you explore the 49th state. Alaska's native peoples—who live across 570,000 square miles of tundra, boreal forest, arctic plains, and coastal rain forest—are undeniably hardy, and their unique artistic traditions are just as resilient and enduring.

TIPS ON CHOOSING AN AUTHENTIC ITEM

1 The Federal Trade Commission has enacted strict regulations to combat the sale of falsely marketed goods; it's illegal for anything made by non-native Alaskans to be labeled as "Indian," "Native American," or "Alaska Native."

2 Some authentic goods are marked by a silver hand symbol or are labeled as an "Authentic Native Handicraft from Alaska."

3 The "Made in Alaska" label, often accompanied by an image of a polar bear with cub, denotes that the handicraft was made in the state.

4 Be sure to ask for written proof of authenticity with your purchase, as well as the artist's name. You can also request the artist's permit number, which may be available.

5 The Alaska State Council on the Arts, in Anchorage, is a great resource if you have additional questions or want to confirm a permit number. Call 907/269–6610 or 888/278–7424 in Alaska.

6 Materials must be legal. For example, only some feathers, such as ptarmigan and pheasant feathers, comply with the Migratory Bird Act. Only Native artisans are permitted to carve new walrus ivory. The seller should be able to answer your questions about material and technique.

THE NATIVE PEOPLE OF ALASKA

There are many opportunities to see the making of traditional crafts in native environments, including the Southeast Alaska Indian Cultural Center in Sitka and Anchorage's Alaska Native Heritage Center.

After chatting with the artisans, pop into the gift shops to peruse the handmade items. Also check out prominent galleries and museum shops.

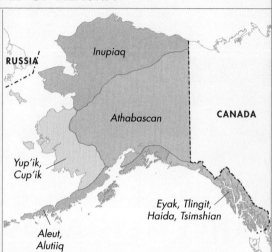

NORTHWEST COAST INDIANS: TLINGIT, HAIDA & TSIMSHIAN

Scattered throughout Southeast Alaska's rain forests, these highly social tribes traditionally benefited from the region's mild climate and abundant salmon, which afforded them a rare luxury: leisure time. They put this time to good use by cultivating highly detailed crafts, including ceremonial masks, elaborate woven robes, and, most famously, totem poles.

TOWERING TOTEM POLES

Throughout the Inside Passage's braided channels and forested islands, Native peoples use the wood of the abundant cedar trees to carve totem poles, which illustrate history, pay reverence, commemorate a potlatch, or cast shame on a misbehaving person.

Every totem pole tells a story with a series of animal and human figures arranged vertically. Traditionally the totem poles of this area feature ravens, eagles, killer whales, wolves, bears, frogs, the mythic thunderbird, and the likenesses of ancestors.

A Tlingit totem reaches for the skies in Ketchikan

K'alyaan Totem Pole

Carved in 1999, the K'alyaan totem pole is a tribute to the Tlingits who lost their lives in the 1804 Battle of Sitka between invading Russians and Tlingit warriors. Tommy Joseph, a venerated Tlingit artist from Sitka, and an apprentice spent three months carving the pole from a 35-ft western red cedar. It now stands at the very site of the skirmish, in Sitka National Historical Park.

Woodworm: The woodworm—a Tlingit clan symbol—is a wood-boring beetle that leaves a distinctive mark on timber.

Beaver: Sporting a fearsome pair of front teeth, this beaver symbol cradles a child in its arms, signifying the strength of Tlingit family bonds.

Frog: This animal represents the Kik.sádi Clan, which was very instrumental in organizing the Tlingit's revolt against the Russian trespassers. Here, the frog holds a raven helmet—a tribute to the Kik.sádi warrior who wore a similar headpiece into battle.

Raven: Atop the pole sits the striking raven, the emblem of one of the two moieties (large multi-clan groups) of Tlingit culture.

Sockeye Salmon (above) and Dog/Chum Salmon (below): These two symbols signify the contributions of the Sockeye and Dog Salmon Clans to the 1804 battle. They also illustrate the symbolic connection to the tribe's traditional food sources.

TOOLS AND MATERIALS
As do most modern carvers, Joseph used a steel adz to carve the cedar. Prior to European contact—and the accompanying introduction of metal tools—Tlingit artists carved with jade adzes. Totem poles are traditionally decorated with paint made from salmon-liver oil, charcoal, and iron and copper oxides.

ALEUT & ALUTIIQ

The Aleut inhabit the Alaska Peninsula and the windswept Aleutian Islands. Historically they lived and died by the sea, surviving on a diet of seals, sea lions, whales, and walruses, which they hunted in the tumultuous waters of the Gulf of Alaska and the Bering Sea. Hunters pursued their prey in *Sugpiaq*, kayaklike boats made of seal skin stretched over a driftwood frame.

WATERPROOF *KAMLEIKAS*

The Aleut prize seal intestine for its remarkable waterproof properties; they use it to create sturdy cloaks, shelter walls, and boat hulls. To make their famous cloaks, called *kamleikas*, intestine is washed, soaked in salt water, and arduously scraped clean. It is then stretched and dried before being stitched into hooded, waterproof pullovers.

FINE BASKETRY

Owing to the region's profusion of wild rye grass, Aleutian women are some of the planet's most skilled weavers, capable of creating baskets with more than 2,500 fibers per square inch. They also create hats, socks, mittens, and multipurpose mats. A long, sharpened thumbnail is their only tool.

ATHABASCANS

Inhabiting Alaska's rugged interior for 8,000 to 20,000 years, Athabascans followed a seasonally nomadic hunter-gatherer lifestyle, subsisting off of caribou, moose, bear, and snowshoe hare. They populate areas from the Brooks Range to Cook Inlet, a vast expanse that encompasses five significant rivers: the Tanana, the Kuskokwim the Copper, the Susitna, and the Yukon.

BIRCH BARK: WATERPROOF WONDER

Aside from annual salmon runs, the Athabascans had no access to marine mammals—or to the intestines that made for such effective boat hulls and garments. They turned to the region's birch, the bark of which was used to create canoes. Also common were birchbark baskets and baby carriers.

FUNCTIONAL & ORNAMENTED PIECES

Much like that of the neighboring Eskimos, Athabascan craftwork traditionally served functional purposes. But tools, weapons, and clothing were often highly decorated with colorful embroidery and shells. Athabascans are especially well known for ornamenting their caribou-skin clothing with porcupine quills and animal hair—both of which were later replaced by imported western beads.

INUPIAQ, YUP'IK & CUP'IK

Residing in Alaska's remote northern and northwestern regions, these groups are often collectively known as Eskimos or Inupiaq. They winter in coastal villages, relying on migrating marine mammals for sustenance, and spend summers at inland fish camps. Ongoing artistic traditions include ceremonial mask carving, ivory carving (not to be confused with scrimshaw), sewn skin garments, basket weaving, and soapstone carvings.

Thanks to the sheer volume of ivory art in Alaska's marketplace, you're bound to find a piece of ivory that fits your fancy—regardless of whether you prefer traditional ivory carvings, scrimshaw, or a piece that blends both artistic traditions.

IVORY CARVING

While in Alaska, you'll likely see carved ivory pieces, scrimshaw, and some fake ivory carvings (generally plastic). Ivory carving has been an Eskimo art form for thousands of years. After harvesting ivory from migrating walrus herds in the Bering Sea, artisans age tusks for up to one year before shaping it with adzes and bow drills.

KEEP IN MIND

The Marine Mammal Protection Act states that only native peoples are allowed to harvest fresh walrus ivory, which is legal to buy after it's been carved by a native person. How can you tell if a piece is real and made by a native artisan? Real ivory is likely to be pricey; be suspect of anything too cheaply priced. It should also be hard (plastic will be softer) and cool to the touch. Keep an eye out for mastery of carving technique, and be sure to ask questions when you've found a piece you're interested in buying.

WHAT IS SCRIMSHAW?

The invention of scrimshaw is attributed to 18th-century American whalers who etched the surfaces of whale bone and scrap ivory. The etchings were filled with ink, bringing the designs into stark relief.

More recently the line between traditional Eskimo ivory carving and scrimshaw has become somewhat blurred, with many native artisans incorporating both techniques.

TIPS

Ivory carving is a highly specialized native craft that is closely regulated. As it is a by-product of subsistence hunting, all meat and skin from a walrus hunt is used.

Ivory from extinct mammoths and mastodons (usually found buried underground or washed up on beaches) is also legal to buy in Alaska; many native groups keep large stores of it, as well as antique walrus tusk, for craft purposes. Many of the older pieces have a caramelized color.

major fault lines, too; half of the pipeline runs aboveground and is held aloft by 78,000 vertical supports that proved their ability to withstand sudden, violent ground shifts, including a 7.9-magnitude earthquake along the Denali Fault.

GETTING HERE AND AROUND

Drive north out of Fairbanks and keep your compass needle pointed to the pole. That will get you to the Dalton, America's northernmost road.

Sights

Coldfoot

TOWN | At Coldfoot, more than 250 miles north of Fairbanks, the summer-only Arctic Interagency Visitor Center provides information on road and backcountry conditions, along with recent wildlife spottings. The in-house bookstore is a good place to stock up on reading material about the area. A picnic area and a large, colorful sign mark the spot where the road crosses the Arctic Circle. ⊠ *Coldfoot* ☎ *907/678–5209 summer visitor center, 800/437–7021 winter BLM office* ⊕ *www.blm.gov/ak* ⊗ *Closed mid-Sept.–late May.*

Dalton Highway

SCENIC DRIVE | The Trans-Alaskan Pipeline is the main attraction for many who travel the Dalton. Thousands of 18-wheelers drive the formerly private highway each year, but since 1994 they've shared it with sightseers, anglers, and other travelers. That doesn't mean the Dalton is an easy drive, however. The road is narrow, often winding, and has several steep grades. Sections may be heavily potholed, and the road's coarse gravel is easily kicked up into headlights and windshields by fast-moving trucks. If you drive the Dalton in your own car, make sure you have windshield-replacement insurance, because it's highly likely you'll need to make a repair when you return. There are few visitor facilities along the Dalton, and almost nowhere to get help if something goes wrong. With tow-truck

charges of up to $5 per mile both coming and going, a vehicle breakdown can cost hundreds of dollars even before repairs. Before setting out, make sure everything in your car is working properly, and know how to change tires. Public access ends at **Deadhorse,** just shy of the Arctic coast. This town exists mainly to service the oil fields of Prudhoe Bay. The only lodging options are down-at-the-heels motels and camps that cater to truck drivers and other workers, or wilderness campgrounds. ⊕ *www.blm.gov/visit/dalton-highway.*

■**TIP**➜ **There are no services between Coldfoot and Prudhoe Bay, a distance of nearly 250 miles.**

Activities

Although this is not a prime fishing area, fish, mostly grayling, populate the streams along the Dalton. You'll do better the farther you hike from the road, where less-motivated fishermen are weeded out. Lakes along the road contain grayling, and some have lake trout and arctic char. The Alaska Department of Fish and Game's pamphlet "Sport Fishing along the Dalton Highway" is available at the Alaska Public Lands Information Center and online at ⊕ *adfg.alaska.gov.*

Alaskan Arctic Turtle Tours

TOUR—SPORTS | This outfit conducts year-round Dalton Highway–area tours in 15-passenger vans. Pickups are available from all area lodgings. Driving the Dalton yourself is difficult and hard on the car; if you're not feeling up to it, these tours are a great alternative. ⊠ *Box 60866* ☎ *907/457–1798* ⊕ *www.wildalaska.info* ⊠ *From $199.*

Alaska Fly-In Fishing

FISHING | This company offers fly-ins to remote lakes for northern pike, rainbow trout, grayling, and silver salmon. Day trips and overnights are both available. ⊠ *1255 Shypoke Dr., Fairbanks* ☎ *907/479–5684* ⊕ *www.alaskaflyinfishing.com* ⊠ *From $315.*

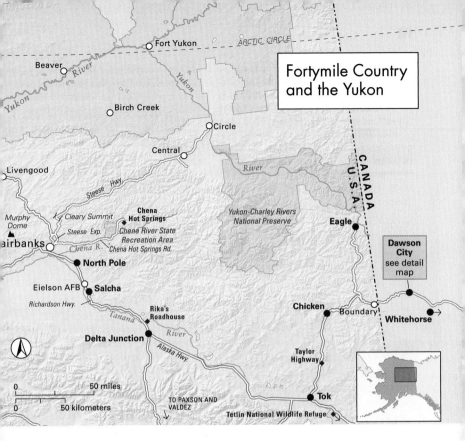

Coyote Air

TOUR—SPORTS | The family-run Coyote Air bush-plane service specializes in scenic flights, backcountry trip support, and fall hunting trips in the Brooks Range. ✉ *Mile 175, Dalton Hwy., Coldfoot* ☎ *907/678–5995* ⊕ *www.flycoyote.com.*

Northern Alaska Tour Company

TOUR—SPORTS | The most established Dalton Highway tour company, Northern Alaska operates trips to the Arctic Circle and beyond, some with fly-drive options offered year-round. ✉ *Fairbanks* ☎ *907/474–8600, 800/474–1986* ⊕ *www. northernalaska.com.*

🛏 Hotels

Here are the most accessible options for the trip north. ⇨ *For details on options in Prudhoe Bay or Deadhorse, see Prudhoe Bay.*

Coldfoot Camp

$$$ | HOTEL | Fuel, tire repairs, and towing are available here, along with basic and clean rooms built from surplus pipeline-worker housing. **Pros:** guided outdoor activities; boxed lunches available for on-the-go adventurers; café is staffed 24 hours a day. **Cons:** basic rooms; greasy road food; fee for Wi-Fi. Ⓢ *Rooms from: $239* ✉ *Mile 175, Dalton Hwy., Coldfoot* ☎ *866/474–3400, 907/474–3500* ⊕ *www. coldfootcamp.com* ⇗ *106 rooms.*

Yukon River Camp

$$$ | HOTELHOTEL | The motel, built from surplus pipeline-worker housing, is basic and clean; there's a tire-repair shop, and you can buy gasoline, diesel, and propane here. **Pros:** tire-repair shop handy for those driving; great hosts to answer questions; a far better restaurant than you'd expect this far north. **Cons:** no private baths; expensive for what you

get; extremely basic accommodations.
⑤ *Rooms from: $219* ⊠ *Mile 56, Dalton Hwy.* ☎ *907/474–3557* ⊕ *www.yukonrivercamp.com* ☻ *Closed mid-Sept.–mid-May* ⬋ *42 rooms* ⦿ *No meals.*

North Pole and Salcha

North Pole, 14 miles southeast of Fairbanks, may be a featureless suburb, but you'd have to be a Scrooge not to admit that this town's year-round acknowledgment of the December holiday season is at least a little bit of fun to take in. The Santa Claus House Gift Shop (on St. Nicholas Drive, of course) is a must-see stop. Sixteen miles farther along in Salcha, the Knotty Shop is a burl-lover's paradise.

🛍 Shopping

The Knotty Shop
STORE/MALL | This shop has a large selection of Alaskan handicrafts as well as a mounted wildlife display and a yard full of spruce-burl sculptures that photographers find hard to resist. Burls are actually caused by parasites in the living tree, and they create beautiful patterns in the wood. Soft drinks, coffee, and ice cream are served over a spruce-burl counter. ⊠ *Mile 332, 6565 Richardson Hwy., Salcha* ✛ *32 miles south of Fairbanks* ☎ *907/488–3014.*

Santa Claus House Gift Shop
STORE/MALL | If you stop in North Pole, don't skip this shop. Look for the world's largest Santa statue and the Christmas murals on the side of the building, as well as the year-round department-store style display windows. Inside, you'll find toys, gifts, Alaskan handicrafts, and, of course, Christmas cookies. Santa is on duty to talk to children in summers and during the holiday season. Also in summers, visit Antler Academy inside the red reindeer barn, where guests can interact with Santa's sleigh team. And

yes, you can get your mail sent with a genuine North Pole postmark, a service offered since 1952. ⊠ *101 St. Nicholas Dr.* ☎ *907/488–2200, 800/588–4078* ⊕ *www.santaclaushouse.com.*

Delta Junction

100 miles southeast of Fairbanks, 108 miles northwest of Tok.

Delta is not only a handy stop on the Richardson Highway, it's the official western terminus of the Alaska Highway. In summer, Delta, the largest agricultural center in Alaska, becomes a bustling rest stop for road-weary travelers. The town is known for its access to good fishing and its proximity to the Delta Bison Range. Don't expect to see the elusive 500-strong bison herd, though, as the animals roam freely and generally avoid people.

GETTING HERE AND AROUND
Delta Junction is at the junction of the Alaska and Richardson highways, a little less than a two-hour drive from Fairbanks and a five- to six-hour drive from Valdez.

👁 Sights

Delta Junction Visitor Center
INFO CENTER | In addition to finding out what's up in Delta Junction, you can purchase an "I Drove the Alaska Highway" certificate ($2) here—technically, the Alcan ends in Delta because there was already a road this far from Fairbanks. Across the street is the Sullivan Roadhouse Historical Museum (ask about hours at the visitor center). If you're in town on a Wednesday or Saturday between mid-May and early September, check out the wonderfully named Highway's End Farmer's Market, open both days from 10 to 5. ⊠ *2855 Alaska Hwy.* ☎ *907/895–5068* ⊕ *www.deltachamber.org* ☻ *Visitor center closed Sept.–May.*

Alaska Highway History

It's hard to overestimate the importance of the Alaska Highway in the state's history. Before World War II there was no road connection between the Alaskan Interior and the rest of North America. Alaska's population center was in the coastal towns of Southeast's Panhandle region, and most of the state's commerce was conducted along its waterways. Access to the Interior was via riverboat until 1923, when the railroad connection from Seward through Anchorage and into Fairbanks was completed.

The onset of the Second World War changed everything. An overland route to the state was deemed a matter vital to national security, to supply war material to the campaign in the Aleutians, and to fend off a potential invasion by Japan. In a feat of amazing engineering and construction prowess (and hubris—the United States started construction in Canada without bothering to ask the Canadian government if it was okay with them), the 1,500-mile-long route was carved out of the wilderness in eight months in 1942. Three regiments of black soldiers—nearly a third of the highway's laborers—worked alongside white troops, and the Highway is credited for moving the military toward racial integration.

The original road was crude but effective (the first truck to travel it made a blazing average speed of 15 mph), and has been undergoing constant maintenance and upgrading ever since. Today the highway is easily traversed by every form of highway vehicle imaginable, from bicycles and motorcycles to the biggest, lumbering RVs, known not so affectionately by locals as "road barns."

Rika's Roadhouse

HISTORIC SITE | The landmark Rika's Roadhouse, part of the 10-acre Big Delta State Historical Park, is a good detour for the free tours of the beautifully restored and meticulously maintained grounds, gardens, and historic buildings. In the past, roadhouses were erected at fairly regular intervals in the north, providing everything a traveler might need. Rika's, which operated from 1913 to 1947, is far and away the prettiest and best preserved of the survivors. It's a great place to get out, stretch, and buy homemade sandwiches, pies, and soft-serve ice cream. ⊠ *Mile 275, Richardson Hwy.* ☎ *507/884–9103* ⊕ *www.dnr.alaska. gov/parks/units/deltajct/bigdelta* ⊠ *Free* ⊘ *Closed mid-May–mid-Sept.*

Tok

12 miles west of Tetlin Junction, 175 miles southwest of Dawson City, 200 miles southeast of Fairbanks.

Loggers, miners, old sourdoughs (Alaskan for "colorful local curmudgeons"), and hunting guides who live and work along Tok's streams or in the millions of acres of spruce forest nearby come here for supplies. The population of Tok is 1,250 year-round, but its residents are joined each summer by thousands of travelers, among them adventurers journeying up the Alaska Highway from the Lower 48. Tok is more of a gateway to nearby attractions, such as the Tetlin National Wildlife Refuge, than a destination in itself, but its visitor center is worth a visit. The town also has markets, fueling stops, and some restaurants and hotels.

GETTING HERE AND AROUND

Tok sits at the junction of the Glenn and Alaska highways. 40-Mile Air serves the town from Fairbanks with three flights per week and flies to the Tetlin National Wildlife Refuge and other wilderness locations. The refuge lies south of the Alaska Highway southeast of Tok.

A huge loop driving tour starting in Tok takes in many of Alaska's terrific landscapes. Head down the Tok Cutoff to the Richardson Highway and continue south to Valdez. From there, catch the ferry to Whittier, Cordova, or Seward. Explore the Kenai and Anchorage, then head north on the Seward Highway to the parks, to Denali, Fairbanks, and beyond. Loop back to Tok and you will have experienced most of what can be seen from the road system.

ESSENTIALS

AIRLINE CONTACT 40-Mile Air ✉ *Mile 1313, Alaska Hwy.* ☎ *907/883–5191* ⊕ *fortymileair.com.*

 ## Sights

Taylor Highway

SCENIC DRIVE | The 160-mile Taylor Highway runs north from the Alaska Highway at Tetlin Junction, 12 miles east of Tok. It's a narrow rough-gravel road that winds along mountain ridges and through valleys of the Fortymile River. The road passes the tiny community of Chicken and ends in Eagle at the Yukon River. This is one of only three places in Alaska where the Yukon River can be reached by road. A cutoff just south of Eagle connects to the Canadian Top of the World Highway leading to Dawson City in the Yukon Territory, which is the route many Alaskans take to Dawson City. That route is far more scenic, and shorter, than the alternative of taking the Alcan to Whitehorse and then turning north, but it's another

Border Crossing 👁

Crossing into Interior Alaska from the Lower 48 or from the ferry terminals in Southeast requires border crossings into Canada and then into Alaska. Be very certain of all the requirements for crossing an international border before you travel, including restrictions on pets and firearms and the need for adequate personal identification for every member of the party. Even citizens of Canada and the United States traveling between Alaska and Canada are required to have a passport—and they will be checked.

of those stretches for which it's good to make sure your insurance policy covers towing and windshield replacement. The highway is not plowed in winter, so it is snowed shut from fall to spring. If you're roughing it, know that the Bureau of Land Management also maintains three first-come, first-served campsites (as all BLM campsites are) on the Taylor Highway between Tetlin Junction and Eagle at Miles 49, 82, and 160.

Tetlin National Wildlife Refuge

NATURE PRESERVE | This 700,000-acre refuge has most of the charismatic megafauna that visitors travel to Alaska to see, including black and grizzly bears, moose, Dall sheep, wolves, caribou, and tons of birds. Just south of the Alaska Highway east of the town of Tok all the way to the U.S.–Canada border, the refuge has a visitor center at Mile 1,229. A large deck here has spotting scopes, and inside are maps, books, and wildlife exhibits, as well as a board with information on current road conditions. At Mile 1,240 you can hike a 1-mile raised-plank boardwalk through lowland forest to scenic Hidden

Lake. Basic and seasonal lakefront campgrounds can be found at Miles 1,249 and 1,256. ⊠ *Visitor Center, Mile 1,229, Alaska Hwy.* ☎ *907/883–5312* ⊕ *www. fws.gov/refuge/tetlin* ⊠ *Free* ☉ *Visitor center closed mid-Sept.–mid-May.*

Tok Main Street Visitor Center

INFO CENTER | To help with your planning, stop in at Tok's visitor center, which has travel information covering the entire state, as well as wildlife and natural-history exhibits. This is one of Alaska's largest info centers, and the staff is quite helpful. ⊠ *Mile 1,314, Alaska Hwy.* ☎ *907/883–5775* ⊕ *www.tokalaskainfo. com* ⊠ *Free* ☉ *Closed Oct.–Apr.*

🍴 Restaurants

Fast Eddy's Restaurant

$$ | AMERICAN | Not the greasy fast-food joint its name might suggest, this relaxing place serves surprisingly interesting cuisine. Portions are sizable—that prime rib dinner will induce a nap—and the variety provides welcome relief from the roadhouse burgers served by most Alaska Highway restaurants. **Known for:** deep-fried mushrooms; blueberry milk shakes; massive menu for a tiny town. ⑤ *Average main: $15* ⊠ *Mile 1,313, Alaska Hwy.* ☎ *907/883–4411* ⊕ *www. fasteddysrestaurant.com.*

🛏 Hotels

Burnt Paw and Cabins Outback

$$ | B&B/INN | One of Tok's nicer lodgings, Burnt Paw has seven comfortable, sod-roof cabins—each with two beds, a private bath, a microwave, a refrigerator, Wi-Fi, satellite TV, and adorable sled-dog puppies. **Pros:** cozy cabins; good breakfast; best location in town. **Cons:** no kitchenettes; fee for pets; not for those who don't enjoy dogs. ⑤ *Rooms from: $149* ⊠ *Mile 1,314.3, Alaska Hwy.* ☎ *907/883–4121* ⊕ *www.*

On the Defensive 👁

Ft. Greely, which is 5 miles south of Tok toward Valdez, contains a growing number of underground silos with missiles that are part of the Ballistic Missile Defense System. The missiles are connected to tracking stations elsewhere and would be launched to try to shoot down enemy missiles in space if the United States were ever so attacked.

burntpawcabins.com ☉ *Closed Dec.–Feb.* ⊅ *7 cabins* ⦿ *Breakfast.*

Cleft of the Rock Bed & Breakfast

$ | B&B/INN | This family-run inn has picturesque private cabins and a comfortable apartment in a home. **Pros:** comfortable cabins; close to town; bikes and kayaks available for guests. **Cons:** no guided activities; no kitchenettes in cabins; some cabins not handicap-accessible. ⑤ *Rooms from: $140* ⊠ *0.5 Sundog Trail, off Alaska Hwy. Mile 1,316.5* ☎ *907/883–4219* ⊕ *cleftoftherock.net* ☉ *Cabins closed late Sept.–mid-May, apt. available year-round* ⊅ *5 cabins, 1 room* ⦿ *Breakfast.*

Chicken

78 miles north of Tok, 109 miles west of Dawson City.

Chicken was, and still is, the heart of the southern Fortymile Mining District, and many of these works are visible along the highway. The second town in Alaska to be incorporated (Skagway was the first), the town got its name (or so the story goes) after its residents, who wanted to call it "Ptarmigan," couldn't figure out how to spell that. Chicken has only a handful of permanent residents, mostly miners and trappers, creating an authentic frontier atmosphere.

Chicken is far from a prime shopping stop, but what it lacks in infrastructure, it makes up for in atmosphere. The town is small, so you don't have far to go to find everything you need. If you like bluegrass music, be sure to check out the Chickenstock Music Festival (⊕ *www.chickenstockmusicfest.com*) if you're passing through in mid-June.

GETTING HERE AND AROUND

Chicken sits off the Taylor Highway, a packed gravel road that closes in winter. The town is accessible only by car or bush plane—or, during winter, dogsled or snowmachine. No major commercial flights come here. Most people fly to Fairbanks and drive the five hours or so to Chicken, or visit as part of a longer road trip.

Overland travel between Chicken and Dawson City winds along a gravel road. Some drivers love it, some white-knuckle it.

◉ Sights

Chicken Creek RV Park & Cabins

TOUR—SIGHT | Free gold panning and in-season tours of a historic schoolhouse (offered daily at 10 am and 2 pm) are among the activities offered through this RV park's gift shop. The shop also has free Wi-Fi and an ATM. The RV park has gas and diesel, hostel rooms, camping sites, and cabins. ⊠ *Mile 66.8, at Chicken Creek Bridge* ☎ *907/505–0231* ⊕ *www.townofchicken.com* ☽ *Closed mid-Sept.–mid-May.*

Chicken Gold Camp & Outpost

HISTORIC SITE | Finder's keepers is the name of the game at the Gold Camp, where you can pan for gold and tour a historic dredge. The Pedro Dredge scooped up 55,000 ounces of gold from Chicken Creek between 1959 and 1967, but apparently plenty was left behind in the creek and elsewhere. Guests can stay in the Gold Camp's cabins, campground, or RV park, but anyone can roam the associated historic buildings for free. Day trips, kayaking, and other activities can also be arranged. Hungry gold seekers can fill up in the café on wood-fired pizzas, sandwiches, and baked goods, or fuel up with an espresso. Bluegrass lovers appreciate the family-friendly Chickenstock Music Festival, held the second weekend in June. ⊠ *Airport Rd. off Taylor Hwy.* ☎ *907/782–4427 Apr.–Oct., 907/399–0005 in winter* ⊕ *www.chickengold.com* ☽ *Closed mid-Sept.–mid-May.*

Downtown Chicken

TOWN | The longest-running business in town has classic wooden porches and provides multiple services. A fun place to explore, the complex includes the Chicken Creek Café, an eight-stool saloon, liquor store, and gift emporium. Free camping and overnight RV parking are available, with cabins and wall tents for rent. Gas and diesel are available from 7:30 am until the bar closes. The café serves baked wild Alaskan salmon for lunch and dinner, as well as scratch chicken pot pie and buffalo chili. ⊠ *Airport Rd. off Taylor Hwy.* ⊕ *www.chickenalaska.com.*

⚡ Activities

Fortymile River

CANOEING/ROWING/SKULLING | The beautiful Fortymile River offers everything from a 38-mile run to a lengthy journey to the Yukon and then down to Eagle. Its waters range from easy Class I to serious Class IV (possibly Class V) stretches. Only experienced canoeists should attempt boating on this river, and rapids should be scouted beforehand. Several access points can be found off the Taylor Highway. ⊠ *Chicken* ⊕ *www.rivers.gov/rivers/fortymile.php.*

Eagle

95 miles north of Chicken, 144 miles northwest of Dawson City. Road closed in winter.

Eagle was once a seat of government and commerce for the Interior. An Army post, Ft. Egbert, operated here until 1911, and territorial judge and noted Alaska historian James Wickersham had his headquarters in Eagle until Fairbanks began to grow from its gold strike. The population peaked at 1,700 in 1898. Today there are fewer than 200 residents. Although the majority of the population is gone, the town still retains its frontier and gold-rush character. John McPhee's providing a fascinating account of life in Eagle during the 1970s in his renowned Alaska travelogue *Coming into the Country.*

A flood devastated much of Eagle in 2009, but most historic structures were left undamaged. The local historical society has information about this town so influenced by the Yukon River, which in the days before cars and trucks was also a vital mode of transportation.

GETTING HERE AND AROUND

Eagle is accessible only by car or bush plane or, during winter, dogsled or snowmachine. Commercial flights don't serve Eagle.

◉ Sights

Eagle Historical Society

MUSEUM | The society has a two- to three-hour walking tour that takes in historic buildings and includes tales of the famous people—among them Arctic explorer Roald Amundsen and aviation pioneer Billy Mitchell—who have passed through this historic Yukon River border town. The society also maintains an extensive archive, photo collection, and museum store stocked with regional history books and locally made items. Call ahead to schedule an appointment. ⊠ *1st*

and Berry St. ☎ *907/547–2325* ⊕ *www. eaglehistoricalsociety.com* ✉ *$7.*

National Park Service and BLM Visitor Center

INFO CENTER | If you're even thinking of heading into the wilderness, this interagency center, the headquarters of the 2.5-million-acre Yukon–Charley Rivers National Preserve, should be your first stop. Informal interpretive programs and talks take place here, and there are videos you can watch to prepare. You can also peruse maps and visit the reference library, and there are helpful books for sale. ⊠ *100 Front St., off 1st Ave. by airstrip* ☎ *907/547–2233 June–Sept., 907/457–5752 Oct.–May* ⊕ *www.nps. gov/yuch* ✉ *Free* ☉ *Closed Oct.–May.*

Dawson City

109 miles east of Chicken.

Beautiful Dawson City is the prime specimen of a Yukon gold-rush town. Since the first swell of hopeful migrants more than 100 years ago, many of the original buildings have disappeared, victims of fire, flood, and weathering. But plenty remain, and it's easy to step back in time, by attending a performance at the Palace Theatre, erected in 1899, or stepping into a shop whose building originally served stampeders. In modern Dawson City, street paving is erratic, and the place maintains a serious frontier vibe. But it's also a center for the arts—the town's yearly summer music festival is one of Canada's biggest—and as the last touch of civilization before the deep wild, it's where hikers share tables with hard-core miners at quirky local restaurants.

Today Dawson City is home to about 1,300 people, 360 or so of whom are of First Nations descent. The city itself is now a National Historic Site of Canada. Besides being one of the hippest, funkiest towns in the north, Dawson also serves as a base from which to explore

Dawson City

KEY

- 1 Exploring Sights
- 1 Restaurants
- 1 Hotels

Yukon River

Klondike River

1st Avenue

Front Street

Albert Street
Duke Street
York Street
King Street
Queen Street
Princess Street
Harper Street
Church Street
Hanson St.
Firth St.
Turner Street
Dugas Street

2nd Ave.
3rd Ave.
4th Ave.
5th Ave.
6th Ave.
7th Ave.
8th Ave.

Mary McLeod Rd.

Ferry Crossing

Tourist Information

TO
TOMBSTONE
TERRITORIAL PARK →

0 ——— 400 yrds
0 ——— 400 meters

the Tombstone Territorial Park, a natural wonderland with plants and animals found nowhere else, living in the spaces between high, steep mountain ranges.

GETTING HERE AND AROUND

The Alaska Highway starts in Dawson Creek, British Columbia, and stretches almost 1,500 miles to Fairbanks. Numerous bus companies offer package tours or simple shuttle services. Regular air service to Dawson flies from Fairbanks in summer. Air North, Yukon's Airline, in Whitehorse, offers direct service from Whitehorse to Dawson City in summer.

Drivers traveling north- and southbound on the Alaska Highway can make a loop with the Taylor Highway route. This adds 100 miles to the trip but is worth it. Part with the Alaska Highway at Tetlin Junction and wind through the Fortymile Country past the little communities of Chicken and Jack Wade Camp into Canada. The border is open from 8 am to 8 pm in summer. The Canadian section of the Taylor Highway is called Top of the World Highway, and with most of it on a ridgeline between two huge valleys, it really does feel like the top of the world, opening broad views of range after range of tundra-covered mountains stretching in every direction. Join back with the Alaska Highway at Whitehorse.

Dawson City is small enough that you can walk end to end in about 20 minutes—even if you stop and spend 5 of those watching the river flow by. The Visitor Information Centre has an excellent walking map of town, and following it is one of the best things you can do while here. Many old buildings have displays in the windows showing what they once were. A couple of older buildings have also been filled with historic photos and information. Walking tours—in English, French, and Dutch—leave regularly from the center.

ESSENTIALS

AIRLINE INFORMATION Air North, Yukon's Airline ☎ 800/661–0407 ⊕ www. flyairnorth.com.

VISITOR AND TOUR INFORMATION

Klondike Visitors Association ✉ 1102 Front St. ☎ 867/993–5575 ⊕ www.dawsoncity. ca. **Visitor Information Centre** ✉ Front and King Sts. ☎ 867/993–5566 May–Sept., 867/993–5575 Oct.–Apr. ⊕ www.dawsoncity.ca/plan-your-trip.

◉ Sights

Dänojà Zho Cultural Centre

MUSEUM | Its inviting atmosphere makes the center a good stop to explore the heritage of Tr'ondëk Hwëch'in First Nations people. For countless generations Hän-speaking people lived in the Yukon River drainage of western Yukon and eastern Alaska. This specific language group settled around the mouth of the Klondike River. Through annually rotating displays, as well as tours, cultural activities, films, live radio broadcasts, and performances, you can learn about the traditional and contemporary life of "the people of the river." Though somewhat sparse, the historical exhibits convey a sense of what the gold rush was like for the people who were here first. Special summer activities include music events and daily workshops in beading, indigenous medicine, and tea- and jelly-making. The gift shop sells fine First Nations art, clothing, and beaded footwear, and stocks music and books. ✉ 1131 Front St. ☎ 867/993–7100 ⊕ www.trondekheritage.com ☜ C$7 ☾ Closed mid-Sept.–late May and Sun.

Dawson City Museum

MUSEUM | There's a lot going on at this museum with exhibits about the gold rush, the geology and prehistory of the Klondike, and the Yukon region's First Nations peoples. While touring the excellent displays of gold-rush material downstairs, you may find it surprising just how luxurious Dawson was for the lucky few who could call themselves rich. Many visitors zip past the household goods upstairs, but don't miss the piece of mammoth meat on the stairway landing. Four restored locomotives and other railway cars and gear from the Klondike Mines Railway are housed in an adjacent building. The museum also has a library and archives, helpful to those seeking information about gold-rush ancestors, and offers programs and demonstrations daily. ⊠ *Old Territorial Administration Bldg., 595 5th Ave.* ☎ *867/993–5291* ⊕ *www.dawsonmuseum.ca* ▤ *C$9* ⊙ *Closed Sept.–mid-May, except by appointment.*

Diamond Tooth Gerties Gambling Hall

CASINO—SIGHT | Adults-only Gerties presents live entertainment and high-energy performances, including a scintillating cancan three times nightly during the summer. This community nonprofit is the only authentic, legal gambling establishment operating in the entire North (it's also the oldest gambling hall in Canada), though the scene is mostly slots along with a few gaming tables. And there really was a Diamond Tooth Gertie—Gertie Lovejoy, a dance-hall queen who wore a diamond between her two front teeth. ⊠ *Queen St. and 4th Ave.* ☎ *867/993–5525* ⊕ *www.diamondtoothgerties. ca* ▤ *C$12* ⊙ *Closed Sun.–Thurs. late Sept.–mid-May.*

Gold Dredge No. 4

MINE | When this massive wooden-hull gold dredge was in operation (1913–59), it ate rivers whole, spitting out gravel and keeping the gold for itself—on one highly productive day it sucked up 800 ounces. These days the dredge—a Canadian National Historic Site—occupies a spot along Bonanza Creek about 10 miles southeast of Dawson. The dredge is still a stop for a look, even on your own, if only to ponder the geology and economics that made it viable to haul this enormous piece of equipment into the middle of nowhere at a time when gold only brought $20 an ounce. Goldbottom Mine Tours offers seven tours a day in summer, and can provide shuttle service from Front Street. You can pan for gold yourself in Bonanza Creek, where the Klondike Visitors Association offers a free claim for visitors. Bring your own supplies (almost every gift shop in town sells pans). ⊠ *Mile 8, Bonanza Creek Rd.* ⊹ *Exit Klondike Hwy. at Km marker 74* ☎ *867/993–5023* ⊕ *www. goldbottom.com* ▤ *C$20* ⊙ *Closed mid-Sept.–mid-May.*

Jack London Museum

MUSEUM | This reproduction of London's home from 1897 to 1898 is constructed with half the wood from his original wilderness home that was found south of Dawson in the 1930s. The other half was sent to Oakland, California, where a similar structure sits at Jack London Square. The small museum contains photos and documents from London's life and the gold-rush era. Half-hour talks are given twice daily during peak season. ⊠ *8th Ave. and Firth St.* ☎ *867/993–5575* ⊕ *www.jacklondonmuseum.ca* ▤ *C$5* ⊙ *Closed Oct.–Apr.*

Robert Service Cabin

HOUSE | The poet Robert Service lived in this Dawson cabin from 1909 to 1912. From late May to early September, enjoy daily readings outside the cabin or learn the region's history on a guided Parks Canada hike up to Crocus Bluffs. Call ahead for the schedule. ⊠ *8th Ave. and Hanson St.* ☎ *867/993–5566* ▤ *C$7.*

🏃 Activities

Tombstone Territorial Park

HIKING/WALKING | Often described as "the Patagonia of the Northern Hemisphere," Tombstone has some of the best hiking and views of granite peaks in the Yukon. About 56 km (36 miles) northeast of Dawson City and bisected by the Dempster Highway, Tombstone occupies 2,200 square km (850 square miles) of wilderness supporting a vast array of wildlife and vegetation. Backcountry mountaineering and wildlife-viewing options abound, though for the most part the terrain is too difficult for hiking novices. The park maintains day-use trails at Km markers 58.5, 71.5 (two here), 74.4, and 78.2. At Km marker 71.5 is the Tombstone Interpretive Centre and Campground. The center has informative displays and great mountain views. Stop here to get a handle on everything the park has to offer, and to learn how animals make it through the winter here. Flightseeing trips over the jagged Tombstone Range depart from Dawson City. ⊠ *Dawson City* ☎ *867/993–7714 in Dawson City, 800/661–0408* ⊕ *www.env. gov.yk.ca/tombstone* ⊠ *Free.*

🍴 Restaurants

Klondike Kate's
$$$ | CANADIAN | Named for a turn-of-the-century gold rush dancer, this casual café uses local ingredients—like Yukon River salmon and foraged mushrooms—in its familiar yet fresh menu. In addition to the standard soups and sandwiches, Kate's also serves up items like fish tacos, currywurst, and lamb. **Known for:** seasonal sides; five types of poutine; big crowds so waits are expected. ⑤ *Average main: C$21* ⊠ *1102 3rd Ave.* ☎ *867/993–6527* ⊕ *www.klondikekates.ca* ⊘ *Closed mid-Sept.–mid-May.*

Red Mammoth Bistro
$ | BAKERY | This coffee shop and its fresh-baked pastries provide a much-needed dose of warmth in Dawson's winter months. Owner and chef Emilie Aubin's chocolate-almond croissants are a local favorite. **Known for:** outdoor seating in summer; from-scratch cakes and desserts; its namesake massive red coffee machine. ⑤ *Average main: C$5* ⊠ *932 2nd Ave.* ☎ *613/885–8430* ⊘ *Closed weekends.*

🛏 Hotels

Bombay Peggy's
$$$ | B&B/INN | Named and fashioned after one of the last of Dawson's legal madams, Peggy's is done in elaborate Victorian gold-rush style, with heavy, plush draperies and rich color schemes. **Pros:** an engaging step back in time; nice touches such as fresh croissants and "Sherry Hour"; fun on-site pub. **Cons:** no elevator; not all rooms have air-conditioning; three upstairs rooms, known as the Snugs, share a bathroom. ⑤ *Rooms from: C$185* ⊠ *2nd Ave. and Princess St.* ☎ *867/993–6969* ⊕ *www.bombaypeggys. com* ⊅ *7 rooms* ⦿ *Breakfast.*

Eldorado Hotel
$$$ | HOTEL | Though this hotel has a pioneer-style facade, its rooms are outfitted with modern amenities such as high-def TVs and Internet connections, and some suites even have Jacuzzis. **Pros:** in-hotel bar and restaurant; kitchenettes in some rooms; good location. **Cons:** no elevator; free Wi-Fi has data limits; no pets. ⑤ *Rooms from: C$165* ⊠ *902 3rd Ave.* ☎ *867/993–5451, 800/764–3536 from Alaska and the Yukon* ⊕ *www.eldorado-hotel.ca* ⊘ *Closed mid-Dec.–mid-Jan.* ⊅ *62 rooms.*

Triple J Hotel & Cabins
$$ | HOTEL | With a pretty white-and-blue annex of suites and standard rooms as well as a selection of log cabins, Triple J offers choice for everyone from solo travelers to families. **Pros:** free Wi-Fi; in-room kitchenettes in cabins and annex; nice restaurant on-site. **Cons:** smallish showers in cabins; kitchenettes lack ovens; some cabin porches face a gravel parking lot. ⑤ *Rooms from: C$149* ⊠ *5th Ave. and Queen St.* ☎ *867/993–5323, 800/764–3555* ⊕ *www.triplejhotel.com* ⊅ *39 rooms, 23 cabins.*

Whitehorse

337 miles southeast of Dawson City, 600 miles southeast of Fairbanks, 110 miles north of Skagway.

Near the White Horse Rapids of the Yukon River, Whitehorse began as an encampment in the late 1890s, a logical layover for gold rushers heading north along the Chilkoot Trail toward Dawson. The next great population boom came during World War II with the building of the Alcan—the Alaska-Canada Highway. Today this city of about 25,000 residents is Yukon's center of commerce, communication, and transportation, and the seat of the territorial government. It also has the only Tim Hortons café locations for hundreds of miles.

Besides being a great starting point for explorations of other areas of the Yukon, the town has plenty of diversions and recreational opportunities. You can spend a day exploring its museums and cultural displays—research the Yukon's mining and development history, look into the backgrounds of the town's founders, learn about its indigenous First Nations people, and gain an appreciation of the Yukon Territory from prehistoric times up to the present.

GETTING HERE AND AROUND

Air Canada flies to Whitehorse in summer from Anchorage through Vancouver. Air North, Yukon's Whitehorse-based Airline, provides direct, seasonal air service from Whitehorse to several other Canadian cities, including Dawson City, Vancouver, and Calgary. Juneau-based Alaska Seaplanes also operates a service between Alaska's capital and Whitehorse.

To take in all the scenery along the way, you can drive yourself up the Alcan Highway, or let someone else do the driving on a bus tour. Alaska/Yukon Trails provides tours from Whitehorse to Dawson City to Fairbanks. There are multiple rental-car companies, buses, and taxis in Whitehorse; Whitehorse Transit has a city bus circuit that will get you where you need to go. From Whitehorse you can also make your way to Skagway, at the northern end of the Inside Passage—the drive takes about three hours via the Klondike Highway.

ESSENTIALS

AIRLINE CONTACT Air North, Yukon's Airline ☎ *800/661–0407* ⊕ *www.flyairnorth. com.*

BUS CONTACT Alaska/Yukon Trails ☎ *800/770–7275* ⊕ *www.alaskashuttle. com.*

CITY BUS Whitehorse Transit ☎ *867/668– 8396* ⊕ *www.whitehorse.ca/transit.*

TAXI Grizzly Bear Taxi ☎ *867/667–4888.*

VISITOR AND TOUR INFORMATION Whitehorse Visitor Information Centre ✉ *100 Hanson St.* ☎ *867/667–3084, 800/661– 0494* ⊕ *www.travelyukon.com.*

◉ Sights

Canyon City Historic Site

ARCHAEOLOGICAL SITE | This archaeological dig site provides a glimpse into the past of the local First Nations people. Long before Western civilizations developed the Miles Canyon area, the First Nations people used it as a seasonal fish camp. From mid-June to late August, the Yukon Conservation Society sponsors two-hour, kid-friendly natural and historical hikes here that provide the opportunity to experience the surrounding countryside with local naturalists. A bookstore in the society's office specializes in the Yukon's history and wilderness and sells souvenirs, maps, and posters. ✉ *302 Hawkins St.* ☎ *867/668–5678* ⊕ *www.yukonconservation.org* ⌘ *Free.*

MacBride Museum of Yukon History

MUSEUM | The exhibits at the MacBride provide a comprehensive view of the colorful characters and groundbreaking events that shaped the Yukon. An old-fashioned confectionery and an 1898 miner's saloon are among the highlights of the Gold to Government Gallery illuminating gold-rush and Whitehorse history. The gold-related exhibits illustrate particularly well what people went through in quest of a little glint of color. Other displays investigate the Yukon's wildlife and geology, and there are fine collections of photography and First Nations beadwork. Outdoor artifacts include the cabin of Sam McGee, who was immortalized in Robert Service's famous poem "The Cremation of Sam McGee." ✉ *1124 Front St.* ☎ *867/667–2709* ⊕ *www.macbride-museum.com* 🖃 *C$10* ⊙ *Closed Sun. and Mon. early Sept.–mid-May.*

Miles Canyon

NATURE SITE | Both scenic and historic, Miles Canyon is a short drive south of Whitehorse. Although the dam below the canyon makes its waters seem relatively tame, it was this perilous stretch of the Yukon River that determined the location of Whitehorse as the starting point for river travel north. The dam, built in 1958, created a lake that put an end to the infamous White Horse Rapids. Back in 1897, though, Jack London won the admiration—and cash—of fellow stampeders headed north to the Klondike goldfields because of his steady hand as pilot of hand-hewn wooden boats here. You can hike on trails along the canyon or rent a kayak and paddle on through. ✉ *Miles Canyon Rd.*

S.S. Klondike

HISTORIC SITE | You can't really understand the scale of the gold rush without touring a riverboat. The SS *Klondike*, a national historic site, is dry-docked on the bank of the Yukon River in central Whitehorse's Rotary Park, just a minute's drive from downtown. The 210-foot stern-wheeler was built in 1929, sank in 1936, and was rebuilt in 1937. In the days when the Yukon River was the transportation link between Whitehorse and Dawson City, the S.S. *Klondike* was the largest boat plying the river. Riverboats were as much a way of life here as on the Mississippi of

Mark Twain, and the tour of the *Klondike* is a fascinating way to see how the boats were adapted to the north. In the old days they were among the few places that provided indigenous people paying jobs, so there's a rich First Nations and Alaska Natives history as well. You can obtain a self-guided tour brochure for C$2. Guided tours are available through Parks Canada at 10:30 am and 2:15 pm daily (C$6). ✉ *Robert Service Way at 4th Ave., on bank of Yukon River* ☎ *867/667–4511 mid-May–mid-Sept., 800/661–0486* ⊕ *www.pc.gc.ca/ssklondike* 🖃 *Free* ⊙ *Closed early Sept.–mid-May.*

Takhini Hot Pools

HOT SPRINGS | Relax away the driving miles with a dip into Takhini Hot Pools at this complex off the Klondike Highway. Lounge or swim in the two hot spring–warmed pools (suits, towels, and flip-flops are for rent). There's also a campground, with space for both tents and RVs, a restaurant specializing in crepes, and a 20-bed hostel. The pools are open year-round, making for a breathtaking way to take in the wintry outdoors while staying warm and toasty. Private late-night pool rentals give you a good excuse to stay up past your bedtime. There's also a hair-freezing photo contest each February, and discounted admission to the pools on some weeknights in winter. ✉ *Km 10/Mile 6, Takhini Hot Springs Rd.* ⊕ *18 miles north of Whitehorse* ☎ *867/456–8000* ⊕ *www.takhinihot-springs.com* 🖃 *C$12.*

Waterfront Walkway

PROMENADE | The walkway along the Yukon River passes by a few points of interest. Start along the river just east of the MacBride Museum entrance on Front Street. Traveling upstream (south), you'll see the old White Pass and Yukon Route Building on Main Street. The walk is a good way to get an overview of the old town site, and just stretch your legs if you've been driving all day. ✉ *Whitehorse.*

Travel along the highway linking Chicken and Dawson City for some awe-inspiring scenery.

Whitehorse Fishway

DAM | **FAMILY** | Yukon Energy built this fishway to facilitate the yearly chinook (king) salmon run around the Whitehorse Rapids hydroelectric dam. The salmon hold one of nature's great endurance records, the longest fish migration in the world—more than 2,000 miles from the Bering Sea to Whitehorse. There's a platform for viewing the ladder, and TV monitors display pictures from underwater cameras. Interesting interpretive exhibits, talks by local First Nations elders, and labeled tanks of freshwater fish enhance the experience. The best time to visit is August, when hundreds of salmon use the ladder to bypass the dam. ⊠ *Nisutlin Dr.* ☎ *867/633–5965* 🎫 *C$3 suggested donation.*

Yukon Beringia Interpretive Centre

MUSEUM | The story of the Yukon during the last Ice Age comes alive at this center near the Whitehorse Airport. Beringia is the name given to the large subcontinental landmasses of eastern Siberia and Interior Alaska and the Yukon, which stayed ice-free and were linked by the Bering Land Bridge during the latest Ice Age. The area that is now Whitehorse wasn't actually part of this—it was glaciated—but lands farther north, among them what is present-day Dawson City, were in the thick of it, and miners are still turning up mammoth bones. Large dioramas depict the lives of animals in Ice Age Beringia, and there are skeleton replicas. A 26,000-year-old horsehide reveals that horses weren't as big back then as they are now. ⊠ *Mile 886, Alaska Hwy.* ☎ *867/667–8855* ⊕ *www.beringia. com* 🎫 *C$6.*

Yukon Permanent Art Collection

MUSEUM | The lobby of the Government of Yukon Main Administration Building displays selections from the Yukon Permanent Art Collection, featuring traditional and contemporary works by Yukon artists. The space also includes a 24-panel mural by artist David MacLagan depicting the historical evolution of the Yukon. In addition to the collection on the premises, the brochure *Art Adventures on Yukon Time,* available at visitor centers throughout the Yukon, guides you to artists' studios as well as galleries, festivals, and public art locations. ⌂ 2071 2nd Ave. ☎ 867/667–5811 ⊕ www.tc.gov. yk.ca/ypac ✉ Free ⊙ Closed weekends.

Yukon Transportation Museum

MUSEUM | This museum takes a fascinating look at the planes, trains, trucks, and snowmachines that opened up the north. Even if big machines don't interest you, this is a cool place to learn about the innovations and adaptations that transport in the north has inspired. ⌂ 30 Electra Crescent ☎ 867/668–4792 ⊕ www. goytm.ca ✉ C$10 ⊙ Closed Tues.–Sat. Sept.–May, except by appointment.

Yukon Wildlife Preserve

NATURE PRESERVE | The preserve provides a fail-safe way to photograph sometimes hard-to-spot animals in a natural setting. Animals roaming freely here include moose, elk, caribou, mountain goats, musk oxen, bison, mule deer, and Dall and Stone sheep. Bus tours take place throughout the day, and self-guided walking maps are available. ⌂ Mile 5, Takhini Hot Springs Rd., Takhini Hot Springs ☎ 867/456–7300 ⊕ www.yukonwildlife.ca ✉ C$15 self-guided tour, C$22 bus tour ⊙ Closed Mon.–Thurs. Oct.–Apr. except by appointment.

🏃 Activities

Kluane National Park and Reserve

HIKING/WALKING | About 170 km (100 miles) west of Whitehorse, the reserve has millions of acres for hiking. This is a completely roadless wilderness, with hundreds of glaciers and so many mountains over 14,000 feet high that most of them haven't been named yet (one exception: Mt. Logan, Canada's highest peak). Kluane, the neighboring Wrangell–St. Elias National Park in Alaska, and a few smaller parks, constitute the largest protected wilderness in all North America. The staff at the Haines Junction visitor center can provide hiking, flightseeing, and other information. ⌂ Visitor center, 119 Logan St., Haines Junction ☎ 867/634–7250 ⊕ www.pc.gc. ca/kluane.

Yukon Quest International Sled Dog Race

LOCAL SPORTS | Because the terrain is rougher and there are fewer checkpoints, most dog mushers think this 1,000-mile race between Whitehorse and Fairbanks provides more intense competition than the higher-profile Iditarod. The Yukon Quest takes place in February; the starting line alternates yearly between the two cities. Twenty to 30 mushers participate, with most finishing in 9 to 14 days. ⌂ Whitehorse ☎ 867/668–4711 ⊕ www.yukonquest.com.

🍴 Restaurants

The Claim Cafe & Food Co

$$ | CAFÉ | Choose from fresh-baked breads and pastries, homemade soups and sandwiches, and salads and quiches at this charming café and deli. Locals love the chocolate cake, a moist, rich delight. **Known for:** outdoor seating; gluten-free options; chocolate indulgences. ⑤ Average main: C$15 ⌂ 305 Strickland St. ☎ 867/667–2202 ⊕ www.theclaim.ca ⊙ Closed Sun.

★ Klondike Rib & Salmon

$$$$ | AMERICAN | Wild-game dishes such as elk, reindeer, bison, and boar are the Klondike's specialty, but it's also known for halibut, salmon, arctic char, and killer ribs. The restaurant meets vegetarians' needs with pasta and meatless dishes. **Known for:** the best wild game in town; long waits; oldest operating building in Whitehorse. ⑤ Average main: C$29 ⌂ 2116 2nd Ave. ☎ 867/667–7554 ⊕ www.klondikerib.com ⊙ Closed mid-Sept.–mid-May.

★ Midnight Sun Coffee Roasters

$ | CAFÉ | One of the hippest coffee shops you'll ever step foot in—but completely devoid of snobbery—shares space with a bicycle shop, cleverly named Icycle Sport. Service is superfriendly and the coffee is, quite simply, stellar, as are the baked goods. **Known for:** eclectic, family-run energy; small-batch coffee; fantastic flower boxes in summer. ⑤ *Average main: C$5* ✉ *21 Waterfront Pl.* ☎ *888/633–4563, 867/633–4563* ⊕ *www. yukoncoffee.com* ☉ *Closed Sun.*

🛏 Hotels

Coast High Country Inn & Convention Centre

$$$ | B&B/INN | At this downtown hotel you'll find modern, comfortably appointed standard rooms and premium ones with Jacuzzis and kitchenettes. **Pros:** free airport shuttle; central location; on-site dining at Morels. **Cons:** some rooms lack air-conditioning and bathtubs; standard rooms are minimally decorated; some rooms are very small. ⑤ *Rooms from: C$210* ✉ *4051 4th Ave.* ☎ *867/667–4471, 800/554–4471* ⊕ *www.highcountryinn. yk.ca* ⟿ *82 rooms* ⦿ *No meals.*

Edgewater Hotel

$$$$ | HOTEL | Thanks to its small size, comfy bedding, and sophisticated style, the Edgewater has the ambience of a boutique hotel. **Pros:** rich history; one block from the Yukon River; free Wi-Fi. **Cons:** no breakfast; some noise from Main Street; adjacent parking is limited. ⑤ *Rooms from: C$259* ✉ *101 Main St.* ☎ *867/667–2572* ⊕ *www.edgewaterho-telwhitehorse.com* ⟿ *32 rooms* ⦿ *No meals.*

Westmark Whitehorse Hotel & Conference Center

$$$ | HOTEL | Rooms are standard issue but clean (suites have a little more personality) at this full-service downtown property, the largest hotel in the Yukon. **Pros:** laundry facilities; great restaurant and lounge; breakfast buffet available in summer. **Cons:** can get noisy; fee for Wi-Fi; no air-conditioning. ⑤ *Rooms from: C$199* ✉ *201 Wood St.* ☎ *867/393–9700, 800/544–0970 reservations* ⊕ *www. westmarkhotels.com* ⟿ *180 rooms* ⦿ *No meals.*

Chapter 8

THE BUSH

8

Updated by
Dawnell Smith

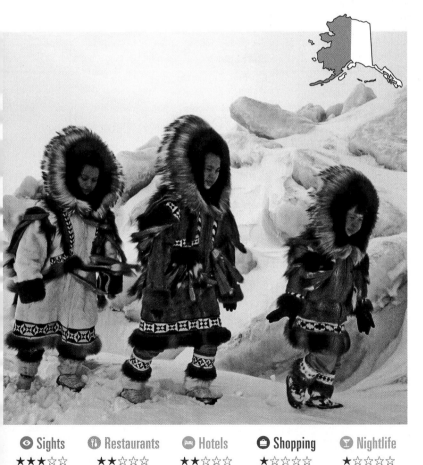

⦿ Sights	🍴 Restaurants	🛏 Hotels	🛍 Shopping	🍸 Nightlife
★★★☆☆	★★☆☆☆	★★☆☆☆	★☆☆☆☆	★☆☆☆☆

WELCOME TO THE BUSH

TOP REASONS TO GO

★ **Bears:** The Alaska Peninsula has the world's largest concentrations of brown bears, which congregate in salmon streams every summer.

★ **Alaska Native cultures:** Native communities celebrate and support their cultural traditions. Come to the Bush to meet and learn about Alaska Native cultures, traditions, and experiences.

★ **Fishing:** You could see (and catch!) 50-pound salmon, 8-pound trout, and be the only one on your block to know what sheefish tastes like.

★ **The land of the Midnight Sun:** Only north of the Arctic Circle is the sun above the horizon 24 hours a day in summer; in Utqiaġvik, the sun doesn't set at all from mid-May to August.

★ **The great outdoors:** Want the world to yourself? Bush Alaska includes millions of acres of remote parklands and wildlife refuges, including the least-visited national park in the United States.

1 Bethel.

2 Yukon Delta National Wildlife Refuge.

3 Wood-Tikchik State Park.

4 Katmai National Park and Preserve.

5 Aniakchak National Monument and Preserve.

6 Becharof and Alaska Peninsula National Wildlife Refuges.

7 Aleutian Islands.

8 Unalaska/Dutch Harbor.

9 Pribilof Islands.

10 Nome.

11 Bering Land Bridge National Preserve.

12 Kotzebue.

13 Kobuk Valley National Park.

14 Noatak National Preserve.

15 Gates of the Arctic National Park and Preserve.

16 Utqiaġvik.

17 Prudhoe Bay.

18 Arctic National Wildlife Refuge.

0 — 100 mi
0 — 100 km

St. Paul Island

PRIBILOF 9
ISLANDS
Saint George
Island

7
ALEUTIAN ISLAN
Dutch Harbor/Unalaska○ 8

When an Alaskan talks about going to the Bush, they usually mean anywhere off the grid, which pretty much includes most of Alaska. However, it also refers to those wild places beyond the state's cities, towns, highways, and railroad corridors, stretching from the Kodiak Archipelago, Alaska Peninsula, and Aleutian Islands in the south to the Yukon-Kuskokwim Delta, the Seward Peninsula, and into the Arctic.

For the sake of this guide, the Bush refers to these remote areas and extends over two-thirds of Alaska, where caribou outnumber people and where the summer sun really does shine at midnight; in fact, at the state's northern edge, the sun remains in the sky for several weeks in June and July, and then disappears altogether for weeks in winter.

If you visit the Arctic plains in the summer, you'll see an array of bright wildflowers growing from a sponge of rich green tundra dotted with pools of melting snow. Willow trees barely an inch tall might be 100 years old while some bushes have berries bigger than the bush they grow on. In the long, dark Arctic winter, a painter's-blue twilight rises from the ice and snowscapes at midday, but the moon can be bright enough to read by, and on a clear night you will have a new appreciation for the depth of the heavens. Spring and fall are fleeting moments when the tundra awakens from its winter slumber or turns briefly brilliant with autumn colors.

Alaskans who live in towns use the Bush as an escape valve, a place to get away. And those who've made the Bush their home are practically heroes to the rest of the state; they're the people who are bold enough to do what the majority of urban Alaskans wish they could do. Bush Alaskans have a deep affection for their raw land that is difficult to explain to strangers. They talk of living with complete independence, "close to nature." A cliché, perhaps, until you realize that these Alaskans reside in the Bush all year long, adapting to brutal winter weather and isolation, preferring to live off the road system. They know a store-bought hamburger will never taste as good as fresh moose meat, and whatever they're missing by not having a cell phone can't possibly be as interesting as the view out the cabin window. They have accepted the Bush for what it is: dramatic, unforgiving, and glorious.

Technically, the Bush is more or less any place in mainland Alaska that can't be reached by road. To outsiders the Bush has three distinct divisions: The Southwest part of the Bush, the Yukon Delta region and Bethel down to the Shelikof Strait, is the preferred territory for sportsmen and those looking to spot big animals. The Aleutian and Pribilof islands and the Alaska Peninsula attract dedicated birders and history buffs. And the northern part of the Bush, from Nome to Point Barrow, is for those who see north as a direction to go. A lot of people may say they're traveling to the Far North for a chance to see the beauty of the tundra or experience the full splendor of the Midnight Sun, but really, most do it for bragging rights.

Of course, venturing to the farthest reaches of Alaska at all is cause enough to boast; each region has its own distinct climates, people, scenery, and activities. Kodiak and Katmai are prime locations for grizzly viewing and birding. Nome is not only the best place for gold-rush history, but is also known for its wildlife and bird-watching in summer, and pristine river systems for paddle adventures. No matter where in the Bush you go, that distinct Alaska culture—created by the simple fact that the only people who live here are people who genuinely want to live here—is abundant, distinct, and welcoming.

A tour of the Bush's Southwest region can begin in Bethel, an important outpost on the Yukon-Kuskokwim Delta ("YK Delta" to locals) surrounded by the Yukon Delta National Wildlife Refuge. Off the mainland coast is the undeveloped wilderness of Nunivak Island.

The Alaska Peninsula juts out between the Pacific Ocean and the Bering Sea; here are the Becharof and Alaska Peninsula National Wildlife refuges, as well as the prime bear-viewing area of Katmai National Park and Preserve. To the northeast of the Alaska Peninsula is the Kodiak Archipelago, where you'll find Kodiak National Wildlife Refuge and Shuyak Island State Park.

Stomping Grounds

Great herds of caribou—including the Western Arctic herd with just under a half million animals, and the Porcupine herd with around 170,000—move slowly across the tundra, feeding and fattening for the next winter and attempting to stay clear of wolves and grizzlies while birthing and nursing their calves. In the Arctic Ocean's Beaufort Sea, polar bears pose on ice floes. One of Alaska's premier wildlands, the Arctic National Wildlife Refuge, protects mountain and tundra landscapes important to grizzlies, wolves, musk oxen, shorebirds, and other animals.

MAJOR REGIONS

The Southwest. The Southwest region, below the Arctic Circle, encompasses some of Alaska's most remote, inaccessible, and rugged land-and-seascapes. Reaching from the Kodiak Archipelago to the Yukon-Kuskokwim Delta, this area contains the world's densest brown bear population and the world's greatest salmon runs. Given all this richness, it's no surprise to learn that Southwest Alaska has some of Alaska's premier parklands and refuges, from Katmai National Park and Wood-Tikchik State Park to Aniakchak National Monument and Preserve and Becharof and Alaska Peninsula National Wildlife Refuges. Here, too, are dozens of rural communities, most of them small Alaska Native villages whose residents gather, hunt, and eat wild foods while relying on technology to stay connected with each other and the world. Many begin their trip in Bethel, an important outpost of the Yukon-Kuskokwim Delta (YK Delta to locals) surrounded by the Yukon Delta National Wildlife Refuge.

Aleutian Islands and Pribilof Islands. Considered part of Southwest, the Aleutians are closer to Japan than to San Francisco. Unalaska and its famed Dutch Harbor is the most population destination in the Aleutian Islands thanks to the hit Discovery Channel show *The Deadliest Catch*; it's also one of the busiest fishing ports in the world. Even more remote, the Pribilof Islands make up the northern edge of traditional Aleut lands and are the seasonal home of hundreds of thousands of seals and breeding birds, some seen nowhere else in North America.

The Northwest and the Arctic. This largely roadless region brings dark, sunless winters and bright summers known for their Midnight Sun, a place where indigenous people have lived for thousands of years and where many continue to hunt, fish, and gather for most of their food. The region also sustains some of the world's largest caribou herds and populations of migrating birds. Other wildlife includes whales and polar bears, along with an array of other mammals, birds, fish, and flora. The area's past and the future are seen in Native villages like Kotzebue and the oil reserves of Prudhoe Bay. Gold and oil stampedes tell some of the story of the region's recent history thanks to towns like Nome and Utqiaġvik, but its true legacy remains in remote parklands such as the Bering Land Bridge National Preserve, Kobuk Valley National Park, Noatak National Preserve, Gates of the Arctic National Park, and Arctic National Wildlife Refuge.

Planning

WHEN TO GO

The best time to visit is June through August, when the weather is mildest (though you should still anticipate cool, wet, windy, and sometimes stormy weather), daylight hours are longest, and the wildlife is most abundant. Because summer is so short, though, things happen fast, and seasonal activities may need to be crammed into just a couple of weeks.

May and August are best for birding. The peak wildflower season is usually short, particularly in the Arctic, when most flowers may not blossom until mid-June and then go to seed by late July.

Salmon runs vary from region to region, so it's best to do your homework before choosing dates. For the most part, though, you're looking at July and August, which is also when the tundra starts turning from its summer hues to autumnal colors. The best times for bear viewing coincide with salmon runs. Note that fishing, bear viewing, and other wildlife exploration often involve licenses and permits that must be secured ahead of time, sometimes many months in advance. Few things about Alaska, especially during the too-short summer season, can be arranged on the fly. Plan ahead for best results.

FESTIVALS

Just because this is a remote area, that doesn't mean there's nothing going on, and some of the festivals and events in the Bush could well sway your decision about when to visit.

Cama-i Dance Festival

ARTS FESTIVALS | FAMILY | Each spring, the Bethel Council on the Arts hosts a regional celebration called the Cama-i Dance Festival (in Yup'ik, *cama-i* means "hello"). Held in the local high school's gym either the last weekend in March or the first two weeks of April, this three-day festival celebrates the food, dance, music, and crafts of the Alaska Native people and draws hoards of visitors from Bethel, surrounding villages, and beyond. ✉ *Bethel High School, 1 Ron Edwards Memorial Dr., Bethel* ⊕ *www.camai.org.*

Heart of the Aleutians Festival

FESTIVALS | FAMILY | The city of Unalaska holds the Heart of the Aleutians Festival every August. A beloved local tradition, this free, two-day festival brings together residents of all ages to peruse arts and crafts, listen to local music, eat specialty foods, participate in fun runs, and much more during a celebration of summer, friends, family, and community. ✉ *Kelty Field, Unalaska* ☎ *907/581–1297* ⊕ *www.ci.unalaska.ak.us/parksrec/page/heart-aleutians-festival.*

Iditarod Trail Sled Dog Race

FESTIVALS | FAMILY | Billed as "The Last Great Race", the Iditarod pulls in spectators (and mushers) from around the world to brave the Alaska winter to witness or to participate as racers and volunteers in this massive feat of endurance for mushers and their dogs. Many visitors watch the dog teams take off from the ceremonial start in Anchorage, and then travel to the finish line in Nome to celebrate as teams cross the finish line. The race, run in March, covers 1,049 snowy, backcountry miles from the official start in Willow, 90 miles north of Anchorage, to Nome. ☎ *907/376–5155* ⊕ *www.iditarod.com.*

Kuskokwim 300 Dog Sled Race

FESTIVALS | FAMILY | Every January, the Kuskokwim 300 dogsled race—"K300" to locals—brings mushers and fans to Bethel, where the 300-mile race both starts and ends. The best known of the middle distance dogsled races, the K300 course commemorates one of the earliest mail routes used in the Bush. The $150,000 or more purse comes as a welcome reward after negotiating the notoriously harsh and difficult weather and trail conditions. Smaller, shorter races happen later in the winter in Bethel as well. ✉ *Downtown, Bethel* ☎ *907/545–3300* ⊕ *www.k300.org.*

GETTING HERE AND AROUND
AIR TRAVEL
Alaska Airlines flies to most major communities in Alaska. Pen Air, Ravn Alaska, Wright Air Service, and Grant Aviation serve the smaller communities on the Alaskan Peninsula, the Aleutian and

Pribilof islands, and parts of the Arctic, Interior, and northwest.

Bush-based carriers such as Bering Air also offer flightseeing tours and, weather and politics permitting, specially arranged charter flights to the Provideniya Airport in the Chukotka Region, on the Siberian coast across the Bering Strait. Currently, it is mandatory for Americans to obtain a visa, migration card, and permission to go to Russia in advance of travel—this can take time, so plan ahead. Applications for visas are available up to 90 days before travel. The process starts at $160 and can take up to 30 business days. The Consulate General of the Russian Federation recommends working through a Russia-sponsored travel agent to secure a travel visa.

Information about certified air-taxi operations is available from the Federal Aviation Administration. Individual parks and Alaska Public Lands Information Centers can also supply lists of reputable air-taxi services. Make your reservations in advance, and always plan for the unexpected; weather often delays a scheduled pickup for days.

AIR CONTACTS Alaska Airlines
☎ *800/252–7522* ⊕ *www.alaskaair. com.* **Bering Air** ☎ *907/443–5464 Nome reservations, 800/478–5422 administration, 907/443–8988 Russian desk* ⊕ *www.beringair.com.* **Federal Aviation Administration** ☎ *907/271–5438* ⊕ *www. faa.gov/airports/alaskan.* **Grant Aviation** ☎ *888/359–4726 general reservations, 907/543–2000 Bethel and Emmonak areas* ⊕ *www.flygrant.com.* **Pen Air** ☎ *907/771–2640, 800/448–4226, 907/771–2599 charter flight reservations* ⊕ *www.penair.com.* **Ravn Alaska** ☎ *907/266-8394 in Alaska, 800/866–8394 outside Alaska* ⊕ *www.flyravn.com.* **Wright Air Service** ☎ *907/474–0502 general reservations, 907/474–0542 charter flight reservations* ⊕ *www.wrightairservice.com.*

BOAT TRAVEL

In the Aleutians, the Alaska Marine Highway, the state's amazing ferry system, makes one trip a month between Kodiak and Dutch Harbor/Unalaska from April through October. It's not for the hurried traveler, however; expect four to five days of travel each way and minimal on-boat luxuries. With many stops in far-flung towns, the ferry is a truly memorable way to get a full taste of Alaska's massive geography, unparalleled natural scenery, and medley of local cultures.

BOAT CONTACTS Alaska Marine Highway ☎ 800/642–0066 from outside Alaska, 907/465–3941 ⊕ www.dot.state.ak.us/amhs.

CAR TRAVEL

The unpaved Dalton Highway connects with the state's paved highway system and traverses the Arctic, but it only leads to the oil fields of Prudhoe Bay. For those looking to tackle the journey north by road, prepare for flat tires, cracked windshields from flying debris, and a slow-going drive. Check with your rental-car company to confirm you are permitted to take the vehicle on the Dalton Highway. If so, consider investing in additional auto insurance as well as a basic roadside repair kit and a satellite phone. Pack extra food, gear, gas, and supplies in case of an accident or breakdown.

HEALTH AND SAFETY

When traveling in the Bush, you should never head out without a decent first-aid kit; you can be a very long way from help out here. The main concern, though, is hypothermia. Always carry more layers than you anticipate needing. Watch out for each other. Encounters with wild animals—bears, moose, caribou, and eagles—are common, if not expected. Stay aware, keep your distance, and remember that these animals are not domesticated pets; they are wild and, in some cases, predatory. However, a much more consistent nuisance than Alaska's mammals and birds are Alaska's insects—until you've experienced it, it's hard to understand just how thick the mosquitoes and other things that bite can get in summer. Bring plenty of DEET.

MONEY

Many small villages don't have bank offices, so visitors should bring cash. Most places within the larger Bush communities accept major credit cards, but don't take that for granted. Always be sure to confirm in advance what sort of payment tour companies, hotels, and restaurants accept. Hub communities that do have bank services are Nome, Bethel, Kotzebue, Barrow, and Unalaska.

TOURS

Package tours are the most common way of traveling to Bush communities, where making your flight connections and having a room to sleep in at the end of the line are no small feats. During peak season (late May through Labor Day) planes, state ferries, hotels, and sportfishing lodges are often crowded with travelers on organized tours; to create a trip on your own can sometimes mean making reservations a year in advance for the really popular destinations. But the Bush is also large enough that there's always somewhere to go, and wherever you end up the odds are it will be amazing and like nothing you've ever seen before.

The type of tour you choose will determine how you get there. In most cases this will be by air, since flying is the only way to access the vast majority of Bush communities. By flying to and from your destination, you can also enjoy an aerial perspective of the Arctic en route. Tours to Arctic towns and villages are usually short—one, two, or three days—so it's easy to combine them with visits to other regions. Road tours up the Dalton Highway are not common, but also not impossible. Northern Alaska Tour Company and Arctic Outfitters offer overland tours on the Dalton Highway, with the latter even renting road-ready vehicles for self-guided land tours. Even more so than usual driving in Alaska, taking to the Dalton Highway on your own can be risky; the road is unpaved, mostly unmaintained, and completely lacks the modern roadside convenience stores and gas stations. Do research first and be prepared for a long, bumpy, and potentially hazardous ride (flat tires and cracked windshields are the norm). Before departing in a rented car, check with your rental car company about any provisions, exclusions, and extra insurance you might need to make the rough drive.

The Bush is home to many Alaska Native communities and people whose families have lived in these areas for thousands of years. Often, Native and local village corporations run tours, hotels, and attractions, and local people sell arts and crafts made from local materials such as bone, animal hair, and baleen. Spending time with local guides and operators can be invaluable to understanding the Bush way of life and the local people's connection to the surrounding lands and waters.

The Northern Alaska Tour Company conducts highly regarded ecotours to the Arctic Circle, the Brooks Range, and Prudhoe Bay that emphasize natural and cultural history, wildlife, and geology. Groups are limited to 25 people on Arctic day tours and to 10 people on Prudhoe Bay overnight trips. Some tours are completely ground-based; others include a mix of ground and air travel. Fairbanks-based Arctic Treks leads small groups on hiking, rafting, and backpacking adventures in places like the Arctic National Wildlife Refuge, Gates of the Arctic National Park, Noatak National Preserve, Kobuk Valley National Park, Cape Krusenstern National Monument, and the Bering Land Bridge National Preserve.

Arctic Outfitters

DRIVING TOURS | This company specializes in providing car rentals equipped for year-round use on the Dalton Highway.

Flying Through the Bush

Roads in the Bush are few, so airplanes—from jetliners to helicopters to small bush planes— are the lifelines. Alaska has 6 times more pilots and 16 times more planes per capita than anywhere else in the country. Flying is truly a way of life here. And the legendary pilots of the Far North are Alaska's counterparts to the cowboy heroes of the Wild West. And, just as in the Wild West, the adventure came with risk: the Bush is where America's favorite humorist, Will Rogers, died in a crash with famed aviator Wiley Post in 1935.

Based out of Fairbanks, Artic Outfitters offers gravel road-ready automobiles, accommodation arrangements, and travel packages on and around the Dalton Highway. ✉ *Fairbanks* ☎ *907/474–3530* ⊕ *www.arctic-outfitters.com* ✆ *From $179 a day.*

★ Arctic Treks

GUIDED TOURS | Based in Fairbanks, Arctic Treks takes small groups into the vast and typically inaccessible wilderness of Alaska's Arctic region. Rafting, backpacking, and camping trips range from 7 to 10 days in some of the most remote and remarkable areas of the Arctic National Wildlife Refuge, the Brooks Range, and Gates of the Arctic National Parks & Preserves. ☎ *907/455–6502* ⊕ *www.arctictreksadventures.com* ✆ *From $4300.*

Explore Tours

ADVENTURE TOURS | This company helps visitors find tour packages from outfitters and vendors across the state. Options range from day trips to longer adventures, and covers every region in Alaska, including the Bush. ☎ *800/523–7405* ⊕ *www.exploretours.com* ✆ *From $99.*

Northern Alaska Tour Company

ADVENTURE TOURS | This company arranges all-season land and/or air adventures into Denali National Park, Alaska's Arctic, and other remote areas outside its hub in Fairbanks. Day or overnight trips include excursions into the Arctic circle and along the Dalton Highway, flights over Denali and the Arctic Ocean, polar bear and Aurora Borealis expeditions, and tours of Alaska Native communities. ☎ *907/474–8600, 800/474–1986* ⊕ *www.northernalaska.com* ✉ *From $189.*

Tundra Tours

ADVENTURE TOURS | **FAMILY** | Operating out of the Top of the World Hotel in Utqiaġvik, Tundra Tours offers half-day excursions that give guests a chance to see wildlife, walk on the tundra, dip a toe in the Arctic Ocean, and learn about Utqiaġvik's cultural and historical sites. ⊠ *Top of the World Hotel, 3060 Eben Hopson St., Barrow* ☎ *907/852–3900* ⊕ *www.tundratoursinc.com* ✉ *From $162 per person.*

Wilderness Birding Adventures

SPECIAL-INTEREST | This Homer-based outfitter takes small groups into the Alaska wilderness to watch birds and wildlife. These eco-adventures last from a few days to a few weeks, and cover a wide range of Alaska from the Alaska National Wildlife Refuge and areas outside of Utqiaġvik and Nome to the Pribilof Islands. They also do private trips that combine birding, hiking, and river-rafting. ⊠ *Homer* ☎ *907/299–3937* ⊕ *www.wildernessbirding.com* ✉ *From $1400.*

RESTAURANTS

Dining options are few when traveling around Alaska's Bush; smaller communities may have one or two eateries, if any at all. On the bright side, you won't need to worry about reservations. If they're open, they'll let you in, and you'll likely be surprised at the variety of foods available. In addition to Alaska seafood, game, and locally grown vegetables, Mexican and Asian fare are standard, even in the state's remotest corners. Most Bush restaurants feature two or three different cuisines, and many deliver. All food prices, including those at small grocery stores, reflect the high transportation charges, so be prepared to pay more than you would back home or even in Anchorage. Since many of these Bush restaurants will shut down for periods of time, particularly during the shoulder seasons, it never hurts to ask a local or call the eatery to confirm it's open before heading over.

HOTELS

Lodging choices in the Bush are limited. Some communities have a single modern hotel while the smallest may have none. Others have a mix of hotels, lodges, and bed-and-breakfasts. As a rule, rooms provide simple furnishing and are often not updated. You may have to share bathroom or kitchen facilities. Rooms go fast during the summer season, so book as far ahead as possible. And it never hurts to carry a tent as backup.

Restaurant and hotel reviews have been shortened. For full information, visit Fodors.com. Restaurant prices are the average cost of a main course at dinner, or if dinner is not served, at lunch. Hotel prices are the lowest cost of a standard double room in high season.

What It Costs			
$	$$	$$$	$$$$
RESTAURANTS			
under $14	$14–$22	$23–$32	over $32
HOTELS			
under $100	$100–$175	$176–$250	over $250

VISITOR INFORMATION

CONTACTS Alaska Department of Fish and Game ⊠ *1255 W. 8th St., Juneau* ☎ *907/267–2253 hunting/wildlife information (statewide), 907/459–7346 sportfishing seasons/regulations (interior contact), 907/465–2376 licenses/permits*

The Southwest

0 ——— 100 miles
0 ——— 150 km

BERING SEA

0 ——— 100 mi
0 ——— 100 km

(statewide) ⊕ www.adfg.alaska.gov.
Alaska Public Lands Information Centers
✉ *605 W. 4th Ave., Suite 105, Anchorage*
☎ *907/644–3678* ⊕ *www.alaskacenters.
gov.* **Alaska State Parks Information** ✉ *550
W. 7th Ave., Suite 1260, Anchorage*
☎ *907/269–8400* ⊕ *www.dnr.alaska.gov/
parks.* **U.S. Fish and Wildlife Service Alaska
Region** ✉ *1011 E. Tudor Rd., Anchorage*
☎ *907/786–3309* ⊕ *www.fws.gov/alaska.*

Bethel

400 miles west of Anchorage.

Spread out on the tundra along the Kuskokwim River, Bethel is a town of about
6,000 year-round residents located in an
area inhabited by the Yu'pik people for
thousands of years (their village is called
Mamterillermiut). During the 19th century, Bethel was a trading post, and it had

a small population of just more than 40
people by the late 19th century. Moravian
missionaries eventually moved the town
to its current spot on the west side of
the Kuskokwim River. Today one of rural
Alaska's most important trading centers
and the largest community in Western
Alaska, it's a hub for 56 native villages
in a region roughly the size of the state
of Oregon. The Yup'ik Eskimo language
and culture are still predominant in this
regional center; Alaska Native people
represent 70% of the town's population.

The surrounding lowland tundra is a rich
green in summer and turns fiery shades
of red, orange, and yellow in autumn,
when plants burst with blueberries, cranberries, blackberries, and salmonberries.
Salmon, arctic grayling, and Dolly Varden
(a species of seagoing trout) fill the area's
many lakes, ponds, and streams, providing excellent fishing just a few miles

outside town. Pretty much everyone in Bethel has smoked, dried, and frozen fish aplenty. The wetlands are also important breeding grounds for more than 60 species of birds, from shrikes to warblers.

Each year on the last weekend in March, Bethel hosts a regional celebration called the Cama-i Dance Festival (in Yup'ik, *cama-i* means "hello"), a great time to experience Native culture.

GETTING HERE AND AROUND
To get to Bethel, take a flight on Alaska Airlines or Ravn. Once you're there, the town itself is walkable.

ESSENTIALS
VISITOR INFORMATION Bethel Chamber of Commerce ✉ *192 Alex Hatley Dr.* ☎ *907/543–2911* ⊕ *www.bethelchamber. org.*

Sights

Nunivak Island
NATURE PRESERVE | Due west of Bethel, and separated from the Yukon-Kuskokwim Delta by the Etolin Strait, Nunivak Island is an important wildlife refuge. Part of this site is noted for its large herd of reindeer, a transplanted herd of musk ox, and the Eskimo settlement of Mekoryuk. For information on the island and travel options, contact the U.S. Fish and Wildlife Service in Bethel. ☎ *907/543–3151* ⊕ *www.fws.gov/refuge/yukon_delta.*

Pinky's Park
CITY PARK | **FAMILY** | Named after Thomas "Pinky" Sekanoff, who walked across the Bering Strait to escape the Russian Revolution in the 1900s, the 22 acres of Pinky's Park remember his life in Bethel and constant goodwill toward the kids in the community. Although he made a very modest living panning for gold in the region, he always managed to have candy for the local children. Take a stroll on the park's nearly 2 miles of wooden boardwalks, decks, and trails; remember that they must be specially engineered to hold up in this brutal climate while not

damaging the tundra underneath. There's also a nice community garden, along with a playground and multiuse sports field that acts as a hub for all of Bethel's July 4 festivities. ✉ *301 Akiachak Ave.* ☎ *907/543–2047* ⊕ *www.cityofbethel. org.*

Yupiit Piciryarait Cultural Center
MUSEUM | **FAMILY** | The center includes a museum along with spaces for workshops and events all year, including classes, movie screenings, summer camps, concerts, and summer Saturday markets. The museum, founded in 1965 as the Bethel Museum, contains more than 2,500 artifacts, photographs, and art pieces from the Athabascan, Cup'ik, and Yup'ik cultures, including display masks, statues, and intricate carvings in ivory, baleen, and whalebone. ✉ *420 Chief Eddie Hoffman Hwy.* ☎ *907/543–4538* ⊕ *www.uaf.edu/bethel/cultural-center/ index.xml.*

🍽 Restaurants

ChopstiX Restaurant
$$ | **JAPANESE** | With its selection of sushi, burgers, and Chinese combo meals, ChopstiX suits the Bush mindset with its range of food styles. If you have to wait, it's likely because locals have ordered for delivery to their doorstep, wherever they might be. **Known for:** to-go sushi; Bento box specials; all-American burgers and sandwiches. ⑤ *Average main: $20* ✉ *320 Tundra St.* ☎ *907/543–4777.*

Fili's Pizza
$$ | **PIZZA** |**FAMILY** | This pizza, burger, and sandwich eatery has nine tables and counter space for dining in. You can choose from a nice selection of beer and wine along with an ample menu of calzones, pizzas, burgers, pastas, sandwiches, and jumbo wings. **Known for:** beer and wine when dining in; famed Fili's Mistake pie; late-night delivery. ⑤ *Average main: $20* ✉ *110 Osage St.* ☎ *907/ 543–7010* ⊕ *www.filispizza.com* ⊘ *Closed Mon. No lunch.*

Hotels

Bentley's B&B
$$$ | **B&B/INN** |**FAMILY** | Hospitality is never in short supply at this two-story, riverfront B&B in downtown Bethel. **Pros:** river views; Wi-Fi available; great breakfast. **Cons:** not for those who want to stay up late making noise; not all rooms have baths; some rooms need updating. ⑤ *Rooms from: $195* ✉ *624 1st St.* ☎ *907/543–3552* ⊕ *www.bentleysbnb. com* ⌁ *30 rooms* ❍*l Breakfast.*

Suite 881
$$$ | **HOTEL** | All 10 units at Suite 881 offer kitchen and work spaces, private baths, washers, dryers, and Internet access. **Pros:** fully stocked kitchen; convenient long-term stays; cable and Wi-Fi. **Cons:** Bethel connectivity means no streaming; some rooms lack great views; decor is generic. ⑤ *Rooms from: $199* ✉ *81 3rd Ave.* ☎ *907/543–3883* ⊕ *www.suite881. net* ⌁ *10 rooms* ❍*l No meals.*

Yukon Delta National Wildlife Refuge

Boundless wildlands and wild waters define the enormous Yukon Delta National Wildlife Refuge that surrounds Bethel. Officially created in 1980 after the consolidation of adjoining refuge lands, the coastal location and climate support nature and habitat on a massive scale. Literally millions of ducks and geese breed here annually, and tens of thousands of caribou roam the hills during fall and winter. Water mammals big and small are prevalent in the adjacent Bering Sea and fish abound in the waters and wetlands created by the delta of the Yukon and Kuskokwim rivers in the midst of the refuge.

GETTING HERE AND AROUND
There are no roads to or in the refuge. The best way to enter the area is to take a commercial flight to Bethel and

Alcohol in the Bush

Many Bush communities have elected to become "dry," aka to prohibit alcohol sales and possession, in order to fight alcohol-abuse problems in the area. Enforcement is strict, and bootlegging is a felony. A few towns are exceptions. Bethel got its first liquor store in 2016 after 40 years without one, while Nome remains "wet" with as many bars as there are churches. Check local laws before bringing any alcohol into Bush communities.

then fly into the refuge by air taxi. If you only want to see the smallest edge of the refuge, or are a very strong hiker, it is also possible to walk in by driving 2 miles down Chief Eddie Hoffman State Highway, the only paved road in town, to the Refuge Office and Visitor Center at the end of the road.

ESSENTIALS
VISITOR INFORMATION Visitor Center
✉ *807 Chief Eddie Hoffman Rd., Bethel* ☎ *907/543–3151* ⊕ *www.fws.gov/refuge/ yukon_delta.*

◉ Sights

Yukon Delta National Wildlife Refuge
NATURE PRESERVE | At 20 million acres, this is the nation's second-largest wildlife refuge, only a little smaller than the Alaska National Wildlife Refuge. Nearly one-third of the refuge is made up of water in the form of lakes, sloughs, bogs, creeks, and rivers, including both forks of the Andreafsky River, one of Alaska's specially designated Wild and Scenic Rivers. Rainbow trout, arctic char, and grayling flourish in upland rivers and creeks; pike, sheefish, and burbot thrive in the lowland streams. These abundant waters are also

spawning grounds for five species of Pacific salmon. Other animal inhabitants include black and grizzly bears, moose, beavers, mink, and Arctic foxes. Occasionally, wolves venture into the delta's flats from neighboring uplands. Given the abundance of fish and wildlife, it's not surprising that the delta holds special importance to surrounding residents. The Yup'ik people have lived here for thousands of years, and continue to hunt and gather their food from the waters and lands. Visitor facilities are minimal in the refuge, and access is only by boat or aircraft. Refuge staff can provide tips on recreational opportunities and recommend guides and outfitters who operate in the refuge ⊕ *www.fws.gov/refuge/yukon_delta*.

🏃 Activities

Opportunities for wildlife watching abound at the Yukon Delta refuge. With so many lakes, ponds, streams, and wetlands, the big thing to do is get in a boat, or hang out on the shore, and watch all the waterfowl. The refuge is also a great place for sportfishing, especially for rainbow trout, salmon, char, pike, grayling, and sheefish. Flat-water paddlers will never run out of water to try, although camping can be a bit marshy and DEET-dependent. Or try hiking and river floating in the uplands of the Andreafsky Wilderness area. You are a long way from help when you're in the refuge; know what you're doing.

Float Alaska

EXCURSIONS | Ambitious travelers looking to set out on a self-guided fishing journey of a lifetime can rent rafts and all camping gear from this outfitter. While they do not offer accompanied tours, their outdoor experts will help visitors plan and prepare for self-guided fishing trips on the remote rivers of the Yukon Delta National Wildlife Refuge. From tackle to first aid to transportation, Float Alaska's team will set up everything for a safe and

Nesting Grounds 👁

one-of-a-kind floating adventure. Actually catching the trout and salmon is up to you, though. ⊠ *198 H-Marker Rd., Bethel* ☎ *208/602–1200* ⊕ *www.floatalaska.com* 🛏 *Raft, tent, and kitchen unit rental, from $140 per day.*

★ **Kuskokwim Wilderness Adventures**
BOAT TOURS | Local expert John McDonald operates seven boats on the Kuskokwim River and its drainages. His company runs boat charters, village trips, cultural tours, wildlife viewing, and rafter pickups. Especially popular are birding tours in May and June, when almost 200 species of birds return to the Yukon-Kuskokwim Delta to breed. Custom five-night trips to Kisaralik Camp include six- to eight-hour guided fishing trips on the Kisaralik River, one of the world's premier trout and salmon streams. The price includes transportation, guided trips, food, and lodging (fishing licenses extra). ⊠ *Bethel* ☎ *907/543–3900* ⊕ *www.kuskofish.com* 🛏 *From $130.*

Papa Bear Adventures
ADVENTURE TOURS | This outfitter provides gear rentals and all transportation

and trip logistics to and from some of the most remote hunting, fishing, and camping locations in the Yukon-Kus-kokwim Delta, Togiak National Wildlife Refuge, and the Yukon Delta National Wildlife Refuge. They specialize in float fishing and rafting, but offer the option to customize trips. Adventures typically depart from the Lakeside Lodge B&B in Bethel, which is owned by Papa Bear's operators. ⊠ *198 H-Marker Lake Winter Rd., Bethel* ☎ *907/543–5275* ⊕ *www. pbadventures.com* ⊠ *From $100.*

Wood-Tikchik State Park

150 miles southeast of Bethel, 300 miles southwest of Anchorage.

The size of Delaware and also Alaska's largest state park, 1.6-million-acre Wood-Tikchik State Park is an angler's dream come true. Five species of salmon as well as rainbow trout abound in the park's pristine waters and attract sportfishers from around the world. South of Wood-Tikchik in the Bering Sea is Walrus Islands State Game Sanctuary, a group of islands known for its—you guessed it—walruses. Access permits and fishing licenses are required in some parts of both the state park and sanctuary, so do your research before hopping in the plane or kayak.

GETTING HERE AND AROUND

Like most of the Bush, there is no road access into Wood-Tikchik State Park. The only way in is either by air taxi or by boat. The entire park is open to private aircraft landings. In the summer months it's not uncommon to see kayakers navigating their way through the river systems, their point of origin in the town of Dillingham or farther away via the waters of Bristol Bay. Kayaking the river system is suggested only for experienced kayakers who have very good navigational skills, as it is quite easy to get lost in the labyrinth of mosquito-infested waters.

ESSENTIALS

VISITOR INFORMATION Walrus Island State Game Sanctuary ☎ *907/267–2189* ⊕ *www.adfg.alaska.gov/index.cfm?ad-fg=walrusislands.main.* **Wood-Tikchik State Park** ☎ *907/842–2641 Dillingham Parks Office, Alekangik Ranger Station, 907/269–8700 Dept. of Natural Resources, Parks, & Outdoor Recreation* ⊕ *www. dnr.alaska.gov/parks/units/wtc.*

⊙ Sights

Walrus Islands State Game Sanctuary

NATURE PRESERVE | Established in 1960 to protect one of the largest North American haul-out sites for the Pacific walrus, this sanctuary protects seven small islands and their adjacent waters in northern Bristol Bay, including Round Island, Summit Island, Crooked Island, High Island, Black Rock and The Twins. The area about 65 miles southwest of Dillingham also nourishes other birds and mammals. Catch a boat from Dillingham or the village of Togiak to Round Island to view the walruses offshore. These giant sea mammals come to the haul-out in such high numbers in the summer that you can barely see the rocks beneath the heaving red blubber. The number of walruses fluctuates from year to year, but more than 14,000 walrus have been counted on Round Island in a single day. The islands also support a large population of Steller sea lions, along with orcas, humpback, and gray whales feeding in the offshore waters. Transportation options to Round Island can be very limited. Day-trip permits can be obtained on the island, but camping permits are limited and must be arranged in advance. Before planning a trip or applying for a permit, check the Alaska Department of Fish and Game website for an updated list of available transportation options and tips. ⊕ *www.adfg.alaska.gov/index. cfm?adfg=walrusislands.main.*

Wood-Tikchik State Park

NATIONAL/STATE PARK | Located in the Bristol Bay region, this park is the nation's largest state park thanks to its 1.6 million acres of water-based wildlands (despite its inland setting). Two separate groups of interconnected lakes, some up to 45 miles long, dominate the park. Grizzlies, caribou, porcupines, eagles, and loons abound in the park's forests and tundra, but Wood-Tikchik is best known for its fish. The park's lakes and streams are critical spawning habitat for five species of Pacific salmon. They also support healthy populations of rainbow trout, arctic char, arctic grayling, and northern pike. Because of this, Wood-Tikchik is a Holy Grail locale for serious anglers and boaters with paddles. Wood-Tikchik has no maintained trails and few visitor amenities. Most campsites here are primitive, and anyone planning to explore the park should be experienced in backcountry travel and camping. Besides the many large lakes and streams, the park's landscape includes rugged mountains, glaciers, and vast expanses of tundra. ⊕ www.dnr.alaska.gov/parks/units/wood-tik.htm.

🏃 Activities

Because it is largely a water-based region, it's easiest to explore Wood-Tikchik by boat, whether via canoe, kayak, or raft. The most popular fly-in float trip is the 90-mile journey from Lake Kulik to Aleknagik, a Yup'ik Eskimo village. Most people doing this trip arrange for drop-off and pickup services with local guides in Dillingham. The lakes are large enough to behave like small inland seas in stormy weather, so boaters need to be cautious when winds are high; always be prepared for bad weather, know proper emergency procedures, and don't ever go out unless somebody knows where you're headed. The water systems also present some of the world's best sportfishing opportunities for salmon and rainbow trout; anglers come from around

the world to stay at wilderness fishing lodges here. Hiking is difficult because of dense brush, except for the uppermost part of the park, where tundra makes on-land travel easier.

★ Tikchik Narrows Lodge

FISHING | This remote lodge caters primarily to sportfishing enthusiasts looking for comfortable housing and delicious gourmet-style meals—and who can afford to pay the princely sum for a week's stay. Packages at the picturesque, waterfront lodge within Tikchik State Park include guided fishing trips via the lodge's floatplane fleet to some of the best headwaters that Alaska—and maybe the world—has to offer. The lodge is owned by Bud Hodson, a guide in the region for decades, also rents kayaks and rafts and provides an air-taxi service into the park's most remote corners. Family-friendly vacation packages are also available. ☎ 907/243–8450 ⊕ www.tikchiklodge.com ✉ From $8700 per week.

Katmai National Park and Preserve

100 miles southeast of Wood-Tikchik, 290 miles southwest of Anchorage.

Katmai is the most famous of Alaska's remote parks for two simple reasons: bears and volcanoes. Although Katmai sees only a fraction of the number of visitors to Denali National Park, its name echoes with mythical force to Alaskans. Katmai is true wilderness Alaska, a place many locals long to visit and very few have. Remote and expensive (even by Alaska travel standards) to reach, with limited visitor facilities (except for a few very nice wilderness lodges), once there you have Alaska to yourself. The price is certainly steep, but guaranteed to buy the trip of a lifetime. Katmai's 4 million acres offer up plenty of opportunities for wildlife viewing and an extraordinary perspective on the awesome power of volcanoes—still active throughout the park. The 1912 eruption sequence was one of the most powerful ever recorded and covered more than 46,000 square miles with ash. Today, this wild, remote area at the northern end of the Alaska Peninsula is home to almost 30 species of mammals, including moose, foxes, lynx, and wolves, all sharing the landscape with bears fishing for salmon from the banks of streams and rivers and along the coast.

GETTING HERE AND AROUND

No roads lead to Katmai National Park. To get to it, at the base of the Alaska Peninsula, it's easiest to arrange a flight from Anchorage, where you can take in the amazing scenery along Cook Inlet, rimmed by the lofty, snowy peaks of the Alaska Range (check out ⊕ www.alaskaair.com for fares and schedules). They land at **King Salmon,** near fish-famous Bristol Bay, where passengers transfer to smaller floatplanes for the 20-minute hop to **Naknek Lake** and **Brooks Camp.** Travel to Brooks from King Salmon is also possible by boat. You are required to check in at the park ranger station, next to Brooks Lodge, for a mandatory bear-safety talk (for the safety of both you and the bears).

◉ Sights

Brooks Falls and Camp

NATURE PRESERVE | At this immensely popular spot, viewing platforms overlook a 6-foot-high cascade where salmon leap to try to make it upstream to spawn while bears stand on the edge of the falls to catch them. An access trail and boardwalk are separated from the river to avoid confrontations with bears. Here, you can see brown bears fishing in July and September. Unlike McNeil River, no special permits are required, though there is a $10 day-use fee at Brooks. Bears are also common along the park's outer coast, where they graze on sedge flats, dig clams and sculpin on the beach at low tide, and fish for salmon. Even

on slow bear days it's a beautiful place to be. Ducks fill the park's rivers, lakes, and outer coast, fussing over nesting space with huge whistling swans, loons, grebes, gulls, and shorebirds. Bald eagles perch on rocky pinnacles by the sea. More than 40 species of songbirds make the area their home during the short spring and summer, and if you fall back into big-mammal mood, Steller's sea lions and a couple of species of seals hang out on the rock outcroppings. From Brooks Lodge, a daily tour bus with a naturalist aboard makes the 23-mile trip through the park to the Valley Overlook. Hikers can walk the 1.5-mile trail for a closer look at the pumice-covered valley floor. (Some consider the return climb strenuous.) ☎ 907/246–4250 King Salmon Visitor Center, 907/246–3305 park headquarters ⊕ www.nps.gov/katm.

Brooks River

NATIONAL/STATE PARK | The Katmai area is one of Alaska's premier sportfishing regions. You can fish for rainbow trout and salmon at the Brooks River, though seasonal closures have been put in place to prevent conflicts with bears and sometimes only fly-fishing is permitted; check locally for the latest information. For those who would like to venture farther into the park, seek out the two other backcountry lodges, or contact fishing-guide services based in King Salmon. A short walk up the Brooks River brings you to Brooks Falls. ☎ 907/246–3305 ⊕ www.nps.gov/katm.

Katmai National Park and Preserve

NATIONAL/STATE PARK | This active volcanic park provides vital habitat for salmon and thousands of brown bears, but Katmai was first established as a monument in 1918 to protect and study the 1912 eruption of Novarupta. Now, people head to the park to watch bears catch salmon from yards away, hike the Valley of Ten Thousand Smokes, and explore the archaeological sites and natural wonders of 4 million acres of mountains, waterways, and coastline. Katmai

officially became a national park in 1980.
☎ *907/246–4250 King Salmon Visitor's Center, 907/246–3305 park headquarters* ⊕ *www.nps.gov/katm/index.htm.*

★ McNeil River State Game Sanctuary

NATURE PRESERVE | At the northern end of the Alaska Peninsula, this game sanctuary protects the world's largest gathering of brown bears. Since 1967, it has earned a reputation as the finest bear-viewing locale in North America, and likely the world. The main focus is where bears come to feed on chum salmon returning to spawn. During the peak of the chum run (July to mid-August) dozens of brown bears congregate at the falls to hunt for and eat fish. As many as 70 bears, including cubs, have been observed along the river in a single day while more than 100 bears roam along the river each season. The bears will play, eat, nap, and nurse cubs within 15 to 20 feet of the falls viewing pad (sometimes even closer) allowing visitors to learn firsthand that bears smell like very wet dogs, at least when fishing. The sanctuary staff make sure that visitors behave in a nonthreatening, nonintrusive way around these wild animals. Only 10 people a day can visit the bear-viewing sites from June 7 through August 25, always accompanied by armed staff. Because demand is so high, an annual drawing is held in mid-March to determine permit winners (Alaska residents get preferential treatment in the lottery). Applications must be received by March 1 to be eligible. Nearly all visitors fly into McNeil Sanctuary on floatplanes, with most arranging air-taxi flights out of Homer on the Kenai Peninsula. Once in the sanctuary, all travel is on foot and closely guided by state biologists. ✉ *Anchorage* ☎ *907/267–2189 Alaska Dept. of Fish and Game, Wildlife Conservation* ⊕ *www.adfg.state.ak.us.*

🏃 Activities

The Katmai region offers an abundance of recreational opportunities, including sportfishing, bear viewing, hiking through the Valley of Ten Thousand Smokes, running the wild and scenic Alagnak River and other clear-water streams, flightseeing, exploring the outer coast, and backpacking through remote and seldom-visited backcountry wilderness.

FLIGHTSEEING

Katmai Air Services

TOUR—SPORTS | This outfitter offers flightseeing tours to the Valley of 10,000 Smokes and other areas of the park, along with one-day bear-viewing trips and charter flights from Anchorage and King Salmon to Brooks Camp. ✉ *4125 Aircraft Dr., Anchorage* ☎ *800/544–0551 reservations, 907/243–5448 in Anchorage* ⊕ *www.katmailand.com* 🖅 *From $275.*

Northwind Aviation

TOUR—SPORTS | This Homer-based air taxi company offers charter flights to Katmai's outer coast and McNeil River in small aircrafts that are limited to three guests. ✉ *1184 Lakeshore Dr., Homer* ☎ *907/235–7482* ⊕ *www.northwindak. com* 🖅 *From $700.*

WILDLIFE VIEWING

Alaska Alpine Adventures–Katmai

ADVENTURE TOURS | This year-round adventure outfitter offers an array of 5- to 10-day excursions into Katmai with packages that include hiking and even family wilderness trips. They also do tours in the Alaska National Wildlife Refuge, Gates of the Arctic National Park, and Aniakchak. ☎ *877/525–2577* ⊕ *www.alaskaalpineadventures.com.*

Katmailand

TOUR—SPORTS | This company offers bear-viewing and fishing packages to Katmai National Park, and trips to Katmai's Valley of 10,000 Smokes. ✉ *4125 Aircraft Dr., Anchorage* ☎ *907/243–5448, 877/708–1391* ⊕ *www.katmailand.com* 🖅 *From $875.*

Alaskan Volcanoes

Earthquakes and Eruptions

Alaskans inhabited Katmai's eastern edge for at least 9,000 years, according to archaeological sites. but on the morning of June 1, 1912, everything changed. After five days of violent earthquakes, the 2,700-foot **Novarupta** blew its top, erupting steadily for the next 60 hours. Rivers of white-hot ash poured into the valley. A foot of ash fell on Kodiak Island, 100 miles away, and more than 46,000 square miles of territory ended up under at least an inch of ash, winds carrying yet more ash to eastern Canada and as far as Texas. While Novarupta was belching away, another explosion occurred 6 miles east. The mountaintop peak of **Mt. Katmai** collapsed, creating a chasm almost 3 miles long and 2 miles wide. The molten andesite that held up Mt. Katmai rushed through newly created fissures to Novarupta and was spewed out. Over 2½ days, more than 7 cubic miles of volcanic material were ejected, and the green valley lay under 700 feet of ash. Miraculously, the people who called this remote region home made it out safely, and no one was killed.

Volcanic Valley Is Born

By 1916 things had cooled off sufficiently to allow scientists to explore the area. A National Geographic Society expedition led by Dr. Robert F. Griggs reached the valley and found it full of steaming fumaroles (holes in the volcanic terrain that emit smoke), creating a moonlike landscape. The report on what Griggs dubbed the **Valley of Ten Thousand Smokes** inspired Congress in 1918 to declare the valley and the surrounding wilderness a national monument. Steam spouted in thousands of fountains from the smothered streams and springs beneath the ash and gave the valley its name. Although the steam has virtually stopped, an eerie sense of earth forces at work remains, and several nearby volcanoes still smolder, or even threaten to blow every couple of years. Anchorage's airport will sometimes get shut down by smoke or ash from the peninsula's active volcanoes.

Katmai Today

The Alaska Native people never returned to their traditional village sites after the eruption, though many now live in nearby communities. They are joined by sightseers, anglers, hikers, and other outdoors enthusiasts who migrate every summer to the Katmai region where the fish and wildlife are plentiful, and a few "smokes" still drift through the volcano-sculpted valley.

Ouzel Expeditions

FISHING | This outfitter does six-day fishing and bear-viewing trips on American Creek in Katmai ($4,800), as well as trips to the Arctic National Wildlife Refuge, the Brooks Range, the Kongakut and Hula Hula Rivers, and Kamchatka. ☎ 907/783–2216, 800/825–8196 ⊕ www.ouzel.com.

🛏 Hotels

All five lodges listed here are on inholdings (privately owned land inside a protected area) within Katmai National Park. Three are inland; Katmai Wilderness Lodge and Hallo Bay Bear Lodge are on the remote outer coast.

★ Brooks Lodge

$$$$ | B&B/INN | Initially a fishing camp, this lodge sits in the midst of Katmai's amazing fish habitat (featuring rainbow trout, lake trout, arctic grayling, and salmon), not to mention its proximity to brown bear viewing and tours of the Valley of 10,000 Smokes. **Pros:** private facilities; bear viewing at Brooks Falls; amazing access to fishing. **Cons:** expensive; requires flying or boating in; bunk beds only. $ *Rooms from: $1000* ☎ *907/243–5448, 877/708–1391* ⊕ *www.katmailand.com/brooks-lodge* ☽ *Closed Sept.–May* ⇄ *16 cabins* ⦿ *No meals.*

Grosvenor Lodge

$$$$ | B&B/INN | Once you arrive by floatplane at Grosvenor Lodge, you have access by motorboat to numerous rivers and streams filled with trout, char, pike, and salmon. **Pros:** great access to fishing; accessible to two spawning streams; only four to six guests at a time. **Cons:** bathhouse is outside the cabin; absolute seclusion not for everyone; often booked far in advance. $ *Rooms from: $3775* ☎ *907/243–5448, 877/708–1391* ⊕ *www.katmailand.com/lodging/grosvenor.html* ☽ *Closed Sept.–May* ⇄ *3 cabins* ⦿ *All meals.*

Hallo Bay Bear Lodge

$$$$ | RESORT | At the northern end of the bay, this is an eco-friendly camp that has been running half-day to multiday bear-viewing trips for more than two decades. **Pros:** truly wild bear viewing; eco-friendly, with solar and wind power and composting toilets; gourmet meals. **Cons:** rustic; shared bathrooms; flights depart from Homer only. $ *Rooms from: $1299* ☎ *907/235–2237, 907/435–7329 Homer office* ⊕ *www.hallobay.com* ☽ *Closed Oct.–mid-May* ⇄ *5 cabins* ⦿ *All meals.*

Katmai Wilderness Lodge

$$$$ | B&B/INN | Built on land owned by the Russian Orthodox Church, this rustic but modern log cabin lodge on Kukak Bay straddles the rugged outer coast of

Campgrounds in Katmai 🛏

Brooks Campground. This National Park Service campground is a short walk from Brooks Lodge, where campers can pay to eat and shower. Designated cooking and eating shelters, latrines, well water, and a storage cache to protect food from the ever-present brown bears are available. It's also surrounded by an electric wire fence. Reservations are required. ☎ *907/246–3305 for info, 877/444–6777 for reservations* ⊕ *www.recreation.gov.*

Katmai National Park, along the shores of Kukak Bay. Mountains, coastal flats, and the waters of Shelikof Strait surround the lodge, where guests stay in private bedrooms with baths and gather to eat gourmet meals in the dining room or, if the weather holds, on outdoor decks. **Pros:** bear viewing guarantee; private rooms and bathrooms; hot showers. **Cons:** pricey; you have to get to Kodiak first; minimum three-night stay. $ *Rooms from: $4160* ☎ *800/488–8767, 907/486–8767 in Alaska* ⊕ *www.katmai-wilderness.com* ☽ *Closed Oct.–mid-May* ⇄ *7 cabins* ⦿ *All-inclusive.*

Kulik Lodge

$$$$ | B&B/INN | Positioned along the gin-clear Kulik River, between Nonvianuk and Kulik lakes, this remote wilderness lodge is reachable only by floatplane. **Pros:** great rainbow-trout fishing; modern facilities; complimentary drinks when telling fish stories. **Cons:** need to bring your own tackle; very fishing focused; minimum stay required. $ *Rooms from: $3495* ☎ *907/243–5448, 877/708–1391* ⊕ *www.katmailand.com/kulik-lodge* ☽ *Closed Sept.–May* ⇄ *12 cabins* ⦿ *All meals.*

Aniakchak National Monument and Preserve

100 miles southwest of Katmai National Park.

Need to check "Visit active volcano" off your bucket list? A trip to Aniakchak will do the trick. The journey to this amazing natural landmark and its enormous caldera is not for the faint of heart or those looking for some laid-back fun in the Alaska sun. The terrain is just as rugged (and bear filled) as it was when the Aniakchak volcano first erupted 3,500 years ago. Travel options to this remote yet phenomenal national park haven't changed much either.

GETTING HERE AND AROUND

Aniakchak National Monument and Preserve is expensive to reach, even by remote Alaska standards. The only easy access is by air, usually from the town of King Salmon. Thus, few people visit this spectacular place—and those who do are likely to have the caldera all to themselves. Needless to say, coming here gives you permanent bragging rights about what you did on your Alaska vacation.

ESSENTIALS

VISITOR INFORMATION Aniakchak National Monument and Preserve Headquarters ☎ *907/246–3305* ⊕ *www.nps.gov/ania.*

◉ Sights

Aniakchak National Monument and Preserve

NATURE PRESERVE | Some 586,000 acres of protected land was established by Congress in 1980 to mark the significance of Aniakchak, an extraordinary living volcano that rises to the south of Katmai. Towering more than 4,400 feet above the landscape, the volcano also has one of the largest calderas in the world, with a diameter averaging 6 miles across and 2,500 feet deep. Although Aniakchak last erupted in 1931, the explosion that formed the enormous crater occurred before history was written. Because the area is not glaciated, geologists place the blowup after the last Ice Age. Aniakchak is wild and forbidding country, with a climate that brews mist, clouds, and serious wind much of the year. The caldera is so big that it can create its own local weather patterns, and it really seems to like the bad stuff. Although the Aniakchak River (which drains Surprise Lake) is floatable, it has stretches of Class III and IV white water navigable only by expert river runners, and you must travel through open ocean waters to reach the nearest community, Chignik Bay (or get picked up by plane, along the coast). In other words, this is not a place for the unprepared or untested. An alternate way to enjoy Aniakchak is to wait for a clear day and fly to it in a small plane that will land you on the caldera floor or on Surprise Lake. But there are no trails, campgrounds, ranger stations, or other visitor facilities here, and it is some serious bear country. ⊕ *www.nps.gov/ania.*

☆ Activities

Alaska Alpine Adventures–Aniakchak

ADVENTURE TOURS | This year-round adventure outfitter offers a 12-day hiking and rafting excursion into Aniakchak Preserve during the summer. Alaska Alpine also operates adventure tours in the Alaska National Wildlife Refuge, Gates of the Arctic National Park, and Katmai National Park. ☎ *877/525–2577* ⊕ *www.alaskaalpineadventures.com* ✉ *From $5495.*

Branch River Air Service

FISHING | Located in King Salmon, Branch River Air Service—"Best in the Bush" is their slogan—offers flightseeing around Bristol Bay and Katmai National Park, as well as customizable charter flights to various remote locations on the Alaska Peninsula, including Aniakchak National Preserve. They will also arrange fishing and bear-viewing trips. ⊠ *King Salmon* ☎ *907/246–3437 June–Sept., 907/248– 3539 Oct.–May* ⊕ *www.branchriverair. com.*

Ouzel Expeditions

FISHING | This experienced outfitter guides weeklong fishing and float trips in Aniakchak National Monument and Preserve. The exursion starts at the caldera and ends in the Pacific ocean. They also do trips in Katmai National Park, Yukon Delta Wildlife Refuge, and Togiak Wildlife Refuge. Outside Southwest Alaska, Ouzel also offers wilderness, white-water rafting, and fishing trips in the Alaska National Wildlife Refuge and other locations on the North Slope and in the Brooks Range. ☎ *907/783–2216, 800/825–8196* ⊕ *www. ouzel.com* ⊠ *From $6150.*

Becharof and Alaska Peninsula National Wildlife Refuges

Adjacent to Aniakchak National Monument and Preserve, 250 miles to 450 miles southwest of Anchorage.

In addition to Aniakchak National Monument and Preserve, the enormous Becharof and Alaska Peninsula National Wildlife Refuges are also prime areas for volcano viewing. Couple these volcano-laden horizons with hundreds of species of birds, fish, and land mammals, and your Alaska experience will be hard to beat. Just be sure to dress appropriately for climate extremes.

GETTING HERE AND AROUND

No visitor facilities are available here, and access is only by boat or plane. Most visitors begin their trips in King Salmon and use guides or outfitters.

ESSENTIALS

VISITOR INFORMATION Becharof National Wildlife Refuge Visitor Center ⊠ *4 Bear Rd., King Salmon* ☎ *907/246–3339*

headquarters, 907/246–4250 visitor center ⊕ www.fws.gov/refuge/becharof.

Sights

Becharof and Alaska Peninsula National Wildlife Refuges

NATURE PRESERVE | Stretching along the southern edge of the Alaska Peninsula, these two refuges encompass nearly 6 million acres of towering mountains, glacial lakes, broad tundra valleys, and coastal fjords. Volcanoes dominate the landscape—14 in all, 9 of them active—and the waters are known for their salmon and trophy grayling. The world-record grayling, nearly 5 pounds (most weigh a pound or less), was caught at Ugashik Narrows in 1981. Remote and rugged, with the peninsula's signature unpredictable weather, the Becharof and Alaska Peninsula refuges draw mostly anglers and hunters. Backpackers, river runners, and mountain climbers also occasionally visit. ☎ *907/ 246–3339 King Salmon office* ⊕ *www.fws.gov/refuge/Becharof/ about.html.*

Aleutian Islands

The Aleutians begin 540 miles southwest of Anchorage and stretch more than 1,400 miles.

Separating the North Pacific Ocean from the Bering Sea, the Aleutian Islands are not a single sequence of islands. Actually, they're a superchain, made of up eight smaller island groups—the Andreanof, Delarof, Fox, Four Mountain, Near, Rat, Shumagin, and Sanak islands. In all, this adds up to more than 275 islands, stretching from the Alaska Peninsula in a southwesterly arc toward Japan. The islands are volcanic in origin, treeless, and alternate between towering (and frequently smoking) volcanic cones, and high tablelands. Separating the islands is some of the wildest, deepest water anywhere: on the Pacific side of the chain the water can be more than 25,000 feet deep, and the north side's Bering Canyon is twice as long as the Grand Canyon and twice as deep, bottoming out at 10,600 feet below the water's surface. The Aleutian Islands and surrounding coastal waters make up one of the most biologically rich areas in Alaska, harboring abundant seabird, marine mammal, and fish populations, the latter supporting one of the world's busiest fishing fleets.

Before the Russians arrived in the mid-1700s, the islands were dotted with Aleut villages, a total population of perhaps 3,000 people; within 100 years that number had dropped to maybe 200 through disease and war. Today's Alaska Native communities include **Nikolski,** on Umnak Island; **Atka**, on Atka Island; and **Cold Bay,** at the peninsula's tip. Like everybody in the Aleutians, the descendants of the original inhabitants mostly work at commercial fishing or in canneries and as expert guides for those who hunt and fish. The settlements are quite small, accommodations are scarce, and year-round travel options are very limited.

Visitors aren't allowed on Shemya Island, which has a remote U.S. Air Force base, without special permission. Because of downsizing, the military has closed its Adak operation, and the base provides the core infrastructure for what now is a small coastal community and commercial fishing port.

Unalaska/Dutch Harbor

On Unalaska Island and neighboring Amaknak Island, the city of Unalaska is by far the most popular destination in the Aleutian Islands. (Dutch Harbor is not a separate town, merely a harbor, albeit a very large one.) Although Unalaska is sometimes called "the Crossroads of the Aleutians," even by Alaska standards people who live here are living remote. Usually referred to simply as "Dutch" (or, by people who spend winter here,

The Alaska Marine Highway System

This much-loved form of Alaskan transport is best known for its routes along the Inside Passage. In summer these ferries also depart from Homer, in Southcentral, and pass by Kodiak on the three-plus-day trip to Unalaska/Dutch Harbor. Though slow-paced and far from luxurious, the ferry (☎ 800/642–0066 ⊕ www.ferryalaska.com) is an unforgettable way to see Southwest's dramatic landscape.

"the gulag"), the islands of Unalaska are connected by a bridge that spans a narrow channel between the two landmasses. (Locals playfully call the span the "Bridge to the Other Side.") Despite the often-harsh weather—this region is known as the "Cradle of Storms" for good reason—the Aleut people and their ancestors have occupied these islands and others in the Aleutians for thousands of years. Today, Unalaska is the region's tourism center and venue for the annual Heart of the Aleutians Festival. The town's Parks, Culture and Recreation department (PCR) manages eight public parks and an impressive community center, where visitors are also welcome to use the indoor and outdoor sports facilities, and various arts and cultural amenities They also publish an activity guide that includes local events. Dutch Harbor, best known from the Discovery Channel's hit show *Deadliest Catch,* is one of the busiest fishing ports in the world, processing a billion—yes, billion—pounds of fish and crab each year. Scattered around both islands are reminders of history, specifically the "Aleutian Campaign" in World War II: the Japanese bombed Dutch Harbor in June

1942 (unexploded ordnance may still be out there, so don't handle any odd metal objects you see while hiking), and you can still explore concrete bunkers built into mountainsides, gun batteries, and a partially sunken ship left over from the war.

GETTING HERE AND AROUND
Pen Air and Grant Aviation provide daily flights from Anchorage to Unalaska. Alaska Marine Highway ferries sail from Homer to Dutch Harbor once a month, May through September, with a journey time of 3½ days; Dutch Harbor welcomes several cruise ships in season.

ESSENTIALS
VISITOR INFORMATION Department of Parks, Culture & Recreation (PCR) ⊠ *37 S. 5th St., Unalaska* ☎ *907/581–1297* ⊕ *www.ci.unalaska.ak.us/parksrec.* **Unalaska–Dutch Harbor Convention and Visitors Bureau (CVB)** ⊠ *5 E. Broadway Ave., Unalaska* ☎ *907/581–2612, 877/581–2612* ⊕ *www.ci.unalaska.ak.us/community/page/convention-and-visitor-bureau.*

◉ Sights

It's worth the trip here on the ferry purely for the scenery along the way, but when travelers finally reach the islands they discover a surprisingly gentle landscape of tawny, rolling hills sheltering a town that is built for work, not beauty. Which is not to say the town lacks pretty things; on a sunny day the natural scenery is glorious. The island's extensive trails are a hiking and mountain-running dream. Don't worry about opening hours: if the ferry (or a cruise ship) is in, the town's attractions are open.

Aleutian World War II National Historic Area and Visitor Center
HISTORIC SITE | Through old newspapers, memorabilia, video footage, and exhibits about the "Aleutian Campaign," this quaint museum outside the Unalaska Airport preserves bits of history from Alaska's little-known role in the war.

The Aleutian Islands saw heavy fighting through much of World War II; at the peak of the war, more than 60,000 servicemen were stationed here in the farthest and most brutal reaches of the United States. On June 3 and 4, 1942, the Japanese bombed Dutch Harbor and landed in the far reaches of the Aleutians a few days later. The Japanese military forces took entire villages and outposts captive in Kiska and Attu, with many of the captured Americans transported to Japan as prisoners of war. The center is within easy walking distance of the ferry terminal. ⊠ *2716 Airport Beach Rd., Unalaska* ☎ *907/581–9944* ⊕ *www.nps.gov/aleu/details.htm.*

Holy Ascension of Our Lord Cathedral
RELIGIOUS SITE | Aside from the spectacular mountains and endless seas, the most dramatic man-made attraction in Unalaska is undoubtedly the Holy Ascension Russian Orthodox Church. The blue, onion-dome chapel right on the edge of Iliuluk Bay is arguably the most perfect Russian church left in Alaska, and possibly the most scenic church anywhere. The extant buildings date to the 1890s, although there has been a church on the site since 1808. Now a National Historic Landmark, Holy Ascension is one of the oldest cruciform-style Russian churches in the nation, and it houses one of Alaska's richest collections of Russian artifacts, religious icons, and artwork. Next to the church is the Bishop's House, which is undergoing continuing restoration. A walk in the graveyard between the two buildings shows the full history of the area: the Aleut culture, sailing history, and the graves of Orthodox parishioners oriented to face the church. Tours of the church can be arranged through the Unalaska-Dutch Harbor Convention and Visitors Bureau. ⊠ *W. Broadway Ave., between 1st and 2nd Sts., Unalaska* ☎ *907/581–5883 parish.*

Museum of the Aleutians

MUSEUM | FAMILY | This small but remarkable museum highlights the cultural, military, and natural history of the Aleutian and Pribilof islands located to the north in the Bering Sea. Find original drawings from Captain Cook's third voyage, a traditional gut parka, and repartriated artifacts from Aleut culture that were once scattered around the world. The exhibits give small glimpses into how the Aleut people lived on the islands for centuries while other artifacts show the impact of the Russian occupation, the gold rush, World War II, and Unalaska/Dutch Harbor's continued importance as a global fishing port. In the summer, the museum sponsors archaeological digs as well as periodic lectures by visiting scientists, historians, and researchers. ⊠ *314 Salmon Way, Unalaska* ☎ *907/581–5150* ⊕ *www.aleutians.org* ⊡ *$7* ⊙ *Closed Sun. and Mon.*

World War II Military Installations

HISTORIC SITE | The impact of World War II on Unalaska/Dutch Harbor is visible practically everywhere you look here: remnants of war bunkers, tunnels, Quonset huts, pillboxes, and other military relics are scattered throughout town. You can explore these pieces of history hands-on when at Bunker Hill, Memorial Park, Unalaska Lake, Mt. Ballyhoo, and other sites. ⊠ *Unalaska.*

🏃 Activities

Miss Alyssa Bering Sea Excursions

CLIMBING/MOUNTAINEERING | Reserve the *Miss Alyssa* and the lands and waters surrounding Unalaska become a true playground. This charter vessel can take up to five passengers on epic backcountry skiing and climbing adventures, whale-watching and scuba-diving expeditions, and halibut fishing trips. The accommodating and experienced crew welcomes other ideas for maritime adventures, too. Day and overnight packages include all meals, gear, and even

drinks. ⊠ *Unalaska* ☎ *907/581–1386, 907/581–2386* ⊕ *www.missalyssa.com* ⊡ *From $1800 a day.*

Ounalashka Corporation

HIKING/WALKING | Much of the land surrounding Unalaska/Dutch Harbor is owned by the Ounalashka Corporation. Before hiking, camping, or exploring off the main roads, purchase a land-use permit online or from the Alaska Native corporation office just around the corner from the Grand Aleutian. You can choose individual or family permits for a day, week, season, or year. ⊠ *400 Salmon Way, Unalaska* ⊕ *www.ounalashka.com/land-use.*

Wilderness Birding Adventures

GUIDED TOURS | The Homer-based outfitter runs small trips to Unalaska/Dutch Harbor in August with the goal of spotting the evasive whiskered auklet. Bringing passionate birders and wilderness enthusiasts to remote locations across Alaska (plus Bhutan) is their speciality. Their guides can also do combined birding, hiking, and river rafting trips. ⊠ *40208 Alpenglow Circle, Homer* ☎ *907/299–3937* ⊕ *www.wildernessbirding.com.*

🍴 Restaurants

Amelia's Restaurant

$$ | INTERNATIONAL | This brightly colored all-day café next door to the Safeway has something for everyone with enormous portions of breakfast fare, burgers, sandwiches, Asian options, house-made milk shakes, and what passes for Mexican this far from the mainland. Strands of beads hang from the ceiling and various other kitschy items cover the walls, in addition to a couple of TVs, giving you a lot to look at while you wait, although it's better still to grab a window seat for a nice view of the Bering Sea. **Known for:** big hearty breakfasts; view of the Bering sea; pretty decent Mexican dishes. Ⓢ *Average main: $22* ⊠ *Biorka Dr. and Airport Beach Rd., Unalaska* ☎ *907/581–2800.*

Cape Cheerful Lounge

$$ | AMERICAN | This casual bar off the main lobby of the Grand Aleutian Hotel is the perfect spot to grab a bite to eat and a cold beer after a long day exploring. The menu is largely the same as the fancier Chart Room directly upstairs, featuring steaks, burgers, salads, and sandwiches, and the bar has a surprisingly good selection of draught and craft beers. **Known for:** standard pub fare; Friday night barbeques; open-mike nights. $ *Average main: $20 ⊠ Grand Aleutian Hotel, 1745 Airport Beach Rd., Dutch Harbor* ☎ *907/581–7130* ⊕ *www.grandaleutian. com* ⊗ *No lunch Mon.–Sat.*

Chart Room

$$$$ | AMERICAN | By far the fanciest restaurant in Unalaska, the Chart Room serves food that very nearly parallels its spectacular views of the surrounding mountains and Margaret Bay. On most nights it's not difficult to grab a table, but consider planning ahead and making a reservation for the famous Wednesday-night seafood buffet or the Sunday brunch buffet. **Known for:** Wednesday seafood buffets; incredible views when the weather's clear; king crab entrées. $ *Average main: $35 ⊠ Grand Aleutian Hotel, 1745 Airport Beach Rd., 2nd fl., Dutch Harbor* ☎ *907/581–7120* ⊕ *www. grandaleutian.com* ⊗ *No lunch weekdays.*

Margaret Bay Café

$$ | AMERICAN | With its lovely waterfront and mountain views, this bright and airy café is a great place to start the day with a traditional American breakfast or weekday lunch. A nice salad bar and litany of other hot and cold items, including sandwiches, bowls, salads and sides, offers something for everyone. **Known for:** crab pot omelet; tasty smoothies; filling lunch bowls. $ *Average main: $15 ⊠ Grand Aleutian Hotel, 1745 Airport Beach Rd., Dutch Harbor* ☎ *907/581–7122* ⊕ *www. grandaleutian.com* ⊗ *Closed Sun. No dinner.*

Hotels

Grand Aleutian Hotel

$$$ | HOTEL | The airy, three-story atrium lobby with a large stone fireplace lends a European chalet sensibility to a hotel with carpeted, brightly lighted rooms decorated with Alaska artwork, many with wonderful views overlooking the water. **Pros:** very clean; helpful and enthusiastic staff; bay-view rooms. **Cons:** interior is a bit generic; doesn't feel very Alaskan; less likely to connect with locals. $ *Rooms from: $199 ⊠ 498 Salmon Way, Box 921169, Dutch Harbor* ☎ *866/581–3844, 907/581–3844* ⊕ *www. grandaleutian.com* ⊟ *No credit cards* ⇆ *116 rooms* ⎢⎥ *No meals.*

Nightlife

Harbor View Bar and Grill

BARS/PUBS | Views, drinks, and a variety of burgers, sandwiches, chili, and standard bar food make the Harbor View Bar and Grill a perfect late night hangout spot. Like with most sports bars, you'll get big screens, pool tables, darts, and live music on weekends. ⊠ *76–94 Gilman Way, Dutch Harbor* ☎ *907/581–7389* ⊕ *www.grandaleutian.com.*

Pribilof Islands

200 miles north of the Aleutian Islands, 800 miles southwest of Anchorage.

What the Bristol Bay region is to fly-fishing, the Pribilof Islands are to birding. Unfortunately, "the Pribs" are quite remote and visiting requires a bit of planning as well as patience and flexibility, since even the best-laid plans fall victim to Mother Nature's whims. Fortunately, once there, you'll likely encounter a medley of people on the hunt for the exact same thing as you: a glimpse of some of the rarest birds on the planet.

GETTING HERE AND AROUND

For most travelers it is much easier and more efficient to sign up for package tours that arrange air travel from Anchorage, lodging, ground transportation on the islands, and guided activities. It can be nearly, if not completely, impossible to arrange such things after you arrive. Guest accommodations in the Pribilofs are very limited, with lodgings only on St. George and St. Paul. The best way to hop between islands is by air on Pen Air, but both islands are notorious fog magnets; you should never plan on getting out quite as scheduled.

ESSENTIALS

AIRLINE CONTACT Pen Air ☎ *907/771–2640, 907/771–2599 charter flight reservations, 800/448–4226* ⊕ *www.penair.com.*

◉ Sights

Pribilof Islands

ISLAND | Rising out of the surging waters of the Bering Sea, the Pribilof Islands are a misty, fog-bound breeding ground of seabirds and northern fur seals, consisting of five islets, all tiny, green, and treeless with rippling belts of lush grass contrasting with volcanic rocks. In early summer, seals come home from far Pacific waters to mate, and the larger islands, St. Paul and St. George, are overwhelmed with frenzied activity. Although St. Paul and St. George are less than 50 miles apart, the island group itself is a 1,600-mile round-trip from Anchorage, over the massive snowy peaks of the Alaska Peninsula and north of the rocky islands of the Aleutian chain. Few visitors go to the Pribilofs, save commercial fishermen and the most dedicated wildlife watchers. Yet together, St. Paul and St. George islands are seasonal homes to hundreds of thousands of fur seals (about 80% of them on St. Paul) and nearly 250 species of birds. Some birds migrate from as far away as Argentina, whereas others are year-round residents.

Bird-Watching in the Bush ◉

Of special interest to birders are the rare vagrant birds of native Asian species, such as the Siberian rubythroat and Eurasian skylark, sometimes blown here by strong winds. But just for day-to-day birding, come here, see a red-legged kittiwake, and make birders back home green with envy.

Most spectacular of all is the islands' seabird population: each summer more than 2 million seabirds gather at traditional Pribilof nesting grounds; about 90% of them breed on St. George ⊕ *www.apiai.org.*

St. George Island

ISLAND | Though home to nearly 2 million nesting seabirds, St. George Island is rarely visited because no organized tours visit here, and accommodations are limited. People who live on St. Paul try to avoid going to St. George because of the weather. Avid bird and wildlife watchers will find plenty to feast the eye, however.

★ St. Paul Island

ISLAND | The largest of the Pribilof Islands at 40 square miles, St. Paul Island is home to the greatest concentration of northern fur seals in the world—500,000 of them—and more than 180 varieties of birds. Certainly it's hard to reach, but it's also a guaranteed treat for adventuresome naturalists. About 500 descendants of Aleut-Russians live in St. Paul year-round, and the community has many elements of Aleut culture, along with the SS. Peter and Paul Russian Orthodox church built in 1907. The local museum provides details on how the U.S. government once controlled seal hunting on the island. ⊕ *www.stpaulak.com.*

⚡ Activities

The Pribilofs are considered a birders' paradise for good reason: species that are seldom, if ever, seen elsewhere in North America frequently show up here, including an array of "Asian vagrants" blown here by westerly winds. Birders can expect to find all manner of shorebirds, waterfowl, and seabirds, including puffins, murres, red- and black-legged kittiwakes, plovers—the list goes on and on. Tour guides are usually hired for their birding skills, but will also show visitors the best places to view seals (well, the seals are kind of hard to miss, since a lot of the adolescent males hang out near the roads) and maybe the occasional whale.

St. Paul Island Tours
BIRD WATCHING | Owned by the Tanadgusix Native Corporation, this tour company takes visitors to St. Paul Island from May to October, with options that include round-trip airfare from Anchorage, ground transportation on St. Paul, lodging at the King Eider Hotel, and tours led by experienced naturalists. ⊠ *St. Paul Island* ☎ *877/424–5637* ⊕ *www.stpaulislandtour.com* ⌲ *From $2375.*

Wilderness Birding Adventures
BIRD WATCHING | This Homer-based operator takes small groups to the Pribilof Islands to see birds during their fall and spring migrations. Pricing includes flights to and from Anchorage, lodging, meals, and guides. The operator also takes travelers to remote locations across Alaska to sight birds and other wildlife. ⊠ *40208 Alpenglow Cir., Homer* ☎ *907/299–3937* ⊕ *www.wildernessbirding.com* ⌲ *From $4550.*

🛏 Hotels

Aikow Inn
$$$ | B&B/INN | Bird and wildlife watchers can get a singular experience at St. George's only hotel, a small, rustic building with a dark-wood interior and a mix of modern and vintage furniture. **Pros:** bird-watcher's paradise; close to seals and other wildlife; European inn flavor in remote Alaska setting. **Cons:** come ready for every weather condition possible, all at once; seals might keep light sleepers awake; must bring your own food. ⑤ *Rooms from: $220* ⊠ *St. George Island* ☎ *907/272–9886 Anchorage office, 907/859–2255 St. George office* ⊕ *www.tanaq.com* ⌲ *10 rooms* ⑩ *No meals.*

King Eider Hotel
$$$ | HOTEL | Close to birding spots and a mile from a seal rookery, the King Eider offers 40 rooms with basic amenities, lodge-style common areas, and a simple gift shop with limited hours. **Pros:** close to airport; proximity to wildlife; comfortable common areas. **Cons:** small rooms; unreliable Wi-Fi and cell service; thin walls between rooms. ⑤ *Rooms from: $250* ⊠ *St. Paul Island* ☎ *907/546–2477* ⊕ *www.stpaulislandtour.com/lodging-and-meals* ⌲ *40 rooms* ⑩ *No meals.*

Nome

540 miles northwest of Anchorage.

More than a century has passed since a great stampede for gold put a speck of wilderness now called Nome on the Alaska map, but gold mining and noisy saloons are still mainstays here. This frontier community on the icy Bering Sea once boasted 20,000 people during the gold stampede in the 1890s, but now has only 3,800 year-round residents. At first glance the town may come off as a collection of ramshackle houses and low-slung commercial buildings—like a vintage gold-mining camp or, because of the spooky, abandoned, monolithic microwave towers from World War II that sit atop Anvil Mountain, the set for an Arctic horror movie—but only a couple of streets back you'll find tidy, modern homes and charming, hospitable shopkeepers. In fact, Nome is one of Alaska's greatest places, very much itself, the kind of town where the grocery store

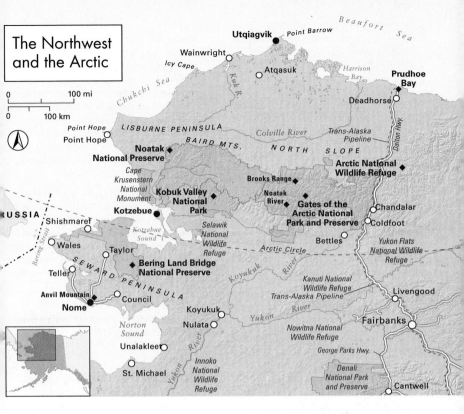

The Northwest
and the Arctic

0   100 mi

0   100 km

Beaufort Sea

Utqiagvik   Point Barrow

Wainwright

Icy Cape

Atqasuk

Harrison Bay

Prudhoe Bay

Chukchi Sea

Deadhorse

Point Hope   LISBURNE PENINSULA   Colville River   Trans-Alaska Pipeline

Point Hope   BAIRD MTS.   NORTH   SLOPE   Dalton Hwy

Noatak
National Preserve

Cape
Krusenstern
National
Monument

Kobuk Valley
National
Park

Kotzebue

Brooks Range

Noatak
River

Arctic National
Wildlife Refuge

Gates of the
Arctic National
Park and Preserve

Chandalar

Coldfoot

USSIA

Shishmaref

Kotzebue
Sound

Selawik
National
Wildlife
Refuge

Arctic Circle

Bettles

Yukon Flats
National Wildlife
Refuge

Wales

Taylor

Bering Strait

SEWARD   PENINSULA

Bering Land Bridge
National Preserve

Koyukuk
River

Kanuti National
Wildlife Refuge
Trans-Alaska Pipeline

Livengood

Teller

Anvil Mountain

Nome   Council

Koyukuk

Yukon River

Fairbanks

Norton
Sound

Nulata

Nowitna National
Wildlife Refuge

Unalakleet

George Parks Hwy.

St. Michael

Yukon River

Innoko
National
Wildlife
Refuge

Denali
National Park
and Preserve

Cantwell

sells ATVs next to the meat counter. "There's no place like Nome" is the city's slogan for good reason.

For centuries before Nome gained fame as a gold-rush town, nomadic Inupiaq Eskimos seasonally inhabited the area in hunting and fishing camps; an archaeological site south of town has the remains of some round pit houses that prove the locals didn't much like corners. The gold stampede—far, far richer than the more famous Klondike strike—occurred in the 1890s and was over relatively quickly, even though gold is still mined by both prospectors and open-pit mining productions.

Nome is best known, however, for the Iditarod Trail. Even though parts of the historic trail from Nome to Anchorage were long used as routes for the Native Eskimos and Athabascans, the full trail gained fame in 1925 when Nome was hit with an outbreak of diphtheria. There was no remedy in town, so the serum was ferried by the Alaska Railroad to Nenana, 250 miles from Anchorage, and then a 20-dog sled team ran it the remaining 674 miles in –50°F temperatures over five days and seven hours; Nome was saved. In 1973, in honor of the original Iditarod (a word derived from the Athabascan word *haiditarod,* meaning "a far, distant place"), an annual race for dog mushers was started. The now world-famous race begins in Anchorage and traverses snow and tundra for 1,049 miles, the odd 49 miles being added to commemorate Alaska's being the 49th state (the actual distance is give or take a few miles, of course; dogsleds don't come with odometers). Thousands of people converge in Nome each and every year (for some Lower-48ers, it's an annual tradition) to watch the dogs and mushers come over the finish line in March. Still more visitors come to Nome in the summer months to take advantage of the beautiful effulgent colors of wildflowers and green grass, its wildlife viewing and birding, and its marvelous end-of-the-world vibe. There is also still a steady flow of those looking to strike it rich panning for gold.

Though at first there doesn't seem to be much to this town on the edge of the Bering Sea, there are many relics of the past in and around the area. There are 44 abandoned gold dredges, enormous constructions of steel that are scattered from the outskirts of town to the surrounding miles of tundra beyond. Just east of town on the road out to Council, a quiet fishing village inhabited by many locals during the summer, you'll stumble across not only fantastic marshlands for birding, but also the Last Train to Nowhere—a railway built to haul gold that was never finished—quietly rusting away. In the opposite direction, northeast of Nome on the road to Taylor, is the Pilgrim Hot Springs, the site of an old settlement including the former Our Lady of Lourdes chapel and orphanage for Eskimo children during the 1918 influenza epidemic. And directly north of Nome is the beautiful Native village of Teller, a subsistence village in Grantley Harbor, which may have one of the most perfect locations in the world, set on a buttonhook spit in a sheltered bay. Teller made the world news in 1926, when Roald Amundsen landed his zeppelin *Norge* here after the first successful flight over the North Pole.

GETTING HERE AND AROUND

Just 165 miles from the coast of Siberia, Nome is considerably closer to Russia than to either Anchorage or Fairbanks. And though you'll find 300 miles of local road system branching out from the town that are well worth exploring, to get to Nome you must either fly or mush a team of sled dogs.

Alaska Airlines flies to Utqiaġvik (formerly Barrow) and Nome. Local arrangements are taken care of by ground operators. The Alaska Travel Industry Association can give tips on air travel and flightseeing opportunities throughout the Bush. From Nome, visitors can access Serpentine Hot Springs, in the Bering Land Bridge National Preserve, by charter plane. These hot springs are well maintained despite their location.

If you're set on doing your own driving, head to Stampede Ventures, which rents cars and vans of various types. ■ TIP→ **Be sure to fill up with gas in Nome, as there are no services once you leave town. And even if the gauge says the tank is full when you rent it, be sure to fill 'er up anyway—sometimes the gauge lies.**

ESSENTIALS

VEHICLE RENTAL Stampede Vehicle Rentals ⊠ *Aurora Inn and Suites, 302 Front St.* ☎ *907/443–3838, 800/354–4606* ⊕ *www. aurorainnome.com.*

VISITOR INFORMATION Nome Convention and Visitors Bureau ⊠ *301 Front St.* ☎ *907/443–6555* ⊕ *www.visitnomealaska.com.*

◉ Sights

Anvil Mountain

MOUNTAIN—SIGHT | Take a summer evening drive to the top of Anvil Mountain, near Nome, for a panoramic view of the old gold town and the Bering Sea. As this is the city's lone peak, anyone in town will be able to direct you there. Be sure to carry mosquito repellent. ⊠ *Nome.*

Carrie M. McClain Memorial Museum

MUSEUM | This museum, located in the Richard Foster Building, holds the long-term exhibit, "Nome: Hub of Cultures and Communities Across the Bering Strait," which centers on five Arctic themes and involves interactive environments such as an Inupiat skin boat and miner's tent, along with hands-on technology to help

Gold Mining in Alaska

The Golden Era

The region's gold stampede began in 1898, when three prospectors—known as the "Lucky Swedes"—struck rich deposits on Anvil Creek, about 4 miles from what became Nome. Their discovery was followed by the formation of the Cape Nome Mining District. More gold was found the following summer on the beaches of Nome, a place no one ever expected to find it. Ordinarily, placer gold sits on bedrock, but here thousands of winter melts washed it down to the sea.

Prospectors' Short-Lived Paradise

Word spread quickly to the south, right about the same time everybody was discovering that all the good spots for gold in the Klondike were staked. When the Bering Sea ice parted the next spring, ships from Puget Sound (in the Seattle area) arrived in Nome with eager stampeders, while miners who struck out in the Klondike arrived via the Yukon River to try again in Nome. An estimated 15,000 people landed in Nome between June and October 1900, bringing the area's population to more than 20,000. Dozens of gold dredges were hauled into the region to extract the metal from Seward Peninsula sands and gravels; more than 40 are still standing, though no longer operating (if you explore them, be sure to call out regularly, as warning to any bears that might have taken shelter inside). Among the gold-rush luminaries were Wyatt Earp, the old gunfighter from the O.K. Corral, who mined the gold of Nome the easy way: by opening a posh saloon and serving drinks to thirsty diggers. Also in Nome were Tex Rickard, the boxing promoter, who operated another Nome saloon (money made there later helped him build the third incarnation of Madison Square Garden, and helped him found the New York Rangers hockey team); and Rex Beach, whose first novel, *The Spoilers*, was based on the true story of government officials stealing gold from the hardworking miners (it was a best seller, letting even people warm and cozy down south experience the stampede).

Incorporation of Nome

The city of Nome was incorporated in 1901, which means it is now Alaska's oldest first-class city, with the oldest continuously operating school district. But the community's heyday lasted less than a decade; by the early 1920s the bulk of the region's gold had been mined, and only 820 or so people continued to live in Nome.

engage the narratives. A second space contains a changing contemporary exhibit that typically features a regional artist(s). ✉ *Richard Foster Bldg., 100 W. 7th Ave.* ☎ *907/443–6630* ⊕ *www.nomealaska.org* 🎫 *$7* ⊘ *Closed Sun.*

Nome Convention and Visitors Bureau
INFO CENTER | Stop by the Nome Convention and Visitors Bureau for a historic walking-tour map, a city map, and information on local activities. The offerings do a good job capturing Nome's historic and current role as a gateway to the vast expanses of western Alaska. ✉ *301 Front St.* ☎ *907/443–6555* ⊕ *www. visitnomealaska.com.*

Activities

Iditarod Trail Sled Dog Race

LOCAL SPORTS | Travelers come from around the world to watch dog teams pass under the burled arch as they finish the 1,049 miles from Anchorage to Nome in the Iditarod, or what's billed as "The Last Great Race." Alaska's most well-known sled dog race pulls in spectators (and mushers) from around the world to brave the Alaska winter to witness or to participate as racers and volunteers in this massive feat of endurance. Many visitors watch the dog teams take off from the ceremonial start in Anchorage, and then travel to the finish line in Nome to celebrate as teams cross the finish line. For sled dog race dates, starting times, and viewing locations, and anything else relating to "The Last Great Race," contact the Iditarod Trail Committee. ✉ *Nome* ☎ *907/376–5155* ⊕ *www. iditarod.com.*

★ Nome Discovery Tours

TOUR—SPORTS | If you want an engaging way to see Nome, look no further than Discovery's "Nome: The People and the Place" day tour. Spend the day with life-long and longtime Nome residents who provide entertaining, informative tours of local sites while offering an intimate perspective on Nome, its history, and its residents. Discovery operates two scheduled tours a day to coincide with arriving flights, but it will also do tours on request. ✉ *Nome* ☎ *907/443–2814* ⊕ *www.exploretours.com/day-trips/ nome-people-place* 🚗 *From $235.*

🍴 Restaurants

★ Bering Tea

$ | **CAFÉ** | This little coffee shop, in a repurposed old A-frame house, is an adorable place and the perfect spot for a breakfast sandwich or midday coffee. Tasty beverages and delicious home-made scones, cinnamon rolls, cupcakes, and muffins are a welcome respite from Nome's wind and industrial surroundings. **Known for:** fresh baked goods; good coffee and tea; hip hangout atmosphere. ⑤ *Average main: $10* ✉ *301 Bering St.* ☎ *907/387–0352* ⊗ *Closed Sun. yr-round and Mon. in winter.*

Milano's Pizzeria

$$ | **PIZZA** | **FAMILY** | This popular Front Street restaurant has a casual atmosphere and offers dine-in service as well as takeout from midmorning to late. They serve pizzas with a wide assortment of toppings, along with steak dinners and Japanese food (including sushi), Korean, and Italian food. **Known for:** arguably the best sushi in town; lots of local customers; good value pizza. ⑤ *Average main: $20* ✉ *2824 Front St.* ☎ *907/443–2924.*

Polar Café

$$ | **DINER** | **FAMILY** | If diner fare with a side of true Nome life is what you're after, this is the spot. Traditional hearty breakfast options are served all day, plus steak, chili, a modest salad bar, and unexpectedly delicious burgers, with everything clearly made to order. **Known for:** breakfast served all day; standard diner fare (with local clientele to match); views of the Bering Sea. ⑤ *Average main: $18* ✉ *224 Front St.* ☎ *907/443–5191.*

🛏 Hotels

Aurora Inn & Suites

$$$ | **HOTEL** | Close to shops, eateries, and local watering holes, this inn offers more than 50 modern rooms within easy walking distance to Nome's historic district. **Pros:** refreshingly clean; ideal location; some rooms have sea views. **Cons:** proximity to the bars means it can get a little rowdy outside; no free Wi-Fi; noise carries easily. ⑤ *Rooms from: $225* ✉ *302 E. Front St.* ☎ *907/443–3838, 800/354–4606* ⊕ *www.aurorainnome.com* 🛑 *No credit cards* 🚗 *54 rooms* ⑩ *No meals.*

Nome Nugget Inn

$$ | **HOTEL** | The architecture and kitschy interiors of the Nugget Inn combine every cliché of the Victorian gold-rush era—authentic it's not, but fun it is. **Pros:** cool atmosphere in public areas; central location; Bering Sea views. **Cons:** dated rooms; bar noise; old hotel idiosyncrasies. $ *Rooms from: $170* ⊠ *315 Front St.* ☎ *877/443–2323* ⊕ *www.nomenuggetinnhotel.com* ⏎ *47 rooms* ⦿ *No meals.*

🛍 Shopping

Nome is one of the best places to buy ivory, because many of the Eskimo carvers from outlying villages come to Nome first to sell their wares to dealers.

Maruskiyas of Nome

CRAFTS | You can get standard tourist souvenirs anywhere in Nome, so go to this shop for its selection of Siberian Yupik and Inupiaq Native art from Northwest Alaska. Items include dolls, baskets, jewelry, masks, and ivory, baleen, and jade sculptures. ⊠ *247 Front St.* ☎ *907/443–2955* ⊕ *www.maruskiyas.com.*

Bering Land Bridge National Preserve

100 miles north of Nome.

A trip to the Bering Land Bridge National Preserve will get you off the beaten path to a place that goes beyond gold rushes and the quest for the end of the road. This expanse of historic tundra contains coastal beach environments, sand dunes, mountains, and lakes created by ancient lava flows. A great diversity of animals, birds, and plants are found throughout this region, with many having origins in Asia. Travelers need to be adventurous and self-reliant; only six cabins offer emergency shelter in an area of nearly 3 million acres.

GETTING HERE AND AROUND

The Bering Land Bridge National Preserve has no trails, campgrounds, or other visitor facilities. Access is largely by air taxi and sometimes by small boat, although there is a road leading from Nome that passes within hiking distance. Winter access is possible by ski-plane, snowmachine, or dogsled.

ESSENTIALS

AIR TAXI CONTACTS Bering Air
☎ *907/443–5464 Nome, 800/478–5422 Nome, 907/478–3943 Kotzebue* ⊕ *www.beringair.com.*

VISITOR INFORMATION Bering Land Bridge Visitor Center ⊠ *214 Front St., Nome* ☎ *800/471–2352* ⊕ *www.nps.gov/bela.*

👁 Sights

Bering Land Bridge National Preserve

NATURE PRESERVE | The frozen ash and lava of the 2.8-million-acre Bering Land Bridge National Preserve lie between Nome and Kotzebue, immediately south of the Arctic Circle, one of the most remote parks in the world. The Lost Jim lava flow is the northernmost flow of major size in the United States, and the paired *maars* (clear volcanic lakes) are a geological rarity.

Of equal interest are the paleontological features of this preserve. Sealed into the permafrost are flora and fauna—bits of twigs and leaves, tiny insects, small mammals, even the fossilized remains of woolly mammoths—that flourished here when the Bering Land Bridge linked North America to what is now Russia. "Bridge" is something of a misnomer; essentially, the Bering Sea was dry at the time, and the intercontinental connection was as much as 600 miles wide in places. Early people wandered through this treeless landscape, perhaps following sources of food and materials, such as the musk ox, whose descendants still occupy this terrain, or the mammoths and steppe bison, which are both long gone. Flowering plants thrive in this seemingly barren region, about 250 species in all, and tens of thousands of migrating birds can be seen in season. More than 100 species, including ducks, geese, swans, sandhill cranes, and various shorebirds and songbirds, come here from around the world each spring. ⊕ *www.nps.gov/bela.*

Kotzebue

170 miles northeast of Nome.

Most of the 3,000 or so residents of this coastal village are Inupiaq, whose ancestors have lived and moved throughout the region for thousands of years, creating seasonal camps when following caribou, moose, and other wildlife. Even today, the Inupiaq people depend on whales, seals, fish, and the wide variety of berries and other plants for their food and culture. The Inupiaq are skilled providers, craftsmen, and artists, known for their rugged gear, ceremonial parkas, dolls, caribou-skin masks, birch-bark baskets, and whalebone and walrus-ivory carvings.

Built on a 3-mile-long spit of land that juts into Kotzebue Sound, the village lies 33 miles above the Arctic Circle on Alaska's northwest coast. Before Europeans arrived in the region, the Inupiaq name for this locale was Kikiktagruk, later changed to Kotzebue after German explorer Otto von Kotzebue passed through in 1818 while sailing for Russia. Kotzebue is the region's economic and political hub and headquarters for both the Northwest Arctic Borough and the NANA Regional Corporation, one of the 13 regional Native corporations formed when Congress enacted the Alaska Native Claims Settlement Act in 1971. Nearby villages also use Kotzebue as a hub for business, services, and travel.

Many people in Kotzebue still fish, hunt, and gather wild food as their main meal source. Some residents also fish commercially. The government and the Native corporation provides most of the jobs in education, health care, utilities, and other services, with other employment opportunities found via small businesses and the area's biggest private employer, the Red Dog Mine. As in many Bush villages, local government here is a blend of tribal government and a more modern borough system.

Kotzebue has dark, cold winters and short, cool summers. The average low temperature in January is −12°F, and midsummer highs rarely reach the 70s. "We have four seasons—June, July, August, and winter," a tour guide jests. But don't worry about the sometimes chilly weather—the local sightseeing company has snug, bright-color loaner parkas for visitors on package tours. And there's plenty of light in which to take in the village and surrounding landscape; in fact, the sun doesn't set for 36 days from June into July. One of summer's highlights is the July 4 parade and fair with contests, food, and games, including a foot race, bike race, blanket toss, and other traditional games.

GETTING HERE AND AROUND

As with pretty much everywhere else in the Bush, the main mode of transportation into Kotzebue is via airplane. Alaska Airlines offers regular flights between Anchorage and Kotzebue. Check the website for more details. The main air-taxi services serve Kotzebue, and there's a daily flight from Anchorage. Cab drivers will take you anywhere in town for reasonable fees, although many destinations will be within walking distance.

👁 Sights

Brooks Range

MOUNTAIN—SIGHT | North and east of Kotzebue is the Brooks Range, one of Alaska's great mountain ranges. Much of the

range is protected by Gates of the Arctic National Park and Preserve, and the Arctic National Wildlife Refuge. The National Park Service website has information on how to access the Brooks Range through the Gates of the Arctic page. ⊠ *Kotzebue* ☎ *907/692–5494* ⊕ *www.nps.gov/gaar/index.htm.*

Permafrost

NATURE SITE | If you're hiking the wildflower-carpeted tundra around Kotzebue, you are entering a living museum dedicated to permafrost, the permanently frozen ground that lies just a few inches below the spongy tundra. Even Kotzebue's 6,000-foot airport runway is built on permafrost—with an insulating layer between the frozen ground and the airfield surface to ensure that landings are smooth. These days, the thawing permafrost can cause problems for communities like Kotzebue: as the ice that binds frozen ground melts, the ground collapses and splits, damaging buildings, roads, and other infrastructure. ⊠ *Kotzebue.*

Wilderness areas

NATURE PRESERVE | Although most people come to Kotzebue on day trips or overnight package tours, the town also serves as a gateway for three exceptional national wilderness areas: Cape Krusenstern National Monument, Kobuk Valley National Park, and Noatak National Preserve. ⊠ *Kotzebue.*

🏃 Activities

Northern Alaska Tour Company

TOUR—SPORTS | This tour company arranges year-round cultural and nature tours of Brooks Range and other Arctic Circle areas, with package tours from Fairbanks or Anchorage. ☎ *800/474–1986, 907/474–8600* ⊕ *www.northernalaska.com* 🎟 *From $359.*

🍴 Restaurants

Bayside Restaurant

$$ | **ECLECTIC** | One of the few restaurants in Kotzebue, Bayside offers breakfast and a menu of American, Italian, and Chinese food for lunch and dinner. There's also free Wi-Fi. **Known for:** varied menu of decent classics; beautiful views; great Asian dishes. ⑤ *Average main: $16* ⊠ *303 Shore Ave.* ☎ *907/442–3600.*

🛏 Hotels

Nullagvik Hotel

$$$$ | **HOTEL** | Although it's been a fixture in town since 1975, the Nullagvik Hotel offers the most modern rooms in town, along with community areas like a meeting room for 100 and a third-floor observation lounge overlooking the Chukchi Sea. Amenities include Wi-Fi, televisions, microwaves, and mini-refrigerators, along with access to an exercise area and a restaurant on the first floor. **Pros:** great views; comfortable rooms; nice amenities. **Cons:** the best lodging in town comes at a price; generic room decor; room windows too small to capture the vast views. ⑤ *Rooms from: $279* ⊠ *306 Shore Ave.* ☎ *907/442–3331* ⊕ *www.nullagvikhotel.com* 🛏 *78 rooms* 🍴 *No meals.*

Kobuk Valley National Park

65 miles east of Kotzebue.

Anything is possible in Alaska's wildlands, even deserts. Kobuk Valley National Park is home to three sets of sand dunes, remnants of retreating glaciers from the Pleistocene epoch. But don't expect the ordinary sandy scenery; Kobuk Valley's dunes are covered with the short trees, shrubs, and lichen typical of the tundra. An aerial tour of the Delaware-size park will display the beautiful winding Kobuk River, endless speckles of lakes, and perhaps also a wandering herd of caribou.

Sights

Kobuk Valley National Park

NATIONAL/STATE PARK | Lying entirely north of the Arctic Circle along the southern edge of the Brooks Range, this park's 1.14 million acres contain remarkable inland deserts. People last lived in the region 12,500 years ago when Asia and North America were still connected by the Bering Land Bridge, and today the area is rich in archaeological history. Like most other remote Alaska parks, Kobuk Valley National Park is undeveloped wilderness with no visitor facilities. It can be a good place for backpacking and river trips for those prepared for the remoteness. In nearby Kotzebue, the National Park Service has a visitor center where staff can provide tips for travel into the park. The villages of Kobuk and Kiana both provide immediate take-off points and have air service. ☎ *907/442–3890 Northwest Arctic Heritage Center* ⊕ *www.nps.gov/kova.*

Noatak National Preserve

20 miles northeast of Kotzebue.

For well-organized and self-reliant adventurers, Noatak National Preserve is an endless playground for those who want to hike, paddle, fish, and view birds and wildlife. Bring bug spray, along with everything else you need to camp and explore. There are no visitor facilities.

Sights

Noatak River

NATURE PRESERVE | Adjacent to Gates of the Arctic National Park and Preserve, the 6.5-million-acre Noatak National Preserve encompasses much of the basin of the Noatak River. This is the largest mountain-ringed river basin in the country, and part of it is designated by the National Park Service as a Wild and Scenic River. The river carves out the "Grand Canyon of the Noatak" over 425 miles and serves as a migration route between arctic and subarctic ecosystems. Its importance to wildlife and plants has resulted in this parkland's designation as an International Biosphere Reserve. The Noatak River also serves as a natural highway for humans, particularly to river runners, thanks to its inviting tundra for camping and the Poktovik Mountains and the Igichuk Hills nearby for good hiking. Birding can be exceptional; horned grebes, gyrfalcons, golden eagles, parasitic jaegers, owls, terns, and loons are among the species you may see. You may also spot grizzly bears, Dall sheep, wolves, caribou, and lynx, as well as the occasional musk ox. The most frequently run part of the river, ending at Lake Machurak, is mostly an easy Class I–III paddle. The mountains around the river make for excellent hiking. As with other parks and preserves in this northwest corner of Alaska, no visitor facilities are available and you are expected to be self-sufficient. Do not neglect the bear precautions. Most trips on the Noatak use the inland town of Bettles as a gateway ☎ *907/442–3890* ⊕ *www.nps.gov/noat.*

Gates of the Arctic National Park and Preserve

180 miles east of Kotzebue.

The most northern national park in the country is a mountain-gazer and trekker's dream. Even by Alaska standards of beauty, Gates of the Arctic National Park and Preserve offers truly epic scenery of endless, cragged peaks (once ancient seabed) and six different "Wild and Scenic" rivers. For instant respect with locals, hike the famed and arduous Anaktuvuk Pass.

Sights

Gates of the Arctic National Park and Preserve

NATIONAL/STATE PARK | Entirely north of the Arctic Circle, in the center of the Brooks Range, this 8.2 million acre park is the size of four Yellowstones. To the north lies a sampling of the Arctic foothills, with colorful tilted sediments and pale green tundra while mountains and tundra cup lovely, albeit buggy, lakes. This landscape, the ultimate wilderness, caught the attention of Arctic explorer and conservationist Robert Marshall in the 1930s. Accompanied by local residents, Marshall explored much of the region now included within Gates of the Artic. He gave names to many of its features, including Frigid Crag and Boreal Mountain, two peaks on either side of the North Fork Koyukuk River. These were the original "gates" for which the park is named. The park nourishes wildlife like barren-ground caribou, grizzlies, wolves, musk oxen, moose, Dall sheep, wolverines, and smaller mammals and birds. The communities of Bettles and Anaktuvuk Pass are access points for Gates of the Arctic, which has no developed trails, campgrounds, or other visitor facilities (though there is a wilderness lodge on private land within the park). You can fly into Bettles commercially and charter an air taxi into the park or hike directly out of Anaktuvuk Pass. The Park Service has rangers stationed in both Bettles and Anaktuvuk Pass; they can provide information for those entering the wilderness, including the mandatory orientation films and the bear-proof canisters necessary for food storage. ☎ *907/692–5494 in Bettles, 907/661–3520 in Anaktuvuk Pass (this station is sometimes unmanned), 907/678–4227 in Coldfoot (open seasonally)* ⊕ *www.nps.gov/gaar.*

Activities

Alaska Alpine Adventures–Gates of the Arctic

ADVENTURE TOURS | This year-round adventure outfitter takes folks out hiking, kayaking, climbing, and skiing by offering multisport adventures and even family wilderness trips. They do a 12-day rafting and hiking trip that combines Gates of the Arctic with the Noatak River and Kobuk sand dunes, and they also run scheduled and custom options in multiple wilderness areas every summer. ☎ *877/525–2577, 907/351–4193 Anchorage office* ⊕ *www.alaskaalpineadventures.com.*

★ Arctic Treks

TOUR—SPORTS | Guided wilderness hikes and backpacking expeditions, sometimes combined with river trips and bird-watching, are available in both Gates of the Arctic and the Arctic National Wildlife Refuge. This well-respected and highly experienced tour operator also offers trips into Noatak National Preserve, Kobuk Valley National Park, Cape Krusenstern National Monument, and Bering Land Bridge National Preserve via Fairbanks. ☎ *907/455–6502* ⊕ *www.arctictreksadventures.com.*

Hotels

Peace of Selby Wilderness

$$$$ | **RENTAL** | On Selby and Narvak lakes within Gates of the Arctic National Park, Peace of Selby offers rustic lodging built of white spruce and surrounded by incredible views. **Pros:** endless outdoor activities; wood-fired hot tub outside; rustic atmosphere. **Cons:** small, so reservations and planning are a must; toilets are outhouses; you pay a price for wilderness comfort. ⑤ *Rooms from: $500* ☎ *907/672–3206* ⊕ *www.alaskawilderness.net* ☉ *Closed end of Sept.–mid-June, except for specially arranged expeditions Mar. and Apr.* ⤢ *1 room, 4 cabins* ⎚ *All meals.*

Utqiaġvik

330 miles northeast of Kotzebue.

The northernmost community in the United States, Utqiaġvik—previously known as Barrow—sits 1,300 miles south of the North Pole, and 10 miles south of the Beaufort Sea and Point Barrow. In 2016, residents voted to change the town's name from "Barrow" to its traditional Inupiaq name; "utqiagvik" refers to a place to gather wild roots. Point Barrow was named in 1825 by British captain Frederick William Beechey, who'd been ordered by the British Navy to map the continent's northern coastline. Beechey wished to honor Sir John Barrow, a member of the British Admiralty involved in exploring the Arctic.

About 4,400 people reside in Utqiaġvik today, making it easily the largest community on the North Slope. Nearly two-thirds of the residents are Inupiaq people who remain deeply rooted in their culture. The community does have a public radio station, cable TV, and Internet access, along with a recreation center. In Utqiaġvik, as in much of Bush Alaska, basketball is the favored sport, played year-round by people of all ages.

Utqiaġvik is the economic and administrative center of the **North Slope Borough,** which encompasses more than 88,000 square miles, making it the world's largest municipal government in terms of area. The village is also headquarters of the **Arctic Slope Regional Corporation,** formed in 1971 through the Alaska Native Claims Settlement Act, as well as the Ukpeagvik Inupiat Corporation, which economically and politically represents the community of Utqiaġvik. Several village councils are also headquartered in the town.

GETTING HERE AND AROUND

Alaska Airlines and other regional airlines fly to Utqiaġvik. The Alaska Travel Industry Association can give tips on air travel and flightseeing opportunities throughout the Bush.

ESSENTIALS

CONTACTS Alaska Travel Industry Association ⊠ *2600 Cordova St., Suite 201, Anchorage* ⊕ *www.travelalaska.com.* **City of Utqiaġvik** ⊠ *2022 Ahkovak St.* ☎ *907/852–5211* ⊕ *www.utqiagvik.us.*

◉ Sights

Non-Natives established a presence at Utqiaġvik in the early 1880s, when the U.S. Army built a research station here. Drawn to the area by the Beaufort Sea's abundant whales, commercial whalers established the **Cape Smythe Whaling and Trading Station** in 1893; a cabin from that operation still stands and is the oldest frame building in Alaska's Arctic. The station is now listed on the National Register of Historic Places (as are the Birnirk dwelling mounds).

By the early 1900s both a Presbyterian church and the U.S. Post Office had been established here. Recalling those days, an Inupiaq elder named Alfred Hopson once recounted that the famed Norwegian explorer Vilhjalmur Stefansson used the church as a base for studies of local residents, including measurements of their head sizes. From then on, Stefansson was known locally as the "head measurer." Oil and gas exploration later brought more people from the Lower 48 to the area; even more came as schools and other government agencies took root in the region. Hopson, too, played a role in the area's development, as he funneled millions of dollars in tax revenues into road building, sanitation and water services, and heath-care services.

Utqiaġvik has opened its annual springtime whale festival to outsiders, and there are several historic sites, including a military installation, points of Native cultural importance, and a famous crash site. The Utqiaġvik airport is where you'll find the **Will Rogers and Wiley Post**

Monument, marking the 1935 crash of the American humorist and his pilot 15 miles south of town.

Drawn by both cultural and natural attractions, visitors to Utqiaġvik usually arrive via Alaska Airlines, the only national carrier serving the area. While in town, visitors often take the informative bus tour of the town's dusty roads and major sights.

Activities

Tundra Tours
TOUR—SPORTS | Year-round tours can be organized through Tundra Tours. The winter tours, offered from mid-September through mid-May, feature visits to a traditional hunting camp, the whaling station, the DEWS site, and opportunities to visit Point Barrow and watch the northern lights. The summer program is highlighted by visits to local historic sites and opportunities to witness traditional cultural activities such as dances, sewing demonstrations, and the blanket toss. In both winter and summer, visitors can purchase locally made Inupiaq arts and crafts. ⊠ *Barrow* ☎ *907/852–3900* ⊕ *www.tundratoursinc.com.*

🛏 Hotels

Airport Inn
$$ | B&B/INN | As the name suggests, this modern and well-appointed property is convenient to the airport (it's only two blocks away). **Pros:** convenient service; fresh-baked bread with breakfast; walking distance of eateries and airport. **Cons:** airplane noise; no restaurant on premises; poor sound insulation. ⑤ *Rooms from: $194* ⊠ *1815 Momeganna St.* ☎ *907/852–2525* ⤴ *16 rooms* ⑩ *Breakfast.*

King Eider Inn
$$ | HOTEL | At the King Eider Inn near the airport, you'll find comfortable rooms with simple furnishings and decor. **Pros:** simple but lovely rooms; Internet

and cable; private sauna rooms. **Cons:** pretty bare-bones; some airport noise; no on-site eatery. ⑤ *Rooms from: $189* ⊠ *1752 Ahkovak St.* ☎ *907/852–4700* ⊕ *www.kingeider.net* ⤴ *19 rooms* ⑩ *No meals.*

Top of the World Hotel
$$$ | HOTEL | On the shores of the Arctic Ocean, this tiered and multicolored frontier hotel is minimalist but comes with the modern conveniences expected by most travelers. **Pros:** laundry room available; restaurant on-site; quick walk to the beach. **Cons:** no elevators (which means you're taking the stairs to the top of the world); a little worn in some places; no frills. ⑤ *Rooms from: $310* ⊠ *1200 Agviq St.* ☎ *907/852–3900* ⊕ *www.tundratoursinc.com* ⊟ *No credit cards* ⤴ *44 rooms* ⑩ *No meals.*

🛍 Shopping

AC Value Center *("Big Store")*
CRAFTS | Known by most as "Stuaqpak" ("Big Store" in Inupiaq), this is the only major market in town. It primarily sells groceries, but it also has a hot food court, and stocks local crafts, including furs, parkas, mukluks, and ceremonial masks (sometimes the artists set up vendor tables outside). For many people, AC Value is a lifeline to the most basic food and clothing supplies that make the extreme reaches of Alaska habitable. If you have time to visit one, you should do so, if for no other reason than to see firsthand the price of milk and bread in the Polar North. ⊠ *4725 Ahkovak St.* ☎ *907/852–6711* ⊕ *www.alaskacommercial.com.*

Prudhoe Bay

250 miles southeast of Barrow.

Most towns have museums that chronicle local history and achievements. Deadhorse is the town anchoring life along Prudhoe Bay, but it could also serve as a

A hiker stands atop a rocky summit at the Arctic National Wildlife Refuge.

museum dedicated to humankind's thirst for energy and its ability to adapt to harsh conditions to appease the need for oil and gas.

The costly, much-publicized Arctic oil-and-gas project is complex and varied. Visitors can survey oil wells, stations, and oil-company residential complexes—small cities in themselves—and might get a chance to spot caribou and wildflowers.

GETTING HERE AND AROUND

In the past, individual travelers rarely turned up in Deadhorse and Prudhoe Bay, but once the Dalton Highway opened as far north as Deadhorse, the more adventurous found their way. Still, rather than driving solo on a couple of hundred miles of gravel road filled with fast driving semitrucks, most people head to Deadhorse on tours. A guided tour is recommended to really explore the area and is necessary to cross the oil fields to get to the Arctic Ocean.

🛏 Hotels

Prudhoe Bay Hotel

$$ | B&B/INN | Near the end of the road at Deadhorse, this hotel is primarily intended for the workers employed in the Prudhoe Bay oil-field complex, but tourists are also welcome. **Pros:** one of the few lodging options in the area; great wildlife viewing; Wi-Fi available. **Cons:** not all rooms have private bathrooms; bare necessities only; dining is buffet-style. ⑤ *Rooms from: $190* ✉ *1 Deadhorse Dr.* ☎ *907/659–2449* ⊕ *www.prudhoebayhotel.com* ➲ *200 rooms* ⑩ *No meals.*

Arctic National Wildlife Refuge

70 miles southeast of Prudhoe Bay.

Enormous even by Alaska standards, the Arctic National Wildlife Refuge encompasses six different eco-zones that support a vast diversity of plants and wildlife. Though difficult to reach, several tour outfits take small groups into the Arctic Refuge.

◉ Sights

Arctic National Wildlife Refuge

NATURE PRESERVE | The Arctic Refuge contains one of the few protected Arctic coastal lands in the United States, as well as millions of acres of mountains and alpine tundra in the easternmost portion of the Brooks Range. Hundreds of thousands of birds, caribou, and other animals move across the Arctic Refuge during their annual migrations, relying on the area to nurse and feed their young, and find refuge from insects and predators. The Gwich'in people consider the coastal plain of the Arctic Refuge a sacred place because it feeds and protects the Porcupine caribou herd, which in turn feeds and provides the cultural foundation for the Gwich'in people.

The quest for oil in the coastal plain has become a divisive issue that pits corporate interests and proponents of development against the traditional way of life of the Gwich'in people and those who care about protecting the water, land, and wildlife of the region. Currently, the coastal plain is being opened to oil and gas leasing. The coastal area of the Arctic Refuge also provides critical denning grounds for polar bears, which spend much of their year on the Arctic Ocean's pack ice. Other wildlife include grizzly bears, Dall sheep, wolves, musk ox, and dozens of varieties of birds, from snowy owls to geese and tiny songbirds. As in many of Alaska's more remote parks and refuges, there are no roads here, and no developed trails, campgrounds, or other visitor facilities. Counterintuitively, for such a notoriously brutal geography, the plants and permafrost are quite fragile. The ground can be soft and wet in summer months so walk with care: footprints in the tundra can last 100 years. You should plan for snow almost any season, and anticipate subfreezing temperatures even in summer, particularly in the mountains. Many of the clear-flowing rivers are runnable, and tundra lakes are suitable for base camps (a Kaktovik or Ft. Yukon air taxi can drop you off and pick you up). ⊠ *North Pole* ☎ *907/456–0250 Fairbanks office, 800/362–4546* ⊕ *www.fws.gov/ refuge/arctic.*

Porcupine Caribou Herd

NATURE PRESERVE | The Porcupine caribou herd, whose numbers reach 169,000, migrate across Alaska's Arctic and into Canada's adjacent Vuntut and Ivvavik national parks, flowing as a wide animal river across the expansive coastal plain, through U-shape valleys and alpine meadows, and over high mountain passes. These migration routes demonstrate how interconnected Arctic places are to each other, and how arbitrary our human boundaries seem.

INDEX

Photo Credits

Front Cover: Hugh Rose / Delimont / AWL Images [Description: Caribou Bluff, White Mountain National Recreation, Alaska]. Back cover, from left to right: orangecrush/Shutterstock; Davidhoffmann photography/Shutterstock; Maxfx | Dreamstime.com. Spine: Darryl Brooks/iStockphoto. Alaskarap (1). Ursocalgirl (2-3). Stephen Frink Collection / Alamy (5). ImageState/Almy Chapter 1: Experience Alaska: Papilio / Alamy (6-7). Emperorcosar/Shutterstock (8). Gleb Tarro/Shutterstock (9). Michael Turner|Dreamstime.com (9). Michele Cornelius |Dreamstime.com (10). reisegraf.ch/Shutterstock (10). Steve Boice/Shutterstock (10). Russ Heinl/Shutterstock (10). Jeanninebryan |Dreamstime.com (11). Darryl Brooks |Dreamstime.com (11). Artincamera/Shutterstock (12). Bob Pool/Shutterstock (12). Paxson Woelber [CC 2.0] / Wikimedia Commons (12). Mikhail Varentsov/Shutterstock (12). Leieng |Dreamstime.com (13). takeshi82/Shutterstock (14). unge255_photostock/Shutterstock (14). FloridaStock (14). Martin Schneiter |Dreamstime.com (14). Suranga Weeratunga |Dreamstime.com (15). Izabela 23 |Dreamstime.com (15). Kondor83/Shutterstock (18). Chrisimages |Dreamstime.com (18). LunaseeStudios/Shutterstock (18). hlphoto/Shutterstock (19). Matyáš Havel [CC 3.0] / Wikimedia Commons (19). Antonov Roman/Shutterstock (20). vitaliy_73/Shutterstock (20). Khritthithat Weerasirirut/Shutterstock (20). The Kobuk Team (21). Reinhardt | Dreamstime.com (21). Gary M. Karl (22). Chase Dekker/Shutterstock (22). Bryan Brazil/Shutterstock (22). Chris McDaniel/Shutterstock (22). Tyler Westhoff (23). Haley Johnston (23). Sergey Yechikov/Shutterstock (23). Tomas Kulaja/Shutterstock (23). Chase Dekker/Shutterstock (23). Tory Kallman/Shutterstock (24). John Coffey (24). Major Marine Tours (24). Julien Schroder (25). Anastasiia Vereshchagina/Shutterstock (25). Walleyelj | Dreamstime.com (25). Wildnerdpix/Shutterstock (25). Shutterspeed800 | Dreamstime.com (26). Ruth Peterkin/Shutterstock (27). VicPhotoria/Shutterstock (28). Hemuli/Shutterstock (29). Chapter 3: Anchorage: Rocky Grimes/Shutterstock (55). HAMediaGroup | Dreamstime.com (64). Jay Yuan/Shutterstock (78), Jeff Schultz (83). Chapter 4: Juneau, the Inside Passage, and Southeast Alaska: Crmarlow (87). Sandy1122 (104). Stephen Frink Collection / Alamy (129). ImageState / Alamy (129). Andoni Canela/age footstock (130). Pieter Folkens (130-131). Michael S. Nolan/age footstock (132). Pieter Folkens (132). Alaska Stock LLC / Alamy (140-141). John Baston/Mountain Travel Sobek (156). Everett Historical/Shutterstock (167). Lembi/Shutterstock (168). James Wickersham / State Historic Sites Collection (169). Pep Roig / Alamy (171). Alaska Stock LLC / Alamy (171). Christian Racich (171). Chapter 5: The Kenai Peninsula and Southcentral Alaska: Izanbar | Dreamstime.com (177). Izanbar | Dreamstime.com (191). Zlex03 | Dreamstime.com (200). Alyssand | Dreamstime.com (212). Rolf Hicker / age footstock (213). Renaud Visage/age footstock (215). Alaska Stock LLC / Alamy (215). Bobby17 | Dreamstime.com (232). Chapter 6: Denali National Park and Preserve: Tyler Westhoff (247). Brett Baunton / Alamy (255). Alissa Crandall/CORBIS (256-257). John Schwieder / Alamy (257). Library of Congress Prints and Photographs Division (258). Jeanninebryan | Dreamstime.com (262). Chapter 7: Fairbanks, the Yukon, and the Interior: Eric Yeager/Bureau of Land Management (271). Patricia Fisher/Fisher Photography (285). Surangaw | Dreamstime.com (298). Bryan & Cherry Alexander Photography / Alamy (303). Walleyelj | Dreamstime.com (304). Sitka National Historical Park (305). Tracy Ferrero / Alamy (305). Alaska State Museum, Juneau (306-307). Pecold/Shutterstock (322). Chapter 8: The Bush: Peter Arnold, Inc. / Alamy (325). Design Pics Inc / Alamy (359). WorldFoto / Alamy (365).

Notes

Notes

Notes

Notes

Notes

Notes

Notes

Notes

Notes

Fodor's ALASKA

Editorial: Douglas Stallings, *Editorial Director*; Margaret Kelly, Jacinta O'Halloran, *Senior Editors*; Kayla Becker, Alexis Kelly, Amanda Sadlowski, *Editors*; Teddy Minford, *Content Editor*; Rachael Roth, *Content Manager*

Design: Tina Malaney, *Design and Production Director*; Jessica Gonzalez, *Production Designer*

Photography: Jill Krueger, *Senior Photo Editor*

Maps: Rebecca Baer, *Senior Map Editor*; David Lindroth and Mark Stroud (Moon Street Cartography), *Cartographers*

Production: Jennifer DePrima, *Editorial Production Manager*; Carrie Parker, *Senior Production Editor*; Elyse Rozelle, *Production Editor*

Business & Operations: Chuck Hoover, *Chief Marketing Officer*; Joy Lai, *Vice President and General Manager*; Stephen Horowitz, *Director of Business Development and Revenue Operations*; Tara McCrillis, *Director of Publishing Operations*

Public Relations and Marketing: Joe Ewaskiw, *Manager*; Esther Su, *Marketing Manager*

Writers: Teekas Ballas, Joey Besl, David Cannamore, Alexander Deedy, Amy Fletcher, and Dawnell Smith

Editors: Amanda Sadlowski (lead editor); Kayla Becker

Production Editor: Jennifer DePrima

36th Edition

ISBN 978-1-64097-116-5

ISSN 0271–2776

Library of Congress Control Number 2018958610

All details in this book are based on information supplied to us at press time. Always confirm information when it matters, especially if you're making a detour to visit a specific place. Fodor's expressly disclaims any liability, loss, or risk, personal or otherwise, that is incurred as a consequence of the use of any of the contents of this book.

SPECIAL SALES
This book is available at special discounts for bulk purchases for sales promotions or premiums. For more information, e-mail SpecialMarkets@fodors.com.

PRINTED IN THE UNITED STATES OF AMERICA

10 9 8 7 6 5 4 3 2 1

About Our Writers

Based in Anchorage, **Teeka Ballas** is the publisher/editor of *F Magazine*, Alaska's only independent statewide arts magazine. For 13 years, she has worked as a freelance writer, staffer and stringer for newspapers, international wire services, travel publications and radio. In addition, Ballas is the director and events coordinator for four statewide arts and media competitions, and directs teen musicals for Alaska Theatre of Youth. She worked on the Kenai Peninsula and Southcentral Alaska chapter this edition.

Joey Besl is a Cincinnati native (and unabashed Ohio-phile) now based in Anchorage, where he plans to continue exploring the North from the state's largest base camp. He works as a staff writer at University of Alaska Anchorage and can be found at the bus stops and bike lanes of the city. He updated the Anchorage and Fairbanks, the Yukon, and the Interior chapters for this guide.

A lifelong Alaskan, **David Cannamore** makes his home in the tiny town of Gustavus on the footsteps of Glacier Bay National Park. After updating the Denali National Park and Preserve chapter this edition, David returned to his cabin, wife, cats, and summer occupation as a kayak guide. When not paddling, David can be found freelance writing, cobbling together a novel, or trying to make his tiny cabin more insulated.

Alexander Deedy is a freelance writer who wrote parts of the Experience chapter this edition.

The catalyst for **Amy Fletcher**'s initial visit to Alaska in 1992 was an enticing two-line description of Juneau's stunning natural beauty in a travel guide. She arrived to find the writer had not exaggerated, and two decades later she still calls the city home. She currently works as the arts editor for the *Juneau Empire*. She updated Juneau, the Inside Passage, and Southeast Alaska and Travel Smart for this guide.

Dawnell Smith has called Alaska home for over 30 years, and currently resides in Anchorage. She makes a living in the nonprofit and gig economy, and has previously worked as a brewer, journalist, nonprofit administrator, communications strategist, bookshop owner, and mom among other things. She writes essays, poems, and other mixed-genre literary work, and has been published in multiple newspapers, magazines, and literary journals. She updated the Bush chapter this edition.